Contents

INTRODUCTION   4

Where to go	6	Things not to miss	12
When to go	10	Itineraries	22

BASICS   24

Getting there	25	Cultural values and etiquette	46
Getting around	27	Shopping	47
Accommodation	32	Travelling with children	50
Eating and drinking	34	Crime and safety	50
The media	39	Health	52
Festivals and public holidays	40	Costs	56
Sport and outdoor activities	42	Travel essentials	58
National parks, reserves and eco-tourism	45		

THE GUIDE   64

1 Colombo and the west coast	64	4 The Cultural Triangle	274
2 The south	138	5 The east	340
3 Kandy and the hill country	194	6 Jaffna and the north	370

CONTEXTS   394

History	395	Ceylon tea	438
Sri Lankan Buddhism	419	Books	441
Sri Lankan Buddhist art and architecture	426	Language	444
Sri Lankan wildlife	432		

SMALL PRINT & INDEX   452

OPPOSITE SIGIRIYA **PREVIOUS PAGE** TRAIN RIDE THROUGH THE HILL COUNTRY

Introduction to
Sri Lanka

Sri Lanka has seduced travellers for centuries. Marco Polo described it as the finest island of its size in the world, while successive waves of Indian, Arab and European traders and adventurers flocked to its palm-fringed shores, attracted by reports of rare spices, precious stones and magnificent elephants. Poised just above the Equator amid the balmy waters of the Indian Ocean, the island's legendary reputation for natural beauty and plenty has inspired an almost magical regard even in those who have never visited the place. Romantically inclined geographers, poring over maps of the island, compared its outline to a teardrop falling from the tip of India or to the shape of a pearl (the less impressionable Dutch likened it to a leg of ham), while even the name given to the island by early Arab traders – Serendib – gave rise to the English word "serendipity".

Marco Polo's bold claim still holds true. Sri Lanka packs an extraordinary variety of attractions within its modest physical dimensions, and few islands of comparable size can boast a natural environment of such beauty and diversity. Lapped by the Indian Ocean, the coast is fringed with idyllic – and often refreshingly undeveloped – **beaches**, while the interior boasts a compelling variety of landscapes ranging from wildlife-rich lowland **jungles**, home to extensive populations of elephants, leopards and rare endemic bird species, to the misty heights of the **hill country**, swathed in immaculately manicured tea plantations. Nor does the island lack in man-made attractions. Sri Lanka boasts more than two thousand years of recorded history, and the remarkable achievements of the early Sinhalese civilization can still be seen in the sequence of ruined cities and great religious monuments that litter the northern plains.

The glories of this early Buddhist civilization continue to provide a benchmark of national identity for the island's Sinhalese population, while Sri Lanka's historic role as the world's oldest stronghold of Theravada **Buddhism** lends it a unique cultural identity that permeates life at every level. There's more to Sri Lanka than just Buddhists, however.

ABOVE POLONNARUWA

FACT FILE

• Lying a few degrees north of the Equator, Sri Lanka is slightly smaller than Ireland and a little larger than the US state of West Virginia.

• Sri Lanka achieved independence from Britain in 1948, and did away with its colonial name, Ceylon, in 1972. The country has had a functioning democracy since independence, and in 1960 elected the world's first female prime minister.

• Sri Lanka's population of 21 million is a mosaic of different ethnic and religious groups, the two largest being the mainly Buddhist Sinhalese (73 percent), and the predominantly Hindu Tamils (17 percent); there are also considerable numbers of Christians and Muslims. Sinhala, Tamil and English are all officially recognized languages.

• Sri Lankans enjoy a healthy life expectancy of 75 years and a literacy rate of 91 percent, though they have also set some less enviable records in recent years, including achieving the world's highest suicide rate and the highest death rate from snakebite.

• The country's main export is clothing, followed by tea; rubber, coconuts and precious gems are also important. Revenues from tourism are vital to the national economy, while remittances from the hundreds of thousands of Sri Lankans working overseas (mainly in the Gulf) are also significant.

The island's geographical position at one of the most important staging posts of Indian Ocean trade laid it open to a uniquely wide range of influences, as generations of Arab, Malay, Portuguese, Dutch and British **settlers** subtly transformed its culture, architecture and cuisine, while the long-established Tamil population in the north have established a vibrant Hindu culture that owes more to India than to the Sinhalese south.

It is, however, this very diversity that has long threatened to tear the country apart. For much of the past three decades the island was the site of one of Asia's most pernicious **civil wars**, as the Sri Lankan Army and the LTTE, or Tamil Tigers, battled it out in the island's north and east, until the final victory of government forces in early 2009. The island is now experiencing **peace** for the first time in a generation, and although the physical, political and human scars of war remain raw in many places, most Sri Lankans are now once again looking to the future with guarded optimism.

Where to go

All visits to Sri Lanka currently begin at the international airport just outside **Colombo**, the island's capital and far and away its largest city – a sprawling metropolis whose contrasting districts offer an absorbing introduction to Sri Lanka's myriad cultures and multi-layered history. Many visitors head straight for one of the **west coast**'s beaches, whose innumerable resort hotels still power the country's tourist industry. Destinations include the package holiday resorts of **Negombo** and **Beruwala**, the more stylish **Bentota**, and the old hippy hangout of **Hikkaduwa**. More unspoilt countryside can be found north of Colombo at the **Kalpitiya peninsula** and in the vast **Wilpattu National Park** nearby, home to leopards, elephants and sloth bears.

Beyond Hikkaduwa, the **south coast** is significantly less developed. Gateway to the region is the marvellous old Dutch city of **Galle**, Sri Lanka's finest colonial town, beyond which lie a string of fine beaches including the ever-expanding village of **Unawatuna** and

ELEPHANTS

No animal is as closely identified with Sri Lanka as the **elephant** – and few other countries offer such a wide range of opportunities to see them both in captivity and in the wild. The kings of Anuradhapura used them to pound down the foundations of their city's huge religious monuments, while the rulers of Kandy employed them to execute prisoners by trampling them to death. During the Dutch era they helped tow barges and move heavy artillery, and under the British they were set to clearing land for tea plantations – even today, trained elephants are used to move heavy objects in places inaccessible to machinery. Elephants also play an integral role in many of the island's religious festivals, and remain revered creatures – killing an elephant was formerly a capital offence, while the death of the great Maligawa Tusker Raja in 1998 prompted the government to declare a national day of mourning.

the quieter stretches of coast at **Weligama**, **Mirissa** and **Tangalla**, as well as the lively provincial capital of **Matara**, boasting further Dutch remains. East of here, **Tissamaharama** serves as a convenient base for the outstanding **Yala** and **Bundala** national parks, and for the fascinating temple town of **Kataragama**.

Inland from Colombo rise the verdant highlands of the **hill country**, enveloped in the tea plantations (first introduced by the British) which still play a vital role in the island's economy. The symbolic heart of the region is **Kandy**, Sri Lanka's second city and the cultural capital of the Sinhalese, its colourful traditions embodied by the famous Temple of the Tooth and the magnificent Esala Perahera, Sri Lanka's most colourful festival. South of here, close to the highest point of the island, lies the old British town of **Nuwara Eliya**, centre of the country's tea industry and a convenient base for visits to the spectacular Horton Plains National Park. A string of towns and villages – **Ella**, **Haputale** and **Bandarawela** – along the southern edge of the hill country offer an appealing mixture of magnificent views, wonderful walks and olde-worlde British colonial charm. Close to the hill country's southwestern edge, the soaring summit of **Adam's Peak** is another of the island's major pilgrimage sites, while the gem-mining centre of **Ratnapura** to the south serves as the best starting point for visits to the elephant-rich **Uda Walawe National Park** and the rare tropical rainforest of **Sinharaja**.

North of Kandy, the hill country tumbles down into the arid plains of the northern dry zone. This area, known as the Cultural Triangle, was the location of Sri Lanka's first great civilization, and its extraordinary scatter of ruined palaces, temples and dagobas still give a compelling sense of this glorious past. Foremost amongst these are the fascinating ruined cities of **Anuradhapura** and **Polonnaruwa**, the marvellous cave temples of **Dambulla**, the hilltop shrines and dagobas of **Mihintale** and the extraordinary rock citadel of **Sigiriya**.

Gateway to **the east** is the characterful, if war-torn, city of **Trincomalee**. The east's huge swathe of pristine coastline itself remains almost completely undeveloped, save for the sleepy villages of **Nilaveli** and **Uppuveli**, just north of Trinco, and the surfing centre of **Arugam Bay**, at the east coast's southern end, although the construction of a huge new resort at **Passekudah** is likely to change that. Even less visited, **the north** is slowly emerging after years of civil war; increasing numbers of visitors are making the long

SRI LANKAN BUDDHISM

Buddhism runs deep in Sri Lanka. The island was one of the first places to convert to the religion, in 247 BC, and has remained unswervingly faithful in the two thousand years since. As such, Sri Lanka is often claimed to be the world's oldest Buddhist country, and Buddhism continues to permeate the practical life and spiritual beliefs of the majority of the island's Sinhalese population. Buddhist temples can be found everywhere, often decorated with superb shrines, statues and murals, while the sight of Sri Lanka's orange-robed monks is one of the island's enduring visual images. Buddhist places of pilgrimage – the Temple of the Tooth at Kandy, the revered "footprint" of the Buddha at Adam's Peak, and the Sri Maha Bodhi at Anuradhapura – also play a vital role in sustaining the faith, while the national calendar is punctuated with religious holidays and festivals ranging from the monthly full-moon poya days through to more elaborate annual celebrations, often taking the form of enormous processions (peraheras), during which locals parade through the streets, often accompanied by elaborately costumed elephants. For more on Buddhism, turn to our Contexts chapter (see p.394).

journey to the absorbing city of **Jaffna**, while a side-trip to remote **Mannar**, closer to India than Colombo, is another adventurous possibility.

When to go

Sri Lanka's climate is rather complicated for such a small country, due to the fact that the island is affected by **two separate monsoons** – though this also means that there is usually good weather somewhere on the island, at most times of the year. It's worth bearing in mind, however, that the basic pattern described below can vary significantly from year to year, and that global warming has disrupted these already complex weather patterns.

The basic rainfall pattern is as follows. The main **southwest ("yala") monsoon** brings rain to the west and southwest coasts and hill country from April/May to September (wettest from April to June). The less severe **northeast ("maha") monsoon** hits the east coast from November to March (wettest from November to December); there's also a **inter-monsoonal period** of unsettled weather preceding the Maha monsoon in October and November during which heavy rainfall and thunderstorms can occur anywhere across the island. In practical terms, this means that the **best time to visit** the west and south coasts and hill country is from December to March, while the best weather on the east coast is from April/May to September.

Sri Lanka's position close to the Equator means that **temperatures** remain fairly constant year-round. Coastal and lowland areas enjoy average daytime temperatures of around 26–30°C (often climbing up well into the 30°Cs during the hottest part of the day). Temperatures decrease with altitude, reducing to a temperate 18–22°C in Kandy, and a pleasantly mild 14–17°C in Nuwara Eliya and the highest parts of the island – nights in the hills can be quite chilly, with temperatures sometimes falling close to freezing. **Humidity** is high everywhere, rising to a sweltering ninety percent at times in the southwest, and averaging sixty to eighty percent across the rest of the island. There is more on Sri Lanka's climate, with a **rainfall and temperature chart**, in our Basics section (see p.58).

OPPOSITE FROM TOP MINNERIYA; NUWARA ELIYA

Author picks

Our much-travelled author has visited every corner of Sri Lanka in order to uncover the very best the island has to offer. Here are some of his own personal highlights.

Classic journeys Ride the hill country train (p.200) through tea plantations to Badulla or drive the long A9 highway (p.378) north to Jaffna.

Multi-faith island Make an eclectic pilgrimage to one of Sri Lanka's great religious melting pots at Kataragama (p.189), Madhu (p.375) or Adam's Peak (p.262), held sacred by Buddhist, Hindus, Muslims and Christians.

Rugged rambling Take a walk on the wild side through the spectacular hill country at Adam's Peak (p.262), Horton Plains (p.246) or the Knuckles Range (p.234) – Sri Lanka at its most scenically dramatic.

Colonial Ceylon Step back in time amid the colonial streetscapes of Galle (p.143) or the old British tea-town of Nuwara Eliya (p.238).

Once more unto the beach Escape the crowds at the unspoilt beaches of Alankuda (p.113), Marakolliya (p.178), Kalametiya (p.181) and Arugam Bay (p.361).

Wildlife on land and at sea Experience Sri Lanka's wonderful range of fauna with highlights including whales at Mirissa (p.168), turtles at Rekawa (p.180), dolphins at Alankuda (p.113), birds in Sinharaja (p.269), elephants at Minneriya (p.306) and leopards at Yala (p.188).

Boutique bliss Crash out in style at one of the island's dazzling array of boutique hotels, ranging from stylish contemporary beachside villas like *Club Bentota* (p.125) to atmospheric old colonial-era lodgings like *The Planter's Bungalow* (p.255).

Flavours of Sri Lanka Dive into a hopper, unpack a *lamprais*, crunch some chilli crab or feast on a classic rice and curry – the Colombo Hilton's *Curry Leaf* (p.94) is a great place to get your taste buds oriented.

> Our author recommendations don't end here. We've flagged up our favourite places – a perfectly sited hotel, an atmospheric café, a special restaurant – throughout the guide, highlighted with the ★ symbol.

25

things not to miss

It's not possible to see everything that Sri Lanka has to offer in one trip – and we don't suggest you try. What follows, in no particular order, is a selective taste of the country's highlights, including astonishing religious and historic sites, unforgettable wildlife, scenery and beaches, and vibrant festivals. All highlights have a page reference to take you straight into the Guide, where you can find out more; the coloured numbers refer to chapters in the Guide section.

1

1 CRICKET
Page 42

Take part in a knock-around on the beach, or join the crowds of cricket-crazy spectators for a Test match in Colombo or Kandy.

2 ADAM'S PEAK
Page 262

One of Sri Lanka's foremost pilgrimage sites, this soaring summit bears the revered impression of what is said to be the Buddha's own footprint, and offers the island's most magical – and enigmatic – views.

2

3 BIG BUDDHAS
Page 426

The Buddha's superhuman attributes are captured in a sequence of massive statues which dot the island, from the majestic ancient figures of Aukana, Sasseruwa and Polonnaruwa's Gal Vihara to the contemporary colossi at Dambulla and Wehurukannala.

4 GALLE
Page 143

Sri Lanka's most perfectly preserved colonial townscape, with sedate streets of personable Dutch-era villas enclosed by a chain of imposing ramparts.

3

4

5 YALA NATIONAL PARK
Page 188

Sri Lanka's most popular and rewarding national park, home to birds, monkeys, crocodiles and elephants, as well as the island's largest population of leopards.

6 WORLD'S END
Page 247

Marking the point at which the hill country's southern escarpment plunges sheer for almost 1km to the plains below, these dramatic cliffs offer one of the finest of the hill country's many unforgettable views.

7 RICE AND CURRY
Page 35

Eat your way through this classic Sri Lankan feast, with its mouthwatering selection of contrasting dishes and flavours.

8 BIRDS
Page 434

Sri Lanka is one of Asia's classic birdwatching destinations, with species ranging from delicate bee eaters and blue magpies to colourful kingfishers and majestic hornbills.

9 KATARAGAMA
Page 189

Join the crowds thronging to the colourful nightly temple ceremonies at this remote pilgrimage town, held sacred by Buddhists, Hindus and Muslims alike.

10

11

12

10 ANURADHAPURA
Page 319
This vast, mysterious ruined city bears witness to the great Sinhalese civilization that flourished here for some two thousand years.

11 BAWA HOTELS
Page 34
With their blend of modern chic and superb natural settings, the hotels of architect Geoffrey Bawa exemplify contemporary Sri Lankan style.

12 SIGIRIYA
Page 297
Climb the towering rock outcrop of Sigiriya, home to the fascinating remains of one of the island's former capitals, complete with ancient graffiti and elaborate water gardens.

13 ELLA
Page 251
Sri Lanka's most beautiful village, offering marvellous views and walks among verdant tea plantations.

14 THE PETTAH
Page 76
Colombo's colourful, chaotic bazaar district offers an exhilarating slice of Asian life.

15 WHALE AND DOLPHIN WATCHING
Page 437
Take to the waves in search of magnificent blue and sperm whales, or pods of acrobatic spinner dolphins.

 POLONNARUWA
Page 307
Quite simply the island's finest collection of ancient Sinhalese art and architecture.

 BENTOTA
Page 122
The unspoilt southern end of Bentota beach is home to a fine selection of luxury beachside hotels.

 KANDY ESALA PERAHERA
Page 208
One of Asia's most spectacular festivals, with huge processions of magnificently caparisoned elephants, ear-splitting troupes of Kandyan drummers and assorted dancers and acrobats.

 SINHARAJA NATIONAL PARK
Page 269
Unique region of pristine rainforest, home to towering trees, opulent orchids and rare endemic birds, lizards and spiders.

 AYURVEDA
Page 118
Sri Lanka's ancient system of healthcare uses herbal medicines and traditional techniques to promote holistic well-being.

ARUGAM BAY
Page 361
This remote east coast village has great sand and surf, lots of local wildlife and an appealingly chilled-out atmosphere.

 KANDYAN DANCING AND DRUMMING
Page 225
Traditional Sinhalese culture at its most exuberant, with brilliantly costumed dancers performing stylized dances to an accompaniment of explosively energetic drumming.

23 DAMBULLA
Page 289
These five magical cave temples are a treasure box of Sri Lankan Buddhist art, sumptuously decorated with a fascinating array of statues, shrines and the country's finest collection of murals.

24 MIRISSA
Page 168
Laid-back beachside village with a fine stretch of sand and world-class whale-watching.

25 KANDY
Page 205
Beautifully situated amidst the central highlands, this historic city remains the island's most important repository of traditional Sinhalese culture, exemplified by the great Esala Perahera festival and the Temple of the Tooth.

24

25

Itineraries

Sri Lanka is one of the biggest little countries in the world. The island's modest size means that it's possible to get a good taste of what's on offer in just a couple of weeks, although, equally, attractions are crammed together so densely that you could easily spend a year in the place and still not see everything.

THE GRAND TOUR

Two weeks suffices to see Sri Lanka's headline attractions, while an extra week would allow you to add on the places listed in the itineraries below.

❶ Kandy Start in Kandy, cultural capital of Sri Lanka and a marvellous showcase of Sinhalese religious art, architecture and dance. **See p.205**

❷ Dambulla Drive north to the cave temples at Dambulla, crammed with Buddhist statues and decorated with Sri Lanka's finest murals. See p.289

❸ Sigiriya The nearby rock citadel at Sigiriya is perhaps Sri Lanka's single most dramatic attraction: the remains of a fifth-century palace perched on the summit of the vertiginous Lion Rock. **See p.297**

❹ Polonnaruwa Another short drive leads to the marvellous ruined city of Polonnaruwa, home to some of medieval Sri Lanka's finest art and architecture, including the giant Buddha statues of the Gal Vihara. **See p.307**

❺ Horton Plains National Park Return to Kandy and then continue to Nuwara Eliya for a trip to Horton Plains National Park, a marvellously rugged stretch of unspoilt hill country culminating in the spectacular view at World's End. **See p.246**

❻ Ella Continue to lively little Ella village, set in a dramatic location amid tea plantations on the edge of the hill country. **See p.251**

❼ Yala National Park Drive south to Yala National Park, home to one of the world's densest populations of leopards, and much more besides. **See p.188**

❽ Mirissa Spend some time on the beach and go on a whale-watching trip at the village of Mirissa. **See p.168**

❾ Galle Continue around the coast to the city of Galle and its time-warped old Dutch Fort – colonial Sri Lanka at its most perfectly preserved. **See p.143**

❿ Colombo Finish with a day or two in the nation's energetic capital. **See p.70**

WILDLIFE AND NATURE

The following itinerary, which picks up on some of the best natural attractions not covered in the Grand Tour, could be done in a week, at a push, allowing plenty of time to combine with other attractions en route during a fortnight's visit to the island.

❶ The Knuckles Range From Kandy you can hike into the rugged Knuckles Range, one of the island's most beautiful and biodiverse areas. See p.234

ABOVE SPOTTED DEER, YALA NATIONAL PARK; MIHINTALE

❷ **Nuwara Eliya** Head south to this venerable old colonial town in the heart of the hill country, with spectacular walks in the surrounding countryside. **See p.238**

❸ **Horton Plains National Park** Sri Lanka's most scenically stunning national park: a misty mix of moorland and cloudforest, home to rare indigenous flora and fauna. **See p.246**

❹ **Haputale** Dramatically perched on the edge of the southern hill country and with fine hiking through the surrounding tea plantations, particularly the walk down from nearby Lipton's Seat. **See p.258**

❺ **Bundala National Park** One of Sri Lanka's premier birdwatching destinations, spread out around a stunning string of coastal lagoons. **See p.183**

❻ **Rekawa** Watch majestic marine turtles haul themselves ashore to lay their eggs on beautiful Rekawa beach. **See p.180**

❼ **Uda Walawe National Park** Superb elephant-watching opportunities, either in the wild or at the attached Elephant Transit Home. **See p.272**

❽ **Sinharaja** Stunning area of unspoilt rainforest, home to an internationally significant array of rare endemic flora and fauna. **See p.269**

BUDDHISM AND BEACHES

A slightly offbeat alternative to the Grand Tour, featuring less mainstream destinations mixing religion, culture and wildlife.

❶ **Kalpitiya** Superb dolphin-watching, kitesurfing and some of the island's finest eco-lodges on beautiful Alankuda Beach. **See p.112**

❷ **Wilpattu National Park** Enormous and very peaceful park famous for its leopards and elephants. **See p.111**

❸ **Anuradhapura** The greatest city in Sri Lankan history, packed with monuments from over a thousand years of the island's past. **See p.319**

❹ **Mihintale** The birthplace of Buddhism in Sri Lanka, with a cluster of absorbing monuments clinging to a jungle-covered hillside. **See p.336**

❺ **Polonnaruwa** Medieval Sri Lankan art and architecture at its finest, from the flamboyant

Vatadage to the brooding statues of the Gal Vihara. **See p.307**

❻ **Batticaloa** Vibrant but little-visited east coast town, famous for its "singing fish" and with a fine beach and lagoon. **See p.354**

❼ **Arugam Bay** This quirky village is one of the most appealing places to hang out for a few days around the coast. **See p.361**

❽ **Kataragama** Vibrant multi-faith pilgrimage town, a holy place for Buddhists, Hindus and Muslims. **See p.189**

❾ **Adam's Peak** The strenuous climb to the top of Adam's Peak is the island's ultimate pilgrimage, rewarded by a glimpse of the Buddha's own footprint at the summit. **See p.262**

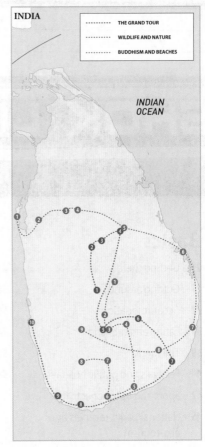

BUS, MATARA

Basics

25 Getting there
27 Getting around
32 Accommodation
34 Eating and drinking
39 The media
40 Festivals and public holidays
42 Sport and outdoor activities
45 National parks, reserves and
    eco-tourism
46 Cultural values and etiquette
47 Shopping
50 Travelling with children
50 Crime and safety
52 Health
56 Costs
58 Travel essentials

Getting there

At present, the only way to get to Sri Lanka is to fly into the island's international airport at Katunayake, just north of Colombo, although the opening of a second international airport in the southern town of Hambantota (scheduled for 2012) and the possible resumption of ferry services between Colombo and India will offer alternative ways of reaching the island in future.

Air fares remain fairly constant year-round – in general, the further ahead you book your flight, the better chance you have of getting a good deal. Another possibility is to pick up a package deal – even if you don't use the accommodation provided (or only use it for a few days), packages can work out reasonable value thanks to the cheap flight.

Flights from the UK and Ireland

The only nonstop **scheduled flights from the UK** to Sri Lanka are with SriLankan Airlines (Wsrilankan .lk) from London Heathrow; flying time to Colombo is around eleven hours. Emirates (Wemirates.com), Qatar Airlines (Wqatarairways.com), Kuwait Airlines (Wkuwait-airways.com), Etihad (Wetihadairways .com) and Oman Air (Womanair.com) all offer one-stop flights from Heathrow via their home cities in the Gulf, while Jet Airways (Wjetairways .com) operates one-stop flights to Mumbai and Delhi. There are also more circuitous routings via various points in Southeast Asia, including Singapore (Wsingaporeair.com), Kuala Lumpur (Wmalaysia-airlines.com), Bangkok (Wthaiair.com), and Hong Kong (Wcathaypacific.com).

Travelling **from Ireland**, you can either make your way to Heathrow and pick up an onward connection there, or fly via one of the various Gulf cities that have direct connections with Colombo – the one-stop route from Dublin to Colombo via Dubai with Emirates is the fastest. Another possibility is to fly via one of the various European cities that have

direct connections with Colombo – these currently include Paris, Frankfurt, Rome and Milan (all served by SriLankan Airlines).

Scheduled **fares** from London to Colombo start at around £500 return year-round. The cheapest tickets are usually offered by Qatar Airways, Jet Airways and SriLankan Airlines.

Flights from the US and Canada

It's a long journey from North America to Sri Lanka, and chances are you'll want to break your flight somewhere or include the island as part of a longer visit to the region. The journey from North America to Sri Lanka takes at least 24 hours, and necessitates at least one change of plane, and probably more like two or three. **From the east coast**, there are various routes via Europe. One possibility is to fly to London and then pick up one of the onward connections described above. Alternatively, you could fly to Paris, Frankfurt, Rome or Milan, all of which have nonstop connections to Colombo with various airlines. There are also various routes via Europe and the Middle East with Gulf Air, Emirates, Etihad and Qatar Airways. Travelling **from the west coast**, the most direct routes go via east and Southeast Asia, flying via Hong Kong, Kuala Lumpur, Singapore, Bangkok or Tokyo, all of which have nonstop connections on to Colombo. **Cathay Pacific** (Wcathaypacific.com), for example, flies from numerous US cities, plus Vancouver and Toronto, to Hong Kong and on to Colombo via Bangkok or Singapore.

Fares to Colombo start from around $1100 from New York and Toronto; from around $1400 from Los Angeles; or about Can$1600 from Vancouver.

Flights from Australia and New Zealand

Flying **from Australia** to Sri Lanka is straightforward, although you'll have to change planes at least once; the most direct routings to Colombo are via Singapore, Kuala Lumpur and Bangkok. There

---

A BETTER KIND OF TRAVEL

At Rough Guides we are passionately committed to travel. We feel that travelling is the best way to understand the world we live in and the people we share it with – plus tourism has brought a great deal of benefit to developing economies around the world over the last few decades. But the growth in tourism has also damaged some places irreparably, and climate change is exacerbated by most forms of transport, especially flying. All Rough Guides' trips are carbon-offset, and every year we donate money to a variety of charities devoted to combating the effects of climate change.

are also a few one-stop options **from New Zealand** via Singapore, Bangkok and Kuala Lumpur. The most regular services are with Qantas (ⓦqantas .com) who operate flights to Singapore (from Sydney, Melbourne, Adelaide, Perth and Brisbane), and to Bangkok and Mumbai (from Sydney), from where there are direct connections to Colombo. Fares from Sydney to Colombo with most carriers generally start at around A$1200, and from Auckland at around NZ$2000, although there are also currently cheaper deals available with low-cost carrier Air Asia (ⓦairasia.com), who fly via Kuala Lumpur.

Flights from the rest of Asia

Sri Lanka isn't normally considered part of the overland Asian trail, although the island is well connected with other countries in **South and Southeast Asia**. There are regular nonstop **flights** with SriLankan Airlines to various places in India, including Delhi, Mumbai (Bombay), Chennai (Madras), Bangalore, Thiruvananthapuram (Trivandrum) and Tiruchirappali; to Bangkok with SriLankan and Thai Air; Kuala Lumpur with SriLankan Airlines, Malaysia Airlines and Air Asia; Singapore with SriLankan and Singapore Airlines; Tokyo with SriLankan; and Hong Kong with SriLankan and Cathay Pacific. There are also direct connections to many places in **the Gulf**, including frequent services to Dubai (Emirates), Abu Dhabi (Etihad), Qatar (Qatar Airways), Muscat (Oman Air) and Kuwait (Kuwait Airways).

Organized tours

Organized guided tours of the island – either with your own car and driver, or as part of a larger tour group – can be arranged through numerous companies both in Sri Lanka and abroad. Tours obviously take virtually all the hassle out of travelling, and some can offer good value in terms of transport and accommodation. The downside is that those offered by foreign companies tend to be much of a muchness – if you want something a bit more unusual you might be better off contacting one of the Colombo-based operators we've listed.

Tours offered by **foreign operators** usually feature a mix of wildlife and culture followed by a few days on the beach, although some are oriented more towards a particular interest, while others offer more adventurous possibilities such as trekking, cycling and whitewater rafting. Many of the operators below can also arrange honeymoon, wedding and cricketing packages, and virtually all of them will customize tours on request. Some tours are by private car, with your own personal chauffeur; others are in larger groups of up to sixteen people travelling by minibus. Note that almost all the leading foreign Sri Lankan tour operators are based in the **UK**; travellers from North America and Australasia shouldn't have any problems booking tours through these companies, although you might have to organize your own flights.

Setting up a tour with a **Colombo-based operator** is a very viable alternative to arranging one at home. They probably won't work out any cheaper than their overseas rivals, but insider knowledge gives several of the following companies a distinct edge over foreign firms.

TOUR OPERATORS IN THE UK

Ampersand Travel ☎ 020 7289 6100, ⓦ ampersandtravel.com.
Luxury island tours (10–23 days) focusing on nature or culture, with accommodation in top-end hotels or luxury villas. Also twin-centre holidays combining Sri Lanka with the Maldives.

Carolanka ☎ 01822 810230, ⓦ carolanka.co.uk. Small Sri Lankan specialist offering two general island tours (15 nights), plus customized itineraries and special-interest trips.

Equinox Travel ☎ 020 7380 0050, ⓦ equinoxtravel.co.uk. Unusual adventure, cultural and wildlife tours visiting a mix of mainstream attractions along with an interesting selection of off-the-beaten-track sites.

THE FERRY FROM INDIA

In June 2011, a long-awaited ferry service was launched between Colombo and Tuticorin, in the southern Indian state of Tamil Nadu – the first scheduled passenger ferry between the two countries since 1983.

Sailings were made twice weekly aboard the Indian-chartered *Scotia Prince*, carrying up to 1000 passengers and taking around 14 hours to make the journey. Sadly, the ferry wasn't the commercial success it was hoped it would be, and just six months after services were launched the *Scotia Prince* was impounded by the Colombo High Court after a claim against the ferry's Indian owners for unpaid bills. Services currently show no sign of restarting. Check online or with the nearest Sri Lankan tourist office (see p.52 & p.90) for latest news.

Explore ☎ 0845 291 4541, 🖥 explore.co.uk. Islandwide trips combining the mainstream highlights with soft adventure activities including cycling, hiking and whitewater rafting.

Insider Tours ☎ 01233 280844, 🖥 insider-tours.com. Sri Lanka specialist offering a range of innovative and ethical customized tours. Run in conjunction with Sri Lankan guides and organizations to create unusual itineraries, tours give a real first-hand taste of the island and provide stimulating encounters with locals.

Mountain Kingdoms ☎ 01453 844400, 🖥 mountainkingdoms .com. Fifteen-day walking tours combining trekking with cultural attractions.

On the Go Tours ☎ 020 7371 1113, 🖥 onthegotours.com. Mainstream but inexpensive five- to fifteen-day tours.

Red Dot Tours ☎ 0870 231 7892, 🖥 reddottours.com. Leading Sri Lankan specialists offering holidays based around wildlife, adventure, culture, cricket, golf and more, along with wedding and honeymoon packages. They also offer cheap flights and have an outstanding selection of properties around the island in most price ranges.

Tikalanka ☎ 020 3137 6763, 🖥 tikalanka.com. Tailor-made tours by small Sri Lanka and Maldives specialist.

Trans Indus ☎ 0844 879 3960, 🖥 transindus.co.uk. Reputable South Asia specialist offering nine- and fourteen-day islandwide tours plus customized trips.

Wildlife Worldwide ☎ 0845 130 6982, 🖥 wildlifeworldwide .com. Wildlife-oriented trips (10–16 days), including whale- and dolphin-watching tours.

Worldwide Holidays ☎ 01202 606160, 🖥 worldwideholidays .co.uk. Various tours ranging from elephant-spotting to golfing.

TOUR OPERATORS IN SRI LANKA

Adventure Asia ☎ 011 536 8468, 🖥 ad-asia.com. One of Sri Lanka's leading outdoor adventure specialists; running biking, climbing, hiking and rafting trips, plus spectacular balloon flights (see p.44).

Aitken Spence Travels ☎ 011 230 8308, 🖥 aitkenspencetravels .com. Travel wing of one of Sri Lanka's top hotel chains, offering various general standard island tours.

Blue Haven Tours and Travels/Rail Tours Fort Railway Station, Colombo ☎ 011 244 0048; 25 D.S. Senanayake Mw, Kandy ☎ 081 222 0572 or ☎ 0777 372 066, 🖥 bluehaventours.com. Reputable agents organizing very inexpensive islandwide tours (around $90–100/day for two people) using train and a/c car (the only travel agents to offer this combination), with accommodation in simple but comfortable guesthouses.

Boutique Sri Lanka ☎ 011 269 9213, 🖥 boutiquesrilanka.com. Huge portfolio of mid- and top-range properties, including a vast selection of villas. Itineraries are customized to suit your interests, from beaches or Ayurveda to nature, surfing and adventure.

Destination Sri Lanka ☎ 0777 840 001, 🖥 dsltours.com. Reliably excellent customized islandwide tours by Nimal de Silva, one of Sri Lanka's most professional and personable driver-guides, and his team.

Eco Team ☎ 011 583 0833, 🖥 srilankaecotourism.com. Specialist eco-tourism and activity holiday operator, offering a vast range of water- and land-based activities at locations islandwide – anything from surfing

and caving to study tours and "nature weddings". Also runs camping trips in national parks through its Mahoora wing (🖥 mahoora.lk).

Jetwing Eco Holidays ☎ 011 238 1201, 🖥 jetwingeco.com. Far and away Sri Lanka's best eco-tourism operator, offering a vast range of wildlife and adventure activities including birdwatching, leopard-spotting, whale-watching, trekking, cycling, whitewater rafting and much more. Nature activities are led by an expert team of guides, including some of Sri Lanka's top naturalists.

Jetwing Travels ☎ 011 471 4830, 🖥 jetwingtravels.com. Travel division of Sri Lanka's largest hotel group, with a range of islandwide tours (7–10 days), including golfing, trekking, diving, cycling and Ayurveda tours.

The Kulu Safari Company ☎ 037 493 1662, 🖥 kulusafaris.com. Luxury tented safaris in or around various national parks. Tents come complete with hot showers, queen-size beds and gourmet cuisine, offering a very civilized (albeit very expensive) way of getting completely off the beaten track.

Sri Lankan Expeditions ☎ 0773 595 411, 🖥 srilankan expeditions.com. Huge range of unusual tours and activites ranging from agro-tourism and rainforest trips to kayaking and windsurfing.

Sri Lanka in Style ☎ 011 239 6666, 🖥 srilankainstyle.com. Luxury tours with unusual and insightful itineraries (either customized or off the peg) and accommodation in some of Sri Lanka's most magical villas and boutique hotels.

Walkers Tours ☎ 011 230 6306, 🖥 walkerstours.com. Large operator offering a good range of islandwide itineraries including wildlife, trekking, camping and golfing tours plus wedding packages.

Wild Holidays ☎ 011 258 8258, 🖥 wildholidaystravel.com. Eco- and adventure-oriented trips including cycling, hiking and birdwatching tours.

Getting around

Given Sri Lanka's fairly modest size, getting around can be a frustratingly time-consuming process. The island's narrow roads, congested with pedestrians, cyclists and tuktuks make bus travel laborious, while in many cases travel by rail is even slower. Even with your own vehicle you shouldn't expect to make rapid progress. Getting from Colombo to Kandy, for instance (a distance of not much over 100km), takes around three hours by bus or train, while the bus trip across the island from Colombo to Arugam Bay takes at least ten hours by public transport for a distance of 320km.

Buses are the standard means of transport. Services reach even the remotest corners of the island, though they're generally an uncomfortable way of travelling. **Trains** offer a more characterful, if

THE FIRST MOTORWAY

Sri Lanka's nineteenth-century highway infrastructure received a long-overdue upgrade in late 2011 with the opening of the country's first genuine motorway, the **E1 Southern Expressway** from Colombo to Galle. The Expressway has transformed access to the west and south coasts, cutting the journey time to Galle from around three hours or more to just one, as well as giving speedy access to other popular tourist spots en route.

The Expressway starts in Kottawa in southern Colombo and finishes on the coast, just east of Galle city centre, with seven intersections en route giving access to Kalutara, Aluthgama, Ambalangoda, Hikkaduwa and other destinations. A toll of Rs.400 is levied to travel the entire length of the highway, with reduced tolls for shorter journeys. An extension of the highway from Colombo to the international airport is expected to open in 2013, while further extensions to Matara and Hambantota are also planned, as is a second expressway from Colombo to Kandy.

generally slower, means of getting about, and will get you to many parts of the country – eventually. If you don't want to put up with the vagaries of public transport, hiring a **car and driver** can prove a reasonably affordable and extremely convenient way of seeing the island in relative comfort. If you're really in a rush, consider SriLankan Airlines' network of "air taxis", which offer speedy (albeit inevitably pricey) connections between Colombo and other parts of the island.

Details of getting around by **bike** and specialist cycle tours are covered in the "Sports and outdoor activities" section (see p.44).

By bus

Buses are the staple mode of transport in Sri Lanka. Buses screech past on the island's major highways every few seconds, and any town of even the remotest consequence will be served by fairly regular connections. That's the good news. The bad news is that bus travel in Sri Lanka is almost uniformly uncomfortable and frequently nerve-racking as well, given the gung-ho driving styles of some drivers. The average Sri Lankan bus journey is a stop-start affair: stomach-tightening bursts of speed alternate with periods of creeping slowness, all played out to an accompaniment of parping horns, blaring Sinhala pop music and the awful noises of mechanical protest as the long-suffering bus careers around yet another corner with every panel rattling – before the inevitable slamming-on of brakes sends everyone lurching forward in their seats. And if you haven't got a seat, so much the worse. If you do, you'll probably find yourself serving as an impromptu armrest to one of the countless unfortunates standing packed in the aisle. The rear seats in large buses are the best place to sit, both because there's usually enough legroom to

stow luggage comfortably under the seat in front, and because you won't have a very clear view of whatever craziness the driver is attempting.

Buses come in a variety of forms. The basic distinction is between government or SLTB (Sri Lanka Transport Board) buses and private services.

SLTB buses

Almost all **SLTB buses** are rattling old TATA vehicles, usually painted red. These are often the oldest and slowest vehicles on the road, but can be slightly more comfortable than private buses (see below) in that the conductor won't feel the same compulsion to squeeze as many passengers on board, or the driver to thrash the vehicle flat out in order to get to the next stop ahead of competing vehicles (accidents caused by rival bus drivers racing one another are all too common).

Private buses

Private buses come in different forms. At their most basic, they're essentially the same as SLTB buses, consisting of large, arthritic old rustbuckets that stop everywhere; the only difference is that private buses will usually be painted white and emblazoned with the stickers of whichever company runs them. Some private companies operate slightly faster services, large buses known variously as "semi-express", "express" or "inter-city", which (in theory at least) make fewer stops en route.

At the top end of the scale, **private minibuses**, often described as "express" and/or "luxury" services (although the description should be taken with a large pinch of salt) offer the fastest way of getting around. These are smaller vehicles with air-conditioning and tinted, curtained windows, though the tiny seats and lack of luggage space (your baggage will often end up on your lap or between your legs) can make them more uncomfortable than SLTB services, especially if you're tall. (If the vehicle isn't packed to capacity you could try paying for an extra seat on which to put your luggage – the conductor might insist you do this anyway.) In theory, express minibuses only make limited stops at major bus stations en route, although in practice it's up to the driver and/or conductor as to where they stop and for how long, and how many people they're willing to cram in.

Fares, timetables and stops

Bus **fares**, on both private and SLTB services, are extremely low. For journeys on non-express buses, count on around Rs.50 per hour's travel, rising to around Rs.80 on express minibuses. Note that on the latter you may have to pay the full fare for the entire route served by the bus, irrespective of where you get off. If you do want to get off before the end of the journey, let the driver/conductor know when you board.

Services on longer and/or less frequently served routes run to fixed **timetables**. Services on shorter or particularly popular routes tend to leave as soon as the vehicle is full. In general, departures on longer-distance routes tend to be more frequent in the morning, tailing off in the afternoon. Seat **reservations** are almost unheard of except on long-distance buses to Jaffna.

Another problem with Sri Lankan buses is the difficulty of finding the relevant service. Most timetables and signs are in Sinhala only, as are many of the destination boards displayed by buses – it's useful to get an idea of the characters you're looking for (see p.448). All bus stations have one or more information booths (although they're often not signposted) where staff can point you in the right direction, as well as providing latest timetable information. If arriving at a larger terminal by tuktuk, it's a good idea to enlist the help of your driver in locating the right bus.

Express services generally only halt at bus terminals or other recognized **stops**. Other types of services will usually stop wherever there's a passenger to be picked up – just stand by the roadside and stick an arm out. If you're flagging down a bus by the roadside, one final hazard is in getting on. Drivers often don't stop completely, instead slowing down just enough to allow you to jump aboard. Keep your wits about you, especially if you're weighed down with heavy luggage, and be prepared to move fast when the bus pulls in – or risk seeing it simply pull off again without you.

By train

Sri Lanka's **train** network, built by the British during the nineteenth century and little changed since, offers a characterful way of getting around the island, and for many visitors a trip aboard one of these chuntering old relics (especially on the marvellously scenic hill country line) is a highlight of a trip to Sri Lanka. Travel by rail is, however, generally slower than by bus, and the charm of the experience often involves a fair dose of frustration – delays are the norm and progress can be incredibly laborious, and can seem even more tedious if you end up standing up in an overcrowded carriage. Nonetheless, Sri Lankan trains are worth experiencing, if only once.

The train network

The network comprises three principal lines: the **coast line**, which runs along the west coast from Puttalam in the north, heading south via Negombo, Colombo, Kalutara, Bentota, Beruwala, Aluthgama, Ambalangoda, Hikkaduwa and Galle to Weligama and Matara (with an extension as far as Kataragama currently under construction). The **hill country line** runs from Colombo to Kandy then on to Hatton (for Adam's Peak), Nanu Oya (for Nuwara Eliya), Haputale, Bandarawela, Ella and Badulla. The **northern line** runs from Colombo through Kurunegala to Anuradhapura and Vavuniya before terminating at Omantai. Two additional branches run off this line: the first to Polonnaruwa and Batticaloa, the second to Trincomalee.

Types of train

Trains comprise three classes. Most services consist exclusively of **second-** and **third-class** carriages. There's not actually a huge amount of difference between the two: second-class seats are slightly more padded and comfortable, and there are fans in the carriages, but the main bonus is that the carriages tend to be (very slightly) less overcrowded. **First class** covers three different types of seating, which are only available on selected trains. These are seats on inter-city trains and in the observation car (see p.30) on hill country trains; seats in the air-conditioned carriage on trains to Anuradhapura and Batticaloa; and sleeping berths on overnight services. The smallness of the island means that, unlike in neighbouring India, there are only a few **overnight trains**. These comprise first-class sleeping berths and second- and third-class "sleeperettes" (fold-down seats), plus ordinary seats.

OBSERVATION CARS AND TOURIST CARRIAGES

All inter-city services on the hill country route from Colombo to Kandy and Badulla carry a special carriage, the so-called **observation car**, with large windows and what passes for plush seating. All seats are reservable, and get snapped up quickly – you'll be lucky to get seats anything less than a week in advance, especially on the popular Colombo to Kandy run.

Booking observation car seats is slightly complicated. They are available from fourteen days in advance of the date of travel. There are 24 seats in the observation car; twenty of these are sold in Colombo and the other four in Kandy. You can buy tickets over the counter at Kandy or Colombo (it's possible to buy tickets in Colombo to travel from Kandy, and vice versa). If you want to reserve an observation car seat from other stations along the line, they'll have to be ordered through either of those two cities, which obviously requires time and a degree of pre-planning.

As well as the traditional observation car, two independent companies – Expo Rail (☏011 522 5050, ⓦexporail.lk) and Rajadhani Express (☏071 0355 355, ⓦblueline.lk) – have recently started running special **tourist carriages** on the main hill country express trains, plus a few services to Anuradhapura, Vavuniya, Trincomalee and Batticaloa. Carriages are modern, comfortable and air-conditioned, with fares starting at around Rs.750 from Colombo to Kandy – about twice the price of a seat in the traditional observation car, but probably worth it. Tickets can be bought over the phone or online.

Fares and booking

Despite recent price increases, **fares** are still extremely cheap. A ticket from Colombo to Kandy in second class, for instance, is currently Rs.190, while even an overnight first-class air-conditioned sleeping berth from Colombo to Batticaloa costs just Rs.900. **Advance bookings** are only available for first-class seats and sleeper berths, and for second-class sleeperettes and seats on inter-city express services between Colombo and Kandy. Reservations can be made up to ten days in advance at the Berths Booking Office (Mon–Sat 8.30am–3.30pm, Sun 8.30am–noon) at Fort Railway Station in Colombo. You can also make reservations at other stations, though they'll have to contact Colombo, so try to reserve as far ahead of the date of travel as possible. Tickets for all other types of seat can only be bought on the day of travel.

Timetables can be checked online at ⓦrailway .gov.lk/ⓦgic.gov.lk (although these may not be completely up to date) and are also sometimes posted at ⓦbest6daytoursinsrilanka.com or ⓦblue haventours.com.

By air

If time is of the essence, SriLankan Airlines' **air taxi** service (ⓦsrilankan.com/airtaxi) offers convenient high-speed connections between Colombo and many other places around the country. All these flights use Twin-Otter water planes (carrying up to fifteen passengers), which are able to land on convenient lakes and lagoons, giving access to destinations without a fixed runway. Scheduled flights currently run between Colombo and Trincomalee, Ampara, Arugam Bay, Tissamaharama, Hambantota, Dikwella, Koggala, Bentota, Kandy, Nuwara Eliya and Dambulla (with more destinations in the north and east planned). There are also thirty-minute scenic flights from Colombo, Kandy and Dambulla. The only other scheduled domestic air services in Sri Lanka at present are Expo Air's flights to Jaffna (see p.385).

If money's no object and you're really in a hurry, you can charter a **helicopter** or **private plane** through Deccan Aviation (ⓦsimplifly.com).

By car

As Sri Lankans say, in order to **drive** around the island you'll need three things: "good horn, good brakes, good luck". Although roads are generally in quite good condition, the myriad hazards they present – crowds of pedestrians, erratic cyclists, crazed bus drivers and suicidal dogs, to name just a few – plus the very idiosyncratic set of road rules followed by Sri Lankan drivers, makes driving a challenge in many parts of the island.

Self-driving

If you're determined to drive yourself, you'll need to bring an **international driving licence**, and then acquire an additional permit to drive in Sri Lanka. These can be obtained from the Automobile Association of Ceylon (☏011 242 1528), 3rd floor, 40 Sir Macan Markar Mawatha, just off Galle Face Green in Colombo (a few metres from the *Ramada* hotel). They cost Rs.1500, are valid for up to twelve months and are issued on the spot.

It's also worth equipping yourself with a good **map or atlas** (such as the *Arjuna's Road Atlas*). In terms of driving rules, it's worth remembering that, in Sri Lanka, might is right: drivers of larger vehicles (buses especially), will expect you to get out of the way if they're travelling faster than you. In addition, many drivers overtake freely on blind corners or in other dangerous places. Expect to confront other vehicles driving at speed on the wrong side of the road on a fairly regular basis.

Reliable **car hire companies** include Malkey (Ⓦmalkey.lk) and Quickshaws (Ⓦquickshaws.com), both of which have a good range of cars at competitive rates, with or without driver.

Car and driver

Given the hassle of getting around by public transport, a large proportion of visitors opt to tour Sri Lanka by hiring a **car and driver**, which offers unlimited flexibility and can be less expensive than you might expect. Some drivers will get you from A to B but nothing more; other are qualified "chauffeur-guides", government-trained and holding a tourist board licence, who can double up as **guides** at all the main tourist sights and field any questions you might have about the country.

The main problem with drivers is that many of them work on **commission**, which they receive from some, but not all, hotels, plus assorted restaurants, shops, spice gardens, jewellers and so on. This means that you and your driver's opinions might not always coincide as to where you want to stay and what you want to do – some drivers will always want to head for wherever they get the best kickbacks (and you'll also pay over the odds at these places, since the hoteliers, restaurateurs or shopkeepers have to recoup the commission they're paying the driver). If you find you're spending more time stressing out about dealing with your driver than enjoying your holiday, find another one – there are plenty of decent drivers out there.

To make sure you get a good driver, it pays to go with a reputable company which employs only Sri Lanka Tourist Board **accredited** chauffeur-guides. Make sure your driver speaks at least some English and emphasize from the outset where you do and don't want to go. Some drivers impose on their clients' good nature to the point of having meals with them and insisting on acting as guides and interpreters throughout the tour. If this is what

you want, fine; if not, don't be afraid to make it clear that you expect to be left alone when not in the car.

Cars and drivers can be hired through any of our recommended **Colombo tour operators** (see p.27), or from many other tour companies and travel agents around the island – we've listed the most reliable outfits in the relevant places in the Guide. Alternatively, most hotels and guesthouses can fix you up with a vehicle.

Prices depend more on quality than size of transport – a posh air-conditioned car will cost more than a non-air-conditioned minivan. Rates start from around $30 per day for the smallest cars, plus drivers' fees and living allowances. All top-end hotels provide meals and accommodation for drivers either for free or for a small additional charge. If you're staying in budget or mid-range places, you'll have to pay for your driver's room and food – as ever, it's best to try to establish a daily allowance for this at the outset of your trip to avoid misunderstandings and arguments later. Your driver will probably also expect a tip of $5–10 per day, depending on how highly trained they are. You'll also probably have to pay for **fuel** – now very expensive in Sri Lanka – which can add significantly to the overall cost. In addition, most companies only offer a decidedly mean 100km per day **free mileage**, which doesn't go far on the island's twisty roads, so you may well have to stump up for some excess mileage as well.

Finally, if this all sounds too stressful (and it can be, unfortunately), you could always just hire vehicles **by the day** as you go round the island. The actual vehicle-hire cost may be a bit higher, but you won't have to worry about having to house and feed your driver, and they're less likely to put pressure on you to visit their favourite shops, restaurants and spice gardens.

By rickshaw

The lines of motorized **rickshaws** that ply the streets of every city, town and village are one of Sri Lanka's most characteristic sights. Known by various names – tuktuks, three-wheelers, trishaws or (rather more optimistically) "taxis" – they are the staple means of travelling short distances in Sri Lanka, principally short hops within towns, although they can also be useful for excursions and can even, at a pinch, be handy for long journeys if you get stranded or can't be bothered to wait around for a bus. The vehicles themselves are mainly Indian-made Bajaj rickshaws, often decorated by their drivers with whimsical fluorescent stickers, statuettes, plastic flowers or other items decorative or talismanic.

It's impossible to walk far in Sri Lanka without being solicited for custom by the owner of one of these vehicles. If you do need a ride, rickshaws are extremely convenient and can even be fun, in a slightly nerve-racking way, as they weave through the traffic, often at surprising speeds. In addition, the sheer number around means that you always have the upper hand in bargaining – if you can't agree a decent fare, there'll always be another driver keen to take your custom.

Rickshaws do have their **drawbacks**, however. They're not particularly comfortable for long journeys, and you can't see much. In addition, tuktuks' diminutive size compared with the buses and lorries they share the road with (and the often gung-ho attitudes of their drivers) can put you at a certain risk, and you're likely to experience at least a couple of near misses with speeding traffic if you use them consistently for longer journeys.

Sri Lankan rickshaws are usually unmetered (although there are now growing numbers of metered rickshaws in Colombo); the **fare** will be whatever you can negotiate with the driver. *Never* set off without agreeing the fare beforehand. The majority of Sri Lanka's tuktuk drivers are more or less honest, and you'll often be offered a decent fare without even having to bargain; a small minority, however, are complete crooks who will (at best) simply try to overcharge you or, at worst, set you up for some kind of scam (see p.51). Given the wildly varying degrees of probity you'll encounter, it's often difficult to know exactly where you stand. A basic fare of Rs.50 per kilometre (which is what metered taxis in Colombo currently charge) serves as a general rule of thumb, though unless you have ironclad bargaining powers you'll probably pay more than this, especially in big cities and heavily touristed areas. Also bear in mind that the longer the journey, the lower the per-kilometre rate should be.

Finally, beware of rickshaw drivers who claim to have **no change** – this can even apply when trying to pay, say, for a Rs.70 fare with a Rs.100 note, with the driver claiming (perhaps truthfully) to have only Rs.10 or Rs.20 change, and hoping that you'll settle for a few rupees less. If you don't have change, check that the driver does before you set off. If you make the position clear from the outset, you're guaranteed that your driver will go through the hassle of getting change for you rather than risk losing your fare.

Accommodation

Sri Lanka has an excellent range of accommodation in all price brackets, from basic beachside shacks to elegant colonial mansions and sumptuous five-star resorts – indeed staying in one of the country's burgeoning number of luxury hotels and villas can be one of the principal pleasures of a visit to the island, if you can afford it.

Types of accommodation

Travellers on a budget will spend most of their time in **guesthouses**, usually family-run places either in or attached to the home of the owners. Some of the nicer guesthouses can be real homes from home, with good food and sociable hosts. Rooms at most places cost between $20 and $30, although you'll sometimes find cheaper deals, especially around the coast.

Hotels come in all shapes, sizes and prices, from functional concrete boxes to luxurious establishments that are virtual tourist attractions in their own right. Some of the finest hotels (particularly in the hill country) are located in old colonial buildings, offering a wonderful taste of the lifestyle and ambience of yesteryear, while the island also boasts a number of stunning modern hotels, including many designed by Sri Lanka's great twentieth-century architect **Geoffrey Bawa** (see p.126). The coastal areas are also home to innumerable **resort hotels**, the majority of which – with a few honourable exceptions – are fairly bland, populated largely by European package tourists on full-board programmes and offering a diet of horrible buffet food and plenty of organized fun.

Sri Lanka is gradually waking up to its massive **eco-tourism** potential, and now boasts a few good eco-oriented hotels and lodges. You can also stay in bungalows or camp within most of the island's

---

ACCOMMODATION PRICES

The accommodation **prices** quoted in this Guide are based on the cost of the least expensive double room in the **high season** (roughly Dec–April on the west and south coasts and hill country, May–July on the east). Outside these periods rates often fall considerably. All taxes and service charges have been included in the prices quoted.

TEN MEMORABLE PLACES TO STAY

Amanwella Tangalla. See p.178
Bar Reef Resort Kalpitiya. See p.114
Club Villa Bentota. See p.125
Galle Fort Hotel Galle. See p.151
Helga's Folly Kandy. See p.221

Heritance Kandalama Dambulla. See p.295
Jetwing Vil Uyana Sigiriya. See p.303
The Kandy House Kandy. See p.222
The Tea Factory Nuwara Eliya. See p.244
Tintagel Colombo. See p.92

national parks, although this can be difficult to arrange (see p.45). The national parks are the only places in Sri Lanka with official **campsites**, and elsewhere camping is not a recognized activity. Pitching your tent unofficially in rural areas or on the beach is likely to lead to problems with local landowners and villagers.

Sri Lanka also boasts a huge (and continually increasing) number of **villas** and **boutique hotels**, many set in old colonial villas or old tea estate bungalows (see p.240) and offering stylish and luxurious accommodation.

Hotels are **classified** using the usual one- to five-star system. In addition, some smaller hotels and guesthouses are officially approved by the Sri Lanka Tourist Board, though it must be said that such approval means absolutely nothing – indeed, if anything, approved places often tend to be worse than their non-approved rivals.

Note that there are no **youth hostels** in Sri Lanka.

Finding a room

Sri Lanka has its fair share of accommodation **touts**. One way of avoiding hassle is to ring ahead; most guesthouses will pick you up for free from the local bus or train station if given advance warning. If travelling with a driver, ring ahead in person – don't let your driver do it for you.

What you'll need from your room depends on where you are in the island; basic necessities change as you move up into the hill country and things become progressively colder. Virtually all accommodation in Sri Lanka comes with **private bathroom** (we've mentioned any exceptions in the relevant listings). In **lowland areas**, you should also always get a **fan** (usually a ceiling fan; floor-standing fans are much less common, and much less effective) – don't stay anywhere without one, unless you're happy to sleep in a puddle of sweat. It's also worth checking that the fan works properly (both that it runs at a decent speed and doesn't make a horrible noise). In lowland areas, room size and ceiling height are both important in determining how hot somewhere will be – rooms with low ceilings can become unbearably stuffy. In some

areas (notably Arugam Bay) many places are built with their roofs raised slightly above the top of the walls, so that cool air can circulate freely through the gap (although, equally, it provides free access to insects). Smarter places will also usually have air-conditioning and/or hot water; the cheapest places in the lowlands are unlikely to have either – we've mentioned any exceptions in the listings (though given how humid it is, cold-water showers are no particular hardship). **Mosquito nets** are provided in most places, although it's well worth carrying your own.

In the cooler climes of the **hill country**, most places in all categories have hot water (again, we've mentioned any exceptions). As a general rule, you'll need a fan in all places up to and including Kandy, and hot water in Kandy and anywhere higher. In the highest parts of the island, particularly Nuwara Eliya, you'll usually need some form of **heating** and/or a good supply of **blankets**. Few hill country establishments provide mosquito nets, which isn't generally a problem – these irritating little creatures shouldn't (in theory at least) be able to survive at these altitudes, though in practice you might be unlucky enough to have an unusually hardy specimen buzzing in your ear anywhere in the island.

There are a few other things worth bearing in mind when choosing a room. Check how many lights there are and whether they work: Sri Lankan hoteliers have a penchant for twenty-watt bulbs, and rooms can be very dingy. And if you're staying in a family guesthouse, keep an eye out for loud children, dogs or television sets in the vicinity of your room; and make sure you get a room away from any noisy nearby roads.

Finally, remember that most Sri Lankans go to bed early. If you're staying at a small guesthouse and you go out for dinner and a few beers, it's not uncommon to find yourself locked out on your return – any time after 9pm. Let your hosts know when to expect you back.

Room rates

Room rates in lower-end places reflect Sri Lanka's **bargaining culture** – exact rates are often

GEOFFREY BAWA HOTELS

Avani Bentota Bentota. See p.125
Avani Kalutara Resort Kalutara.
   See p.116
Bentota Beach Hotel Bentota. See p.125
Blue Water Kalutara. See p.116
Club Villa Bentota. See p.125
Heritance Ahungalla Ahungalla. See p.128

Heritance Ayurveda Maha Gedara
   Beruwala. See p.119
Heritance Kandalama Dambulla. See p.295
Jetwing Beach Negombo. See p.104
Jetwing Lighthouse Galle. See p.152
Lunuganga Bentota. See p.125
Paradise Road The Villa Bentota. See p.125

somewhat notional, as owners will vary prices to reflect the season, levels of demand and how rich they think you look. It's always worth bargaining, even in top-end places, especially if you're planning to stay a few nights, or if business is slow. If you're travelling on your own, you'll have to work harder to get a decent price since many establishments don't have **single rooms or rates** (and where they exist, they're still usually two-thirds to three-quarters of the price of a double). Try to establish what the price of a double would be, and bargain from there.

In many places, your hotel or guesthouse will also be the place you're most likely to eat, and **half- and full-board rates** are common. These can often work out to be extremely good value, though the food can be bland; obviously, the appeal of all-inclusive options depends on the presence or absence of other places to eat in the vicinity.

Prices in most coastal areas are also subject to **seasonal variations**. The most pronounced seasonal variation is along the west coast, where rates at almost all places rise (usually by between 25 and 50 percent) from November 1 through to mid- or late April. Some places along the south coast also put up their prices during this period. East coast places tend to raise rates from around April through to September. Rates in particular towns also rise if there's a big festival or other event going on locally – as during the Esala Perahera at Kandy – or during important holidays, as during the Sinhalese New Year in Nuwara Eliya, when accommodation prices everywhere treble or quadruple.

Room rates at mid- and top-end places are often quoted in **dollars** for convenience, but are payable in rupees only (a few places along the west coast quote prices in euros, again usually payable in rupees). Make sure you clarify whether any **additional taxes** will be added to the bill or are already included in the quoted price (the so-called "nett" rate). Cheaper hotels and guesthouses tend to quote nett rates; upmarket places are more likely to quote rates excluding taxes and service charge, although there's no hard and fast rule. Many places

add a ten percent "service charge" while there are also several other government taxes which may or may not be figured into the quoted price, but which can potentially add up to 27 percent to the total bill – a nasty surprise when you come to check out, especially since these taxes will most likely also have been added to your food and drink bill.

Finally, note that many hotels operate a **dual-pricing system** whereby foreigners pay more (sometimes significantly more) than locals. If you have a resident's visa, you may be eligible for local rates.

SRI LANKAN ACCOMMODATION ONLINE

Between them, the following Sri Lankan specialists cover pretty much all the best mid-range and top-end places in the island, including numerous gorgeous little villas and tea estate bungalows which you might not hear about otherwise, as well as more mainstream hotels.

Boutique Sri Lanka Ⓦ boutiquesrilanka.com
Eden Villas Ⓦ villasinsrilanka.com
Red Dot Tours Ⓦ reddottours.com
Sri Lanka in Style Ⓦ srilankainstyle.com

Eating and drinking

Sri Lanka boasts a fascinatingly idiosyncratic culinary heritage, the result of a unique fusion of local produce with recipes and spices brought to the island over the centuries by Indians, Arabs, Malays, Portuguese, Dutch and English.

The staple dish is **rice and curry**, at its finest a miniature banquet whose contrasting flavours – coconut milk, chillies, curry leaves, cinnamon, garlic and "Maldive fish" (an intensely flavoured pinch of sun-dried tuna) – bear witness to Sri Lanka's status as one of the original spice islands. There are plenty of other unique **specialities** to explore and enjoy – hoppers, string hoppers, *kottu rotty*, *lamprais* and *pittu* – as well as plentiful **seafood**.

Sri Lankan cuisine can be incredibly fiery – sometimes on a par with Thai, and far hotter than most Indian cooking. Many of the island's less gifted chefs compensate for a lack of culinary subtlety with liberal use of **chilli** powder; at the same time, as a tourist you'll often be seen as a weak-kneed individual who is liable to faint at the merest suspicion of spiciness. You'll often be asked how hot you want your food; "medium" usually gets you something that's neither bland nor requires the use of a fire extinguisher. If you do overheat during a meal, remember that water only adds to the pain of a burnt palate; a mouthful of plain rice, bread or beer is much more effective.

Sri Lankans say that you can't properly enjoy the flavours and textures of food unless you **eat with your fingers**, although tourists are almost always provided with cutlery by default. As elsewhere in Asia, you're meant to eat with your right hand, although this taboo isn't really strictly observed – if you'd really prefer to eat with your left hand, you're unlikely to turn heads.

Costs are generally reasonable (though no longer the bargain they were a few years ago). You can get a filling rice and curry meal for a couple of dollars at a local café, while main courses at most guesthouse restaurants usually cost around $5–7, and even at the island's poshest restaurants it's usually possible to find main courses for under $15. Note that many places add a ten percent service charge to the bill, while more upmarket restaurants may add additional government taxes of varying amounts (usually 13–15 percent) on top of that.

Be aware that the typical vagaries of Sri Lankan **spelling** mean that popular dishes can appear on menus in a bewildering number of forms: *idlis* can become *ittlys*, *vadais* turn into *wadais*, *kottu rotty* transforms into *kotturoti* and *lamprais* changes to *lumprice*. You'll also be regaled with plenty of unintentionally humorous offerings such as "cattle fish", "sweat and sour" or Adolf Hitler's favourite dish, "nazi goreng".

Where to eat

Although Sri Lankan cooking can be very good, few **restaurants** really do justice to the island's cuisine. There's no particular tradition of eating out and, except in Colombo, few independent restaurants of note. Locals either eat at home or patronize the island's innumerable scruffy little cafés, often confusingly signed as "hotels", which serve up filling meals for a dollar or two: rough-and-ready portions

of rice and curry, plus maybe hoppers or *kottu rotty*. However as the food is usually pretty ordinary, eating in local cafés is more of a social than a culinary experience.

Given the lack of independent tourist restaurants, most visitors end up taking the majority of their meals in their **hotel** or **guesthouse**. The sort of food and setting you'll encounter varies wildly, from the big bland restaurants at the coastal resorts to the cosy guesthouses of Ella and Galle, where you can experience the sort of home cooking that rarely makes its way onto menus at larger hotels. In general, however, choice is limited, with most places offering a standard assortment of fried noodles or rice, a small range of seafood and meat dishes (usually including a couple of devilled options) and maybe a few kinds of curry.

Most of the island's **independent restaurants** can be found in Colombo and, to a lesser extent, Kandy, Galle and Negombo, where tourism has inspired the growth of a modest local eating scene. The most common independent restaurants are aimed at tourists, with a mix of Sri Lankan, seafood and Western dishes; you'll also find a few South Indian-style places, especially in Colombo.

If you want to eat like the locals, you'll find **lunch packets** on sale at local cafés and street stalls all over the country between around 11am and 2pm. These usually include a big portion of steamed rice along with a piece of curried chicken, fish or beef (vegetarians can get an egg), some vegetables and *sambol* (see p.36). At less than two dollars, they're the cheapest way to fill up in Sri Lanka, although probably best avoided until your stomach and tastebuds are properly acclimatized to the local cooking.

Rice and curry

The island's signature dish is the ubiquitous **rice and curry**, the staple food of almost every Sri Lankan man, woman and child, served up in just about every café and restaurant across the land. A really good Sri Lankan rice and curry can be a memorable experience, although it's worth noting that the dish bears zero resemblance to the classic curries of North India. Typical Sri Lankan curry sauces (known as *kiri hodhi*, or "milk gravy") are made from coconut milk infused with chillies and various other spices – much more like a Thai green or red curry than anything you'll find in India.

Basic rice and curry (not "curry and rice" –the rice is considered the principal ingredient), as served up in local cafés islandwide, consists of a plate of rice topped with a few dollops of veg curry, a hunk of chicken or fish and a spoonful of *sambol*. More sophisticated versions comprise the inevitable mound of rice accompanied by as many as fifteen side dishes (a kind of miniature banquet said to have been inspired by Indonesian *nasi padang*, which was transformed by the Dutch into the classic *rijsttafel*, or "rice table", and introduced to Sri Lanka sometime in the eighteenth century). These generally include a serving of meat or fish curry plus accompaniments such as curried pineapple, potato, aubergine (*brinjal*), sweet potatoes, okra (lady's fingers) and dhal. You'll probably also encounter some more unusual **local vegetables**. Curried jackfruit is fairly common, as are so-called "drumsticks" (*murunga* – a bit like okra). Other ingredients you might encounter include ash plantain (*alu kesel*), snake gourd (*patolah*), bitter gourd (*karawila*) and breadfruit (*del*), along with many more outlandish and unpronounceable types of regional produce. Another common accompaniment is **mallung**: shredded green vegetables, lightly stir-fried with spices and grated coconut.

Rice and curry is usually served with a helping of **sambol**, designed to be mixed into your food to give it a bit of extra kick. *Sambols* come in various forms, the most common being *pol sambol* (coconut *sambol*), an often eye-watering combination of chilli powder, chopped onions, salt, grated coconut and "Maldive fish" (salty, intensely flavoured shreds of sun-dried tuna). Treat it with caution. You might also come across the slightly less overpowering *lunu miris*, consisting of chilli powder, onions, Maldive fish and salt; and the more gentle, sweet-and-sour *seeni sambol* ("sugar sambol").

Funnily enough, the **rice** itself is often fairly uninspiring – don't expect to find the delicately spiced pilaus and biryanis of North India. Sri Lanka produces many types of rice, but the stuff served in restaurants is usually fairly low-grade, although you may occasionally come across the nutritious and distinctively flavoured red and yellow rice (a bit like brown rice in taste and texture) that are grown in certain parts of the island.

Other Sri Lankan specialities

Sri Lanka's tastiest snack, the engagingly named **hopper** (*appa*) is a small, bowl-shaped pancake traditionally made from a batter containing coconut milk and palm toddy, and is usually eaten either at breakfast or, most commonly, dinner. Hoppers are cooked in a small wok-like dish, meaning that most of the mix sinks to the bottom, making them soft and doughy at the base, and thin and crisp around the edges. Various ingredients can be poured into the hopper. An egg fried in the middle produces an egg hopper, while sweet ingredients like yoghurt or honey are also sometimes added. Alternatively, plain hoppers can be eaten as an accompaniment to curry. Not to be confused with the hopper are **string hoppers** (*indiappa*), tangled little nests of steamed rice vermicelli noodles, often eaten with a dash of dhal or curry for breakfast.

Another rice substitute is **pittu**, a mixture of flour and grated coconut, steamed in a cylindrical bamboo mould – it looks a bit like coarse couscous. Derived from the Dutch *lomprijst*, **lamprais** is another local speciality: a serving of rice baked in a plantain leaf along with accompaniments such as a chunk of chicken or a boiled egg, plus some veg and pickle.

Muslim restaurants are the place to go for **rotty** (or *roti*), a fine, doughy pancake – watching these being made is half the fun, as the chef teases small balls of dough into huge sheets of almost transparent thinness. A dollop of curried meat, veg or potato is then plonked in the middle and the *rotty* is folded up around it; the final shape depends on the whim of the chef – some prefer crepe-like squares, others opt for samosa-style triangles, some a spring roll. *Rottys* can also be chopped up and stir-fried with meat and vegetables, a dish known as **kottu rotty**. You'll know when *kottu rotty* is being made because of the noise – the ingredients are usually simultaneously fried and chopped on a hotplate using a large pair of meat cleavers, producing a noisy drumming sound – part musical performance, part advertisement.

Devilled dishes are also popular, and can be delicious. These are usually prepared with a thick, spicy sauce plus big chunks of onion and chilli, though the end product often isn't as hot as you might fear (unless you eat the chillies). Devilled chicken, pork, fish and beef are all common – the last is generally considered the classic devilled dish and is traditionally eaten during drinking binges. Another local staple is the **buriani**. This has little in common with the traditional, saffron-scented North Indian biryani, being nothing more than a mound of rice with a hunk of chicken, a bowl of curry sauce and a boiled egg, but it makes a good lunchtime filler and is usually less fiery than a basic plate of rice and curry.

VEGETARIAN FOOD IN SRI LANKA

Surprisingly for such a Buddhist country, **vegetarian** food as a concept hasn't really caught on in Sri Lanka. Having said that, a large proportion of the nation's cooking is meat-free: vegetable curries, vegetable *rottys*, hoppers and string hoppers – not to mention the bewildering variety of fruit on offer. Colombo's numerous pure veg South Indian restaurants are a delight, while if you eat fish and seafood, you'll have no problems finding a meal, especially around the coast.

South Indian food

Sri Lanka also boasts a good selection of "pure vegetarian" **South Indian restaurants** (vegetarian here meaning no meat, fish, eggs or alcohol); they're most common in Colombo, although they can be found islandwide wherever there's a significant Tamil population. These cheerfully no-nonsense places cater to a local clientele and serve up a delicious range of South Indian-style dishes at giveaway prices. The standard dish is the **dosa**, a crispy rice pancake served in various forms: either plain, with ghee (clarified butter), onion or, most commonly, as a masala dosa, folded up around a filling of curried potato. You'll also find **uttapam**, another (thicker) type of rice pancake that's usually eaten with some kind of curry, and **idlis**, steamed rice cakes served with curry sauces or chutneys.

Some South Indian places (again, particularly in Colombo) serve a fascinating array of **sweets**, luridly coloured and heavily spiced.

Short eats

Another classic Tamil savoury which has entered the Sri Lanka mainstream is the **vadai** (or *wadaî*), a spicy doughnut made of deep-fried lentils – no train or bus journey is complete without the sound of hawkers marching up and down the carriage or vehicle shouting "Vadai-vadai-vadai!". Platefuls of *vadais*, *rottys* and bread rolls are often served up in cafés under the name of **short eats** – you help yourself and are charged for what you eat, though be aware that these plates are passed around and their contents indiscriminately prodded by all and sundry, so they're not particularly hygienic.

Other cuisines

There are plenty of **Chinese restaurants** around the island, though many are just glorified local drinking holes serving up plates of fried rice and noodles. Genuine places, as listed in the Guide, are often good, although the predominantly Cantonese-style dishes are usually spiced up for Sri Lankan tastes. As usual, Colombo has easily the best range of such places.

Indonesian dishes introduced by the Dutch are also sometimes served in tourist restaurants – most commonly *nasi goreng* (fried rice with meat or seafood, topped with a fried egg) and *gado gado* (salad and cold boiled eggs in a peanut sauce), although these rarely taste much like the Indonesian originals.

Other cuisines are restricted to Colombo. **Thai** food has made some limited inroads, while **Japanese** cuisine is also modestly popular. Colombo is also where you'll find Sri Lanka's surprisingly small number of decent **North Indian** restaurants, along with a few excellent European places. Smarter hotels all over the island make some attempt to produce **European** cuisine, though with wildly varying results.

Seafood

Not surprisingly, **seafood** plays a major part in the Sri Lankan diet, with fish often taking the place of meat. Common fish include tuna, seer (a firm-bodied white fish), mullet and the delicious melt-in-the-mouth butterfish, as well as pomfret, bonito and shark. You'll also find lobster, plentiful crab, prawns and cuttlefish (calamari). The Negombo lagoon, just north of Colombo, is a particularly prized source of seafood, including gargantuan jumbo prawns the size of a well-fed crab.

Seafood is usually a good bet if you're trying to avoid highly spiced food. Fish is generally prepared in a fairly simple manner, usually fried (sometimes in breadcrumbs) or grilled and served with a twist of lemon or in a mild garlic sauce. You will, however, find some fiery fish curries, while chillied seafood dishes are also fairly common – chilli crab is particularly popular.

Desserts and sweets

The classic Sri Lankan dessert is **curd** (yoghurt made from buffalo milk) served with honey or **kitul** (a sweet syrup from the kitul palm). When boiled and left to set hard, kitul becomes **jaggery**, an all-purpose Sri Lanka sweet or sweetener. Other characteristic desserts are **wattalappam**, an egg pudding of Malay origins which tastes faintly like crème caramel, but with a sweeter and less slippery texture. **Kiribath** is a dessert of rice cakes cooked in milk and served with jaggery – it's also traditionally made for weddings, and is often the first solid food fed to babies. A South Indian dessert you might come across is **faluda**, a colourful cocktail of milk, syrup, jelly, ice cream and ice served in a tall glass like an Indian knickerbocker glory. **Ice cream** is usually factory made, and safe to eat; the most widely available brand is Elephant House. You'll also find a wide selection of **cakes**, often in fluorescent colours and in a bizarre variety of curried flavours.

Fruits

Sri Lanka has a bewildering variety of **fruits**, from the familiar to the less so, including several classic Southeast Asian fruits introduced from Indonesia by the Dutch. The months given in brackets below refer to the periods when each is in season (where no months are specified, the fruit is available year-round). Familiar fruits include pineapple, mangoes (April–June & Nov–Dec), avocados (April–June) and coconuts, as well as a wide variety of **bananas**, from small sweet yellow specimens to enormous red giants. **Papaya** (pawpaw), a distinctively sweet and pulpy fruit, crops up regularly in fruit salads, but the king of Sri Lankan fruits is undoubtedly the **jackfruit** (April–June & Sept–Oct), the world's largest fruit, a huge, elongated dark-green monster, rather like an enormous marrow in shape, whose fibrous flesh can either be eaten raw or cooked in curries. **Durian** (July–Sept) is another outsized specimen: a large green beast with a spiky outer shell. It's very much an acquired taste: though the flesh smells rather like blocked drains, it's widely considered a great delicacy, and many also believe it to have aphrodisiac qualities. The strangest-looking fruit, however, is the **rambutan** (July–Sept), a delicious, lychee-like fruit enclosed in a bright-red skin that's covered in tentacles. Another prized Sri Lankan delicacy is the **mangosteen** (July–Sept), which looks a little like a purple tomato, with a rather hard shell-like skin that softens as the fruit ripens. The delicate and delicious flesh tastes a bit like a grape with a slight citrus tang. Equally distinctive is the **wood apple**, a round, apple-sized fruit covered in an indestructible greyish bark, inside which is a red pulpy flesh, rather bitter-tasting and full of seeds. It's sometimes served with honey poured over it. You might also come across **custard apples**: greenish,

apple-sized fruits with knobbly exteriors (they look a bit like artichokes) and smooth, sweet white flesh; **guavas**, smooth, round yellow-green fruits, usually smaller than an apple and with slightly sour-tasting flesh around a central core of seeds. Other exotic fruits you might encounter include soursop, lovi-lovi, sapodilla, rose apple, and beli fruit (not to be confused with nelli fruit, a kind of Sri Lankan gooseberry). Finally, look out for the tiny **gulsambilla** (Aug–Oct), Sri Lanka's strangest fruit – like a large, furry green seed enclosing a tiny, tartly flavoured kernel.

Drink

It's best to avoid tap water in Sri Lanka (see p.53). **Bottled water** is available everywhere, sourced from various places in the hill country and retailed under a baffling range of names. Check that the seal hasn't been broken – but note that they're all usually pretty grubby.

Soft drinks

International brands of **soft drinks** – Pepsi, Coca-Cola, Sprite – are widely available and cheap, but it's much more fun (and better for the Sri Lankan economy) to explore the glorious range of outlandish soft drinks produced locally by Olé, Lion and Elephant. These include old-fashioned favourites like cream soda and ginger beer, and unique local brands like Portello (which tastes a bit like Vimto) and the ultra-sweet, lollipop-flavoured Necta. **Ginger beer** is particularly common, and very refreshing – the Elephant brand uses natural ginger, which is meant to be good for the stomach and digestion.

The slightly sour-tasting **coconut water** (*thambili*) isn't to everyone's taste, although it's guaranteed safe, having been locked up in the heart of the coconut. It's also claimed to be an excellent hangover cure thanks to its mix of glucose and potassium, which also makes it good to drink if you're suffering from diarrhoea.

Tea and coffee

Despite the fame of Sri Lanka's **tea**, most of the stuff served up is usually fairly bland – and you won't find the marvellous masala teas of India. Normal tea is often called "milk tea" (ask for "milk and sugar separate" if you want to add your own or you might end up with a cupful of supersweet bilge). "Bed tea" is just ordinary tea brought to your room for breakfast. **Coffee** is sometimes a better bet. This is generally either Nescafé or locally produced coffee – the latter is usually unexciting but perfectly drinkable, although you're normally left with a big layer of silt at the bottom of the cup. Proper machine-made coffee is increasingly available.

Alcoholic drinks

Sri Lanka has a strong drinking culture – beer was introduced by foreign captives during the Kandyan period, and the islanders have never looked back. The island's two staple forms of alcohol are lager and arrack. **Lager** is usually sold in large (625ml) bottles; draught lager is rare. There's not a great choice of brands; all clock in with an alcohol content of just under five percent. The staple national tipple, the ubiquitous Lion Lager, is uninspiring but perfectly drinkable. More palatable beers include Carlsberg (brewed under licence in Sri Lanka), the delicately malty Three Coins, and Three Coins Riva, a good wheat beer. Anchor beer is also becoming increasingly popular: soft, creamy and a bit bland. Lion also brews a very dense stout, Lion Stout, which is virtually a meal in itself, as well as Lion Strong (eight percent a.b.v.), beloved by local alcoholics. As you'd expect, lager is relatively expensive in Sri Lankan terms, ranging from around Rs.120 in a liquor shop to Rs.250–400 or more in most bars and restaurants. Imported beers, on the rare occasions you can find them, come with a hefty mark-up.

Two more distinctively local types of booze come from the versatile coconut. **Toddy**, tapped from the flower of the coconut, is non-alcoholic when fresh but ferments into a beverage faintly reminiscent of cider – it's sold informally in villages around the country, though unless you're travelling with a Sinhala-speaker it's difficult to track down. When fermented and refined, toddy produces **arrack** (33 percent proof), Sri Lanka's national beverage for the strong-livered – you won't go far before finding a group of voluble Sri Lankan men clustered around a bottle. Arrack is either drunk neat, mixed with coke or lemonade or used in tourist-oriented bars and restaurants as a base for cocktails. It's available in various grades and is usually a darkish brown, though there are also clear brands like White Diamond and White Label; the smoother, double-distilled arrack tastes faintly like rum. Imported **spirits** are widely available, but are predictably expensive. There are also locally produced versions of most spirits, including rather rough whisky, brandy, rum and vodka, as well as various brands of quite palatable lemon gin.

Where to drink

Most people drink in their hotel bar or guesthouse. There are a few decent **bars** and English-style **pubs** in Colombo, Kandy and a few tourist resorts, but most local bars are gloomy and rather seedy places, and very much a male preserve. Alcohol is available from supermarkets in larger towns. In smaller places, there are usually a few rather disreputable-looking **liquor shops** – usually a small kiosk, piled high with bottles of beer and arrack and protected by stout security bars. You're technically not allowed to buy alcohol on full-moon (poya) days, although tourist hotels and bars often discreetly serve visitors.

The media

Sri Lanka has an extensive English-language media, including numerous newspapers and radio stations, though journalistic standards are not especially high, thanks at least partly to heavy-handed state control exercised over large sections of the media. Numerous journalists were threatened, abducted or even murdered during the final phase of the civil war (see p.418), and government repression of outspoken media critics remains a reality of the current regime, leading to the largely tame press you see today.

There are also several good, independent **online** resources for Sri Lankan news. The recently established Colombo Telegraph (ⓦcolombotelegraph .com), run by a group of expatriate journalists, is particularly good, while the BBC's ⓦbbc.co.uk/news has a huge searchable archive of stories dating back to around 1997, while ⓦbbc.co.uk/sinhala offers a dedicated portal for breaking Sri Lankan news. In addition, ⓦtheacademic.org has comprehensive links to Sri Lanka-related news stories across the web.

Newspapers and magazines

Sri Lanka has a good spread of **English-language newspapers**, including three dailies – The Island (ⓦisland.lk), the Daily Mirror (ⓦdailymirror.lk) and the Daily News (ⓦdailynews.lk) – and three Sunday papers, the Sunday Observer (ⓦsundayobserver.lk), the Sunday Times (ⓦsundaytimes.lk) and the Sunday Leader (ⓦthesundayleader.lk) – the last is particularly known for its outspoken criticism of the government, which led to the killing of its editor,

Lasantha Wickramatunga, in 2009. The *Daily News* and *Sunday Observer* are both owned by the government and are little better than feeble, fifth-rate propaganda. Standards are higher in the independent papers, though all devote the majority of their coverage to domestic politics and cricket and tend to be generally cautious in criticism of the government, for obvious reasons.

There are also a fair number of English-language **magazines** available. The long-running *Explore Sri Lanka* has decent, tourist-oriented articles about all aspects of the island, while it's also worth looking out for back copies of the excellent (though now sadly defunct) *Travel Sri Lanka*. The business-focussed *Lanka Monthly Digest* (Wlmd.lk) also sometimes runs interesting general features on the island. *Hi!!* magazine (Whi.lk) – Sri Lanka's answer to *Hello!* – is essential reading for anyone seeking an insight into the Colombo cocktail-party circuit.

Radio

There are a surprising number of **English-language radio stations** in Sri Lanka, although reception can be hit and miss outside Colombo and most stations broadcast on a confusing variety of frequencies in different parts of the island. Most stations churn out a predictable diet of mainstream Western pop, sometimes presented by hilariously inept DJs. The main broadcasters include TNL Rocks (101.7 FM; Wtnlrocks.com), Yes FM (101.0 FM; Wyesfmonline.com), Lite FM (89.2 FM in Colombo, 90.0 FM islandwide; Wlitefm.me), E FM (100.4 FM in Colombo; Wefm.lk), plus Gold FM (99.9 FM in Colombo and Kandy; Wgoldfm.lk), which dishes up retro-pop and easy listening. One **Sinhala-language station** that you might end up hearing a lot of (especially if you're travelling around by bus) is Shree FM (99.0 and other frequencies; Wshree.fm), beloved of bus drivers all over the island and offering a toe-curling diet of Sinhala pop inter-spersed by terrible adverts. For a more interesting selection of local music, try Sirasa FM (88.8 FM, 106.5 FM and other frequencies; Wsirasa.com).

Television

You're not likely to spend much time watching **Sri Lankan television**. There are three state-run channels (Rupavahini, Channel Eye and ITN), which broadcast almost entirely in Sinhala and Tamil, plus various local satellite TV channels which offer a small selection of English-language programming – though this is a fairly deadly mixture of shopping programmes, children's shows, pop music, soaps and the occasional duff film. Rooms in most top-end (and some mid-range) hotels have **satellite TV**, usually offering international news programmes from the BBC and/or CNN along with various channels from the India-based Star TV, including movies and sports.

Cinema

Sri Lankan **cinema** has a long history, although it continues to struggle to escape the huge shadow cast by the film industry in neighbouring India; the increasingly wide availability of television poses another challenge. The first Sinhala-language Sri Lankan film was *Kadawunu Poronduwa* (Broken Promise), premiered in 1947, although the first truly Sinhalese film is generally considered to be Lester James Peries' *Rekawa* (Line of Destiny), of 1956, which broke with the Indian all-singing all-dancing model and attempted a realistic portrayal of Sri Lankan life. Peries went on to score further triumphs with films like *Gamperaliya* (Changing Village), based on a novel by Martin Wickrama-singhe (see p.163), and served as a role model for a new generation of Sri Lankan directors. Modern Sri Lankan filmmakers have tended to focus on themes connected with the country's civil war, most famously in Prasanna Vithanage's *Death on a Full Moon Day* (1997), which portrays a blind and naive father who refuses to accept the death of his soldier son. At present, about a hundred films are released each year in Sri Lankan cinemas, with offerings in English, Tamil, Sinhala and Hindi. Sri Lankan-made films are almost exclusively in Sinhala, apart from a few in Tamil.

There are only a very modest number of **cinemas** on the island, concentrated largely in Colombo. A couple show recent Hollywood blockbusters in English; others specialize in Tamil, Hindi and Sinhala releases, and are easily spotted by their huge adver-tising hoardings showing rakish, moustachioed heroes clutching nubile heroines. Tickets for all movies cost around a dollar. You might also catch screenings of more highbrow Sri Lankan movies at cultural centres in Colombo and Kandy.

Festivals and public holidays

It's sometimes claimed that Sri Lanka has more festivals than any other country in

the world, and with four major religions on the island and no fewer than 25 public holidays, things can seem to grind to a halt with disconcerting frequency.

Virtually all the festivals are religious in nature and follow the **lunar calendar**, with every full moon signalling the start of a new month (an extra month is added every two or three years to keep the solar and lunar calendars in alignment). As a result, most festival **dates** vary somewhat from year to year, apart from a couple (such as Thai Pongol and Sinhalese New Year). Muslim festivals also follow a lunar calendar but without the corrective months which are inserted into the Buddhist lunar calendar, meaning that the dates of these festivals gradually move backwards at the rate of about eleven days per year, completing one annual cycle roughly every 32 years.

Buddhist festivals revolve around the days of the full moon – or **poya days** – which are official public holidays as well as having special religious significance (the Buddha urged his disciples to undertake special spiritual practices on each poya day, and according to traditional belief he himself was born, attained enlightenment and died on the poya day in the lunar month of Vesak). On poya days, Sri Lankan Buddhists traditionally make offerings at their local temple and perform other religious observances, while the less pious section of the population marks the occasion with riotous behaviour and widespread drunkenness. The island's most important Buddhist festivals are traditionally celebrated with enormous **peraheras**, or parades, with scores of fabulously accoutred elephants accompanied by drummers and dancers. People often travel on poya days, so transport and accommodation tend to be busy; there's also (in theory) a ban on the sale of alcohol, although tourist hotels and guesthouses will usually serve you.

Sri Lanka's main **Hindu festivals** rival the island's Buddhist celebrations in colour – in addition to the ones listed below, there are numerous other local temple festivals across the Jaffna peninsula. Sri Lanka's **Muslim festivals** are more modest affairs, generally involving only the Muslim community itself, with special prayers at the mosque. The three main celebrations (all of which are public holidays) are the Milad un-Nabi (Jan 25, 2013; Jan 13, 2014; Jan 3, 2015), celebrating the Prophet's birthday; Id ul-Fitr (Aug 8, 2013; July 28, 2014; July 10, 2015), marking the end of Ramadan; and Id ul-Allah (Oct 15, 2013; Oct 4, 2014; Sept 24, 2015), marking the beginning of pilgrimages to Mecca.

A festival calendar

Public holidays in the listings below are marked "(P)".

JANUARY

Duruthu Poya (P) Marks the first of the Buddha's three legendary visits to Sri Lanka, and celebrated with a spectacular perahera (parade) at the Raja Maha Vihara in the Colombo suburb of Kelaniya. The Duruthu poya also marks the beginning of the three-month pilgrimage season to Adam's Peak.

Thai Pongol (Jan 14/15) (P) Hindu festival, honouring the sun god Surya, Indra (the bringer of rains) and the cow, in no particular order. It's marked by ceremonies at Hindu temples, after which the first grains of the new paddy harvest are ceremonially cooked in milk in a special pot – the direction in which the liquid spills when it boils over is thought to indicate good or bad luck in the coming year.

Galle Literary Festival (late Jan/early Feb). Eminent local and international wordsmiths and culture vultures descend on Galle (see p.145).

FEBRUARY

Navam Poya (P) Commemorates the Buddha's announcement, at the age of 80, of his own impending death, celebrated with a major perahera at the Gangaramaya temple in Colombo. Although this dates only from 1979, it has become one of the island's biggest festivals, featuring a procession of some fifty elephants.

Independence Day (P) Celebrates Sri Lanka's independence on February 4, 1948, with parades, dances and games.

Maha Sivarathri (Feb/March) (P) Hindu festival dedicated to Shiva, during which devotees perform a one-day fast and an all-night vigil.

MARCH

Medin Poya (P) Marks the Buddha's first visit to his father's palace following his enlightenment.

Good Friday (March/April) (P) An Easter Passion play is performed on the island of Duwa, near Negombo.

Galle/Jaffna Music Festival Three-day music festival held in Galle and Jaffna on alternate years and featuring an impressive line-up of local and international folk musicians, dancers and other performers.

APRIL

Bak Poya (P) Celebrates the Buddha's second visit to Sri Lanka.

Sinhalese and Tamil New Year (P) Coinciding with the start of the southwest monsoon and the end of the harvest season, the Buddhist and Hindu New Year is a family festival during which presents are exchanged and the traditional kiribath (rice cooked with milk and cut into diamond shapes) is prepared. Businesses close, rituals are performed, new clothes are worn and horoscopes are cast. April 13 is New Year's Eve; April 14 is New Year's Day.

MAY

Labour Day (May 1) (P) The traditional May Day bank holiday.

Vesak Poya (P) The most important of the Buddhist poyas, this is a threefold celebration commemorating the Buddha's birth, enlightenment and death, all of which are traditionally thought to have happened on the day of the Vesak Poya. In addition, the last of the Buddha's three alleged visits to Sri Lanka is claimed to have been on a Vesak poya day. Lamps are lit in front of houses, and pandals (platforms decorated with scenes from the life of the Buddha) are erected throughout the country. Buses and cars are decorated with streamers, and free food (from rice and curry to Vesak sweetmeats) is distributed in roadside booths (dansal). Meanwhile, devout Buddhists visit temples, meditate and fast. The day after the Vesak Poya is also a public holiday. Vesak also marks the end of the Adam's Peak pilgrimage season. The sale of alcohol, meat and fish in public restaurants is prohibited for a six-day period around the poya day, though hotels and guesthouses may be able to circumvent this when serving their own guests.

JUNE

Poson Poya (P) Second only in importance to Vesak, Poson Poya commemorates the introduction of Buddhism to Sri Lanka by Mahinda, marked by mass pilgrimages to Anuradhapura, while thousands of white-robed pilgrims climb to the summit of Mihintale.

JULY

Esala Poya (P) Celebrates the Buddha's first sermon and the arrival of the Tooth Relic in Sri Lanka. The lunar month of Esala is the season of festivals, most notably the great Esala Perahera in Kandy (see p.208), Sri Lanka's most extravagant festival. There are also festivals at Kataragama (see below), Dondra and Bellanwila (a southern Colombo suburb) and a big seven-day celebration at Unawatuna, during which thousands descend on the village and beach.

Kataragama Festival Festival at Kataragama during which Hindu devotees fire-walk and indulge in various forms of ritual self-mutilation, piercing their skin with hooks and weights, and driving skewers through their cheeks and tongues.

Hikkaduwa Beach Festival (July/Aug) Three-day beach bash with international DJs.

Vel (July/Aug) Colombo's most important Hindu festival, dedicated to Skanda/Kataragama and featuring two exuberant processions during which the god's chariot and *vel* (spear) are carried across the city from the Pettah to temples in Wellawatta and Bambalapitiya.

AUGUST

Nikini Poya (P) Marks the retreat of the Bhikkhus following the Buddha's death, commemorated by a period of fasting and of retreat for the monastic communities.

SEPTEMBER

Binara Poya (P) Commemorates the Buddha's journey to heaven to preach to his mother and other deities.

Dussehra (Sept/Oct) Also known as Durga Puja, this Hindu festival honours Durga and also commemorates the day of Rama's victory over Ravana.

OCTOBER

Vap Poya (P) Marks the Buddha's return to earth and the end of the Buddhist period of fasting.

Deepavali (late Oct/early Nov) (P) The Hindu Festival of Lights (equivalent to North India's Diwali), commemorating the return from exile

of Rama, hero of the Ramayana (holy scripture), with the lighting of lamps in Tamil households, symbolic of the triumph of good over evil, and the wearing of new clothes.

World Spice Food Festival (late Oct/early Nov) Ten days of culinary events at assorted venues around Colombo.

NOVEMBER

Il Poya (P) Commemorates the Buddha's ordination of sixty disciples.

DECEMBER

Unduvap Poya (P) Celebrates the arrival of the Bo tree sapling in Anuradhapura, brought by Ashoka's daughter, Sangamitta.

Christmas (25 Dec) (P)

Christian New Year's Eve (31 Dec)

Sport and outdoor activities

Sri Lanka's unspoilt environment and variety of landscapes offer all sorts of possibilities for outdoor and activity holidays. Water-based activities like diving and surfing are well covered, while there are plenty of other ways to get active, ranging from mountain biking and trekking to ballooning and yoga. As for spectator sports, if you're lucky enough to coincide with a match, a trip to watch Sri Lanka's cricket team in action – always an occasion of huge national excitement – is an absolute must.

Cricket

Of all the legacies of the British colonial period, the game of **cricket** is probably held dearest by the average Sri Lankan. As in India and Pakistan, cricket is undoubtedly king in the Sri Lankan sporting pantheon. Kids play it on any patch of spare ground, improvising balls, bats and wickets out of rolled-up bits of cloth and discarded sticks, whilst the country virtually grinds to a halt during international matches, with excitable crowds clustered around every available radio or television set.

Although the national team is a relative newcomer to international cricket – they were only accorded full Test status in 1982 – they've more than held their own since then. It's in the **one-day game**, however, that Sri Lanka has really taken the world by storm, capped by their triumph in the 1996 World Cup, when their fearsomely talented batting line-up – led by elegant left-hander Aravinda da Silva and the explosive Sanath Jayasuriya – blasted their way to the title (a feat they almost repeated during the 2007 and 2011 World Cups, when they reached the final).

Not surprisingly, the success of the Sri Lankan team has proved an important source of national pride and cohesion. Although Sinhalese players have traditionally dominated the squad, the Tamil population has provided perhaps Sri Lanka's finest ever player, **Muttiah Muralitharan** (or "Murali", as he's often popularly known). One of the world's most lethal spin bowlers, Muralitharan retired in 2010 after capturing an astonishing 800 wickets in test cricket, a record which is unlikely to be broken for many years. Other star players include world-class batsmen Mahela Jayawardene and Kumar Sangakkara, both of whom currently average over fifty in test matches.

Watching a match

If you get the chance, it's well worth taking in a cricket match, particularly a one-day or **Twenty20** – the vociferous crowds and carnival atmosphere are a world away from the rather staid ambience of most English cricket grounds. The island's principal Test-match **venues** are the Sinhalese Sports Club in Colombo (see p.99), Pallekele International Cricket Stadium in Kandy and the cricket ground in Galle. One-day and Twenty20 internationals are mainly held at Kandy, Galle, the Premadasa Stadium in Colombo, and the new cricket stadiums in Dambulla and Hambantota. Tickets for matches are available from the relevant venues. Note also that many of the tour operators we recommend (see p.26), Red Dot Tours in particular, offer cricketing tours to Sri Lanka. For more on Sri Lankan cricket, check out ⓦ srilankacricket.lk.

Surfing

Many of the waves that crash against the Sri Lankan coast have travelled all the way from Antarctica, and not surprisingly there are several excellent surfing spots. The outstanding destination is **Arugam Bay** on the east coast, the one place in Sri Lanka with an international reputation amongst surfheads. Other leading **surf spots** include the south coast village of Midigama, nearby Medawatta (on the edge of Matara), and Hikkaduwa. Boards are available to rent at all these places. Various places in Arugam Bay and Hikkaduwa arrange surfing trips around the coast, sometimes combined with visits to other

attractions. The surfing **season** runs from April to October at Arugam Bay, and from November to April at Midigama and Hikkaduwa.

Whitewater rafting and other watersports

The island's premier spot for **whitewater rafting** is around Kitulgala, where the Kelani Ganga river comes tumbling out of the hill country, creating boulder-strewn grade 3–4 rapids. You can either arrange trips locally or plan something in advance – reputable local operators include Jetwing Eco Holidays (ⓦ jetwingeco.com), Action Lanka (ⓦ actionlanka.com) and Adventure Asia (ⓦ ad-asia .com), all of whom can also arrange **kayaking** and **canoeing**.

Sri Lanka's watersports capital is **Bentota**, whose lagoon provides the perfect venue for all sorts of activities, including jet-skiing, speed-boating, water-skiing, inner-tubing and banana-boating – **windsurfing** is also particularly good here. You can also arrange watersports in Negombo through the *Jetwing Beach* hotel and various other ad hoc operators. **Kitesurfers** head either to Negombo or to Kalpitiya peninsula, which offers superb wind conditions and a mix of sea and more sheltered lagoon. **Wakeboarding** is also beginning to take off. Negombo is one of the main centres, along with Hikkaduwa.

Diving and snorkelling

Sri Lanka isn't usually thought of as one of Asia's premier **diving** destinations, and although you probably wouldn't come here specifically to dive, there are enough underwater attractions to make a few days' diving a worthwhile part of a visit – ⓦ divesrilanka.com offers a handy overview of what's available. Sri Lanka is also a good and cheap place to learn to dive, with schools in Bentota, Beruwala, Hikkaduwa, Unawatuna, Weligama and Uppuveli – see the relevant Guide accounts for details. Diving **packages** and **courses** are good value compared to most other places in the world. A three-day Open-Water PADI course goes for around $375, and single dives for around $30.

The **west coast** has a well developed network of schools and dive sites. Marine life is plentiful, while there are also some fine (and often technically challenging) underwater cave and rock complexes, and a string of wrecks. Diving on the **east coast** remains relatively less developed, although that is changing rapidly with the opening up of new sites and some superb wrecks, including that of the *Hermes*, near Batticaloa, a 270m-long aircraft carrier sunk during World War II and lying at a depth of 60m.

The diving **season** on the west coast runs roughly from November to April, and on the east coast from May to October; pretty much all the island's diving schools shut up out of season, although if you're really keen and don't mind diving in rough seas with poor visibility you might be able to find someone willing to take you out.

There's not a lot of really good **snorkelling** around Sri Lanka: little coral survives close to the shore, although this lack is compensated by the abundant shoals of tropical fish that frequent the coast. The island's better snorkelling spots include the beach at Polhena, Pigeon Island ant Uppuveli and, if you don't mind the boats whizzing around your ears, the Coral Sanctuary at Hikkaduwa.

Trekking

Sri Lanka's huge **trekking** potential remains largely unexploited. The hill country, in particular, offers the perfect hiking terrain – spectacular scenery, marvellous views and a pleasantly temperate climate – while trekking through the wildlife-rich lowland jungles can also be a deeply rewarding experience. A few of the tour operators we've listed (see pp.26–27) offer **walking tours**. Alternatively, good **local guides** include Sumane Bandara Illangantilake and Ravi Desappriya in Kandy (see p.226), and Neil Rajanayake in Nuwara Eliya (see p.226). In addition, shorter guided walks are often organized from eco-lodges and eco-oriented hotels, some of whom have resident guides to lead guests on walks.

Cycling

So long as you avoid the hazardous main highways, **cycling** around Sri Lanka can be a real pleasure, and the island's modest dimensions and scenic diversity make it great for touring, especially the hill country, with its cooler climate, relative lack of traffic and exhilarating switchback roads. The major caveat is **safety**: as a cyclist you are extremely vulnerable – bus and truck drivers consider cyclists a waste of valuable tarmac, and as far as they're concerned you don't really have any right to be on the road at all: be prepared to get out of the way quickly (in fact, it's generally safest to get off the tarmac completely and ride along the dirt shoulder). You are at risk not only from traffic coming from behind, but also from oncoming vehicles overtaking another vehicle, who will think nothing of forcing you into the ditch, even though they're on what is technically your side of the road.

Bikes are available for **hire** in most tourist towns (alternatively, just ask at your guesthouse – they'll probably have or know someone who has a spare bike knocking around, or who will be prepared to surrender their own to you for a small price). In some places it's also possible to hire good-quality mountain bikes. **Costs** vary wildly, but will rarely be more than a few dollars a day, often much less.

A number of the operators we've listed (see pp.26–27) offer cycling or mountain-biking **tours**, usually including a mixture of on- and off-roading and with a backup vehicle in support. Other good options include Ride Lanka (🌐ridelanka.com), Jetwing Eco Holidays (🌐jetwingeco.com), Action Lanka (🌐actionlanka.com) and Adventure Asia (🌐ad-asia.com).

Yoga and meditation

Yoga isn't nearly as established in Sri Lanka as it is in India, although many of the island's numerous Ayurvedic centres now offer classes as part of their treatment plans, and it's sometimes possible to enrol for them without taking an Ayurveda course. Otherwise, your options are pretty limited. Serious students of yoga might consider signing up for a stay at Ulpotha (🌐ulpotha.com), a wonderful rural retreat in the Cultural Triangle near Embogama (not far from the Sasseruwa and Aukana Buddhas), attracting leading international yoga teachers; prices start at around $1300 per person per week inclusive of accommodation, meals and tuition.

Meditation courses are mainly concentrated around Kandy (see p.222).

Other activities

Balloon trips are offered by various companies, offering a spectacular bird's-eye view of the island. Most flights are around the Cultural Triangle, particularly in the Dambulla and Sigiriya area, though flights are also sometimes offered in other areas, particularly the south coast. Flights generally last roughly an hour and cost around $165 per person. The leading operator is Adventure Asia (🌐ad-asia .com), who pioneered ballooning in the island. Other operators include Air Magic (🌐airmagic.lk) and Sun Rise Ballooning (🌐srilankaballooning.com).

Horseriding day-trips and longer tours can be arranged through Sri Lanka Horse Safaris

(@horsesafarissrilanka.com) at various locations around the island, including Dambulla, Sigiriya, Nuwara Eliya, Tissamaharama, Kalpitiya and Bentota. Prices are around $200 per person per day.

Sri Lanka has three gorgeous **golf courses**, at Colombo (see p.99), Kandy (see p.227) and Nuwara Eliya (see p.244); a number of operators offer special golfing **tours** (see pp.26–27).

National parks, reserves and eco-tourism

Nature conservation has a long and illustrious history in Sri Lanka – the island's first wildlife reserve is said to have been established by King Devanampiya Tissa in the third century BC, while many of the national parks and reserves that make up today's well-developed network date back to colonial times and earlier.

Administered by the **Department of Wildlife Conservation** (@dwc.gov.lk), these protected areas cover almost fifteen percent of the island's land area and encompass a wide variety of terrains, from the high-altitude grasslands of Horton Plains National Park to the coastal wetlands of Bundala. Almost all harbour a rich selection of wildlife and birds, and several are also of outstanding scenic beauty.

Sri Lanka's 22 **national parks** include two marine parks at Hikkaduwa and Pigeon Island. The most touristed are Yala, Uda Walawe, Horton Plains, Bundala, Minneriya and Kaudulla. A number of parks lie in areas affected by the civil war, and several were closed for long periods during the fighting, including Maduru Oya, Gal Oya, Wilpattu and Kumana (formerly Yala East), although all have now reopened, while a new park is being established at Mullaitivu in one of the expanses of jungle which once sheltered the LTTE.

There are numerous other protected areas dotted across the island that are run under government supervision. These are categorized variously as **nature reserves**, **strict nature reserves** (entry prohibited) and **sanctuaries**. In general these places possess important botanical significance but lack the wildlife found in the national parks, as at (to name just one example) the unique, World Heritage-listed Sinharaja Forest Reserve, Sri Lanka's last undisturbed pocket of tropical rainforest.

Visiting national parks

All national parks keep the same **opening hours**: daily from 6.30am to 6.30pm. Other than in Horton Plains, where you're allowed to walk, you'll have to hire a jeep (or boat) to take you around. There are usually jeeps (plus drivers) for hire at park entrances, although it's generally easier to hire one at the place you're staying to take you to and from the park, as well as driving you around it. Count on around $30–45 for half a day's jeep (and driver) hire, or $60–80 for a full day.

All vehicles are allocated an obligatory "tracker", who rides with you and acts as a **guide**. Some are very good, but standards do vary considerably and unfortunately many trackers speak only rudimentary English. One way of insuring yourself against the chance of getting a dud tracker is to go with a good jeep **driver** – the best are expert wildlife trackers and spotters in their own right, and may also carry binoculars and wildlife identification books. Note that except at designated spots, you're supposed to stay in your vehicle at all times; in Yala, you're also obliged to keep the hood on your jeep up.

The basic **entrance charge** per person ranges from between $10 at the less popular parks up to $15 at Yala and Uda Walawe and $20 at Horton Plains (locals, by contrast, pay entrance fees of around $0.25). This basic charge is significantly inflated by the various **additional charges** which are levied, including a "service charge" ($8/vehicle), which covers the services of your tracker, a "vehicle charge" (Rs.250/vehicle); plus tax on everything at fifteen percent (the exact entrance cost per person thus becomes slightly cheaper the more people you share a vehicle with). Children aged 6–12 pay half price; under-6s get in free. The bottom line is that, once you've factored in the cost of transport as well, you're looking at something like **$75–100** for two people for a half-day visit to a national park.

It's also possible **to stay** in many national parks, most of which are equipped with simple but adequate bungalows for visitors. Unfortunately these are difficult to book – they have to be reserved in person at the Department of Wildlife Conservation, which is inconveniently located on the outskirts of Colombo at 811A Jayanthipura Rd, Battaramula (☎011 288 8585) – the best ones tend to get snapped up very quickly. The extra charges levied on foreigners are a further disincentive. As well as paying the basic bungalow fee (around $25–30/person), you'll have to pay two days' park entrance fees, plus a raft of other massively inflated add-ons (including "service charge" and "linen charge"), and tax on everything at fifteen percent. It typically costs around $150/night for two people to stay in a park bungalow – significantly more expensive than the price of a room in one of Colombo's cheaper five-star hotels – and this is before you've even begun to cover your transport costs to, from and around the park.

You can also **camp** in any of the national parks: again you'll have to pay two days' entrance charges, plus around $15 in camping fees (plus, of course, your transport costs). You'll also have to pre-book a camping space through the Department of Wildlife Conservation in Colombo. Alternatively, Eco Team and Kulu Safari (see p.27) run (expensive) camping trips to various national parks.

Eco-tourism

Sri Lanka is one of the world's most biodiverse islands, and **eco-tourism** is beginning to play an increasingly major role in the island's tourism industry. The island has some splendid eco-lodges and eco-oriented hotels (see box below); the best general eco-tourism tour operator is Jetwing Eco Holidays (☏011 238 1201, ⊕jetwingeco.com). For more on the island's wildlife, turn to the Contexts section (see p.432).

Birdwatching is well established, and even if you've never previously looked at a feathered creature in your life, the island's outstanding range of colourful birdlife can prove surprisingly fascinating. A number of companies run specialist tours (see pp.26–27), while bird-spotting usually forms a significant part of trips to the island's national parks – although you'll see birds pretty much everywhere you go, even in the middle of Colombo.

Elephants can be seen in virtually every national park in the country, at the famous Pinnewala Elephant Orphanage and in temples and at work on roads around the country. For **leopards**, the place to head for is Yala National Park, while **whale-watching** trips start from Mirissa, just down the coast, or alternatively from Uppuveli on the east coast. There's also superb **dolphin-watching** at

Kalpitiya (plus the chance of seeing more whales). Sri Lanka is also an important nesting site for **sea turtles**; turtle watches are run nightly at the villages of Kosgoda and Rekawa.

Cultural values and etiquette

Sri Lanka is the most Westernized country in South Asia – superficially at least – and this, combined with the widespread use of English and the huge tourist industry, can often lure visitors into mistaking the island for something more familiar than it actually is. Scratch the surface, however, and examples of cultural difference can be found everywhere.

Behaving yourself

They are all very rich, and for a thing that costs one shilling they willingly give five. Also they are never quiet, going here and there very quickly, and doing nothing. Very many are afraid of them, for suddenly they grow very angry, their faces become red, and they strike any one who is near with the closed hand.

From *The Village in the Jungle*, by Leonard Woolf

Sri Lankans place great emphasis on politeness and **manners**, as exemplified by the fabulously courteous staff at top-end hotels – raising your voice in a dispute is usually counterproductive and makes you look foolish and ill-bred.

Sri Lankans are very proud of their country – "Sri Lanka good?" is one of the questions most commonly asked of visitors – and they tend to take a simple and unquestioning pride in their island, its national achievements and (especially) their cricket team.

A few Western concepts have yet to make their way to the island. Nudity and toplessness are not permitted on any Sri Lankan beaches. Overt physical displays of affection in public are also frowned upon – Sri Lankan couples hide behind enormous umbrellas in the quiet corners of parks and botanical gardens. You should eat and shake hands with people using your right hand. For more on money and bargaining, see "Costs" (p.56).

Temple etiquette

All visitors to Buddhist and Hindu temples should be appropriately dressed. In **Buddhist temples**

FIVE TOP ECO-LODGES AND HOTELS

Palagama Kalpitiya. See p.114
Jetwing Vil Uyana Sigiriya. See p.303
Ranweli Holiday Village Waikkal. See p.109
Samakanda near Galle. See p.156
Tree Tops Jungle Lodge Buttala. See p.369

this means taking off shoes and headgear and covering your shoulders and legs. Beachwear is not appropriate and can cause offence. In large temples, the exact point at which you should take off shoes and hats is sometimes ambiguous; if in doubt, follow the locals. Finally, note that walking barefoot around temples can sometimes be more of a challenge that you might imagine when the tropical sun has heated the stone underfoot to oven-like temperatures – no one will mind if you keep your socks on.

Though you should never have yourself photographed posing with a Buddha image (that is, with your back to the image), there are two other traditional Buddhist observances that are only loosely followed in Sri Lanka: the rule about not pointing your feet at a Buddha image is not as widely followed as in, say, Thailand, though you occasionally see people sitting in front of Buddhas with their legs neatly tucked under them. Equally, the traditional Buddhist rule that you should only walk around dagobas in a clockwise direction is not widely observed.

The same shoe and dress rules apply in **Hindu temples**, with a couple of twists. In some, non-Hindus aren't permitted to enter the inner shrine; in others, men are required to take off their shirt before entering, and women are sometimes barred entirely.

In some temples (Buddhist and Hindu) you will be shown around by one of the resident monks or priests and expected to make a donation. At other places, unofficial "guides" will sometimes materialize and insist on showing you round – for a consideration. Try not to feel pressured into accepting the services of unofficial guides unless you want them.

Begging, bon-bons and schoolpens

Whether or not you decide to give to **beggars** is of course a personal decision, though there's nothing wrong with handing out a few coins to the obviously old and infirm, who often congregate outside temples, churches and mosques. What is important, however, is that you do not contribute to a cycle of excessive dependence or create unrealistic expectations of foreign beneficence. For this reason, be sparing in the amounts you distribute (it's always better to give small amounts to lots of people rather than a big sum to a single unfortunate who catches your fancy) and never give handouts to children. In addition, avoid giving to beggars who specifically target tourists.

What is unfortunately widespread is a kind of pseudo-begging practised by perfectly well-to-do schoolchildren (and sometimes teenagers and even adults). This generally takes the form of requests for bon-bons (sweets), schoolpens or money (often in the form of "one foreign coin?"). Sadly, this behaviour is the result of the misguided munificence of previous visitors, who have handed out all of the above in the mistaken belief that they are helping the local population, but who have instead created a culture of begging that both demeans Sri Lankans themselves and creates hassles for all the visitors who follow in their wake. If you really want to help local communities, make your donation to a local school or contribute to a recognized charitable agency working in the area.

"Where are you going?"

Western concepts of **privacy** and solitude are little understood or valued in Sri Lanka, whose culture is based on extended family groupings and closely knit village societies in which everyone knows everyone else's business. Natural curiosity usually expresses itself in the form of endless repeated questions, most often "Where are you going?", closely followed by "What is your country?" and "What is your name?". These may drive you slightly crazy if you're spending a long time in Sri Lanka, but it's important to stay polite and remember how potentially negative an impact any rudeness or impatience on your part will have on perceptions of foreigners, and on the treatment of those who follow in your wake. A smile (even through gritted teeth) and a short answer ("Just walking. England. John.") should suffice. If you really can't bear it any more, a little surreal humour usually helps relieve the tension ("To Australia. Mars. Lord Mountbatten.") without offending local sensibilities – Sri Lankans usually take great pleasure in being given first-hand proof of the generally recognized fact that all foreigners are completely mad.

Shopping

Sri Lankan craftsmanship has a long and vibrant history, and a visit to any museum will turn up objects testifying to the skill of the island's earlier artisans, who have for centuries been producing exquisitely manufactured objects in a

wide variety of media, ranging from lacework and ola-leaf manuscripts to carvings in ivory and wood and elaborate metalwork and batiks.

Unfortunately, despite these fine traditions, much modern Sri Lankan craftsmanship has largely degenerated into the mass production of a few stereotypical items, and shopping is something of a disappointment compared to nearby countries such as India or Thailand. The decline in creativity is exemplified by the nation-wide chain of government-run **Laksala** shops, whose outlets are stuffed to the gills with a predictable assortment of clumsily painted wooden elephants, kolam masks, ugly batiks and other tourist tat. It's not all bad news, however, and there are still a few worthwhile exceptions, especially in **Colombo**, which is also the best place to buy everything else Sri Lanka has to offer, from books to tea and discount clothing.

All larger shops have fixed, marked **prices**, although if you're making a major purchase or buying several items, a polite request for a "special price" or "small discount" might knock a few rupees off, especially for gems or jewellery. The smaller and more informal the outlet, the more scope for bargaining there's likely to be – if you're, say, buying a sarong from an itinerant hawker on the beach, you can haggle to your heart's content.

Finally, there are a couple of things you shouldn't buy. Remember that buying **coral** or **shells** (or any other marine product) contributes directly to the destruction of the island's fragile ocean environment; it's also illegal, and you're likely to end up paying a heavy fine if you try to take coral out of the country. Note that it's also illegal to export **antiques** (classified as anything over fifty years old) without a licence (see below).

The superb **website** ⓦ craftrevival.org (follow the Sri Lanka link under "Crafts") has copious information on all the island's traditional arts and crafts.

Handicrafts

The most characteristic – and clichéd – Sri Lankan souvenirs are brightly painted **masks**, originally designed to be worn during kolam dances or exorcism ceremonies (see p.130) and now found for sale wherever there are tourists (though the sheer quantity churned out means that many are of indifferent quality and sloppily painted). Masks vary in size from the tiny to the huge; the vast majority depict either the pop-eyed Gara Yaka or the bird demon Gurulu Raksha, though if you hunt around you may find other designs. Some masks are artificially but attractively aged to resemble antiques – a lot easier on the eye than the lurid colours in which most are painted. The centre of mask production is Ambalangoda, where there are a number of large shops selling a wide range of designs, some of heirloom quality.

Second in popularity are **elephant carvings**. These range from small wooden creatures painted with bright polka-dot patterns to the elegant stone carvings sold at places like Paradise Road in Colombo. **Batiks** (an art introduced by the Dutch from Indonesia) are also widespread. Designs are often stereotypical (the Sigiriya Damsels and naff beach scenes are ubiquitous), though a few places produce more unusual and interesting work.

A number of other traditional crafts struggle on with a little help from the tourist trade. **Metalwork** has long been produced in the Kandy area, and intricately embossed metal objects such as dishes, trays, candlesticks and other objects can be found in all the island's handicraft emporia, though they're rather fussy for most foreign tastes. **Leatherwork** can also be good, and you'll find a range of hats, bags, boots and footrests (the shops at Pinnewala Elephant Orphanage have a particularly good selection). **Lacquerware**, a speciality of the Matale area, can also sometimes be found, along with Kandyan-style **drums** and, occasionally, **carrom boards** (see box below). **Wooden models** of tuktuks and other vehicles are another

---

CARROM

A kind of hybrid of pool, marbles and draughts (checkers), **carrom** is played throughout Sri Lanka. The game's origins are obscure: some say that it was invented by the maharajas of India, although many Indians claim that it was actually introduced by the British, while Burma, Egypt and Ethiopia are also touted as possible sources.

The game is played using a square wooden board with a pocket at each corner; the aim is to flick all your pieces (which are very similar to draughtsmen) into one of the pockets, using the heavier "striker" piece. Carrom can be played by either four or (more usually) two people. If you get hooked, a carrom board makes an unusual, if bulky, souvenir.

local speciality and make good souvenirs or children's toys. They're most commonly found in Negombo, but are also increasingly available in Colombo and elsewhere on the island.

Finally, if you've a day in Colombo, it's well worth seeking out the **modern handicrafts** found at a few Colombo boutiques, such as Paradise Road, *The Gallery Café* or, especially, Barefoot, whose range of vibrantly coloured fabrics have become synonymous with modern Sri Lankan style.

Religious items

Wood or stone **Buddha carvings** of varying standards are common. For something a bit more unusual, the brightly coloured **posters** or strip-pictures of Buddhist and Hindu deities which adorn tuktuks and buses across Sri Lanka are sold by pavement hawkers and stationers' shops everywhere and make a cheap and characterful souvenir, while a visit to Kataragama or a trawl along St Anthony's Mawatha in Colombo (see p.78) will uncover an entertaining assortment of other **religious kitsch**, from bleeding Catholic saints to illuminated Ganesh clocks.

Tea and spices

Most top-quality **Ceylon tea** is exported, but there's still plenty on sale that is likely to satisfy all but the most dedicated tea-fancier. The main local brand is the Dilmah (W dilmahtea.com), though look out too for the Tea Tang range (W teatang.com), comprising a first-rate selection of speciality teas, ranging from standard Sri Lankan blends through to some rare connoisseur varieties. Alternatively, for a real taste of Sri Lanka, look for unblended ("single estate") high-grown teas – a far cry from the heavily blended and homogenized teabags that pass muster in Europe and the US. You'll also find a wide range of flavoured teas made with a huge variety of ingredients, including standard offerings like lemon, orange, mint and vanilla, as well as the more unusual banana, rum, kiwi fruit or pineapple.

The best (and cheapest) place to buy tea is in a local supermarket; Cargills supermarkets islandwide usually have a good selection, including unblended single-estate teas. The specialist Mlesna tea shop chain has branches in Colombo, Kandy, Bandarawela and at the airport, although they concentrate on more touristy offerings including boxed tea sets, flavoured teas and the like.

Sri Lanka's **spice gardens**, mostly concentrated around Kandy and Matale, pull in loads of visitors on organized tours and sell packets of spices, often at outrageously inflated prices. You'll find identical stuff in local shops and supermarkets at a fraction of the price.

Gems and jewellery

Sri Lanka has been famous for its **precious stones** since antiquity, and gems and jewellery remain important to the national economy even today. This is nowhere more obvious than at the gem-mining centre of **Ratnapura**, where locally excavated uncut gems are traded daily on the streets. All foreign visitors to the town will be offered stones to buy, but unless you're an expert gemologist there's a strong chance that you'll end up with an expensive piece of coloured glass. Another variant on this scam is that you will be persuaded to buy gems at a special "cheap" price, with assurances that you will be able to resell them back home for several times the price you paid for them. Again, unless you're an expert, steer well clear of these deals.

Ratnapura apart, you'll find **gem and jewellery shops** all over the island – the major concentrations are in Negombo, Galle and Colombo. These include large chains, such as Zam Gems or Sifani, and smaller local outfits. If you are going to buy, it's worth doing some homework before you arrive so you can compare prices with those back home. You can get gems tested for authenticity in Colombo (see p.97).

For silver and, especially, **gold** jewellery, try Sea Street in Colombo's Pettah district, which is lined with shops. These see few tourists, so prices are reasonable, although the flouncy designs on offer aren't to everyone's taste.

Clothes and books

Sri Lanka is a bit of a disappointment when it comes to **clothes**, and doesn't boast the gorgeous fabrics and nimble-fingered tailors of, say, India and Thailand. Having said that, the island is a major garment-manufacturing centre for overseas companies, and there are lots of good-quality Western-style clothes knocking around at bargain prices. In Colombo, places to try include the fancy Odel department store (see p.98) or the more downmarket House of Fashions (see p.98) and Cotton Collection (see p.98). Colourful but flimsy beachwear is flogged by shops and hawkers at all the major west-coast resorts – it's cheap and cheerful, but don't expect it to last much longer than your holiday. Most Sri Lankan women now dress Western-style in skirts and blouses, but you can still find a few shops in Colombo and elsewhere selling beautiful saris and *shalwar kameez* (pyjama suits) – these shops are usually easily spotted due to their enormous picture windows stuffed with colourfully costumed mannequins.

Books are relatively cheap: new paperbacks are about two-thirds of European and North American prices, and there are also lots of colourful coffee-table books and weird and wonderful works on Sri Lankan history, culture and religion that you won't find outside the island. The Vijitha Yapa bookshop has branches islandwide, and there are a number of other good bookshops in Colombo – Barefoot's (see p.98) is the best.

Travelling with children

Sri Lankans love children, and travelling with kids more or less guarantees you a warm welcome wherever you go. Locals will always do whatever they can to help or entertain – there's certainly no need to worry about disapproving stares if your baby starts crying or your toddler starts monkeying around, even in quite posh establishments.

Having said that, travelling with **babies** may prove stressful. Powdered milk is fairly widely available, but disposable nappies and baby food are rare, while things like baby-sitting services, nursery day-care, changing facilities, high chairs and microwaves for sterilizing bottles are largely unheard of; car seats will also probably have to be brought from home. Breast-feeding in public, however discreet, is also not something that Sri Lankan women usually do, while prams are virtually useless, since there are no decent pavements to push them on – the common sight of mothers burdened with a tiny baby on one arm and a small child in the other scrambling on and off packed buses or fighting their way across busy roads is one of Sri Lanka's more stomach-churning sights. The heat, and the associated dangers of dehydration, are another concern, not to mention the risks of mosquito-borne diseases such as malaria and dengue fever (see p.53).

Older children will get a lot out of a visit to the island. Sri Lanka's **beaches** are likely to provide the main attraction, with endless swathes of golden sand to muck around on and warm waters to splash

about in – though you should always check local swimming conditions carefully and guard carefully against the very real possibility of sunburn and dehydration. Beaches apart, the outstanding kids' attraction is the **Elephant Orphanage** at Pinnewala, a guaranteed child-pleaser, especially for its cute babies – this is one of the few places in the world where children can see elephants that are even smaller than themselves. There are further elephant-spotting opportunities around Kandy, while a visit to any of the **national parks** is also likely to stimulate budding zoologists; Yala, where there's a good chance of sighting crocodiles, peacocks, flamingos and other wildlife, is a particularly good choice, as is Uda Walawe, where you'll find another elephant orphanage. **Activity sports**, such as banana boating or kayaking at Bentota, may also appeal, while the island's varied forms of **transport** – whether a tuktuk ride, a train trip through the hill country or a boat cruise along one of the island's rivers or lagoons – should also keep little ones entertained. Energetic kids with a head for heights might also enjoy the challenge of clambering up **Sigiriya** and its rickety iron staircases. And if you've exhausted all the preceding possibilities, you can always go **shopping**: there are plenty of fun handicrafts to be had, with gruesome masks, painted elephants and wooden toys aplenty – if you're in Colombo, don't leave without bagging a colourful cuddly stuffed-toy animal from the Barefoot (see p.98).

Crime and safety

The good news is that Sri Lanka is a remarkably safe place to travel in, and violent crime against foreigners is virtually unheard of – this is still a place where, despite 25 years of brutal civil war, in parts of the country the theft of two bicycles is considered a crime wave. The only bad news is that scams and aggressive touting are widespread in a few places.

Petty theft is less common than in many other parts of Asia (and rarer than in most European and American cities), though you should still take sensible care of your belongings. Pickpockets sometimes work in crowded areas, while thefts from hotel rooms are occasionally reported. Many hotels and guesthouses ask guests to deposit valuables in their safe, and it's sensible to do so when you can. **Muggings** are very rare, though single travellers (especially women) should avoid dark beaches late at

COMMON SCAMS

Taking you for a ride Many scams involve gaining your trust, then getting you into a tuktuk to visit some temple/"elephant festival"/handicraft shop or other attraction. Having driven you around for a while, you will be dumped in some remote and seedy part of town at which point the tuktuk driver will demand a wildly inflated fare for the ride. *Never* get into a tuktuk without agreeing a fare beforehand.

Free tea You are offered free tea by someone claiming to own or work on a plantation, on condition you pay a "small sum" to cover the export duty or postage. Needless to say, the tea never arrives.

Fake charity collectors Often elderly and respectable-looking gents with clipboards and official-looking letters; especially common around the lake in Kandy, but also in Colombo and on beaches everywhere. Real Sri Lankan charities do not collect on the streets.

Having a drink You fall into conversation with a friendly local who asks if you would like to have a drink with him. Having taken you to some obscure drinking den, he claims to have forgotten his wallet, leaving you to pay the (usually vastly inflated) bill. Once you've gone, he will return to collect his share of your money from the bar staff.

The card trick Someone asks you where you plan to stay. When you tell them, they produce a business card (purloined) from the relevant establishment and claim that they work there/are related to the owner. They then tell you that the said guesthouse or hotel is closed/full/undergoing renovations, then propose you come with them to their own guesthouse, or one where they earn commission.

Milk powder A plausibly ragged-looking local engages you in conversation and tells you about the shocking poverty he lives in. He insists, however, that he doesn't want any money for himself, but desperately needs a tin of milk powder so that he can at least feed his hungry baby. You are then led to a chemist, where a (surprisingly expensive) tin of milk powder is produced. Once you've left, he'll be back to return the powder and split the proceeds.

night – Negombo and Hikkaduwa have particularly bad reputations. In addition, make sure you keep a separate record of all your bank card details (along with the phone numbers needed in case of their loss) and passport information; it's worth taking a photocopy of the pages from your passport that contain your personal details.

If you do have anything stolen, you'll need to report it to the **police** – there's little chance that they will be able to recover it for you, but you'll need a report for your insurance claim. Given the fact that you might not find any English-speaking policemen on duty, you might try to get someone from your guesthouse to come along as an interpreter. The process of reporting a crime is usually a laborious affair, with much checking of papers and filling in of forms. Unfortunately, although tourist police offices have been set up in a few parts of the island, they're not much cop.

Dangers

Following the end of the **civil war** in May 2009, the entire island is now at peace for the first time in almost thirty years and almost all travel restrictions have been lifted, with the exception of a few remote areas in the north which remain out of bounds. No LTTE attacks have been reported since the end of the fighting, although the landmines and UXO (see p.372) pose a risk in remote areas.

An altogether more prosaic but much more serious source of danger in Sri Lanka is **traffic**. Be particularly careful when walking near busy roads and treat buses, in particular, with respect: as a pedestrian you're at the very bottom of the food chain in the dog-eat-dog world of Sri Lankan road use.

Drowning is the second most common cause of death amongst tourists in Sri Lanka (after road accidents). Currents can be strong and beaches may shelve off into deep waters with unexpected steepness – and there are no lifeguards to come and pull you out if you get into trouble. Always ask local advice before venturing in the water anywhere that is obviously not a recognized swimming spot. Conditions can vary radically even within a few hundred metres, so don't assume that because lots of people are swimming at one end of the beach, the other, deserted, end will be safe. The only warning signs of dangerous swimming conditions are the red flags posted on the beaches outside major resort hotels. Sensible precautions include always keeping within your depth and making sure that someone on the shore knows that you're in the water. Never swim under the influence of alcohol – newspaper stories of locals washed out to sea after too many bottles of arrack are an almost weekly occurrence.

Scams and hassles

Sri Lanka has an unfortunate but well-deserved reputation for **hassle**, ranging from tuktuk drivers, gem shop owners and guesthouse touts to virtuoso scam merchants who run well-oiled schemes to entrap the unwary. At its simplest, you'll encounter low-level hassle from people who want you to visit their shop, stay in their guesthouse or be your guide (or, alternatively, who want to take you to a shop or guesthouse where they'll receive commission). Tuktuk drivers are the main source of this sort of pressure, although it can come from pretty much anyone with even a few words of English.

Fortunately, the island's virtuoso **con artists** who formerly plagued places like Galle, Kandy and, especially, Colombo's Galle Face Green are now far less numerous than they once were, although it still pays to be aware of the classic scams (see p.51). Convincing you of their trustworthiness is an important part of any scam, and con artists will often attempt to boost their own credentials by claiming to be a member of a professional elite (a SriLankan Airlines pilot; a former international cricketer). A standard ploy in Colombo is for con artists to claim to be visiting from the Maldives, thereby implying that they too are visitors and thus to be trusted. Another common introductory ploy is for a con artist to claim to be a cook, gardener or other backroom member of staff at your hotel, hoping thereby to gain your confidence.

You shouldn't get too paranoid about these characters, and it's important not to stop talking to people because you're afraid they're going to rip you off. The vast majority of Sri Lankans who approach you will be perfectly honest, and simply keen to have a chat – or at least find out which country you are from (see p.47). Look out for the classic scams and, if you suspect that you are being set up, simply withdraw politely but firmly from the situation.

Health

Sri Lanka is less challenging from a health point of view than many other tropical countries: standards of hygiene are reasonable, medical care is of a decent standard and even malaria has now been largely eliminated. Nevertheless, the island does play host to the usual gamut of tropical diseases, and it's important to make sure you protect yourself against serious illness.

You should start **planning** the health aspect of your trip well in advance of departure, especially if you're having vaccines for things like rabies or Japanese encephalitis, which need to be administered over the course of a month. Vaccinations and medical advice are available from your doctor or – more conveniently but expensively – a specialist travel clinic. It's also crucial to have adequate medical insurance.

Ensure that you're up to date with the following standard **vaccinations**: diphtheria, tetanus, hepatitis A and polio. Other jabs you might consider are tuberculosis, meningitis and typhoid.

The best way to avoid falling ill is to look after yourself. Eat properly, make sure you get enough sleep and don't try to cram too much strenuous activity into your holiday, especially in the first few days before you've acclimatized to the sun, water and food, and while you're probably still suffering jetlag. Luckily, standards of medical care in Sri Lanka are good. Most **doctors** speak English and a significant number have trained in Europe, North America or Australia. All large towns have a hospital, and you'll also find **private medical clinics** in Colombo. If you pay for treatment, remember to get receipts so that you can claim on your insurance policy. All larger towns have well-appointed **pharmacies** (signed by a red cross on a white circle) and can usually produce an English-speaking pharmacist. If stuck, any reputable hotel or guesthouse should be able to put you in touch with a local English-speaking doctor.

There is more on **Ayurveda**, Sri Lanka's remarkable home-grown system of holistic medical care, in our Beruwala account (see p.118).

TRAVEL ADVISORIES

For current information on the security situation in Sri Lanka, visit one of the sites listed below.

Australian Department of Foreign Affairs ⓦ dfat.gov.au
British Foreign & Commonwealth Office ⓦ fco.gov.uk
New Zealand Ministry of Foreign Affairs ⓦ mfat.govt.nz
US State Department ⓦ travel.state.gov

Water and food

Avoid drinking **tap water** in Sri Lanka. Although it's generally chlorinated and safe to drink, the unfamiliar micro-organisms it contains (compared with what you're used to at home) can easily precipitate a stomach upset. Also avoid ice, unless you're sure that it's been made with boiled or purified water. Mineral water is widely available, although always check that the seal hasn't been broken – it's not unknown for bottles to be refilled with tap water. Whatever precautions you take, however, you're still likely to come into contact with local water at various points – your eating utensils will be washed in it, and it will probably be used without your knowledge in things like fruit juices – so it's not worth getting paranoid about.

Though Sri Lankan standards of **food hygiene** are reasonable, it still pays to be careful, and the old travellers'adage usually applies: if you can't cook, boil or peel something, don't eat it (although if you can't peel something, you can always wash it thoroughly in purified water). Stick to hot food that has been freshly prepared. Avoid salads and anything which looks like it has been sitting uncovered for a while; short eats (see p.37) are particularly likely to be old and to have been poked by many fingers. The busier the establishment, the less probability that the food's been sitting around all day. Obviously you'll need to use your discretion: the buffet at a five-star hotel has more chance of being OK than a local café's tureen of curry, which has been keeping the flies fat since dawn. Finally, remember that refrigerators stop working during power cuts, so unless you're eating at a place with its own generator, avoid any food (including meat and ice cream) that might have been unfrozen and then refrozen.

Diarrhoea, dysentery and giardiasis

Diarrhoea remains the most common complaint amongst tourists visiting Sri Lanka. It can have many causes, including serious diseases like typhoid or cholera, but in the vast majority of cases diarrhoea is a result of contaminated food or drink and will pass naturally in a few days. Such diarrhoea is also often accompanied by cramps, nausea and vomiting, and fever in more severe cases.

You should seek medical advice if diarrhoea continues for more than five days or if there is blood mixed up in the faeces, in which case you could be suffering from giardiasis or amoebic dysentery (see opposite).

Treatment

One of the biggest problems with diarrhoea, particularly in a hot country like Sri Lanka, is **dehydration**; it's vital you keep topped up with fluids – aim for about four litres every 24 hours (the colour of your urine is the best guide). If you're having more than five bouts of diarrhoea a day or are unable to eat, take **oral rehydration salts** to replace lost salt and minerals. These can be bought ready-prepared in sachets from camping shops; alternatively, you can make your own by mixing eight teaspoons of sugar and half a teaspoon of salt in a litre of purified water. Coconut water is a good alternative, especially if you add a pinch of salt; flat cola or lemonade with a pinch of salt also work. **Children** with diarrhoea dehydrate much more quickly than adults, and it's even more vital to keep them hydrated. If you have to go on a long journey where you won't have access to a toilet, you can temporarily bung yourself up with a blocking drug like lomotil or loperamide, though these simply suppress symptoms and have no curative value. Whilst recovering, stick to bland foods (rice and yoghurt are traditionally recommended, and bananas help replace lost potassium) and get plenty of rest – this is not the moment to go rushing up Adam's Peak.

If you have persistent diarrhoea, you may be suffering from giardiasis or amoebic dysentery. With **giardiasis** you may suffer stomach cramps, nausea and a bloated stomach. In **amoebic dysentery**, diarrhoea is severe, with bloody stools and fever. If any of the above symptoms apply, see a doctor.

Malaria

The incidence of **malaria** in Sri Lanka has fallen dramatically in recent years – from over 200,000 reported cases in 2000 to just 736 in 2010 – although of course it's always possible that the incidence of the disease may rise again in the future.

At present, the main **risk areas** are in the north and northeast (see the malaria maps at Ⓦ fitfortravel.nhs.uk/destinations/malariamaps /srilanka.htm and Ⓦ cdc-malaria.ncsa.uiuc.edu). It's recommended that you talk to your doctor or, even better, a travel health specialist, although be aware that different doctors and travel health resources may offer different, often conflicting advice.

If you do decide to take anti-malarial drugs, there are various options including the traditional combination of **proguanil** (Paludrine) plus **chloroquine** (trade names Nivaquin or Avloclor) –

although some sources claim that chloroquine is no longer effective in the island. Alternative anti-malarials include **doxycycline** and **Malarone** (a combination of atovaquone and proguanil). The stronger **mefloquine** (Lariam) isn't usually prescribed for Sri Lanka.

The disease itself has a typical incubation period of nine to sixteen days, sometimes longer – hence the importance of continuing with the medication once you get home. Initial **symptoms** are virtually indistinguishable from severe flu. If you think you might have malaria, have a blood test done as soon as possible.

Avoiding bites

Even if you're on medication, it's important to avoid being bitten, since no antimalarial offers total protection, and mosquitoes in Sri Lanka also transmit other diseases such as dengue fever and Japanese encephalitis. Malarial mosquitoes come out at dusk and remain active throughout the night. Standard avoidance techniques are to wear light-coloured clothing with long sleeves; use a **repellent** containing DEET on exposed parts of your body; and (if your room's not air-conditioned) always sleep under a net. You might also want to spray your clothing with a permethrin spray; burning a mosquito coil in your room or putting one under the table while you eat is also recommended. An alternative to coils are the Pyrethroid tablets that you place on a tray and put in a plug; the electricity heats the tray and vaporizes the Pyrethroid. Citronella oil (available from many chemists in Sri Lanka) is also thought to be good for repelling mosquitoes.

Dengue fever

More widespread than malaria, and equally serious, is the mosquito-borne disease **dengue fever**, regular outbreaks of which continue to plague the island, causing numerous fatalities. Dengue is a predominantly **urban disease** – Colombo is particularly at risk. As mosquitoes lay their eggs in water, dengue outbreaks tend to peak during or after periods of rain. There are four subtypes of dengue fever, so unfortunately it's possible to catch it more than once. The disease is typically characterized by the sudden onset of high fever accompanied by chills, headache, a skin rash and muscle or joint pains (usually affecting the limbs and back, hence dengue fever's nickname "break-bone fever"). The fever usually lasts three to seven days, while post-viral

weakness, lethargy and sometimes depression can persist for anything up to several weeks. A rare but potentially fatal complication is **dengue haemor-rhagic fever** (DHF), which is almost entirely confined to children under fifteen who have previously been infected with dengue fever.

There is no **vaccine** for dengue fever, which makes avoiding getting bitten in the first place (see opposite) all the more important. Unfortunately, the mosquitoes that transmit dengue bite during the day, making them harder to guard against than malarial mosquitoes. If you think you've contracted dengue fever, go to a doctor.

Japanese encephalitis

A third mosquito-borne disease is **Japanese encephalitis** (JE), a virus transmitted by mosquitoes which bite at night. It's particularly associated with **rural areas**, as the virus lives in wading birds, pigs and flooded rice fields. JE is most prevalent following periods of heavy rainfall resulting in large areas of stagnant water.

JE is an extremely dangerous disease, with mortality rates of up to forty percent (though tourists are only rarely affected). As with malaria, you won't contract JE if you don't get bitten (see opposite). **Symptoms** include drowsiness, sensitivity to light and confusion. An effective vaccine exists for JE (three shots administered over 28 days), though the standard advice is that it's only worth considering if you're travelling in high-risk areas during the monsoon for a period of over a month, especially if you'll be spending a lot of time in the country and/or camping out a lot.

Sun

The potential health risks associated with the **sun** are easily underestimated – especially since a desire to soak up the rays is often a major reason to come to Sri Lanka in the first place. Sunscreen should always be applied to exposed skin when outdoors; young children are particularly vulnerable to burns and should be kept out of the sun at all times. Older kids should wear the highest factor sunblock and a hat. For all ages, eyes also need to be protected by proper sunglasses. If you do get sunburnt, take plenty of warm (not cold) showers, apply calamine lotion or aloe vera gel, and drink lots of water.

A common but minor irritant is **prickly heat**, usually afflicting newly arrived visitors. It's caused by excessive perspiration trapped under the skin, producing an itchy rash. Keep cool (a/c is good), shower frequently, use talcum powder on the affected skin and wear loose (ideally cotton) clothing. At its worst, prolonged exposure to the sun and dehydration can lead to **heatstroke**, a serious and potentially life-threatening condition. Symptoms are a lack of sweat, high temperature, severe headaches, lack of coordination and confusion. If untreated, heatstroke can lead to potentially fatal convulsions and delirium. If you're suffering from heatstroke, get out of the sun, get into a tepid shower and drink plenty of water.

Marine hazards

Besides the risks of drowning (see p.51), swimmers are also at a small potential risk of **marine stings**. Jellyfish are common, and some can inflict painful stings; coral scratches and cuts can also be painful (although more of a problem for the coral itself, which dies on contact). Occasionally people develop quasi-allergic reactions to stings; if you start to wheeze or swell up around the face, go to hospital immediately.

The other thing you need to think about is how **clean** the water is: beaches in the vicinity of town centres are obviously prone to pollution. In addition, parts of some beaches are filthy. Look out for broken glass, fishing hooks, syringes and other rubbish; dog shit is also common. If you cut your foot, disinfect it immediately and seek medical advice, since you may need a tetanus booster and/ or a hepatitis B vaccine.

Hepatitis

Hepatitis is an inflammation of the liver. The disease exists in various forms, though with a shared range of symptoms, typically jaundiced skin, yellowing of the whites of the eyes and a general range of flu-like symptoms. **Hepatitis A** and **hepatitis E** are spread by contaminated food and water. If you become infected, there's little you can do except rest – unfortunately, it can take a couple of weeks or more to shake off the effects. The much more serious **hepatitis B** can result in long-term liver damage and liver cancer. Like the HIV virus, it's spread via infected blood or body fluids, most commonly through sex or needle sharing. **hepatitis C and D** are similar.

You can (and should) be **vaccinated** against hepatitis A. The hepatitis B vaccine is usually only recommended to those at especially high risk, such as health-care workers. There are no vaccines for other types of hepatitis.

Rabies

Rabies, an **animal disease** transmitted to humans by bites, scratches or licking is usually associated with dogs, but can also be transmitted by cats, monkeys, bats or any other warm-blooded animal. Rabies, once symptoms have developed, is fatal. You are at risk if you suffer a bite that draws blood or breaks the skin, or if you are licked by an animal on an open wound. Bites to the face, neck and fingertips are particularly dangerous.

Fortunately, a safe and effective **vaccine** exists (three shots over 28 days). Casual tourists on short holidays to the island may well feel that they are not sufficiently at risk to go through the hassle of a rabies vaccine, but if you're going for a long period or are likely to be in close contact with animals, you might decide it's worth the trouble. In general, Sri Lankan dogs are fairly well behaved, and it's rare that you'll encounter the sort of aggressive and unpredictable strays that you sometimes find in other parts of Asia.

Regardless of whether you've been vaccinated or not, if you're bitten or scratched (or licked on an open wound) by an infected animal, clean the wound thoroughly with disinfectant as soon as possible. Iodine is ideal, but alcohol or even soap and water are better than nothing. If you've already been vaccinated, you'll need two booster shots three days apart. If you haven't been vaccinated, you will need to be given five shots of the rabies vaccine over 28 days (the first must be administered as soon as possible after you've been bitten), along with a single injection of rabies antibody serum.

Other diseases

Typhoid is a gut infection caused by contaminated water or food, and which leads to a high fever and diarrhoea. Oral and injected vaccines are available and usually recommended. A vaccination against **meningitis** is also available. This cerebral virus, transmitted by airborne bacteria, can be fatal. Symptoms include a severe headache, fever, a stiff neck and a stomach rash. If you think you have it, seek medical attention immediately. Sri Lanka has experienced occasional outbreaks of **cholera**, although this typically occurs in epidemics in areas of poor sanitation, and almost never affects tourists.

Initial symptoms of **tetanus** ("lockjaw") can be discomfort in swallowing and stiffness in the jaw and neck, followed by convulsions – potentially fatal. The vaccination is a standard childhood jab in developed countries. **Typhus** is spread by the bites of ticks, lice and mites. Symptoms include fever, headache and muscle pains, followed after a few days by a rash, while the bite itself often develops into a painful sore. A shot of antibiotics will shift it.

Chikungunya fever is another mosquito-borne disease, outbreaks of which are sometimes reported in various parts of the country. Symptoms include fever, joint pains, muscle aches, severe headaches and a rash, usually lasting around a week – sometimes much longer. There is no vaccine, although the disease is hardly ever fatal.

Animals and insects

Leeches are common after rain in Sinharaja, Adam's Peak and elsewhere in the hills. They're difficult to avoid, attaching themselves to your shoes and climbing up your leg until they find flesh, and are quite capable of burrowing through a pair of socks. Once latched on, leeches will suck your blood until sated, after which they drop off of their own accord – perfectly painless, but not terribly pleasant. You can make leeches drop off harmlessly with the end of a lighted cigarette or the flame from a lighter, or by putting salt on them. Don't pull them off, however, or bits of leech might break off and become embedded in your flesh, increasing the risk of the bite becoming infected.

Sri Lanka has the dubious distinction of having one of the highest number of **snakebite** fatalities, per capita, of any country in the world, and any form of bite should be treated as quickly as possible. The island boasts five species of poisonous snake, all relatively common, especially in northern dry zones; they include the cobra and the extremely dangerous Russell's viper. Avoid wandering through heavy undergrowth in bare feet and flipflops; wear proper shoes or boots, socks and long trousers. If you're bitten, you should wrap up the limb, as for a sprained ankle, and immobilize it with a splint – this slows down the speed at which venom spreads through the rest of the body; keeping as still as possible also helps. Popular advice recommends catching and killing the snake so that the doctor knows what type of antivenin to administer, although it's unlikely you'll be able to do this, and you'll probably have to settle for a description of the creature. Unfortunately, reliable antivenins have not yet been developed for all types of snake – that for the Russell's viper, for instance, has been developed from the Indian Russell's viper, and is not always effective in treating bites administered by the Sri Lankan sub-species.

STDs, HIV and AIDS

Sexually transmitted diseases (STDs) are common in the chilled-out, uninhibited and scantily clad world of the average Sri Lankan tourist beach. Practise safe sex, or you might come home with an unwelcome souvenir of your visit.

Compared to other parts of Asia, Sri Lanka has relatively few reported **HIV** and **AIDS** cases – around 0.1 percent of the population. Again, there are obvious risks if you have unprotected sex. Contaminated needles are not considered a problem in Sri Lanka, so there's no need to carry your own – but ask to have the packet opened in your presence if you want to check this for yourself. Contaminated blood poses a potentially greater risk – blood transfusions should only be accepted in an absolute emergency.

Medical resources

International Society for Travel Medicine Ⓦ istm.org. A full list of travel health clinics.

UK AND IRELAND

Hospital for Tropical Diseases Travel Clinic Ⓦ thehtd.org.
MASTA (Medical Advisory Service for Travellers Abroad) Ⓦ masta.org.
Tropical Medical Bureau Ireland Ⓦ tmb.ie.

NORTH AMERICA

Canadian Society for International Health Ⓦ csih.org. Extensive list of travel health centres.
CDC Ⓦ cdc.gov/travel. The official US government travel health site.

AUSTRALASIA AND SOUTH AFRICA

Travellers' Medical and Vaccination Centre Ⓦ tmvc.com.au. Lists travel clinics in Australia, New Zealand and South Africa.

Costs

Rampant inflation over recent years means that Sri Lanka is no longer the bargain it once was, although prices remain comparable to other places in South and Southeast Asia. How much you spend is entirely up to you. Stay on the beach in a cheap cabana and eat meals in budget cafés and you could probably get by on $20 (£12.50) per person per day, travelling as a couple or larger group. Check into one of the island's top hotels or villas, however, and

then add in the cost of touring with your own car and driver, and you could easily spend $500 a day, or more.

If you're **on a budget**, Sri Lanka can still be fairly inexpensive, so long as you stick to using local transport and staying in cheap guesthouses – you can still travel by bus from one end of the island to the other for around $20, get a filling meal at local cafés for a couple of dollars, and find a decent double room for $20 per night or less. Taking a tour or renting a vehicle will obviously bump costs up considerably – a car and driver normally goes for around $55–70 (£35–45) a day. Entrance fees for archeological sites and national parks can also strain tight budgets – a day-ticket to Sigiriya, for example, currently costs $30, while the cost of visiting the country's national parks works out at somewhere around $80 per couple per day once you've factored in entrance fees and transport.

Note that some hotels and restaurants levy a ten percent **service charge**, while various government taxes also apply, although no two places seem to calculate them the same way: some places include all taxes in the quoted priced (the so-called "nett" rate), others charge one or more taxes separately. These taxes include twelve percent VAT, a one percent Tourist Development Tax, and a two percent "Nation-Building Tax" in more upmarket hotels. It's always worth checking beforehand what is and isn't included – the extra twenty-five percent added at a top hotel can add a nasty twist to the bill if you're not expecting it.

Tourist prices

Another thing to bear in mind is that many places on the island apply official **tourist prices**. At all national parks and reserves, and at government-run archeological sites, the authorities operate a two-tier price system whereby foreigners pay a significantly higher entrance fee than locals, sometimes almost a hundred times more than Sri Lankan nationals. At the national parks, for example, locals pay an entrance fee of around 25 cents, while overseas visitors pay around $25 once various taxes and additional charges have been taken into account. A similar situation obtains at the sites of the Cultural Triangle – at Anuradhapura, for instance, foreigners pay $25, while locals pay nothing. This makes visiting many of Sri Lanka's biggest sights a pricier prospect than in other parts of the subcontinent, a fact of life that many visitors grumble about – although the most vociferous critics are local Sri Lankan hoteliers, drivers and others involved in the tourist trade, who have seen their businesses suffer as many visitors vote with their feet and stay on the beach.

Bargaining

As a tourist, you're likely to pay slightly over the odds for a range of things, from rickshaw rides to market groceries. It's worth remembering, however, that many prices in Sri Lanka are inherently fluid – there's often no such thing as a "correct price", only a "best price". Many hoteliers, for instance, chop and change their prices according to demand, while the price of anything from a tuktuk ride to an elephant carving may depend on anything from the time of day to the weather or the mood of the seller. Given this, it's always worth **bargaining**. The key to effective bargaining here (as throughout South Asia) is to retain a sense of humour and proportion. There is nothing more ridiculous – or more damaging to local perceptions of foreign visitors – than the sight of a Western tourist arguing bitterly over the final few rupees of a budget room or an item of shopping. The fact is that even the most cash-strapped Western backpacker is, in Sri Lankan terms, extremely rich, as their very presence in the country proves. And however tight one's budget, it's important to realize the difference that even a few rupees can make to a guesthouse owner who is struggling by on a handful of dollars a day.

On the other hand, it's also important not to be outrageously **overcharged**. Visitors who lack a sense of local prices and pay whatever they're asked contribute to local inflation, pushing up prices both for other tourists and (more importantly) for locals – the implications of just one tourist paying $10 for a tuktuk ride that should cost $1 can have serious implications for the local economy.

Tipping

Tipping is a way of life in Sri Lanka – visitors will generally be expected to offer some kind of remuneration for most services, even on top of agreed fees, and the whole business of what to give and to whom can be a bit of a minefield. Many hotels and restaurants add a ten percent service charge to the bill, although it's worth bearing in mind that the staff who have served you won't necessarily see any of this money themselves. If a service charge hasn't been added, a tip won't necessarily be expected, although it is of course always appreciated. If you tour the island by car, your driver will expect a tip of around

$5–10 per day, depending on his level of expertise, though you shouldn't feel obliged to give anything unless you're genuinely pleased with the service you've received (and if you're *not* happy, it's well worth explaining why). If touring a site with an official guide, you should always agree a fee in advance; additional tips should only be offered if you're particularly pleased with the service. When visiting temples, you'll probably be shown around by a resident monk or priest; it's polite to offer them something at the end of the tour – some will take this money themselves (despite the fact that Buddhist monks aren't meant to handle money); others will prefer you to place it in a donation box. Whatever happens, a dollar or two should suffice. Occasionally, unofficial "guides" (usually bored teenagers or other local hangers-on) will materialize to show you around temples – and will of course expect a tip for their troubles. Again, a dollar or two is almost certainly sufficient. Anyone else who assists you will probably welcome some kind of gratuity, though of course it's impossible to generalize and visitors will have to make (sometimes difficult) decisions about whether to offer money or not.

Travel essentials

Climate

Reflecting Sri Lanka's position close to the equator, average **temperatures** remain fairly constant year round. The main factors shaping local weather are altitude and the two **monsoons**. There is more on the island's climate in the Introduction (see p.10).

Customs regulations

Entering Sri Lanka you are allowed to bring in 1.5 litres of spirits and two bottles of wine. You're not allowed to bring cartons of duty-free cigarettes into Sri Lanka, although it's unlikely you'll be stopped at customs and searched. If you are caught "smuggling", your cartons will be confiscated and you'll be fined Rs.6000. There are no duty-free cigarettes on sale at the airport on arrival, either.

Leaving Sri Lanka you are permitted to export up to 10kg of tea duty-free. In theory, you're not allowed to take out more than Rs.250 in cash, though this is rarely checked. If you want to export **antiques** – defined as anything more than fifty years old – you will need authorization from the Archeological Department (Sir Marcus Fernando Mw, Colombo 7 ☎011 269 5255, Ⓦarchaeology.gov.lk) depending on exactly what it is you want to export. The export of any coral, shells or other protected marine products is prohibited; taking out flora, fauna or animal parts is also prohibited.

Electricity

Sri Lanka's electricity runs at 230–240V, 50 cycles A/C. Round, three-pin **sockets** are the norm, though you'll also sometimes find square

AVERAGE MONTHLY TEMPERATURES AND RAINFALL

COLOMBO

	Jan	Feb	Mar	Apr	May	Jun	Jul	Aug	Sep	Oct	Nov	Dec
Max/min (°C)	31/22	31/23	32/24	32/25	31/25	30/25	30/25	30/25	30/25	30/24	30/23	30/23
Max/min (°F)	88/72	88/73	89/75	89/76	88/78	87/78	86/77	86/77	86/77	86/75	86/74	87/73
Rainfall (mm)	62	69	130	253	382	186	125	114	236	369	310	168

NUWARA ELIYA

	Jan	Feb	Mar	Apr	May	Jun	Jul	Aug	Sep	Oct	Nov	Dec
Max/min (°C)	20/9	21/9	22/10	23/11	21/13	19/13	18/13	19/13	19/12	20/12	20/11	19/11
Max/min (°F)	68/49	70/49	72/50	73/52	70/55	66/56	65/55	66/55	67/54	68/53	68/53	67/52
Rainfall (mm)	107	75	71	151	178	176	174	159	176	228	215	194

TRINCOMALEE

	Jan	Feb	Mar	Apr	May	Jun	Jul	Aug	Sep	Oct	Nov	Dec
Max/min (°C)	28/24	29/24	31/25	33/26	34/26	35/26	34/26	34/25	34/25	32/25	29/24	28/24
Max/min (°F)	82/76	85/76	88/77	91/78	94/79	95/79	94/78	94/78	93/77	89/76	85/76	83/76
Rainfall (mm)	132	100	54	50	52	26	70	89	104	217	334	341

three-pin sockets, especially in more upmarket hotels; adaptors are cheap and widely available. Power cuts, once frequent, are now much less common, while most top-end places have their own generators.

Emergencies

For police assistance in an emergency, call ☎119 in Colombo or ☎118 anywhere else on the island. The emergency number for Emergency Medical Services is ☎110.

Entry requirements

Citizens of all countries apart from the Maldives and Singapore require a **visa**, or "ETA" (Electronic Travel Authorization) to visit Sri Lanka. Visas can be obtained online in advance at ⓦeta.gov.lk or on arrival at the airport. The visa (prices are charged in $) is valid for thirty days and for two entries and currently costs $20 if bought online ($10 for citizens of SAARC countries) or $25 if bought on arrival; you can also buy a thirty-day business visa online (also $20). Your passport must be valid for six months after the date of your arrival.

This thirty-day visa can be **extended** to three months at the Department of Immigration (Mon–Fri 8.30am–2pm; ☎011 532 9300, ⓦimmigration .gov.lk) at 41 Ananda Rajakaruna Mw, Punchi Borella, Colombo 10, on the east side of the city centre beyond Colombo General Hospital. You can extend your visa as soon as you get to Sri Lanka; the month included in your original visa is included in the three months. You'll need to bring one passport photo. Fees for three-month visa extensions (again, these are quoted in $) can be checked at ⓦimmigration.gov.lk; they're currently $54 for UK nationals, $16 for citizens of the Republic of Ireland, $30 for Australians, $34.50 for New Zealanders, $50 for Canadians, and $100 for US citizens. Conditions for extensions are an onward ticket and proof of

sufficient funds, calculated at $15 a day, although a credit card will probably suffice.

Foreign embassies and consulates are virtually all based in Colombo (see p.99).

SRI LANKAN EMBASSIES AND CONSULATES

Australia and New Zealand ⓦ slhcaust.org.
Canada ⓦ srilankahcottawa.org.
UK and Ireland ⓦ srilankahighcommission.co.uk.
US ⓦ slembassyusa.org.

Gay and lesbian travellers

There is little understanding of gay issues in Sri Lanka – gays and lesbians are generally stigmatized and homosexuality is technically **illegal** (although no one has been arrested since 1950), so discretion is advised, and the whole scene remains rather secretive. ⓦequal-ground.org is a good first port of call for information about the local scene, while ⓦutopia-asia.com/tipssri.htm has further links, as well as listings of gay-friendly accommodation and general travel information.

Insurance

It's essential to take out **insurance** before travelling to cover against theft, loss and illness or injury. A typical travel insurance policy usually provides cover for loss of baggage, tickets and – up to a certain limit – cash or cheques, as well as cancellation or early curtailment of your journey. Most of them exclude so-called dangerous sports unless an extra premium is paid: in Sri Lanka this can mean scuba diving, whitewater rafting, windsurfing and trekking. Many policies can be chopped and changed to exclude coverage you don't need – for example, sickness and accident benefits can often be excluded or included at will. When securing baggage cover, make sure that the per-article limit – typically under £500 – will cover your most

---

ROUGH GUIDES TRAVEL INSURANCE

Rough Guides has teamed up with WorldNomads.com to offer great travel insurance deals. Policies are available to residents of over 150 countries, with cover for a wide range of adventure sports, 24hr emergency assistance, high levels of medical and evacuation cover and a stream of travel safety information. Roughguides.com users can take advantage of their policies online 24/7, from anywhere in the world – even if you're already travelling. And since plans often change when you're on the road, you can extend your policy and even claim online. Roughguides.com users who buy travel insurance with WorldNomads.com can also leave a positive footprint and donate to a community development project. For more information go to ⓦroughguides.com/shop.

valuable possession. If you need to make a claim, you should keep receipts for medicines and medical treatment, and in the event you have anything stolen, you must obtain an official statement from the police.

Internet

Most towns in Sri Lanka now have at least one or two places offering **internet** access, either in proper cybercafés, in communications bureaux or in guesthouses – details are given throughout the Guide. Costs vary widely, from as little as Rs.1 per minute in Colombo and Kandy up to Rs.6 per minute or more in less well-connected areas. An increasing number of places also have **wi-fi**. If you have a laptop and need to be constantly connected, all Sri Lanka's telecom providers (see p.61) offer various mobile broadband packages.

Laundry

Most guesthouses and hotels offer a **laundry** service. Washing usually takes 24 hours and usually costs around Rs.50–75 for a shirt or blouse and around Rs.100 for a pair of trousers or a light dress. There are no public coin-operated launderettes anywhere on the island.

Mail

Postal services from Sri Lanka (Ⓦ slpost.gov.lk) are fairly reliable, at least if you stick to airmail, which takes three to four days to reach the UK and US. Surface mail is about half to one-third the cost of airmail but is horribly slow and offers lots of potential for things to get lost or damaged in transit. A postcard to the UK, Australasia and North America costs Rs.25. An airmail parcel to the UK costs around $25 for up to 0.5kg, plus around $12.50 for each additional 0.5kg up to a maximum weight of 20kg (rates to North America are similar; to Australia, slightly cheaper). Parcels heavier than 20kg have to be sent by EMS Speed Post (see below). If you want to send a parcel home from Sri Lanka, you must take the contents unwrapped to the post office so that they can be inspected before wrapping (all larger post offices have counters selling glue, string and wrapping paper).

Another option is **EMS Speed Post**, slightly faster (and more expensive) than airmail – a 0.5kg package to the UK costs around $27 (slightly less to North America and Australia). Alternatively, a number of reputable international **couriers** have offices in Colombo – try Fedex at 300 Galle Rd, Kollupitiya (Ⓣ 011 452 2222).

Maps

There are several good **maps** of Sri Lanka. The best and most detailed is the *Rough Guide Sri Lanka Map* (1:500,000); it's also printed on indestructible water-proof paper so it won't disintegrate in the tropics and can even be used as an emergency monsoon shelter, at a pinch. Otherwise, the entire island is covered by a series of 92 1:50,000 maps – detailed, but somewhat dated. These are only available from the Survey Dept on Kirulla Rd, Havelock Town, Colombo 5 (Mon–Fri 10am–3.30pm); you'll need to show your passport to get in. In Colombo, *Arjuna's A–Z Street Guide* is generally useful, if not always totally accurate.

Money

The Sri Lankan **currency** is the rupee (abbreviated variously as R., R/ or R/-, and, as in this book, as Rs.). **Coins** come in denominations of Rs.1, 2, 5 and 10. **Notes** come in denominations of Rs.10, 20, 50, 100, 200, 500, 1000, 2000 and 5000. Try to avoid accepting particularly dirty, torn or disreputable-looking notes, and break big notes and stock up on change whenever you can – don't expect to be able to pay for a Rs.50 cup of tea with a Rs.5000 note.

At the time of writing, the **exchange rate** was around Rs.130 to $1, Rs.175 to €1, and Rs.210 to £1; you can check current exchange rates at Ⓦ xe .com. The Sri Lankan rupee continues to devalue steadily against hard currencies. To guard against the effects of this devaluation, top-end hotels always give their prices either in **US dollars** or (occasionally) in euros, though you'll be expected to pay in rupees, with the bill converted at the current bank exchange rate. Many other tourist services are also often priced in dollars – anything from entrance tickets at archeological sites to tours, balloon trips or diving courses – though, again, payment will be expected in rupees.

Sri Lanka is well supplied with **banks**. The six main chains (most larger towns will have a branch of at least three or four of these) are the Bank of Ceylon, Hatton National Bank, Sampath Bank, Commercial Bank, People's Bank and Seylan Bank. All are open Monday to Friday from 8 or 9am in the morning until 2 or 3pm in the afternoon, and all shut at weekends. Exchange rates for foreign currency, whether travellers' cheques, cash or making withdrawals by credit or debit card, are fairly uniform; you may get fractionally better rates if you shop around, but you won't make any dramatic savings. If you need to change money **outside banking hours**, head to the nearest top-end hotel – most change cash or travellers' cheques, though at rates that are up to ten percent poorer than bank rates. Failing this, you could try at local guesthouses or shops – the more tourist-oriented the place you're in, the better your chances, though you'll probably have to accept poor rates. All towns of any consequence now have at least one bank **ATM** that accepts foreign debit and credit cards; details are given throughout the Guide. ATMs at the Commercial Bank (which accept both Visa and MasterCard) are usually the most reliable, followed by those at the Hatton National Bank.

Despite the usefulness of plastic, you might still feel it's worth taking at least a few **travellers' cheques**. These can be changed rapidly and painlessly at any bank in Sri Lanka. Sterling-, euro- and dollar-denominated travellers' cheques are all universally accepted, but take a standard brand (Amex, Thomas Cook or Visa) to avoid problems.

You might also want to carry some **cash** with you for emergencies. US dollars, euros, pounds sterling and Australian dollars are all widely recognized and easily changed. New Zealand or Canadian dollars might occasionally cause problems, but are generally accepted in most banks.

Opening hours

Most businesses, including banks and government offices, work a standard **five-day working week** from Monday to Friday 9/9.30am to 5/5.30pm. Major post offices generally operate longer hours (typically 7am–9pm), and stay open on Saturdays as well. Many museums shut on Fridays, while Hindu temples stay shut until around 4pm to 5pm, when they open for the evening puja. Buddhist temples, by contrast, generally stay open from dawn until dusk, or later.

Phones

Phoning home from Sri Lanka is straightforward, and relatively inexpensive, although if you're planning a long trip and are likely to be making a lot of calls, using your own **mobile** is probably the most cost-effective option. Ask your service provider whether your handset will work abroad and what the call costs are. Most UK, Australian and New Zealand mobiles use GSM, which works well in Sri Lanka, but US mobiles (apart from tri-band phones) won't work. While some foreign mobile providers have reciprocal arrangements with local operators and offer surprisingly cheap rates using your existing SIM card – you might like to check tariffs before you travel – it's generally cheaper to **replace the SIM card** in your phone with a new SIM from a Sri Lankan company (assuming your phone isn't locked). This will give you a Sri Lankan phone number and you will be charged domestic rates – as low as Rs.15 per minute for international calls, and around Rs.5 for local calls. SIM cards can be picked up for around $10 or less from the myriad phone shops which have sprung up to cater to the Sri Lankan mobile boom; these places also sell chargers and adaptors for Sri Lankan sockets, and cards with which you can top up your airtime (or look for any shop displaying the relevant sticker). The **main operators** are Dialog (Ⓦ dialog.lk), Mobitel (Ⓦ mobitel.lk), Etisalat (Ⓦ etisalat.lk), Airtel (Ⓦ airtel.lk) and Hutch (Ⓦ hutch.lk). You can get a mobile signal pretty much everywhere on the island apart from a few remote rural locations, most notably Kudawa, in Sinharaja.

Without a mobile, the easiest way to make a call is to go to one of the island's innumerable **communications bureaux**, little offices offering phone, fax and photocopying services, and sometimes email as well (look out for signs advertising IDD calls); there will usually be at least a couple on the main street of even the smallest town. You make your call, either from a private cubicle or from a phone at the counter, and then pay the bill at the end. Some places have phones with built-in LCD timers so you can see exactly how long you've been on the line for; in other places they just use a stop-watch. Calls to the UK, Australasia and North America cost from around Rs.75 per minute; calls within Sri Lanka cost around Rs.5 per minute.

There are very few **public payphones** in Sri Lanka. If you can't get to a communications bureau, you could possibly phone from your **hotel room**, though this is expensive.

To **call home from Sri Lanka**, dial the international access code (☎ 00), then the country code (UK ☎ 44; US & Canada ☎ 1; Ireland ☎ 353; Australia ☎ 61; New Zealand ☎ 64; South Africa ☎ 27), then the area code and subscriber number. Note that the initial zero is omitted from the area code when dialling the UK, Ireland, Australia and New Zealand from abroad.

To **call Sri Lanka from abroad**, dial your international access code then the country code for Sri Lanka (☎ 94), then the area code, minus the initial zero, then the subscriber number.

Photography

Sri Lankans love having their photo taken – though it's obviously polite to ask and, if you're using a digital camera, to show them the results afterwards. A few of the island's more photogenic inhabitants might expect to be paid to be photographed, particularly stilt fishermen, when you can find them, and (occasionally) tea pickers in the highlands. You're not allowed to pose for photographs with Buddha images (standing with your back to the image), and photography is also generally not permitted inside Hindu temples. In addition, note that flash photography can damage old murals; if you're asked not to take flash photos, don't. And of course photographing soldiers or military installations is asking for trouble.

There are camera shops in most main towns, plus a few places in Kandy and Colombo where you can burn digital images to CD and which also sell memory cards (at Western prices). If you're using slide or black-and-white **film** it's best to bring it from home. If you buy film in Sri Lanka, check the expiry date on the box and don't buy film that has been left lying around in the sun. Processing is widely available, though won't always match the standards you're used to back home.

Time

Sri Lanka is five hours and thirty minutes ahead of **GMT**; it doesn't follow Daylight Savings Time.

Tourist information

Considering the importance of tourism to the national economy, there are surprisingly few sources of official **tourist information** either in Sri Lanka itself or abroad – only the UK currently boasts a properly equipped overseas tourist office (3rd floor, 1 Devonshire Square, London EC2M 4WD; ☎0845 880 6333). For detailed information about specific areas, the best sources are the independent tour operators (see pp.26–27) and staff at hotels and guesthouses.

In addition to a number of magazines that feature listings and articles of local interest (see p.40), the free monthly *Travel Lanka*, available from the tourist office in Colombo (see p.90), contains listings of accommodation, shops, services and transport in the capital and across the island.

Good **online** sources of information include the Sri Lanka Tourist Board's site (Ⓦsrilanka.travel).

You might also like to have a browse through Ari Withanage's Sri Lanka pages at Ⓦmembers .tripod.com/~withanage and the eclectic Lanka Library (Ⓦlankalibrary.com), which has loads of background on sites, culture, history and cuisine. The websites dedicated to **current affairs** in Sri Lanka are also worth a look (see p.39).

Travellers with disabilities

Awareness of the needs of **disabled people** remains extremely low in Sri Lanka, and there's virtually no provision for disabled travellers. Few hotels, restaurants or tourist sites are wheelchair-accessible, although there are plenty of one-storey guesthouses that might be usable – though more by accident than design. Public transport is enough of a challenge for able-bodied passengers, and completely useless for wheelchair users, so you'll need your own vehicle and a driver who is sympathetic to your needs – and even then the lack of specially adapted vehicles can make getting in and out difficult.

Pavements – where they exist – are generally uneven, full of potholes and protected by high kerbs, while the anarchic traffic presents obvious dangers to those with only limited mobility.

Volunteering in Sri Lanka

There are all sorts of **voluntary work projects** in Sri Lanka – anything from teaching football to mucking out elephants – and a quick trawl on the internet will turn up dozens of possibilities. Note, however, that although volunteering is richly rewarding, it demands a real commitment of time and energy, and most placements cost at least as much as you'd expect to pay on an equivalent-length backpacking holiday on the island, and sometimes rather more. The following organizations give a good idea of what's available.

VOLUNTEER ORGANIZATIONS

Children's Hope Habaraduwa, Sri Lanka ☎091 493 4440, Ⓦvolunteersvillage.com or Ⓦchildrenshope.lk. Opportunities for teaching and working in a local deaf and blind children's school, as well as assisting with other projects around Galle.

Global Crossroad US ☎1 866 387 7816, UK ☎0800 310 1821; Ⓦglobalcrossroad.com. Two- to twelve-week projects, ranging from placements in orphanages to elephant conservation and teaching English to Buddhist monks.

IMPAKT Aid Trust Sri Lanka ☎011 250 7099, Ⓦimpaktaid.com. Well-regarded Sri Lankan specialists working with tsunami survivors and widows.

i to i International Projects UK ☎ 01892 886 166, ⓦ i-to-i.com. Two- to eight-week placements including conservation work with elephants and turtles, and community projects with kids in Colombo.
Millennium Elephant Foundation Sri Lanka ☎ 035 226 3377, ⓦ millenniumelephantfoundation.org. This leading elephant sanctuary near Kandy (see p.204) offers one- to six-month placements. Volunteers are expected to contribute fundraising, public relations and other administrative support, as well as to work with the elephants and the local community.
Outreach International UK ☎ 01458 274957, ⓦ outreach international.co.uk. Wide variety of placements – anything from art therapy and football coaching to working in the Unawatuna Old People's Home.
Travellers Worldwide UK ☎ 01903 502595, ⓦ travellers worldwide.com. Varied range of projects (two weeks to six months) including English teaching, football coaching and placements at Colombo zoo and Wasgomuwa National Park.

Weddings

Sri Lanka is one of the world's leading honeymoon destinations, and many couples go a step further and actually get married on the island – beach **weddings** are particularly popular. Arranging the ceremony independently and dealing with the attendant paperwork and bureaucracy can be difficult, however, and it's much easier to leave the details to a specialist operator. Most large hotels and a number of tour operators (see p.204) can arrange the whole wedding for you, including (if you fancy) extras like Kandyan drummers and dancers, plus optional elephants and a chorus of local girls.

Colombo and the west coast

70 Colombo

100 Negombo

106 Around Negombo

109 North of Negombo

112 Kalpitiya peninsula

114 South of Colombo

SEEMA MALAKA TEMPLE, COLOMBO

1

Colombo and the west coast

Sri Lanka's west coast is the island's front door and – via the international airport at Katunayake just outside Colombo – the point of arrival for all visitors to the country (at least pending the opening of the new international terminal at Hambantota). This is Sri Lanka at its most developed and populous: the busiest, brashest and most Westernized region in the country, home to the capital city and the principal coastal resorts, which have now all but fused into an unbroken ribbon of concrete which meanders along the seaboard for over a hundred kilometres.

Situated about two-thirds of the way down the west coast, Sri Lanka's sprawling capital, **Colombo**, is usually low on visitors' list of priorities, although beneath the unprepossessing surface lies an intriguing and characterful city which offers a fascinating microcosm of contemporary Sri Lanka. North of Colombo is the busy resort of **Negombo**, whose proximity to the airport makes it a popular first or last stop on many itineraries, while further up the coast is the idyllic **Kalpitiya peninsula**, with deserted beaches and superb dolphin-watching, and – a short drive inland – the vast **Wilpattu National Park**, now slowly regaining its former glory after decades of upheaval during the civil war.

South of the capital lie the island's main beach resorts. The principal areas – **Kalutara**, **Beruwala** and **Bentota** – are home to endless oversize hotels catering to vacationing Europeans on two-week packages. Pockets of serenity remain, even so, along with some characterful hotels and guesthouses, while further south lies **Hikkaduwa**, Sri Lanka's original hippy hangout, now rather past its best, though it does retain a certain down-at-heel charm and (by sleepy Sri Lankan standards at any rate) a refreshingly upbeat atmosphere thanks to the backpackers who still flock here for cheap sun, sand and surf.

GETTING AROUND

By train and bus Getting around the west is straightforward. There are regular train services along the coast, while endless buses ply the main coastal highway, the Galle Road – though the clogged traffic and antiquated trains mean that it can take a surprisingly long time to cover relatively short distances. The opening of the new Southern Expressway (see p.28) has helped speed travel up, and will do so even further once the new airport extension is completed.

Colombo: getting oriented see p.70
Area numbers and street names see p.72
Henry Steel Olcott: American Buddhist see p.76
Green Path art gallery see p.84
Principal train departures from Colombo Fort see p.89
The Karavas see p.101
Boat trips, watersports and diving see p.102

Tour guides in Negombo see p.103
Rama, Shiva and Munnesvaram see p.110
Kitesurfing at Alankuda see p.113
Ayurveda: the science of life see p.118
Ayurveda and health resorts in Beruwala and Bentota see p.119
Diving and watersports see p.124
Geoffrey Bawa see p.126
Turtle hatcheries see p.128
Low-country dancing see p.130
Watersports at Hikkaduwa see p.133

CLUB VILLA, BENTOTA

Highlights

❶ The Pettah Colombo's absorbing bazaar district, stuffed full of every conceivable type of merchandise, from mobile phones to Ayurvedic herbs. **See p.76**

❷ Gangaramaya and Seema Malaka Step out of the urban melee of Colombo into the serene enclosures of these two contrasting Buddhist temples. **See p.82**

❸ Wilpattu National Park Huge and very peaceful national park, home to significant populations of leopards, elephants and sloth bears. **See p.111**

❹ Kalpitiya peninsula Superb dolphin-watching, intriguing colonial remains, a beautiful lagoon and the island's most alluring cluster of boutique eco-resorts on idyllic Alankuda Beach. **See p.112**

❺ Bentota With an idyllic sandy beach and a string of elegant small-scale hotels, the southern end of Bentota offers an oasis of style and tranquillity among the brash west coast package resorts. **See p.122**

❻ Hikkaduwa Popular backpacker hangout, with good surfing, snorkelling and diving, and one of the liveliest beach scenes anywhere on the coast. **See p.131**

HIGHLIGHTS ARE MARKED ON THE MAP ON PP.68–69

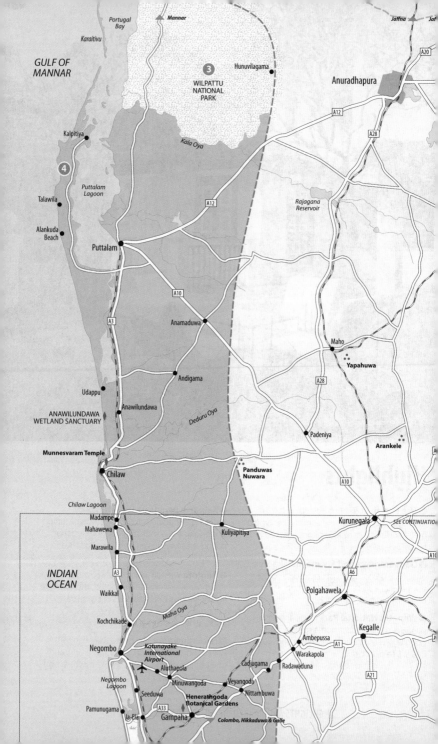

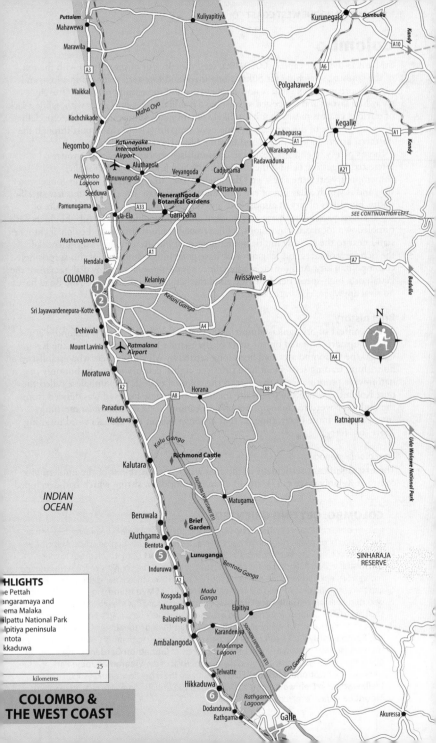

Puttalam
Mahawewa
Marawila
Waikkal
Kochchikade
Negombo
Kuliyapitiya
Kurunegala
Dambulla
Polgahawela
Ambepussa
Warakapola
Radawaduna
Kegalle
Katunayake International Airport
Aluthapola
Veyangoda
Cadjugama
Nittambuwa
Vinuwangoda
Negombo Lagoon
Seeduwa
Henerathgoda Botanical Gardens
Pamunugama
Ja-Ela
Gampaha

A3
A10
A6
A1
A21
A33
A1

SEE CONTINUATION LEFT

Muthurajawela
Hendala
COLOMBO
Kelaniya
Avissawella
Sri Jayawardenepura-Kotte
Dehiwala
Mount Lavinia
Ratmalana Airport
Moratuwa
Panadura
Wadduwa
Horana
Ratnapura

Kalu Ganga
Kelani Ganga

A7
A1
A4
A4
A8
A2
A8

INDIAN OCEAN

Kalutara
Richmond Castle
Matugama
Beruwala
Brief Garden
Aluthgama
Bentota
Lunuganga
Induruwa
Kosgoda
Madu Ganga
Ahungalla
Balapitiya
Elpitiya
Karandeniya
Ambalangoda
Madampe Lagoon
Telwatte
Hikkaduwa
Dodanduwa
Rathgama
Rathgama Lagoon
Galle
Akuressa

Bentota Ganga
Gin Ganga

Southern Expressway (E1)

SINHARAJA RESERVE

Uda Walawe National Park
Badulla

N

① ②
⑤
⑥

HLIGHTS
e Pettah
angaramaya and
ema Malaka
Ilpattu National Park
Ipitiya peninsula
ntota
kkaduwa

25
kilometres

COLOMBO & THE WEST COAST

1

Colombo

Sri Lanka's dynamic capital, **COLOMBO**, seems totally out of proportion with the rest of the country, stretching for 50km along the island's western seaboard in a long and formless urban straggle that is now home to around three million people. The city's sprawling layout and congested streets make it difficult to get to grips with, while a lack of obvious charms means that it's unlikely to win many immediate friends, especially if your first taste of the capital is via the hour-long drive from the airport through the northern breeze-block suburbs and hooting files of weaving traffic.

There's plenty to enjoy beneath the unpromising exterior, especially if you're interested in getting behind the tourist clichés and finding out what makes contemporary Sri Lanka tick – it's definitely a place that grows on you the longer you stay, and is worth a day out of even the shortest itinerary. The city musters few specific sights, but offers plenty of atmosphere and quirky character: a heady admixture of Asian anarchy, colonial charm and modern chic. Shiny office blocks rub shoulders with tumbledown local cafés and shops, while serene Buddhist shrines and colonial churches stand next to the garishly multicoloured towers of Hindu temples – all evidence of the rich stew of races and religions that have gone into the making of this surprisingly cosmopolitan city. And for sheer adrenaline, a walk through the crowded bazaars of the Pettah or a high-speed rickshaw ride amid the kamikaze traffic of the Galle Road have no rival anywhere else in the country.

Brief history

In the context of Sri Lanka's almost 2500 years of recorded history, Colombo is a relative upstart. Situated on the delta of the island's fourth-longest river, the Kelani Ganga, the Colombo area had been long settled by Muslim traders who established a flourishing trading settlement here from the eighth century onwards, but only rose to nationwide prominence at the start of the colonial period. The Sinhalese called the port Kolamba, which the poetically inclined Portuguese believed was derived from the Sinhalese word for mango trees (*kola* meaning "leaves", and *amba* meaning "mango"); it's more likely, though, that *kolamba* was an old Sinhala word meaning "port" or "ferry".

The colonial period

The first significant settlement in the area was 13km northeast of the modern city centre at **Kelaniya** (see p.87), site of a famous Buddhist shrine which had developed

---

COLOMBO: GETTING ORIENTED

Colombo is a confusing city. There's no single focal point, and it's more helpful to think of it as a collection of disparate neighbourhoods than as a single, coherent urban space. At the heart of the old colonial city, the moribund and bomb-afflicted **Fort** district, Colombo's former administrative and financial centre, offers a stark reminder of the conflicts which have beset modern Sri Lanka, while to the east and south lie the bustling mercantile district of the **Pettah** and the engaging temples and old-fashioned street life of **Slave Island**. From here, it's a short walk or tuktuk ride to **Galle Face Green** – perfect, after a hard day's exploring, for an evening stroll along the seafront promenade and a sundowner at the historic *Galle Face Hotel*.

South of the Green, the sulphurous **Galle Road** runs through the suburbs of **Kollupitiya** and **Bambalapitiya**, the heart of the modern city, and home to many of Colombo's best shopping and eating venues. Inland, the leafy streets of **Cinnamon Gardens** conceal further places to stay, eat and drink, as well as the tropical oasis of the **Viharamahadevi Park** and the city's excellent **National Museum**. Further south are the more downmarket suburbs of **Wellawatta** and **Dehiwala**, home to the national zoo, and the attractive beachside suburb of **Mount Lavinia**, 10km from the city centre.

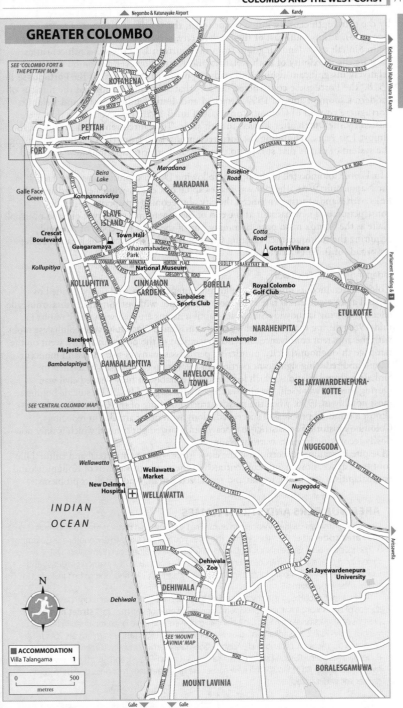

GREATER COLOMBO

◀ Negombo & Katunayake Airport   ▲ Kandy

SEE 'COLOMBO FORT & THE PETTAH' MAP

KOTAHENA

Dematagoda

AVISSAWELLA ROAD

PETTAH

Fort

FORT

Beira Lake

Maradana

MARADANA

Baseline Road

Galle Face Green

Kompannavidiya

SLAVE ISLAND

Crescat Boulevard

Gangaramaya

Viharamahadevi Park

Town Hall

Cotta Road

Gotami Vihara

Kollupitiya

National Museum

KOLLUPITIYA

CINNAMON GARDENS

BORELLA

Royal Colombo Golf Club

ETULKOTTE

Sinhalese Sports Club

NARAHENPITA

Barefoot

Majestic City

Bambalapitiya

BAMBALAPITIYA

Narahenpita

HAVELOCK TOWN

SRI JAYAWARDENEPURA-KOTTE

SEE 'CENTRAL COLOMBO' MAP

NUGEGODA

Wellawatta

Wellawatta Market

New Delmon Hospital

WELLAWATTA

Nugegoda

INDIAN OCEAN

Dehiwala Zoo

Sri Jayewardenepura University

DEHIWALA

Dehiwala

SEE 'MOUNT LAVINIA' MAP

BORALESGAMUWA

N

MOUNT LAVINIA

■ **ACCOMMODATION**

Villa Talangama   **1**

0   500

metres

▼ Galle   ▼ Galle

1

by the thirteenth century into a major town; the nearby settlement of **Kotte** (see p.88), 11km southeast of the modern city, served as the capital of the island's main Sinhalese lowland kingdom from the fourteenth to the sixteenth centuries. Despite the proximity of both Kelaniya and Kotte, however, Colombo remained a relatively insignificant fishing and trading port until the arrival of the **Portuguese** in 1518. The Portuguese constructed the fort that subsequently formed the nucleus of modern Colombo and, in 1597, attacked and destroyed both Kotte and Kelaniya. Portuguese control of Colombo only lasted until 1656, however, when they were ousted by the **Dutch** after a seven-month siege. The Dutch remained in control for almost 150 years, rebuilding the fort, reclaiming land from the swampy delta using the system of canals that survive to this day, and creating spacious new tree-lined suburbs.

In 1796, Colombo fell to the **British**, following Dutch capitulation to the French in the Napoleonic Wars. The city was made capital of Ceylon, while new road and rail links with Kandy further enhanced the city's burgeoning prosperity. With the construction of a new harbour at the end of the nineteenth century, Colombo overtook Galle as the island's main port, becoming one of the great entrepôts of Asia and acquiring the sobriquet the "Charing Cross of the East" thanks to its location at the crossroads of Indian Ocean trade.

Independence and civil war

Colombo retained its importance following **independence**, and has continued to expand at an exponential rate ever since, though not without sometimes disastrous side effects. Growing islandwide Sinhalese–Tamil tensions erupted with tragic results in mid-1983, during the month subsequently christened **Black July**, when Sinhalese mobs, with the apparent connivance and encouragement of the police and army, went on the rampage throughout the city, murdering perhaps as many as two thousand innocent Tamils and reducing significant portions of the Pettah to ruins – a watershed in Sinhalese–Tamil relations which led, almost inevitably, to fully fledged civil war. During the **civil war** itself, the city was repeatedly targeted by LTTE suicide bombers, most notably in 1996, when the massive truck-bombing of the Central Bank killed almost a hundred people and succeeded, along with other attacks, in reducing Colombo's historic Fort district to a heavily militarized ghost town which is only now slowly recovering from its wartime trauma.

Despite its traumatic recent past, the city's irrepressible commercial and cultural life continues apace, now mainly concentrated in the southern suburbs of Kollupitiya and Bambalapitiya, and in the rebuilt and revitalized Pettah. And for all its problems,

---

AREA NUMBERS AND STREET NAMES

Greater Colombo is divided into fifteen numbered suburbs, and districts are often identified by their **area code** rather than their name. The ones you're most likely to encounter are: Colombo 1 (Fort); Colombo 2 (Slave Island); Colombo 3 (Kollupitiya); Colombo 4 (Bambalapitiya); Colombo 5 (Havelock Town); Colombo 6 (Wellawatta); Colombo 7 (Cinnamon Gardens); and Colombo 11 (Pettah). Mount Lavinia isn't technically part of Colombo, and so isn't included in the numbering system.

The fact that suburbs in the city are known by both name and number is one possible source of confusion. Another is provided by ongoing changes to the city's **street names**. Dozens of streets have now lost their colonial monikers and have been renamed in honour of various polysyllabic Sri Lankan notables. Five of the most important renamings are R.A. de Mel Mawatha (formerly Duplication Rd); Ananda Coomaraswamy Mawatha (Green Path); Dr Colvin R. de Silva Mawatha (Union Place); De Soysa Circus (Lipton Circus); and Ernest de Silva Mawatha (Flower Rd). Many of the new names are only erratically recognized, with the old names still widely used.

Colombo remains a fascinating melting pot of the island's Sinhalese, Tamil, Muslim, Burgher and expatriate communities, who combine to give the place a uniquely forward-thinking and outward-looking character quite unlike anywhere else in the island – one which gives a glimpse of what a multi-ethnic, twenty-first-century Sri Lanka might become, communal tensions permitting.

Fort

Fort district lies at the heart of old Colombo, occupying (as its name suggests) the site of the now-vanished Portuguese defences. Under the British, Fort developed into the centrepiece of the colonial capital, adorned with handsome Neoclassical buildings and boasting all the necessities of expatriate life in the tropics, right down to the inevitable clocktower and statue of Queen Victoria. Following independence, Fort retained its position as Colombo's administrative and financial hub until the onset of the civil war, when repeated LTTE attacks – most notably the massive **bomb** that was detonated outside the Central Bank in 1996 – all but killed off the life of the district.

Despite these reverses, **southern Fort** retains something of its former commercial importance, with a clutch of five-star hotels and an optimistically modernist skyline presided over by the two soaring towers of the World Trade Center. A block north, **central Fort** remains one of Sri Lanka's strangest urban spaces, its moribund streets lined with the grandiose shells of semi-derelict nineteenth-century buildings and carved up by security barriers and wire-mesh fences into a perplexing maze of blocked-off streets and security checkpoints. Some of area's fine old buildings are finally receiving long overdue renovations, although a significant portion of the district remains off- limits to visitors thanks to the proximity of the harbour and the president's official residence.

Around the clocktower

Thanks to the presence of the President's House, much of the western side of Fort is currently closed to visitors. Aside from the places described here, the area's few sites of interest are now largely out of bounds. More or less at the centre of the district is the quaint **clocktower-lighthouse**, ignominiously hemmed in on three sides by security fences and now a rather forlorn sight. The clocktower was originally constructed in 1857, apparently at the behest of the punctilious wife of Governor Henry Ward as a result of her exasperation with oriental standards of timekeeping. Ten years later, a lighthouse-style beacon was constructed on top of the clock, and it served simultaneously as timekeeper and as a signal for approaching shipping for a century until the surrounding buildings grew so high that they blocked out the lighthouse's beam (a new lighthouse now stands on the seafront just to the west). East of the clocktower, **Chatham St** and **Mudalige** and **Sir Baron Jayatilaka mawathas** are lined with an impressive medley of grandiose colonial buildings, many of them in advanced states of crumbling decay, although a few are now undergoing belated and badly needed renovations.

York Street and Cargills

The area north of the clocktower, home to the zealously guarded President's House, is closed to the general public, with the only exit from the clocktower being east along Chatham Street to **York Street**, at the edge of the high-security zone. A block north of here is the stolidly mercantile frontage of **Cargills** department store, whose expansive red-brick facade is one of Fort's most famous landmarks. Inside, the wood-panelled fittings and display cases look as though they haven't changed since the store's opening in 1906, though the disconcertingly bare shelves appear not to have been restocked since independence.

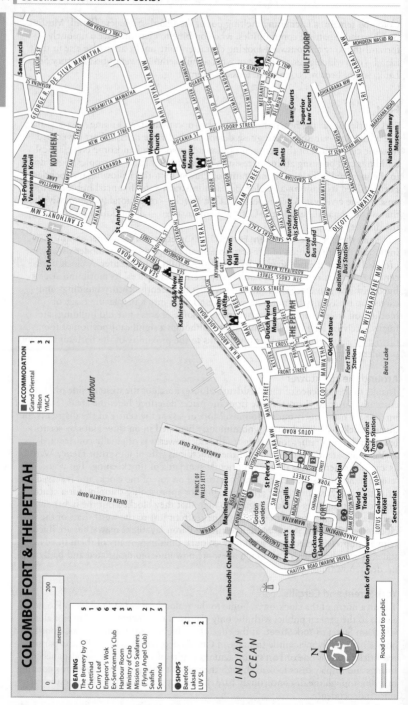

COLOMBO FORT & THE PETTAH

ACCOMMODATION
Grand Oriental	1
Hilton	3
YMCA	2

● EATING
The Brewery by O	5
Chettinad	1
Curry Leaf	6
Emperor's Wok	6
Ex-Serviceman's Club	4
Harbour Room	3
Mission to Seafarers (Flying Angel Club)	5
Ministry of Crab	2
Seafish	7
Semondu	5

● SHOPS
Barefoot	2
Laksala	1
LUV SL	2

Road closed to public

INDIAN OCEAN

Harbour

QUEEN ELIZABETH QUAY

Prince of Wales Jetty

BANDARANAIKE QUAY

KOTAHENA

HULFTSDORP

THE PETTAH

FORT

Beira Lake

N

1

The port and Grand Oriental Hotel
North from Cargills, York Street becomes increasingly down-at-heel before reaching Colombo's **port**, hidden behind high walls and strictly off-limits. Until the early twentieth century, the island's main port was Galle, but Colombo's improved road and rail links with the rest of the country and Sri Lanka's strategic location on Indian Ocean sea routes between Europe, Asia and Australasia encouraged the British to invest in a major overhaul of the city's rather unsatisfactory harbour, during which they constructed three new breakwaters (the largest, built in 1885, is over a kilometre long).

Opposite the main entrance to the port stands the famous old **Grand Oriental Hotel** – passengers arriving in Colombo would stagger straight off their ocean liner into the palatial hotel foyer, to collapse over a revivifying cocktail. Little of the establishment's former colonial splendour remains, though its *Harbour Room* restaurant-bar affords marvellous port views.

St Peter's Church
Church St • Daily 7am–5pm • Free
The area east of the *Grand Oriental Hotel* is currently out of bounds, though you can duck through the checkpoint to visit **St Peter's Church**, next door to the hotel. Occupying an old Dutch governor's residence of 1680, this was converted into a church in 1821, its plain little Neoclassical facade squeezed into a narrow space between surrounding buildings. The interior is almost completely bare, the only decoration being the wall memorials to various British notables who ended their lives in Ceylon – a strangely time-warped and atmospheric little spot, which seems a million miles away from the decaying Sri Lankan streets outside.

Southern Fort and the Dutch Hospital
Southern Fort is dominated by a trio of five-star **hotels**, the slender, cylindrical **Bank of Ceylon Tower** and the twin towers of the unfortunately named **World Trade Center**, whose high-rise modern outlines offer a sharp contrast to the colonial appearance of the rest of the district. Opposite the World Trade Center sits the newly restored and reopened **Dutch Hospital**. Dating (probably) from the seventeenth century, the complex comprises a neat cluster of low-slung ochre buildings arranged around a pair of rectangular courtyards, now home to an excellent selection of restaurants, cafés, bars and shops.

Sambodhi Chaitiya
Chaitiya Rd • No fixed hours • Free
West of the Dutch Hospital, **Chaitiya Road** (Marine Drive) sweeps north along the oceanfront, passing Fort's modern lighthouse en route to the **Sambodhi Chaitiya**, a huge dagoba on stilts, built in 1956 to mark the 2500th anniversary of the Buddha's death. Looking a bit like a gigantic lava lamp, this thoroughly peculiar structure is quite the oddest thing in Colombo. Some 260 (admittedly very shallow) steps climb up to the top, offering sweeping views of port and Fort and of the roofline of the huge white President's House sulking in trees below. It's also possible to go inside the hollow dagoba itself, painted with scenes showing scenes from the Buddha's life and the history of the religion in the island.

Maritime Museum
Chaitiya Rd • Daily 10am–7pm • Free
The city's modest **Maritime Museum**, a few steps beyond the Sambodhi Chaitiya, has some rather tenuous exhibits featuring large (and largely conjectural) models of the ships on which various significant personages – Prince Vijaya, Fa-Hsien, Ibn Battuta – arrived in the island, plus later colonial vessels, along with miscellaneous bits of

1

maritime bric-a-brac, including an enormous sling once used to load elephants onto ships. You're now close to the main entrance to the port and the *Grand Oriental Hotel*, though roadblocks bar further progress.

The Pettah

East of Fort, the helter-skelter bazaar district of the **Pettah** is Colombo's most absorbing area, and feels quite unlike anywhere else in Sri Lanka. The crush and energy of the gridlocked streets, with merchandise piled high in tiny shops and on the pavements, holds an undeniable, chaotic fascination, although exploring can be a slow and rather exhausting process, made additionally perilous by the barrow boys and porters who charge through the crowds pulling or carrying huge loads and threatening the heads and limbs of unwary tourists.

Shops in the Pettah are still arranged in the traditional **bazaar layout**, with each street devoted to a different trade: Front Street, for example, is full of bags, suitcases and shoes; 1st Cross Street is devoted to hardware and electrical goods; 3rd Cross Street and Keyzer Street are stuffed with colourful fabrics, and so on. The wares on display are fairly mundane – unless you're a big fan of Taiwanese household appliances or fake Barbie dolls – although traces of older and more colourful trades survive in places.

Unlike the rest of Colombo, the district retains a strongly **Tamil** (the name Pettah derives from the Tamil word *pettai*, meaning village) and **Muslim** flavour, as evidenced by its many pure veg and Muslim restaurants, quaint mosques, Hindu temples and colonial churches (many Sri Lankan Tamils are Christian rather than Hindu). Even the people look different here, with Tamil women in gorgeous saris, Muslim children dressed entirely in white and older men in brocaded skullcaps – a refreshing change from the boring skirts and shirts which pass muster in the rest of the city.

Dutch Period Museum

Prince St • Tues–Sat 9am–5pm • Rs.500

A couple of blocks north of the station on Prince Street, among some of the most densely packed of the Pettah's bazaars, the **Dutch Period Museum** occupies the old Dutch town hall, a fine colonnaded building of 1780. The mildly interesting displays on the Dutch colonial era feature the usual old coins, Kandyan and Dutch artefacts,

---

HENRY STEEL OLCOTT: AMERICAN BUDDHIST

On the south side of the Pettah, in front of Fort Railway Station, stands a statue of **Henry Steel Olcott** (1842–1907), perhaps the most influential foreigner in the modern history of Sri Lanka. Olcott was an American Buddhist and co-founder (with Madame Blavatsky, the celebrated Russian clairvoyant and spiritualist) of the Theosophical Society, a quasi-religious movement which set about promoting Asian philosophy in the West and reviving oriental spiritual traditions in the East, to protect them from the attacks of European missionary Christianity. The society's utopian (if rather vague) objectives comprised a mixture of the scientific, the social, the spiritual and the downright bizarre: the mystical Madame Blavatsky, fount of the society's more arcane tenets, believed that she had the ability to levitate, render herself invisible and communicate with the souls of the dead, as well as asserting that the Theosophical Society was run according to orders received from a group of "masters" – disembodied tutelary spirits who were believed to reside in Tibet.

In 1880, Blavatsky and Olcott arrived in Ceylon, formally embracing Buddhism and establishing the **Buddhist Theosophical Society**, which became one of the principal driving forces behind the remarkable worldwide spread of Buddhism during the twentieth century. Olcott spent many of his later years touring the island, organizing Buddhist schools and petitioning the British colonial authorities to respect Sri Lanka's religious traditions, though his most visible legacy is the multicoloured Buddhist flag (see p.422) which he helped design, and which now decorates temples across the island.

military junk and dusty European furniture, plus a couple of miserable-looking waxworks of colonists dressed in full velvet and lace despite the sweltering heat. The main attraction, however, is the wonderfully atmospheric mansion itself, whose groaning wooden floors and staircases, great pitched roof and idyllic garden offer a beguiling glimpse into the lifestyle enjoyed by the eighteenth century's more upwardly mobile colonists.

Main Street and Jami ul-Aftar

Main St • Not open to non-Muslims

Cutting through the heart of the Pettah, the district's principal thoroughfare **Main Street** is usually a solidly heaving bedlam of vehicles and pedestrians, with porters weaving through the throng pushing carts piled high with every conceivable type of merchandise. On the far side of the road is Colombo's most eye-catching mosque, the **Jami ul-Aftar**, a gloriously kitsch red-and-white construction of 1909 which rises gaudily above the cluttered shops of Main Street like a heavily iced cake.

The Old Town Hall

Kayman's Gate • No fixed hours • Free

East of the Jami ul-Aftar (and a memorably malodorous fish market) is the intersection known as **Kayman's Gate** – the name probably refers to the crocodiles (or caimans) which were once kept in the canals surrounding Slave Island and in the fort moat to deter slaves from attempting to escape. Kayman's Gate is dominated by the fancifully Moorish-style **Old Town Hall** of 1873. Following an incarnation as a public market, the building was reopened in 1984 as a now-defunct municipal museum. The wrought-iron market building to one side still houses various marooned pieces of industrial and municipal hardware – including a steamroller, old street signs and a former van of the Colombo Public Library – which you can peek at through the railings. The doors into the town hall itself are usually left open, allowing you to walk up the fine Burma teak staircase to the old council chambers, whose austere wooden fittings and stalled fans exude a positively *Marie Celeste*-like charm. The small room next door houses a petrified huddle of waxwork figurines sitting around a table re-enacting a council meeting of yesteryear – unquestionably one of Colombo's most surreal sights.

The fruit and veg sellers who line the western side of the town hall building make this one of the most photogenic sections of the Pettah, while just behind lies another half-submerged remnant of colonial times in the form of an elaborate wrought-iron **market building**, now occupied by a miscellany of shops. Just behind here, **4th Cross Street** is usually full of colourful lorries loading and unloading: great sacks of chillies clutter the pavements, while merchants sit behind huge ledgers and piles of spices inside the picturesque little office-warehouses that line the street.

Sea Street

North of the town hall, the crowds begin to thin. The south side of **Gabo's Lane** is home to a few easily missed shops selling Ayurvedic ingredients: outlandish-looking sacks and pallets sit outside shops stuffed with bark, twigs and other strange pieces of vegetable matter. North of here, **Sea Street**'s eye-catching selection of fluorescent Sinhala signs advertise a long line of small jewellers' shops, usually full of local women haggling over ornate gold rings, earrings and necklaces.

Sea Street's middle section is dominated by the colourful **New Kathiresan** and **Old Kathiresan kovils**, whose three gateways fill one side of the street with a great clumpy mass of Hindu statuary. The temples are dedicated to the war god Skanda and are the starting point for the annual Vel Festival (see p.42); they're usually shut during the day, but become a hive of activity after dark, when bare-chested, luxuriantly bearded priests conduct evening puja amid the hypnotic noise of drumming and dense swirls of smoke.

1

Kotahena

The suburb of **Kotahena**, northeast of the Pettah, is one of the most ecclesiastical in Colombo, home to numerous colonial churches and small but brightly coloured Hindu temples. Walking north along St Anthony's Mawatha, you'll pass a string of colourful shops selling Hindu and Christian religious paraphernalia before reaching **St Anthony's Church**, where people of all faiths come to pay homage to a statue of St Anthony which is said to work miracles in solving family problems.

Santa Lucia

St Lucia's St • No fixed hours • Free

Foremost among Kotahena's many places of worship is the grand cathedral of **Santa Lucia**, perhaps the most imposing church in Sri Lanka, a fifteen-minute walk from St Anthony's Church along Jampettah, Kotahena and St Lucia's streets. Built between 1873 and 1910, and sporting a stately grey classical facade inspired by St Peter's in Rome, it seats some six thousand people, though not since the pope conducted a service here in 1994 has it been even half-full. Inside, the tombs of three French bishops of Colombo are about as exciting as it gets. Two further Neoclassical buildings – a Benedictine monastery and a convent – sit by the cathedral, creating an unexpectedly impressive architectural ensemble in this out-of-the-way corner of the city.

Wolfendahl Church

Wolfendahl St • No fixed hours • Free

Sitting unobtrusively in a quiet side street at the southern edge of Kotahena, the Dutch Reformed **Wolfendahl** (or Wolvendaal) **Church** of 1749 is Colombo's oldest church and one of Sri Lanka's most interesting colonial relics. Its rather severe Neoclassical exterior conceals an attractive period-piece interior complete with old tiled floor, simple stained glass, wicker seating and wooden pews, organ and pulpit. Numerous finely carved eighteenth-century floor tablets in the south transept commemorate assorted Dutch officials, including various governors whose remains were moved here from Fort in 1813. The whole structure exudes a sense of beautiful quiet and longevity which seems to have survived in a curious bubble amid the ramshackle surrounding streets. Ask the caretaker to show you the church's impressive collection of old Dutch church silver, if he's around.

Hulftsdorp

Various religious edifices dot the suburb of **Hulftsdorp**, named after Dutch general Gerard Hulft, who was killed in 1656 during the siege of the Portuguese fort in Colombo. These include a number of small, fanciful-looking mosques – the largest (but plainest) is the **Grand Mosque** on New Moor Street, the most important in the city, which hides behind shyly latticed orange walls. The large and striking modern building with the hat-shaped roof you can see from here is the **Superior Law Courts** (the original Neoclassical courts stand stolidly next door, two dumpy little buildings with dour Doric facades). Opposite the law courts rises the soaring spire of the pale grey Gothic Revival church of **All Saints**.

National Railway Museum

Olcott Mw, Maradana • Mon–Fri 10am–4pm • Rs.500 • ⓦ railwaymuseum.lk

Due south of Hulftsdorp in the suburb of Maradana, the former Colombo Terminus Station (which served as the main railway terminus in Colombo until it was closed in 1906 and replaced by the nearby Maradana station) now provides a home for the **National Railway Museum**, showcasing an engaging selection of old Sri Lanka Railways rolling stock, including a couple of fine old steam locomotives.

1

The Green has also traditionally been one of the city's main hang-outs for local **con artists** (see pp.51–52), and although the situation has improved markedly in recent years, it's still worth being on your guard.

Galle Face Green

The grassy sweep of **Galle Face Green**, running along the seafront south of Fort, is one of Colombo's best-loved landmarks, bounded to the north by the modern towers of Fort and to the south by the sprawling facade of the *Galle Face Hotel*. The Green was created by Sir Henry Ward, governor from 1855 to 1860 (an easily missed memorial plaque to him stands halfway along the promenade, in which the Green is "recommended to his successors in the interest of the Ladies and Children of Colombo"), and such is its place in the city's affections that even the rail line south – which elsewhere runs straight down the coast – was rerouted inland to avoid it. The Fort end of the Green is bounded by the ponderous Neoclassical **Secretariat**, now dwarfed by the *Galadari* hotel and the World Trade Center towers which rise behind it. Statues of independent Sri Lanka's first four prime ministers stand in front; in the centre is a purposefully moustachioed D.S. Senanayake, the first post-independence PM, who died in 1952 from injuries sustained when he fell from his horse on the Green.

A turn along the Green's seafront promenade makes a pleasantly salty stroll, with the waves crashing a few feet below and breezy views along the coast and out to sea, where lines of gargantuan tankers and container ships line up waiting to enter the harbour. Late in the day is the best time to visit, when half the city seems to come here to gossip, fly kites and eat the curious-looking snacks served up by the line of hawkers stretched out along the front.

Slave Island

Immediately east of Galle Face Green is the area known as **Slave Island** (although it's not actually an island), encircled on three sides by **Beira Lake**, whose various sections are connected by stagnant, pea-green canals. The name dates back to its Dutch-era title, **Kaffir Veldt**, from the African slaves (Kaffirs) who worked in the city – at one time there were as many as four thousand of them here. After a failed insurrection in the seventeenth century, the Dutch insisted that all slaves were quartered overnight in the Kaffir Veldt, and stocked the surrounding waterways with crocodiles in order to discourage attempts to escape.

Parts of Slave Island preserve a ramshackle charm, especially around Rifle Street, Akbar Mawatha and Malay Street, dotted with scruffy little cafés and assorted churches, mosques and temples, including several built during the colonial era for soldiers from Malaya and India serving in the British army, who were garrisoned on the island.

Sri Subramanian Kovil

Kew Rd • Usually closed except during morning and evening pujas (around 8–9am & 5–6pm) • Free

Constructed for Indian troops stationed here during the colonial era, the **Sri Subramanian Kovil** is one of Colombo's most imposing Hindu temples. The entrance, just off Kumaran Ratnam Road, is marked by a towering gopuram, a great mountain of kitsch masonry flanked with incongruously Victorian-looking miniature clocktowers. The temple is dedicated to the god Subramanian (or Kataragama, as he is known to the Sinhalese; see p.191), whose peacock symbol you will see at various places inside. The interior follows the standard pattern of Sri Lankan Hindu temples, with an inner shrine constructed from solid stone enclosed within a shed-like ambulatory, and an eclectic array of images including conventional Hindu gods – many blackened images of the maleficent Durga

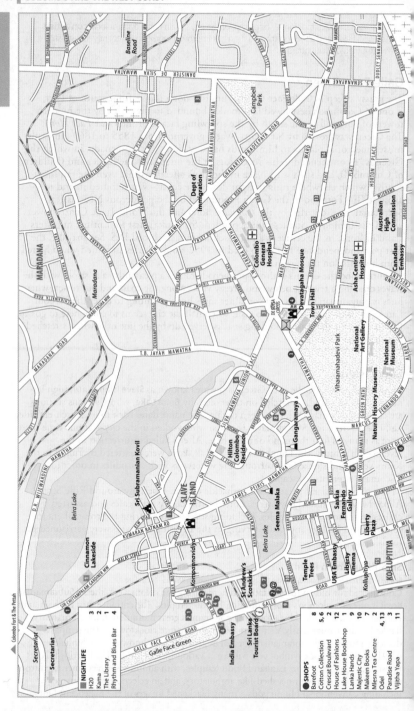

◀ Colombo Fort & The Pettah

Secretariat

■ NIGHTLIFE

H2O	3
Kama	2
The Library	1
Rhythm and Blues Bar	4

● SHOPS

Barefoot	8
Cotton Collection	5, 6
Crescat Boulevard	12
House of Fashions	1
Lake House Bookshop	9
Lanka Hands	7
Majestic City	10
Makeen Books	2
Mlesna Tea Centre	4, 13
Odel	3
Paradise Road	11
Vijitha Yapa	

MARADANA

Baseline Road

Campbell Park

Dept of Immigration

Colombo General Hospital

Devatagaha Mosque

Town Hall

Asha Central Hospital

Australian High Commission

Canadian Embassy

National Art Gallery

National Museum

Natural History Museum

Viharamahadevi Park

Maradana

T.B. JAYAH MAWATHA

Beira Lake

Sri Subramanian Kovil

SLAVE ISLAND

Gangaramaya

Hilton Colombo Residence

Seema Malaka

Cinnamon Lakeside

Temple Trees

USA Embassy

Liberty Cinema

Saskia Fernando Gallery

Liberty Plaza

KOLLUPITIYA

Kollupitiya

St Andrew's Scotskirk

India Embassy

Sri Lanka Tourist Board

Galle Face Green

GALLE FACE CENTRE ROAD

KUMARAN RATNAM RD

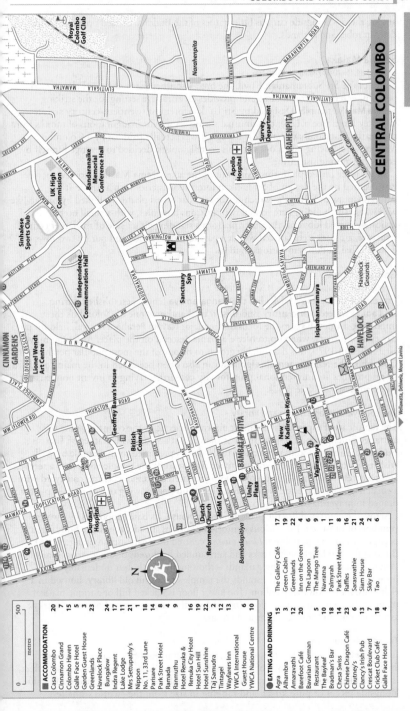

1

among them – alongside curious little statues of the Buddha, dressed up like a Hindu deity in robes and garlands.

Seema Malaka
Sir James Peiris Mw • Daily 7.30am–11.30pm • Free

South of the Sri Subramanian Kovil, the breezy southern arm of Beira Lake attracts pelicans, egrets and cormorants and provides an attractive setting for the striking **Seema Malaka** temple. Designed by Sri Lanka's foremost twentieth-century architect, Geoffrey Bawa (see p.126), this unusual shrine is used for inaugurations of monks from the nearby Gangaramaya temple – though it was actually paid for by a Colombo Muslim who, having fallen out with his co-religionists, decided to revenge himself by endowing a Buddhist shrine.

Set on three linked platforms rising out of the lake, Seema Malaka's novel structure was inspired by the design of Sri Lankan forest monasteries such as those at Anuradhapura and Ritigala, which feature similar raised platforms linked by bridge-like walkways. The buildings are roofed with lustrous blue tiles, with a small bo tree and delicately carved kiosk on the outer platforms standing either side of the larger central structure, an intricately latticed wooden pavilion lined inside and out by two rows of delicate Thai Buddhas in various mudras.

Gangaramaya
Just off Sir James Peiris Mw • Daily 7.30am–11.30pm • Rs.100

Just east of the Seema Malaka lies the **Gangaramaya** temple, established during Sri Lanka's nineteenth-century Buddhist revival and now one of Colombo's most important shrines. It's also the focus of the major **Navam Perahera** festival, held on poya day every February, when up to fifty elephants descend on the place. Although only established in 1979, this has quickly grown to be one of the most popular peraheras in Colombo. The resident **temple elephant** can also often been seen in the main courtyard – and provides an unintentional prop for city con-artists trying to invent non-existent "elephant festivals" (see p.52).

The courtyard, image house and library

The temple itself is probably the most bizarrely eclectic in the country, home to a strange hotchpotch of objects from Sri Lanka and abroad, with statues of Thai Buddhas, Chinese Bodhisattvas and Hindu deities presented to the temple by well-wishers scattered randomly here and there. The heart of the temple comprises a serene, and relatively traditional, group of buildings clustered around a central courtyard with a small dagoba at its centre and a venerable old **bo tree** growing out of a raised platform draped in prayer flags.

Across the courtyard lies the principal **image house**, its base supported by dwarfs (symbols of prosperity) in various contorted positions. Inside, the entire building is occupied by an eye-popping *tableau vivant*, centred on a gargantuan orange seated Buddha flanked by elephant tusks and surrounded by dozens of other larger-than-life Buddhas and devotees bearing garlands – thoroughly kitsch, but undeniably impressive. Next to the bo tree stands the temple's beautiful old **library**, housed in a richly decorated wooden pavilion. The lower floor is stacked full of antique ola-leaf manuscripts, while the upper floor (reached via the bo tree terrace) houses a quirky assortment of Buddhist artefacts and curios.

The temple museum

Just off the courtyard, the temple's entertaining **museum** fills a large room with an astonishing treasure trove of weird and wonderful bric-a-brac. The overall effect is rather like a vast Buddhist car-boot sale, with objects of great delicacy and value alongside pieces of pure kitsch and ranging in size from the "world's smallest

Buddha statue" (properly visible only through a magnifying glass) to a stuffed elephant.

Cinnamon Gardens

South of Slave Island stretches the much more upmarket suburb of **Cinnamon Gardens**, named for the plantations which flourished here during the nineteenth century. The capital's most sought-after area, the leafy streets here preserve their aura of haughty Victorian privilege – along with their colonial street names – and are lined with elite colleges and rambling old mansions (most now occupied by foreign embassies and government offices) concealed behind dauntingly high walls.

The most exclusive part of the district is contained by the rectangle of streets between Ward Place and Gregory's Road, the latter home to a whole string of embassies in spectacularly opulent colonial residences. South of here, Maitland Place runs down to the **Sinhalese Sports Club**, whose engagingly old-fashioned stadium, complete with antiquated manually operated scoreboard, serves as Colombo's principal venue for Test cricket. Just south of here at the end of Independence Avenue lies the bombastic **Independence Commemoration Hall**, an overblown stone replica of the wooden Audience Hall at Kandy.

Viharamahadevi Park and De Soysa Circus

Viharamahadevi Park • Daily 6am–6pm • Free

Hugging the northern edge of Cinnamon Gardens lies Colombo's principal open space, **Viharamahadevi Park**, originally called Victoria Park but renamed with characteristic patriotic thoroughness in the 1950s after the famous mother of King Dutugemunu (see p.185). The park boasts gorgeous tropical trees and plentiful birdlife and is also a magnet for local courting couples, who sit discreetly snogging under umbrellas.

Facing the north side of the park stands Colombo's **Town Hall** (1927) – a functional white Neoclassical structure looking something like a cross between the US Capitol and a municipal waterworks. A large **gilded Buddha** sits opposite, while immediately to the north lies lively **De Soysa Circus** – still widely known by its old name of Lipton Circus – one of central Colombo's major intersections and home to a couple of the city's best shops, the huge Osu Sala state pharmacy and the eye-catching **Devatagaha Mosque**, a big, white Moorish-looking structure that adds a quaint touch of architectural whimsy to the otherwise functional junction.

The National Museum

Entrance from Marcus Fernando Mw • Daily 9am–6pm • Rs.500 • No phones or cameras

Immediately south of Viharamahadevi Park stands the well-presented **National Museum**, in an elegant white Neoclassical building dating from 1877 and housing a large and absorbing collection of Sri Lankan artefacts from prehistoric times to the colonial era.

The **entrance lobby** is dominated by a famous eighth-century limestone Buddha from Anuradhapura – a classic seated image in the meditation posture and whose simplicity, serenity, lack of decoration and very human features embody much that is most characteristic of Sri Lankan art. Turn right from here to reach **room 1**, which offers a good overview of Sri Lankan **prehistory** with modest exhibits including a few human bones, the fossilized shells of assorted snails (which apparently formed a significant part of the diet of early Sri Lankans) and the teeth of extinct species of rhino and hippo which once roamed the island – along with conjectural artistic impressions of what these early wild beasts and even wilder humans would have looked like.

1

Rooms 2 to 5

Home to the museum's finest collection of artefacts, **rooms 2 to 5** showcase the full range of Sri Lankan artistry from the Anuradhapura period through to the Kandyan era. Room 2 is devoted to **Buddha images** and related iconography, showing changing representations of the master through the centuries, starting with early symbolic portrayals – sacred footprints (*sri pada*), dagobas – followed by portraits of the master in wood and stone, exemplifying the transition in Buddhist art from the abstract to the figurative. Another important strand in Sri Lankan art is shown by the superb collection of **Hindu images** in room 3, most of them twelfth-century bronzes from the Shiva Devale no. 1 at Polonnaruwa, proof of the strength of Hindu influence on this avowedly Buddhist city. Figures include a fine Shiva *nataraja* (dancing Shiva) and several voluptuous, wasp-waisted Parvatis – hauntingly exotic compared to the chaste Buddha images in the previous room.

The exhibits in rooms 4 and 5 leap abruptly into the **Kandyan era**, with a range of luxury items showing the incredibly intricate levels of craftsmanship, in a variety of materials, which were achieved by the kingdom's artisans – look out in particular for the stunning silver sword made for Bhuvanekabahu I, of Gampola (room 4), with its jewel-encrusted dragon's head handle. Most impressive, however, is the glittering **regalia** of the kings of Kandy (room 5) – one of the museum's highlights – which was surrendered to the British during the handover of power in 1815 and kept in Windsor Castle until being returned by George V in 1934.

The rest of the museum

Exiting room 5 brings you to a small **veranda** which is home to a display of "urinal stones", including a superb example from Anuradhapura – sumptuously decorated carvings on which monks would formerly have relieved themselves in order to demonstrate their contempt for worldly riches. Beyond here lies the large **room 6**, or "Stone Antiquities Gallery", home to an impressive selection of eroded pillars, friezes and statues salvaged from archeological sites across the island, and ranging in time from third-century Anuradhapura through to various colonial coats of arms and tombstones. The majority of pieces come from Anuradhapura and Polonnaruwa, and include a sequence of pillar inscriptions which were commonly used to record administrative decrees and grants of land.

The **first floor** is currently undergoing extensive refurbishment and was closed at the time of writing, though it's planned to incorporate galleries devoted to coins, jewellery and crafts, bronzes, anthropology, painting, ceramics and epigraphy.

The Natural History Museum

Horton Place • Daily except Fri 9am–5pm • Rs.300

Just behind the National Museum (although only accessible from Horton Place), the **Natural History Museum** fills three gloomy and labyrinthine floors with exhibits ranging from stuffed leopards and pickled snakes to quaintly didactic presentations on the island's ecology and economy ("Easy Ways To Make Agricultural Chemical Safe for You And Everyone Else", and the like). It all looks like the sort of thing you'd have expected to find in Communist Bulgaria, although the vast quantity of stuffed animals posed in moth-eaten pomp is enough to turn a conservationist's hair grey.

GREEN PATH ART GALLERY

Right next to the National Art Gallery, Nelum Pokuna Mawatha (still generally referred to by its colonial name of Green Path) is home to an enjoyable impromptu **open-air art show** every weekend, when local students and other part-time painters descend on the area, hanging their canvases from the railings along the side of the road. All artworks on display are for sale, often at very affordable prices.

National Art Gallery

Horton Place • Daily except Fri 9am–5pm • Free

Next door to the Natural History Museum, Sri Lanka's **National Art Gallery** comprises a single large room full of twentieth-century paintings by Sri Lankan artists (along with assorted portraits of various island notables), showing the influence of a range of European styles and including several rather Matisse-like canvases by George Keyt (1901–93), Sri Lanka's foremost twentieth-century painter. Sadly there are no labels, and exhibits are roped off, so you can't get close enough to read the signatures or even look at the paintings in any detail, making the whole experience rather unedifying.

Southern Colombo

The backbone of southern Colombo, the fumy **Galle Road** runs purposefully south from Galle Face Green, bisecting a string of coastal suburbs – **Kollupitiya**, **Bambalapitiya**, **Wellawatta** and **Dehiwala** – before reaching Mount Lavinia. Much of the commercial activity driven out of Fort by repeated bombings has now established itself in this part of the city, moving Colombo's centre of gravity decisively southwards and transforming Galle Road – the area between Kollupitiya and Bambalapitiya especially – into the city's de facto high street.

Kollupitiya

Immediately south of Galle Face Green, Galle Road has a decidedly military atmosphere, with the heavily fortified compounds of the US and Indian embassies and **Temple Trees**, the prime minister's official residence, all but hidden behind sandbagged gun emplacements and high walls topped by army watchtowers. The only spot of architectural relief is supplied by the quaint Gothic **St Andrew's Scotskirk** of 1842, just north of Temple Trees. Continuing south, Colombo's ordinary commercial life resumes as Galle Road passes through **central Kollupitiya**, with strings of cafés, banks and assorted shops. Many of the buildings here are functionally nondescript, with lots of the reflective glassy facades favoured by modern Sri Lankan architects, though the occasional dog-eared little café, colourful sign or curious shop survives among the bland modern office blocks.

Geoffrey Bawa's house

No.11, 33rd Lane • Mon–Fri 9am–5pm (last tour 4pm) • Rs.750 • Ⓦ geoffreybawa.com

Hidden away in a tiny lane off Bagatelle Road is one of Colombo's buried treasures, **No.11, 33rd Lane**, the former Colombo residence of architect Geoffrey Bawa (see box, p.126). The house comprises what were originally four tiny bungalows, which Bawa gradually acquired between 1959 and 1968 and then set about dramatically remodelling, knocking the four bungalows together and constructing a magical little labyrinth of rooms, courtyards, lightwells, verandas and passageways which feels far larger than the modest space it actually occupies, festooned with colourful artworks and artefacts – a kind of architectural sketchbook in miniature of many of the themes which can be seen in Bawa's other work around the island.

Bambalapitiya

The helter-skelter commercial suburb of **Bambalapitiya** is more workaday than the posher suburbs to the north, but generally a lot livelier. Following the decline in Fort's fortunes, the area around Bambalapitiya Junction (where the Galle Road meets Bauddhaloka Mawatha) has now to all intents and purposes become the centre of modern Colombo. It's a slightly anarchic mix of the old and new, ranging from the large Majestic Plaza shopping mall to little lopsided shops selling household items or packets of spices, while a series of determinedly local cafés and South Indian restaurants

1

brighten the fume-filled Galle Road with their fanciful signs. This is one of the busiest areas of Colombo: the pavements are clogged during daylight hours with office workers, beggars and tuktuk drivers touting for custom, while the handcarts of *vadai*-sellers and modest piles of merchandise laid out by street hawkers – anything from Buddha posters to recycled computer innards – add to the congestion.

Wellawatta

The Galle Road becomes progressively more ramshackle and down-at-heel as it continues south into the suburb of **Wellawatta**, popularly known as "Little Jaffna" thanks to its large Tamil population. This is one of the most characterful suburbs in southern Colombo, an interesting area full of colourful local cafés and picturesque (in a grubby kind of way) shops selling saris, "fancy goods" and all sorts of other paraphernalia.

Dehiwala Zoo

Dharmapala Mw, Dehiwala • Daily 8.30am–6pm • Rs.500 • Catch any bus running along Duplication Rd/Galle Rd to Dehiwala, and then either walk or take a tuktuk

Some 10km south of Fort in the suburb of Dehiwala, **Dehiwala Zoo** is home to a good range of Sri Lankan, Asian, African and South American wildlife. Sri Lankan species here include cute sloth bears, monkeys, porcupines, jungle- and fishing-cats, lots of birds and a number of leopards, part of the zoo's good collection of **big cats**, which also includes jaguars, lions, tigers and cheetahs. The zoo is also home to a number of Asian and a couple of African **elephants**; they can be seen performing during the infamous "elephant dance" (daily at 4.30pm) during which these surprisingly agile pachyderms perform various party tricks to the never-failing delight of local schoolchildren and other elephant-fanciers.

The zoo's large assortment of **monkeys** includes examples of all the native primates, such as purple-faced leaf monkey, grey langur and toque macaque. There's also a wide array of other mammals, from African giraffes and springboks or South American guanacos and tapirs to Australian red-necked wallabies and giant red kangaroos – plus a cage full of rabbits. The excellent range of **birdlife** on display includes some fabulously large and fluffy owls and there's also huge walk-in aviary full of Sri Lankan species – a good place to practise your bird-spotting skills. In addition to the caged birdlife, a flooded quarry at one end of the zoo serves as a magnet to Colombo's aquatic birds, which are fed daily at around 3.30pm. Egrets, herons and pelicans from all over the city flock here – a fine sight at feeding times, when hundreds swoop down onto the water. If you feel like some food yourself, there's a **restaurant** inside the zoo, as well as plenty of kiosks selling drinks and snacks.

Mount Lavinia

The leafy beachside suburb of **Mount Lavinia**, 10km south of Colombo Fort, is bounded by the small headland (the so-called "Mount") that is one of the few punctuating features on the coastline near the capital. This area supposedly takes its name from a certain Lavinia, the lady friend of British Governor Sir Thomas Maitland, who himself established a residence here in 1806.

Maitland's residence was subsequently expanded by successive governors before being turned into the **Mount Lavinia Hotel**, now one of the most venerable colonial landmarks in Sri Lanka and the main reason most foreign visitors come here, while the suburb provides a handy bolthole if you want to escape the bustle of central Colombo for a day or two.

Mount Lavinia is also home to Colombo's closest half-decent **beach**, and on Sunday afternoons half the city seems to come here to splash around in the water, play cricket and smooch under umbrellas. The proximity of the city means that the water is borderline for swimming, while the beach itself is a bit messy, with piles of fishing

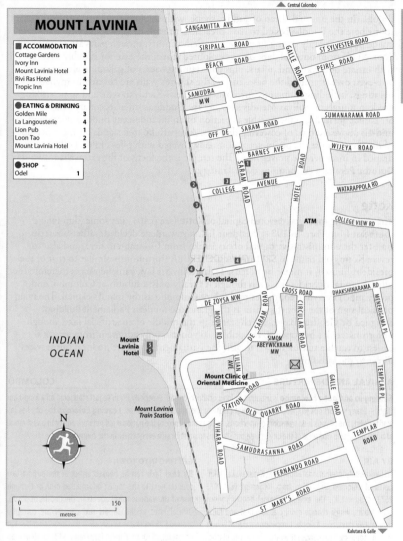

MOUNT LAVINIA

■ ACCOMMODATION
Cottage Gardens	3
Ivory Inn	1
Mount Lavinia Hotel	5
Rivi Ras Hotel	4
Tropic Inn	2

● EATING & DRINKING
Golden Mile	3
La Langousterie	4
Lion Pub	1
Loon Tao	2
Mount Lavinia Hotel	5

● SHOP
Odel	1

INDIAN OCEAN

Mount Lavinia Hotel

Footbridge

Mount Clinic of Oriental Medicine

Mount Lavinia Train Station

N

0   150
metres

Kalutara & Galle ▼

tackle scattered here and there, but does have a decent stretch of sand and a certain scruffy charm, especially at night, with the lights of the towers in central Colombo twinkling away to the north, and the more modest illuminations of the *Mount Lavinia Hotel* framing the beach to the south.

Kelaniya Raja Maha Vihara

Catch any bus to Kelaniya from Olcott Mw, outside Bastian Mawatha bus station

Ten kilometres east of Fort lies Colombo's most important Buddhist shrine, the **Kelaniya Raja Maha Vihara** – the Buddha himself is said to have taught at this spot on the last of his three visits to the island. Various temples have stood on the site; the present structure dates from the eighteenth and nineteenth centuries. A fairly modest

1

dagoba (in the unusual "heap of paddy" shape, with sloping shoulders) marks the exact spot where the Buddha is said to have preached, though it's upstaged by the elaborate **image house** (mainly dating from the twentieth century, though parts are older), next door. Made from unusual dark orange-coloured stone, the exterior is richly decorated, with ornate doorways and pillars, plus entertaining friezes of galloping elephants and pop-eyed dwarfs around the base. Inside, the shrine's walls are covered in myriad paintings, including numerous strip panels in quasi-Kandyan style and some striking modern murals by Soliyas Mendis showing the Buddha's three legendary visits to Sri Lanka, including a memorable depiction of an incandescent Buddha floating in mid-air above a crowd of cowering demons. A superb **bo tree** stands on the other side of the image house, its perimeter wall usually covered with piles of floral offerings and draped in innumerable prayer flags. The temple is the focus of the extravagant two-day **Duruthu Perahera** celebrations every January.

Kotte

The site of the medieval regional capital of **Kotte** (see p.401) lies some 7km inland southeast from Fort. In 1984, President J.R. Jayawardene decided, rather bizarrely, to transfer the administrative capital of Sri Lanka from Colombo to here, and also to revive Kotte's old name of **SRI JAYAWARDENEPURA** (fortuitously similar to that of the president himself, it might be noted). Technically, Sri Jayawardenepura is therefore the official capital of Sri Lanka, even though it's really only a suburb of Colombo, and pretty much everyone continues to think of Colombo as the island's capital. The main physical sign of the suburb's status is the grandiose modern **Parliament Building**, designed by Geoffrey Bawa, which stands in the middle of an artificial lake, though unfortunately it's not open to the public, so you can only admire it from afar. It's easiest to catch a tuktuk or taxi to visit the parliament; there are no local bus services direct to the building.

ARRIVAL AND DEPARTURE	COLOMBO

Getting in and out of Colombo is usually one long gridlocked drag, especially if you've just staggered off a long-haul flight – many visitors opt to spend their first night close to the airport in Negombo. **Leaving Colombo** the city has (as you'd expect) the island's best transport connections, lying at the centre of the national rail network and with a vast range of buses departing from one of the city's three bus stations to pretty much everywhere in the country.

BY AIR

Sri Lanka's only international airport is at Katunayake, 30km north of Colombo and 10km from Negombo (☎01973 2677, ⓦairport.lk). The arrivals terminal houses various bank kiosks, which change money at identical and fairly competitive rates, plus a single, temperamental ATM – best to bring some cash to change rather than relying on plastic.
Airlines Cathay Pacific, 186 Vauxhall St, Slave Island ☎011 233 4145; Emirates, Hemas House, 75 Braybrooke Place, Slave Island ☎011 470 4070; Malaysia Airlines, c/o Hemas Air Services, 81 York St, Fort ☎011 234 2291; Oman Air, 400 Deans Rd, Maradana ☎011 446 2222; Qatar Airlines, Level 3, West Tower, World Trade Center, Fort ☎011 557 0000; Qantas, Air Global Ltd, Cinnamon Lakeside hotel, 115 Chittampalam Gardiner Mawatha ☎011 476 7767; SriLankan Airlines, Levels 3, East Tower, World Trade Center, Fort ☎019 733 5500 (reservations), ☎019 733 1627 (enquiries); Thai Airways, Hilton Colombo Residence, 200 Union Place, Slave Island ☎011 230 7100.

GETTING INTO TOWN

By taxi Taxis can be booked either at the airport taxi counter next to the tourist information desk or through one of the various travel agents in the booths opposite. Official fares at the airport taxi counter are currently around $25 for the tediously slow trip into Colombo (1hr or more), $70 to Kandy (3hr) and $13 to Negombo (20min); you may be able to get a cheaper deal through one of the travel agents, though don't count on it. Several of these agents also offer very cheap islandwide tours with car and driver, although these places don't have the best reputation and you're better off sorting something out in Negombo or Colombo.
By bus Free shuttle buses run every 30min from just outside the terminal building to Averiwatte bus station, about 1.5km away, from where there are regular services on to Colombo (1hr or more) and Negombo (30min), plus less frequent buses to Kandy.

PRINCIPAL TRAIN DEPARTURES FROM COLOMBO FORT

Note that train timetables are subject to constant change, so if possible it's always best to check current departure times before travelling. In addition to the services listed below, there are regular trains from Colombo north to **Negombo** (15 daily; 1hr–1hr 30min) plus trains to Vavuniya (5 daily; 4–6hr) and a few (not very fast or useful) services to Polonnaruwa (2 daily; 6hr), Batticaloa (2 daily; 8–9hr) and Trincomalee (1 daily; 8hr 30min). Intercity services are marked with an asterisk (*).

WEST AND SOUTH COAST

Colombo	06.50	08.35	10.30	14.05	15.50	16.45	17.25	18.00	19.20
Galle	09.55	11.20	13.25	17.40	18.35	19.15	20.45	21.10	22.45
Matara	11.00	13.10	14.25	19.05	19.30	20.10	–	22.25	–

All services call at Kalutara South (approximately 1hr from Colombo), Aluthgama (1hr 20min), Ambalangoda (1hr 50min) and Hikkaduwa (2hr 10min). All Matara trains also call at Weligama.

COLOMBO TO KANDY

Colombo	07.00*	10.35	12.40	15.35*	16.35	17.40
Kandy	09.30	13.50	16.10	18.05	20.00	21.00

HILL COUNTRY TRAINS

Colombo	05.55	09.45	19.00
Peradeniya	08.40	12.20	23.00
Nanu Oya	12.30	16.00	03.00
Badulla	16.00	19.10	07.10

All services to Badulla call at Hatton (for Adam's Peak; approximately 2hr 30min from Kandy), Nanu Oya (for Nuwara Eliya; 4hr), Haputale (5hr 30min), Bandarawela (6hr) and Ella (6hr 30min).

CULTURAL TRIANGLE

Colombo	05.45	06.50	10.00	13.45	16.20*
Anuradhapura	09.40	10.00	16.00	18.40	20.10

All Anuradhapura services call at Kurunegala (2hr–2hr 30min).

INTERNAL FLIGHTS

Ratmalana airport Expo Air flights to Jaffna leave from Sri Lanka's domestic airport at Ratmalana, south of Mount Lavinia.

BY TRAIN

Colombo is the hub of the Sri Lankan rail system, with direct services to many places in the country (see box above).

Fort Railway Station Long-distance services arrive at and depart from Fort Railway Station (actually in Pettah, not Fort). Different ticket windows sell tickets to different destinations – the helpful enquiries window (no. 10) by the entrance on the left will point you to the right one. The station is conveniently close to the cluster of top-end hotels in Fort and around Galle Face Green, but some way from the city's southern areas, although there are fairly regular suburban trains from here south via Kollupitiya and Bambalapitiya to Mount Lavinia (see p.86).

BY BUS

Buses arrive at and depart from one of the city's three bus stations – Saunders Place, Bastian Mawatha or the Central Bus Stand – which lie side by side about 500m to the east of Fort station in Pettah; lack of space in the terminals means that some services drop off passengers in the surrounding side streets. Wherever you're deposited, there are always plenty of tuktuks hanging around. The locations of the three terminals are shown on the Fort and Pettah map (see p.74). For buses to Jaffna, see the Jaffna section of the guide (see p.385).

Bastian Mawatha (BM) handles private buses to Kandy, Nuwara Eliya, the airport and south along the coast; it's cramped but relatively orderly, with several wire-mesh information kiosks if you get stuck. For south coast destinations beyond Matara you may find it easier to catch a Matara bus and change there if you can't immediately find a bus direct to your destination. Buses to Matara will also drop you off at other coastal destinations en route such as Unawatuna, Weligama, Midigama and so on, assuming you know where to get off.

1

Saunders Place Bus Station (SP) handles all other long-distance private buses. This station is utterly chaotic, and potentially quite dangerous, with far too many vehicles jockeying for position in too small a space. Watch your back. There's little signage – you'll probably have to ask around to find your bus.

Central Bus Stand handles all CTB bus departures islandwide, which follow a broadly similar pattern to private services; for information, call ☎011 258 1120. It's well laid out and spacious, although it's generally quicker to take a private bus when leaving Colombo.

Destinations Airport (BM: every 15min; 50min); Ambalangoda (BM: every 15min; 2hr); Anuradhapura (SP: every 30min; 5hr); Arugam Bay/Pottuvil (SP: 3 daily; 10hr); Badulla (SP: hourly; 7hr); Bandarawela (SP: every 20min; 6hr 30min); Batticaloa (SP: 4 daily; 9hr); Beruwala, Aluthgama and Bentota (BM: every 15min; 1hr 30min–1hr 45min); Dambulla (SP: every 20min; 4hr); Hambantota (BM: every 30min; 5hr); Haputale (SP: every 30min; 6hr); Hikkaduwa (BM: every 15min; 2hr 15min); Galle (BM: every 15min; 2hr 30min); Kalutara (BM: every 15min; 1hr); Kandy (BM: every 10–15min; 3hr); Kurunegala (SP: every 15min; 2hr);

Matara (BM: every 15min; 3hr 30min); Negombo (SP: every 10min; 1hr); Nuwara Eliya (BM: every 30min; 4hr 30min); Polonnaruwa (SP: every 30min; 6hr); Ratnapura (SP: every 15min; 3hr); Tangalla (BM: every 30min; 4hr 30min); Tissamaharama (BM: every 30min; 5hr 30min); Trincomalee (SP: hourly; 7hr).

BY CAR

Car with driver for airport or other short tours/ transfers can be hired (expensively) through the travel desks at any of the major hotels or (more cheaply) through a local car-hire agent – reliable options include Malkey Rent-A-Car (see p.31) and Quickshaws (☎ quickshaws.com) – or travel agent (try George Travel, c/o Pan International, 82 Bristol St, Fort ☎011 293 9782, or one of the little travel agents under the arches of the Galle Face Court Building on the corner of Galle Road and Sir M.M. Markar Mw at the southern end of Galle Face Green). Count on around $25 for a trip to the airport, or $70–80 for transfers or day tours to Galle and Kandy. For longer tours it's better to arrange something before you arrive with one of the larger tour operators listed in Basics (pp.26–27).

GETTING AROUND

By tuktuk The city has a superabundance of tuktuks, and in many parts of the centre it's impossible to walk more than a few metres without being solicited for custom. Colombo also has Sri Lanka's only (at the time of writing) metered tuktuks, found in increasing numbers across the city, and offering cheaper fares than you'd normally be able to achieve by bargaining (assuming the meter doesn't magically stop working the moment you sit down inside). At the time of writing metered tuktuks were sporting signs advertising a fixed fare of Rs.30/km but actually charging Rs.50/km (although this figure may well have increased by the time you read this), with a minimum fare of Rs.50, although it's worth keeping an eye on the map to make sure they don't follow a convoluted route in order to bump up the fare.

By taxi For longer journeys, metered taxis offer a more comfortable alternative to hunting out a tuktuk. There are plenty of firms operating taxis, usually only bookable by phone, although you may be able to wave a vehicle down on the street. Conventional radio-taxi companies include Kangaroo Cabs (☎011 258 8 588, ☎2588588.com) and GNTC (☎011 268 8688); fares are around Rs.75/km. Alternatively, a growing number of companies have launched taxi services using the tiny Indian-made Tata Nano cars, which can nip easily through the city traffic;

fares in these "nanocabs" are only slightly higher than in a metered tutuk (around Rs.60/km). Companies include Nano Cabs ☎011 267 6767, Budget Cabs ☎011 759 2592 and Budget Taxi ☎011 729 9299.

By bus Endless lines of buses chunter along Colombo's major thoroughfares, though given the difficulty of working out routes, they're of little use to the casual visitor (and if you've got luggage, forget it). The only time you might want to catch a bus is to get up and down the Galle Rd in the southern half of the city between Kollupitiya and Mount Lavinia. Buses tear up and down between Galle Face Green and the southern suburbs literally every few seconds (although southbound buses were being diverted inland along Duplication Rd on their way through Kollupitiya at the time of writing); stops are marked by signs showing a picture of a bus set in a blue border.

By suburban train Suburban trains are a useful way of reaching the southern part of the city, although they can get packed at rush hours (roughly Mon–Fri 7.30–9.30am & 4.30–6.30pm). Trains run roughly every 30min (less frequently on Sun) from Fort Railway Station, calling at Kollupitiya, Bambalapitiya, Wellawatta, Dehiwala and Mount Lavinia. The journey from Fort to Mount Lavinia takes around 30min.

INFORMATION

Tourist information The city's tourist office (Mon–Fri 8.30am–4pm; ☎011 243 7055, ☎ srilanka.travel) is just south of the *Galle Face Hotel* at 80 Galle Rd, Kollupitiya. Staff

can assist with general queries and also dish out copies of the free monthly tourist guide, *Travel Lanka*. For listings of forthcoming events, see ☎ whatsupcolombo.lk.

ACCOMMODATION

Colombo has an over-supply of top-end hotels aimed at business travellers, plus a growing number of chic boutique hotels. Unfortunately, there's a paucity of good budget options. It pays to **book in advance**, especially if you're planning on staying at one of the smaller guesthouses, when you may need to reserve a week or more ahead. Never turn up at a small family-run guesthouse unannounced; you're unlikely to find a vacancy and the owners won't appreciate having unexpected visitors on their doorsteps, especially if you arrive at some ungodly hour of the night or morning.

FORT

The landmark *Ceylon Continental* was closed for extensive renovations at the time of writing, but will hopefully have reopened for business by sometime in 2014.

Grand Oriental York St ☎ 011 232 0320, ✉ goh @sltnet; map p.74. Famous old establishment (see p.75), with superb port views from its fourth-floor restaurant, though the building itself has lost most of its colonial charm and the setting at the end of ramshackle York St is rather cheerless. Rooms are decent value, however: characterless but spacious, with satellite TV, fridge, a/c and town or (in deluxe rooms) fine harbour views. $89; deluxe $114

Hilton Sir Chittampalam A. Gardiner Mw ☎ 011 254 4644, ⊛ hilton.com; map p.74. Flashy but rather dated five-star, with heavily marbled public areas and heaps of facilities including health club, swimming pool (non-guests an exorbitant Rs.1500) and a good selection of in-house restaurants. Rooms are spread over nineteen floors and get more expensive the higher you go – and with increasingly superb views – although the decor's uninspiring. $220

YMCA Bristol St ☎ 011 232 5252; map p.74. The cheapest place in town, this dingy, labyrinthine institution offers a range of very basic doubles with or without private bathroom, very cheap singles (Rs.550) sharing clean communal bathrooms, and a men-only dormitory (Rs.165/ person). Fills up quickly with locals, so book ahead or arrive early. **Rs.750**; en-suite **Rs.1150**

GALLE FACE GREEN

★ **Galle Face Hotel** Galle Face Green ☎ 011 254 1010, ⊛ gallefacehotel.com; map p.80. The city's most famous hotel, this oceanfront landmark has bags of colonial charm and slightly quirky character. Rooms in the old building, now known as the Classic Wing, are older but more atmospheric (the deluxe rooms are generally better value than the overpriced standard rooms – and avoid those overlooking the noisy Galle Rd). Those in the modern Regency Wing are kitted out in neo-colonial style and combine modern comforts with traditional decor. All rooms come with a/c, satellite TV and minibar, and there's also a romantic seafront bar, a small pool (non-guests Rs.1000) and an attractive spa. $130; deluxe $140

Ramada (formerly the Holiday Inn) 30 Sir M.M. Markar Mw ☎ 011 242 2001, ⊛ holidayinn.lk; map p.80. Tucked away in a quiet side street just off the bottom of Galle Face Green, this pleasantly low-key hotel doesn't have the style of its near neighbours, but offers an excellent location and larger-than-average (albeit slightly drab) and well-equipped rooms at relatively inexpensive rates. There's also a swimming pool (non-guests Rs.750) and the good *Alhambra* Indian restaurant (see p.94). $121

Taj Samudra 25 Galle Face Centre Rd ☎ 011 244 6622, ⊛ tajhotels.com; map p.80. One of Colombo's smartest hotels, this immense five-star palace is set in lush grounds straddling the eastern side of Galle Face Green. Rooms (some sea-facing) are attractively furnished, if a tad small, while facilities include a health club and swimming pool (guests only), plus a decent selection of places to eat and drink. $215

KOLLUPITIYA

★ **Cinnamon Grand** 77 Galle Rd ☎ 011 243 7437, ⊛ www.cinnamonhotels.com; map p.80. Colombo's glitziest five-star, with swanky public areas and a big array of facilities including a medium-sized pool (non-guests Rs.800), the halcyon Angsana Spa (see p.99), and the capital's best selection of hotel restaurants. Rooms are modern and stylish; those higher up the building have great views over downtown Colombo. $210

Colombo Haven 262/3 Galle Rd (entered from Galle Rd via the small lane running down the right-hand side of the Carnival Ice Cream Parlour) ☎ 011 230 1672, ⊛ colombohaven.com; map p.80. Recently opened guesthouse run by a retired tour guide with four cosy doubles (all with a/c, hot water and fridge) of varying sizes and prices – the fancy showers, with disco lights and built-in radio, are a sight to behold. Free wi-fi. Advance booking highly recommended. $50

Indra Regent 383 R.A. de Mel Mw (Duplication Rd) ☎ 011 257 7405, ⊛ indraregent.net; map p.80. Simple modern hotel with small, functional rooms, all with a/c, satellite TV, hot water and minibar, though not all have windows – and avoid those near the noisy main road. Conveniently located, although a bit expensive for what you get. $60

Lake Lodge 20 Alwis Terrace ☎ 011 232 6443, ⊛ taruhotels.com; map p.80. Smooth modern guesthouse by leading Sri Lankan designer Taru, with stylish rooms, a central but peaceful location (equally convenient for Kollupitiya, Cinnamon Gardens and Slave Island) and surprisingly affordable rates. B&B **Rs.9696**

1

No.11 33rd Lane, off Bagatelle Rd ☎ 011 433 7335, ✉ leopold@eureka.lk; map p.80. A chance to stay in the marvellous former Colombo residence of Geoffrey Bawa (see p.85). There are just two rooms, sharing a common lounge, and guests also have use of the third-floor loggia and fourth-floor viewing deck. B&B **$120**

Ranmuthu 112 Galle Rd ☎ 011 243 3986; map p.80. Downmarket local hotel with absolutely no frills, but in an excellent location. Rooms (some with a/c and hot water) are basic and not always very clean, but are large and decent value at the price. Those at the back are particularly good, remarkably quiet and with fine sea-views and breezes. **Rs.2464**; a/c **Rs.3757**

Hotel Renuka & Renuka City Hotel 328 Galle Rd ☎ 011 257 3598, ⦿ renukahotel.com; map p.80. Smart mid-range hotel in two adjoining buildings (each, confusingly, with a different name) offering modern a/c rooms with satellite TV and minibar – though get a room away from the noisy Galle Rd. The rather swanky rooms in the newly refurbished *City Hotel* wing are the ones to go for, and only a few dollars more than those in the slightly older *Renuka* wing. There's also small swimming pool, wi-fi and the good in-house *Palmyrah* restaurant (see p.95). **$90**

Hotel Sun Hill 26 Palmyrah Ave ☎ 011 250 4376; map p.80. Attached to a breezy Chinese restaurant right on the seafront, with a mix of smallish fan rooms and larger and brighter a/c rooms. **Rs.2900**; a/c **Rs.4400**

YWCA National Centre 7 Rotunda Garden ☎ 011 232 8589, ✉ natywca@sltnet.lk; map p.80. Soothingly tranquil place, with a rather convent-school atmosphere and clean, attractive private rooms with hot water set around a courtyard garden, as well as very cheap double "cubicles" (Rs.550/person) with shared bathroom. Couples are admitted, but not single men. Good value, and an excellent location. **Rs.3300**; a/c **Rs.5500**

SLAVE ISLAND

Nippon 123 Kumaran Ratnam Rd ☎ 011 243 1887; map p.80. Situated in an interestingly down-at-heel part of town in the characterful, colonnaded Mannings Mansion of 1883, with neat and spacious a/c rooms and equally large but somewhat shabby fan rooms (while all rooms at the front suffer from serious traffic noise). Excellent value, although planned renovations may lead to price hikes. **Rs.2250**; a/c **Rs.3250**

Park Street Hotel 20 Park St ☎ 011 243 9977, ⦿ anilana .com; map p.80. Elegant new boutique hotel in a sensitively restored 250-year-old villa. There are two very spacious, eye-wateringly expensive colonial-style suites ($440/550) in the villa itself, plus more contemporary-looking rooms in the converted warehouse at the back, unusually large, although somewhat lacking in windows. All come with the full array of mod-cons, and there's also an idyllic courtyard with pool, small gym and attractive bar and restaurant. **$275**

YWCA International Guest House 393 Colvin R. De Silva Mw (Union Place) ☎ 011 232 4181; map p.80. Atmospheric old Dutch colonial mansion with antique furniture scattered around the veranda, a fruit-tree-filled garden and with plenty of olde-worlde charm. The twenty rooms are simple but clean, though road noise can be a problem at the front, and fan rooms are decidedly overpriced. B&B: **Rs.4070**; a/c **Rs.5500**

CINNAMON GARDENS

Parisare 97/1 Rosmead Place (no sign; it's behind the UNHCR building) ☎ 011 269 4749; map p.80. In a family house in a very quiet location in the heart of Cinnamon Gardens, with just three simple but comfortable rooms (although the walls don't reach the ceiling in two of them, meaning that they're cool but not very private). Rates are an absolute steal, although you'll probably have to reserve well in advance. **Rs.2200**

★ **Tintagel** 65 Rosmead Place ☎ 011 460 2121, ⦿ paradiseroadhotels.com; map p.80. Superb new boutique hotel set in a stunning colonial mansion which was formerly the family home of the Bandaranaike family, who have provided Sri Lanka with three prime ministers since Independence, including the world's first woman prime minister; S.W.R.D. Bandaranaike was shot here on the veranda in 1959 (see p.407). The mansion has now been lavishly restored by Shanth Fernando of Paradise Road (see p.98), with ten spacious and beautiful suites in muted colours, a picture-perfect little infinity pool, in-house restaurant (but no alcohol, although guests are welcome to bring their own). **$280**

Wayfarers Inn 77 Rosmead Place (no sign) ☎ 011 269 3936, ⦿ wayfarers-inn.com; map p.80. Set in a quiet residential area, this attractive colonial-style guesthouse has a range of comfortable fan and a/c doubles with satellite TV, hot water and fridge, plus a studio apartment with kitchen ($50). There's also free wi-fi and internet, and a lovely garden. Advance booking almost always necessary. **$40**; a/c **$45**

BORELLA

Garden Guest House (Mrs Fonseka's) 7 Karlsruhe Gardens ☎ 071 702 0007, ⦿ gardenguesthousecolombo .com; map p.80. Long-running family guesthouse, overseen by the charming Mrs Fonseka assisted by her very cute dog, Bimbo, in a quaint house full of shiny porcelain, silk flowers and other eye-catching chintz. There are just three cosy rooms (including one family room for $70), all with a/c and hot water, and meals are available. It's a fair way east of the centre, but worth the journey. **$57**

BAMBALAPITIYA

Casa Colombo 231 Galle Rd, Bambalapitiya ☎ 011 452 0130, ⦿ casacolombo.com; map p.80.

Striking boutique hotel, occupying a two-hundred-year-old mansion given a very contemporary twist, with a mix of colonial chintz and contemporary pazzazz. The twelve funky suites come complete with all sorts of digital mod-cons and off-the-wall artworks and bric-a-brac. There's also a small pool, plus swanky indoor and outdoor restaurants, and a spa. **$186**

Greenlands Hotel 3A Shrubbery Gardens, off Galle Rd, ☎ 011 258 5592, ✉ greenlandshotel@gmail.com; map p.80. Located above the famous *Greenlands* vegetarian restaurant (see p.95), with simple and old-fashioned but reasonably well-maintained rooms, some with a/c and hot water, at rock-bottom prices. **Rs.2000**; a/c **Rs.2600**

★ **Mrs Settupathy's** 23/2 Shrubbery Gardens (directly behind the Church of Christ), Bambalapitiya ☎ 011 258 7964, ✉ jbs@slt.lk; map p.80. Long-running and reliably excellent family guesthouse, with six spacious, clean rooms, all with hot water and (optional) a/c, plus a nice upstairs communal seating area, a kitchen for guests' use and free wi-fi. Rates are a bargain, although advance bookings are strongly recommended, and check-in is between 8am and 6pm only. **Rs.2100**; a/c **Rs.2700**

Hotel Sunshine 5A Shrubbery Gardens ☎ 011 401 7676, ✉ sunshine.shrubbery@gmail.com; map p.80. Functional modern hotel with spacious tiled rooms and small bathrooms (all with hot water) – looking a bit worn in places, but decent value at current rates, non a/c rooms in particular. **Rs.2000**; a/c **Rs.3750**

HAVELOCK TOWN

★ **Havelock Place Bungalow** 6 Havelock Place, Havelock Town (turn down the side road by the petrol station) ☎ 011 258 5191, ✉ havelockbungalow.com; map p.80. One of Colombo's more alluring places to stay, despite the slightly inconvenient location, set in a pair of intimate and colonial villas which combine old-fashioned charm with all modern amenities (including a/c and wi-fi). There's also a small pool, a beautiful garden and a peaceful garden café. **$140**

MOUNT LAVINIA

Cottage Gardens 42–48 College Ave ☎ 011 271 9692, ✉ cottagegardenbungalows.com; map p.87. Five large

and attractively furnished detached cottages (each sleeping two) with kitchenette and optional a/c, dotted around a peaceful and very private walled garden. **$33**; a/c **$38**

★ **Ivory Inn** 21 De Saram Rd ☎ 011 271 5006, ✉ ivoryinn@hotmail.com; map p.87. One of Mount Lavinia's best cheapies, with spotless, nicely furnished rooms with private balcony (plus optional a/c and hot water) in an attractive modern red-brick building in a quiet location. B&B **Rs.2750**; a/c **Rs.3250**

Mount Lavinia Hotel 100 Hotel Rd ☎ 011 271 1711, ✉ mountlaviniahotel.com; map p.87. Famous old landmark hotel which retains engaging touches of colonial style, despite comprehensive modernization, and enjoys a superb location atop its little oceanfront promontory – although the whole place is often very busy with wedding parties and events and isn't the most relaxing spot in town. Rooms are modern and fairly characterless, though with all the usual five-star mod cons; most have sea views. There's also a biggish swimming pool, a serene modern beachfront spa, and a huge stretch of idyllic private beach if you want to escape from the hoi polloi (non-guests can use both pool and private beach for Rs.600). **Rs.19,000**

Rivi Ras Hotel 50/2 De Saram Rd ☎ 011 271 7786, ✉ rivirashotel.com; map p.87. Attractive hotel occupying a series of detached, colonnaded red-brick buildings set in very spacious gardens. Rooms are large and minimally but pleasantly furnished; all have hot water, and a few have a/c and satellite TV. B&B **$55**; a/c **$65**

Tropic Inn 30 College Ave ☎ 011 273 8653, ✉ tropicinn.com; map p.87. Pleasant and very peaceful small hotel, with attractive wood and wrought-iron decor. Rooms (all with hot water and a/c) are cool, clean, modern and nicely furnished. **$45**

THE OUTSKIRTS

Villa Talangama Hokandara ☎ 011 789 5810 (or ☎ 0870 231 7892 in the UK), ✉ reddottours.com; map p.71. The ultimate Colombo hideaway, this superb three-room contemporary-colonial-style villa is set in a tranquil location on the eastern edge of the city, a 30min drive from the centre, complete with its own swimming pool and garden overlooking the birdlife-rich Talangama wetlands. **$120**

EATING

Colombo is far and away the best place to eat in Sri Lanka – the city boasts pretty much the full range of Asian and European cuisines, including an excellent selection of **Sri Lankan**, **Chinese** and **Indian** (both north and south) restaurants. If your stomach's acclimatized, there are innumerable lively little **local cafés** – clustered all over Slave Island, down Galle Rd and around the Pettah – which really come alive after dark. **Lunch packets** are sold by pavement stalls and cafés all over the city – a decent-sized helping of simple rice and curry costs around Rs.150–200.

FORT, PETTAH AND SLAVE ISLAND

Chettinad 293 Sea St, Pettah; map p.74. This no-frills locals' café makes a good lunch stop in the depths of the

Pettah, dishing up delicious and dirt-cheap South Indian food – dosas, *vadais*, *uttapam* – in an authentically Subcontinental atmosphere, complete with banana-leaf

1

"plates", metal utensils and a colourful display of sweets in the entrance. Most mains under Rs.250. Daily 8am–8pm.

Curry Leaf Hilton hotel, Sir Chittampalam A. Gardiner Mw, Fort ☎011 254 4644; map p.74. Tucked away in the *Hilton* grounds in a rather naff faux-jungle village construction. The nightly buffet (Rs.2800) is pricey but provides Colombo's best introduction to the full range of Sri Lankan cuisine – string hoppers, hoppers, *kottu rotty*, *wattalapan*, plus all sorts of rice and curries, as well as fresh seafood. Daily 7pm–midnight.

Emperor's Wok Hilton hotel, Sir Chittampalam A. Gardiner Mw, Fort ☎011 254 4644; map p.74. Showy Chinese restaurant whose Hong Kong chef cooks up an enormous range of Cantonese and Sichuan dishes (from around Rs.900), from abalone to bean curd and shredded duck, along with all the usual standards, plus special dim sum menus. Gets busy, so best to book. Daily noon–2.30pm & 7–11pm.

Ministry of Crab Dutch Hospital ☎011 234 2722, ⓦministryofcrab.com; map p.74. If you like crab, you'll love this place, with its unrepentantly crab-centric menu showcasing the famous Sri Lankan crustacean in an array of culinary styles ranging from the ever-popular chilli crab through to a variety of Asian-influenced styles – as well as a few (significantly less expensive) prawn, fish and chicken dishes. It's not cheap, however, with your average dish going for around Rs.4000. Daily 6–10pm.

Park Street Mews 50/1 Park St, Slave Island ☎011 230 0133; map p.80. Popular with Colombo's alternative creative types, this funky urban café wouldn't look out of place in London or New York with its stripped-down, wood-and-brick warehouse-style decor. There's a good selection of breakfasts, plus meat and seafood international mains (Rs.1250–1500) and cheaper pasta dishes, sandwiches and salads and a good dessert selection – but no booze. Free wi-fi. Daily 8am–11pm (Fri–Sun from 9am).

Seafish 15 Sir Chittampalam A. Gardiner Mw, Fort; map p.74. This low-key little restaurant is the place for good and relatively inexpensive fish and seafood, and there are also a few meat, noodle and pasta options, plus curries. Mains from around Rs.700. Daily noon–3pm & 6–11pm.

Semondu Dutch Hospital, Fort ☎011 244 1590; map p.74. Owned by SriLankan Airlines, this place is in danger of giving airline catering a good name with its well-prepared selection of mainly Sri Lankan and Asian meat and seafood dishes served up in one of Colombo's most attractive dining rooms. Dinner mains go for around Rs.900–1800, or there's a good-value express lunch for just Rs.890. Daily noon–2.30pm & 7–10.30pm.

AROUND GALLE FACE GREEN

Alhambra Ramada hotel, 30 Sir M.M. Markar Mw; map p.80. Long-running North Indian restaurant (despite the Moorish name and decor), with a solidly prepared and

refreshingly inexpensive range of North Indian standards, including Mughlai dishes, biryanis and tandooris, plus plenty of vegetarian options. Mains from around Rs.600 (veg)/Rs.750 (non-veg). Daily noon–2.45pm & 7–11pm.

Bavarian German Restaurant 11 Galle Face Court 2, Galle Rd; map p.80. A rustic interior full of chunky wooden furniture provides a suitably Bavarian setting for hearty Central European dishes like goulash, pickled beef, pepper steak, Wiener schnitzels, and bratwurst, plus a few seafood, pasta and vegetarian options. Mains around Rs.1100–1650. Daily noon–3pm & 6–11pm.

Navratna Taj Samudra hotel, Galle Face Centre Rd ☎011 244 6622; map p.80. Colombo's swankiest North Indian restaurant, offering an inventive and unusual selection of regional dishes from across the Subcontinent – anything from Goan fish curry to Rajasthani *ghatta* (dumplings) – including an excellent vegetarian selection. Mains from around Rs.800. Daily 12.30–3pm & 7–11pm.

KOLLUPITIYA

Amaravathi 2 Mile Post Ave; map p.80. Functional but deservedly popular a/c restaurant serving up an eclectic and inexpensive medley of veg and non-veg dishes from Sri Lanka and India (both north and south) ranging from curries and *kottu rotty* through to dosas and tandooris. Mains Rs.550–700. Daily 11.30am–3.30pm & 6.30–11pm.

★ **Barefoot Café** Barefoot, 704 Galle Rd; map p.80. Set in the beautiful courtyard at the back of Colombo's most personable shop (see p.98), with a short but excellently prepared selection of international café-style fare (mains a very reasonable Rs.500–700), plus tempting daily lunch specials and more-ish desserts and cakes. The live jazz sessions (most Sundays 1–4pm) are a city institution. Mon–Sat 10am–7pm, Sun 11am–4pm.

Chesa Swiss 3 Deal Place, corner of R.A. de Mel Mw (Duplication Rd) ☎011 257 3433, ⓦchesaswiss.com; map p.80. Chic, pricey Swiss restaurant in a gorgeous colonial villa, with garden or indoor a/c seating, offering a classy selection of nourishing middle-European specialities ranging from fondues and *rösti* to pickled beef and barley soup as well as Australian steaks and a reasonable vegetarian selection. Mains around Rs.1250–2500. Mon–Sat noon–2.30pm & 7–10.30pm, Sun 7–10.30pm.

★ **Chutneys** Cinnamon Grand ☎011 249 7372; map p.80. The most original restaurant in Colombo, showcasing the lesser-known culinary byways and, particularly, street food of Southern India, with a tempting assortment of little-known dishes from Kerala, Tamil Nadu, Andhra Pradesh and Karnataka. There's a good range of meat dishes, plus a superb vegetarian selection, all prepared with hearty infusions of chilli, tamarind and coconut milk, served with feisty chutneys and backed up by a range of traditional street drinks ranging from tamarind *juice* to panna (sweet and sour raw mango). Given the quality, prices are a steal, with mains around Rs.625–800. Daily 7pm–midnight.

Crescat Boulevard Galle Rd; map p.80. The food court in the basement of Colombo's smartest shopping mall teems with fast-food outlets dishing up everything from Mongolian to Sri Lankan, Indian, Chinese and Malaysian cuisine, plus pizza, pasta, wraps and ice cream. Daily 10am–10pm.

★ **Cricket Club Café** 34 Queen's Rd, off R.A. de Mel Mw (Duplication Rd) ☎011 250 1384; map p.80. This shrine to cricket is deservedly popular with expats, tourists and locals alike, with memorabilia ranged around the walls and nonstop matches on the TV. The menu features a mix of tasty and unpretentious light meals like burgers and salads (from around Rs.550) plus more elaborate international mains (from Rs.950), all named after famous men in white (Ganguly's grill, Freddie's fillet o' fish, and so on). Daily 11am–11pm.

Gallery Café 2 Alfred House Rd ☎011 258 2162, ⓦparadiseroad.lk; map p.80. Colombo's most stylish café, occupying a beautiful villa which formerly housed the offices of architect Geoffrey Bawa. The outer courtyard hosts temporary exhibitions, while the inner courtyard is home to the café itself, with open-air seating and a big menu of reasonably prepared international mains (around Rs.1000–1600) – anything from pork chops to prawn curry. There's also a huge range of calorie-busting puddings, plus a good wine and cocktail list, although the whole place is sometimes let down by seriously lousy service – all the more disappointing given the top-dollar prices. Daily 10am–11.30pm.

Green Cabin 453 Galle Rd; map p.80. Cheap and cheerful local place on Galle Rd serving up above-average rice and curry, *lamprais* and other Sri Lankan offerings, plus *kottu rotty*, hoppers and string hoppers in the evening. Unlicensed. Mains Rs.250–450. Daily 11am–3pm & 6–11pm.

★ **The Lagoon** Cinnamon Grand hotel, 77 Galle Rd ☎011 243 7437; map p.80. Colombo's best seafood, served up in a bright glass-sided restaurant permeated with salty marine smells. Choose what you want from the superb display of fish and seafood (including all sorts of fish, and prawns the size of small lobsters), and have it prepared in any one of over 25 different cooking styles, ranging from Sri Lankan and Indian to Chinese, Thai and Continental. Mains from around Rs.1200. Daily noon–3pm & 7pm–midnight.

Palmyrah Hotel Renuka, 328 Galle Rd ☎011 257 3598; map p.80. This unpretentious basement restaurant is one of Colombo's better places for Sri Lankan cuisine, with tasty curries, hoppers, *pittu* and *kottu rotty*, plus rich Jaffna-style meat and fish *poriyals* and a few Indian dishes. Mains from around Rs.550. Daily noon–2.30pm & 7–10.30pm.

Raffles 35 Bagatelle Rd ☎011 255 9846, ⓦrafflescolombo.com; map p.80. Set in a gracious old colonial house, this relaxed restaurant dishes up a well-prepared array of meat, fish and vegetarian dishes – mainly Italian-cum-European, plus a few Asian offerings. Mains Rs.600–700. Daily noon–3pm & 7–11pm.

★ **Tao** Cinnamon Grand hotel, 77 Galle Rd ☎011 243 7437; map p.80. The beautiful gardens of the *Cinnamon Grand*, with twinkling fairy lights and floodlit palm trees, provide an idyllic setting for superb fusion cuisine which blends Sri Lankan, Asian and European influences. The inventive and beautifully prepared food ranges from mainstream seafood and meat dishes to more unusual mixes like the combination plate of red curry chicken, grilled lamb chops and spiced tiger prawns. Most mains from around Rs.1000. Daily 7pm–midnight.

CINNAMON GARDENS

Agra Sri Lanka Foundation Mw ☎011 535 3333; map p.80. Romantic Indian restaurant with one of the prettiest interiors in the city and a fine selection of classic North Indian and Mughlai cuisine, including plenty of kebabs, tandoori dishes and a good spread of vegetarian options, all reasonably priced. Mains from around Rs.600. Daily 11.30am–3pm & 6.30–11pm.

The Bayleaf 79 Gregory's Rd ☎011 269 5920; map p.80. Smart Italian restaurant in a gracious colonial villa on one of Colombo's most exclusive streets, with seating inside and out. The menu features a big selection of home-made pastas, plus a few meat and fish options and some of the best cocktails in the city. Mains from around Rs.1000. Daily 11am–11pm (or later on Fri & Sat).

★ **The Mango Tree** 82 Dharmapala Mw ☎011 587 9790; map p.80. Sleek North Indian restaurant with attractive modern decor and a well-prepared range of meat, seafood and vegetarian dishes with the emphasis on tandooris, tikkas, kebabs and hearty Punjabi-style cuisine. Mains from around Rs.700. Daily noon–3pm & 7–11pm.

BAMBALAPITIYA

Chinese Dragon Café 11 Milagiriya Ave, off Galle Rd ☎011 780 8080; map p.80. One of the city's liveliest and longest-running Chinese restaurants, tucked away in a rambling old mansion off Galle Rd. The extensive menu includes a decent range of Chinese standards prepared with the usual dash of Sri Lankan spice, plus local favourites like chilli crab and devilled chicken. Mains from Rs.500. Daily 11am–3pm & 6–11pm.

★ **Greenlands** 3A Shrubbery Gardens, off Galle Rd; map p.80. A Colombo institution, hidden away in an old colonial house, this sedate South Indian vegetarian restaurant offers a big range of excellent, dirt-cheap food (virtually all mains under Rs.150) including *vadais* (masala, ulundu, curd), dosas (paper, ghee, onion) and

1

other goodies including *idlis*, *pooris* and *bonda* (a kind of bhaji). Very popular, so service can be slow. Unlicensed. Daily 8am–10pm.

Saraswathie Galle Rd; map p.80. This long-established, no-nonsense South Indian vegetarian restaurant is ultra-cheap, interestingly hectic and offers a quintessential slice of Colombo life. Food includes various types of dosa (plain, masala, onion, ghee), string hoppers, veg burianis, potato curry, *idlis* and *vadais*, all at virtually giveaway prices, with most dishes under Rs.200. Daily 8am–10pm.

Siam House 17 Melbourne Ave ☎ 011 259 5944; map p.80. The most convivial Thai restaurant in the city, with smooth modern decor and a big menu featuring all the usual favourites – red and green curries, fish curries, spicy salads, *pad thai* – all served in big portions. Mains from around Rs.750. Daily 11am–1pm.

MOUNT LAVINIA

Golden Mile ☎ 011 273 3997; map p.87. The ritziest place on the beach, with a beautiful oceanside location and seating either outside on the sand or inside the big two-storey wooden building. Food is mainly fish and seafood,

plus a few European-style meat dishes (mains around Rs.850–1000). Daily 11am–midnight.

La Langousterie map p.87 Attractive open-air restaurant, set in a beachfront pavilion and with a decent range of well-prepared and moderately priced seafood and Sri Lankan dishes for around Rs.500–750. Daily 10am–10pm.

Loon Tao ☎ 011 272 2723; map p.87. Rustic beach restaurant specializing in Chinese seafood, with a vast menu offering fish and seafood in every conceivable style – Sichuan, Cantonese, Thai and Malaysian – as well as an extensive range of meat and vegetarian options. Mains around Rs.600–850. Daily 11am–3pm & 6–11pm.

Mount Lavinia Hotel 100 Hotel Rd ☎ 011 271 1711; map p.87. There are a range of eating options at this landmark hotel. The *Governor's Restaurant* does a vast and better-than-average buffet spread nightly (Rs.2250), though the number of guests can mean it's a bit like eating in the middle of a rush hour. Alternatively, the informal and more sedate *Seafood Cove* (daily 7–11pm) on the hotel's private beach offers a range of freshly caught fish, cooked to suit.

DRINKING AND NIGHTLIFE

Colombo's **nightlife** is gradually recovering some modest momentum following the conclusion of the war and increasingly relaxed security situation. There's a fair spread of places to drink, although nightclubs are more or less nonexistent.

BARS AND PUBS

Bradman's Bar Cricket Club Café, 34 Queen's Rd, off R.A. de Mel Mw (Duplication Rd), Kollupitiya; map p.80. Cosy little pub-style bar at one of the city's most popular cafés (see p.95); gets packed with expats and locals most nights. Daily 11am–11pm.

The Brewery by O Dutch Hospital, Fort; map p.74. Convivial new bar in the Dutch Hospital complex serving up the inevitable Lion and Carlsberg (both bottled and draught) along with a range of unusual "beer cocktails" and a decent selection of snacks and bar meals. Bar 11am–2pm & 5–11pm; restaurant daily 11am–11pm.

Clancy's Irish Pub 29 Maitland Crescent, Cinnamon Gardens; map p.80. Lowbrow but consistently popular pub-cum-club hosting a mix of live music and DJs, plus a weekly quiz (usually Tues). There's also passable pub food and Guinness in cans – although otherwise it's about as Celtic as chicken tikka masala. Entrance around Rs.500 for men, depending on the night; free for ladies. Daily except Sun noon–late.

Ex-Serviceman's Club Bristol St, Fort; map p.74. The down-at-heel bar and beer garden here serves up the cheapest beer in Colombo (just Rs.170 for a bottle of Lion), and is usually full of voluble locals getting smashed on Johnnie Walker – unaccompanied ladies may feel uncomfortable. Daily 11am–2pm & 5–9pm.

Galle Face Hotel Galle Face Green; map p.80. Romantic, colonial-style veranda bar overlooking the courtyard of this atmospheric old hotel, with the Indian Ocean breaking just beyond. Wildly popular with honeymooners. Daily 10am–midnight.

Harbour Room Fourth floor, Grand Oriental Hotel, York St, Fort; map p.74. The food is nothing special, but it's worth coming for a drink for the magnificent views over the port below from the tiny outside terrace, particularly spectacular after dark. Daily 10am–midnight.

Inn on the Green Galle Face Hotel (entrance outside, on the Galle Rd opposite the German Restaurant), Kollupitiya; map p.80. Decent stab at a traditional English pub with a reasonable selection of local tipples and decent pub food. Daily 4pm–midnight.

Lion Pub Galle Rd, Mount Lavinia; map p.87. Entered via a gaping lion's mouth, this popular drinking hole attracts Sri Lankans and Westerners alike, with pleasant outdoor seating, cheap beer and a party atmosphere – expect spontaneous outbreaks of singing from boozed-up locals. Daily 10am–11.30pm.

Mission to Seafarers (Flying Angel Club) 26 Church St, Fort; map p.74. Aimed mainly at visiting sailors from the adjacent port, this homely little place (it looks like someone's sitting room) is a pleasant spot for a beer or soft drink. Internet access (Rs.100/hr) and free wi-fi. Daily 9am–9.30pm.

Skky Bar 42 Sir Mohamed M. Markar Mw, Kollupitiya ☎ 0775 523 316; map p.80. Fancy new open-air rooftop bar on top of the AA Building just off Galle Face Green (the spot formerly occupied by the popular but now defunct *Tantra*), with moody lighting, chilled-out music and a cool local crowd supping on cocktails and shots. When you leave, try saying the full name of the street – Sir Mohamed Macan Markar Mawatha – to find out how drunk you are. Daily 5pm–1am.

LIVE MUSIC AND NIGHTCLUBS
Forthcoming events are listed at ⓦ whatsupcolombo.lk.

H2O 447 Union Place; map p.80. The city's best-equipped nightclub, with a glass dance floor and a decent sound system; check the local press for upcoming events.

Kama 32B 1/1 Sir M. M. Markar Mw, Kollupitiya ☎ 011 233 9118, ⓦ kamacolombo.com; map p.80. Small, stylish nightclub with Sri Lanka's first multi-coloured laser lighting system and one of the city's posiest crowds. Don't expect much to be happening any time before 11pm. Daily 10pm–2/3am.

The Library Cinnamon Lakeside, Slave Island; map p.80. More a bar-lounge than a club – though there's also a small dancefloor and the atmosphere can get slightly lively later on once the nightly DJ cranks things up. Daily 10am–midnight (Thurs–Sat until 2am).

Rhythm and Blues Bar 19/1 Daisy Villa Ave, R.A. de Mel Mw (Duplication Rd), Bambalapitiya; map p.80. Relaxed and completely unpretentious bar-cum-live music venue with a mix of live bands and DJs, plus a couple of pool tables and a long drinks list. Daily 7.30pm–2am.

ARTS AND ENTERTAINMENT

Barefoot Gallery 704 Galle Rd, Kollupitiya, ☎ 011 250 5559, ⓦ barefootgallery.com; map p.80. Next to the excellent *Barefoot* café (see p.94), this intimate little gallery hosts a roster of excellent, regularly changing exhibitions by local and international artists and photographers, along with a lively programme of concerts, talks and other events.

Lionel Wendt Art Centre Guildford Crescent, Cinnamon Gardens ☎ 011 269 5794; map p.80. Named after the famous Sri Lankan photographer and musician

and hosting a varied programme of dance, music and drama, along with regularly changing exhibitions, mainly photographic.

Saskia Fernando Gallery 61 Dharmapala Mw, Cinnamon Gardens ☎ 011 742 9010, ⓦ saskiafernando gallery.com; map p.80. State-of-the-art modern gallery hosting regularly changing exhibitions, usually concentrating on the work of living Sri Lankan artists, or foreign artists particularly associated with the island. Daily 10am–7pm.

SHOPPING

Colombo has a good range of shops, and a day trawling through the city's handicrafts emporia and chic boutiques can be an enjoyable way to end a visit and offload surplus rupees. You'll find the best of Sri Lanka's modest traditional **handicraft** production on sale at various places around the city, as well as at characterful modern shops, such as Barefoot, which offer chic contemporary takes on traditional designs – everything from stationery and stuffed toys to fabrics and kitchenware – and all at bargain-basement prices. The only fly in the soup is the fact that in virtually all establishments (except Barefoot) you'll be tailed obsessively during your browsing by the shops' under-employed sales assistants – though whether this is so that they can be of immediate service when required or because they suspect all foreigners of being closet shoplifters remains unclear. Colombo also boasts an excellent selection of **bookshops**, a plethora of **jewellers** and, of course, plenty of **tea shops**. When buying handicrafts, remember that the export of **antiques** (classified as any object more than fifty years old) is prohibited without a licence (see p.58).

GEMS AND JEWELLERY
There are gem and jewellery shops all over the city, particularly along Sea Street in the Pettah and on Levels 4 and 5 of the World Trade Center in Fort at the so-called Sri Lanka Gem and Jewellery Exchange, which is also home to a useful gem-testing laboratory (Mon–Fri 9am–4.45pm; tucked away at the back of level 4) run by the National Gem and Jewellery Authority. Staff here can tell you whether a stone is what it's claimed to be, and if it's natural, but they don't offer valuations. Tests are carried out on the spot and are free (you can buy a basic certificate of authenticity for Rs.285, or a more detailed one for Rs.856). The obvious drawback is that it will be difficult to

get something tested without buying it first, although you might be able to persuade Colombo jewellers to send a representative with you and the gem(s) before you part with your cash.

DEPARTMENT STORES AND SHOPPING MALLS
Crescat Boulevard Galle Rd, Kollupitiya, next to the Cinnamon Grand hotel. Sri Lanka's ritziest mall – if you've spent some time out in the sticks, you might appreciate the crisp a/c and bland consumerism of it all. Home to branches of the Vijitha Yapa Bookshop, Mlesna and Dilmah tea shops, as well as a Keells supermarket, a

1

good food court (see p.95) and the smart icafe internet café (see p.100).

Majestic City Galle Rd, Bambalapitiya. The city's flagship shopping centre until the opening of Crescat, this is now looking very dated, but retains a loyal following among Colombo's teenage mall rats. Lots of shoe and clothes shops (including branches of Odel and Cotton Collection), a big Cargills supermarket, internet café and Colombo's best cinema.

Odel 5 Alexandra Place, just off De Soysa Circus (Lipton Circus), Cinnamon Gardens ☎ 011 462 5800, ⓦ odel.lk. A popular expat haven, this chic emporium stocks a good range of clothes, along with assorted homeware and all sorts of other stuff. There's also a Dilmah Tea Shop and a good bookshop (see opposite). There are other branches across the city including Majestic City (see above), though it only sells clothes; Dickman's Rd in Bambalapitiya; Galle Rd in Mount Lavinia and elsewhere. Daily 10am–8pm.

CLOTHES

Cotton Collection Dharmapala Mw ☎ 011 237 2098, ⓦ cottoncollection.lk. Popular local chain selling cut-price rejects from Sri Lanka's garment industry along with its funky own-label clothes, including fun T-shirts, colourful ladieswear and lots of kids clothes. There are smaller branches at 26 Ernest de Silva Mw (Flower Rd), Cinnamon Gardens; at Majestic City (see above) and in the *Hilton* hotel. Mon–Sat 10am–7pm, Sun 10am–5pm.

House of Fashion R. A. de Mel Mw (Duplication Rd), Bambalapitiya, corner of Visaka Rd ☎ 011 250 4639, ⓦ houseoffashions.lk. Huge and incredibly popular store which acts as a clearing house for the surplus production of Sri Lanka's massive garment industry, with three floors stuffed full of all sorts of clothing and sportswear at giveaway prices, including Western labels at under a tenth of their retail price back home. Can be a bit hit-and-miss, though, depending on which orders have been over-fulfilled recently, while taller and larger foreigners may struggle to find much that fits. Mon–Sat 10am–8.30pm, Sun 10am–5pm.

HANDICRAFTS AND SOUVENIRS

Barefoot 706 Galle Rd, Kollupitiya ☎ 011 258 9305, ⓦ barefootceylon.com; map p.80. Colombo's most interesting and original shop, and a serene retreat from the pollution and noise of Galle Rd (the sense of escape is enhanced by the deliberate lack of street-facing windows). It's best known for its vibrantly coloured woven fabrics, sold on their own or made into all sorts of objects including clothes, tablecloths, fabric-covered stationery, marvellous soft toys (grown-ups will love them too), and much more besides. There's also an excellent little bookshop (see opposite) and café (see p.94). Interesting temporary exhibitions are often held here, while a local weaver can

often be seen at work in the courtyard at the back. Mon–Sat 10am–7pm, Sun 11am–5pm.

Laksala 60 York St, Fort ☎ 011 232 3513 (map p.74). The flagship store of the national chain of government-run handicrafts shops, this cavern of kitsch is worth visiting just to get an idea of the tat that often passes for Sri Lankan craftsmanship: shiny orange Buddhas, shoddy masks, herds of gruesomely coloured wooden elephants and similar monstrosities. Other offerings include woodcarvings, metalware, a mixed selection of batiks, jewellery, tea and drums. Daily 9am–9pm.

Lanka Hands 135 Bauddhaloka Mw, Kollupitiya ☎ 011 451 2311. An upmarket alternative to the ubiquitous Laksala, selling similarly touristy stuff, but of a somewhat higher quality. Wares include decent woodcarvings, brasswork, lacquered bowls, a mixed bag of batiks, better-than-average *kolam* masks and cute elephants. Also has a reasonable selection of Western and Sri Lankan CDs upstairs. Daily 9.30am–6.30pm, Sun until 6pm.

LUV SL Dutch Hospital, Fort ☎ 011 244 8873 (map p.74). Offshoot of the pioneering Odel chain (see opposite), stocking a fun range of accessories, clothes and unusual souvenirs. Daily 10am–7pm.

Paradise Road 213 Dharmapala Mw, Cinnamon Gardens ☎ 011 268 6043, ⓦ paradiseroadsl.com. Set in a lovely, chintzy colonial villa, this is one of the top names in Colombo chic, stocking a range of superior household items alongside miscellaneous bric-a-brac and souvenirs. There's also a nice little café upstairs. They have a second branch around the corner from the *Gallery Café* (see p.95), called Paradise Road Studio (Mon–Fri 10am–8pm, Sat & Sun 10am–7pm). Daily 10am–7pm.

TEA

Mlesna Tea Centre Crescat Boulevard (plus branches at Majestic City, Bambalapitiya; and the Hilton in Fort) ⓦ mlesnateas.com. Fancy packs of souvenir teas and other tea-making paraphernalia – nice for a present or chintzy souvenir, although for real local tea at cheap prices you'll do much better in a local supermarket such as Cargills or Keells. Daily 10am–6pm.

BOOKSHOPS

New English-language books are sold in Sri Lanka for about two-thirds of the retail price in Europe and North America, though the stock is often rather dog-eared. All the city's bookshops also offer huge selections of Sri Lanka-related titles, ranging from gorgeous coffee-table volumes to arcane tomes on a baffling range of historical, cultural and religious topics. The best selection can be found on Galle Rd between Kollupitiya and Bambalapitiya; there are also small bookshops in most of the big hotels.

Barefoot 706 Galle Rd, Kollupitiya ☎ 011 258 9305, ⓦ barefootceylon.com. The bookshop here manages to cram an excellent range of titles into a relatively small space, including the city's best selection of English-language fiction, plus lots of gorgeous coffee-table books and loads of volumes on Sri Lankan art, culture and history. Mon–Sat 10am–7pm, Sun 11am–5pm.

Lake House Bookshop Sir Chittampalam A. Gardiner Mw, Slave Island (map p.80). Large bookshop with a huge selection of Sri Lanka-related volumes, plus a passable selection of English-language novels. Mon–Sat 10am–6pm.

Makeen Books 430–432 Galle Rd ☎011 237 5930. Decent selection of English-language novels and Sri Lanka-related titles. Mon–Sat 9.30am–6.30pm.

Odel 5 Alexandra Place, just off De Soysa Circus (Lipton Circus), Cinnamon Gardens ☎011 462 5800, ⓦodel.lk. Excellent outlet in the city's flashest department store, particularly good for glossy coffee-table tomes, and with a decent selection of local and foreign magazines. Daily 10am–8pm.

Vijitha Yapa ⓦvijithayapa.com. The island's main bookshop chain has branches in the basement of Unity Plaza (next door to Majestic City; see p.98), Crescat Boulevard (see p.97) and Thurston Rd, and a small branch at the British Council (see below). All four branches have a good range of books on Sri Lanka, plus a middling selection of English-language novels and local magazines.

AYURVEDA AND SPAS

Ayurveda There's a surprising lack of Ayurveda facilities in Colombo, although an increasing number of spas (see opposite). The best place in town is the Mount Clinic of Oriental Medicine, 38b Station Rd, Mount Lavinia (☎011 272 3464, ⓔmtclinic@sti.lk), run by a doctor qualified in both Ayurveda and Chinese medicine with the main emphasis on the serious treatment of chronic conditions, rather than on "soft" Ayurveda massages and baths. A hundred different therapies are offered – perhaps the largest range of anywhere in Sri Lanka – including 25 different types of Ayurvedic massage and four Chinese, plus medieval-sounding treatments including

blood-letting and cauterization with fire (so-called "moxibustion"), as well as the rare *ashtakarma* (eightfold treatment). Individual treatments from around $30.

Spas There are good spas at the *Galle Face* and *Mount Lavinia* hotels. Right in the city centre, the tranquil new Angsana City Club and Spa, Crescat City (next to the *Cinnamon Grand* hotel ☎011 242 4245, ⓦangsanaspa .com), offers a range of massages, facials, manicures and pedicures, and has treatment rooms for couples, steam bath and sauna, as well as a gym, café and a large rooftop infinity swimming pool, which you can use if you have a treatment.

SPORT

Cricket Most Test matches are played at the Sinhalese Sports Club (SSC), centrally located on Maitland Place in Cinnamon Gardens, although one match a year is held at the P. Sara Oval (aka the "Colombo Oval"), west of the centre in Borella. One-day internationals are played at the Premadasa Stadium in Dematagoda. Tickets are available direct from the stadia.

Diving Underwater Safaris, 25C Barnes Place, Cinnamon Gardens (☎011 269 4012, ⓦunderwatersafaris.org) is the oldest diving school in Sri Lanka, offering PADI

courses and reef and wreck dives at local sites. Another possibility is Colombo Divers (☎077 8787 291, ⓦcolombodivers.com).

Golf The beautiful Royal Colombo Golf Club is a short drive from the city centre at 223 Model Farm Rd, Colombo 8 ☎011 269 5431, ⓦrcgcsl.com. Green fees are around $50/75/day (weekdays/weekends).

Swimming Many of the city's hotel pools can be used by non-guests for a fee. See the accommodation listings (pp.91–93) for details.

DIRECTORY

Banks and exchange There's at least one bank on virtually every city block across Colombo; all change cash and traveller's cheques, and almost all now have 24hr ATMs, many of which accept foreign Visa and MasterCards.

British Council 49 Alfred House Gardens, Kollupitiya ☎011 452 1521, ⓦbritishcouncil.org/srilanka (Tues–Sat 9am–6pm, Sun 9am–4.30pm). Has a good library, a small cafeteria and a branch of the Vijitha Yapa bookshop chain; also stages occasional talks, readings, concerts and exhibitions.

Cinema Colombo's only modern cinema is the Majestic Cineplex, on the fourth floor of the Majestic City mall (see p.98), which shows the latest Hollywood and Bollywood

blockbusters on its one and only screen (four screenings daily; Rs.460).

Couriers DHL, 148 Vauxhall St, Slave Island ☎011 230 4304, ⓦdhl.com.lk; FedEx, 93 1/1 Chatham St, Fort ☎011 254 4357, ⓦfedex.com/lk/dropoff.

Embassies and consulates Australia, 21 Gregory's Rd, Cinnamon Gardens ☎011 246 3200; Canada, 33A, 5th Lane, Kollupitiya ☎011 522 6232; India, 36–38 Galle Rd, Kollupitiya ☎011 242 1605; UK, 389 Bauddhaloka Mw, Cinnamon Gardens ☎011 539 0639; USA, 210 Galle Rd, Kollupitiya ☎011 249 8500.

Hospitals and health clinics If you need an English-speaking doctor, first ask at your hotel or guesthouse (or at the nearest large hotel). For more serious problems, head to one of the city's reputable private hospitals. These include Asha Hospital, Horton Place, Cinnamon Gardens ☎ 011 269 6412; Apollo Hospital, Narahenpita ☎ 011 453 0000; and Durdans Hospital, 3 Alfred Place, Kollupitiya ☎ 011 257 5205.

Internet access Reliable places (from north to south) include: Mission to Seafarers (Flying Angel Club), Church St, Fort (daily 8am–8pm; Rs.100/hr); icafe, Ground Floor, Crescat Boulevard, Galle Rd, Kollupitiya (daily 9.30am–9.30pm; Rs.180/hr); Berty's, Galle Rd, Kollupitiya (Mon–Sat 7am–5pm; Rs.100/hr); ATEC Internet Cafe, 3rd Floor, Majestic City, Bambalapitiya (daily 9am–8.30pm; Rs.100/hr); Hanna Communications, corner of Galle Rd and De Fonseka Place, Bambalapitiya (daily 8.30am–9pm; Rs.50/hr).

Left luggage There's a left-luggage office (signed "cloak room"; daily 5am–10pm) at Fort Railway Station, outside the station to the left of the entrance.

Pharmacies Union Chemists (7am–11pm; open 365 days a year); or the City Dispensary (daily 8.30am–8.30pm), both close by at the eastern end of Union Place. Another large City Dispensary (daily 8am–8pm) is on Bambalapitiya Junction, Galle Rd, and there are also well-stocked pharmacies in Cargills on York St, Fort, and in the basement of Majestic City, Kollupitiya.

Photos The reliable Millers Digital Imaging Centre (Kodak Express) has branches in Majestic City (see p.98) and on York St in Fort (in the street-facing side of the Cargills building; see p.73).

Post office The main post office on Bristol St in Fort (Mon–Sat 7am–6pm) offers free poste restante service (post is held for only fourteen days). There are agency post offices all over the city, especially along Galle Rd.

Supermarkets The main chains are Cargills, which has branches at York St, Fort (see p.73) and in the basement of Majestic City (see p.98); and Keells, in the basement of Crescat Boulevard (see p.97).

Negombo

Sprawling **NEGOMBO** is of interest mainly thanks to its proximity to the international airport, just 10km down the road – many visitors stagger off long-haul flights straight into one of the beach hotels here, or stay here as a last stop before flying home. Negombo's **beach** is very wide in places, but rather shabby compared to the more pristine resorts further south, although the surrounding resort area is often one of the liveliest places around the coast if you're in search of cheap beer and late nights. A couple of miles south of the beach, **Negombo Town** offers an interesting introduction to coastal Sri Lankan life, with a lively fish market, a dash of olde-worlde colonial charm and hundreds of colourful wooden boats.

Brief history

The hordes of international tourists who descend on the town annually are merely the latest in the long line of foreign visitors who have done so much to shape Negombo's decidedly cosmopolitan history. The town was one of the first to be taken by the Portuguese, who converted many of the local Karavas (see box opposite), and the area remains a stronghold of **Christian Sri Lanka**, as borne out by the imposing churches and florid wayside Catholic shrines scattered about the town and its environs. The Dutch transformed Negombo into an important commercial centre, building a canal (and a fort to guard it) on which spices – particularly the valuable cinnamon which grew profusely in the surrounding areas – were transported from the interior to the coast prior to being shipped abroad. Nowadays much of the town's economy revolves around tourism, although fishing also remains vitally important, with the sea providing plentiful supplies of tuna, shark and seer, while the Negombo lagoon, backing the town, is the source of some of the island's finest prawns, crabs and lobster.

The fort and fish market

The heart of the old town is situated on the tip of a peninsula enclosing the top of the Negombo lagoon. Close to the western end of the peninsula lie the very modest remains of the old Dutch **fort**, mostly demolished by the British to make way for the prison that still stands behind the gateway. There's little to see beyond a weed-covered

archway emblazoned with the date 1678 and a very short section of ramparts topped with a miniature clocktower added by the British.

Just north of here sits the town's time-warped old rest house and more modern **fish market**, with endless lines of fish laid out to dry on the sand (and even bigger flocks of crows attracted by the smell). The market is busiest early in the morning, but keeps going right on into the afternoon.

Around the lagoon

South of the fort, the narrow channel leading into the Negombo lagoon stretches alongside Custom House Road, with myriad multicoloured fibreglass boats tied up under huge tropical trees. A couple of hundred metres down the road, a bridge crosses to the diminutive island of **Duwa**, offering photogenic views of long lines of colourful

---

THE KARAVAS

The people of Negombo are **Karavas**, Tamil and Sinhalese fishermen who converted en masse to Catholicism during the mid-sixteenth century under the influence of Portuguese missionaries, taking Portuguese surnames and becoming the first of Sri Lanka's innumerable de Silvas, de Soysas and Pereras.

The Karavas are also famous for their unusual fishing boats, known as **oruwas**, distinctive catamarans (a word derived from the Tamil *ketti-maran*) fashioned from a hollowed-out trunk attached to an massive sail. Hundreds of these small vessels remain in use even today, and make an unforgettable sight when the fleet returns to shore.

1

BOAT TRIPS, WATERSPORTS AND DIVING

Local boatmen sometimes hang out on the beach touting for custom and offering pricey **oruwa trips** either out to sea or into the Negombo lagoon (count on around Rs.3000–4000 for 1hr, although prices are highly susceptible to bargaining). Some guesthouses and tour operators arrange **boat trips** along the Dutch canal north of Negombo. These usually include a visit to a coir factory and some low-level birdwatching along with the chance to watch local toddy tappers at work, and perhaps to sample some of the resulting brew – Negombo's very own booze cruise. None of these trips, however, is as interesting at the boat ride through the nearby Muthurajawela wetlands (see p.108).

The watersports and diving centre between the *Jetwing Beach* and *Jetwing Blue* hotels (☎031 227 3500) offers diving, sailing, surfing, windsurfing and kitesurfing tuition, and also has kayaks, sailing boats, boogie-boards and other equipment for hire. Diving can also be arranged through Colombo Divers (☎077 8787 291, ⓦcolombodivers.com). Negombo is particularly good for **kitesurfing** (best Jan–March), including a fine, 8km-long downwinder along the coast from Waikkal to Negombo.

---

wooden boats tied up along the mouth of the lagoon. Duwa is also the venue for a big Passion play, staged here every Easter.

St Mary's

Main St • No set hours • Free

Towering aristocratically above the low-rise streets of the old town centre, **St Mary's** is one of the finest of Negombo's many churches: a grandiose custard-yellow Neoclassical edifice, constructed over fifty years from 1874 onwards. The interior is decorated with dozens of colourful statues of po-faced saints and tableaux showing the Stations of the Cross – the importance ascribed to religious images in both Catholicism and Hinduism was doubtless a useful factor in persuading the local Karavas to switch allegiance from one faith to the other.

Main Street and the Dutch Canal

Running in front of St Mary's is the old town's principal thoroughfare, **Main Street**. The stretch west of St Mary's is attractively old-fashioned, lined with string of lawyers' offices interspersed with fine old colonial-era verandaed mansions and chintzy villas decorated with elaborately carved *mal lali* eaves, shutters and wooden balconies. East of St Mary's stretches the town's main commercial area, bounded on its west side by the old **Dutch canal** (known here as Hamilton Canal) which arrows north, continuing all the way to Puttalam. The canal was once the major conduit for Dutch trade in the area, although it now looks rather forlorn.

ARRIVAL AND DEPARTURE   **NEGOMBO**

The **bus** and **train** stations are close to one another in the town centre, some way from most of Negombo's accommodation. A tuktuk from either station to Lewis Place/Porutota Rd should cost around Rs.200–250, but you might have to bargain hard; drivers here are used to taking advantage of newly arrived tourists.

By car/taxi All Negombo's guesthouses should be able to arrange taxis for onward travel; the trip to the international airport currently costs around Rs.1500; to Kandy, around $70. If you're travelling in your own car or taxi between Negombo and Colombo, it's well worth travelling via the more scenic coastal road through Pamunugama and Hendala (see p.106) rather than along the main road.

By train Services between Negombo and Colombo are frustratingly slow; it's easier and just as quick (or quicker) to catch the bus. If you want to reach Kandy by train without travelling via Colombo, head to Veyangoda about 25km inland (around 45min and Rs.1800 by tuktuk; also served by infrequent buses), and pick up the train from there.

Destinations Chilaw (11 daily; 1hr 15min); Colombo (11 daily; 1hr–1hr 30min); Puttalam (4 daily; 2hr 45min).
By bus Services leave from Negombo's swanky new bus station in the town centre. For the Pinnewala Elephant Orphanage take a Kandy bus to Udamulla, just past Kegalle, and then follow the route described in chapter 3 (see p.204). To reach the Cultural Triangle, take a bus to Kurunegala, from where there are regular onward services to Dambulla and Anuradhapura. Heading towards the south coast, you'll probably have to change in Colombo.
Destinations Airport (every 20min; 40min); Chilaw (every 15min; 1hr 15min); Colombo (every 10–15min; 1hr); Kandy (every 30min; 3hr 30min); Kurunegala (every 30min; 2hr 15min); Puttalam (every 15min; 2hr 15min).

ACCOMMODATION

There's heaps of **accommodation** in Negombo, ranging from inexpensive guesthouses through to a growing range of chic modern resorts – although some of the cheaper hotels remain stuck very much in the 1970s, catering to an endless supply of all-inclusive package tourists who appear to demand nothing more of Sri Lanka than cheap beer, execrable quasi-European cuisine and ping-pong tournaments. Most of the **budget** places are in Lewis Place, at the southern end of the beach area; more **upmarket** options are concentrated to the north along (or just off) Porutota Rd in the suburbs of Ettukala and Palangatura. The landmark *Brown's Beach Hotel* had been demolished at the time of writing; it will eventually be rebuilt and reopen as a posh new five-star in around 2014. All the places listed below appear on the Negombo Beach map (p.104).

LEWIS PLACE

Ayubowan Guest House 47/55 School Lane, Ettukala ☎031 223 8673, ⓦsmoothhound.co.uk/sri-lanka/hotels/ayubowan. Tucked away on a quiet back street, this UK-owned guesthouse has just four homely rooms in a very peaceful villa set in a gorgeous little garden with a small pool. Free wi-fi and internet, and singles at half the double rate. B&B <u>$72</u>

Camelot Beach Hotel 345 Lewis Place ☎031 222 2318, ⓦcamelothotelnegombo.com. Large old-fashioned resort hotel – looking its age in places, although rooms (all a/c) are well maintained, rates are competitive and there are spacious grounds to crash out in and a nice big pool (non-guests Rs.1000). <u>$72</u>

Dephani 189/15 Lewis Place ☎031 223 8225, ⓦdephanie.com. Attractive old budget stalwart, set back behind a pretty little beachfront garden and with comfortable rooms boasting big frame-nets and old-fashioned wooden furniture – although service is lacklustre, and the occasional smile wouldn't go amiss. <u>Rs.2000</u>; a/c <u>Rs.2500</u>

★ **The Icebear** 103 Lewis Place ☎031 223 3862, ⓦicebearhotel.com. Tranquil and comfortable Swiss-owned place with a range of attractive rooms with rather arty furnishings (most with a/c and hot water) of various sizes and prices scattered around an idyllic beachfront garden. <u>$40</u>

Jeero Guest House 239 Lewis Place ☎031 223 4210, ⓔsilversands@dialogsl.net. Small family guesthouse with four bright, spacious and attractively furnished modern tiled rooms. All have hot water, while two come with sea views and one with a/c. <u>Rs.2600</u>; a/c <u>Rs.3300</u>

Ocean View 104 Lewis Place ☎031 223 8689, ⓦoceanview-negombo.com. Run by excellent local guide Mark Thamel (see below), this cheery and well-organized guesthouse offers a range of neat and trim fan and a/c rooms (all with hot water) either fronting the small garden downstairs or on the breezy balcony above. The only drawback is that it's on the road, not the beach. Fan <u>$20</u>; a/c <u>$30</u>

★ **Silver Sands** 95 Lewis Place ☎031 222 2880, ⓦsilversands.go2lk.com. Negombo's most appealing budget option, set in attractive white arcaded buildings running down to the beach. Rooms (a few with a/c) are old but well maintained, with private balconies and unusual but effective hooped mosquito nets. Fan <u>Rs.1760</u>; a/c <u>Rs.3630</u>

TOUR GUIDES IN NEGOMBO

All the larger hotels and various tour operators along the main road can arrange day-tours or transfers to Kandy, Colombo, Pinnewala Elephant Orphanage or pretty much anywhere else you fancy (count on around $70 to Kandy, $40 to Colombo) or longer tours islandwide. There are also several reputable independent CTB-registered **guides** in town, including the excellent and extremely professional Mark Thamel at the *Ocean View* guesthouse (see above), who can customize tours to suit either with himself or other reliable local CTB-registered guides; expect to pay around $60–70 per day for a couple, excluding accommodation). Other local guides include Terry at the *Jeero* guesthouse (see above) and Lakshman Bolonghe (a.k.a. "Lucky") at 146 Lewis Place (☎077 357 8487, ⓔlucky_tour55@hotmail.com). Lucky also leads specialist birdwatching excursions, including interesting half-day trips to Chilaw.

1

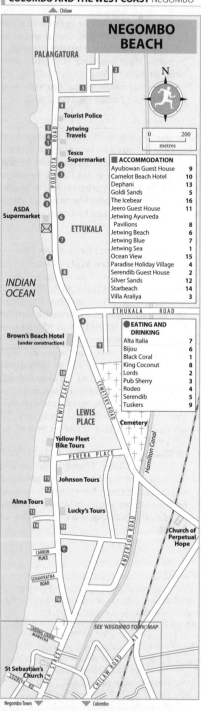

NEGOMBO BEACH

Chilaw

PALANGATURA

N

0   200
metres

Tourist Police

Jetwing Travels

Tesco Supermarket

ASDA Supermarket

ETTUKALA

INDIAN OCEAN

ETHUKALA ROAD

Brown's Beach Hotel
(under construction)

LEWIS PLACE

Cemetery

Yellow Fleet Bike Tours

PERERA PLACE

Hamilton Canal

Johnson Tours

Alma Tours

Lucky's Tours

CARRON PLACE

@

SENAVIRATNA ROAD

CARDINAL COORAY MAWATHA

SEE 'NEGOMBO TOWN' MAP

St Sebastian's Church

SOORIYA RD

SEA STREET

CHILAW ROAD

Church of Perpetual Hope

ANDERSON ROAD

CEMETERY ROAD

PORUTOTA ROAD

Negombo Town   Colombo

ACCOMMODATION
Ayubowan Guest House	9
Camelot Beach Hotel	10
Dephani	13
Goldi Sands	5
The Icebear	16
Jeero Guest House	11
Jetwing Ayurveda Pavilions	8
Jetwing Beach	6
Jetwing Blue	7
Jetwing Sea	1
Ocean View	15
Paradise Holiday Village	4
Serendib Guest House	2
Silver Sands	12
Starbeach	14
Villa Araliya	3

● EATING AND DRINKING
Alta Italia	7
Bijou	6
Black Coral	1
King Coconut	8
Lords	2
Pub Sherry	3
Rodeo	4
Serendib	5
Tuskers	9

Starbeach 83/3 Lewis Place ☎031 222 2606, ⓦ starbeachnegombo.com. Very similar to the adjacent *Dephani*, with simple but comfortable rooms (more expensive ones with hot water and sea views), plus a nice beachfront garden. **Rs.1650**; a/c **Rs.3630**

ETTUKALA AND PALANGATURA
Goldi Sands Porutota Rd ☎031 227 9021, ⓦ goldisands.com. Airy modern hotel with attractive rooms, simply designed in black and white decor and with sea-facing balconies overlooking a good stretch of clean and quiet beach, plus a decent size pool (non-guests Rs.990). Good value, although less memorable than the slightly pricier Jetwing hotels nearby. **$143**

Jetwing Ayurveda Pavilions Porutota Rd ☎031 227 6719, ⓦ jetwinghotels.com. Luxurious little hideaway with twelve gorgeous miniature villas set in a pretty little ochre huddle, each concealed behind high walls with its own private garden and open-air bathroom. The focus here is on Ayurveda, with two doctors, eleven therapists and a sitar-playing music therapist on hand to balance your *doshas*; courses cost $255 for three days, or select from a range of individual therapies (also available to non-guests). There's no obligation to take treatments, however, if you just want to stay here. B&B **$230**

★ **Jetwing Beach** Porutota Rd ☎031 227 3500, ⓦ jetwinghotels.com. Negombo's only five-star, set at the quiet northern end of the beach in attractively landscaped grounds. Rooms are superbly designed and equipped, with lots of dark wood, white linen, glass-walled bathrooms and all the facilities you'd expect for around $250 a night. Facilities include a heavenly (but relatively affordable) spa, an unusual tree-studded pool (non-guests Rs.750), resident naturalist, watersports centre, childcare facilities and the suave *Black Coral* restaurant (see opposite). B&B **$260**

Jetwing Blue (formerly the Blue Oceanic) Porutota Rd ☎031 227 9000, ⓦ jetwinghotels.com. This dated old package-tour stalwart has recently been given a comprehensive makeover and now rivals the standards (and prices) of the adjacent *Jetwing Beach* hotel (whose watersports centre and childcare facilities it shares), with stylishly chic rooms, cool interiors, a superb swathe of beautifully tended beach, plus a good-sized pool (non-guests Rs.750) and attractive spa. B&B **$260**

Jetwing Sea (formerly the Seashells hotel) Palangatura ☎031 227 7140, ⓦ jetwinghotels.com. At the quiet northern end of the beach, this is another old Jetwing package resort which has now reinvented itself as a rather chic contemporary hotel, with airy white interiors and well-equipped modern rooms at a surprisingly affordable price. The beach here is large and very peaceful, best enjoyed from the attractively rustic *Lellama* seafood restaurant. B&B **$175**

Paradise Holiday Village 154/9 Porutota Rd ☎ 031 227 4588, ⓦ paradiseholidayvillage.com. Bright, modern hotel with spacious and sparklingly clean tiled rooms and apartments (all with a/c, wi-fi, minibar, fridge, satellite TV and safe), a medium-size pool and cheery blue and white decor. $65; apartments $100

Serendib Guest House 106/8 St Joseph St, Palangatura ☎ 031 227 4440, ⓦ serendibguesthouse.com. Hidden away in a peaceful backstreet of Porutota Rd, this UK-owned guesthouse has three neat rooms (with optional a/c for Rs.500) in a pleasant modern house, plus a small garden with tiny pool (for sitting rather than swimming). Free wi-fi and internet. Good value. B&B Rs.3500

★ **Villa Araliya** 154/10 Porutota Rd, Palangatura ☎ 0712 728 504, ⓦ villaaraliya-negombo.com. One of Negombo's most characterful places to stay (though slightly away from the beach), set in a pair of rambling red-brick buildings around a neat garden and swimming pool. Rooms (mostly a/c) are attractively furnished in contemporary colonial style; no two are exactly the same, so have a look around before choosing. B&B: $55; a/c $70

AROUND NEGOMBO

The Wallawwa Kotugoda ☎ 077 363 8381, ⓦ thewallawwa.com. Stylish boutique hotel in converted old walauwe (manor house) tucked away just down the road from Henerathgoda Botanical Gardens (see p.109) in the village of Kotugoda (15min drive from the airport, 25min from Negombo). Rooms are elegantly designed and come with rainshowers, four-poster beds, widescreen TVs and wi-fi, and there's also a spa and a good restaurant. $250

EATING

Negombo has one of Sri Lanka's better selections of **places to eat** – although disappointingly, most are strung out along the main road, rather than on the beach itself, and the majority are identikit tourist dives with largely undistinguished cooking and ambience. The town's proximity to the Negombo lagoon, source of some of the island's finest prawns and crabs, also makes it a good place for **seafood**. All the places below appear on the Negombo Beach map (opposite) apart from the *Icebear Century Café* and *New Rest House*, which are shown on the Negombo town map on p.101. Some restaurants close down in the sleepier months from May to October.

Alta Italia 36 Porutota Rd ☎ 031 227 9206. Pleasant Italian-managed place which makes a decent stab at producing authentic Italian cuisine in the tropics using imported ingredients. Mains (Rs.650–950) include gnocchi, risotto, lasagne, pizzas, heaps of handmade pasta dishes and fresh seafood, including the signature *pesce spada alla griglia* (grilled swordfish), plus tiramisu and Italian coffee. Daily 9am–3pm & 5–11pm.

★ **Bijou** 44 Porutota Rd ☎ 031 531 9577. This homely Swiss-managed place has a tempting menu of excellent Central European dishes like pepper steak, Wiener schnitzel and fondues (order in advance), plus a range of perfectly prepared seafood. Mains Rs.800–1300. Daily 9am–11pm in theory, although often closes out of season.

Black Coral Jetwing Beach hotel, Porutota Rd ☎ 031 227 3500, ⓦ jetwinghotels.com. Negombo's most upmarket restaurant, with smooth modern decor (or seating on terrace outside) and vaguely fine-dining pretensions. The menu focuses on modern European-style cooking with Asian touches and ingredients such as the signature *Meerpura Issan Hindala* (Negombo prawn and herb-crusted sole fish). Mains Rs.1250–4000. Daily 7.30–10.30pm.

★ **Icebear Century Café** Main St, on corner of 3rd Cross St, Negombo town. Set in a gorgeously renovated colonial mansion in the heart of the old town, this chic little café is one of Negombo's most unexpected surprises, serving up shakes, juices, sandwiches, soups and cakes, plus breakfasts and bargain business lunches (Rs.260), along with excellent coffee and speciality teas. Mon–Sat 9am–6pm.

King Coconut 11 Porutota Rd ☎ 031 227 8043. A hungry-looking fibreglass T-rex welcomes you to one of Negombo's few independent beachfront restaurants (although on a rather shabby bit of sand). The main draw is the fresh seafood, although there's also the usual rice and curry and Chinese dishes, plus not very authentic pasta and pizza. Most mains Rs.600–750. Daily noon–11pm.

★ **Lords** Porutota Rd ☎ 0777 234 721, ⓦ lords restaurant.net. This chic modern restaurant brings a welcome dash of style to Negombo's scruffy main road, with sleek decor and beautifully presented cuisine. The wide-ranging menu offers all sorts of tempting international fare with a strong Asian flavour, including a good vegetarian selection, ranging from Thai fish cakes and crispy lemon chicken to button mushroom, cashew nut and raisin curry. Most mains around Rs.850. Free wi-fi. Daily 11am–2.30pm & 6–9.30pm.

New Rest House 14 Circular Rd, Negombo town ☎ 031 222 2299. This time-warped rest house in a fine old Dutch colonial mansion has gone downhill somewhat since Queen Elizabeth stayed here in 1958 but remains a tremendously atmospheric place for a meal or drink – a taste of old Ceylon a million miles from the brash beach. Locals come for the big rice and curry spreads (from a paltry Rs.200), and there also a selection of other standard Sri Lankan mains (Rs.400–500). You can also stay here, although rooms are fairly unappealing. Daily 6am–11pm.

1

Serendib 35a Porutota Rd (immediately south of Rodeo) ☎031 227 9129, ⓦserendibnegombo.com. Large and usually lively restaurant with seating either indoors or in the spacious (if not particularly attractive) garden at the back. The menu features all the usual suspects – seafood, devilled dishes, pizza and pasta– reasonably prepared and served in generous portions. Most mains Rs.660–880. Daily 11am–11pm.

★ **Tuskers** Lewis Place ☎031 222 6999. Top-notch new restaurant, in a pleasant pavilion-style structure open to the breezes but screened from the road. Food comprises a small range of mainly European-style meat and fish dishes (and pasta), plus some Chinese and Sri Lankan-style mains – all excellently prepared and attractively presented. Surprisingly affordable given the quality, with mains from Rs.770. Free wi-fi. Daily 10am–10pm.

DRINKING

During the season, Negombo is usually the liveliest of the west coast resorts, with most action concentrated along the northern end of the strip around the *Rodeo* bar and *Pub Sherry* – about as rowdy as Sri Lanka gets, which isn't very.

Pub Sherry 74 Porutota Rd. Larger and usually a bit more laid-back than *Rodeo*, with seating either at the bar or in the small garden and a decent drinks list including cocktails, plus imported spirits and beers including rum, tequila, Corona beer, Red Bull and – yes – sherry. Reasonable food also available. Daily 11am–2pm.

Rodeo Porutota Rd. A large streetside cactus announces this small, vaguely Wild-West themed bar, which is usually the liveliest drinking spot in town despite the complete lack of space and uncomfortable bench seats. Daily 11am–midnight/1am.

DIRECTORY

Ayurveda Ayurveda treatments are available at the beautiful *Jetwing Ayurveda Pavilions*, as well as at the *Jetwing Beach*, *Jetwing Blue* and *Jetwing Sea* hotels.

Banks There are numerous banks with ATMs accepting foreign cards in Negombo town, but none in the beach area – although plenty of shopkeepers along the main beach road will offer to change money if you can't be bothered to go into town.

Bookshop There's a modest branch of the Vijitha Yapa bookshop near the train station.

Internet There's free wi-fi in many of the town's hotels and restaurants, while numerous places along Lewis Place and Porutota Road in the beach area offer internet access and wi-fi – the best-equipped is the H20 internet café (Rs.180/hr; daily 7.30am–10.30pm, Sun from 8.30am) at 84/A Lewis Place, just south of the *Golden Star Beach Hotel*.

Motorbike and car rental Alma Tours (217 Lewis Place ☎031 487 3624), Yellow Fleet Bike Tours, 279 Lewis Place and Johnson Tours (182b Lewis Place ☎0777 825750) all have a range of scooters and larger bikes for rent for around $10–30/day. Alma Tours have various other vehicles available, including self-drive cars and minivans, and also rent out bicycles.

Post office Main St, Negombo town. There's also a handy agency post office on Porutota Rd just south of the ASDA Supermarket.

Shopping There are heaps of handicraft shops all along the main road – the best selection is along Porutota Rd around the *Jetwing Blue* hotel.

Swimming pools Most hotels allow non-guests to use their pools for a fee. See the accommodation listings (pp.103–105) for details.

Around Negombo

There are a number of low-key attractions scattered around Negombo including the fine wetlands of **Muthurajawela**, the **Henerathgoda Botanical Gardens** and a couple of temples, any of which make for a pleasant half-day excursion.

Pamunugama and Hendala

South of Negombo, the main coastal highway runs through an unbroken swathe of ugly modern development all the way to Colombo, though you can escape the fumes and concrete by taking the **old coastal road** through **Pamunugama** and **Hendala**, which runs along the narrow spit of land dividing Negombo lagoon from the ocean. This bumpy little palm-fringed road is infinitely preferable to the main highway, with occasional glimpses of the sea and an eye-catching sequence of florid, improbably

FROM TOP MASKS, AMBALANGODA (P.129); DWARFS, KELANIYA (P.87) >

1

grandiose nineteenth-century Catholic churches. The whole area is remarkably tranquil considering its proximity to Colombo, and the last few miles of road are particularly lovely, running alongside the Dutch canal, with colourful little wooden boats tied up along the banks. Then, at Elakanda Junction in the suburb of Hendala, the road turns a corner and deposits you suddenly back on the main coastal highway among the mayhem of the northern Colombo suburbs.

Muthurajawela

Around 15km south of Negombo (and 20km north of Colombo), at the southern end of the Negombo lagoon and close to the southern edge of the airport, **Muthurajawela** comprises a considerable area of saltwater wetland which attracts a rich variety of water-loving **birds**, including various species of colourful kingfisher, assorted herons, egrets, moorhen, duck, painted stork and many others, as well as crocodiles, macaque monkeys and a large population of water monitors. The small Muthurajawela **visitor centre** is the starting point for rewarding two-hour boat trips through the wetlands; it's best to ring in advance to make sure there's a boat available when you arrive, especially on Sundays, when lots of locals visit. Trips take you up along the idyllic old Dutch canal before reaching the Negombo lagoon itself, which you'll skirt while exploring the surrounding wetlands and mangroves.

ARRIVAL AND DEPARTURE   MUTHURAJAWELA

By car or tuktuk The trip from Negombo, including transport and boat tour, costs around Rs.1800 in a tuktuk, or Rs.3500 in a car, and can be arranged through most of the town's guesthouses and travel agents.

By train Catch a train to Ja-Ela, on the main Colombo to Negombo line, and take a tuktuk from there for the

three-kilometre trip to the visitor centre; turn west off the main Colombo highway down Bopitiya Road (signposted to the *Villa Palma* hotel).

Boat tours Boat trips (daily 7am–4pm; Rs.800/person including guide); a boat can be reserved by calling ☎011 403 0150 (office hours) or ☎0777 043 447 (mobile).

Angurukaramulla Temple

4km east of Negombo • Donation • Tuktuk drivers in Negombo offer a combined tour of this and Aluthapola Temple (see below), plus a Negombo city tour, for around Rs.2500

A short drive inland from Negombo, the eye-catching **Angurukaramulla Temple** serves as a rare beacon of Buddhism in an overwhelmingly Christian area. The temple is best known for its huge Buddha statue, built in 1980 and showing the master seated in the *samadhi* (meditation) pose. There are also various garish Buddhist *tableaux vivants*, along with a ramshackle subsidiary building filled with portraits or statues of all the major Sinhalese kings, topped with an unusual modern vatadage (circular shrine).

Aluthapola Temple

Around 15km from Negombo, on the road between Kimbulapitiya and Minuwangoda • Tuktuk drivers in Negombo offer a combined tour of this and Angurukaramulla Temple (see above), plus a Negombo city tour, for around Rs.2500

East of Angurukaramulla Temple, the **Aluthapola Temple** is said to date back to the reign of King Valagamba, creator of the famous temples at Dambulla. Like Dambulla, Aluthapola is a cave temple, built into the side of a huge rock outcrop, topped by an old Dutch survey tower and with mesmerizing views over the endless green treetops of the so-called "Coconut Triangle" (the area between Negombo, Puttalam and Kurunegala). Inside the temple there's a large reclining Buddha said to date back to 1792, though heavily restored since.

Henerathgoda Botanical Gardens

Daily 8am–5pm • Rs.600

Some 15km inland from Aluthapola, just outside the town of Gampaha on the main Colombo–Kandy railway, the historic **Henerathgoda Botanical Gardens** are famous as the place where rubber was first grown in Asia, during the 1870s, using seeds smuggled out of Brazil – some of the original trees can still be seen in situ. The rest of the gardens have recently received some long-overdue care and attention, and are well worth a brief visit, although admittedly nowhere near as extensive or spectacular as those at Peradeniya.

North of Negombo

North of Negombo, the coastline becomes increasingly rocky and wild, with narrow beaches and crashing waves that make swimming impossible for most of the year. Not surprisingly, the area remains largely undeveloped, although there are a cluster of appealing places to stay just north of Negombo in peaceful **Waikkal**. Heading north brings you to the bustling fishing town of **Chilaw** and the interesting **Munnesvaram Temple**, one of the island's most important Hindu shrines, while further up the coast the idyllic **Kalpitiya Peninsula** is home to the island's best dolphin-watching and a superb cluster of small-scale eco-resorts on beautiful Alankuda Beach – which also provide a convenient jumping-off point for the nearby **Wilpattu National Park**.

Waikkal

Twelve kilometres north of Negombo, the small village of **WAIKKAL** is a major **tile-making** centre, thanks to the good clay found hereabouts, and the area is dotted with quaint tile factories sporting tall chimneys attached to barn-like buildings with sloping sides and huge roofs, with great mounds of freshly baked tiles stacked up beneath them. The village also has a several good **places to stay**.

ACCOMMODATION **WAIKKAL**

★ **Ging Oya Lodge** Kammala North, Waikkal (signed turn on right just before you reach the turn-off for the Club Dolphin hotel) ☎ 031 227 7822, ⓦ gingoya.com. Very peaceful retreat, with seven rooms on a little peninsula surrounded on three sides by the Ging Oya river and screened from neighbouring houses by a swathe of jungle. Accommodation is in individual a/c chalets in the rambling, tree-studded grounds, all well-equipped and furnished in attractive colonial style with open-air bathrooms. It's a 10min walk to the beach, or you can paddle there in a similar time in one of the guesthouse's free kayaks. There's also a neat little bar and good-sized pool. Excellent value. B&B **$62**

★ **Ranweli Holiday Village** ☎ 031 227 7359, ⓦ ranweli.com. Idyllic eco-friendly resort squeezed in between the ocean and the lagoon, with rustic but stylish a/c rooms set in low red-brick buildings connected by covered walkways. Activities include yoga and Ayurveda courses, boat trips on the lagoon, bike trips and birdwatching with the hotel's excellent naturalist, and there's also a big pool overlooking the beach. B&B **$152**

Villa Suriyagaha About 200m from Ranweli Resort ☎ 0779 206 184, ⓦ villa-suriyagaha.com. Soothing little British-owned villa with six spacious and well-equipped rooms set around an attractive garden and surprisingly large pool. B&B **$70**

Marawila to Madampe

Twenty kilometres north of Negombo, the strongly Catholic village of **MARAWILA** has several large churches and produces good batiks – a trade introduced by the Dutch from Indonesia. The Eric Suriyasena and Buddhi Keerthisena showrooms on the main road are both good places to hunt for local creations.

1

Beyond Marawila, the beautiful coastal road runs north through an endless succession of fishing villages, past toppling palms, Christian shrines and cemeteries, palm shacks and prawn hatcheries. A few kilometres north of Marawila is **MAHAWEWA**, also renowned for its batiks. There are various tiny "factories" dotted around the village if you want to buy, or just watch how the cloth is made.

A few kilometres further north the small town of **MADAMPE** is home to the handsome **Tanniyan-valla Bahu temple**, right next to the main road. Fronting the road, the main courtyard is notable for its unusual statue of a rearing, riderless horse – said to commemorate a former traveller who once rode past the temple without paying his respects and was thrown to the ground by his mount as a result – whereupon the chastened rider vowed to erect a statue to atone for his insolence. A most plausible (if less colourful) explanation is that the horse belonged to a certain King Tanniawalaba, after whom the temple is named, and a statue of whom stands nearby, usually garlanded with flowers and surrounded by offerings.

Chilaw and around

Some 32 kilometres north of Negombo lies the town of **CHILAW** (pronounced, Portuguese-style, "Chilao"), home to a big fish market and dominated by the eye-catching, orange-pink **St Mary's Cathedral** – testimony to the town's large Catholic population which has led to its popular nickname of "Little Rome".

Munnesvaram Temple
4km east of Chilaw • No set hours • Donation

Just inland from Chilaw, the **Munnesvaram Temple** is one of the four most important Shiva temples on the island and an important pilgrimage centre. Its origins are popularly claimed to date back to the mythical era of the *Ramayana* (see box below), though the original temple was destroyed by the Portuguese, and the present building dates from the British era. A lively local **festival** is celebrated here each year in either August or September, with fire-walking; tour operators in Negombo might be able to give you information about precise timings.

Munnesvaram follows the usual plan of Sri Lankan Hindu temples, with a solidly built inner shrine of stone enclosed within a larger, barn-like wooden structure, its stout outer walls painted in the traditional alternating red and white stripes. The darkly

---

RAMA, SHIVA AND MUNNESVARAM

According to legend, **Munnesvaram temple** was established by none other than **Rama** himself, after he defeated and killed Rawana, as related in the *Ramayana*. Following the final battle with Rawana, Rama was returning to India in his air chariot (the *Dandu Monara*, or "Wooden Peacock" – often claimed to be the earliest flying machine in world literature – whose stylized image formerly adorned the tailfins of all Air Lanka planes) when he was overcome by a sudden sense of guilt at the bloodshed occasioned by his war with Ravana. Seeing a temple below he descended and began to pray, whereupon Shiva and Parvati appeared and ordered him to enshrine lingams (symbolic of Shiva's creative powers) in three new temples: at Konesvaram in Trincomalee, Thiruketheswaram in Mannar, and at Munnesvaram.

The belief that these three temples were thus established by Rama – an incarnation of the great Hindu god Vishnu – lends each an additional aura of sanctity, though the fact that they were created to enshrine a trio of lingams serves as a subtle piece of propaganda asserting the superiority of Shiva over his greatest rival in the Hindu pantheon. The paradox is that, despite Sri Lanka's close association with Vishnu in his incarnation as Rama, almost all the island's Hindu temples are dedicated to Shiva, or to deities closely related to him, and hardly any to Vishnu himself.

1

impressive **inner shrine** (*cella*) is very Indian in style; a large gilded *kodithambam* (a ceremonial pillar carried in procession during the temple festival, and a standard element of all Sri Lankan Hindu temples) stands in front of the entrance door. The **outer building** is a fine old wooden structure, slightly adulterated by bits of modern bathroom-style tiling. To the left of the entrance are various chariots used to carry images and other paraphernalia during temple festivities; more festival chariots can be found at the rear of the inner shrine, including a peacock (for Skanda), a Garuda (Vishnu) and a lion (Parvati). On the other side of the inner shrine are images of various gods – Vishnu flanked by Garuda and Hanuman; Sarasvati playing a sitar; Kali killing a buffalo; and Lakshmi. The huge chariot used in the festival is usually parked in the courtyard outside.

Anawilundawa Wetland Sanctuary

10km north of Chilaw • Open access 24hr • Free

North of Chilaw lies the lushly beautiful but little-visited **Anawilundawa Wetland Sanctuary**. The sanctuary consists of an ancient "cascading irrigation tank system", dating from the twelfth century AD and designed to irrigate surrounding paddy fields, along with a stretch of beach. Paths crisscross the sanctuary and you can wander freely between lotus-strewn tanks and the wide and beautifully unspoilt stretch of empty beach by the Hamilton Canal.

Uddapu

Beyond Chilaw the landscape becomes increasingly rural, with endless coconut plantations lining the main highway. Just under 20km north of Chilaw a turn-off from the village of Butul Oya (between the 96km and 97km post) leads to **UDDAPU** (or Uddapuwa), a small and impoverished Tamil village of sandy streets and palm-thatch fishermen's shacks which provides an unlikely home for the dramatic **Draupadi Amman Temple**, whose massive gopuram towers majestically over the surrounding low-rise houses. The village is also home to a sizeable Muslim minority, with a mosque (and church, tending to local Tamil Christians) standing in the lee of the temple – the mixture of local Tamil women in colourful saris and Muslims in flowing white robes lends the village a decidedly exotic appeal, quite unlike other settlements hereabouts.

The temple is also the focus of a remarkable 18-day Hindu festival (held late July/early August; see ⓦudappu.org) culminating in the **Tee Mithi** ceremony, during which the entire male population of the village walk barefoot over a bed of red-hot coals.

ARRIVAL AND DEPARTURE

By bus Buses run from Colombo and Negombo to Chilaw every half-hour or so.

ACCOMMODATION

The Mudhouse Around 30km northeast of Chilaw near the town of Anamaduwa ⓣ0773 016 191, ⓦthemudhouse.lk. Appealingly rustic eco-retreat set within two hectares of jungle beside a lotus-strewn lake,

CHILAW AND AROUND

By train Around 11 trains daily from Colombo and Negombo (2hr–2hr 30min).

with accommodation in simple but comfortable huts made entirely of natural local materials. Rates include full board and local activities and excursions (excluding transport). Minimum stay two nights. **$240**

Wilpattu National Park

Entrance at Hunuvilagama, about 40km west of Anuradhapura and 25km northeast of Puttalam • Tours can be arranged through guesthouses and hotels in Alankuda and Anuradhapura; jeeps can be hired for tours of the park at the entrance • Daily 6am–6pm • $10 per person, plus the usual additional charges and taxes (see p.45)

Occupying a vast swathe of land stretching all the way up to the border of the Northern Province, **Wilpattu National Park** is the largest in Sri Lanka, and was

1

formerly the most popular until the onset of the civil war, when its position straddling the frontline between Sinhalese and Tamil areas led to the widespread destruction of local infrastructure and killing of wildlife. The park finally reopened in 2009 and its wildlife is now gradually recovering, although the effects of long-term poaching mean that the overall density of wildlife remains significantly lower than in parks such as Yala, Uda Walawe and Minneriya, although there's a small but significant chance of spotting the leopards and sloth bears for which the park was once famous, not to mention elephants, deer, and many types of bird. Equally, the lack of visitors and the size of the area open to visitors (around eight times larger than that at Yala, for instance) means that it's also supremely peaceful compared to many other parks.

An unusual feature of Wilpattu's topography are its numerous **villus**. These look like lakes (indeed the park's name derives from *villu-pattu*, "Land of Lakes"), though they're actually just depressions filled with rainwater which expand and contract with the seasons, attracting a range of water-birds and wildlife.

ACCOMMODATION   **WILPATTU NATIONAL PARK**

In addition to the places listed below, Kulu Safaris and Mahoora (see p.27) both operate (pricey) tented safaris inside the park.

Hotel Leopard Den (formerly the Preshamel Safari Hotel) Near the turn-off to the park from the main Puttalam–Anuradhapura highway, 7km from the park entrance ☏ 025 325 9128, ⊛ wilpattuleopardden .com. Long-established hotel, with a mix of simple fan rooms and slightly smarter a/c doubles with hot water. You can also arrange trips into the park from here.

Rs.1320; a/c Rs.3850
Park View Bungalow Near the park entrance ☏ 025 490 1475, ⊛ parkviewwilpattu.com. Four simple fan doubles set in attractive modern bungalows amid shady gardens. Jeep tours of the park can also be arranged here. B&B Rs.3000

Kalpitiya peninsula

North of Chilaw (and about 8km before reaching the town of Puttalam), a side road branches off west, threading its way across the beautiful, windswept **Kalpitiya peninsula**, fringed with unspoilt beaches and bounded on opposite sides by sea and lagoon. The peninsula's considerable tourist potential (especially given its relative proximity to the international airport) remains largely unexploited as yet, and government plans to establish a $4 billion tourist zone near Kalpitiya town, complete with luxury resort, golf course and airstrip, have thankfully so far come to naught. For the time being, tourism remains low-key, centred on the marvellous cluster of eco-resorts at beautiful **Alankuda Beach**.

North to Kalpitiya town

Heading north across the peninsula, the main road skirts the southern edge of the Puttalam Lagoon, with views across the water to an impressive line of wind turbines opposite. After about 25km you'll pass the turn-off to Alankuda Beach (see opposite) followed, around 10km further on, by the side-road to the important Catholic shrine at the nineteenth-century church of **St Anne**, almost on the seafront at the village of **Talawila**, site of an important festival in March and again in July/August.

From here it's just under 20km to Kalpitiya town, close to the northernmost tip of the peninsula: a watery, end-of-the-world sort of place, home to the modest ruins of an old **Dutch fort** and the rustic little Dutch-era **St Peter's Kirk**.

Alankuda Beach

On the western, sea-facing side of the peninsula, idyllic **Alankuda Beach** is one of Sri Lanka's newest and most magical tourist destinations, offering a winning combination of dolphin-watching, kitesurfing, and beachcombing, along with the island's finest cluster of boutique eco-resorts (which also make a good base for visits to Wilpattu National Park, an hour's drive away). The beach itself is long, idyllic and largely unspoilt – even the massive new Chinese-built coal-fired power station just down the coast intrudes much less than you might expect.

Dolphin- and whale-watching

Early-morning dolphin-watching tours (around 90min) bookable through any of the eco-resorts around Alankuda, leave at around 7am daily (whale-watching tours can also be arranged through any of the resorts) • $30

Alankuda's principal attraction is as Sri Lanka's prime **dolphin-watching** destination, with dolphin sightings virtually guaranteed on the tours available. On a good morning you might see literally hundreds of these beautiful creatures (mainly spinner dolphins) coasting through the waves in every direction as far as the eye can see, occasionally launching themselves clean out of the water and spinning acrobatically through the air. **Whale-watching** is also a possibility (best during Nov–April). You might be lucky enough to spot whales during a dolphin-watching trip.

The eco-resorts

Apart from marine life, Alankuda's other major draw is the wonderful cluster of upmarket, low-key **eco-resorts** which have sprung up along the beach here: a rambling assortment of mud-brick cabanas, palm-thatch pavilions and rustic villas scattered among the endless dunes and trees – like a kind of anti-resort, and the polar opposite of brash Negombo or Beruwala down the coast. The various resorts are technically separate, and each has its own style and identity, although they're also connected by common design elements – rustic cabanas and huge verandas littered with colourful cushions; palm-thatch *ambalama* pavilions (inspired by traditional pilgrims' resthouses); tables made from old boats and so on – giving the whole development the feel of a rather surreal, but very chic, traditional Sri Lankan village. In addition there are no walls between the various properties and guests are encouraged to wander between them at will and to use facilities at any of them – alternating, for example, between the saltwater pool at *Bar Reef Resort* and the freshwater pool at *Palagama* as the fancy takes.

KITESURFING AT ALANKUDA

Alankuda is also a prime spot for **kitesurfing**, thanks to the strong winds which blow down either side of the peninsula: beginners head for the calmer waters of the lagoon; more advanced kiters head out onto the ocean waves. There are two kitesurfing schools, one at *Bar Reef Resort* (May–Oct), and the independent Kitekuda (☎072 223 2952, ⓦsrilankakiteschool.com), offering equipment and tuition from beginners to advanced levels, plus a kite camp with inexpensive bungalow accommodation. The best time for kiting is from May to September, when the winds gust most strongly; kiting at other times of year is also possible apart from April and November, when the winds die away to nothing.

In addition to kitesurfing, a range of other watersports including **snorkelling**, **kayaking** and **deep-sea fishing** can also be arranged. There's particularly good diving in the nearby **Bar Reef**, home to some of Sri Lanka's most pristine and biodiverse coral gardens, home to over 150 types of coral and almost 300 species of tropical fish.

Note that much of the accommodation below – the cabanas at *Bar Reef* and *Palagama* especially – is very open to surrounding nature and the elements; beguilingly peaceful, but not the place to come if you want a/c, satellite TV and 24hr room service. As well as the places listed below more properties are expected to open over the coming years and there's also the attractive **Khomba House** to rent, sleeping up to 10 people ($300). For a handy overview of the beach, see ⓦ alankuda.com.

★ **Bar Reef Resort** (formerly the Alankuda Beach Resort) ☎ 0777 352 200, ⓦ barreefresort.com. Alankuda's original eco-retreat, arranged around a picture-perfect infinity pool pointing towards the sea, surrounded by a trio of rustic thatched *ambalamas* and tables made out of old boats. Accommodation is in one of six cabanas, with faux-mudbrick ochre walls and thatched roofs, or two stunning villas (sleeping up to ten people), resembling a pair of glamorous Indonesian longhouses. Rustic eco-chic at its very best. B&B $155

Dolphin Beach ☎ 032 738 8050, ⓦ dolphinbeach.lk. A bit different from the other Alankuda resorts, with accommodation in well-equipped and very comfortable Rajasthani-style a/c tents (including four family tents containing two bedrooms), with attractive cushioned sit-outs in front. Meals (including real wood-fired pizza) are served in the breezy thatched dining pavilion, and there's a lovely chill-out zone in the circular beachfront *ambalama*. A pool and spa are planned. Pricier than other places here,

although rates fall almost fifty percent in low season. B&B $225

★ **Palagama** ☎ 0777 352 200, ⓦ palagamabeach .com. Next door to *Bar Reef Resort*, and sharing many of the same features, including a sea-facing infinity pool surrounded by *ambalamas* and accommodation scattered around lush grounds and the beachfront. Accommodation is in a string of quaint wooden cabanas – ingeniously designed (by owner and architect Cecil Balmond) in a range of styles using local woods, palm-thatch and other local materials. There's also more conventional lodging in a pair of homely villas, and a small spa. $137

Udekki ☎ 0777 446 135, ⓦ udekki.com. The funkiest of the Alankuda resorts, arranged around a wonderful "jungle" courtyard stuffed with all manner of trees and a cute little H-shaped pool. Accommodation is in a trio of whitewashed a/c villas decorated with eclectic bric-a-brac and artworks along with recycled windows, doors and cast-iron bathtubs. $165

South of Colombo

The coast **south of Colombo** is home to Sri Lanka's biggest concentration of resort hotels, catering particularly to a German and, increasingly, Russian clientele. This is the best-established package-holiday area on the island, and some parts, notably the main stretches of beach at **Kalutara**, **Beruwala** and **Bentota**, have largely sold out to the tourist dollar – if you're looking for unspoilt beaches and a taste of local life, these aren't the places to find them. Away from the big resort areas, pockets of interest can still be found, particularly at the lively town of **Aluthgama**, backing the Bentota lagoon, and **Ambalangoda**, the main centre for the production of the island's eye-catching masks. Further south lies the old resort of **Hikkaduwa**, still one of the liveliest places along the coast, with good surfing, snorkelling and diving.

Heading **south out of Colombo**, the heaving Galle Road passes through a seemingly endless succession of ragtag suburbs before finally shaking itself clear of the capital, though even then a more or less continuous ribbon of development straggles all the way down the coast – according to Michael Ondaatje in his celebrated portrait of Sri Lanka, *Running in the Family*, it was said that a chicken could walk along the roofs of the houses between Galle and Colombo without once touching the ground. The endless seaside buildings mean that although the road and rail line run close to the

---

The best season for **diving** and **swimming** on the west coast is roughly November to mid-April; at other times, heavy breakers and dangerous undertows mean that it can be risky to go in beyond chest height. For more about swimming and other marine hazards, see p.51 and p.55.

coast for most of the way, you don't see that much of the sea, beaches or actual resorts from either.

Kalutara

Just over 40km from Colombo, bustling **KALUTARA** is the first town you reach travelling south to retain a recognizably separate identity from the capital. It's one of the west coast's largest settlements, but the long stretch of beach north of town remains reasonably unspoilt, dotted with a string of upmarket hotels. Sitting next to the broad estuary of the Kalu Ganga, or "Black River", from which it takes its name, Kalutara was formerly an important spice-trading centre, controlled at various times by the Portuguese, Dutch and British. Nowadays, it's more famous as the source of the island's finest **mangosteens** (in season June–Sept).

Gangatilaka Vihara

Kalutara announces its presence via the immense white dagoba of the **Gangatilaka Vihara**, immediately south of the long bridge across the Kalu Ganga. Built during the 1960s on the site of the former Portuguese fort, the dagoba has the distinction of being the largest entirely hollow stupa in the island. You can go inside the cavernously echoing interior, whose walls are ringed by a strip of 75 murals depicting various scenes from the Buddha's life; windows above the murals offer fine views of the Kalu Ganga and out to sea. Outside, the line of donation boxes flanking the roadside are fed with huge quantities of small change by local motorists, who stop here to say a prayer and offer a few coins in the hope of a safe journey.

The remainder of the temple buildings are situated in a compound on the other side of the road, featuring the usual bo tree enclosures and Buddha shrines. It's a lively complex, and a good place to watch the daily rituals of Sri Lankan Buddhism: the Buddha images here are "fed" three times a day (rather like the package tourists at the nearby resorts); devotees place food in boxes in front of the images, as well as offering flowers, lighting coconut-oil lamps, tying prayers written on scraps of cloth to one of the bo trees (sometimes with coins wrapped up inside them) or pouring water into the conduits which run down to water the bo trees' roots.

Richmond Castle

Palatota • Daily 9am–4pm • Rs.200

A few kilometres inland along the lagoon-side road immediately south of the Gangatilaka temple, near the village of Palatota, stands the imperious **Richmond Castle**. A striking hybrid of Indian and British architectural styles, the house was built at the end of the nineteenth century by a wealthy landowner and spice-grower Don Arthur de Silva Wijesinghe Siriwardena; it now serves as an educational centre for underprivileged local children. Sitting proud atop a hill at the centre of a 42-acre estate, the two-storey mansion is constructed on a lavish scale – two entire shiploads of teak from Burma were used during its construction, some of which can be seen in the finely carved wooden pillars in the main hall. Hotels sometimes arrange trips to the house by canoe down the old Dutch canal – a pretty journey between nodding palm trees which is at least half the fun of a visit to the house.

Wadduwa

Kalutara's **beach** extends north of the bridge all the way to the village of **WADDUWA**, some 8km distant, backed by a string of large but discreetly spread-out resort hotels. The coast is edged with a fine – if in places rather narrow – strand of golden sand, and remains surprisingly unspoilt and quiet given the proximity of Colombo, although (as along much of the west coast) the sea can be rough, and most people swim in their hotel pools.

1

By bus The bus stand is a few minutes' walk south of the Gangatilaka Vihara on Main St.

Destinations Aluthgama (every 15min; 30–45min), Ambalangoda (every 15min; 1hr–1hr 20min); Colombo (every 15min; 1hr–1hr 20min); Hikkaduwa (every 15min;

1hr 15min–1hr 45min); Galle (every 15min; 1hr 45min–2hr 30min).

By train The train station, Kalutara South, is 100m west of the bus stand; see the timetable (p.89) for details of services.

ACCOMMODATION AND EATING

Most **accommodation** in Kalutara straggles up the beach north of the lagoon, spreading from Kalutara itself to **Wadduwa**. Distances are given from the bridge across the Kalu Ganga at the north end of Kalutara. There are a number of rather dismal **budget guesthouses** in the impoverished fishing village at the southern end of the beach, but if funds are tight it's really much better to press on south to Aluthgama or Hikkaduwa. You'll most likely eat in your hotel, although there are a few informal cafés dotted along the beach.

KALUTARA

★ **Avani Kalutara Resort and Spa** (formerly the Kani Lanka) 1.5km south of Kalutara ☏ 034 222 6537, ⊛ kanilanka.com. Stylish, Geoffrey Bawa-designed hotel in a breezy location on a narrow spit of land between the ocean and the Kalutara lagoon, with fine views over the town to one side and the ocean to the other. Rooms are elegantly furnished in minimalist style, and diversions include various watersports on the adjacent lagoon, yoga classes and an attractive spa. $120

Hibiscus Beach Hotel 3.5km north of Kalutara ☏ 034 508 2222, ⊛ hibiscusbeachhotel.com. Well-run resort attractively set in a palm grove threaded with colonnaded walkways. The comfortable, wood-furnished rooms all have TV and minibar, while the superior split-level villas boast gorgeous, partly open-air bathrooms with private pools and jacuzzis. B&B $90; villas $140

Royal Palms 3km north of Kalutara ☏ 034 222 8113, ⊛ tangerinehotels.com. Upmarket resort hotel, with rather grand public areas sporting eye-catching, quasi-Indian touches, plush but bland rooms, and an enormous, serpentine pool set amid spacious grounds. Guests can also use the Ayurveda centre in the sister *Tangerine Beach Hotel* next door. B&B $235

Tangerine Beach Hotel 3km north of Kalutara ☏ 034 223 7282, ⊛ tangerinehotels.com. Above-average resort hotel, the stereotypical design enlivened with quirky statues, fancy wooden doors and other whimsical touches. Rooms (some with sea views) are cheerfully furnished, and there's a big pool and spacious grounds, plus Ayurveda spa. B&B $200

WADDUWA

The Blue Water 11km north of Kalutara ☏ 038 223 5067, ⊛ bluewatersrilanka.com. This large Geoffrey Bawa-designed five-star resort manages to combine size and understated style, with classically simple buildings set behind a vast, imaginatively landscaped pool. The attractive rooms have all mod cons and sea-facing balconies or terraces, and there's also a gorgeous little spa. $205

Reef Villa 8km north of Kalutara ☏ 038 228 4442, ⊛ reefvilla.com. A sumptuous mix of colonial charm and modern luxuries set in a lush three-acre garden. Accommodation is in seven huge, high-ceilinged suites, beautifully furnished in updated Raj-era style complete with antique canopied beds and Indian ceiling punkah fans. Spectacular – and spectacularly expensive. $490

DIRECTORY

Banks Plenty of banks along Main St in Kalutara have ATMs which accept foreign cards.

Beruwala

BERUWALA is Sri Lanka's resort destination par excellence, perfect if you're looking for an undemanding tropical holiday with hot sun, bland food and characterless accommodation. Big resort hotels stand shoulder to shoulder along the main section of the broad and still attractive **beach** – Beruwala's so-called "Golden Mile" – often separated by stout fences and security guards from contact with the ordinary life of Sri Lanka outside.

That, at least, is the normal state of affairs, although at present Beruwala is undergoing a temporary hiatus thanks to major redevelopment all along the seafront. A couple of landmark hotels (the *Riverina* and *Tropical Villas*) are currently closed for renovations, while several new hotels, including the massive Chaaya Bey, are under construction further up the beach on the site of resorts destroyed in the tsunami. Much of the strip is

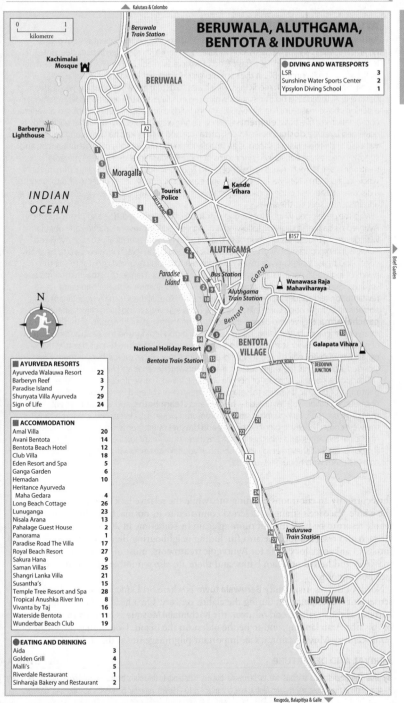

Kalutara & Colombo

BERUWALA, ALUTHGAMA, BENTOTA & INDURUWA

0   1
kilometre

Beruwala
Train Station

Kachimalai
Mosque

BERUWALA

A2

Barberyn
Lighthouse

Moragalla

**INDIAN
OCEAN**

Kande
Vihara

Tourist
Police

B157

ALUTHGAMA

Paradise
Island

Bus Station

Ganga

Wanawasa Raja
Mahaviharaya

Aluthgama
Train Station

Bentota

N

National Holiday Resort

Bentota Train Station

**BENTOTA
VILLAGE**

Galapata Vihara

ELPITIYA ROAD

DEDDUWA
JUNCTION

Brief Garden

● DIVING AND WATERSPORTS
LSR	3
Sunshine Water Sports Center	2
Ypsylon Diving School	1

■ AYURVEDA RESORTS
Ayurveda Walauwa Resort	22
Barberyn Reef	3
Paradise Island	7
Shunyata Villa Ayurveda	29
Sign of Life	24

■ ACCOMMODATION
Amal Villa	20
Avani Bentota	14
Bentota Beach Hotel	12
Club Villa	18
Eden Resort and Spa	5
Ganga Garden	6
Hemadan	10
Heritance Ayurveda Maha Gedara	4
Long Beach Cottage	26
Lunuganga	23
Nisala Arana	13
Pahalage Guest House	2
Panorama	1
Paradise Road The Villa	17
Royal Beach Resort	27
Sakura Hana	9
Saman Villas	25
Shangri Lanka Villa	21
Susantha's	15
Temple Tree Resort and Spa	28
Tropical Anushka River Inn	8
Vivanta by Taj	16
Waterside Bentota	19
Wunderbar Beach Club	19

A2

Induruwa
Train Station

INDURUWA

● EATING AND DRINKING
Aida	3
Golden Grill	4
Malli's	5
Riverdale Restaurant	1
Sinharaja Bakery and Restaurant	2

1

AYURVEDA: THE SCIENCE OF LIFE

Ayurveda – from the Sanskrit, meaning "the science of life" – is an ancient system of healthcare which is widely practised in India and Sri Lanka. Its roots reach back deep into Indian history – descriptions of a basic kind of Ayurvedic medical theory are found as far back as the second millennium BC, in the sacred proto-Hindu texts known as the Vedas.

Unlike allopathic Western medicines, which aim to determine what's making you ill, then destroy it, Ayurveda is a holistic system which regards illness as the result of a derangement in a person's basic make-up. The Ayurvedic system holds that all bodies are composed of varied combinations of five basic **elements** – ether, air, fire, water and earth – and that each body is governed by three **doshas**, or life forces: **pitta** (fire and water); **kapha** (water and earth); and **vata** (air and ether). Illness is seen as an imbalance in the proportions of three influences, and specific diseases are considered symptoms of more fundamental problems. Ayurvedic treatments aim to rectify such imbalances, and Ayurveda doctors will typically examine the whole of a patient's lifestyle, habits, diets and emotional proclivities in order to find the roots of a disease – treatment often consists of establishing a more balanced lifestyle as much as administering specific therapies.

With the developed world's increasing suspicion of Western medicine and pharmaceuticals, Ayurveda is gaining a growing following among non-Sri Lankans – it's particularly popular with Germans, thousands of whom visit the island every year specifically to take Ayurvedic cures. Genuine courses of Ayurveda treatment need to last at least a week or two to have any effect, and treatment plans are usually customized by a local Ayurveda doctor to suit the needs of individual patients. Programmes usually consist of a range of herbal treatments and various types of baths and massages prescribed in combination with cleansing and revitalization techniques including yoga, meditation, special diets (usually vegetarian) and abstention from alcohol. Some of the more serious Ayurveda resorts and clinics offer the **panchakarma**, or "five-fold treatment", comprising the five basic therapies of traditional Ayurveda: therapeutic vomiting; purging; enema; blood-letting; and the nasal administration of medicines – a rather stomach-turning catalogue which offers the serious devotee the physical equivalent of a thorough spring-cleaning. A few places offer other yet more weird and wonderful traditional therapies such as treatments with leeches and fire ("moxibustion").

Although a sizeable number of people visit Sri Lankan Ayurvedic centres for the serious treatment of chronic diseases, the majority of treatments offered here are essentially cosmetic, so-called "soft" Ayurveda – **herbal** and **steam baths**, and various forms of **massage** are the overwhelming staples, promoted by virtually every larger resort hotel along the west coast. These are glorified beauty and de-stress treatments rather than genuine medicinal therapies, and whether there's anything truly Ayurvedic about many of them is a moot point, but they're enjoyable enough, if you take them for what they are and don't confuse them with genuine Ayurveda.

thus currently an enormous building site, while the relative lack of visitors means that the whole place feels strangely deserted compared to its normal bustling self. Expect the whole resort to be back up and running again by sometime in 2014.

Beach and resorts aside, the area (including neighbouring Bentota) has also developed into Sri Lanka's major centre for **Ayurvedic treatments**; most of the larger hotels offer massages and herbal or steam baths, and there are also a number of specialist resorts (see box opposite).

North of the resorts, scruffy **Beruwala town** is where Sri Lanka's first recorded Muslim settlement was established, during the eighth century. On a headland overlooking the harbour at the northern end of town, the **Kachimalai Mosque** is believed to mark the site of this first Arab landing, and to be the oldest on the island. Containing the shrine of a tenth-century Muslim saint, it's an important pilgrimage site at the end of Ramadan.

ARRIVAL AND DEPARTURE   BERUWALA

By bus The nearest bus stations are in Beruwala town, 2–4km north of the various resorts, and Aluthgama, a similar distance to the south; both are served by regular buses (every 10–15min) running between Colombo and Galle/Matara.

Alternatively you could jump off the bus between Beruwala town and Aluthgama on the main road close to the resorts, but it's difficult to know exactly where to get off – it's easier to go to one of the two stations and catch a tuktuk from there.

By train The nearest train station is in Beruwala town, though it's served only by irregular, slow services. It's easier to go to Aluthgama and catch a tuktuk from there. See the timetable (p.89) for full details.

ACCOMMODATION

Recommendable accommodation in Beruwala is surprisingly thin on the ground at present, pending the reopening of the *Riverina* and *Tropical Villas* hotels and the completion of the huge new *Chaaya Bey* resort, all of which should have come into service by 2014 – until then, you can get much more for your money in Bentota, just down the coast. A couple of the places listed below have a strong Ayurveda emphasis; for specialist **Ayurveda resorts**, see the box below.

Eden Resort and Spa Beruwala ⓣ 034 227 6075, ⓦ lolcleisure.com. Glitzy five-star resort that doubles as a spa and health club. The huge list of treatments includes Ayurveda, herbal baths, reflexology, massages and yoga lessons, and there's also a vast pool (non-guests Rs.1000) and spacious grounds, although for all its rather brash luxury (and seriously meaty price tag) the place has all the style and atmosphere of a second-rate shopping mall. **$252**

Heritance Ayurveda Maha Gedara (formerly the Neptune) ⓣ 034 555 5000, ⓦ heritancehotels.com. This long-running, rather Andalucian-looking establishment has now reinvented itself as a pseudo-Ayurveda hotel, but remains the nicest place to stay hereabouts even if you're just after the beach. Rooms are bright and attractive, and there's a big pool and fine gardens. Rates include one Ayurveda treatment per day (chosen for you by a resident doctor), and there are Ayurveda packages and individual treatments. Rates include obligatory full board, although the Ayurveda food provided contains no beef, pork, prawns, chilli or oil – those in search of good food may prefer to stay elsewhere. **$215**

Pahalage Guest House ⓣ 034 227 6406, ⓦ pahalage.com. Neat little guesthouse (patronized mainly by German visitors) set in an attractive walled garden with pool and comfortable rooms. Also offers simple Ayurveda treatments and packages. **$45**; a/c **$50**

Panorama ⓣ 034 227 7091. The cheapest accommodation hereabouts, set just back from the relatively quiet and unspoilt (though narrower) stretch of beach north of the main resorts. Accommodation is in nine comfortable rooms (all with hot water, one with a/c) set in a family home – all are clean and comfortable, while four have partial sea views. **Rs.3600**; a/c **Rs.3850**

AYURVEDA AND HEALTH RESORTS IN BERUWALA AND BENTOTA

Ayurveda Walauwa Resort Bentota ⓣ 034 227 5372, ⓦ sribudhasa.ch. In a chintzy old walauwe (manor), set amid peaceful, tree-filled gardens and with soothingly old-fashioned rooms. All-inclusive seven-day treatment courses per person **$1100**

Barberyn Reef Ayurveda Resort Beruwala ⓣ 034 227 6036, ⓦ barberyn.com. The oldest of the area's Ayurveda resorts, and still one of the best, with immaculate rooms set amid tranquil, frangipani-shaded grounds. Courses go for around $660/week on top of accommodation; room rates include vegetarian Ayurvedic meals and free yoga and meditation classes. Full board (excluding treatments) **$140**

Paradise Island Bentota ⓣ 034 227 5354, ⓦ sribudhasa.ch. Slightly more expensive sister establishment to the *Ayurveda Walauwa Resort*, in a fine location near the tip of Paradise Island, with accommodation in neat little red-brick chalets scattered around flower-filled gardens. Six-day complete treatment courses per person including accommodation (based on two people sharing) and meals **$1300**

Shunyata Villa Ayurveda Next to Temple Tree resort, just south of the 66km post ⓣ 034 227 1944, ⓦ shunyata-villa.net. Idyllic little Ayurveda retreat in serene modern beachfront premises. Rooms sport deliciously cool Zen-like decor, with white walls, and rock-crystal jacuzzi bathrooms. There's also a nice little pool, while Ayurveda treatments are administered in a homely little palm-leaf shack in the beautiful garden. Longer Ayurveda packages also available – see the website. **$150**

Sign of Life (formerly the Niroga Herbal Resort) Bentota ⓣ 034 227 0312, ⓦ sign-of-life-resort. Next to *Saman Villas*, this homely little Ayurveda resort offers good-value courses including accommodation in bright white a/c rooms, Ayurvedic meals and free yoga classes. The emphasis here is on the treatment of specific complaints – anything from obesity to alcohol addiction – with treatment plans personally customized after an initial doctor's consultation. Twelve-day all-inclusive courses around **$1200**

1

EATING

Riverdale Restaurant Galle Rd. Plush but surprisingly inexpensive little restaurant serving up a wide à la carte menu (most mains Rs.400–800) ranging from reasonably priced rice and curry through to fillet steak or chicken cordon bleu, plus pasta and pizza; it also has a small separate bar and coffee shop. Daily 7am–10pm.

DIRECTORY

Banks The larger hotels all change money or traveller's cheques at lousy rates; if you want a bank (or a post office), you'll have to go down the road to Aluthgama or up to Beruwala Town.

Aluthgama

Dividing Beruwala from Bentota, the lively little town of **ALUTHGAMA** offers a welcome dose of everyday life amid the big resorts, and remains refreshingly unaffected by the local package-tourist industry. The main street is a colourful succession of trades: a fish market straggles part way up its west side, with all sorts of seafood lined up on benches supervised by machete-wielding fishmongers, while at the south end of the road, local ladies flog great piles of lurid factory-made cloth. A photogenic vegetable market is held just south of here, past the Nebula supermarket – Mondays are particularly lively.

Aluthgama's other attraction is its good and relatively cheap selection of **guesthouses**; these places aren't actually on the beach, but slightly behind it across the beautiful lagoon at the mouth of the Bentota River – in many ways just as attractive a location as the oceanfront, especially at night, when the lights of the northern Bentota resorts twinkle prettily in the darkness across the waters. If you want the beach, it's a ten-minute walk, or a quick tuktuk ride, to the nearest section of sand at Bentota.

Kande Vihara

About 1km inland from Aluthgama (head north along the main road towards Beruwala, then turn right, opposite the road to the Club Bentota jetty, just before the bridge over the narrow Kaluwamodera Ganga) • No fixed hours • Donation

A short walk or tuktuk ride inland from Aluthgama town, the pretty hilltop **Kande Vihara** temple is home to one of Sri Lanka's **tallest Buddha statues**, completed in 2007. Seated in the *bhumisparsha* mudra ("earth witness" pose), the colossus looms impassively over the pretty white buildings of the temple below, which also include an ornate eighteenth-century image house, a relic chamber with some well-preserved Kandyan-era murals, plus a pair of resident elephants and a herd of deer.

Brief Garden

Daily 8am–5pm • Rs.500 including guided tour

About 10km inland from Aluthgama, the idyllic **Brief Garden** comprises the former house and surrounding estate of the writer and artist **Bevis Bawa**, elder brother of the architect Geoffrey Bawa; the name alludes to Bawa's father, who purchased the land with the money raised from a successful legal brief. Bevis Bawa began landscaping the five-acre gardens in 1929 and continued to work on them almost up until his death in 1992, creating a series of terraces which tumble luxuriantly down the hillside below the house – Bevis's work here served as an important inspiration to brother Geoffrey in encouraging him to embark on a career in architecture and landscape design. The gardens are nice for a stroll, but the main attraction is the **house**, a low-slung orange building stuffed with quirky artworks, some by Bawa himself, plus several pieces (including two entertaining aluminium sculptures and a big mural of Sri Lankan scenes) by the Australian artist Donald Friend, who came to Brief for a week's visit and ended up staying five and a half years. Other exhibits include a fascinating collection of photographs of the imposing Bawa himself (he was six foot seven inches

1

tall), both as a young man serving as a major in the British Army and as one of Sri Lanka's leading social luminaries, posing with house guests such as Laurence Olivier and Vivien Leigh.

ARRIVAL AND DEPARTURE — ALUTHGAMA

Aluthgama is the area's major transport hub, with **train and bus stations** close to one another towards the northern end of the town centre. Count on Rs.150–200 for a tuktuk to places in Bentota and the main section of Beruwala beach, or Rs.200–250 to the northern end of Beruwala beach.

By bus Buses head north and south along the Galle Rd every ten to fifteen minutes.
Destinations Ambalangoda (every 15min; 30–45min); Colombo (every 15min; 1hr 30min–2hr); Galle (every 15min; 1hr 30min–2hr); Hikkaduwa (every 15min; 45min–1hr); Kalutara (every 15min; 30–45min).
By train for details of train services, see the timetable (p.89).

ACCOMMODATION

Ganga Garden Off Galle Rd, behind the Sinharaja Bakery ⓣ034 227 1770, ⓦganga-garden.com. UK-owned lagoon-side guesthouse. Rooms (all with a/c and hot water) are scrupulously maintained, while the communal veranda and the surrounding gardens are perfect for idle lounging. **$60**

★ **Hemadan** 25 River Ave ⓣ034 227 5320, ⓦhemadan.dk. Welcoming and well-run guesthouse with a pleasantly soporific atmosphere and a neatly kept garden running down to the lagoon, plus free boat transfers to the beach opposite. The airy, high-ceilinged rooms are unusually spacious and attractively furnished, and there's also good food in the pleasant terrace restaurant, and free wi-fi. Excellent value. **Rs.3000**

Sakura Hana 34 Padmini Pieris Mw (the side road opposite Sunshine Watersports) ⓣ034 227 5739. Attractive modern guesthouse with seven spotless and very competitively priced white rooms (all with hot water; five with optional a/c) in a smart modern family home. **Rs.2000**; a/c **Rs.2500**

Tropical Anushka River Inn 97 River Ave ⓣ034 227 5377, ⓦanushka-river-inn.com. Friendly guesthouse on the edge of the lagoon with six clean and very comfortable rooms (all with a/c and hot water, some with fine lagoon views), attractively kitted out with old-fashioned teak furniture. There's also a small Ayurveda centre, a breezy roof terrace and good food in the attractive restaurant, cantilevered right out over the waters of the lagoon. A bit expensive at quoted rates, though discounts may be available during quiet periods. Free wi-fi. **$65**

EATING

The *Tropical Anushka River Inn* and *Hemadan* both do good food – alternatively you're just a short walk from several good restaurants in neighbouring Bentota (see p.127).

Sinharaja Bakery and Restaurant Galle Rd, north end of town. Spacious bakery-cum-café offering a good selection of short eats and snacks downstairs, and simple noodle and rice and curry lunches and dinners upstairs – a refreshing and package-tourist-free pocket of local life. Daily 6am–10pm.

DIRECTORY

Banks There are several banks north of the bus station with ATMs accepting foreign cards.
Shopping Various scruffy shops at the southern end of the main road through Aluthgama stock a surprisingly good selection of handicrafts, principally *kolam* masks and woodcarvings; it's also worth checking out the well-stocked Aluthgama Wood Carvers shop, on River Ave just south of the *Hemadan* guesthouse.

Bentota and around

South of Aluthgama, **BENTOTA** offers a further clutch of package resorts, plus an outstanding selection of more upmarket places. The **beach** divides into two areas. At the **north** end, facing Aluthgama, lies **Paradise Island** (as it's popularly known), a narrow spit of land beautifully sandwiched between the choppy breakers of the Indian Ocean and the calm waters of the Bentota lagoon, though sadly none of the few hotels here really lives up to the setting. Backing Paradise Island, the tranquil **Bentota Ganga** provides the setting for Sri Lanka's biggest range of watersports (see p.124), along with interesting boat trips up the river. The **southern end of Bentota beach** (south of Bentota train station) comprises a wide stretch of sand backed by dense thickets of corkscrew palms – one of the most attractive beaches on the island, although somewhat spoilt by the unsightly amounts of litter that get dumped here. This is also where you'll find one of Sri Lanka's finest clusters of top-end hotels and villas, set at discreet intervals from one another down the coast. Many of the hotels in the area are the work of local architect **Geoffrey Bawa** (see p.126) – it's well worth splashing out to stay in one of his classic creations, whose artful combination of nature and artifice offers an experience both luxurious and aesthetic.

Despite the number of visitors, Bentota beach remains surprisingly quiet, particularly south of the station. Unlike Hikkaduwa or Unawatuna, there's virtually no beachlife here, and the oceanfront lacks even the modest smattering of impromptu cafés, handicraft shops and hawkers you'll find at Beruwala – it's this somnolent atmosphere which either appeals or repels, depending on which way your boat's pointing. If you're staying at Aluthgama or Beruwala and fancy a day on the beach here, you can eat and drink at all the guesthouses and hotels listed below; most also allow non-guests to use their pools for a modest fee.

Bentota village

Sprawling under an endless canopy of palm trees between the lagoon and the land-side of the busy coastal highway, sleepy **Bentota village** has a smattering of low-key sights, although the place is full of opportunistic locals hanging around waiting to pounce on tourists – harmless but tiresome. You might be offered a village tour, which could include seeing a local toddy tapper in action or a visit to one of the village's many small coir factories, where coconut husks are turned into rope (you'll see huge piles of coconut husks piled up around the village, waiting for processing).

There are also two village temples. At the eastern end of the village, next to the lagoon, is the **Wanawasa Raja Mahaviharaya**, a large and unusually ugly building full of kitsch pictures, dayglo statues and a memorable model of Adam's Peak equipped with a kind of flushing mechanism which sends water streaming down the mountainsides at the tug of a lever. Further south, also on the lagoon side, is the much more attractive **Galapata Vihara**, a venerable temple which dates back to the twelfth century and sports interesting wall paintings, peeling orange Buddhas and a large boulder outside carved with a long extract from the *Mahavamsa*, written in Pali.

Bentota River safaris

Trips can be arranged through some Bentota or Aluthgama guesthouses and hotels, through local watersports centres (see box, p.124), or through the Rainbow Boat House, next to the bridge over the mouth of the lagoon • Around $10 per person per hour in a group of four people, proportionately more in a couple or on your own

The Bentota lagoon is the last section of the broad **Bentota River** (Bentota Ganga), a popular spot for boat safaris along the river, which meanders inland for a few kilometres from the Bentota bridge before losing itself in another mazy lagoon dotted with tiny islands and fringed with tangled mangrove swamps. These trips aren't the greatest natural adventure you're likely to have: the boats themselves are usually noisy and smelly, and the standard of guiding pretty hopeless. Even so, you should see a fair selection of aquatic birds – herons, cormorants and colourful kingfishers – as well as a few water monitors, while your boatman might also ferry you right in among the mangroves themselves, a mysterious and beautiful sight as you drift though still, shaded waters beneath huge roots. You're unlikely to see much of interest on a one-hour trip, but the longer the trip and the further upriver you travel, the more unspoilt the scenery becomes. Longer excursions usually include extras such as trips to coconut factories or handicrafts shops, and you may also be taken to visit the Galapata Vihara (see above).

1

DIVING AND WATERSPORTS

The calm waters of the Bentota lagoon provide a year-round venue for all sorts of **watersports** including waterskiing, jetskiing, speed-boating, sailing, windsurfing, canoeing, lagoon boat trips, deep-sea fishing and banana-boating. There's also good **diving** along the coast here and decent **snorkelling** around Lighthouse Island off the northern end of Beruwala beach – trips can be arranged with local boatmen who tout for custom along this stretch of beach (around Rs.1500 for the boat plus Rs.750 for snorkelling equipment). The following are the main operators, although there are plenty of other smaller outfits dotted around the area.

LSR (Lanka Sportreizen) Marine Bentota hotel (just north of Bentota Beach Hotel) ☎ 0777 732 019, ⓦ LSR-srilanka.com. Wide range of watersports, boat cruises, sailing and snorkelling, plus PADI dive centre. There's a second, less well equipped branch in the grounds of the *Bentota Beach Hotel* itself.

Sunshine Water Sports Center Aluthgama, just north of the *Hemadan* guesthouse ☎ 034 428 9379 or ☎ 0777 941 857, ⓦ sunshinewatersports.net. Full range of watersports, and particularly good for windsurfing and waterskiing, with tuition available

from two former and one current Sri Lankan champion. Other offerings include jetskiing, body-board hire, snorkelling trips, deep-sea fishing, Bentota river cruises and lagoon- and sea-kayaking, as well as diving. Rough Guide readers are promised a ten percent discount.

Ypsylon Diving School Ypsylon Tourist Resort, Beruwala ☎ 034 227 6132, ⓦ ypsylon-srilanka.de. One of the area's longest-established dive schools, offering the usual range of individual dives, PADI courses, night dives, introductory "discovery" dives and wreck dives.

Lunuganga

About 6km inland from Bentota along the Elpitiya road (turn right at Dedduwa Junction after 4km and ask locally for "Geoffrey Bawa's house") • Garden tours daily 9am–5pm • Rs.1250

Inland up the Bentota River lie the magical house and gardens of **Lunuganga**, one of the west coast's most beguiling attractions, rambling over two small hills surrounded by the tranquil waters of Dedduwa Lake. Lunuganga was the creation of seminal Sri Lankan architect Geoffrey Bawa (see p.126) who acquired the estate – at that time nothing more than "an undistinguished bungalow surrounded by 25 acres of rubber trees" (according to his biographer David Robson) – in 1948, and gradually transformed it over the subsequent five decades, inspired by the example of his brother Bevis's work at Brief Garden (see p.120). The original house was systematically modified and expanded and new gardens created in place of the old rubber plantation, with intertwining terraces, a sculpture gallery and strategically placed artworks, opening up at moments to reveal carefully planned vistas, such as that over Cinnamon Hill, framing the distant Katakuliya temple. Like much of Bawa's work, Lunuganga manages to feel both captivatingly artful and refreshingly natural at the same time, while the various buildings offer an intriguing overview of the Bawa style in miniature, from the tiny little hip-roofed "Hen House", built sometime during the 1970s, to the serene Cinnamon Hill House of 1992.

You can combine a visit to the gardens with tea on the terrace or lunch, while if you want to explore the house in more depth you can also stay here (see opposite).

ARRIVAL AND DEPARTURE   BENTOTA

By bus Arriving by bus, it's easiest to get off at the terminal in Aluthgama and catch a tuktuk for the short ride south to Bentota unless you know exactly where you want to be set down.

By train Bentota has its own train station served by some (but not all) express services; alternatively, get off at Aluthgama station and catch a tuktuk.

ACCOMMODATION

For Ayurveda resorts in Bentota, see the box on Ayurveda resorts (p.119).

Amal Villa ☎ 034 227 0746, ⓦ amal-villa.com. Neat upmarket guesthouse on the landside of the Galle Rd, set amid attractive palm-shaded gardens with a delectable little infinity pool and small Ayurveda spa. Rooms are comfortable if unremarkable, and the beach is just a couple of minutes' walk away over the road, which is also where you'll find the villa's attractive upstairs open-air pavilion restaurant, nestled between the treetops. Half-board only. **$90**; a/c **$100**

★ **Avani Bentota** (formerly the Serendib Hotel) ☎ 034 494 7878, ⓦ avanihotels.com. Serene Geoffrey Bawa-designed resort, recently given a stylish upgrade complete with big new pool (guests only), smooth spa and very chic rooms with wooden floors and huge flatscreen TVs – a far cry from your average bucket-and-spade resort. Slightly more expensive than other places nearby, but worth the extra cash. B&B **$281**

Bentota Beach Hotel ☎ 034 227 5176, ⓦ johnkeellshotels.com. One of the west coast's oldest resort hotels, and the first designed by Geoffrey Bawa (see p.126), whose distinctive pagoda-style main building still serves as the area's major local landmark. Sadly only a few elements of the original design survive, such as the stunning batik ceiling in reception and the frangipani-studded courtyard pool. What remains is a slightly bland but perfectly acceptable (albeit overpriced) four-star, surrounded by large, rambling grounds and with comfortable rooms with either sea or lagoon views. There's also a spa, while the attached LSR centre (see box opposite) provides a big range of watersports. **$254**

★ **Club Villa** ☎ 034 227 5312, ⓦ club-villa.com. One of Sri Lanka's most personable small hotels, this intimate Geoffrey Bawa-designed establishment occupies a tranquil location at the southern end of Bentota beach. The fifteen rooms occupy a cluster of serene colonial-style modern buildings enlivened with strategically placed artworks and colourful furnishings, which manage to combine memorable design with a sense of homeliness. There's also a small swimming pool and an attractive restaurant. Half- and full-board rates only. **$275**

★ **Lunuganga** ☎ 034 428 7056, ⓦ lunuganga.com. Now an exquisite boutique hotel and restaurant, Geoffrey Bawa's former country house and its extensive gardens (see opposite) offer a privileged insight into the estate to whose beautification Bawa devoted most of his adult life. There are six sublime rooms: three in the main house, plus more expensive lodgings in Bawa's converted private art gallery and the two-room Cinnamon Hill House. **$230**

Nisala Arana ☎ 0777 733 313, ⓦ nisalaarana.com. Homely boutique hotel in an extensive secluded fruit and palm garden, 3km inland from the beach. Accommodation is in three colonial-style two-suite villas: the gorgeously restored nineteenth-century "Doctor's House" bungalow; the treetop Mango Wing; and the newer Coconut Wing. Local tours are run in an open-top Morris Minor. **$150**

Paradise Road The Villa (formerly The Villa Mohotti) ☎ 011 460 2060, ⓦ paradiseroadhotels.com. This gorgeous 1880s colonial mansion, with extensions by Geoffrey Bawa, has recently reopened after a stylish contemporary makeover by *Paradise Road* (see p.98) guru Shanth Fernando, now boasting 15 well-equipped rooms and suites each individually designed in a variety of styles ranging from smooth contemporary-colonial to funky liquorice-and-peppermint stripes. **$225**

Saman Villas By the 66km post ☎ 034 227 5435, ⓦ samanvilla.com. Luxurious boutique hotel, superbly situated on an isolated headland 3km south of Bentota bridge. Rooms come with every conceivable mod con, including private plunge pools in deluxe rooms – as you'd expect for $500 or more a night (although rates can halve in low season) – and there's also a gorgeous spa and spectacular swimming pool, seemingly suspended in mid-air above the sea. **$500**

Shangri Lanka Villa 23 De Alwis Rd, Horanduwa, Bentota ☎ 034 227 1181, ⓦ shangrilankavilla.com. Welcoming and intimate guesthouse run by Anglo-Sri Lankan couple, with just three cheerfully furnished rooms (all with TV, DVD and laptop) in an attractive little garden with pool. **$100**

★ **Susantha's** ☎ 034 227 5324, ⓦ hotelsusanthas .com. Set immediately behind the train station around a shady courtyard garden, this excellent guesthouse is one of Bentota's cheapest options – although still rather pricey. All rooms are clean and nicely furnished, and there's also a decent restaurant, plus bargain treatments in the frill-free Ayurveda centre, featuring an ingeniously designed (if rather uncomfortable-looking) steam bath. **Rs.4200**; a/c **Rs.4900**

Vivanta by Taj (formerly the Taj Exotica) ☎ 034 555 5555, ⓦ vivantabytaj.com. Set in magnificent isolation on a beautiful headland at the southern end of Bentota beach, this vast hotel, all gleaming marble, rather overwhelms its tranquil natural setting, although it has plenty of swanky and rather ostentatious style, and the full range of five-star comforts and facilities, including an attractive spa. B&B **$300**

Waterside Bentota Yathramulla ☎ 034 227 0080, ⓦ bentotawaterside.com. Intimate boutique hotel in an attractive cluster of whitewashed, red-tiled buildings overlooking the Bentota river, 1km inland (a 5min ride on the hotel's free boat to the beach). The six rooms are smartly furnished with satellite TV, minibar and a/c, and there are sweeping gardens running down to the water with a good-sized pool. Half-board and full board only. Half-board **$150**

Wunderbar Beach Club ☎ 0777 908 640, ⓦ hotel-wunderbar.com. Pleasant mid-range beachside resort, with very spacious, nicely furnished rooms (all with a/c, satellite TV and minibar) plus pool and a rather grand upstairs wooden pavilion restaurant. Free wi-fi. B&B **$100**

1

GEOFFREY BAWA

We have a marvellous tradition of building in this country that has got lost. It got lost because people followed outside influences over their own good instincts. They never built right "through" the landscape…You must "run" with the site; after all, you don't want to push nature out with the building.   Geoffrey Bawa

One of the twentieth century's foremost Asian architects, **Geoffrey Bawa** (1919–2003) was born to a wealthy family of Colombo Burghers (see p.146) boasting English, Dutch, German, Sinhalese and Scottish ancestors – a heady cocktail of cultures which mirrors the eclectic mix of European and local influences so apparent in his work.

Bawa spent a large proportion of his first forty years abroad, mainly in Europe. Having studied English at Cambridge and law in London, Bawa finally dragged himself back to Sri Lanka and followed his father and grandfather into the legal profession, though without much enthusiasm – his only positive experience of the law seems to have been driving around Colombo in his Rolls-Royce whilst wearing his lawyer's robes and wig. After scarcely a year he threw in his legal career and went to Italy, where he planned to buy a villa and settle down.

Fortunately for Sri Lanka, the Italian villa didn't work out, and Bawa returned, staying with his brother Bevis at the latter's estate at Brief Garden (see p.120). Inspired by his brother's example, Bawa decided to do something similar himself, purchasing the nearby house and gardens which he christened **Lunuganga** (see p.124), and beginning to enthusiastically remodel the estate's buildings and grounds. The architectural bug having finally bitten, Bawa returned to England to train as a professional **architect**, finally qualifying at the advanced age of 38, after which he returned to Colombo and flung himself into his new career.

Bawa's early leanings were modernist, encouraged by his training in London and by his close working relationship with the Danish architect Ulrik Plesner, a keen student of functional Scandinavian design. The style of his early buildings is often described as "**Tropical Modernism**", but local conditions gradually changed Bawa's architectural philosophy. The pure white surfaces favoured by European modernists weathered badly in the tropics, while their flat rooflines were unsuitable in monsoonal climates – and in any case, shortages of imported materials like steel and glass encouraged Bawa to look for traditional local materials and indigenous solutions to age-old architectural conundrums.

The result was a style in which the strong and simple forms of modernism were softened and enriched by local influences, materials and landscapes. Bawa revived the huge overhanging tiled roofs traditionally used by colonial architects in the tropics, whose broad eaves and spacious verandas offered protection against both sun and rain, while buildings were designed to blend harmoniously with their surrounding landscape (Bawa often and famously designed buildings to fit around existing trees, for example, rather than just cutting them down). In addition, the use of open, interconnecting spaces avoided the need for air-conditioning as well as blurring the distinction between interior and exterior spaces, allowing architecture and landscape to merge seamlessly into one.

The arrival of package tourism in the 1960s brought with it the need for modern hotels, a genre with which Bawa became inextricably associated – see Basics (p.34) for a list of his principal hotels. His first major effort, the **Bentota Beach Hotel**, established a style which many hotels across the island would subsequently follow. The main wooden pavilion, topped by a hipped roof, used natural local materials throughout and paid distant homage to traditional Kandyan architecture in its overall shape and conception; at its centre lay a beautifully rustic courtyard and pond set within a cluster of frangipani trees, giving the sense of nature not only being around the building, but also within.

Around a dozen other hotels followed – most notably the *Kandalama* in Dambulla (see p.295) and the *Lighthouse* in Galle (see p.152) – as well as major public commissions including the mammoth new **Sri Lankan Parliament** building in Kotte. Bawa's architectural practice became the largest on the island during the 1970s, and most of Sri Lanka's finest young architects started their careers working for him. Many took his influence with them when they left, and buildings (hotels especially) all over the island continue to show the trappings of the Bawa style, executed with varying degrees of competence and imagination.

1

EATING

Most visitors here eat at their guesthouses – the restaurants at *Club Villa* and *Amal Villa* are particularly good – while Bentota also boasts a surprisingly good, rather upmarket spread of independent restaurants.

Aida By the bridge over the lagoon. Spacious and attractive open-air pavilion restaurant directly above the lagoon serving up a well-prepared selection of touristy European meat dishes – chicken in a basket, pepper steak, beef stroganoff – plus a decent range of seafood. Mains Rs.770–1100. Daily 8am–10pm.

Golden Grill National Holiday Resort ☎034 227 5455, ⓦ goldengrill.lk. This long-running lagoonside restaurant looks disconcertingly like a Sri Lankan wedding, complete with dressed chairs, a surfeit of pink napkins and flowers on every table, and a chuntering soundtrack of *baile* in the background. Food, fortunately, is better than the decor, with an above-average selection of tourist standards,

including lots of grilled things – fish, prawns, chicken and sizzling steaks – plus Sri Lankan standards and seafood. Mains Rs.750–1000. Daily 10am–1pm (last orders).

Malli's On the railway lines opposite The Surf hotel ☎077 851 4894. Unexpectedly smart little restaurant tucked away above a line of shops by the railway tracks just down from the station – pricey, but a distinct cut above your average Sri Lankan beach restaurant. The menu focuses on international fare with an Asian slant – Thai red prawn curry, chicken satay, risotto with mussels, panfried mahi-mahi with *rösti* and saffron sauce – plus good Sri Lankan curries and fresh seafood. Mains Rs.1200–1650. Daily 11.30am–10.30pm.

Induruwa

Immediately south of Bentota, the straggling village of **INDURUWA** is backed by a stretch of wide and beautiful beach which, compared to the more developed stretches of sand further north, remains clean and mercifully tout-free, while an offshore reef makes swimming safer here than in most places further up the coast. This winning combination is attracting more and more visitors to its increasingly upmarket accommodation, though the general atmosphere remains deeply somnolent.

ARRIVAL AND DEPARTURE   INDURUWA

By bus Frequent buses run up and down the Galle Rd past the various hotels and guesthouses; if arriving by bus try to get the conductor to put you off in the right place – the hotels are spread out and can be difficult to spot from the

road as you whizz past.
By train There's a train station in the middle of the village too, but only slow services stop here.

ACCOMMODATION AND EATING

You'll probably eat where you're staying, although the hotels and guesthouses of southern Bentota, including *Club Villa* (see p.125), are only a short tuktuk ride away if you want to venture out. The following places are shown on the map on p.117.

★ **Long Beach Cottage** Next door to Royal Beach Resort ☎034 227 5773, ✉hanjayas@yahoo.de. This cosy, laid-back beachside guesthouse, tenderly looked after by an enchanting elderly Sri Lankan/German couple, has operated pretty much unchanged for over thirty years. The spotlessly white rooms are comfortable and a real steal – other guesthouses offer half as much for twice the price. Rs.2000
Royal Beach Resort ☎034 227 4351, ⓦroyal beachresortsrilanka.com. This quirky beach hotel has a decidedly theatrical atmosphere, from the frothing mermaid and map of Sri Lanka in the patio pond to the camp design, with sweeping staircases and kitsch architectural touches,

which gives the whole place the look of a stage set for a 1930s Hollywood musical. Rooms are large and comfortable, with a/c, satellite TV, hot water, minibar and ocean views, and there's also a decent-sized pool. B&B $110
Temple Tree Resort and Spa Just south of the 66km post ☎034 227 0700, ⓦtempletreeresortandspa.com. This top-dollar boutique hotel is a real architectural fashion statement, with stylishly (if rather severely) minimalist rooms sporting big picture windows, smooth wood finishes and polished concrete galore. There's also a gorgeous pool, a delightful spa and excellent Asian-fusion cuisine. Awfully nice, but seriously expensive. $380

Kosgoda

About 8km south of Induruwa, the four-kilometre stretch of beach close to the village of **KOSGODA** is the most important **sea turtle nesting site** along the west coast. All five

1

species of turtle that visit Sri Lanka's beaches lay eggs here, and the **Turtle Conservation Project** (TCP; ⓦtcpsrilanka.org), in association with the Wildlife Department, has set up a community-based watch scheme along a one-kilometre stretch to protect the eggs from poaching by local villagers.

Turtle watches (Rs.750; if you don't see a turtle, then donation only) currently take place nightly from 8pm, starting from the TCP's beach hut just behind the *Kosgoda Beach Resort*, though the scheme periodically stops running: it's best to call in advance to check. As at the longer-established programme at Rekawa on the south coast (see p.180), local villagers (often former beach touts) have been trained as guides, and keep lookout along the beach in anticipation of the first, laboured arrival. During the season (Jan–May), if you're patient (the turtles may not pitch up till the early hours), you should get to see at least one nesting turtle fighting its way up the beach. On April nights, the peak month, the appearance of up to eight or even ten of the creatures is not unusual; outside these months, luck plays a greater role and it's not uncommon to go two or three nights without a sighting.

ACCOMMODATION   **KOSGODA**

Heritance Ahungalla Ahungalla, 6km south of Kosgoda (and 9km north of Ambalangoda) ☎091 555 5000, ⓦheritancehotels.com. This vast, Geoffrey Bawa-designed five-star resort sprawls along a considerable section of unspoilt beach. It's luxurious but surprisingly intimate and low-key given its size, with attractive landscaping, stylish rooms, a fine (if pricey) spa and one of Sri Lanka's largest and most spectacular pools, which

blends almost imperceptibly with the ocean. $\overline{\$250}$
Kosgoda Beach Resort Kosgoda ☎091 563 8177, ⓦkosgodabeachresort.com. Appealingly low-key resort in a tranquil setting between the ocean and Kosgoda lagoon, with attractively furnished rooms in a mix of low-slung colonial-style chalets and pretty brick cottages set amid palm-studded gardens. Half-board and full board only. Half-board $\overline{\$150}$

Balapitiya

Some 8km south of Kosgoda, and about 5km north of Ambalangoda, the village of **BALAPITIYA** is the starting point for interesting boat safaris along the **Madu Ganga**, a good place to spot water monitors and a wide array of birdlife, including myriad colourful kingfishers. No fewer than 64 islands dot this stretch of river; one is home to a large Buddhist temple adorned with lurid modern paintings and sculptures. Ninety-minute boat trips along the river cost around Rs.2000 per person, although you need to make your own way to the river. Local hotels can arrange round trips.

ACCOMMODATION   **BALAPITIYA**

The River House Balapitiya ☎011 576 9500, ⓦtheriverhouse-balapitiya.com. Occupying a fine position above the Madu Ganga, this superb villa houses

five large, very stylish suites, each with a private garden and plunge pool. An exquisite blend of traditional craftsmanship and modern comforts. $\overline{\$285}$

TURTLE HATCHERIES

A familiar sight along the Galle Road between Bentota and Hikkaduwa, particularly in Kosgoda, are the numerous battered signs for an ever-growing multitude of **turtle hatcheries** set up in recent years in response to the rapidly declining numbers of turtles visiting Sri Lanka's beaches. Staffed by volunteers, and funded by tourist donations, the hatcheries buy the turtles' eggs (at above market value) from local fishermen and rebury them in safe locations; once hatched, the babies are kept in concrete tubs for a few days before being released into the sea. Despite the hatcheries' (mostly) laudable aims however, questions have long been raised over their effectiveness – it is almost impossible to replicate the turtles' natural incubation and hatching conditions, and as a consequence the overwhelming majority succumb to disease or predators – and there is little evidence that they have helped to reverse the turtles' declining fortunes.

Ambalangoda

Some 25km south of Bentota, the bustling, workaday coastal town of **AMBALANGODA** is the island's major production centre for the demonic wooden **masks** which leer at you from doorways and handicrafts shops across the island. These were originally designed to be worn by performers in exorcism ceremonies and *kolam* dances (see box, p.130), and although the dances themselves are now rarely performed, the masks have acquired a new lease of life as souvenirs, while many locals hang a Gurulu Raksha mask outside their houses to ward away demons (the Gurulu is a fearsome mythical bird, believed to prey on snakes and related demonic beings). Masks are made out of the light and easily carved Sri Lankan balsa wood, *kaduru* (*Nux vomica*), and come in all sorts of different sizes, costing anything from a few hundred rupees up to several hundred dollars – larger masks can take up to six weeks to carve and paint. Some are artificially aged to resemble antiques, their colours skilfully faded to a lustrous, mellow patina which makes a more aesthetic alternative to the lurid, day-glo tones of the standard items.

The main outlets are the two museums-cum-shops (see below) which face one another across the coastal highway at the northern end of the town centre, set up by two sons of the late mask-carver Ariyapala Wijesuriya, who was largely responsible for establishing Ambalangoda as a centre of mask-carving. There are a number of other mask-making workshops dotted around the northern end of town, the best being **Southland Masks at** 353 Main Street (the side road which runs behind the Ariyapala and Sons Mask Museum; daily 8am–5pm), which has a fine selection of beautifully crafted masks in a wide range of designs.

Ariyapala and Sons Mask Museum

Galle Rd, north end of town · Daily 8.30am–5.30pm · Donation

The larger and more interesting of the two mask museums, the **Ariyapala and Sons Mask Museum** comprises two well-laid-out rooms focusing on *kolam* dances and *sunni yakuma* healing dances respectively, with masks and photos of performances. The shop upstairs sells the island's biggest selection of masks, featuring all the characters you'll have encountered in the museum. The quality here can be variable, however: masks are churned out in the workshop next door (which you can also visit) in industrial quantities for the endless tour groups that stop here, and you might find better craftsmanship in the smaller workshops around town, in Hikkaduwa, or even in Kandy or Colombo.

Ariyapala Traditional Masks

Galle Rd, north end of town · Daily 8.30am–6pm · Donation

Opposite the Ariyapala and Sons Mask Museum, the more modest **Ariyapala Traditional Masks** shop-cum-museum is home to a small display featuring large puppets of the last king of Kandy, Sri Wickrama Rajasinha, and his queen, plus a gruesome *tableau vivant* showing the execution of the family of Prime Minister Ehelepola. The items for sale upstairs are of a similarly variable standard to those over the road.

Bandu Wijesuriya School of Dance

Galle Rd, north end of town

Dance performances are staged around half a dozen times a year at the **Bandu Wijesuriya School of Dance**, a couple of doors along from the Ariyapala and Sons Mask Museum. If no performance is scheduled, you can usually visit the school to see students rehearsing (Mon–Fri at around 3.30pm; Sat 8am–4pm; donation) or even enrol in dance classes yourself.

Ambalangoda town and beach

Masks and dancing aside, Ambalangoda also boasts a fine expanse of almost completely untouristed **beach** and a picturesque fishing harbour. It's also worth wandering down

1

LOW-COUNTRY DANCING

The masks you'll see at Ambalangoda (and elsewhere around the island) were originally produced to be worn by performers in low-country (southern) dances, either in devil dances or *kolam*. Many Sri Lankans still believe that diseases and illness can be caused by demons, and the purpose of the **devil dance** – more strictly known as an exorcism ceremony (*bali*) or healing dance (*sunni yakuma*) – is to summon up the demons who are causing a person sickness, make offerings to them and then politely request that they leave their victim in peace. There are various groups of demons – five *yakka* demons, twelve *pali* demons and eighteen *sanni* demons; each is believed to be responsible for certain diseases, and each is represented by its own mask, which is worn by a dancer during the exorcism ceremony (all 35 individual masks are sometimes combined into a single enormous medicine mask). Devil dances are still occasionally performed in rural villages, although you'd have to be very lucky to see one.

The origins of the **kolam** dance-drama are popularly claimed to date back to the mythical Queen Menikpala, who while pregnant developed a craving to witness a theatrical performance. Vishvakarma, the god of craftsmen and artists, is said to have given the king the first *kolam* masks and the plot of the entire entertainment. The traditional *kolam* performance features a sequence of dances held together by a rather tenuous plot based around the visit of the pregnant Queen Menikpala and her husband, King Maha Sammatha, to a village. The performance traditionally comprises a medley of satirical and royal dances, featuring characters such as the king's drunken drummer, a lecherous village clerk, assorted village simpletons, a couple of propitious demons, a lion and, of course, the royal couple themselves. Unfortunately, complete *kolam* performances are no longer staged, so it's impossible to experience this unique Sri Lankan medley of folk tale, demonic superstition and history (laced with a touch of Buddhism) – though you can at least still enjoy the masks.

As well as *kolam* and devil dances, the south is also home to a range of populist **folk dances** – though nowadays you're more likely to see them performed in one of Kandy's nightly cultural shows (see p.225) than anywhere in the south itself. Popular dances include the stick dance (*leekeli*), harvest dance (*kulu*), pot dance (*kalageldi*) and the ever-popular *raban* dance, during which small *raban* drums (they actually look more like thick wooden plates than musical instruments) are spun on the fingers or on sticks balanced on the hands or head – an experienced performer can keep as many as eight *rabans* twirling simultaneously from various parts of his or her body.

Main Street, an interesting and relatively traffic-free little thoroughfare whose southern end is lined by attractive shops selling everything from huge sacks of rice to shiny new motorbikes, and whose pavements are taken over most days by a lively fish, fruit and veg market.

Galagoda Sailathalaramaya temple

No set hours • Donation (around Rs.250–500 requested)

About 6km inland from Ambalangoda at the village of Karandeniya, the obscure **Galagoda Sailathalaramaya temple** is the unlikely home of Sri Lanka's longest reclining Buddha, measuring some 35m in length (the precise dimensions remain unknown, since it's considered sacrilegious to measure it), which fills the entire length of an extremely ramshackle building at the back of the temple. The statue is said to be more than two hundred years old and has now lost most of its original red and saffron paint, though its delicately moulded features – with wide-awake eyes and aquiline nose – remain perfectly preserved. Karandeniya is on the Elpitiya road; the temple itself is off the main road down a tiny road on the left (no sign).

ARRIVAL AND DEPARTURE   AMBALANGODA

By bus Buses run up and down the coast along the Galle Rd every 15mins or so, serving all destinations between Colombo and Galle/Matara. Note that many buses don't actually go into the bus station but simply stop on the road outside.

Destinations Aluthgama (every 15min; 30–40min); Colombo (every 15min; 2hr–2hr 30min); Galle (every 15min; 1hr–1hr 20min); Hikkaduwa (every 15min; 20–30min); Kalutara (every 15min; every 15min; 1hr–1hr 30min). **By train** Regular trains on the coastal line stop here – see the timetable (p.89).

ACCOMMODATION

Ambalangoda has a couple of excellent **places to stay**. For **food**, the *Nirodh Tourist Restaurant*, on Main Street opposite the Bank of Ceylon, is a pleasant spot with standard tourist grub at standard prices, although rather popular with local flies.

Shangrela Beach Resort 38 Sea Beach Rd ☎091 225 8342, ⓦshangrela.de. Overlooking the pretty harbour breakwater, this attractive and well-run place has bright, spacious and good-value tiled rooms (some with a/c) and a lush garden; they also run local boat trips. $26; a/c $35

Sumudu Tourist Guest House 418 Main St (down the side road behind the Ariyapala and Sons Mask Museum) ☎091 225 8832. Very friendly family-run establishment with six simple but pleasant, high-ceilinged rooms (fan and a/c), some with hot water, in a characterful old colonial villa. B&B: Rs.2000; a/c Rs.2200

DIRECTORY

Banks Several banks along the main road have ATMs accepting foreign cards.

Hikkaduwa

Back in the 1970s, **HIKKADUWA** was Sri Lanka's original hippy hangout, a budget alternative to the fancier resort hotels at Beruwala and Bentota. Subsequent decades were not kind to the town: rampant over-development led to the systematic erosion of the beach and the creation of a memorable line of concrete eyesores masquerading as hotels, while the famous Coral Gardens were reduced to a circus of boats chasing traumatized fish through a labyrinth of dead coral.

Over the past few years, however, Hikkaduwa has begun to rise, cautiously, from its own ashes, as the tourist hordes have largely ignored the town, flocking to newer and less spoilt destinations further south, allowing Hikkaduwa to recapture some of its former sleepy, slightly hippified charm. The much abused beach and Coral Gardens are now being gradually rehabilitated, while following the tsunami many of the town's bomb-shelter resort hotels were demolished or renovated, and the whole place is now looking better than it has for years, while even the formerly hectic and noxious traffic along the Galle Road has lessened somewhat following the opening of the Southern Expressway.

It's still far from unspoilt, but compared to the somnolent resorts further north Hikkaduwa remains refreshingly lively, with plenty of restaurants, bars and shops to tempt you off the beach, and a crowd of predominantly young and independent travellers keeping things busy. Things are particularly lively during the annual **Hikkaduwa Beach Fest**, a three-day beach party in July/August with visiting international DJs and crowds of hedonistic locals and foreigners partying on the beach. Other attractions include excellent local **surf**, plus good **diving** and **snorkelling**. Beach and sea aside, there are also several interesting Buddhist temples **around Hikkaduwa**, all easily reachable by tuktuk or bicycle – though be *very* careful cycling along the treacherous Galle Road.

Hikkaduwa Marine National Park

Daily 7am–6pm • Rs.30; glass-bottomed boat tours Rs.1750/25min per person

Hikkaduwa Marine National Park (still popularly known as the **Coral Sanctuary**) was established in 1979 to protect the small, shallow area of reef, never more than 5m deep, which stretches from the beach a couple of hundred metres out to sea, now enclosed and protected by a string of rocks. The once-beautiful coral has suffered significant depredations over the years, but is now slowly growing back following concerted replanting efforts following the tsunami. Clumps of reviving coral can now be seen in

1

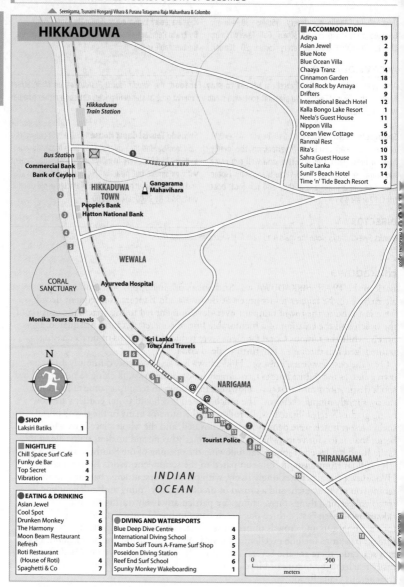

Seenigama, Tsunami Honganji Vihara & Purana Totagama Raja Mahavihara & Colombo

HIKKADUWA

Hikkaduwa
Train Station

Bus Station
Commercial Bank
Bank of Ceylon

BADDEGAMA ROAD

HIKKADUWA
TOWN

People's Bank
Hatton National Bank

Gangarama
Mahavihara

WEWALA

Ayurveda Hospital

CORAL
SANCTUARY

Monika Tours & Travels

Sri Lanka
Tours and Travels

GALLE ROAD

NARIGAMA

N

Tourist Police

THIRANAGAMA

INDIAN
OCEAN

■ ACCOMMODATION

Aditya	19
Asian Jewel	2
Blue Note	8
Blue Ocean Villa	7
Chaaya Tranz	4
Cinnamon Garden	18
Coral Rock by Amaya	3
Drifters	9
International Beach Hotel	12
Kalla Bongo Lake Resort	1
Neela's Guest House	11
Nippon Villa	5
Ocean View Cottage	16
Ranmal Rest	15
Rita's	10
Sahra Guest House	13
Suite Lanka	17
Sunil's Beach Hotel	14
Time 'n' Tide Beach Resort	6

● SHOP

Laksiri Batiks	1

■ NIGHTLIFE

Chill Space Surf Café	1
Funky de Bar	3
Top Secret	4
Vibration	2

● EATING & DRINKING

Asian Jewel	1
Cool Spot	2
Drunken Monkey	6
The Harmony	8
Moon Beam Restaurant	5
Refresh	3
Roti Restaurant (House of Roti)	4
Spaghetti & Co	7

● DIVING AND WATERSPORTS

Blue Deep Dive Centre	4
International Diving School	3
Mambo Surf Tours A-Frame Surf Shop	5
Poseidon Diving Station	2
Reef End Surf School	6
Spunky Monkey Wakeboarding	1

0   500
meters

places, while the gardens are also home to a rich population of tropical **fish** including myriad colourful species such as parrotfish, unicornfish, trunkfish, angelfish, grunts, fusilierfish and balloonfish. Around full moon time you may also be fortunate enough to see **turtles**, a majestic sight, though as soon as one is spotted, every boatman in the vicinity is likely to go chasing after the poor creature.

A popular way of seeing the sanctuary is to take an expensive trip in a **glass-bottomed boat**, although at busy times the flotilla of boats chasing round the waters in search of big fish and turtles lends the park all the charm of a marine motorway. **Snorkelling** is much more eco-friendly, and you'll see more, although the number of boats tearing around can make it a bit unnerving. You can rent snorkelling equipment from one of the dive centres listed below; count on around Rs.400–500 for an hour to so and check carefully for leaks.

Gangarama Mahavihara

The closest temple to town, just 500m inland from the bus station along Baddegama Road, is the **Gangarama Mahavihara**, an attractive modern Buddhist temple perched atop a large terrace, whose pretty ensemble of neat white buildings is often busy with devout locals, including many old ladies in white saris making offerings at the bo tree and various shrines – a far cry from the bedlam of Hikkaduwa town just down the road.

Seenigama Temple

About 2km north of town stands the diminutive **Seenigama Temple**, an eye-catching little white building squeezed onto a tiny island just offshore. Unusually, the temple is dedicated to Dewol, a malevolent deity who is approached by those seeking revenge.

WATERSPORTS AT HIKKADUWA

DIVING AND SNORKELLING

Hikkaduwa has the largest selection of **diving schools** in Sri Lanka – the three operators listed below are the best-established, although other outfits come and go. As usual, the dive season runs from November to April. There's a good range of dives close by, including **reef dives** down to 25m at the labyrinthine Hikkaduwa Gala complex, a well-known spot with swim-through caves, and the rocky-bottomed area of Kiralagala (22–36m deep). There are also some sixteen **wrecks** in the vicinity, including a much-dived old steam-driven oil tanker from the 1860s known as the *Conch*; the *Earl of Shaftesbury* sailing ship, wrecked in 1848; and the *Rangoon*, which sank near Galle in 1863. All the following also rent out **snorkelling** equipment.

Blue Deep Dive Centre *Coral Reef Hotel* ☎ 077 315 0726, ⓦ bluedeepdiving.com.

International Diving School *Coral Sands Hotel* ☎ 071 725 1024, ⓦ internationaldivingschool.com.

Poseidon Diving Station Hikkaduwa town, immediately south of the *Hikkaduwa Beach Hotel* ☎ 091 227 7294, ⓦ divingsrilanka.com.

SURFING AND OTHER WATERSPORTS

After Arugam Bay and Midigama, Hikkaduwa has some of the best **surfing** in Sri Lanka. A number of places along the beach offer tuition, trips and rent out surf boards (around Rs.300/hr or Rs.1000/day) and slightly cheaper body boards. Three kilometres inland from town, the broad, breezy **Hikkaduwa lagoon** is a popular spot for wakeboarding.

Mambo Surf Tours A-Frame Surf Shop Narigama ☎ 091 227 5202, ⓦ mambo.nu. Facing the main surf point, this is Hikkaduwa's longest-established surf shop and school. Offerings include board hire, surfing tuition for beginners ($20/hr) and 24hr board repairs, plus one-day surfing tours along the south coast, two-day surf and safari trips to Yala, plus longer trips to Arugam Bay – count on around $50/person/day.

Reef End Surf School Narigama, next to *Rita's* guesthouse ☎ 0777 043 559, ⓔ reefend@yahoo.com.

Another reliable surf stop, running beginner's five-day packages ($20, including an hour's personal instruction) and budget trips to Arugam Bay during Hikkaduwa's off-season.

Spunky Monkey Wakeboardcamp in front of *Kalla Bongo Lake Resort* (see p.136) ☎ 0779 613 926, ⓦ wakeboardcamps.com. Offers five-day courses in **wakeboarding** on the lagoon (October–May), and can also arrange windsurfing, wakeskating and waterskiing.

1

Tsunami Honganji Vihara

Hikkaduwa was badly hit by the 2004 tsunami, and the scruffy stretch of coast north of town is one of the few areas where evidence of the disaster remains. Around 500m north of Seenigama (on the land-side of the main coastal road) stands the **Tsunami Honganji Vihara**, erected with Japanese assistance as a memorial to those who perished in the tragedy and unveiled on December 26, 2006, the second anniversary of the catastrophe. The centrepiece of the memorial is a towering, eighteen-metre-high Buddha statue standing on a platform at the centre of a small lake – the tallest standing Buddha in Sri Lanka and supposedly modelled on one of the images at Bamian in Afghanistan which were destroyed by the Taliban in 2001. The location of the memorial is telling, just a couple of minutes' walk from where the *Samudra Devi* ("Queen of the Sea") train, en route to Matara, was washed away by the tsunami, killing at least 1700 people – the world's worst-ever railway disaster, and a potent symbol of the tsunami's terrible destructive power.

Purana Totagama Raja Mahavihara

Just north of the Tsunami Honganji Vihara a turn-off (at a rather battered sign for a non-existent Tsunami Museum) heads inland for a few hundred metres across the rail tracks to reach the **Purana Totagama Raja Mahavihara**, or Telwatta Monastery. This was a celebrated centre of learning as far back as the fifteenth century – the great teacher and poet Sri Rahula Maha Thera, celebrated both for his verse and for his powers of exorcism, lived here; he's commemorated with a bright modern copper statue. The original temple was destroyed by the Portuguese; the present buildings date from 1805, an atmospheric complex with well-preserved murals, peeling reclining Buddhas and fine *makara toranas*.

Kumarakanda Vihara

Around 4km south of Hikkaduwa, the traffic-plagued town of **DODANDUWA** is home to the chintzy little **Kumarakanda Vihara**, looking for all the world like a Baroque Portuguese church rather than a Buddhist temple. The temple is on the inland side of the Galle Road just north of the rail line, from where a long flight of steps leads up to the principal shrine, which contains a reclining Buddha and various modern murals.

Rathgama lagoon

Inland from here (take the road immediately south of the temple and ask for directions) a sylvan country lane runs to **Rathgama lagoon**, one of the many that dot the southwestern coast. The Blue Lagoon Boat House down by the waterside offers **lagoon trips** (Rs.2000 for two people for 2hr) in primitive wooden catamarans – late afternoon is the best time to see birds and other wildlife, including monkeys. They'll also take you to the two retreats on the lake, one for men, one for women. You may be offered similar trips but at much higher prices by touts at Dodanduwa.

ARRIVAL AND DEPARTURE   HIKKADUWA

The **bus** and **train** stations are at the northern end of Hikkaduwa town. A tuktuk from here to Wewala will cost around Rs.100, to Narigama around Rs.150 and to Thiranagama around Rs.150–200. When catching a tuktuk look out for vehicles carrying a "Hikkaduwa Tourist Supplier Provided Association Approved Tourist-Friendly Tuktuk" sticker (these tuktuks also have their own parking bays up and down the main road). The scheme was introduced to protect local drivers and visitors from the unscrupulous behaviour of outside tuktuk drivers descending on the town. All tourist-friendly tuktuks are registered with the local police (drivers can provide ID on request) and should provide a hassle-free, and possibly cheaper, ride than non-registered vehicles.

By bus Note that many buses heading north don't leave from the bus station itself, but from the ocean-side of the main road, about 50m south of the station.
Destinations Aluthgama (45min–1hr); Ambalangoda (20–30min); Colombo (2hr 15min–3hr); Kalutara (1hr 15min–1hr 45min); Galle (30–45min).
By train Regular trains run up and down the coast – see the timetable (p.89).

GETTING AROUND

Bicycle rental A number of places along the main road have knackered old bikes for rent.
Car and motorbike rental Sri Lanka Tours and Travels (@0772 965 270) hires out cars or jeeps for $35–40/day self-drive, or $60/day with driver. They also have a range of mopeds and motorbikes for Rs.600–2000/day, depending on size; you don't need a licence, but you'll have to leave your passport or plane ticket (should you have one) as a deposit.

ACCOMMODATION

Accommodation in Hikkaduwa is relatively pricey, but all much of a muchness. Guesthouses sprawl down the coast for a considerable distance. **Wewala**, immediately south of ramshackle Hikkaduwa town, is the most developed section, with assorted upmarket hotels, restaurants and other amenities. Further south, **Narigama** is more backpacker-oriented, centred on a lively cluster of guesthouses and beach restaurants around *Neela's* and *Rita's*. Past here is sleepy **Thiranagama**, notably quieter than areas further north. **Out of season**, room rates can fall by as much as fifty percent, though this is of largely academic interest, since apart from festival time Hikkaduwa during the monsoon is best avoided: from mid-April to the beginning of November many places close for repairs, and the entire town has all the charm and atmosphere of a building site.

HIKKADUWA TOWN
Coral Rock by Amaya 340 Galle Rd @ 091 227 7021, @amayaresorts.com. This brand-new hotel is the smartest option in Hikkaduwa at present, in a fine location overlooking the Coral Gardens and with a selection of chic and spacious (although rather austere) rooms with minimalist, arctic-white decor and polished concrete floors. More expensive rooms overlook the sea, although cheaper rooms are uncomfortably close to the noisy Galle Rd. There's also a skinny pool right above the beach and small pool terrace, plus stylish restaurant. $195

WEWALA
Blue Note 424 Galle Rd @ 091 438 3052, @eureka.lk /bluenote. Comfortable concrete bungalows (with TV, minibar and optional a/c) ranged around a sandy courtyard next to the beach. There's also a decent roadside bar-café with draught beer and satellite TV, plus a quieter beachside restaurant – although it's pricey for what you get. $35; a/c $44
Blue Ocean Villa 420 Galle Rd @091 227 7566. Intimate modern place with a Mediterranean feel, painted in pleasing shades of blue and peach. Rooms (all with hot water) are spacious, high-ceilinged and immaculately maintained; best-value are the two breezy sea-facing rooms upstairs (and make sure you get a room away from the road). Rs.2800; a/c Rs.4500
Chaaya Tranz (formerly the Coral Gardens hotel) Galle Rd @ 091 227 7023, @www.chaayahotels.com. This large, long-established hotel (looking like a cross between a Chinese pagoda and a multistorey car park) has recently been scrubbed up and rebranded with wacky

murals and staff in silly porkpie hats – allegedly reflecting Hikkaduwa's alternative beach scene and "tranz" music (geddit?). The "concept" is lame, although the hotel itself is OK, with spacious a/c rooms, all sea-facing with balcony – perfectly comfortable, albeit perfectly anonymous. Facilities include a pool (non-guests Rs.1000), gym and spa. $200
Nippon Villa 412d Galle Rd @091 438 3095, @nipponvillabeach.com. Modern hotel in cheery strains of blue and orange set around a pleasant two-storey courtyard with a small pool and a mix of bright, comfy rooms; some have satellite TV, minibar and four-posters, and the larger ones at the front have sea views. Could be cheaper, though. $45
Time 'n' Tide Beach Resort 412 Galle Rd @091 227 7781, @time-n-tide.com. Comfortable, reasonable-value rooms with pretty terraces and balconies. The level of luxury increases as you go up – the high-ceilinged rooms at the top have a/c, satellite TV and hot water. Rs.3500; a/c Rs.4500

NARIGAMA AND THIRANAGAMA
Cinnamon Garden Galle Rd @091 227 7081, @cinnamongardenhotel.com. Peaceful guesthouse set in a pair of attractive, low-slung buildings overlooking a sizeable garden and the sea, with a breezy open-air restaurant and spacious, high-ceilinged rooms (all with a/c and hot water). B&B $77
Drifters Hotel 602 Galle Rd @ 091 227 5692. Pleasant guesthouse, slightly smarter and more expensive than other places nearby and with a small pool and attractive beachside resto. Rooms are neat and comfortable – the

1

two with private balcony overlooking the beach are the best. Free wi-fi. $38; a/c $82

International Beach Hotel Galle Rd ☎091 227 7202, ⊕ibhsrilanka.com. Functional modern guesthouse next to the *Drunken Monkey* restaurant. There's a wide spread of rooms including simple but cheapish fan rooms and relatively expensive ones with a/c – nothing special, but ok at the price. Rs.3000; a/c $70

★ **Neela's Guest House** 634 Galle Rd ☎091 438 3166, ⊕neelasguesthouse.com. Long-established and very welcoming guesthouse at the heart of the Narigama action – one of Hikkaduwa's few stand-out accommodation options. The comfortable and well-maintained rooms here are among the best bargains in Hikkaduwa, and there's also a pleasant beachside restaurant. Advance booking recommended. $25; a/c $45.

★ **Ocean View Cottage** Galle Rd ☎091 227 7237, ⊕oceanviewcottage.net. Bright modern guesthouse in a sea-facing modern block overlooking a grassy garden and decent-sized pool (non-guests Rs.500). The spacious tiled rooms (most with a/c) come with hot water, minibar, and free wi-fi. Excellent value by Hikkaduwa standards. $32; a/c $41

Ranmal Rest Galle Rd ☎091 227 5474, ⊕ranmal-rest .com. Large, colourful guesthouse occupying two cheery yellow blocks built around a garden with a mix of simple fan rooms, smarter a/c rooms (all with terrace or balcony plus hot water) and a couple of wooden beachfront cabanas. Rs.3000; a/c Rs.6000

Rita's Galle Rd ☎091 227 7496, ⊕ritashotel.com. Functional beachfront guesthouse with a mix of comfortable modern fan rooms and smarter a/c offerings (including some at the front with fabulous sea views for $60), plus a breezy restaurant. Free wi-fi. $30; a/c $45

Sahra Guest House Galle Rd ☎091 227 6093 or ☎0773 542 880, ✉anildmp@yahoo.com. One of the cheapest options in town; acceptable enough if you don't mind the simple rooms and rather ageing furniture. B&B Rs.2500

Suite Lanka Galle Rd ☎091 227 7136, ⊕suitelanka .de. Refreshing oasis of olde-worlde charm, with bijou rooms kitted out with colonial-style furniture (including four-poster beds) and a shady garden with small pool, although overpriced at current rates. $160

Sunil's Beach Hotel Galle Rd ☎091 227 7186, ⊕sunilsbeach.com. Large and slightly old-fashioned hotel. Rooms (most with a/c) are a bit past their best, but are clean and spacious and there's also a pool and a decent in-house bar and restaurant. B&B: $45; a/c $55

AROUND HIKKADUWA

Aditya Rathgama, 5km south of Hikkaduwa ☎091 226 7708, ⊕aditya-resort.com. Intimate and personable small luxury hotel, set in a shady, hammock-strewn garden on its own stretch of deserted beach. Each of the twelve huge suites is a harmonious blend of indoor and outdoor space, with cool, deliciously light interiors featuring distinctive antiques and artwork, and with plunge pools and private gardens or expansive balconies outside. There's also a fine restaurant, glorious pool and a seductive spa. $410

Asian Jewel Baddegama Rd, 3km inland from town ☎091 493 1388, ⊕asian-jewel.com. Overlooking the serene Hikkaduwa lagoon, this beguiling little British-run hideaway offers a mix of boutique luxury and homestay hospitality. Accommodation is in five well-equipped a/c rooms (including a family suite) kitted out with chintzy wooden furniture, plus private balcony, TV and DVD. There's also a pool and excellent restaurant (see below). Minimum stay 3–5 nights depending on season. B&B $120

Kalla Bongo Lake Resort Baddegama Rd, 3km inland ☎091 438 3234, ⊕kallabongo.com. Occupying a spacious hilly garden plot with magnificent views over the Hikkaduwa lagoon, this chilled-out place is a popular hangout for the young Hikkaduwa crowd. There's also a cute pool, open-air restaurant, cosy lagoon-side bar and watersports with the attached Spunky Monkey Wakeboardcamp (see p.133). $75; a/c $82

EATING

Asian Jewel Baddegama Rd, 3km inland from town ☎091 493 1388. The veranda restaurant at this welcoming hotel (see above) is ideal if you've had your fill of rice and curry, with a menu including cottage pie, fish and chips, and even Sunday roasts alongside Indian dishes and Thai curries; diners can also use their inviting pool. Mains around $10. Daily 8am–9pm (last orders).

Cool Spot 327 Galle Rd, Wewala. Cute little place that's been dishing up big portions of dirt-cheap tourist grub for almost forty years, with a decent selection of seafood alongside a good range of cheap breakfasts and assorted snacks, plus the usual curries and noodles. Mains Rs.600–800. Daily 9am–9.30pm.

Drunken Monkey Galle Rd, Narigama, at the International Beach Hotel. Popular and pleasantly crashed-out beach café, set in an attractive two-storey wooden pavilion right on the sands, with a decent range of cheap tourist standards. Mains Rs.600–700. Daily 8am–11pm.

The Harmony/Top Secret The Harmony Guest House, Galle Rd, Narigama. Chilled-out and very popular beachside café, with mats and scatter cushions laid out on the sand beneath funky low Moroccan-style lanterns – although food (mains Rs.700–900) is predictable. Daily 8am–10pm.

Moon Beam Restaurant Moon Beam Hotel, Galle Rd, Narigama. One of the nicest beach restaurants, in a big wooden pavilion with a beer garden to one side and offering a long menu of well-prepared, if rather pricey, tourist standards (mains Rs.900–1000). Daily 7.30am–late.

Refresh 384 Galle Rd, Wewala ☎091 505 8108, ☯refreshrestaurant.com. Set on a romantic, lantern-dotted terrace running down to the sea, Hikkaduwa's most popular independent restaurant has a menu the size of a telephone directory, offering everything from gazpacho to gnocchi and enchiladas. The food is pricey (most mains Rs.900–1000) and gets very mixed reviews, although the rice and curry is usually a reliable bet. Free wi-fi. Daily 9am–11.30pm.

Roti Restaurant 373 Galle Rd, Wewala. Unassuming little café serving up *rotty* in over a hundred different combinations (Rs.80–220), from simple banana *rotty* to more ambitious concoctions featuring decidedly untraditional ingredients like salami, avocado and prawns. Daily 8am–10pm.

Spaghetti & Co Galle Rd, Thiranagama. Italian-owned and -managed place, occupying an attractive colonial-style villa and garden on land-side of the Galle Rd and offering a good range of well-prepared homemade pasta dishes and pizza cooked in a genuine wood-fired oven. Most mains Rs.880–990. Daily 6–10.30pm.

NIGHTLIFE

The town has a certain amount of tourist-inspired **nightlife** during the season, with a number of crashed-out places to drink along the beach. Most nights out in Hikkaduwa are in any case fairly impromptu and mainly revolve around drinking; for specific events, looks out for flyers and posters around the village.

Chill Space Surf Café Narigama, next to the A-Frame Surf Shop. Perennially popular and laid-back venue complete with modest indoor dancefloor (with Saturday disco; 10pm–6am). Daily 7pm until late.

Funky de Bar Galle Rd, Narigama. Tiny venue right over the waves with a diminutive dancefloor hosting a once-weekly night house club. Thurs 9pm–2am.

Top Secret The Harmony Guest House, Galle Rd, Narigama. Sometimes lively beach bar with nightly DJ playing a mix of pop, house and chill-out (daily 8pm–late) at the popular *The Harmony* beach café – see opposite.

Vibration Narigama, land-side of Galle Rd near the Moon Beam Hotel. One of Hikkaduwa's more happening venues. Friday is the big night with DJs in the garden out the back. Fri 9.30pm–6am.

SHOPPING

A load of places along the Galle Rd offer all sorts of collectables, including plenty of *kolam* masks (the quality is actually often as high here as in Ambalangoda) and more unusual wooden sculptures.

Laksiri Batiks 400m down Baddegama Rd, behind the bus station (just before the Gangarama Mahavihara). Local batik factory; the attached showroom

has a decent range of pieces from around $5, as well as clothes and sarongs.

DIRECTORY

Ayurveda There are numerous little ad hoc Ayurveda centres dotted around Wewala and Thiranagama, though they're all very low-key compared with the flashy resorts at Beruwala and Bentota – although also much cheaper.

Banks and exchange Hikkaduwa town has several banks with ATMs accepting foreign cards, although nowhere in Wewala, Narigama or Thiranagama.

Internet A number of places along the Galle Rd offer internet access. There's a handy cluster of places just north of *Rita's* in Narigama including the Netflora Internet Café (daily 8am–midnight; Rs.100/hr; also has wi-fi) and a couple of other places. Further north, in Wewala, Sri Lanka

Tours and Travels has a number of machines (Rs.60/hr). Wi-fi is available free at an increasing number of cafes and restaurants.

Post office Baddegama Rd, 150m east of the bus station (Mon–Sat 8am–6pm).

Travel agents Monika Tours and Travels (☎0773 372 144, ☯monika_shyamali@hotmail.com), next to *Refresh*, is one of the more reliable of the many travel agents in town, offering islandwide guided tours for around $100/person/day, including transport and half-board accommodation. The tours arranged by Lalith at *Drifters Hotel* also have a good reputation.

The south

143 Galle

155 Around Galle

156 Unawatuna

161 Dalawela and Thalpe

163 Koggala to Midigama

165 Weligama

168 Mirissa

170 Matara and around

174 Dondra

175 Dickwella and around

176 Tangalla and around

181 Hambantota

183 Bundala National Park

184 Tissamaharama

188 Yala National Park

189 Kataragama

MEERA JUMMA MOSQUE, GALLE FORT

The south

In many ways, the south encapsulates Sri Lanka at its most traditional. Stretched out along a great arc of sun-baked coastline from Galle in the west to Tissamaharama in the east, the area remains essentially rural: a land of a thousand sleepy villages sheltered under innumerable palms, where the laid-back pace of life still revolves around coconut farming, rice cultivation and fishing (the last still practised in places by the distinctively Sri Lankan method of stilt-fishing). Culturally, too, the south remains a bastion of Sinhalese traditions exemplified by the string of temples and giant Buddha statues which dot the coast, and by the colourful festivals celebrated throughout the region, which culminate in the exuberant religious ceremonies enacted nightly at the ancient shrine of Kataragama.

The south's physical distance from the rest of the island, and from the hordes of Indian invaders who periodically overran the north, meant that the ancient kingdom of **Ruhunu** (or Rohana) – a name still often used to describe the region – evolved into one of the heartlands of traditional Sinhalese culture. In later centuries, despite the brief importance of the southern ports of Galle and Matara in the colonial Indian Ocean trade, Ruhunu preserved this separation, and with the rise of Colombo and the commercial decline of Galle and Matara in the late nineteenth century, the south became a relative backwater – as it remains, despite the more recent incursions of tourism.

The region's varied attractions make it one of Sri Lanka's most rewarding areas to visit. Gateway to the south – and one of its highlights – is the atmospheric old port of **Galle**, Sri Lanka's best-preserved colonial town, while beyond Galle stretch a string of picture-perfect beaches including **Unawatuna**, **Weligama**, **Mirissa** and **Tangalla**. Nearby, the little-visited town of **Matara**, with its quaint Dutch fort, offers a further taste of Sri Lanka's colonial past, while ancient **Tissamaharama** makes a good base from which to visit two of the country's finest national parks: the placid lagoons and birdlife-rich wetlands of **Bundala**, and **Yala**, famous for its elephants and leopards. Beyond Tissamaharama lies the fascinating religious centre of **Kataragama**, whose various shrines are held sacred by Buddhists, Hindus and Muslims alike.

Principal train departures in the south see p.143

Galle festivals see p.145

Dutch Burghers see p.146

A walk around the ramparts see p.149

Tours in and around Galle see p.151

Villas along the south coast see p.152

Diving, snorkelling and surfing at Unawatuna see p.160

Stilt fishermen see p.162

Whale-watching in Mirissa see p.168

Snorkelling and surfing around Matara see p.172

Swimming and diving at Tangalla see p.178

A Malay enclave see p.182

Queen Vihara Maha Devi see p.185

Tours from Tissa see p.186

Wildlife in Yala see p.188

Kataragama see p.191

The evening puja see p.192

MULKIRIGALA CAVE TEMPLE

Highlights

❶ **Galle** Sri Lanka's most perfectly preserved colonial town, its time-warped streets lined with historic Dutch villas hidden behind formidable ramparts. **See p.143**

❷ **Unawatuna** Crash out on Sri Lanka's most popular beach at the personable little village of Unawatuna. **See p.156**

❸ **Whale-watching, Mirissa** Mirissa's picturesque harbour is the jumping-off point for exhilarating boat trips to see Sri Lanka's newest attraction: blue whales. **See p.168**

❹ **Mulkirigala** Absorbing sequence of richly decorated cave temples carved into the flanks of a spectacular rock outcrop. **See p.179**

❺ **Bundala National Park** A wide range of bird-life – including great flocks of flamingoes – and other fauna inhabit this scenic string of coastal lagoons. **See p.183**

❻ **Yala National Park** Sri Lanka's foremost national park, with marvellous scenery and abundant wildlife, from peacocks to leopards. **See p.188**

❼ **Kataragama** Join the crowds for the evening puja at Kataragama, one of Sri Lanka's most colourful religious spectacles, at a shrine held sacred by Buddhists, Hindus and Muslims alike. **See p.189**

HIGHLIGHTS ARE MARKED ON THE MAP ON P.142

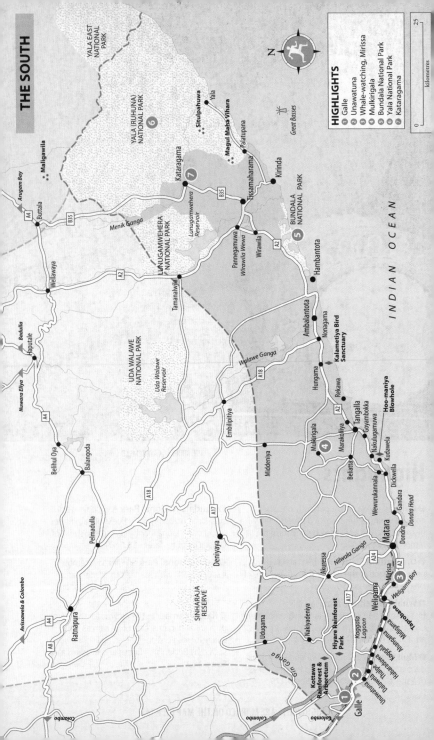

THE SOUTH

HIGHLIGHTS

1. Galle
2. Unawatuna
3. Whale-watching, Mirissa
4. Mulkirigala
5. Bundala National Park
6. Yala National Park
7. Kataragama

N

0 — 25 — kilometres

YALA EAST NATIONAL PARK

YALA (RUHUNA) NATIONAL PARK 6

• Situlpahuwa

• Magul Maha Vihara

Yala

Palatupana

Great basses

Maligawila •

Arugam Bay

Buttala

A4

B35

Wellawaya

Maliyadeniya

Menik Ganga

LUNUGAMWEHERA NATIONAL PARK

Lunugamwehera Reservoir

Kataragama 7

B35

Tissamaharama

Palatupana

Kirinda

A2

BUNDALA NATIONAL PARK

5

Tamanalwila

Panegamuwa

Wirawila Wewa

Wirawila

Hambantota

Badulla

Haputale

A4

Nuwara Eliya

Belihul Oya

Balangoda

UDA WALAWE NATIONAL PARK

Uda Walawe Reservoir

Walawe Ganga

A18

Ambalantota

Nonagama

Kalametiya Bird Sanctuary

INDIAN OCEAN

Pelmadulla

A18

Embilipitiya

Middeniya

Hungama

Rekawa

A2

Tangalla

Hoo-maniya Blowhole

Goyambokka

Nakulugamuwa

Kudawela

Avissawela & Colombo

A4

Ratnapura

A8

Deniyaya

A17

Mulkirigala 4

Marakolliya

Beliatta

Dickwella

Wewurukannala

Gandara

Dondra Head

SINHARAJA RESERVE

Nakiyadeniya

Hiyare Rainforest Park

Udugama

Gin Ganga

Koggala Lagoon

Akuressa

Nilwala Ganga

A24

Matara

Dondra

Mirissa

A2

Weligama

Weligama Bay

3

Taprobane

Kottawa Rainforest & Arboretum

1

2

Galle

Unawatuna

Dalawela

Thalpe

Habaraduwa

Koggala

Ahangama

Midigama

Colombo

Colombo

PRINCIPAL TRAIN DEPARTURES IN THE SOUTH

Note that train timetables are subject to constant change, so if possible it's always best to check latest departure times locally before travelling. For details of services south from Colombo to Galle and Matara, see the timetable in chapter 1 (p.89).

Matara	04.35	05.55	06.10	09.55	13.25	14.25	14.45
Galle	05.25	06.35	07.13	10.50	14.10	15.28	15.25
Colombo	08.15	08.50	10.05	13.20	17.15	18.40	18.05

All services from Matara also call at Weligama (roughly 30min from Matara), Hikkaduwa (1hr 30min), Ambalangoda (1hr 45min), Aluthgama (2hr 15min) and Kalutara (3hr).

GETTING AROUND

Getting around the south is straightforward: most of the places covered in this chapter are strung out along the main coastal highway, and principal towns are served by innumerable buses; in addition, the southern coastal railway connects Galle, Weligama and Matara with Colombo (with an extension as far as Kataragama currently under construction).

Galle

Perched on the coast close to the island's southernmost point, the venerable port of **GALLE** (pronounced "Gaul") has grown from ancient origins into Sri Lanka's fourth largest city. At the heart of the modern city – but strangely detached from it – lies the old Dutch quarter, known as the **Fort**, Sri Lanka's best-preserved colonial townscape, enclosed within a chain of huge bastions which now guard the area from modernization as effectively as they once protected Dutch trading interests from marauding adventurers. The Fort is Sri Lanka at its most magically time-warped, its low-rise streets lined with Dutch-period villas, many of which retain their original street-facing verandas and red-tiled roofs, and dotted with a string of imposing churches and other colonial landmarks. There's not actually much to see (a few unusual museums excepted): the main pleasure here is just ambling round the atmospheric old streets and walls, savouring the easy pace of life and refreshing absence of traffic – you won't find a quieter town anywhere else in the island.

Brief history

Galle is thought to have been the Biblical **Tarshish**, from whence King Solomon obtained gold, spices, ivory, apes and peacocks, and the combination of its fine natural harbour and strategic position on the sea routes between Arabia, India and Southeast Asia made the town an important trading emporium long before the arrival of the Europeans. In 1589, the Portuguese established a presence here, constructing a small fort named Santa Cruz, which they later extended with a series of bastions and walls. The **Dutch** captured Galle in 1640 after a four-day siege, and in 1663 expanded the original Portuguese fortifications to enclose the whole of Galle's sea-facing promontory, establishing the street plan and system of bastions which survive to this day, as well as introducing marvels of European engineering such as an intricate subterranean sewer system which was flushed out daily by the tide and is still in use today.

The **British** took Galle in 1796 during the islandwide transfer of power following Dutch defeat in the Napoleonic Wars (see p.405) – ironically, after all the ingenuity and labour they had invested in the town's defences, Galle was finally surrendered with hardly a shot being fired. The city continued to serve as Ceylon's principal harbour for much of the nineteenth century but Colombo's growing commercial importance and improvements to its harbour gradually eroded Galle's trade. By the early twentieth century, Galle had become an economic backwater, lapsing into a tranquil decline

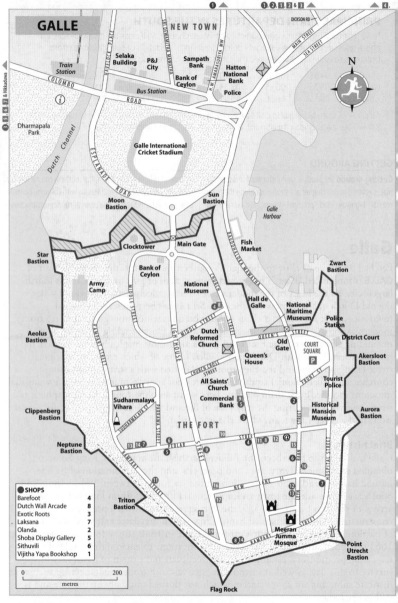

GALLE

NEW TOWN

Train Station

Selaka Building
P&J City
Sampath Bank
Bank of Ceylon
Hatton National Bank
Police

COLOMBO ROAD
Bus Station

Dharmapala Park

Dutch Channel

Galle International Cricket Stadium

ESPLANADE ROAD

Moon Bastion
Sun Bastion
Galle Harbour

Clocktower
Main Gate
Fish Market
Zwart Bastion

Star Bastion
Army Camp
Bank of Ceylon
National Museum
Hall de Galle
National Maritime Museum
Police Station
District Court

Aeolus Bastion
Dutch Reformed Church
Queen's House
Old Gate
COURT SQUARE
Akersloot Bastion

Clippenberg Bastion
Sudharmalaya Vihara
All Saints' Church
Commercial Bank
THE FORT
Historical Mansion Museum
Tourist Police
Aurora Bastion

Neptune Bastion
BAY STREET
PEDLAR STREET
RAMPART STREET

Triton Bastion
NEW LANE
Meeran Jumma Mosque
Point Utrecht Bastion

Flag Rock

0   200
metres

● SHOPS
Barefoot	4
Dutch Wall Arcade	8
Exotic Roots	3
Laksana	7
Olanda	2
Shoba Display Gallery	5
Sithuvili	6
Vijitha Yapa Bookshop	1

■ ACCOMMODATION
Amangalla	8
Beach Haven (Mrs N.D. Wijenayake's)	16
Closenburg Hotel	4
The Dutch House (Doornberg)	1
Fort Fifty Inn	15
Fort Inn	12
Galle Fort Hotel	9
Galle Heritage Villa	17
Jetwing Kurulubedda	5
Jetwing Lighthouse	7
Khalid's	14
Ocean View Guest House	18
Pedlar 62	10
Rampart View	19
Tamarind Hill	2
The Fort Printers	11
The Lady Hill	3
The Sun House	3
Weltevreden	13

● EATING & DRINKING
Amangalla	4
Dick's Bar	2
Fort Printers Restaurant	8
Galle Fort Hotel	5
Harbour Bar	1
Heritage Café	9
Indian Hut	14
Jetwing Lighthouse	3
Khalid's	7
Mamas Roof Café	13
Pedlar's Inn Café	6
Rampart Hotel	11
Royal Dutch Café	12
Serendipity Arts Café	10
The Sun House	2

which happily, if fortuitously, allowed the old colonial townscape of the Fort to survive almost completely intact.

Independence and revival

In the years **since independence**, Galle has recovered some of its lost dynamism. Despite playing second fiddle to Colombo, Galle's port still receives significant quantities of shipping and there are usually a few enormous container ships parked offshore waiting to dock. Most significant, however, has been the dramatic revival in the Fort's fortunes over the past decade, as **expats** (mainly British) and members of the Colombo elite have bought up and renovated many of the area's historic properties. This remarkable influx of foreigners and cash has transformed the formerly sleepy and slightly scruffy old town into Sri Lanka's most cosmopolitan enclave, home to a sizeable foreign population and now awash with boutique hotels, cute cafes and chic shops – a fitting turn of events for Sri Lanka's most European settlement.

The Fort

The principal entrance to the Fort is through the **Main Gate**, one of the newest parts of the fortifications, added by the British in 1873 to allow easier vehicular access. The section of ramparts facing the new town is the most heavily fortified, since it protected the Fort's vulnerable land-side. The Dutch substantially enlarged the original Portuguese fortifications here, naming the new defences the **Sun, Moon** and **Star bastions**. The sheer scale of theses bastions is brutally impressive, if not particularly aesthetic – a fitting memorial to Dutch governor Petrus Vuyst (1726–29), who was largely responsible for their construction and whose cruelty and abuse of power was such that he was eventually recalled to Jakarta and executed by the Dutch authorities. The ugly clocktower on top of the bastions was erected by the punctilious British in 1883.

The National Museum

Church St • Tues–Sat 9am–5pm • Rs.300 (camera Rs.250, video camera Rs.2000)

From the Main Gate, go left at the roundabout to reach one of the Fort's two main north–south thoroughfares, the atmospheric **Church Street** (originally Kerkstraat), named after a long-demolished Dutch church. An attractive old colonial building near the top of the street holds the **National Museum**, a wildly over-optimistic name for three dark rooms of rather sorry-looking exhibits which give only the faintest sense of the exotic and luxurious items which would formerly have passed through Galle's harbour; save your money.

Amangalla

Church St

The large and rather stately white building next door to the National Museum was originally built for the Dutch governor in 1684; it was subsequently converted into the

---

GALLE FESTIVALS

Proof of Galle's burgeoning cultural credentials is provided by the string of new festivals which have been held here over the past few years. Pride of place goes to the **Galle Literary Festival** (late Jan; ⓦ galleliteraryfestival.com), founded in 2007, which has established itself as a major item on the global literati circuit – the 2012 festival attracted a string of luminaries ranging from Tom Stoppard and Joanna Trollope through to Simon Sebag Montefiore and Richard Dawkins. The other big event in town is the recently launched **Galle Music Festival** (ⓦ gallemusicfestival.org), a three-day music event alternating between Galle (even-numbered years) and Jaffna (ⓦ jaffnamusicfestival.org) and showcasing local and international folk musicians, dancers and other performers.

venerable *New Oriental Hotel* in 1863 and then, following a massive makeover, reopened in 2005 as the ultra-luxurious **Amangalla** hotel (see p.151), though the exterior has survived almost unchanged including the spacious old veranda – a perfect venue for afternoon tea.

Dutch Reformed Church

Church St • Daily 8am–5pm • Donation

Galle's most striking colonial building, the graceful **Dutch Reformed Church** (or Groote Kerk) was built on the site of an earlier Portuguese Capuchin convent in around 1755. The delicate, slightly Italianate lines of the facade belie the severity of the **interior**, in which the only decorative concessions are the huge canopy over the pulpit (presumably for acoustic effect) and the attractive organ loft, reached by an elegant flight of balustraded stairs. The floor is covered in ornately carved **memorials** to the city's Dutch settlers, the earlier examples in Dutch (moved here from two earlier Dutch cemeteries which were dismantled by the British in 1853), later ones in English, many of them bearing witness to the lamentably brief life expectancy of Ceylon's early European colonists. Most striking, however, is the carved memorial, hanging on the southern wall, to **E.A.H. Abraham**, Commander of Galle, complete with a miniature skull, a medieval-looking armoured helmet and the remains of his baptism shirt.

A few steps further down the road is the dilapidated but still functioning **post office**, whose Dickensian-looking interior is worth a peek. Diagonally opposite stands

---

DUTCH BURGHERS

Many of the tombstones which cover the floor and fill the small churchyard of the Dutch Reformed Church bear Dutch names – Jansz, De Kretser, Van Langenberg and the like – dating from the colonial period right up to modern times. These commemorate the families of Sri Lanka's smallest, and oddest, minority: the **Dutch Burghers** – Sri Lankans of Dutch or Portuguese descent.

At the time of Independence the Burgher community numbered around fifty thousand, based mainly in Colombo. Burghers had held major government posts under the British as well as running many of the island's trading companies, although their numbers declined significantly in the 1950s, when as many as half the country's Burgher families, disillusioned by Sinhalese nationalist laws based on language and religion, left for Australia, Canada or Britain.

Despite their Dutch (or Portuguese) ancestry, the Burghers have for centuries spoken English as their first language. Burgher culture preserves strong Dutch elements, however, and they would be horrified to be confused with the British, despite a certain amount of intermarriage over the years (not only with the British, but also with the Sinhalese and Tamils). Not that there is really such a thing as a single Burgher culture or community. Many of the wealthier Burghers arrived in Ceylon as employees of the Dutch East India Company, while working-class Burghers, more often from Portugal, came to help build the railways and settled largely on the coast between Colombo and Negombo. And to make things a little more confused, there are thousands of Sri Lankans with Dutch or Portuguese names, adopted during the years of occupation, yet who have no connection at all with Europe.

Over the past five decades, the Burghers have particularly made their mark in the arts, both in Sri Lanka and beyond. **Geoffrey Bawa** (see p.126), arguably Asia's greatest twentieth-century architect, belonged to the community (though his family, in typical Burgher style, also claimed Malay descent). **George Keyt** (1901–93), Sri Lanka's foremost modern painter, was also a Burgher, as are two of Sri Lanka's leading contemporary artists, **Barbara Sansoni**, founder of the Barefoot company in Colombo (see p.98), and designer **Ena de Silva**. Overseas, the best-known Burgher is Canada-based novelist **Michael Ondaatje**, whose memoir of island life, *Running in the Family*, gives a wonderful picture of Burgher life in the years before Independence.

OPPOSITE GALLE FORT (P.145) >

2

Queen's House, originally the offices of the Dutch city governor (it's still sometimes called the Old Dutch Government House) and now belonging to *Amangalla*.

All Saints' Church

Church St • Daily 8am–5pm • Donation

Immediately south of the Dutch Reformed Church is the Fort's principal Anglican place of worship, **All Saints' Church**, a Romanesque basilica-style structure whose stumpy steeple provides one of the area's most distinctive landmarks. The church was begun in 1868 on the site of a previous courthouse – the town's gallows might (as a sign outside gruesomely points out) have stood on the site of the current high altar; otherwise, the bare interior gives disappointingly little insight into the history of the British in Galle.

The National Maritime Museum

Queen's St • Daily 9am–4.30pm • Rs.575 • No photography

Queen's Street, a short walk east from All Saints' Church, is dominated by the imposing bulk of the **Great Warehouse**, one of Galle's most striking colonial buildings: a long, barn-like structure punctuated by barred windows cloistered behind black shutters, which was formerly used to store ships' provisions and valuable commodities such as cowries, sappan wood and cinnamon.

The warehouse now provides a large and rather gloomy setting for Galle's new **National Maritime Museum**. Opened with great fanfare in 2010, this is without doubt the worst museum in Sri Lanka, and quite possibly in the whole of South Asia – it's not often you see so much money spent to produce something quite this bad. The paucity of actual exhibits appears to be in inverse proportion to the amount of space they occupy: a few catamarans (which you can see on the beach in Negombo for free); assorted Chinese pots; a few utterly random historical artefacts; a smattering of feeble mannequins; and so on. The only vaguely interesting items on display are a few artefacts recovered from colonial-era shipwrecks and a pair of battered wooden Buddhas which were washed ashore during the tsunami, having apparently been transported by the waves all the way from some unknown part of Southeast Asia. Most of the remaining space is filled with an interminable waffle of signboards in barely functioning English offering information from the merely mundane ("Ropes were used by the sailors on board") via the curiously surreal ("Canons are huge and heavy guns … they were operated by foot") to the totally incomprehensible ("as it unfolds the rich experience of trans-oceanic connectivity having a long antiquity and enriched the multi cultural ethos of Sri Lanka"). Save your time. And cash.

The Old Gate

Queen's St

On the eastern side of the Maritime Museum stands the **Old Gate**, the only entrance to the Fort until the construction of the Main Gate in 1873. The fully restored arch on the Fort side of the gate is dated 1669 and inscribed with the coat of arms of the **VOC** (Vereenigde Oost-indische Compagnie, or Dutch East India Company), showing two lions holding a crest topped by the inevitable cockerel; the distinctive VOC symbol at its centre – with the O and C dangling off the arms of the V – is sometimes claimed to be the world's oldest corporate logo. The mossy arch on the exterior, port-facing side is decorated with the date 1668 and a British crest, emblazoned with the words "Dieu et mon droit", which was added in 1796.

Court Square

The northeastern corner of the Fort is occupied by the park-like **Court Square**, almost completely surrounded by handsome old Indian rain trees, one of which is being dramatically engulfed by an enormous banyan. Local courts flank either side of the square, while south of here, the top of **Leyn Baan Street** (Rope Walk St) is home to dozens of lawyers' offices, a few still sporting their picturesque old hand-painted signs.

Historical Mansion Museum
Leyn Baan St • Daily 9am–6pm; closed for prayers Fri noon–2pm • Donation

One of Galle's quirkier attractions, the entertaining **Historical Mansion Museum** is the result of the efforts of a certain Mr Gaffar, who for over forty years has accumulated an enormous collection of antiques, bric-a-brac and outright junk. The overall effect of this Aladdin's cave of curiosities is strangely compelling, even when it becomes obvious that at least part of the aim of the entire museum is to lure you into Mr Gaffar's gem shop. The museum also employs a number of local artisans – including a lacemaker, gem-cutter and jewellery-maker – who can be seen at work in the courtyard, and whose creations are also sold in the shop.

Hospital Street and the eastern ramparts

Bounding the eastern side of the Fort, **Hospital Street** is flanked by another stretch of well-preserved **fort ramparts**. They're largely hidden behind buildings until the junction with Pedlar Street, though you can see parts of the **Zwart Bastion** (Black Fort), which incorporates the remains of the original Portuguese fortress of Santa Cruz, making it the town's oldest surviving section of fortification. Its neighbour to the south, **Akersloot Bastion** (1789) is named after the birthplace of Admiral Wilhelm Coster, the Dutch captain who captured Galle from the Portuguese in 1640. At the southern end of Hospital Street is **Point Utrecht Bastion**, topped by a slender white **lighthouse** of 1938; the ruined structure standing below it was a British powder magazine.

Meeran Jumma Mosque
Rampart St • Not open to the public

Standing opposite the lighthouse is the large, early twentieth-century **Meeran Jumma Mosque** – although it actually looks much more like a European Baroque church (and is actually built on the site of the former Portuguese cathedral), with only a couple of tiny minarets and a token scribble of Arabic betraying its true function. The mosque stands at the heart of Galle's **Muslim quarter**, often busy with crowds of white-robed, skull-capped locals on their way to or from prayers.

From here the path along the top of the ramparts (see box below) heads west to Flag Rock, usually busy with a few hawkers and the local snake charmer, who will fire his python into life at the merest hint of an approaching tourist. The veranda of the *Indian Hut* café (see p.153) provides a convenient vantage point from which to enjoy the scene.

Flag Rock

At the southernmost point of the Fort, **Flag Rock** is the most imposing of Galle's bastions – the name derives from the Dutch practice of signalling approaching ships to warn them of offshore hazards hereabouts (the warning signals would have been backed up by musket shots, fired from the huge Pigeon Rock, which you can see just offshore). If you're lucky, you might catch one of the clearly potty "**fort jumpers**" in action, who (anticipating a sizeable tip) fling themselves freestyle off the bastion down the sheer

---

A WALK AROUND THE RAMPARTS

From the lighthouse it's possible to **walk** clockwise around the top of the ramparts all the way to the main town-facing bastions – a good way to get oriented and an enjoyable stroll at any time of day but particularly at sunset, when half the town seems to take to the bastions to fly kites, play cricket or simply shoot the breeze.

2

thirteen-metre drop into the terrifyingly narrow space between the rampart and the deadly rocks just offshore.

The section of ramparts beyond here gives a clear idea of how the original Dutch fortifications would have appeared. Look closely at the stones and you'll see that many are actually formed from coral, which was hewed and carted into place by slaves. The next bastion along, the **Triton**, comes alive around dusk, as the townsfolk turn out en masse to promenade along the walls and take in the extraordinary red-and-purple sunsets.

The western bastions

Guarding the ramparts' southwestern face, the **Neptune** and **Clippenberg bastions** give increasingly fine views over the Fort, with the stumpy spire of All Saints' prominent among the picturesque huddle of red-tiled rooftops. Closer to hand stands the neat white dagoba of the 1889 **Sudharmalaya Vihara**, looking bizarrely out of place in its colonial surroundings. The path peters out north of here as the **Aeolus Bastion** is still in military use, meaning that you'll have to descend briefly from the walls and detour around it. Just beyond here, the modest **tomb** of a Muslim saint lies in solitary splendour beneath the ramparts. From here you can continue up to the Star Bastion and back across to the Main Gate.

The new town

On the north side of the Fort by the Main Gate, you have a fine view of Galle's compact **Galle International Cricket Stadium**, occupying the site of the former British racecourse, and one of Sri Lanka's three principal Test match venues. To the east, the **harbourside** is normally busy with fishing boats, their owners noisily bartering over piles of tuna, seer and crab. Beyond here the **new town** straggles northwards in an indeterminate confusion of hooting buses and zigzagging rickshaws. The most interesting place for a wander is the relatively traffic-free section of **Main Street** past the junction with Sea Street, where lines of small shops and local pavement traders cut a colourful dash.

ARRIVAL AND DEPARTURE   **GALLE**

Galle's bus and train stations are in the new town, just north of the fort. A tuktuk from either the train or bus station to any of the Fort guesthouses shouldn't cost more than Rs.100.

By bus The opening of the new Southern Expressway (see p.28) has revolutionized travel between Galle and Colombo, reducing travel times from over 3hr via the coastal highway to just over an hour. There are currently four superluxury buses daily (Rs.400) along the expressway (although services are likely to increase in frequency); these drop you in the southern Colombo suburb of Maharagama from where it's easy to catch a tuktuk or local bus to central Colombo. Services (local and express) in both directions along the main coastal road leave roughly every 15min. If you're heading to Tangalla, Hambantota, or Tissamaharama you may find it quicker to catch a bus to Matara and change there, rather than waiting for a through bus. To reach Sinharaja, you'll need to take a bus to Akuressa then change for Deniyaya (every 30min from Akuressa), although there are also a few direct buses to Deniyaya. Reaching the hill country from Galle is a laborious process. The easiest way to get to Kandy from Galle is to return to Colombo, while there are a few early-morning direct services to Badulla via Bandarawela, and to Nuwara Eliya.

Alternatively, catch the bus to Tissa, then another to Wellawaya, from where there are frequent services to Ella, Haputale and Badulla.

Destinations Akuressa (every 10min; 1hr); Aluthgama (every 15min; 1hr 30min); Badulla (2 daily; 8hr); Colombo (via coastal highway: every 15min; 3hr–3hr 30min; via Southern Expressway: 4 daily; 1hr 15min); Deniyaya (4 daily; 4hr); Hambantota (every 30min; 3hr 30min); Hikkaduwa (every 15min; 30min); Kalutara (every 15min; 2hr 15min); Kataragama (5 daily; 5hr); Matara (every 15min; 1hr 15min); Nuwara Eliya (2 daily; 8hr); Tangalla (every 30min; 2hr 30min); Tissamaharama (every 30min; 4hr 15min).

By train For further details, see the timetable at the beginning of the chapter (p.143).

Destinations Aluthgama (7 daily; 1hr–1hr 30min); Ambalangoda (7 daily; 40min–1hr); Colombo (7 daily; 2hr 15min–3hr 30min); Hikkaduwa (7 daily; 30min); Kalutara (7 daily; 1hr 15min–1hr 45min); Matara (7 daily; 40min–1hr); Weligama (7 daily; 30min).

TOURS IN AND AROUND GALLE

An amble through the Fort's sleepy backstreets is an obligatory part of visiting the city, but for an opportunity to peep behind the crumbling Dutch facades and meet some of the town's engaging residents, it's well worth joining one of the insightful guided walks led by Juliet Coombe, author of *Around the Fort in 80 Lives* (see p.441). Themed **walking tours** of the Fort (Rs.1500; 1hr 30min; ☎0776 838 659, ⓦsriserendipity.com/walking_tours.html), starting from (and bookable at) the *Serendipity Arts Café* at 65 Leyn Baan St, are adapted to individual interests, whether wildlife, architecture, food, history (visiting the otherwise inaccessible Fort prisons and clambering *inside* the ramparts) – or simply meeting some of the characters featured in the book.

Venturing further afield, highly enjoyable guided **bike rides** are run in the lush countryside around Galle by Idle Tours (☎0777 906 156, ⓦidletours.com). Trips, on good-quality mountain bikes, range in length from 12km to 40km through a variety of terrains – see the website for details. Custom-made tours can also be arranged. They also run foodie and tea tours, plus canoeing trips on the nearby Ginganga River.

2

INFORMATION

Tourist information The Tourist Information Centre (Mon–Fri 9am–4.30pm; ☎091 224 7676), in the park opposite the train station, is staffed on an ad hoc basis by English-speaking guides, and provides free general information.

ACCOMMODATION

Galle has a good selection of both budget and luxury accommodation, though few mid-range places. Galle has its fair share of **touts** – all the usual cautions (see p.51) apply. None of the Fort's guesthouses is clearly signed, so if you take a tuktuk to reach one, check the address to make sure you're actually being taken to the right place; some guesthouse owners will pick you up from the bus station if you ring in advance.

THE FORT

Amangalla 10 Church St ☎091 223 3388, ⓦaman resorts.com. Occupying the premises of the former *New Oriental* (see p.145), Galle's most famous colonial hotel, this superb Aman resort has remained extremely faithful to that famous old establishment's decor and style, with sensitively updated rooms and facilities (including an exquisite spa and gorgeous residents-only *Sunset Bar*) which manage to combine olde-worlde charm with the last word in contemporary luxury – albeit at predictably stratospheric prices. $625

★ **Beach Haven** (Mrs N.D. Wijenayake's) 65 Lighthouse St ☎091 223 4663, ⓦbeachhaven-galle .com. Very welcoming and sociable guesthouse right in the middle of the Fort, offering a varied range of good-value fan and smarter a/c rooms. There's also a pleasant upstairs sitting area and communal veranda overlooking the street – good for idle people-watching – tasty home-cooked meals, plus internet and free wi-fi. Rs.1200; a/c Rs.3500

Fort Fifty 50 Leyn Baan St ☎091 224 8711, ⓦfortfiftyinn.com. Seven modern rooms of varying sizes and prices (all with a/c, hot water and satellite TV) in an attractive townhouse. Downstairs rooms are smaller and darker; upstairs rooms are bigger, brighter and a bit more expensive. There's also free wi-fi and a kitchen for guests'

use, plus a nice little streetside café under the veranda at the front. Decent value, and rates may be susceptible to bargaining. Downstairs Rs.2500; upstairs Rs.4000

The Fort Printers 39 Pedlar St ☎091 224 7977, ⓦthefortprinters.com. Immaculately renovated old colonial building (formerly the town printers) with huge whitewashed rooms, creaking teak floorboards and timber ceilings – the austerity relieved with brightly coloured fabrics and modern artworks. $175

★ **Galle Fort Hotel** 28 Church St ☎091 223 2870, ⓦgalleforthotel.com. Set in a spectacularly restored former gem merchant's mansion, this UNESCO Heritage Award-winning hotel is every bit as memorable as nearby *Amangalla*, and at less than a third of the price. Accommodation is in a mix of elegant rooms and enormous suites, all individually designed, with tasteful neo-colonial decor enlivened by quirky personal touches. There's also superb food (see p.153), and an atmospheric bar and pool. $200

Galle Heritage Villa 71 Lighthouse St ☎091 223 4384, ⓦjetwinghotels.com. Recently opened villa-cum-boutique hotel in a historic (albeit heavily restored) 200-year-old mansion. The four rooms are spacious and attractively furnished in contemporary colonial style, and there's also an attractive little garden, streetside veranda and communal lounge. $200

2

Khalid's 102 Pedlar St ☏0773 177 676, ⓦgallefort guesthouse.com. This long-established guesthouse was undergoing a major upgrade at the time of writing but should have reopened by the time you read this, with four attractive and competitively priced rooms (all with a/c, hot water and free wi-fi) in a fine colonial house, plus good food (see p.154). No alcohol. B&B **$60**

Ocean View Guest House 32 Rampart St/80 Lighthouse St ☏091 224 2717, ⓔjewelgem@sltnet.lk. One of the Fort's more upmarket family guesthouses, set in an immaculately restored colonial villa. Rooms (all with hot water and a/c, some with sea views for about $10 extra) are pleasantly wood-furnished, though some are rather small for the price. There's also a cute rooftop garden (with real grass) and free wi-fi, but no alcohol. **$44**

Pedlar 62 62 Pedlar St ☏0773 182 389, ⓔpedlar62@yahoo.com. Uninspiring but good-value lodgings bang in the middle of the Fort, with big and clean (if rather bare) white rooms, some with a/c, and a modest rooftop café. **Rs.2500**; a/c **Rs.3000**

Rampart View 37 Rampart St ☏091 492 8781, ⓦgallefortrampartview.com. Modern house right by the ramparts with five neat tiled rooms (including one family room) with hot water, a nice little breezy veranda, plus a grassy rooftop terrace with great views over Flag Rock. Free wi-fi. **Rs.2000**; a/c **Rs.4000**

★ **Weltevreden** 104 Pedlar St ☏091 222 2650 ⓔpiyasena88@yahoo.com. Welcoming and peaceful family-run place set in an attractive Dutch house arranged around a neat flower-filled courtyard garden. Rooms (all with hot water; some with TV) are a little dark, but comfortable and good value, and there's tasty home-cooking available. **Rs.2500**

OUTSIDE THE FORT

Closenburg Hotel Megalle ☏091 222 4313, ⓦclosenburghotel.com. Occupying a rambling

nineteenth-century villa tucked away in a bay 3km east of Galle, this handsome old colonial-style hotel has modern a/c rooms with sea-facing balconies plus a few atmospheric and old-fashioned "colonial suites" (non a/c) complete with chunky teak furniture. B&B **$150**

The Dutch House (aka Doornberg) 23 Upper Dickson Rd ☏091 438 0275, ⓦthedutchhouse.com. Opposite *The Sun House* and under the same management, this meticulously restored Dutch villa of 1712 has four huge suites complete with reproduction antique furniture and all the amenities you'd expect at $400 a night. Outside there's an immaculately manicured garden with croquet hoops, and a gorgeous L-shaped infinity pool. B&B **$400**

Jetwing Kurulubedda Mahamodera ☏091 222 3744, ⓦjetwinghotels.com. Reached via a short but atmospheric boat ride through the mangroves from *Jetwing Lighthouse* (see below), this magical hideaway feels out in the wilds – though you're just on the edge of the city. Accommodation is in a pair of luxurious private eco-lodges, stylishly designed in dark wood and featuring lap-style plunge-pools and open terraces enveloped by the tree canopy. Rates vary considerably but are often surprisingly affordable, given the style. B&B **$225**

Jetwing Lighthouse Dadella ☏091 222 3744, ⓦjetwinghotels.com. On the main road 2km west of town, this very stylish Geoffrey Bawa-designed hotel is perched on a rather wild stretch of coast in an elegantly understated, slightly Tuscan-looking ochre building. The sixty rooms are masterpieces of interior design, complete with all mod cons, and there are plenty of facilities, including two pools, a gym and an attractive spa. Good food, too (see p.154). **$225**

The Lady Hill 29 Upper Dickson Rd ☏091 224 4322, ⓦladyhillsl.com. Galle's best mid-range option, set in a modern five-storey building atop the highest hill in Galle. Rooms are on the small side, but come with a/c, minibar, TV and private balconies from where (on higher floors

VILLAS ALONG THE SOUTH COAST

The past decade has seen a massive explosion in Sri Lanka's **holiday villa** market, with literally hundreds of properties being offered by owners keen to jump onto a potentially lucrative bandwagon. The biggest concentration of villas is in and around Galle (including upwards of twenty historic houses available in the Fort alone, and a dense concentration in Thalpe, about 10km east), though properties dot the coastline as far as Tangalla, and increasing numbers of tea plantation bungalows in the hill country are also becoming available (see p.240). There's plenty of choice, with villas sleeping anything between two and sixteen people and ranging in price from less than $100 per night in low season up to $2000 for a large villa over Christmas and New Year. Many occupy stunning natural settings, often on unspoilt stretches of private beach, while some show contemporary Sri Lankan design at its finest. In all, the emphasis is on intimacy, style and self-indulgence.

Good places to start browsing include ⓦvillasinsrilanka.com, ⓦboutiquesrilanka.com and ⓦreddottours.com and ⓦsrilankainstyle.com, with offer a vast array of properties, many of which can be viewed and booked online.

especially) there are superlative views over the town, coast and hills inland. There's also a small swimming pool, fine rooftop bar and wi-fi. **$95**

★ **The Sun House** 18 Upper Dickson Rd ☎ 091 438 0275, ⊚ thesunhouse.com. One of Sri Lanka's most magical places to stay, in a restored 1860s planter's villa perched on a hillside and offering memorable views across a sea of palm trees. Rooms are lovingly furnished and brimful of character (albeit a couple are rather small); best is the Cinnamon Suite, occupying the whole first floor of the main house. There's also marvellous food (see p.154).

and a small pool set in an enchanting, frangipani-studded garden. B&B **$220**

Tamarind Hill Dadella ☎ 011 576 9500, ⊚ tamarindhill -gallehotel.com. Elegant boutique hotel, 2km west of town, occupying a stylishly refurbished nineteenth-century walauwe. Highlights are the vast, colonial-style Admiral's and Captain's suites, which take up an entire floor of the imposing main building. Rooms, enclosing the neat garden courtyard, are less grand but equally full of exquisite design touches; behind, the fine pool stretches out towards a lush canopy of palms. **$210**

EATING

The ongoing gentrification of the Fort has given Galle a long-overdue injection of culinary sophistication, and there's now a good range of **restaurants**, although most are expensive. If you're on a budget, several of the Fort's guesthouses dish up good local cooking, as do a handful of homespun **cafés**, most of which offer lunchtime rice and curry as well as Western light meals and snacks.

CAFÉS

Heritage Café 53 Lighthouse St. The latest in Galle's array of chic new villa cafés, occupying the former town bakery, complete with original brick oven. It's not quite as atmospheric as other nearby cafés, but considerably more spacious, with a choice of indoor, streetside veranda and garden seating and a wide-ranging selection of international fare (most mains Rs.770–880) – rice and curry, spaghetti carbonara, southern fried chicken and so on – plus soups, salads, sandwiches. Free wi-fi. Unlicensed. Daily 9am–9pm.

Indian Hut 54 Rampart St, Fort. Inexpensive and no-frills Indian café occupying a breezy upstairs terrace overlooking the ramparts and sea. Food features a decent range of Indian, Pakistani and Chinese dishes including tandoori kebabs and breads in the evenings from 6pm – but no pizza, despite the pseudo-Pizza Hut logo and name. Unlicensed. Daily 11.30am–10pm.

Mamas Roof Café 76 Leyn Baan St ☎ 091 222 6415. Breezy rooftop café occupying an attractive – if rather cramped – plant-filled terrace. Rice and curry is the speciality, often featuring unusual ingredients depending on what's available in the market (sour mango, jackfruit, bitter gourd, and so on), although the actual cooking can be disappointingly bland. Also does wraps, soups, salads, sandwiches, plus assorted pan-Asian-style stir-fries and curries. Mains around Rs.650. Daily 6.30–10pm.

Pedlar's Inn Café 92 Pedlar St. Attractive little café in an old Dutch villa, with seating either on the streetside veranda or in the small courtyard garden within. The menu features assorted Western breakfasts, sandwiches, salads, snacks and good coffee, plus pasta and other international mains (Rs.600–900). Daily 9am–9.30pm.

Royal Dutch Café 72 Leyn Baan St. This tiny veranda café is the quaintest place in the Fort for a drink or snack with an unusual menu featuring quirky creations like

chocolate and coconut sandwiches or flavoured coffees and teas – including the house speciality ginger tea – along with more substantial burianis and rice and curry (Rs.500–600). Owner Fazal is a fount of information about the Fort, and the attached batik and sari shop is also worth a quick browse. Daily 8.30am–8pm or later.

★ **Serendipity Arts Café** 65 Leyn Baan St. Popular café with arty decor plus books and magazines to browse. There's a good range of breakfasts plus a short list of tasty international mains (Rs.660–930) at lunch and dinner with a pronounced Asian slant – anything from rice and curry to Vietnamese prawn soup – as well as lighter meals and snacks and tempting cakes, juices, Lavazza coffee and the reassuringly calorific icecream with Mars bar sauce. Unlicensed. Daily 7.30am–9.30pm.

RESTAURANTS

★ **Amangalla** 10 Church St ☎ 091 223 3388. Even if you can't afford to stay here – and you probably can't (see p.151) – this superbly revamped landmark hotel is worth visiting for a meal to lap up something of its dreamy atmosphere. Light lunches go for around $12–15, or come for afternoon tea ($8–15) on the veranda or an evening meal of finely prepared Sri Lankan or international cuisine, including a magnificent rice and curry (mains $30–50). Daily 7.30am–10pm.

Fort Printers Restaurant 39 Pedlar St ☎ 091 224 7977, ⊚ thefortprinters.com. Tucked away in a courtyard garden of this boutique hotel (see p.151), this neat little restaurant serves up a good range of international dishes with Mediterranean influences (mains around Rs.1200 at lunch, Rs.1500–2000 at dinner). Daily 11.30am–3pm & 6.30–11.30pm.

★ **Galle Fort Hotel** 28 Church St ☎ 091 223 2870. Food is a major attraction at this gorgeous hotel, which dishes up some of the best non-Sri Lankan cooking you'll

2

find on the island. Light lunchtime meals go for around $10, while the daily changing gourmet evening menu (3 courses for around $35) features delicately flavoured contemporary pan-Asian cooking, rounded off with the best puddings in the Fort. Daily 12.30–6 & 7.30–9.30pm (last orders).

Jetwing Lighthouse Dadella, 2km west of Galle ☎091 222 3744, ⊛jetwinghotels.com. This landmark hotel (see p.152) provides the five-star setting for some excellent Sri Lankan and international cuisine, either in the stylish *Cinnamon Room* restaurant (mains around $10–15) or the less formal *Cardamom Café*. Cinnamon Room daily 8am–10.30pm; Cardamom

Café open 24hr.

Khalid's 102 Pedlar St ☎0773 177 676. Set evening meals (served daily at 6pm) featuring good home-cooked rice and curry and Sri Lankan-style Muslim dishes like mutton buriani (Rs.700–1000). Non-guests should book at least an hour ahead. No alcohol.

★ **The Sun House** 18 Upper Dickson Rd ☎091 438 0275. The candlelit garden veranda of this magical colonial villa provides an incomparably romantic setting for daily-changing three-course set meals (around $35), featuring fabulous Sri Lankan cuisine with Indian, Malay, Dutch and Portuguese influences. Daily 7–10pm; book by 4pm for dinner.

DRINKING

Several of the town's hotels make an atmospheric venue for a sunset **drink**, while it's easy enough to head out to Unawatuna or Dalawela for an evening's lounging by the beach; a tuktuk should cost around Rs.200 each way, and (in Unawatuna at least) there are plenty hanging around for the return trip until quite late at night.

Dick's Bar The Sun House, 18 Upper Dickson Rd. This intimate and sociable lounge-style bar is the toast of Galle's expat community, with a good range of international beers, single malts and an impressive array of (pricey) cocktails. Daily noon–10pm.

Galle Fort Hotel 28 Church St. The perfect place to indulge your Somerset Maugham fantasies, the *Galle Fort's* colonial-style veranda bar is the most memorable place in town for a drink, with a long list of expertly mixed cocktails. Daily noon–10pm.

Harbour Bar Lady Hill Hotel, 29 Upper Dickson Rd.

It's well worth the climb up to this hilltop hotel bar before dark, when there's a marvellous view on one side out over the red-tiled roofs of the Fort and, on the other, across miles of palm trees stretching away inland to the Hill Country. Drinks are reasonably priced. Daily noon–11pm.

Rampart Hotel 31 Rampart St. Though they also serve (average) food, the main attraction here is the pleasantly breezy location overlooking the western ramparts, making it the ideal venue for a (rather pricey) sunset beer. Daily 8am–8.30pm (or a bit later).

SHOPPING

The rush of cash into Galle has sparked a miniature consumer revolution in town, with an increasing number of funky little boutiques and galleries springing up around the Fort.

Barefoot 49 Pedlar St. Galle outpost of the famous Colombo shop, stocking the same distinctive range of clothing, fabrics, stationery, toys and books. Mon–Sat 10am–7pm, Sun 11am–5pm.

Dutch Wall Arcade 54 Rampart St. Modelled on Olanda, this rampart-side old Dutch warehouse houses a fascinating collection of colonial-era bric-a-brac – anything from old phones and cutlery through to religious artefacts and grandfather clocks – picked up from local houses and laid out in glass cabinets. Daily 9.15am–7pm.

Exotic Roots 32 Church St. Attractive little boutique showcasing the quirky and colourful paintings and pottery of owner Catherine Hewapathirana, featuring colourful modern takes on traditional Sri Lankan subjects like elephants and stilt fishermen, along with other crafts including jewellery and homeware. Daily 9.30am–6.30pm.

Laksana 30 Hospital St. Of Galle's many jewellers, this is

perhaps the most reputable and reliable, crammed full of a wide range of stunning local gems – sapphires in various colours; dazzling quartz and amethysts; and semi-precious stones like moonstone, aquamarine. They also copy designs. Daily 9am–6.30pm.

Olanda 30 Leyn Baan St. This atmospheric shop is almost a sight in its own right, occupying a huge old Dutch warehouse stuffed full of bits and pieces of colonial furniture and other objects salvaged from local villas, from chairs and wardrobes to carriages and clocks. Daily 9am–noon & 2–5pm.

Shoba Display Gallery 67A Pedlar St. Women's cooperative showcasing the skills of local lacemakers and other artesans including individual lace pieces plus pretty cotton bags, handpainted fabrics, patchwork embroidery and toys. They also run workshops during which you can learn basic lace-making techniques, as well as courses in papercrafts and fabric painting. Daily 9.30am–7pm.

Sithuvili 56 Leyn Baan St. Quality Sri Lankan art and crafts by Ambalangoda artist Janaka de Silva, including a good range of masks and well-executed reproductions of Kandyan-style temple paintings – along with a few genuine Kandyan and Jaffna antiques. Daily 9am–6pm.

Vijitha Yapa 12 H.W. Amasuriya Mw. Galle branch of national bookshop chain with a reasonable selection of English-language titles. Daily 9am–7pm.

DIRECTORY

Banks Several banks in the new town (see map, p.144) have ATMs which accept foreign Visa and MasterCards. In the Fort, there are ATMs accepting foreign cards at the Bank of Ceylon on Middle St, and the Commercial Bank on Church St.

Hospital General Hospital ☎ 091 222 2261.

Internet Many of the Fort's guesthouses have internet and wi-fi, and there's also a small internet café at 19 Pedlar St (daily 8am–9pm; Rs.100/hr).

Pharmacies Steuart Remedica, on the ground floor of the Selaka Building immediately north of the bus station.

Police The tourist police have an office on Hospital St in the Fort (open 24hr).

Spas The superb The Baths spa at *Amangalla* is open to non-guests, with steam rooms, saunas and gorgeous hydrotherapy pools, as well as a full range of massages and treatments, plus Ayurveda rituals. The spa at the *Jetwing Lighthouse* has a similarly comprehensive list of treatments.

Supermarket There's a Cargills supermarket in the P&J City Building in the new town immediately north of the bus station.

Around Galle

Most visitors to Galle stick to the town and surrounding beaches, although there are a handful of rewarding inland excursions if you fancy a change from the coast, all attesting to Galle's self-proclaimed status as "Rainforest Capital of Sri Lanka" (for more on local rainforest tours, visit Rainforest Rescue International's website Ⓦ rainforestrescueinternational.org/ecotours).

Kottawa Rainforest and Hiyare Rainforest Park

Both parks: Daily 8am–5pm • Rs.700 • Guided tours by Rainforest Rescue International Rs.2500–3500 per person, depending on group size, including entrance charge • Ⓦ rainforestrescueinternational.org/ecotours

Around 16km from the city along the road to Udugama, the compact **Kottawa Rainforest and Arboretum** provides an easily accessible introduction to the Sri Lankan rainforest, with a wide one-kilometre walking trail shaded by giant dipterocarps towering up to 45m high. Resident mammals include purple-faced langurs and giant squirrels, plus rather more shy muntjac and sambur, and there's an impressive array of colourful endemic birds and (rather less polychromatic) reptiles. Leeches can be ferocious in the wet season, so bring appropriate gear. Buses run every fifteen minutes or so between Galle and Udugama, taking about half an hour to reach Kottawa; the ticket office is by the side of the road, near the 14km post. Prices include transport, guide, entry fees and lunch.

You'll need your own transport to reach **Hiyare Rainforest Park**, around 8km from Kottawa and 4km off the Galle–Udugama road back towards the city. Centrepiece of the park is the picturesque Hiyare Reservoir, while the surrounding rainforest is home to a small population of rare hog deer and over fifty species of birds.

Samakanda

Udugama road, close to Nakiyadeniya village, around 22km north of Galle • Rs.500 (book in advance on ☎ 0777 424 770) • Ⓦ samakanda.org

The low-lying hills inland from Galle are also home to **Samakanda** (Ⓦ samakanda.org), a sixty-acre organic farm developed on the site of an abandoned tea estate by British environmentalist Rory Spowers, who recorded its creation in his highly readable *A Year in Green Tea and Tuk-Tuks* (see p.442). Defined as a "bio-versity" project,

Samakanda provides an exemplary model of sustainable living and eco-tourism in action. It's possible either to stay here (see below) or just visit for the day, giving you the chance to explore the estate, go swimming in the local river and enjoy a traditional rice and curry lunch (Rs.1000). There's also a programme of regular activities including nature hikes, bike rides and cookery workshops (advance booking required; see the website for details).

ACCOMMODATION AND EATING   **AROUND GALLE**

Samakanda ☎ 0777 424 770, ⓦ samakanda.org. If you fancy staying the night at *Samakanda*, accommodation is available in a trio of comfortable solar-powered bungalows (each sleeping 4–6 adults). Full board per person $60

Unawatuna

Five kilometres southeast of Galle, the ever-expanding village of **UNAWATUNA** is now firmly established as Sri Lanka's most popular resort for independent travellers and remains a pleasant spot to while away a few days, even if rampant commercialization and ever-growing hordes of visitors have now significantly eroded the village's former sleepy charm. If you don't mind the increasing hustle and bustle, there's still plenty to enjoy, including a decent, if heavily developed, stretch of beach, a good selection of places to stay and eat, plus varied activities ranging from surfing and diving through to yoga and cookery classes, while in recent years Unawatuna has begun to compete with Hikkaduwa as Sri Lanka's beach-party capital, with noisy discos thumping out beats along parts of the beach during the season. The resort also remains busy all year round, making it a good place to visit if you're on the west coast during the monsoon.

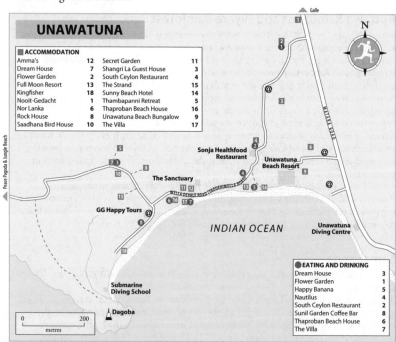

UNAWATUNA

ACCOMMODATION			
Amma's	12	Secret Garden	11
Dream House	7	Shangri La Guest House	3
Flower Garden	2	South Ceylon Restaurant	4
Full Moon Resort	13	The Strand	15
Kingfisher	18	Sunny Beach Hotel	14
Nooit-Gedacht	1	Thambapanni Retreat	5
Nor Lanka	6	Thaproban Beach House	16
Rock House	8	Unawatuna Beach Bungalow	9
Saadhana Bird House	10	The Villa	17

Galle

Peace Pagoda & Jungle Beach

Sonja Healthfood Restaurant

Unawatuna Beach Resort

The Sanctuary

WELLA DEVALE ROAD (YADDEHIMULLA ROAD)

GG Happy Tours

INDIAN OCEAN

Unawatuna Diving Centre

Submarine Diving School

Dagoba

0   200
metres

● EATING AND DRINKING	
Dream House	3
Flower Garden	1
Happy Banana	5
Nautilus	4
South Ceylon Restaurant	2
Sunil Garden Coffee Bar	8
Thaproban Beach House	6
The Villa	7

The beach

Unawatuna **beach** is small and intimate: a graceful semicircular curve of sand, not much more than a kilometre from start to finish, set snugly in a pretty semicircular bay and picturesquely terminated by a dagoba on the rocky headland to the northwest, while the sheltered bay gives safe year-round swimming, and a group of rocks 150m offshore further breaks up waves (though it can still get a bit rough during the monsoon).

Unfortunately, the devastating effects of the tsunami allied to years of unchecked development before and after have now destroyed much of Unawatuna's former appeal, while a massive government-sponsored clearance of illegal structures on the beach in late 2011 has left parts of the bay looking (for the time being at least) a complete mess. The western end of the beach, around the *Hot Rock* café, is now lined with the skeletons of half-demolished cafes and huge piles of debris, although hopefully by the time you read this the rubble will have been cleared away and the beach hereabouts restored. In the meantime, most of the action has shifted east, to the area around the *Full Moon* and *Happy Banana*, which remains lively and loud until late most nights.

At the northern end of the beach, a footpath leads up to a small **dagoba** perched on the rocks above the bay, offering fine views over Unawatuna and north to Galle.

Rumassala

Unawatuna's most striking natural feature is **Rumassala**, an incongruously grand outcrop of rock whose sides rise up sheer behind the village; it's popularly claimed to be a fragment of the chunk of mountain carried from the Himalayas by the monkey god **Hanuman**. As recounted in the Ramayana, Hanuman was sent by Rama to collect a special herb from the Himalayas which was needed to save the life of Rama's wounded brother, Lakshmana. Arriving in the Himalayas, the absent-minded Hanuman realized he had forgotten the name of the required plant, so ripped up an entire chunk of mountainside in the hope that the necessary plant would be found somewhere on it. He then carried this fragment of mountain back to Sri Lanka, dropping a bit in Ritigala, in the north of the island, and another piece at Unawatuna. The rock still sports a large collection of medicinal herbs as well as entertaining troupes of boisterous macaque monkeys, Hanuman's latter-day relatives, who periodically descend from the rock to raid the villagers' papaya trees.

The peace pagoda

Around the headland from Unawatuna, high up on the Rumassala hillside, is a gleaming white **peace pagoda** – actually a colossal dagoba – constructed by Japanese Buddhists in 2004. The views from here, particularly at sunset, are magical, with the mosque and clocktower of Galle Fort clearly visible in the distance to the west and, to the east, the carpet of thick jungle that separates the pagoda from Unawatuna. The peace pagoda is a fifteen-minute drive across Rumassala's beautiful countryside from Unawatuna (Rs.500 in a tuktuk), though it's much more easily (and prosaically) accessed from the Matara Road – there's a turning at the 120km post just opposite the cement factory.

ARRIVAL AND DEPARTURE   UNAWATUNA

By bus Unawatuna is hidden away off the coastal Matara Rd some 5km east of Galle. Take any bus heading east from Galle and ask to be dropped at the turn-off for the village, Wella Devale Rd (also known as Yaddehimulla Rd and Beach Access Rd), which runs from the Matara Rd for 500m down to the beach (no buses actually go into the village itself). The village isn't signposted and is easy to miss – make sure the conductor knows where you're getting off (coming from Galle the turning is just after the prominently signposted *Nooit-Gedacht*, on the right-hand side of the road). Heading east from Unawatuna, you should be able to flag down a bus to Weligama, Mirissa or Matara along the main Matara Road, though the local tuktuk drivers may deny that buses stop at Unawatuna in an attempt to get you into their vehicle.

By tuktuk A tuktuk to or from Galle costs around Rs.350. If you're heading west from Unawatuna, it's easiest to take a tuktuk to Galle and pick up a bus or train there (see p.150). Tuktuks to Weligama shouldn't cost more than Rs.750.

ACCOMMODATION

There are heaps of places to stay in Unawatuna, though the resort's ongoing popularity and increasing gentrification has pushed up prices. Note that parts of the beach can be noisy well into the small hours at weekends as there's usually a late-night disco going on, and you'll usually pay over the odds for a beachfront location; the best-value accommodation is in any case away from the water. **Seasonal variations** and fluctuations in demand keep prices fluid, though there are few steals. High season runs roughly from November to mid-April; outside this period rates fall by up to thirty percent in many places, though at any time of year it's worth bargaining if trade is quiet.

Amma's ☎ 091 222 5332. Functional block set slightly back from the sea amid rather bare gardens. Rooms are simple and uninspiring, but as cheap as it gets this close to the beach. <u>Rs.2000</u>

Dream House ☎ 091 438 1541, ⓦ srilanka -dreamhouse.com, ⓔ dreamhouse@libero.it. Italian-owned establishment in an attractive old colonial villa, with four characterful if rather small rooms (fan only) with wooden floors and period furniture, plus good Italian cooking (see p.161) – very pleasant, if a bit pricey. B&B <u>$71</u>

Flower Garden ☎ 091 222 5286, ⓦ hotelflowergarden srilanka.com. Idyllic (if rather pricey) little hideaway set in an abundant flower-filled garden with accommodation in neat little chalets and cabanas (all with hot water and optional a/c). There's also a small Ayurveda centre, a decent-sized pool and good European cuisine. <u>$68</u>; a/c <u>$75</u>

Full Moon Resort ☎ 091 223 3091, ⓦ fullmoon resortunawatuna.com. Attractive guesthouse right on the beach, with cheery modern concrete cabanas and a range of pleasant rooms (some with a/c), plus a good seafront restaurant with an Italian slant and free wi-fi. Can be noisy, though, when there's a disco (currently Fri) at next-door *Happy Banana*. <u>$40</u>; a/c <u>$50</u>

Kingfisher ☎ 091 225 0312, ⓦ kingfisherunawatuna .com. Formerly Unawatuna's best beachside restaurant, *Kingfisher* has now, following recent beach clearances, reinvented itself as a svelte modern boutique hotel, with just four neat (if rather bare) rooms. A new restaurant and bar were under construction at the time of writing. <u>$100</u>

Nooit-Gedacht ☎ 091 222 3449, ⓦ sriayurveda.com. Set in spacious gardens with two pools around a delectable colonial mansion of 1735, this long-running Ayurveda resort has bags of character and a wide range of rooms (all with a/c and hot water), ranging from rather uninspiring budget rooms to smart modern accommodation furnished in colonial style in the new wing. The Ayurveda centre here is one of the best on the south coast; a one-week course costs around $760, inclusive of accommodation and all treatments. B&B <u>$55</u>; new wing <u>$110</u>

Nor Lanka ☎ 091 222 6194, ⓦ norlanka.com. Attractive and very professionally run Norwegian/Sri Lankan-owned guesthouse set in peaceful gardens a couple of minutes from the beach. The spacious and attractively furnished white rooms all come with fridge and hot water, while some also have a/c and four-poster beds. B&B <u>$50</u>; a/c <u>$67</u>

Rock House ☎ 091 222 4948, ⓔ rockhouse2002 @hotmail.com. A range of bright, modern rooms of varying size and standard (some with hot water and a/c), including three mini-apartments in Unawatuna's highest building, perched atop the flanks of Rumassala with fabulous views down to the bay across a sea of palms. <u>Rs.3500</u>; a/c <u>$50</u>

Saadhana Bird House ☎ 091 222 4953. Low-key little family guesthouse surrounded by trees and twittering birds with a small selection of neat, competitively priced fan and a/c rooms of various sizes and standards (some with hot water). <u>Rs.2000</u>; a/c <u>Rs.4000</u>

★ **Secret Garden** ☎ 091 224 1857, ⓦ secretgarden unawatuna.com. Exactly as the name suggests, with a tiny door leading into a wonderful concealed walled garden full of trees, birds and the occasional monkey. Accommodation is either in the old colonial villa (all beautifully furnished in period style, and with outdoor bathrooms) or in the less characterful modern bungalow. There's also a pretty little yoga dome (with classes at 9am and 5pm), plus Ayurveda treaments. Bungalow <u>$68</u>; villa <u>$87</u>

★ **Shangri La Guest House** ☎ 091 438 4252, ⓦ shangrila.lk. Deservedly popular South African/Sri Lankan-owned guesthouse set in rambling, hammock-strewn gardens. There's an excellent range of accommodation, from spotless, homely rooms in the main building to attractive wooden cabanas with open-air showers, plus a pair of two-bedroom cottages, each sleeping four, and a cute African hut. There's also cheap internet and decent food. Rooms <u>$25</u>; cabanas <u>$25</u>

South Ceylon ☎ 0779 526 824, ⓦ southceylon restaurant.com. A handful of brand-new rooms attached to this ever-popular café (see p.161). The larger "premium" rooms (a/c planned) come with hot water, big frame nets and fridge; smaller "budget" rooms downstairs are simpler but good value. There's also a chill-out zone cum meditation terrace (classes daily at 8.30am), plus free laundry and wi-fi. Budget <u>Rs.2000</u>; premium <u>Rs.5000</u>

★ **The Strand** ☎091 222 4358, ⊕homestay-strand .net. Welcoming guesthouse occupying an attractive old 1920s colonial-style house and surrounding modern buildings all set within a tranquil garden – very peaceful, despite its proximity to the village centre. Rooms come in various styles, sizes and standards (some with hot water, one with a/c); better ones, such as "The Nest", boast attractive period touches. Free wi-fi. Rs.3000–4500; a/c Rs.5500

Sunny Beach Hotel ☎091 438 1456 ⊖upnagasinghe @yahoo.com. Modern two-storey building set right above the waves, with a breezy seafront terrace restaurant. Rooms (fan only) are a mixed bag – ask to see a few – but among the cheapest available right on the beach. Rs.3500

Thambapanni Retreat ☎091 223 4588, ⊕thambapannileisure.com. Inviting hotel tucked away in thick jungle at the foot of Rumassala – more rainforest retreat than beachside resort. Accommodation (all with a/c, minibar and satellite TV) ranges from the comfortable but relatively humdrum standard rooms through to more characterful deluxe and superior categories. There's also a small swimming pool, Ayurveda treatments and yoga classes. B&B $55; deluxe $85

★ **Thaproban Beach House** ☎091 438 1722, ⊕thambapannileisure.com. Much-loved Unawatuna landmark, right on the beach in the middle of the village. The attractive rooms (all with a/c, minibar and balcony) come in various sizes, styles and prices – smarter ones, elegantly furnished in light wood and bamboo, add a touch of boutique style. There's also internet, wi-fi and an excellent restaurant (see opposite). Fills up quickly, so book ahead. B&B: $55

★ **Unawatuna Beach Bungalow** ☎091 222 4327, ⊕unawatuna-beachbungalow.com. One of the nicest small guesthouses in Unawatuna, with spotless and very comfortable modern tiled rooms (all with hot water) just a few steps from the beach. B&B: $43; a/c (and free wi-fi) $48

The Villa ☎091 224 7253, ⊕villa-unawatuna.com. Right on the beach in Unawatuna's most shamelessly kitsch building – it's like staying in an enormous cuckoo clock. The six rooms are nicely equipped with big walk-in nets, colonial-style furniture and colourful blue bathrooms, plus a/c, hot water, minibar, satellite TV and free wi-fi; all have sea views. Also has a good restaurant (see opposite). B&B $80

EATING AND DRINKING

Unawatuna is easily the best of the south-coast resorts for food, with dozens of inviting **restaurants** lining the beachfront and Wella Devale Road – fish and seafood are predictably good. A number of places, including *Happy Banana* (Fri) host regular **discos** in season; ask around when you arrive.

Bong Spice Chili Café. Budget-conscious backpacker place, offering a wide range of travellers' favourites at below-average prices including salads, sandwiches, noodles, pancakes and pasta (most under Rs.500), plus

---

DIVING, SNORKELLING AND SURFING AT UNAWATUNA

Unawatuna has a modest range of diving, snorkelling, surfing and other watersports on offer, with two good diving schools: **Submarine Diving School** (☎0777 196 753, ⊕divinginsrilanka .com), at the western end of the beach, and **Unawatuna Diving Centre** (☎091 224 4693, ⊕unawatunadiving.com; Oct–April only), around the bay to the east. Both offer the usual range of PADI courses, plus single and introductory dives and wreck and deep dives (there are no fewer than eight wrecks in the vicinity, including an old wooden English ship, the *Rangoon*, lying at a depth of 30m), though they're rather more expensive than in nearby Hikkaduwa. Diving is best between October and April.

You can **snorkel** off the beach at Unawatuna, although it's not wildly exciting; you might see a few colourful tropical fish, and there's a little patch of live coral where the waves break in front of the Submarine Diving School. The best two snorkelling spots are **Rock Island**, about 1km offshore, and around the headland facing Galle at **Jungle Beach**, where you'll find live coral and fish. For the former you'll need to hire the Submarine Dive School's **glass-bottomed boat** (Rs.2600 for two people for ninety-odd minutes), which can also be used to reach Jungle Beach (two people Rs.5000 for 3hr trip). Alternatively, Jungle Beach is reachable by tuktuk, or by foot (though it's a convoluted 45-min walk, and very easy to get lost; ask for directions locally). Submarine rent out expensive snorkelling equipment (Rs.300/hr or Rs.1000/day), as do a couple of cheaper shacks on the beach nearby. Check all equipment carefully, as there are plenty of dud masks and snorkels in circulation.

A lot of locals **surf** at Unawatuna, though the waves aren't nearly as good as at nearby Hikkaduwa or Midigama. Boards can be rented at the Submarine Diving School (Rs.300/hr or Rs.1500/day).

more expensive seafood dishes and a good cocktail list. Daily 8am–late.

Dream House ☎ 091 438 1541. Some of the south coast's best Italian cooking – pasta, meat and seafood – served up on the intimate terrace of this upmarket guesthouse when the Tuscan owners are in residence (Dec–March & Aug), using imported ingredients, although quite reasonably priced (mains Rs.600–800). Advance bookings recommended. Daily except Mon 7–10pm.

Flower Garden ☎ 091 222 5286. Attractive open-sided restaurant, serving an excellent range of beef steaks, plus plenty of pasta and fish and an extensive wine list. Mains Rs.900–1500. Daily 11am–3pm & 7–10pm.

Happy Banana ☎ 091 225 0252. Lively and perennially popular beachfront restaurant, particularly on Fridays when it hosts a noisy disco. The menu features a bit of everything – pizza, pasta, seafood, Chinese and Sri Lankan, plus assorted snacks – with mains around Rs.750–1000. Daily 7am–late.

Nautilus ☎ 0779 110 090. This neat little streetside restaurant is perhaps the best place in Unawatuna for a traditional rice and curry, using authentic ingredients and spices – try the *ambul thiyal* (sour fish curry). Also dishes up all the other usual local standards, plus pizza, pasta and a good range of Sri Lankan and western breakfasts. Mains Rs.500–900. Daily 8.30am–4pm & 6–11pm.

★ **South Ceylon Restaurant** ☎ 0779 526 824. In a quaint rickety wooden building on the main road through the village, this place does an unusual selection of international vegetarian dishes ranging from *gado gado* and Sri Lankan *pittu* to enchiladas and chilly con veggy – not always totally authentic, but generally tasty and good value, with all mains at Rs.660, although service can be painfully slow. Also a good place for breakfast. Daily 8am–10pm.

Sunil Garden Coffee Bar Attractive little garden café with tables tucked away between the trees, plus a cute little pavilion. There's a good little menu of pancakes, sandwiches and other snacks (around Rs.500) plus ice cream, home-made cake and pricey but excellent Lavazza coffee and free wi-fi. Daily 8.30am–10pm.

★ **Thaproban Beach House** ☎ 091 438 1722. The nicest restaurant in the village, with above-average cooking, smooth decor and welcoming service. The reasonably priced menu (mains Rs.600–1000) focuses on seafood, with offerings fresh from the day's catch, plus Sri Lankan classics and a few international offerings ranging from pasta to chicken korma – and the pizzas aren't bad either. Dine either in the attractive dining room or right over the waves on the beachfront terrace outside. Free wi-fi. Daily 7.30am–10.30pm.

The Villa ☎ 091 224 7253. Pleasant and quietly civilized beachfront restaurant serving the usual island standards (including Sri Lankan breakfasts – order the day before), plus a few international dishes such as *nasi goreng* and mutton *rogan josh*. Mains mostly Rs.600–800. Free wi-fi. Daily 7.30am–10.30pm.

DIRECTORY

Ayurveda and spa Expert Ayurveda treatments are available at the *Nooit-Gedacht* Ayurveda resort. Another possibility is The Sanctuary, 136 Wella Devale Rd (☎ 0773 078 583; book in advance), tucked away in a shady garden behind the *Dhammika* hotel, with reasonably priced Ayurveda, plus spa, reflexology and aromatherapy treatments in a pretty little garden.

Banks The nearest banks are in Galle.

Cookery courses A number of places around the village now run half-day cookery classes, offering the chance to get behind an apron and learn some of the secrets of Sri Lankan chefs, and perhaps also visit a local market to purchase ingredients. The two best are the Sonja Healthfood Restaurant (Rs.3000; ☎ 091 224 5815) and the *Nautilus* restaurant (see above) (Rs.3000/Rs.2500 with/without market visit; ☎ 0779 110 090). You'll need to book a day in advance at both places.

Internet Many restaurants and guesthouses offer free wi-fi. If you haven't got your own machinery try the reliable but overpriced GG Happy Tours (daily 8.30am–9.30pm; Rs.240/hr) or the smaller but cheaper The Hub (daily 8am–9pm; Rs.2120/hr) further up Beach Rd.

Tour operators At least half a dozen travel agents are dotted around the village, all offering assorted local and island-wide tours including general information about the area and tours to nearby places like Balapitiya and Koggala, as well as day-trips to Sinharaja and Uda Walawe. Try the helpful GG Happy Tours right in the middle of the village (☎ 091 223 2838, ◍ gghappytours.com).

Yoga and meditation Secret Garden guesthouse runs daily yoga classes (9am and 5pm), while the South Ceylon café runs free daily meditation classes at 8.30am (and may also run yoga classes in future).

Dalawela and Thalpe

A few kilometres east of Unawatuna, the beautiful and unspoilt beaches at **DALAWELA** and **THALPE** are becoming increasingly popular with visitors turned off by the hustle and bustle of Unawatuna. Dalawela is home to a handful of good mid-range

2

STILT FISHERMEN

The section of coast between Dalawela and Ahangama is the best place to witness one of Sri Lanka's most emblematic sights, **stilt fishermen**. The stilts consist of a single pole and crossbar planted out in the sea, on which fishermen perch while casting their lines when the currents are flowing in the right direction (most likely to happen between Oct and Dec, especially at sunset). Positions are highly lucrative thanks to the abundant supplies of fish, even close to shore, and are handed down from father to son.

guesthouses and hotels while a succession of high walls on the ocean-side of the Matara road at Thalpe, 2km further on, conceals a raft of luxury beachfront villas belonging to (mostly) foreigners and available for rent; there are also a few small upmarket hotels.

Accommodation aside, there's very little to either village apart from the beach and a few clusters of fishing stilts – perfect for Robinson Crusoe types who enjoy counting palm trees and also hugely popular with Galle's expats, who flock here for a trio of lively beach hangouts.

ARRIVAL AND DEPARTURE   DALAWELA AND THALPE

By bus/tuktuk Buses running along the main coastal highway pass right by all the places listed below, although as most aren't prominently signposted it can be tricky knowing where to get off. It's much easier to take a tuktuk from Unawatuna or Galle.

ACCOMMODATION

The following places are listed in the direction you reach them travelling east from Unawatuna.

Shanthi Guest House Dalawela, 2km east of Unawatuna ☎ 091 228 3550, ⓦ shanthiguesthouse.com. Large and good-value modern guesthouse in an attractive beachfront location right next to the village's main cluster of stilt-fishing posts, with a natural swimming pool formed by a protective reef. There's a big selection of rooms of varying standards (all with hot water, some with a/c), plus simpler wood or concrete cabanas, and bikes for hire. $35; a/c $40

Sri Gemunu Beach Resort Dalawela, 2km east of Unawatuna ☎ 091 228 3202, ⓦ sri-gemunu.com. Next door to the *Shanthi*, the stilt-fishing posts and the natural pool, this modern beach hotel, set in attractive gardens, has comfortable (if rather randomly furnished) standard rooms with hot water, plus deluxe rooms with a/c, satellite TV and minibar, although rates are on the high side thanks to the obligatory half-board. $76; deluxe $96

★ **Wijaya Beach** Dalawela, 2.5km east of Unawatuna ☎ 091 228 3610. The nicest budget place in Dalawela, with a friendly and laid-back atmosphere. Rooms are modern, tiled and very comfortable, and there's a terrific beachfront restaurant (see opposite) and safe swimming thanks to a reef just offshore. *Wijaya Beach* is easy to miss: coming from the west, if you've reached the drab *Point de Galle* you've gone too far. $30

Star Light Hotel Thalpe, 3km east of Unawatuna ☎ 091 228 2216, ⓦ starlighthotel.lk. Comfortable and well-run (if uninspiring) modern hotel with fourteen large, comfortably furnished rooms (all with a/c, satellite TV, minibar, bath tub and hot water), plus a good-sized pool.

Reasonable value, though some rooms are very close to the main road and there's not actually much of a beach here. **Rs.6160**

Frangipani Tree Thalpe, 3km past Unawatuna, at the 125km post (about 200m east of the Star Light Hotel) ☎ 091 228 3711, ⓦ thefrangipanitree.com. Intimate boutique hotel arranged around a spectacular lap pool that extends the length of the immaculate frangipani-studded lawn. Rooms are stylish and minimalist, with built-in cement furniture and outdoor bath tubs. There's also a sliver of sand and a few stilt fishing posts at the end of the garden, and turtles can sometimes be seen. B&B $250

Jetwing Era Beach Thalpe, 3.5km east of Unawatuna, just east of the 125km post (and about 200m east of Frangipani Tree) ☎ 091 228 2302, ⓦ jetwinghotels .com. New boutique hotel in an attractive Dutch colonial-style building running down to a narrow strip of sand, with a neat pool sandwiched between the two accommodation wings. The eight rooms come with either garden or (for $80 extra) sea view. $230

Apa Villa Thalpe, 3.5km east of Unawatuna (about 100m east of Jetwing Era Beach) ☎ 091 228 3320, ⓦ villa-srilanka.com. This beautiful (albeit pricey) beachfront property comprises three stunning colonial-style villas, containing seven minimally furnished but very stylish suites (each sleeping two), set in spacious gardens around a gorgeous pool. A sister property, *Illuketia*, lies 5km inland in a beautifully recreated plantation house with six slightly cheaper suites. $250

EATING

Why Beach Club and Restaurant Thalpe, 4km east of Unawatuna (there's no sign – look for the large letters "WB" on the entrance doors, set in a big white gateway) ⓣ 077 698 0000, ⓦ whybeach.com. Backing onto a gorgeous stretch of beach, this is a fine place to chill either by day or after dark, strewn with funky outdoor sofas and serving up a daily-changing selection of quality Mediterranean cuisine, plus a fine array of cocktails. Advance bookings are essential for both lunch and dinner, and there are also a few rooms available for rent if you're really taken with the place. Daily 10am–11pm.

★ **Wijaya Beach** Always lively with local expats, this smooth beachfront café-restaurant is usually packed out from lunchtime onwards, dishing up a creative range of daily specials, excellent desserts and the south coast's best pizza, as well as good beers and cocktails. Mains around Rs.800–900. Daily 8.30am–11pm.

Koggala to Midigama

Around 12km east of Unawatuna lies the small and unprepossessing town of **KOGGALA**, dominated by a pair of military themed constructions with two very different purposes: a military airbase, hurriedly built here during World War II against the threat of Japanese attack, and the spectacular new *Fortress* hotel. The town is also home to one of the island's more rewarding museums, erected in honour of the famous Sinhalese writer **Martin Wickramasinghe**, and close to the fascinating **Handunugoda Tea Estate** and **Kataluwa Purvarama Mahavihara** temple, while **Koggala lagoon** is just a couple of kilometres away.

Martin Wickramasinghe Museum

Daily 9am–5pm • Rs.200 • ⓦ martinwickramasinghe.org

Directly opposite *The Fortress*, the excellent **Martin Wickramasinghe Museum** is inspired by – and partly devoted to – the life, works and ideas of Martin Wickramasinghe, one of the most important Sinhalese cultural figures of the twentieth century. A prolific writer, Wickramasinghe penned fourteen Sinhala-language novels and eight collections of short stories, plus some forty non-fiction books on subjects ranging from Buddhism to cultural anthropology – all of which played an important part in establishing Sinhala as a viable literary alternative to English at a time when the language was particularly threatened by Western influence. Wickramasinghe was deeply attached to Koggala and remained very much a local boy at heart – his birthplace and grave (both now part of the museum) lie just a few metres apart – although the traditional rural village which he grew up in (and idealized in his work) has now largely vanished.

Folk Museum

The site is divided into several different sections. The excellent **Folk Museum** houses an absorbing selection of exhibits pertaining to the daily practical and spiritual life of the Sinhalese – everything from catching a fish to chasing off malevolent spirits. You'll also find an excellent collection of traditional masks depicting assorted characters, including an unusual pair of red-faced British officers, and a couple of "sand boards"– trays of sand which were used to practise writing – the Sri Lankan equivalent of a blackboard.

The house and hall

Behind the Folk Museum is a display of traditional modes of transport, including a high-speed bull-racing cart, while at the rear of the grounds stands the **house** in which Wickramasinghe was born and grew up with his nine sisters. The **Hall of Life**, attached to the house, is devoted to Wickramasinghe's life, though it gives disappointingly little information on the man himself. Wickramasinghe's simple **grave** stands right by the side of the house.

Koggala lagoon

Around $40 for the 3hr trip for two people

Spreading north of Koggala town, the extensive **Koggala lagoon** is dotted with islands and fringed with mangroves. It's good for birds and boat trips, although factories associated with the nearby Free Trade Zone have sullied the waters somewhat. You might be able to arrange a boat or catamaran trip here locally (ask around at the Folk Museum in Koggala or one of the hotels).

Kataluwa Purvarama Mahavihara

Around 5km east of Koggala lies one of the south's most absorbing temples, the **Kataluwa Purvarama Mahavihara**. The temple is interesting principally for the remarkable Kandyan-style **wall paintings** in the main shrine, dating from the late nineteenth century – a resident monk will probably materialize to explain some of the most notable panels. The four walls were painted by different artists in competition (no one seems to know who won) and illustrate various Jatakas and other cautionary Buddhist tales, peopled with detailed crowds of meticulously executed figures including various colonial bigwigs and – strangely enough – a rather lopsided, characteristically dour Queen Victoria, placed here to commemorate her support for native Buddhism in the face of British missionary Christianity. The inner shrine (mind your head: the doors are built purposefully low to force you to bow as you enter the presence of the Buddha) contains further Buddha figures, as well as a black Vishnu and a blue Kataragama.

The temple lies about 3km inland from the coastal highway; various side roads (a couple of them signed) lead to it from the main road, though the road layout is slightly confusing, so you'll have to ask for directions locally.

Ahangama

The road from Koggala to Midigama runs close to the ocean for much of the way, in many places squeezing the beach into a narrow ribbon of sand between the tarmac and the waves. A few kilometres beyond Koggala, the town of **AHANGAMA** is famous for having the greatest concentration of **stilt fishermen** (see box, p.162) along the entire coast, and also has some decent surf. Thanks to the proximity of the highway to the sea, this is one of the few areas along the south coast where there's still evidence of tsunami damage.

Handunugoda Tea Estate

Tittagalla, Ahangama • Daily 7am–6pm • Free • ⓦ devostea.com

The **Handunugoda Tea Estate**, around 4km inland from the Kataluwa junction, is renowned locally for the remarkably high quality of its teas given such low altitude. It's particularly celebrated as one of Sri Lanka's few producers of highly prized "white tea" (or "silver tips") – produced using delicate young buds and leaves which are allowed to wither in natural sunlight before they are lightly processed (without crushing) to avoid the oxidation produced during traditional tea-processing techniques. It's also one of the planet's most expensive brews, retailing at around $1400 per kilo. Rubber and cinnamon, as well as coconuts, are also grown here, and guided tours of the plantation provide an informative overview of the production and treatment of all four crops; the highlight is a tea-tasting session of over twenty varieties (with cake) at the main plantation bungalow overlooking the estate.

Midigama

A couple of kilometres further on, the scattered village of **MIDIGAMA** has some of the best **surfing** in the island, though the village is very small and sleepy and apart from at ts far eastern end the beach is rather narrow and exposed – unless you're here to surf, there's not a lot to do.

ACCOMMODATION   KOGGALA TO MIDIGAMA

West of tiny Midigama village, a clutch of low-key guesthouses straggle along the beach and road (which are very close together here); the quaint little clocktower at the village's centre makes a useful landmark when you're trying to work out where to get off the bus. *Subodanee* and a few other guesthouses rent out **surfboards** at around Rs.300/hr or Rs.1200/day. Note that most places tend to close during the low season (mid-April to Oct), or are turned upside down with repairs.

KOGGALA

The Fortress ☎ 091 438 9400, ⊛ thefortress.lk. This sprawling new super-luxury resort is one of the island's grandest recent hotel projects, sitting on a prime stretch of beach and occupying a huge verandaed building looking a bit like an old colonial Dutch villa on steroids – lots of them. The 50-odd rooms come equipped with state-of-the-art amenities, while facilities include a spectacular 74-metre infinity pool, a fine spa (focusing mainly on Ayurveda treatments) and three swanky restaurants. The hotel is also proud purveyor of "The World's Most Expensive Dessert", selling at a whopping $14,000 and including a large diamond in its list of ingredients. Overall, however, the whole place feels like a classic example of substance trumping style. Rates vary wildly, but are never cheap. $275

★ **Kahanda Kanda** Anugulugaha, 5km inland from Koggala ☎ 091 494 3700, ⊛ kahandakanda.com. Perched in a magnificent position above Koggala lagoon. One of Sri Lanka's most beguiling small hotels, with eight eclectic, individually designed suites housed in a series of imaginatively landscaped pavilions. Facilities include a fabulous infinity pool, gym and massage room, and there's also superb food, well worth the trip even if you're not staying (a three-course lunch or dinner costs Rs.3700; non-guests are advised to book in advance). B&B $380

Villa Modarawattha Kataluwa, 200m inland from the coastal highway ☎ 091 228 3975, ⊛ modarawattha .com. Idyllic rural bolthole occupying an attractive, 200-year-old (although comprehensively restored) villa in spacious gardens with a small pool overlooking Koggala lagoon. There are just four rooms, all attractively furnished in colonial style, although it's probably worth paying a bit more for one of the two larger superior rooms. Deluxe $125; superior $150

AHANGAMA

Kabalana Boutique Hotel 500m west of the 133km post ☎ 091 228 3294, ⊛ kabalana.com. Ahangama's smartest option, close to its best surfing point, and with stilt fishing posts and a bit of beach at the end of the garden. Accommodation is either in rooms in the main building or beachfront cabanas, all furnished in a colonial idiom with antique-style furniture, plus a/c, satellite TV, free wi-fi and minibar, and there's also a good-sized pool and surfboards to rent. B&B and cabanas $130

MIDIGAMA

Ram's Surfing Beach At the 139km post, 300m east of the clocktower ☎ 041 225 2639. Lively hangout, perennially popular with visiting surfdude-types and with a mix of cheap and basic rooms (some with shared bath) plus smarter modern doubles, though it's right on the main road so can be noisy. Rs.1000; en-suite Rs.1500

Subodanee Down the side road from the clocktower, diagonally opposite the train station ☎ 091 228 3383. Cheap and cheerful surfers' place with a mix of basic budget rooms (some with shared bath) and smarter modern doubles. Also has a further selection of modern tiled rooms and attractive cabanas a couple of minutes' walk inland. Surfing lessons available. Rooms Rs.1000; cabanas $25

Villa Tissa 200m after the 140km post, 100m off the main road ☎ 041 225 3434, ⊛ villatissa.com. Attractive and peaceful small hotel set in three interconnecting reproduction Dutch-style villas at the picturesque eastern end of Midigama Bay, with stilt posts and a safe, reef-protected swimming area just offshore. Rooms (fan only) are nicely furnished in colonial style, and there's also a pool in the neatly tended garden. Rs.6600

Weligama

Twenty-three kilometres east of Unawatuna, the sleepy fishing town of **WELIGAMA** ("Sandy Village") meanders around a broad and beautiful bay, dotted with rocky outcrops and fringed with fine golden sand. It's an attractive spot, though one which has never really caught on with foreign tourists – although this may change with the forthcoming arrival of the vast new *Courtyard by Marriott* hotel, rising (at the time of writing) like an enormous concrete bombsite on the beach just west of town. For now, however, things remain pretty somnolent and there's not much to do other than stare at the sea – which may be exactly what you're after.

Weligama itself is surprisingly attractive as Sri Lankan towns go: quiet and relatively traffic-free, its modest commercial centre trailing off into lush streets of pretty gingerbread villas decorated with ornate *mal lali* wooden fretwork, while along the well-tended seafront road ladies sit out in front of their houses hunched over pieces of lace, a local speciality since Dutch times.

Kusta Raja

At the western edge of Weligama, near the rail line, stands a large megalith carved (probably sometime during the eighth or ninth centuries) with a three-metre figure known as **Kusta Raja**, the "Leper King", usually thought to show an unknown Sinhalese monarch who was miraculously cured of leprosy by drinking nothing but coconut milk for three months. An alternative theory claims it as a depiction of a Mahayana Bodhisattva, possibly Avalokitesvara or Samantabhadra – a claim lent credence by the carvings of meditating Buddhas in the figure's tiara.

Weligama Bay

The waters of **Weligama Bay** are relatively exposed, and suffer from pollution close to the town – ask at your guesthouse about where's safe to swim. The bay's most prominent feature is the minuscule island of **Taprobane**, just offshore, virtually invisible under a thick covering of luxuriant trees. The island was owned during the 1930s by the exiled French Count de Maunay, who built the exquisite white villa that still stands, its red-tiled roof poking up through the trees; the whole lot is available for rent via *The Sun House* in Galle (see p.153). The prettiest part of the bay is around

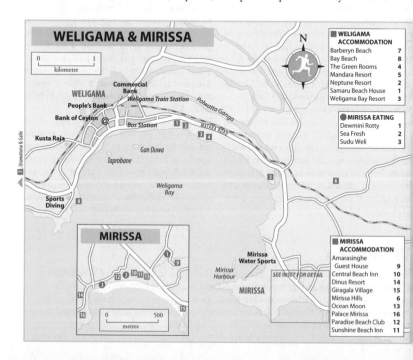

Taprobane, where dozens of colourful outrigger **catamarans** pull up on the beach between fishing expeditions; you may be able to negotiate a trip round the bay with one of the local fishermen.

ARRIVAL AND DEPARTURE WELIGAMA

By bus Buses stop at the bus station in the centre of Weligama, a block inland from the bay. Few services originate in Weligama (most are in transit between Galle, Matara and Colombo), so you'll have to take your chances with what's passing through. There should be at least one bus in each direction every 15min or so.

Destinations Colombo (every 15min; 3hr 45min); Galle (45min); Hambantota (every 15min; 3hr); Matara (every 15min; 30min); Tangalla (every 15min; 1hr 45min); Tissamaharama (every 30; 3hr 20min).

By train Weligama is also a major stop on the Matara–Colombo railway; the train station is in the town centre a block inland from the bus station. See the timetable (p.143) for details.

Destinations Aluthgama (7 daily; 1hr 30min–2hr); Ambalangoda (7 daily; 1hr–1hr 40min); Colombo (7 daily; 2hr 45min–4hr); Galle (7 daily; 30min); Hikkaduwa (7 daily; 1hr); Kalutara (7 daily; 1hr 45min–2hr 15min); Matara (7 daily; 20min).

ACCOMMODATION AND EATING

Weligama has a good range of accommodation, spread out along the beach – while the arrival of the new *Courtyard by Marriott* hotel (on the seafront just east of the centre), likely to open in late 2013, will provide the town with a major new upmarket option. There's nowhere much to eat in town, though all the hotels and guesthouses offer food. The places below are marked on the map opposite.

Barberyn Beach 4km west of Weligama ☎041 225 2994, ⓦ barberynresorts.com. An offshoot of the long-established *Barberyn Reef* in Beruwala, this idyllic if slightly pricey Ayurveda resort has sixty rooms in extensive beachfront grounds and a huge range of treatments for around $85/day. Full board only. **$190**

Bay Beach ☎041 225 0210, ⓦ baybeachhotel.com. This extremely faded resort hotel has seen better days and is looking significantly worse for wear. The location is the best in town, however, at the top end of the bay with marvellous views of myriad colourful fishing boats moored just offshore. Rooms (all a/c with hot water; seaview Rs.1000 extra) are old-fashioned and a bit shabby, but surprisingly cheap, and there's also a pool, breezy restaurant and modest Ayurveda centre. **Rs.3800**

The Green Rooms ☎077 111 9896, ⓦ thegreen roomssrilanka.com. Pleasantly laid-back beach hangout, aimed mainly at surfers, directly opposite Weligama's best break. Accommodation is in four cute but fairly basic wooden and concrete cabanas while activities include surfing tuition and cookery lessons. Ten percent of profits go local causes, although it's a bit pricey for what you get. **$75**

Mandara Resort ☎041 225 3993, ⓦ mandараresort .com (next to the 147km post). Upmarket resort in a fine location at the eastern end of the bay. Design follows the

stereotypical sub-Bawa template, with spacious rooms in attractive, minimalist style, although overall the whole place feels a bit underwhelming – particularly at current, inflated rates. B&B **$250**

★ **Neptune Resort** ☎041 225 0803, ⓦ neptune -resort.com. Bright and welcoming place, with spacious, nicely furnished hexagonal a/c cabanas plus cheaper rooms in the attractive main building. There's also an appealingly rustic, coir-canopied restaurant, plus internet, wi-fi, surfboard rental and boat trips on the Polwatta Ganga. B&B: rooms **$40**; cabanas **$89**

Samaru Beach House ☎041 225 1417, ⓦ guesthouse -weligamasamaru.com. The top budget option in town, right on the beach, with spotless modern rooms outside the main building or darker and simpler rooms inside – all good value. There are also surfboards and bikes for rent, and they can arrange surfing lessons and surfing trips to Midigama, Mirissa and Hikkaduwa. **Rs.2200**

Weligama Bay Resort ☎041 225 3920, ⓦ weligama bayresort.com. Weligama's top option, with luxurious lodgings either in rooms in the main building or in larger and pricier garden villas leading down to the inviting beachside pool (non-guests Rs.500). Pleasant enough, but, as with most places in town, overpriced at current rates. B&B **$250**

DIRECTORY

Banks There are branches of the Commercial Bank, People's Bank and Bank of Ceylon in the town centre, all of which have ATMs accepting foreign cards.

Diving, surfing and boat trips Diving trips can be

arranged through Sports Diving (on the side road leading to the *Bay Beach* hotel ☎041 225 0799, ⓦ freewebs.com/padisportdiving), who offer dives to local coral reefs and the spectacular underwater Yala Rock complex. There's also some good surfing in the centre of the bay between December and April; equipment can be rented from *Neptune Resort* and *Samaru Beach House*, both of which also offer lessons. Several of the guesthouses also offer boat trips on the Polwatta Ganga, which flows behind the town a few hundred metres inland.

Mirissa

A couple of kilometres beyond Weligama, the village of **MIRISSA** is one of the most appealing places to spend a few days next to the sea in southern Sri Lanka. The beach here is one of the nicest along this stretch of coast, with a fine swathe of sand tucked away into a pretty little bay, backed by a dense thicket of coconut palms – particularly lovely at night, when the lights go on and the sands transform into a magical tangle of fairy lights. It's not exactly unspoilt, but development remains refreshingly low-key for the moment, confined to a string of fairly rustic little restaurants and modest guest-houses, with a merciful absence of big resorts and a lively but pleasantly low-key atmosphere, attracting a youngish crowd of mainly independent travellers.

Mirissa has also developed into Sri Lanka's leading **whale-watching centre** (see box below), with excellent chances of seeing blue and sperm whales close to shore. There's reasonable **swimming**, though conditions vary considerably along different parts of the beach, so it's worth asking at your guesthouse about where's safe to swim before venturing into the water. You can also **snorkel** here, though you won't see much apart from the occasional pretty fish. Snorkelling "safaris" and numerous **other watersports**, including sport fishing and sea kayaking, as well as cruises around the bay and beyond, can be arranged with Mirissa Water Sports (ⓦmirissawatersports.com).

ARRIVAL AND DEPARTURE   **MIRISSA**

Mirissa village is mostly packed into a compact area between the harbour to the west, headland to the south and Matara road to the north and east. **Buses** whizz up and down the Matara road every few minutes; when arriving, make sure the conductor knows to let you off, since Mirissa is easily missed. When leaving, you'll have to flag something down along the main road. The village has its own **train** station, though as only slow services stop here and it's a bit of a way from the village, it's easier to catch the bus.

> ## WHALE-WATCHING IN MIRISSA
>
> Over the past five years, Sri Lanka has emerged as one of the world's major **whale-watching destinations**, thanks largely to the work of pioneering British marine biologist Charles Anderson, who in 1999 first proposed the theory that there was an annual migration of blue and sperm whales between the Bay of Bengal and around the coast of Sri Lanka to the Arabian Sea (heading west in April, and returning in the opposite direction in Dec/Jan). Anderson's theory led to the dramatic discovery that Sri Lanka was sitting alongside one of the world's great cetacean migratory routes, with sightings of these majestic creatures almost guaranteed for large parts of the year, and the possibility of seeing both sperm and blue whales (as well as spinner dolphins) in a single trip.
>
> Mirissa is perfectly placed for whale-watching expeditions, being where the continental shelf on which Sri Lanka sits is at its narrowest, with ocean depths of 1km within 6km of the coast – ideal whale country. Sightings are most regular from December to April (with Dec & April being the best months). A growing number of operators around the village now offer whale-watching trips in a range of boats seating between 25 and 50 people. Most trips leave early in the morning (around 6.30–7am), last 3–4hr and cost around $50–65 per person. Two of the main operators are Mirissa Water Sports (☎0773 597 731, ⓦmirissawatersports.com; Rs.5750; minimum four people), the original whale-watching pioneers in the village, located at Mirissa Harbour around 1km west of the beach; and Mirissa Whale Watching, c/o *Paradise Beach Club* ☎041 225 0380, ⓦmirissawhalewatching.com.
>
> For more on the island's whales and dolphins, see p.437.

ACCOMMODATION

Amarasinghe Guest House 500m inland from the coastal highway, signposted from almost opposite the *Ocean Moon* guesthouse ☎041 225 1204, ⓦ amarasingheguesthouse.com; map p.166. Some distance from the beach, but the idyllic rural location, surrounded by lush gardens full of birds and the occasional monkey, is ample compensation. Accommodation is in a range of rooms (in the family house) and bungalows (in the garden) of varying sizes and prices. There's also Internet and free wi-fi, and daily cookery classes on request. Rooms Rs.1000; cottages Rs.2500

Central Beach Inn ☎041 225 1699; map p.166. Budget guesthouse with a mix of simple rooms plus a handful of smarter and pricier concrete cabanas – all set in attractive flowering gardens. Rs.2500

Dinus Resort ☎041 225 3610, ⓦ dinumirissa.com; map p.166. Rambling guesthouse at the western end of the bay with various accommodation options ranging from rather pricey a/c rooms with hot water in the main building to cheaper and better-value fan rooms in the bright white modern two-storey annexe. Rs.2500; a/c Rs.5000

Giragala Village ☎041 225 0496, ⓦ giragala.com; map p.166. Refreshingly breezy location on the grassy defile at the eastern end of the beach, with comfortable if slightly pricey rooms (some with a/c and hot water) dotted around attractive gardens, plus a small spa. The bay here is safe for swimming and snorkelling, and there's a surf point directly In front of the hotel (with surfboards and snorkelling gear available for hire). Rs.5000; a/c Rs.6000

Mirissa Hills ☎041 225 0980, ⓦ mirissahills.com (turn-off from the coastal road signed between km147 and 148); map p.166. Superb retreat set on a working cinnamon plantation on a hillside 2km inland from the beach. Accommodation is spread over three buildings: The Bungalow, a restored walauwe, The Museum and, best (and most expensive), the superb Mount Cinnamon villa (sleeps eight; you can rent the whole thing), complete with stunning views and contemporary Sri Lankan artworks galore (including an extraordinary sculpture by Laki Senanayake). $150; Mount Cinnamon rooms $250; rental of whole villa $850

Ocean Moon ☎041 225 2328; map p.166. Friendly place with a selection of comfortable and reasonably priced modern concrete cabanas and a few cheaper and more basic rooms. Rooms Rs.2000; cabanas Rs.3000

Palace Mirissa ☎041 225 1303, ⓦ palacemirissa .com; map p.166. Mirissa's smartest option, set in a magnificent position on a rocky headland overlooking Mirissa Bay, a steep climb up from the beach. Scattered among rambling gardens, accommodation is in spacious and attractive concrete cabanas, all with a/c, TV and fine views. There's also a kidney-shaped pool and very average food. Good value, despite the compulsory half-board rates. $90

Paradise Beach Club ☎041 225 0380, ⓦ paradise mirissa.com; map p.166. This popular, laid-back albeit rather bland establishment is the closest Mirissa gets to a proper resort. Accommodation is either in simple, slightly cramped concrete cabanas (fan only) scattered around attractive gardens by the beach, or the newer, more comfortable and more expensive two-storey a/c block behind. The main drawback is the average buffet food and compulsory half-board. $58; a/c $90

Sunshine Beach Inn ☎041 225 2282; map p.166. One of the cheapest beachside options, with 16 rooms in a modern three-storey block; downstairs rooms are cheapest – although they could do with a lick of paint. Rs.2500

EATING

The beach is backed by a long string of low-key **café-restaurants**, particularly pretty after dusk when tables are set out on the sands and hundreds of fairy lights twinkle in the darkness. Most places are much of a muchness, and food at most is generally reliable rather than spectacular, with all the usual seafood suspects and other touristy classics, although the freshness and quality of the produce can't be faulted, and many places lay out big trays of iced seafood to tempt you inside – huge jumbo prawns, deep crimson red snapper, pointy snouted barracuda, butterfish, seer fish, red and white mullet, calamari, and so on. If you fancy manipulating a skillet yourself, **cookery courses** are run by the *Amarasinghe* guesthouse (Rs.2500) and *Dewmini Rotty* café (Rs.2000); book the day before.

Dewmini Rotty On the south side of the side road leading to the Amarasinghe guesthouse. Peaceful little garden café serving up a great selection of tasty *rottys* (Rs.40–200) in many guises – plain, coconut, pineapple, chocolate, chicken, and so on – plus Western and Sri Lankan breakfasts. Daily 7.30am–8pm or later.

Sea Fresh Attractive little place halfway along the with beach, particularly pretty after dark when it's illuminated with fairy lights dangling from the surrounding trees. The menu covers all the usual seafood bases, plus touristy snacks, with decent service and big portions. Mains Rs.500–900. Daily 8am–late.

Sudu Weli Usually one of the beach's livelier places, and with one of its better soundtracks, set on a wobbly covered wooden deck above the sand. The menu (mains Rs.600–900) features a little bit of absolutely everything, all reasonably prepared, although service can be lackadaisical unless you're young, beautiful and, crucially, female. Daily 8am–late.

2

Matara and around

Close to the southernmost point of the island, the bustling town of **MATARA** (pronounced "*maat*-rah" the middle syllable is virtually elided) provides a taste of everyday Sri Lanka that may (or may not) be welcome if you've spent time in the coastal resorts. Standing at the terminus of the country's southern rail line, the town is an important transport hub and a major centre of commerce – a lively place given a youthful touch by the presence of students from the nearby **Ruhunu University**. Matara preserves a few Dutch colonial buildings, an atmospheric old fort area and an attractive seafront (though you wouldn't want to swim here). A couple of kilometres either side of town, the low-key beachside suburbs of **Polhena** and **Medawatta** offer good snorkelling and surfing respectively, while the area **around Matara** boasts a couple of mildly interesting and little-visited sights, including the giant Buddha at **Weherehena** and the town of **Dondra**, whose slender lighthouse marks the island's southernmost point.

Matara itself (from Mahatara, or "Great Harbour") is an ancient settlement, though no traces of anything older than the colonial era survive. The Portuguese used the town intermittently, but it was the Dutch, attracted by the deep and sheltered estuary of the Nilwala Ganga, who established a lasting presence here, fortifying the town and making it an important centre for cinnamon and elephant trading.

As at Galle, Matara divides into two areas: the **modern town** and the old Dutch colonial district, known as the **Fort**. The two are separated by the **Nilwala Ganga**, a fine and remarkably unspoilt stretch of water, edged by thick stands of palm trees and spanned by the town's most impressive modern construction: the six-lane **Mahanama Bridge**, constructed with Korean help and unveiled in December 2007 on the third anniversary of the tsunami.

The Fort

Matara's main **Fort** lies on the narrow spit of land south of the river, its eastern side bounded by a long line of stumpy **ramparts**, built by the Dutch in the eighteenth century and topped by the inevitable ugly white British clocktower of 1883. At the north end of the ramparts, a dilapidated **gateway** (dated 1780) marks the original entrance to the Fort, while a short walk brings you to the restored **Dutch Reformed Church**, one of the earliest Dutch churches in Sri Lanka – a large and rather austere gabled structure sheltered beneath a huge pitched roof. The interior is largely bare, save for a few battered old wooden pews, a clapped-out harmonium and various florid British and Dutch gravestones inserted into the floor, the oldest dating back to the very beginning of the eighteenth century.

The rest of the Fort comprises an interesting district of lush, tree-filled streets dotted with fine old colonial-era houses in various stages of picturesque disrepair: some are surprisingly palatial, with grand colonnaded facades and sweeping verandas, although heavy-handed development is beginning seriously to erode the area's character. At the far west end of the Fort, the peninsula tapers off to a narrow spit of land at the confluence of the Nilwala Ganga and the sea, where there's a pretty new harbour.

2

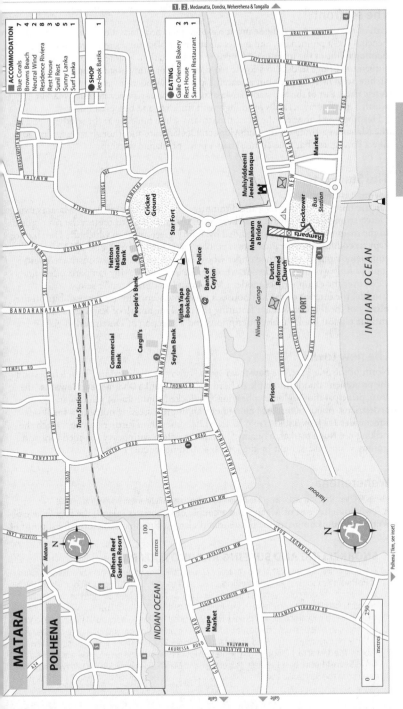

■ ACCOMMODATION
Blue Corals	7
Browns Beach	4
Neutral Wind	2
Residence Riviera	8
Rest House	3
Sunil Rest	6
Sunny Rest	5
Surf Lanka	1

● SHOP
Jez-look Batiks	1

◆ EATING
Galle Oriental Bakery	2
Rest House	3
Samannal Restaurant	1

MATARA

POLHENA

Polhena Reef
Garden Resort

INDIAN OCEAN

Matara

N

0   100
metres

Train Station

Commercial
Bank

Cargill's

People's Bank

Hatton
National
Bank

Seylan Bank

Vijitha Yapa
Bookshop

Bank of
Ceylon

Police

Star Fort

Cricket
Ground

Muhiyiddeenil
Jeelani Mosque

Market

Clocktower

Bus
Station

Ramparts

Mahanam
a Bridge

Dutch
Reformed
Church

FORT

Prison

Harbour

Nilwala Ganga

INDIAN OCEAN

N

Nupe
Market

BANDARANAYAKA MAWATHA

TEMPLE RD

STATION ROAD

ST THOMAS RD

ST YEHIYA ROAD

UDYANA ROAD

NEW LANE

ARALIYA MAWATHA

JAYASUMANARAMA MAWATHA

MAHAMAYA MAWATHA

SEA BEACH ROAD

TANGALLA ROAD

NEW

MAIN STREET

LAWRENCE ROAD

KACHCHERI ROAD

C.A. ARIYATHILAKE MW

KUMARATUNGA

ANAGARIKA

DHARMAPALA

MAWATHA

RAHULA ROAD

KATHUTA ROAD

TEMPLE RD

DIKWANDA MW

RAHULA ROAD

SRI DHARMA

YSALAMULLA

WILMOT BALASURIYA MAWATHA

ELGIN BALASURIYA MW

H.C.W. JAYASURIYA MW

UYANWATTE ROAD

AKURESSA ROAD

GALLE ROAD

JAYAMAHA VIHARAYA RD

SUJATHA LANE

Galle

Galle

Polhena (1km, see inset)

0   250
metres

INDIAN OCEAN

2

The seafront

East of the the ramparts, the **seafront** has been prettified since the tsunami with park benches and a promenade, and makes an attractive place for a stroll if you don't mind the hooting traffic of the main road. Opposite the bus station, a rather wobbly pedestrian suspension bridge leads across to the red-tiled roofs of a tiny **island temple**, of no great architectural merit in itself but a peaceful spot with wonderful views of the ocean behind. A few paces east of the bus station, Matara's cacophonous indoor morning **market** is worth a quick foray, its stalls piled high with fruit, veg and bug-eyed fish.

Heading north towards the river, the striking white building at the southern end of the Mahanama Bridge is the **Muhiyiddeenil Jeelani** mosque, though it looks far more like a Portuguese Baroque church than a place of Islamic worship.

The Star Fort

Daily except Tues 8am–5pm • Donation

On the north side of the river the diminutive **Star Fort** is the smaller of Matara's two Dutch strongholds, a quaint little hexagonal structure built to protect the river crossing to the main Fort area and surrounded by a dirty-green moat in which the Dutch once kept crocodiles. The entrance gate is emblazoned "Redoute Van Eck 1763", commemorating the governor under whose administration it was constructed, and sports a fully working wooden drawbridge. A circuit of the tiny ramparts offers fine views over the cacophony of modern Matara and its unruly traffic below.

Inside, the interior of the fort houses a small **museum**, with modest exhibits on the history of the fort and Matara featuring the usual mishmash of Kandyan artefacts, antique ola-leaf books, tablet inscriptions and a selection of Dutch period glass.

The new town

North of the Star Fort, the **new town** sprawls away in all directions. Turn left beyond the prominent Buddhist temple to head down **Anagarika Dharmapala Mawatha**, the area's principal thoroughfare, a heaving, gridlocked confusion of vehicles and pedestrians. About 500m west along here, an unprepossessing house in a small side street hides **Jez-look Batiks** (see p.174), while some 500m further on you'll reach the striking old **Nupe Market**, a quaint, T-shaped pavilion with heavy red-tiled roof and stumpy white pillars, built by the Dutch sometime around 1780.

Weherehena

Take bus #349 from Matara bus station (every 30min; 20min) or a tuktuk (around Rs.700 return, including waiting time)

A few kilometres east of Matara and a couple of kilometres inland, the tiny village of **WEHEREHENA** is home to one of the island's largest Buddha statues, the focal point of

SNORKELLING AND SURFING AROUND MATARA

A couple of kilometres west of the centre of Matara, the rather down-at-heel beachside suburb of **Polhena** has some good **snorkelling** straight off the beach, with lots of colourful fish and a small section of live coral; swimming conditions and visibility are best outside the monsoon period. Snorkelling equipment can be rented from *Sunil Rest* for Rs.200 per day, and the knowledgeable local snorkelling guides Titus (c/o *Hotel TK Green Garden*; ☎041 222 2603) and Nishantha (c/o *Blue Corals*) charge around Rs.400 (including equipment) for ninety-minute trips.

At the picturesque eastern end of Matara Bay, about 1.5km east of the town, another low-key suburb, **Medawatta**, is popular with long-term surfers who come here to ride waves of up to 4m at **Secret Point**, best between November and March. Surfboards (Rs.1000/day) can be hired from the *Surf Lanka* hotel.

a sprawling modern temple complex constructed on the site of a hidden underground temple built in the seventeenth century to escape the evangelical attentions of the Portuguese. Thirty-nine metres tall and set within a rather ugly shelter, the giant Buddha figure itself, shown in the seated *samadhi* position, is a thing of impressive size, if no particular beauty. Most of the temple is actually buried underground, with endless corridors decorated with around twenty thousand cartoon-style depictions of various Jatakas. Right underneath the giant Buddha, a monk will take your donation (Rs.200 is "suggested") and point out a mirror below in which you can see reflected a cache of precious gold and stone Buddhas buried in an underfloor vault. From here steps lead up to the giant Buddha itself – you can climb all the way up to the head, although there's not much to see. A big **perahera** is held here on the Unduvap poya day in early December.

2

ARRIVAL AND DEPARTURE

MATARA AND AROUND

By bus Matara is the south's major transport hub. The bus station (next to the old ramparts and convenient for the *Rest House* and *Browns Beach Hotel*) is unusually orderly, with clearly marked bays and a helpful information office (not signposted) in the outside corridor in the corner near the statue of a woman holding a baby. Eastbound services leave from the eastern side of the terminal; westbound services from the west. As ever, it pays to check the latest schedules in the information office in advance.

Destinations Akuressa (for Deniyaya and Sinharaja; every 10min; 45min); Bandarawela (5 daily; 6hr); Badulla (2 daily; 6hr); Colombo (every 15min; 4hr–4hr 30min); Deniyaya (4 daily; 3hr); Embilipitiya (every 20min;

2hr 30min); Galle (every 15min; 1hr 15min); Hambantota (every 15min; 2hr 30min); Kataragama (5 daily; 3hr 30min, alternatively change at Tissa); Monaragala (2 daily; 5hr); Nuwara Eliya (3 daily; 8hr); Ratnapura (5 daily; 4hr); Tangalla (every 15min; 1hr 30min); Tissamaharama (every 15min; 3hr); Weligama (every 15min; 30min).

By train The train station is just north of the town centre. Matara stands at the end of the southern rail line from Colombo; see p.143 for details of services.

Destinations Aluthgama (7 daily; 2hr–2hr 30min); Ambalangoda (7 daily; 1hr 20min–2hr); Colombo (7 daily; 3hr–4hr 30min); Galle (7 daily; 40min–1hr); Hikkaduwa (7 daily; 1hr 30min); Kalutara (7 daily; 2hr–2hr 45min); Weligama (7 daily; 20min).

ACCOMMODATION

Matara town suffers from a chronic lack of places to stay, and most visitors stay in the suburbs of **Polhena**, a couple of kilometres west of town, or **Medawatta**, about 1.5km east.

MATARA TOWN

Brown's Beach 39B Beach Rd ☎ 041 222 6298. Reliable old seafront restaurant, with comfortable and inexpensive, if slightly shabby, rooms and decent rice and curry in the downstairs restaurant itself. If it's full, the adjacent *Wijetunga Sea View Inn* offers a similar, if slightly less appealing, alternative. Rs.1870

Rest House Fort ☎ 041 222 2299, ☻ resthousematara .com. Painstakingly rebuilt after being flattened by the tsunami, this attractive seafront rest house still has plenty of old-school charm, with attractively furnished rooms (all with hot water), shady verandas, a decent restaurant and refreshing sea breezes. Good value. Rs.2400; a/c Rs.4000

POLHENA

Blue Corals ☎ 0777 600 803. Three modern, very cheap but rather shabby tiled rooms close to the beach. The owner, Nishantha, runs snorkelling (see box opposite) and diving trips, and can also arrange boat tours along the Nilwala Ganga (Rs.6000/six-person boat) and rents out

motorbikes (Rs.800/day) and bikes (Rs.200, or free for guests). Rs.1000

Residence Riviera 67 Beach Rd ☎ 0777 424 114, ☻ riviera.lk. Offshoot of *Sunil Rest*, set in a big modern house right on the seafront (although there's not much of a beach). The five rooms are spacious and spotless, albeit rather bare, with smart bathrooms (all with hot water) and sea-facing balconies. There's also a fun TV room with local instruments including a *serpina* (a kind of accordion), *dholak* and *tablas* to mess around on. Good value for fan rooms, less so for a/c. Rs.3000; a/c Rs.5000

★ **Sunil Rest** ☎ 077 943 4193, ☻ sunilrestpolhena @yahoo.com. Polhena's friendliest, liveliest and best-organized guesthouse, with a range of inexpensive and comfortable rooms, a range of day-trips, bikes for hire (Rs.250/day) and free internet. Rs.1500

Sunny Lanka ☎ 041 222 3504, ☻ sunnyamare@yahoo .com. Long-running budget stalwart, with large, clean and nicely furnished rooms – exceptionally good value at current prices. Rs.900

MEDAWATTA

Neutral Wind ☎ 0777 621 160. Small and friendly family-run place, popular with long-term surfers, with clean rooms in a cheerfully painted house; those downstairs are a bit pokey; the more expensive upstairs rooms are newer, nicer and a lot brighter. **Rs.2000**

Surf Lanka ☎ 041 222 8190, ⊛ surf-lanka.com. The smartest place in Medawatta, with a range of bright and spacious (if rather expensive) rooms in a functional white building right above Secret Point; more expensive ones have a/c, hot water, TV and jacuzzis. Also has surfboards for rent (Rs.1000/day). Fan **$45**, a/c **$56**

EATING

Galle Oriental Bakery Anagarika Dharmapala Mawatha. The most characterful place in town, this pleasantly old-fashioned local establishment (with charmingly antiquated, white-smocked waiters) serves up very cheap food including the usual basic rice and curry and short eats, though with enough chilli in them to reduce you to tears. Daily 8am–8pm.

Rest House Fort ☎ 041 222 2299, ⊛ resthousematara .com. Sedate, old-fashioned dining room with a well-prepared selection of all the usual Sri Lankan classics. Mains around Rs.500–700. Daily 8am–11pm.

Samanmal Restaurant Edmond Samarasekara Mw. Immediately north of the cricket ground, this serves primarily as a local drinking hole, although the Sri Lankan-style Chinese food is cheap (mains Rs.300–500) and surprisingly good – even if it's so gloomy inside you can hardly see what you're eating. Daily 8.30am–11pm.

SHOPPING

Jez-look Batiks 12 St Yehiya St ☎ 041 222 2142. One of the best batik workshops in the island, run by the charming Jezima Mohamed. The batiks produced here are far superior to the usual tourist junk, with a wide range of striking original designs, and they also make gorgeous silk and even jute batiks, as well as clothes. Jezima's girls can also make up pieces according to your own designs if you fancy, or you can even stay and study batik-making here if you get really enthused. Daily 9am–6pm.

DIRECTORY

Banks Various banks are scattered across town with ATMs that accept foreign Visa and MasterCards. See the map (p.171).

Dondra

Around 5km southeast of Matara, the sleepy little town of **DONDRA** was formerly one of the south's most important religious centres, known as **Devi Nuwara** ("City of the Gods") and housing a great temple dedicated to Vishnu, among the most magnificent on the island until it was destroyed by the Portuguese in 1588. Nothing of the temple now survives apart from one ancient shrine, the **Galge**, a small, plain rectangular structure thought to date back to the seventh century AD, making it the oldest stone building in Sri Lanka. The shrine lies half a kilometre inland from the main crossroads in the middle of Dondra; turn left down a narrow lane just after the clocktower. After 400m you'll reach a rather flouncy modern white temple; the Galge lies up a short flight of steps in a grassy field on the slope immediately above.

The diminutive Galge pales into insignificance next to modern Dondra's main temple, the sprawling roadside **Devi Nuwara Devalaya**, right in the middle of town by the main road, complete with a huge standing Buddha (a copy of the Aukana Buddha – see p.296). One of the south's major festivals, the **Devi Nuwara Perahera**, is held at the temple every year on the Esala poya day (late July/early Aug).

Dondra lighthouse

Daily 9am–6.30pm • Rs.500 (though you may be able to bargain this down)

Just over a kilometre south of Dondra, the fifty-metre-high **Dondra lighthouse**, built in 1889, marks the **southernmost point** in Sri Lanka. You can climb the 222 steps to the top of the lighthouse for huge views up and down the coast and a close look at the beam's beautifully maintained colonial machinery, still used to illuminate Dondra Head for the benefit of local shipping. Look south of here, and there's nothing but sea between you and Antarctica, over fifteen thousand kilometres distant.

To reach Dondra, take any **bus** heading eastwards out of Matara; you'll have to either walk or catch a tuktuk to the lighthouse itself.

ACCOMMODATION   DONDRA

★ **Talalla Retreat** Gandara, 4km east of Dondra chalets, with plenty of simple rustic chic and outdoor
☎ 041 225 9171, ⑩ talallaretreat.com. Wonderfully bathrooms throughout. Also has a simple spa, surfing and
tranquil retreat set in extensive gardens next to a huge stretch snorkelling equipment, and runs yoga and surfing classes.
of unspoilt beach. Accommodation is in attractive two-storey Rates fall considerably during low season. B&B $115

2

Dickwella and around

Around 15km east of Dondra on the coastal highway, the small town of **DICKWELLA** is home to an attractive resort (see p.176) and, diagonally opposite, **Dickwella Lace** (daily 9am–5pm), a women's cooperative set up to protect and revive the art of *beeralu*, or bobbin lace-making, one of the area's traditional industries. Women from local villages are trained up here and provided with the skills to earn an income from their craft. As well as demonstrations of lace-making techniques, there's also a small lace museum, and assorted bags, dolls, toys, tablecloths and linen for sale.

Wewurukannala

2km north of Dickwella • Rs.500 • Buses from Tangalla to Matara via Beliatta pass directly by the temple; alternatively, take any bus along the coastal highway and get off at Dickwella, then 2km on foot or by tuktuk

Just inland from Dickwella, the entertainingly kitsch temple at **Wewurukannala** is home to the largest Buddha statue on the island, a fifty-metre concrete colossus constructed in the late 1960s. The rather supercilious-looking Buddha is shown in the seated posture, draped in orange robes with his head crowned by a gaudy, polychromatic *siraspata* (the Buddhist equivalent of the halo) – supposedly representing the flame of wisdom, though on this occasion it looks more like an enormous dollop of ice cream. Immediately to the rear of the statue is a seven-storey building, which the Enlightened One appears to be using as a kind of backrest. You can walk up the steps inside the building, past a big collection of cartoon-style Jataka paintings, and peer into the Buddha's head.

The main **image house** dates from the late nineteenth century and contains an impressive ensemble of huge Buddhas in various poses. Outside and to the left of the main shrine is the oldest part of the temple, a small shrine some 250 years old, decorated with faded murals and housing a seated clay Buddha. Next door, another image house houses a kind of Buddhist **chamber of horrors** showing the punishments awaiting wrongdoers in the afterlife. The gruesome collection of life-size statues here depicts unfortunates being sawn in half, boiled in oil and impaled on stakes by rather jolly-looking devils. The corridor past the statues shows a long series of paintings (many unfinished): the upper panels depict various sins – everything from slapping your mother to urinating in front of a temple – and the corresponding panel underneath shows the relevant punishment. You have been warned.

Hoo-maniya blowhole

Kudawela • Rs.500 • Direct bus from Tangalla to Matara along the coast road to turn-off to Kudawela, just beyond Nakulugamuwa, then 2km on foot or by tuktuk

Around 8km east of Dickwella, the **Hoo-maniya blowhole** is one of the south's more uncomplicated tourist attractions – the fanciful name derives from the low, booming

"Hoo" sound which it produces prior to spouting water. The blowhole is formed from a deep, narrow cleft in the cliff which funnels plumes of water up into the air in great jets by some mysterious action of water pressure – it's most impressive during the monsoon (May–Sept; June is reckoned to be best), when the jets can reach heights of 15m. At other times it can be slightly underwhelming, though a push-button contraption at the **visitor centre** gives an entertaining recreation of the blowhole's jetstream even when the real thing's decided not to perform. The blowhole is a popular spot with locals and gets busy at weekends, when the sight of great crowds of sari-clad ladies screaming and hopping around the rocks as they try to avoid getting drenched is at least as entertaining as the blowhole itself.

ACCOMMODATION   DICKWELLA

Dickwella Resort Coastal highway, between km179 and 180 ☎ 041 225 5271, ⓦ dickwella.net. Upmarket resort in a superb location on a headland flanked by two gorgeous beaches, with stylish rooms scattered around extensive gardens. Diving, surfing and other watersports are available, and there's a large salt-water swimming pool, a spa, and good food including a Neapolitan-standard pizzeria. Half-board rates only. **$168**

Tangalla and around

Strung out along one of the south's most stunning stretches of coastline, **TANGALLA** (or **Tangalle**) is among the region's more developed beach destinations, with a string of simple guesthouses – and a handful of upmarket hotels and villas – dotted along the coves and beaches which line the oceanfront here. Tourism has never taken off quite as much as the entrepreneurial locals would like, however, and Tangalla remains resolutely low-key compared to the resorts further west. What gives Tangalla added appeal, however, is the number of rewarding attractions in the surrounding countryside, including the **Hoo-maniya blowhole**, the giant Buddha and gaudy shrines of **Wewurukannala**, and the magnificent rock temples of **Mulkirigala**, all of which can be combined into a rewarding half-day excursion. In addition, the nearby beach at **Rekawa** is Sri Lanka's premier site for turtle-watching, while dedicated ornithologists might also fancy a trip to the little-visited **Kalametiya Bird Sanctuary**, which can be combined with a visit to the mysterious plateau at **Ussangoda**.

The beaches

Tangalla's beaches stretch for several kilometres either side of **Tangalla town**, a busy but unremarkable provincial centre with a dusty selection of shops and cafés plus the obligatory clocktower and anarchic bus station. The most developed section of coast, though still very somnolent, is to the east of town, along **Medaketiya and Medilla beaches**, a long, straight stretch of golden sand lined with a string of guesthouses opened in anticipation of a flood of tourists who have yet to arrive. Beyond Medilla, around 4km northeast of Tangalla town, the coastline tapers to little more than a sandspit at idyllic Kapuhenwala beach in **Marakolliya**, backed by the mangrove-fringed Rekawa lagoon.

Though just as sleepy, the coast immediately west of town, known as **Pallikaduwa**, is quite different in character, made up of a sequence of pretty rocky coves – much more scenic than Medaketiya and Medilla, but with little sand. The rocky shoreline here has prevented building directly on the beach, so most of Pallikaduwa's accommodation is set back behind the main road.

The most striking section of Tangalla coastline can be found a couple of kilometres further west at the village of **Goyambokka**, with a superb rocky promontory flanked by two gorgeous beaches – to the west of the headland, Godellawela Beach (or "Silent

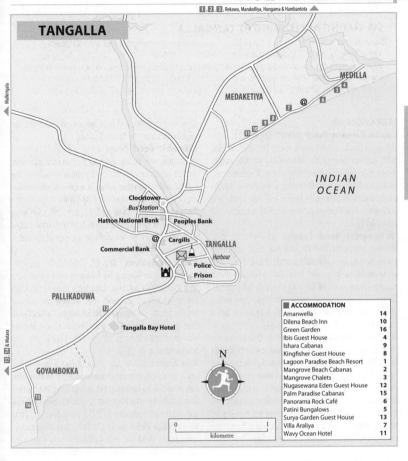

ACCOMMODATION

Amanwella	14
Dilena Beach Inn	10
Green Garden	16
Ibis Guest House	4
Ishara Cabanas	9
Kingfisher Guest House	8
Lagoon Paradise Beach Resort	1
Mangrove Beach Cabanas	2
Mangrove Chalets	3
Nugasewana Eden Guest House	12
Palm Paradise Cabanas	15
Panorama Rock Café	6
Patini Bungalows	5
Surya Garden Guest House	13
Villa Araliya	7
Wavy Ocean Hotel	11

Beach", as it's popularly known) is an absolute picture, though you'll have to share it with guests from the superb *Amanwella* hotel.

ARRIVAL AND DEPARTURE   TANGALLA

By bus Buses stop at the station right in the middle of town by the clocktower.

Destinations Colombo (every 15min; 5hr–5hr 30min); Embilipitiya (every 30min; 1hr 30min); Galle (every 15min; 2hr 30min); Hambantota (every 15min; 1hr 30min); Matara (every 15min; 1hr 30min); Tissamaharama (every 15min; 2hr); Weligama (every 15min; 1hr 45min).

ACCOMMODATION AND EATING

The biggest concentration of budget guesthouses is north of Tangalla at **Medaketiya**, while, further north, **Medilla** and particularly Kapuhenwala beach at **Marakolliya** (accessed by car from the main road only; take the small side road between km200 and 201) boast some more characterful alternatives. South of Tangalla there are further options at **Pallikaduwa** and **Goyambokka** – the rustic accommodation at the latter is significantly more expensive, though given the idyllic setting you might be prepared to cough up the extra rupees. In addition to the places listed below, the landmark *Tangalla Bay Hotel* in Pallikaduwa was undergoing renovations during 2012 but may have reopened by the time you read this. The nicest places **to eat** are the string of seafront guesthouses in Medaketiya and Medilla – the restaurants at the *Ibis Guest House* and *Dilena Beach Inn* are usually two of the better and livelier places.

2

SWIMMING AND DIVING AT TANGALLA

Swimming in Tangalla can be hazardous: Kapuhenwala, Medaketiya and Medilla beaches shelve steeply into the sea and there are dangerous currents in places, although the coves south of town at Pallikaduwa and Goyambokka are pleasantly sheltered. Always check at your guesthouse before venturing into the water: conditions vary considerably even within a few hundred metres. **Diving** can be arranged through the PADI dive school at the *Ibis* guesthouse.

MARAKOLLIYA

Lagoon Paradise Beach Resort ☎ 047 224 2509, ⊛ lagoonparadisebeachresort.com. Set in rambling palm gardens next to the Rekawa lagoon, this largish resort-style complex offers comfortable if characterless accommodation in spacious rooms and cabanas. Kayaks can be rented for trips on the lagoon and there's a big new pool complete with underwater music. $35; a/c rooms and cabanas $75

★ **Mangrove Beach Cabanas** ☎ 0777 906 018, ⊛ beachcabana.lk. One of Tangalla's most appealing places to stay, on a gorgeous stretch of beach and with accommodation in quaint beachside wood-and-thatch cabanas (*douze points* for guessing where the bathroom is). There's also an attractive restaurant, night-time turtle-watches and free canoes to explore the lagoon – or take a catamaran trip with a local fisherman. $47

Mangrove Chalets ☎ 0777 906 018, ⊛ beachcabana .lk. Bounded on three sides by water and accessed via a cute bridge (or rope ferry) across the Rekawa lagoon, this place makes full use of its superb position close to where the lagoon meets the sea. Accommodation is in neat chalets dotted around the extensive palm-studded grounds, and there's a big new pavilion-style restaurant and ship-shaped bar, plus safe swimming in a natural rock pool in front of the resort and catamaran tours of the lagoon. $63

MEDAKETIYA AND MEDILLA

Dilena Beach Inn ☎ 047 224 2240, @ dilenabeachinn @yahoo.com. One of the nicer cheapies hereabouts, with four simple but clean rooms of varying sizes and prices in two little concrete buildings behind the attractive seafront restaurant. Rs.1500

★ **Ibis Guest House** ☎ 047 567 4439, ⊛ guesthouse -ibis.de. Medilla's most welcoming guesthouse, with a mix of spacious, comfortable and attractively furnished rooms and cabanas in the main building and hammock-slung garden. There's also an above-average restaurant, free wi-fi and internet, plus local cycling, catamaran and kayak tours, snorkelling, windsurfing and kitesurfing equipment for rent and Tangalla's only dive centre. The owners also run the nearby Eliya Children´s Home (⊛ eliya-kinderheim -srilanka.com); guests interested in seeing a local social project in action are welcome to visit. Rs.4500

Ishara Cabanas ☎ 071 895 0747. Four simple but cheerful rooms in a cute pair of matching concrete cabanas,

all with hot water and little terraces or balconies, set slightly back from the beach. Rs.2500

Kingfisher Guest House ☎ 047 224 2472. Friendly guesthouse with shabby and basic (but very cheap) rooms, and an attractive little thatched pavilion restaurant. The helpful and informative owner is a mine of information about local attractions and tours. Rs.1000

Panorama Rock Café ☎ 0777 620 092. Six neat, modern, tiled rooms and a breezy little restaurant tucked away in a verdant garden, right on the edge of the water. Good value. Rs.2500

Patini Bungalows ☎ 0777 402 038, ⊛ patini bungalows.com. French-Sri Lankan-owned guesthouse with four sparklingly clean, attractively furnished modern beach bungalows set amid lush gardens on unspoilt Medilla beach – extremely peaceful, but only a short walk from the livelier Medaketiya area. The owners can arrange local tours and catamaran trips, and also have bicycles and scooter for rent. Rs.4500

Villa Araliya ☎ 047 224 2163, ⊛ ferien-in-sri-lanka .com. Medaketiya's most characterful place to stay, with two attractive bungalows set in lush gardens and another room inside the main house, all furnished in quasi-colonial style – plus a friendly dog. Rs.2725; bungalows Rs.3300

Wavy Ocean Hotel ☎ 047 224 0629. One of the better-value places along the main Medaketiya strip. Rooms are simple and unexciting but comfortable enough (those upstairs are slightly brighter and more expensive), and there's also a nice downstairs restaurant. Rs.1980; upstairs Rs.2200

PALLIKADUWA AND GOYAMBOKKA

Nugasewana Eden Guest House ☎ 047 224 0389, ⊛ nugasewana.com. The setting, right next to the main road, isn't great, but rooms (all with hot water, some with a/c) are among of the best in town at this price: modern, tiled, nicely furnished and scrupulously clean. Free wi-fi and internet. Rs.2500, a/c $45

★ **Amanwella** ☎ 047 224 1333, ⊛ amanresorts.com. Set on Godellawela Beach (or "Silent Beach", as it's generally known), this utterly captivating if very expensive resort offers a model of how beach hotels in Sri Lanka should be done, with a stylishly understated, low-impact design which blends magically with the surrounding palm trees and water. The rooms are works of art in themselves, with all mod-cons including large plunge pools and superb ocean views through huge French windows, plus a sensational infinity pool overlooking the beach. Note that room rates vary considerably, rising almost to $1000 for even the cheapest room during certain periods. $680

Green Garden Cabanas ☎077 624 7628, ✉lanka tangalla@yahoo.com. Welcoming guest house with assorted rooms and concrete cabanas scattered among attractive gardens, just a couple of minutes' walk from a neat little beach in the bay below. Rooms $30; a/c $40; cabanas $35

Palm Paradise Cabanas ☎047 224 0338, ⓦpalmparadisecabanas.net. Popular place tucked into a corner of the bay, with accommodation in simple wooden

cabanas set in shady beachside gardens and with safe swimming nearby, There's also pricey internet access (but free wi-fi), Ayurvedic massages and bike rental. Half-board rates only. $72

WEST OF TANGALLA

Surya Garden Guest House Seenimodera (Sugar Bay), 6km west of Tangalla ☎0777 147 818, ⓦsrilanka -vacanze.com. Laid-back Italian-owned guesthouse close to a fine stretch of beach, with accommodation in stylish bungalows with outdoor bathrooms, dotted around shady gardens. The rustic restaurant serves good Italian food, and there's also a small Ayurveda centre. $75

DIRECTORY

Banks The Commercial Bank, People's Bank and Hatton National Bank in the middle of town all have ATMs which accept foreign cards.

Internet Sawsiri Communications, on the southern side of the town centre (Mon–Sat 8am–5pm, Sun 8am–1pm;

Rs.100/hr), provides (slow) internet access; alternatively you can get online at the *Blue Horizon* guesthouse (Rs.100/ hr), at the top end of Medaketiya beach. A growing number of guesthouses also now have free wi-fi.

Around Tangalla

A rewarding half-day trip from Tangalla combines the **Hoo-maniya blowhole** (see p.175), the **Wewurukannala** temple (see p.175) with its enormous Buddha statue and the absorbing rock temples of **Mulkirigala**. All local guesthouses should be able to arrange a combined round-trip by tuktuk to these three places; the current going rate is around Rs.2500 for two people. Other interesting local excursions include evening trips to spot turtles coming ashore at **Rekawa**, while Tangalla can also be used as a base for trips to the little-visited wetlands of the **Kalametiya Bird Sanctuary** en route to Hambantota.

Mulkirigala

Daily 6am–6pm • Rs.500 (guide available for additional tip) • Bus from Tangalla to Beliatta (every 15min; 30min), then catch any onward bus to Middeniya, taking you directly past the site

Sixteen kilometres north of Tangalla lies the remarkable temple-monastery of **Mulkirigala**, the only monument in the south to rival the great ancient Buddhist sites of the Cultural Triangle. Mulkirigala (also spelt "Mulgirigala") consists of a series of **rock temples** carved out of the face of a huge rock outcrop which rises sheer and seemingly impregnable for over 200m out of the surrounding palm forests; the temples date back to the third century BC, but were completely restored during the eighteenth century under the patronage of the kings of Kandy. The overall effect is rather like a cross between the far better known Dambulla and Sigiriya, though even if you've visited those sites, climbing Mulkirigala is well worth the effort, both for the temples themselves and for the magnificent panoramas out over the surrounding countryside.

Terrace one

Immediately beyond the ticket office lies **terrace one**, home to two rock temples and a small dagoba; the unusual structures standing on elephant feet outside are oil lamps dating from the beginning of the twentieth century. The temple nearest the entrance contains a reclining Buddha, plus paintings (along the side wall nearest the entrance) of Vishnu, Kataragama (by the door) and Vibhishana (the demonic blue figure with fangs), while the wall between the two doors into the first temple is decorated with pictures of *arhats* (enlightened Buddhist monks). The second cave here is one of

2

Mulkirigala's finest, with vivid Kandyan-style paintings dating back to the eighteenth-century restoration – the wall between the two doors, decorated with Jataka stories, is particularly striking.

Terraces two and three

Retrace your steps past the ticket office to reach the steep flight of steps that lead up to **terrace two**, with a single rock temple housing a reclining Buddha flanked by two disciples. Further steps lead up to **terrace three**, the most interesting section of the complex. There are four temples here, ranged side by side, with a small rock pool at the left-hand end. Immediately behind the pool is the smallest of the four temples (you have to go through the adjacent temple to reach it), the so-called **Naga** or **Cobra temple**, named after the fearsome snake painted on the door at the rear.

The next temple along sports a gaudy reclining Buddha in its inner shrine, while the third temple, known as the **Raja Mahavihara**, is Mulkirigala's finest. The vestibule, paved with old Dutch floor tiles and supported by Kandyan-style wooden pillars, contains an antique chest which was once used to hold ola-leaf manuscripts of religious and other texts. It was in this chest, in 1826, that the British official and antiquarian **George Turnour** discovered a clutch of ancient manuscripts which enabled him to translate the *Mahavamsa* (see p.396), the first time Sri Lanka's famous historical chronicle had been deciphered in the modern era. The shrine itself holds yet another sleeping Buddha, its feet intricately decorated. The fantastically kitsch final temple is home to Mulkirigala's only *parinirvana* Buddha – that is to say a dead, rather than a merely sleeping, Buddha (see p.427), surrounded by a lurid tableau of grieving figures.

Terrace four

Next to the Raja Mahavihara, steps lead up again, past a set of treacherously narrow and steep rock-cut steps to **terrace four**, at the very summit of the site. There's not much to see here, apart from two young bo saplings, both grown from cuttings taken from the famous tree at Anuradhapura, and a small dagoba at the top of the site; the main attraction is the wonderful views – scramble down the path behind the dagoba onto the open rock for an unobstructed panorama over a sea of palms.

Rekawa

4km off the coastal highway, signposted just east of the 203km post • Turtle watches nightly, starting around 8pm from the TCP hut on Rekawa beach • Rs.1000; a tuktuk from Tangalla will cost around Rs.1300

The 2km beach at **REKAWA** village, 10km east of Tangalla, is home to one of the most important **sea turtle nesting sites** in Sri Lanka, visited by five different species which lay their eggs in the sand here most nights throughout the year. The nesting sites along the beach are protected by the Turtle Conservation Project (TCP; ☏0777 810 508, ⊛tcpsrilanka.org), which conducts research into visiting turtles, pays local villagers to protect eggs from poachers and trains some as tourist guides.

Turtle watches are held nightly, with villagers keeping watch up and down the beach for their arrival – when one appears (the vast majority are green turtles), it first crawls across the beach, away from the sea, leaving behind a remarkable trail which looks as if a one-wheeled tractor has driven straight up out of the water. This takes an exhausting thirty minutes, since turtles are very badly adapted for travel on land. Having reached the top of the beach, the turtles then spend about another 45 minutes digging a huge hole; you'll hear periodic thrashings and the sound of great clouds of sand being scuffed up. As laying begins, you're allowed in close to watch, although all you actually see is the turtle's backside with eggs – looking just like ping-pong balls – periodically popping out in twos and threes. The eggs are then taken by staff to be reburied in a secure location. The turtle then rests, fills in the hole and eventually crawls back down to the sea. It's an epic effort, the sight of which makes the whole evening-long experience worthwhile.

The **best time** to see the animals is between March and June; periods when there's a full or fullish moon are also good throughout the year, because there are both more turtles and more light to see them by. Rekawa's record is apparently 23 turtles in one night, and most nights from March to June at least one will appear, though you might have to wait until around midnight for a sighting.

ACCOMMODATION — REKAWA

Buckingham Place ☎ 047 348 9447, 🌐 buckingham place.lk. Striking modern boutique resort, a stone's throw from Rekawa's turtle beach, with just eleven rooms and suites in a series of elegant cubist buildings attractively situated on a bluff above the lagoon. The cool minimalist rooms feature lots of polished stone and crisp white walls enlivened with colourful artworks and fabrics, plus sweeping lagoon views through big picture windows. There are free bikes for guests, plus canoe trips and turtle watching – although it's also rather nice just to sit and enjoy the view. Rooms $\overline{\$225}$; suites $\overline{\$295}$

Kalametiya Bird Sanctuary

Open access • Free

Roughly equidistant between Tangalla and Hambantota, the **Kalametiya Bird Sanctuary** (best Nov–March) comprises an area of coastal lagoons and mangroves, similar to that found in Bundala, and rich in marine and other birdlife. There are various entrances to the sanctuary, perhaps most conveniently from the road leading to the *Turtle Bay* resort and *AquaBeach Cabanas* (see below), both of which can organize catamaran trips on the sanctuary's picturesque **Lunama lagoon** (around Rs.2500 for up to four people).

ACCOMMODATION — KALAMETIYA

To reach the places listed below, take the turning off the main coastal highway towards the coast at Gurupokuna junction, 2km west of Hungama (signed 4km to Kalametiya; it's very close to the 214km post). Follow this road for 3km to reach a fork; the right-hand turning leads to Aqua Beach; the left-hand fork leads to *Turtle Bay*.

AquaBeach Cabanas ☎ 047 492 0554, 🌐 aqua-beach .com. Set in a sandy palm garden on an endless stretch of deserted beach, this tranquil retreat has just four simple but very comfortable wooden cabanas, plus a seawater swimming pool, yoga pavilion and regular "wellness" programmes. Half-board only $\overline{\$73}$

Turtle Bay ☎ 047 788 7853, 🌐 turtlebay.lk. Serene, classy new boutique hotel in an idyllic, picture-perfect setting on Kalametiya beach, with sweeping coastal views and a very peaceful, Robinson Crusoe ambience. There are just seven rooms with almost all mod-cons (but no TVs), kitted out with suave modern wooden decor, plus a small garden and neat little pool almost lapping against the beach. Turtles can often be spotted on the beach here during season (Nov–April), and it's just 5min walk to Kalametiya Bird Sanctuary – staff can arrange boat trips through the reserve. B&B $\overline{\$200}$

Hambantota

The area dividing Tangalla and Hambantota marks the transition between Sri Lanka's wet and dry zones, where the lush palm forests of the southwest give way to the arid and scrub-covered savannah that characterizes much of the island. Some 53km east of Tangalla, the dusty provincial capital of **HAMBANTOTA** is the unlikely beneficiary of a remarkable economic regeneration programme sponsored by President Mahinda Rajapakse (who hails from the town) focused around the construction of the island's second international airport and the dredging of a huge new Chinese-sponsored port, along with other projects. The opening of the new airport in late 2012 or early 2013 is likely to bring significant changes to Hambantota, although for the time being it remains an indomitably sleepy little place with little obvious tourist potential except perhaps as an alternative base to Tissamaharama from which to visit Bundala or Yala national parks, or a smattering of other nearby attractions.

A MALAY ENCLAVE

Hambantota was originally settled by Malay seafarers (the name is a corruption of "Sampan-tota", or "Sampan Port", alluding to the type of boat in which they arrived) and the town still has the largest concentration of **Malay-descended people** in Sri Lanka, with a correspondingly high proportion of Muslims and mosques – you really notice the call to prayer here. A few inhabitants still speak Malay, and although you probably won't notice this, you're likely to be struck by the occasional local face with pure Southeast Asian features.

Hambantota is the **salt** capital of Sri Lanka. Salt is produced by letting seawater into the **lewayas**, the sometimes dazzlingly white saltpans which surround the town, and allowing it to evaporate, after which the residue is scraped up and sold.

The fish market and harbour

Hambantota's modest attractions are easily covered in an hour's walk. Starting from the lively **fish market** opposite the bus station, follow the coastal road south, edging the pretty breakwater-fringed **harbour**. The views over the beach, usually lined with colourful fishing boats, and along the coast to the grand, saw-tooth hills around Kataragama away in the distance are magnificent, though the beach itself is scruffy, and strong currents make swimming dangerous.

Old Hambantota

Beyond the harbour, the road meanders around the headland to the attractive old *Rest House*, at the centre of a time-warped little cluster of government buildings and crumbling old villas which is all that survives of colonial Hambantota. The buildings here were formerly home to Hambantota's British government agents, among them **Leonard Woolf**, future husband of Virginia, who spent several years here in the pay of the Ceylon Civil Service – his name is recorded on a board outside the District Secretariat – before returning to England, where following his marriage he published the classic *The Village in the Jungle*, an extraordinarily depressing tale of life in the Sri Lankan backlands.

Nearby sits a neglected old British **Martello tower**, and a black-and-white-striped **lighthouse**. A small plaque by the Martello tower commemorates the laying of the foundation stone for a proposed Fisheries Museum in 1999 by current Sri Lankan president Mahinda Rajapakse (then Minister of Fisheries and Aquatic Resources), although the museum itself has failed singularly to get built.

ARRIVAL AND DEPARTURE   HAMBANTOTA

By bus Buses stop at the terminal right in the middle of town. There are branches of Hatton National Bank, just up from the harbour on Main St, and the People's Bank, opposite the *Rest House*.
Destinations Colombo (every 15min; 6hr); Galle (every

15min; 3hr 30min); Embilipitiya (1hr 30min); Matara (every 15min; 2hr 30min); Tangalla (every 15min; 1hr 30min); Tissamaharama (every 15min; 45min–1hr); Weligama (every 15min; 3hr).

ACCOMMODATION

Peacock Beach Hotel 1km along the road to Tissa ☎047 567 1000, ⍟peacockbeachonline.com. Hambantota's most upmarket option, set behind luxuriant gardens on a rather wild stretch of beach (not safe for swimming) with a pool tucked to one side. Accommodation (all with a/c and satellite TV) comprises a mix of older standard rooms and much nicer deluxe rooms. Local tours

are run in an open-top double-decker bus, and they can arrange jeeps to Bundala (Rs.4500) and Yala (Rs.8000). $95; deluxe $115
★ **Rest House** Murray Rd ☎047 222 0299. Fine old rest house, brimful of colonial character and superbly located on a headland overlooking the harbour, with views of the parched coastline and distant hills from the

lovely veranda. Rooms in the atmospheric old wing (with a/c and hot water) are huge and stuffed full of creaking old furniture; cheaper fan rooms in the "new" wing are much less characterful, but still neat and extremely comfortable. Superb value at current rates. **Rs.1845**; a/c **Rs.3000**

EATING AND DRINKING

Hambantota is not awash with places to eat. For a **drink**, try the breezy, rattan-clad *Lihiniya Bar* at the *Peacock Beach Hotel* (daily 10am–midnight).

Jade Green Opposite the Peacock Beach Hotel ☎ 047 222 0692. Pleasant modern restaurant offering assorted Sri Lankan and western breakfasts and snacks, plus the usual seafood and pseudo-Chinese mains (Rs.500–700) and an above-average lunchtime rice and curry buffet (Rs.550). Daily 7am–10pm.

Kuma Restaurant First floor, vegetable market, just south of the bus stand. Cavernous local restaurant offering all the usual fried Sri Lankan standards at bargain

prices (mains around Rs.200–400). The breezy outdoor terrace is great for watching the goings-on in the fishing harbour below. Daily 8.30am–10pm.

Rest House Murray Rd ☎ 047 222 0299. The attractive colonial-style dining room at Hambantota's time-warped *Rest House* is the prettiest spot in town for lunch or dinner, with a short menu featuring the usual array of rice and curry and other Sri Lankan standards. Mains Rs.400–600. Daily 7am–10pm.

DIRECTORY

Banks Several banks along or just off the main road have ATMs accepting foreign cards.

Internet Hiroda Communications (8.30am–8pm;

Rs.50/hr) on Bazaar St, one block along Main St from the bus stand.

Bundala National Park

Accessed around 15km east of Hambantota (and a similar distance west of Tissa), **Bundala National Park** is one of Sri Lanka's foremost destinations for **birdwatchers**, protecting an important area of coastal wetland famous for its abundant aquatic (and other) birdlife, as well as being home to significant populations of elephants, crocodiles, turtles and other fauna. Although it doesn't have quite the range of wildlife or scenery of nearby Yala National Park, Bundala is much quieter, and makes a good alternative if you want to avoid Yala's crowds.

The park stretches along the coast for around 20km, enclosing five shallow and brackish **lagoons**, or *lewayas* (they sometimes dry up completely during long periods of drought) separated by thick low scrubby forest running down to coastal dunes. Almost two hundred bird species have been recorded here, their numbers swelled by seasonal visitors, who arrive between September and March. The lagoons attract an amazing variety of **aquatic birds**, including ibis, pelicans, painted storks, egrets and spoonbills, though the most famous visitors are the huge flocks of **greater flamingoes**. The Bundala area is the flamingoes' last refuge in southern Sri Lanka, and you can see them here in variable numbers throughout the year; their exact breeding habits remain a mystery, though it's thought they migrate from the Rann of Kutch in northern India. Flamingoes apart, the park's most visible avian residents are its many **peacocks** (or Indian peafowl, as they're correctly known): a memorable sight in the wild at any time, especially when seen perched sententiously among the upper branches of the park's innumerable skeletal *palu* (rosewood) trees.

Bundala is also home to 32 species of **mammals**, including civets, mongooses, wild pigs and giant Indian palm squirrels, as well as black-naped hares, though the most commonly seen mammals are the excitable troupes of grey langur **monkeys**. There are also a few **elephants**, including around ten permanent residents and some twenty semi-resident; larger seasonal migratory herds of up to sixty, comprising animals that roam the Yala, Uda Walawe and Bundala area, also visit the park. All five species of **turtle** (see p.435) lay their eggs on the park's beaches, although there are currently no turtle watches. You'll probably also come across large **land monitors** and lots of enormous **crocodiles**, which can be seen sunning themselves along the sides of the park's lagoons and watercourses.

The **best time to visit** is between September and March, when the migratory birds arrive; early morning is the best time of day, though the park is also rewarding in late afternoon. Take binoculars, if you have them.

2

ARRIVAL AND INFORMATION	BUNDALA NATIONAL PARK

Tours Bundala is about a 20min drive from both Hambantota and Tissa; drivers charge around $45 for a half-day jeep tour from either. Tours from Hambantota are most easily arranged through the *Peacock Beach Hotel*. See the Tissa account below

for information on tours from that town.
Opening hours Daily 6am–6pm.
Entry fee $10/person, plus the usual additional charges and taxes (see p.45).

Tissamaharama

Beyond Bundala National Park the main highway turns away from the coast towards the pleasant town of **TISSAMAHARAMA** (usually abbreviated to **Tissa**). Tissa's main attraction is as a base for trips to the nearby national parks of Yala and Bundala or the temple town of Kataragama, but it's an agreeable place in its own right, with a handful of monuments testifying to the town's important place in early Sri Lankan history when, under the name of **Mahagama**, it was one of the principal settlements of the southern province of Ruhunu. Mahagama is said to have been founded in the third century BC by a brother of the great Devanampiya Tissa (see p.396) of Anuradhapura, and later rose to prominence under **Kavan Tissa**, father of the legendary Dutugemunu (see p.324). A cluster of dagobas and an expansive tank dating from this era lend parts of Tissa a certain distinction and a sense of history which makes a pleasant change from the run-of-the-mill towns which dot much of the southern coast.

Modern Tissa is a bustling but unremarkable local commercial centre – essentially a single thoroughfare, **Main Street**, lined with banks, shops and little cafés. Refreshingly compact, the town is bounded on its northern side by a lush expanse of paddy fields, in

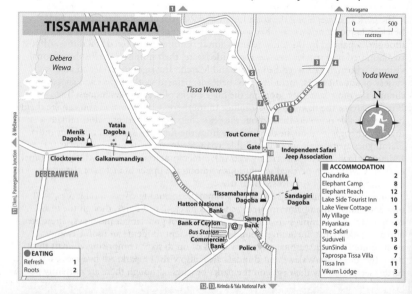

QUEEN VIHARA MAHA DEVI

Early Sinhalese history has many heroes but very few heroines – with the notable exception of the legendary **Queen Vihara Maha Devi**. According to tradition, Vihara Maha Devi's father – a certain King Tissa of Kelaniya – unjustly put to death a Buddhist monk, whereupon the waters of the ocean rose up and threatened to submerge his kingdom. The waters abated only when he sacrificed his pious and beautiful young daughter to the sea, placing her in a fragile boat and casting her off into the waves. The brave young princess, who had patiently submitted to this ordeal for the sake of her father's kingdom, was carried away around the coast and finally washed ashore in Kirinda, near Tissa. The local king, the powerful **Kavan Tissa**, came upon the delectable princess as she lay asleep in her boat, fell in love with her, and promptly married her. Their first son, **Dutugemunu** (see p.324), became one of the great heroes of early Sinhalese history.

Quite what the story of Vihara Maha Devi's sea journey symbolizes is anyone's guess (although since the 2004 tsunami the part of the story describing the catastrophic flooding of Kelaniya – which was previously regarded as a piece of colourful but entirely fanciful story-telling – has acquired a new significance and credibility). Whatever the legend's basis, it provided the Sinhalese's greatest warrior-king with a suitably auspicious parentage, and created Sri Lanka's first great matriarch in the process.

the middle of which stands the most impressive of Tissa's various dagobas, the **Tissamaharama dagoba**, allegedly built by Kavan Tissa in the second century BC and now restored to its original glory, with a "bubble"-shaped dome topped by an unusually large and lavishly decorated harmika and broad spire – a strangely squat and top-heavy-looking construction quite unlike any other dagoba in the island.

A second, much more obviously ancient dagoba, the **Sandagiri dagoba**, stands close by (currently covered in scaffolding) comprising a big, square, high brick base and a slope-shouldered dagoba in the "heap-of-paddy" shape (see p.428), although the harmika has completely vanished. The scant remains of the monastery which formerly stood here can be seen scattered hereabouts.

Tissa Wewa

About 1km north of the modern town lies the beautiful **Tissa Wewa**, an expansive artificial lake thought to have been constructed in the second or third century BC – the shore nearest the town is often busy with crowds of people bathing (including the occasional tourist) and flocks of aquatic birds including bitterns, herons and egrets skimming across the waters. A rewarding walk leads along the massive **bund** (embankment) which bounds the lake's southern shore, lined by majestic old Indian rain trees which were planted throughout the island by the British to provide shade along major trunk roads; you should be able to fix up a **boat trip** on the lake – wonderful for birdlife – along here (around Rs.750/hr). At the far end a track leads to the smaller adjacent lake of **Debera Wewa**, another haven for birdlife, its surface prettily covered in water lilies.

Yatala and Menik dagobas

From the southwest corner of the Tissa Wewa, a short walk along the road back towards the town centre brings you to two large dagobas dating back to the second century BC – each once probably formed part of a large monastery, though little now survives above ground. The first of these, the **Yatala dagoba**, is surrounded by a wall faced with sculpted elephant heads and may once have housed the Tooth Relic. There's a small and only erratically open **museum** here, containing a very modest selection of carvings and masonry rescued from local archeological sites. Continue

2

TOURS FROM TISSA

A horde of local operators offer a wide range of trips from Tissa. Easily the most popular are the half- and full-day trips to **Yala** and **Bundala national parks**, which are best started at either 5.30am or 2.30pm, to be in the parks for dawn or dusk. Some operators also offer **overnight camping trips**; these usually leave at 3.30pm and return at 10.30am the next morning and include two park drives, plus tent, dinner, breakfast and tea. Camping trips don't come cheap (at least $100/person, excluding entrance fees), although staying the night in the park gives you the chance to see nocturnal animals, including snakes, crocs, owls, wild pigs, porcupines (rare) and nocturnal birds. You can arrange similar trips to stay around the edge of the Yala, just outside the boundaries; the terrain is similar, and you might see a bit of wildlife, but by and large this is a watered-down experience compared to visiting the park itself, and costs the same (apart from not having to pay park entrance fees).

Another popular option is the half-day excursion to the rock temple at **Situlpahuwa** followed by a visit to **Kataragama** for the evening puja. The journey to Situlpahuwa passes through the fringes of Yala (though you don't have to pay the entrance fee), so you might spot some wildlife en route, but this is much less interesting than a proper trip to the main portion of the park. Some drivers also offer a combined tour of five different local **tanks**, including Tissa Wewa, Deberawewa and Wirawila Wewa, all rich in birdlife (assuming they haven't dried up, as happens frequently in periods of low rainfall). There's also a third national park nearby, **Lunugamwehera** (entered off the Wellawaya—Tissa road close to the km282 post) although this lacks the appeal of both Yala and Bundala and sees very few visitors.

TOUR OPERATORS AND PRICES

Almost all the town's guesthouses and hotels can fix up tours, though it may be marginally cheaper to organize one yourself with one of the drivers at **tout corner**, by the archway at the southeastern corner of Tissa Wewa. Tissamaharama's 170-plus strong rabble of jeep safari drivers is now loosely organized into a syndicate, the **Independent Jeep Safari Association** with an office (daily 8am–5pm; ☎047 561 7480) on the side road opposite tout corner. Obviously standards vary, but the association does contain some switched-on individuals and by going with a registered driver (who should have an ID card and a numbered badge on the side of his jeep) you should be guaranteed at least a basic level of training and English.

Prices are fixed by the Jeep Safari Association – though you might save Rs.500–1000 booking direct with a driver if business is quiet, as he can then avoid paying commission to a third party. A half-day trip to Yala or Bundala currently costs around $45 (or $55 in a "luxury" jeep with more comfortable seating), or $80 for a full day ($100 in luxury jeep), plus tip (prices are about $5 more to Lunugamwehera National Park). Other half-day trips – such as to Situlpahuwa combined with Kataragama or around five different local lakes – also cost around $45. These prices are for a jeep seating up to six or seven people, so obviously it becomes cheaper if you can get a group together.

It has been known for rogue drivers to collect the Yala entrance fee from their passengers, then to drive them around the edge of the park on the pretence that they're inside it, allowing the driver to pocket the hefty entrance fee. You should only ever hand over entrance fees at the park's visitor centre, to the relevant official.

down the road for 400m or so to reach the **Menik dagoba**. The small cluster of pillars you pass en route is all that remains of the **Galkanumandiya**, thought to be some kind of monastic building.

ARRIVAL AND DEPARTURE   TISSAMAHARAMA

By bus Tissa is a major terminus for buses travelling east along the coastal road, which stop here before heading back west (meaning that you should be able to get a seat); most are old SLTB rustbuckets; if you're heading back to Colombo, you might find it faster and more comfortable to change onto an express bus in Matara. Buses stop at the bus station in the middle of the town; a tuktuk to the guesthouses around Tissa Wewa will cost Rs.75–100. If you're staying around Tissa Wewa and going to Kataragama (every 10min; 20–30min), there's no need to go into the bus station in town; just stand on the main road here, which is also the road to Kataragama, and flag down anything that passes. Tissa is also a convenient place to head up into the hills, though to get there you may have to change buses at Pannegamuwa, a small town located on a major road intersection 5km west of Tissa, and/or at Wellawaya, from where there are plenty of buses to Ella or Haputale. There are also a few

services to Monaragala, from where you can catch a bus to Arugam Bay.

Destinations Colombo (every 15min; 7hr); Galle (every 15min; 4hr–4hr 30min); Hambantota (every 15min; 45min–1hr); Matara (every 15min; 3hr); Monaragala (5 daily; 2hr); Tangalla (every 15min; 2hr); Weligama (every 15min; 3hr 20min); Wellawaya (hourly; 2hr).

2

ACCOMMODATION

Most accommodation in Tissa is north of the town proper, in the area around the placid **Tissa Wewa**. There are also two possibilities near the small temple town of **Kirinda** (15km from Tissa, and around 12km from the entrance to Yala National Park).

TISSA WEWA

Chandrika ☎ 047 223 7143, ⓦ chandrikahotel.com. Pleasantly old-school, mid-range hotel, with comfy a/c rooms (with satellite TV and minibar) facing a pretty palm-studded garden running down to a pool (non-guests Rs.500) and rustic Ayurveda centre. **$75**

Elephant Camp Opposite the end of Court Rd ☎ 047 223 7231, ⓔ jayathunga.herath@yahoo.com. Friendly family guesthouse with five spotless tiled rooms (all with a/c and hot water) in a modern room on the main road (meaning slight traffic noise at front). Free wi-fi, with satellite TV also planned. **Rs.3300**

Lake Side Tourist Inn ☎ 047 223 7216, ⓦ tissalake sidehotel.com. Homely, old-fashioned hotel with pool and dated but comfortably furnished and well-maintained rooms (all with hot water; some with a/c and/or limited lake views). Fan **Rs.2800**; a/c **Rs.3800**

Lake View Cottage 1.5km down Court Rd ☎ 0770 471 717, ⓔ vinolitissa@gmail.com. Next to the lake in a very rural location 1.5km from town, with lovely views of the Tissamaharama dagoba across the water and five smart modern tiled rooms nicely furnished and equipped with a/c, wi-fi, satellite TV and hot water) – those upstairs are brighter and airier. **Rs.3500**

★ **My Village** ☎ 0773 500 900, ⓦ myvillagelk.com. In a peaceful setting far from the madding safari crowds, spread across two buildings each in its own intimate walled garden. The five rooms (all a/c with hot water) are smart and surprisingly stylish for the price – the three slightly more expensive rooms in the main building ($35) are particularly attractive. Free wi-fi. Excellent value at current rates. **$25**

Priyankara ☎ 047 223 7206, ⓦ priyankarahotel.com. The more affordable of Tissa's two top-end hotels, with suave and attractively furnished modern rooms with all mod-cons and private balconies overlooking the paddy fields to the rear, plus a nice pool (non-guests Rs.500, or free if you take a meal). B&B **$120**

The Safari (formerly known as the Tissamaharama Resort) ☎ 047 223 7299, ⓦ ceylonhotels.lk. Right next

to Tissa Wewa, this smartly refurbished former rest house has the most scenic position in town right above the lake and the swankiest rooms in town, with stylish modern decor and all mod-cons. There's also a good-sized pool (non-guests Rs.500). **$155**

SunSinda ☎ 047 223 9078, ⓦ hotelsunsinda.com. Smart and surprisingly inexpensive modern hotel with cheerful orangey decor and pretty rooms furnished in a kind of ethnic-minimalist style. All come with a/c, hot water and balcony (though not much of a view). There's also a large but shallow pool. **Rs.4300**

Taprospa Tissa Villa Court Rd ☎ 047 223 7287, ⓦ taprospa.com. Small, upper mid-range hotel in a superb location overlooking the lake. Rooms (all with a/c, hot water, satellite TV and minibar) are crisply decorated with bright modern decor, polished concrete floors and colourful orange tones, and there's also a chic little restaurant and a small pool. B&B **$85**

Vikum Lodge ☎ 047 223 7585 ⓔ vikumlodge@gmail .com. Tissa's most personable guesthouse, slightly out of the way, but worth the walk. Rooms (some with a/c and hot water) are slightly past their best, but spacious and well maintained, arranged around a pretty garden courtyard with a little vine-covered restaurant in the centre. **Rs.2800**, a/c **Rs.3000**

TISSA TOWN AND DEBERAWEWA

Tissa Inn Deberawewa, 1.5 km west of the Deberawewa clocktower ☎ 047 223 7233, ⓦ tissainn .lk. Pleasantly old-fashioned and good-value hotel set in sprawling gardens, with a homely, low-key atmosphere and twelve clean and comfortable rooms (some with a/c, all with satellite TV and hot water). **Rs.2300**; a/c **Rs.3000**

KIRINDA

Elephant Reach 1.5km outside Kirinda towards Tissa on road ☎ 047 567 7544, ⓦ elephantreach.com. Low-key and peaceful safari-themed resort with accommodation in mud-coloured brick chalets in the spacious gardens or rooms in the main building. All are attractively and comfortably furnished, although with spectacularly dim lighting – don't expect to get much reading done after dark. B&B: rooms $\overline{\$155}$; chalets $\overline{\$175}$

Suduveli 2km outside Kirinda towards Tissa, 200m off the main road ☎0722 631 059, ⓦbeauties-of -nature.net. Friendly and homely little guesthouse in a

very peaceful spot with accommodation either in simple rooms in the main house (a couple with shared bathroom) or in more appealing cabanas in the rambling gardens. There are free bikes for guests, motorbike rental and a free tuktuk from Tissa, plus jeep hire for Yala trips (Rs.4500/half-day). B&B. $\overline{Rs.2300}$; ensuite $\overline{Rs.3300}$; cabanas $\overline{Rs.4500}$

EATING

Refresh Kataragama Rd ☎047 223 7357. Virtually every tourist piles in at some point to the popular *Refresh*, a big, slick operation with seating under a huge open-air pavilion. The big menu majors on seafood, and there's also a good spread of pasta and pizza, plus Sri Lankan and Chinese standards and a few other international dishes. The food gets mixed reviews and is a bit pricey (mains from Rs.1000, some seafood dishes significantly more) although

the huge rice and curry spread is still one of best on the island. Daily 5am–10.30pm.

Roots Restaurant Tissa town, just off Main St. Pleasant open-air restaurant serving up a reasonable selection of cheap Chinese and Sri Lankan food (mains Rs.450–650), including all the usual suspects: simple rice and curry, devilled dishes, fried rice and noodles, plus assorted sandwiches and snacks. Daily 10am–9.30pm.

DIRECTORY

Banks Various banks along Main St have ATMs accepting foreign cards. See the map (p.184).

Internet Sakura Communications (daily 7.30am–10pm;

Rs.50/hr), next to the Commercial Bank on Main St, which also has wi-fi, and the nearby Nemasala (daily 9am–6.30pm; Rs.70/hr), also on Main St opposite the Sampath Bank.

Yala National Park

Around 20km southeast of Tissamaharama lies the entrance to **Yala National Park** (properly known as Yala West or Ruhunu National Park), Sri Lanka's most visited and most rewarding wildlife reserve. Yala covers an area of 1260 square kilometres, although four-fifths of this is designated a Strict Natural Reserve and closed to visitors. On the far side of the Strict Natural Reserve is Yala East National Park (see p.366), which is

WILDLIFE IN YALA

Yala's most famous residents are its **leopards** – the park boasts a higher concentration of these elusive felines than anywhere else in the world (block 1 of the park, the only section currently open to visitors, is thought to be home to around 60–70 animals) and sightings are reasonably common, though you'll stand a much better chance if you spend a full day in the park, which allows you to reach less touristed areas. Leopards can be seen year round, though they might be slightly easier to spot during the latter part of the dry season, when the ground vegetation dies back. Adult leopards are mainly active from dusk until dawn. Most daytime leopard sightings are of cubs and sub-adults, who are dependent on their mother for food. These confident and carefree young animals can provide hours of viewing, often showing themselves to visitors in the same spot for several days running. Much more visible are the resident **elephants**, which can usually be seen on most trips, though they can be a bit easier to spot during the dry season (May–Aug), when they congregate around the park's waterholes. Other resident **mammals** include sambar and spotted deer, wild boar, wild buffaloes, macaque and langur monkeys, sloth bears, jackals, mongooses, pangolins, porcupines, rabbits and (rare) wild cats, as well as plentiful **crocodiles**.

Yala also offers outstanding **birdwatching** year round, although from October to March visitors have the added bonus of seeing thousands of migratory species arrive to escape the northern winter. Around 130 species have been recorded here. Peacocks are ubiquitous throughout the park, while you should also spot at least a couple of jungle fowl, a singularly inelegant, waddling creature, like a feral hen, which has been adopted as the national bird of Sri Lanka.

only accessible via Arugam Bay. There's no public transport to Yala, and you're only allowed into the park in a vehicle, so you'll have to hire a jeep.

The park's dry-zone **landscape** is impressively wild and unspoilt, especially when viewed from the vantage points offered by the curious rock outcrops which dot the park. From these you can look out over a seemingly endless expanse of low scrub and trees dotted with brackish lakes next to the dune-covered coastline – particularly magical from Situlpahuwa. In addition, the park's wildlife has its own distinctive charm, with huddles of colourful painted storks perched on the edge of lagoons between the supine shapes of dozing crocodiles; fan-tailed peacocks kicking up clouds of dust while monkeys chatter in the treetops; or the incongruously conjoined sight of elephants marching sedately through the bush while rabbits scamper through the undergrowth.

Situlpahuwa and Magul Maha Vihara

Yala also has significant historic interest. The remains of extensive settlements that once dotted the area during the Ruhunu period can still be seen, most notably the monastery at **Situlpahuwa**, which may once have housed over ten thousand people and remains an important site of pilgrimage en route to nearby Kataragama. The temple comprises two rock-top dagobas separated by a small lake; there's a faded Pali inscription at the base of the first rock. The main draw, though, is the temple's lost-in-the-jungle setting and the marvellous views it affords of pretty much the entire park, with scarcely a single sign of human presence interrupting the majestic swathe of scrub and forest receding into the saw-tooth hills further away up the east coast. South of Situlpahuwa are the very modest remains of the first-century BC **Magul Maha Vihara**. Although these two temples lie within the national park, you can visit them without paying the entrance fee; combined with Kataragama, they make a good half-day excursion from Tissa.

ARRIVAL AND INFORMATION   YALA NATIONAL PARK

Visiting the park The entrance to the park is at Palatupana, 27km from Tissa (about a 45min drive), where there's a well-designed and informative visitor centre. See the "Tours from Tissa" box (p.186) for details about arranging a tour to the park.

Opening hours Daily 6am–6pm (although the park is usually closed Sept 1–Oct 15).

Entry fee $15, plus the usual additional charges and taxes (see p.45).

Park rules All vehicles entering the park are assigned an obligatory tracker. You're meant to stay inside your vehicle (except on the beach), keep your jeep's hood up, stick to roads and avoid all noise, although you are allowed to drive freely around the park, following whichever track takes your fancy.

ACCOMMODATION

Chaaya Wild Yala (formerly Yala Village) ☎047 223 9450, ⌨chaayahotels.com. If you want to stay in the countryside around the park your best option is the luxurious *Chaaya Wild Yala*, a couple of kilometres from the park entrance, which has appealing chalets equipped with all mod-cons (if you get bored of looking for elephants from the hotel's elevated observation deck) scattered around ten acres of jungle between the sea and lagoon. Nice, but overpriced at current rates. **$230**

Kataragama

Nineteen kilometres further inland from Tissa lies the small and remote town of **KATARAGAMA**, one of the three most venerated religious sites in Sri Lanka (along with Adam's Peak and the Temple of the Tooth at Kandy), held sacred by Buddhists, Hindus and Muslims alike – even Christians sometimes visit in search of divine assistance. The most important of the town's various shrines is dedicated to the god **Kataragama** (see box, p.191), a Buddhist-cum-Hindu deity who is believed to reside here.

2

Buttala & Wellawaya

KATARAGAMA

Dutugemunu Statue

Kiri Vihara

Maha Devale

Kataragama Museum

SELLAKATARAGAMA ROAD

SACRED PRECINCT

ul-Khizr Mosque

Shiva Kovil

Menik Ganga

NAGARA ST

Commercial Bank

Main Entrance

Detagamuwa Wewa

Bank of Ceylon

Hatton National Bank

Clocktower

People's Bank

Police Station

Bus Station

TISSA ROAD

PUSADEWA MAWATHA

DEPOT ROAD

SITULPAHUWA RD

HANSA MW

KAYANTISSA ROAD

DHAMMARAKKHITHA MW

SARDHATISSA MAWATHA

MAWATHA

0   200
metres

5, 6, 7 & Tissamaharama

ACCOMMODATION

CeyBank Rest	3
Chamila	5
Mandara Rosen	7
National Holiday Resort	1
Robinson	6
Sunflower	2
Sunil's Rest	4

EATING

Jayanthie Hotel	1

Kataragama is easily visited as a day-trip from Tissa, but staying the night means you can enjoy the evening puja in a leisurely manner and imbibe some of the town's backwater charm and laid-back rural pace. The town is at its busiest during the **Kataragama festival**, held around the Esala poya day in July or August. The festival is famous for the varying forms of physical mortification with which some pilgrims express their devotion to Kataragama, ranging from crawling from the river to the Maha Devale to gruesome acts of self-mutilation: some penitents pierce their cheeks or tongue with skewers; others walk across burning coals – all believe that the god will protect them from pain. During the festival devotees flock to the town from all over Sri Lanka, some walking along the various pilgrimage routes which converge on Kataragama from distant parts of the island – the most famous route, the **Pada Yatra**, leads all the way down the east coast from Jaffna, through the jungles of Yala, and is still tackled by those seeking especial religious merit. Most of today's visitors, however, come on the bus.

Kataragama town spreads out over a small grid of tranquil streets shaded by huge Indian rain trees – outside poya days and puja times, the whole place is incredibly sleepy, and its quiet streets offer a welcome alternative to the dusty mayhem that usually passes for urban life in Sri Lanka. During the **evening puja** (see box, p.192), Kataragama is magically transformed. Throngs of pilgrims descend on the Sacred Precinct, while the brightly illuminated stalls which fill the surrounding streets do a brisk trade in garlands, fruit platters and other colourful religious paraphernalia, as well as huge slabs of gelatinous oil cake and other unusual edibles.

KATARAGAMA

Perhaps no other deity in Sri Lanka embodies the bewilderingly syncretic nature of the island's Buddhist and Hindu traditions as clearly as the many-faceted **Kataragama**. The god has two very different origins. To the Buddhist Sinhalese, Kataragama is one of the four great protectors of the island. Although he began life as a rather unimportant local god, named after the town in which his shrine was located, he gained pan-Sinhalese significance during the early struggles against the South Indian Tamils, and is believed to have helped Dutugemunu (see p.324) in his long war against Elara. To the Hindu Tamils, Kataragama is equivalent to the major deity **Skanda** (also known as Murugan or Subramanian), a son of Shiva and Parvati and brother of Ganesh. Both Buddhists and Hindus have legends which tell how Kataragama came to Sri Lanka to battle against the *asuras*, or enemies of the gods. While fighting, he became enamoured of Valli Amma, the result of the union between a pious hermit and a doe, who became his second wife. Despite Kataragama's confused lineage, modern-day visitors to the shrine generally pay scant attention to the god's theological roots, simply regarding him a powerful deity capable of assisting in a wide range of practical enterprises.

Kataragama is often shown carrying a **vel**, or trident, which is also one of Shiva's principal symbols. His colour is red (devotees offer crimson garlands when they visit his shrines) and he is frequently identified with the peacock, a bird which was sacrificed to him. Thanks to his exploits, both military and amorous, he is worshipped both as a fearsome warrior and as a lover, inspiring an ecstatic devotion in his followers exemplified by the kavadi, or peacock dance (see box, p.192), and the ritual self-mutilations practised by pilgrims during the annual Kataragama festival (see opposite) – a world away from the chaste forms of worship typical of the island's Buddhist rituals.

The Sacred Precinct

The town is separated by the Menik Ganga ("Gem River") from the so-called **Sacred Precinct** to the north, an area of sylvan parkland overrun by inquisitive grey langurs and dotted with myriad shrines; pilgrims take a ritual bath in the river before entering the precinct itself. The first buildings you'll encounter are the **ul-Khizr mosque** and the adjacent **Shiva Kovil** – the former houses the tombs of saints from Kyrgyzstan and India and is the main focus of Muslim devotions in Kataragama.

Maha Devale

Walk along the main avenue, past a string of gaudy minor shrines, to reach the principal complex, the **Maha Devale**. This exhibits a quintessentially Sri Lankan intermingling of Hindu and Buddhist, with deities and iconography from each religion – trying to work out where one religion begins and the other ends is virtually impossible, and certainly not something which troubles the pilgrims who congregate here every night. The main courtyard is surrounded by an impressive wall decorated with elephant heads, and is entered through an ornate metal gate – both wall and gate are decorated with peacocks, a symbol of the god Kataragama. Inside are three main shrines. Directly opposite the entrance gate is the **principal shrine**, that of Kataragama himself – lavishly decorated, although surprisingly small. **Kataragama** himself is represented inside not by an image, but simply by his principal symbol of a *vel*, or trident. The two rather plain adjacent shrines are devoted to **Ganesh**, often invoked as an intermediary with the fearsome Shiva, and the **Buddha**.

Back towards the main entrance to the complex are two **stones** surrounded by railings, one marked by a trident, the other with a spear – supplicants bring coconuts here as offerings to Kataragama, sometimes setting fire to the coconut first, then holding it aloft while saying a prayer, before smashing it to pieces on one of the stones. It's considered inauspicious if your coconut fails to break when you throw it on the stone, which explains the concentration and determination with which pilgrims perform the ritual. North of the main enclosure stands a secondary complex of subsidiary shrines, including ones to Vishnu and to Kataragama's wife, Valli Amma.

2

THE EVENING PUJA

Kataragama's Sacred Precinct springs to life at **puja** times. Flocks of pilgrims appear bearing the fruit platters as offerings to Kataragama, and many smash coconuts in front of his shrine (see p.191). As the puja begins, a long queue of pilgrims line up to present their offerings, while a priest makes a drawn-out sequence of obeisances in front of the curtained shrine and a huge ringing of bells fills the temple. Musicians playing oboe-like *horanavas*, trumpets and drums perambulate around the complex, followed by groups of pilgrims performing the **kavadi**, or peacock dance, spinning around like dervishes while carrying kavadis, the semicircular hoops studded with peacock feathers after which the dance is named. The music is strangely jazzy, and the dancers spin with such fervour that it's not unusual to see one or two of the more enthusiastic collapsing in a dead faint on the ground. Eventually the main Kataragama shrine is opened to the waiting pilgrims, who enter to deposit their offerings and pay homage to the god, while others pray at the adjacent Buddha shrine or bo trees.

The evening puja starts at 7pm. There's another early-morning puja at around 5am (except on Sat), and a mid-morning one at around 11am, though these are pretty low-key compared to the evening ceremonies.

Next to the Maha Devale, the overpriced and only intermittently open **Kataragama Museum** (daily 8am–5pm in theory, although often closed; $5) houses various bits of religious statuary and other paraphernalia, but really isn't worth the money.

Kiri Vihara

From the rear of the Maha Devale, a road leads 500m past lines of stalls selling lotus flowers to the **Kiri Vihara**, an alternative focus for Buddhist devotions at Kataragama – it's basically just a big dagoba, its only unusual feature being the two sets of square walls which enclose it – but it's a peaceful place, surrounded by parkland and usually far less busy than the Maha Devale. A modern statue of King Dutugemunu astride his faithful elephant Kandula stands just behind.

ARRIVAL AND DEPARTURE   KATARAGAMA

By bus Kataragama is a 20min bus journey north of Tissa. The bus station is right in the centre of town on the Tissa Rd, a 5min walk south of the temples.

ACCOMMODATION

It's best to book ahead during the Kataragama festival, although at other times you shouldn't have problems finding a bed.

CeyBank Rest Tissa Rd ☎ 011 254 4315. Pleasantly old-fashioned rest house with good-value rooms – clean, quiet and spacious. It tends to fill up most weekends and holidays with Bank of Ceylon employees, but there's usually space at other times. Free wi-fi. **Rs.2200**, a/c **Rs.3400**

Chamila Tissa Rd, Detagamuwa, 1km out of town (next door to the Robinson hotel) ☎ 047 223 5294. Rather grand-looking hotel complex, although it's cheaper than you might expect, with a mix of neat, old-fashioned fan rooms and slightly smarter but less good-value a/c rooms. **Rs.2600**; a/c **Rs.3900**

★ **Mandara Rosen** Tissa Rd, Detagamuwa, 1.5km out of town ☎ 047 223 6030, ⊛ rosenhotelsrilanka .com. This smart four-star looks a bit out of place in sleepy Kataragama, but makes an excellent and affordable base from which to explore the area. Rooms (all with a/c, satellite TV and minibar) are set in a pretty building modelled on a traditional pilgrim's rest house and there's also a decent-size swimming pool (non-guests Rs.300) complete with underwater music, plus free wi-fi. **$113**

National Holiday Resort (formerly the Sulanka) Depot Rd ☎ 047 223 5227. Large but peaceful traditional rest house set around shaded gardens. Rooms have been recently renovated but preserve their old-fashioned charm. Half-board (and pure-veg food) only. **Rs.2600**; a/c **Rs.3600**

Robinson Tissa Rd, Detagamuwa, 1km out of town ☎ 047 223 5175, ✉ robinsonhotel@dialogsl.com, ⊛ infotravelsrilanka.com/robinson. Pleasant modern hotel set in shady gardens, with rather old-fashioned fan rooms and smarter a/c rooms with satellite TV, a/c and hot water. Free wi-fi. **Rs.2500**; a/c **Rs.4500**

Sunflower Depot Rd, 1km out of town ☎047 223 5611, ⓦhotelsunflowerlk.com. One of Kataragama's plusher options, with spacious and comfortable modern rooms set in neat gardens with a shallow pool (non-guests Rs.250). **Rs.3355**; a/c **Rs.4345**

Sunil's Rest Tissa Rd ☎047 567 7172, ⓔhotelsunils @gmail.com. Eight clean tiled rooms in a friendly family guesthouse – the more modern a/c rooms come with private balconies overlooking the neighbouring paddy fields. **Rs.2750**; a/c **Rs.3850**

EATING AND DRINKING

All the guesthouses do **food** (usually pure-veg only, owing to religious considerations) and there are numerous simple local places in town serving up dirt-cheap rice and curry and short eats. Note that **alcohol** is prohibited close to the Sacred Precinct: if you can't do without booze, head just outside town to the *Mandara*, *Robinson* or *Chamila* hotels, which are always happy to indulge spiritually imperfect foreign tourists.

Jayanthie Hotel Opposite the bus station (no English sign at present; it's on the right side of the Matara Hotel). Conveniently central local café offering a decent range of devilled dishes, rice and curry and fried rice dishes, including meat and fish, all for under Rs.350. Daily 8am–8pm.

DIRECTORY

Banks The ATMs at the Hatton National Bank and Bank of Ceylon, both just west of the bus station, accept foreign cards.

Information ⓦkataragama.org is an absolute treasure trove of weird and wonderful information about the shrine.

Kandy and the hill country

200 Colombo to Kandy

205 Kandy

234 East of Kandy

237 The southern hill country

ELEPHANTS BATHING IN MA OYA,
PINNEWALA ELEPHANT ORPHANAGE

Kandy and the hill country

Occupying the island's southern heartlands, the sublime green heights of the hill country are a world away from the sweltering coastal lowlands – indeed nothing encapsulates the scenic diversity of Sri Lanka as much as the short journey by road or rail from the humid urban melee of Colombo to the cool altitudes of Kandy or Nuwara Eliya. The landscape here is a beguiling mixture of nature and nurture. In places the mountainous green hills rise to surprisingly rugged and dramatic peaks; in others, the slopes are covered in carefully manicured tea gardens whose neatly trimmed lines of bushes add a toy-like quality to the landscape, while the mist and clouds which frequently blanket the hills add a further layer of mystery.

3

The hill country has been shaped by two very different historical forces. The northern portion, around the historic city of **Kandy**, was home to Sri Lanka's last independent kingdom, which survived two centuries of colonial incursions before finally falling to the British in 1815. The cultural legacy of this independent Sinhalese tradition lives on today in the city's distinctive music, dance and architecture, encapsulated by the **Temple of the Tooth**, home to the island's most revered Buddhist relic, and the exuberant **Kandy Esala Perahera**, one of Asia's most spectacular festivals.

In contrast, the character of the southern hill country is largely a product of the British colonial era, when tea was introduced to the island, an industry which continues to shape the economy and scenery of the region today. At the heart of the tea-growing uplands lies the town of **Nuwara Eliya**, which preserves a few quaint traces of its British colonial heritage and provides the best base for visiting the misty uplands of **Horton Plains** and **World's End**. To the south, in Uva Province, a string of small towns and villages – **Ella**, **Bandarawela** and **Haputale** – offer marvellous views and walks through the hills and tea plantations. At the southwestern corner of the hill country lies the town of **Ratnapura**, the island's gem-mining centre and a possible base for visits to the **Sinharaja** reserve, a rare and remarkable pocket of surviving tropical rainforest, **Uda Walawe National Park**, home to one of the island's largest elephant populations, and **Adam's Peak**, whose rugged summit, imprinted with what is claimed to be the Buddha's footprint, remains an object of pilgrimage for devotees of all four of the island's principal religions.

Principal trains in the hill country p.200	**Kandyan dancing and drumming** p.225
Saradiel: Sri Lanka's Robin Hood p.202	**Tours from Kandy** p.226
Animal rights and wrongs p.203	**Walking the Three-Temples Loop** p.230
Shit happens: pachyderm paper p.204	**The Veddhas** p.237
The Esala Perahera p.208	**Tea estate bungalows** p.240
The Buddha's Tooth p.212	**Spring in Nuwara Eliya** p.240
Hares in the moon p.214	**Tours from Nuwara Eliya** p.245
Maligawa Tuskers p.215	**Walking up Ella Rock** p.253
Pattini p.218	**The walk to Idalgashina** p.260
Hassles in Kandy p.220	**Saman** p.262
Meditation p.222	**Gems of Sri Lanka** p.268
Robert Knox and seventeenth-century Kandy p.224	**Birds of different feathers** p.270

TEMPLE OF THE TOOTH, KANDY

Highlights

❶ Kandy The last independent capital of the Sinhalese, hidden away amid the beautiful central highlands. **See p.205**

❷ Esala Perahera, Kandy Sri Lanka's most spectacular festival, with immense processions of drummers, dancers and richly caparisoned elephants. **See p.208**

❸ Kandyan dancing Watch lavishly costumed dancers performing to an accompaniment of explosively energetic drumming. **See p.225**

❹ Horton Plains and World's End Hike across the uplands of Horton Plains to the vertiginous

cliffs of World's End, which plunge sheer for almost a kilometre to the plains below. **See p.246**

❺ Ella The island's most beautifully situated village, with superb views and country walks. **See p.251**

❻ Adam's Peak The classic Sri Lankan pilgrimage, climbing to the summit of one of the island's most spectacular mountains. **See p.262**

❼ Sinharaja This unique tract of undisturbed tropical rainforest is a botanical treasure trove of international significance. **See p.269**

HIGHLIGHTS ARE MARKED ON THE MAP ON PP.198–199

THE HILL COUNTRY

Batticaloa

MADURU OYA
NATIONAL PARK

Polonnaruwa

Dambana

Kotabakina

Mavaragalpota

Hettipola

Mahiyangana

Wasgomuwa National Park

Hasalaka

Hanyella

A 26

Mimure

KNUCKLES
RANGE

Corbet's Gap

Looloowatte

Rangala

Knuckles
(1863m)

Teldeniya

Hunasgiriya

Victoria
Reservoir

Radenigala
Reservoir

Dambulla

Elkaduwa

Victoria
Dam

Hangurariketa

Dambulla

Matale

A 9

A 9

Katugastota

Kandy

Galaha

Pussellawa

A 5

Ramboda

Ramboda
Falls

St Clair Falls

Nuwara
Eliya

Kandi

Sita Eliya

Dohinda
Falls

Badulla

A 5

Hali Ela

Bogoda
Bridge

Ragala

Sita Amman
Temple

Kandapola

Pidurutalagala
(2555m)

A 10

Peradeniya
Botanical
Gardens

A 5

Kadugannawa
Pass

Gampola

Nawalapitiya

Dimbulla

Devon Falls

A 7

Polgahawela

A 6

Uluwankada
(Castle Rock)

Mawanella

Udamulla

A 1

Bible
Rock

Kitulgala

A 7

Pinnewala
Elephant
Orphanage

Rambukkana

Kegalle

A 21

A 21

Kurunegala

A 10

A 6

A 19

Nelundeniya

A 1

Warakapola

Dedigama

Karawanella

Avissawella

A 4

A 10

Galketigedara
Panavitiya

Methyagane

Dambadeniya

Alawwa

A 6

Ambepussa

A 1

Colombo

Colombo

Puttalam

HIGHLIGHTS
1. Kandy
2. Esala Perahera, Kandy
3. Kandyan dancing
4. Horton Plains and World's End
6. Adam's Peak
7. Sinharaja

> ## PRINCIPAL TRAINS IN THE HILL COUNTRY
>
> Note that railway timetables are subject to constant change, so it's always best to check latest departure times before travelling at the nearest station. In addition to the principal services between Kandy and Badulla listed below, there are also various local services which cover only a part of the line; again, timings change frequently – check at the nearest station. Inter-city services are marked with an asterisk (*). Note that none of the Colombo–Badulla services goes via Kandy; you'll have to catch a train to Peradeniya and pick up the train there. For services from Colombo see p.89.
>
> | | | | | | | |
> |---|---|---|---|---|---|---|
> | **Kandy** | 05.10 | 06.15* | 06.30 | 10.40 | 15.00* | 15.30 |
> | **Colombo** | 08.15 | 08.45 | 10.00 | 13.45 | 17.35 | 18.45 |
> | **Badulla** | 05.45 | 08.50 | 18.00 | | | |
> | **Nanu Oya** | 09.30 | 12.30 | 22.00 | | | |
> | **Peradeniya** | 13.02 | 16.40 | 02.10 | | | |
> | **Colombo** | 15.45 | 19.30 | 05.30 | | | |
>
> All services from Badulla call at Hatton, Haputale, Bandarawela and Ella. Journey times from Badulla are approximately 1hr to Ella, 1hr 30min to Bandarawela, 2hr to Haputale and 5hr to Hatton.

Colombo to Kandy

The 110km journey **from Colombo to Kandy** provides a neat snapshot of Sri Lanka's dramatic scenic contrasts, taking you within just three hours from sweltering coastal lowlands to cool inland hills. Many visitors make the journey **by train**, a classic rail journey (sit on the right-hand side en route to Kandy for the best views) along one of south Asia's most spectacularly engineered tracks, first opened in 1867, which weaves slowly upwards through long tunnels and along narrow ledges blasted by Victorian engineers out of solid rock, with vertiginous drops below. Despite the pleasures of the train trip, however, the journey **by road** (another legacy of British engineering skills, completed in 1825) is in many respects more spectacular, as the main highway rolls uphill and down, before making the final, engine-busting climb up into Kandy, giving a much more immediate sense of the hills' scale and altitude than the rail line's carefully graded ascent – although the long slog through the interminable suburbs of Colombo and Kandy is a drag.

East from Colombo

Heading inland from Colombo along the Kandy road, the urban sprawl continues for the best part of 25km until you pass the turn-off to the large town of Gampaha. Beyond here, a series of roadside settlements exemplify the continuing tendency for Sri Lankan villages (especially in the Kandyan region) to specialize in a particular craft or crop. These include, in order, **Belummahara** (pineapples, stacked up in neat racks by the roadside), **Nittambuwa** (rambutans, when in season), **Cadjugama** (cashew nuts) and **Radawaduna** (cane furniture). Cadjugama, in particular, attracts a steady trade from passing tourists, who stop to sample the cashew nuts, which are collected wild in the nearby jungle and sold by ladies along the road; prices are surprisingly high.

Dedigama

Some 5km beyond Cadjugama, around the village of **Warakapola** (roughly at the midway point between Colombo and Kandy), the appearance of steep-sided, forest-covered hills marks the gradual beginnings of the hill country. A few kilometres beyond Warakapola, at Nelundeniya, a side road from the main highway heads 4km south through a verdant landscape of rubber trees, paddy fields and banana palms to the sleepy village of **DEDIGAMA**. The village was formerly the capital of the semi-autonomous southern kingdom of **Dakkinadesa** and served as one of the island's capitals for a decade or so during the reigns of the brothers Bhuvanekabahu IV (1341–51) and Parakramabahu V (1344–59), who ruled simultaneously from Dedigama and Gampola, although sources disagree on which king reigned from which city. (A pillar inscription erected by Bhuvanekabahu can be found in the grounds of the modern Kota Vihara temple in the middle of the village, though its substance – the pardoning of a rebellion – suggests how slight his hold on power actually was.) The place is better known, however, for its associations with **Parakramabahu the Great** (see p.309), king of Polonnaruwa, who was born here and who later succeeded to the throne of Dakkinadesa – although he quickly hot-footed it off to Panduwas Nuwara, where he established a new capital before launching his bid for islandwide power.

Suthighara Cetiya and Dedigama Museum

Museum Daily except Tues 8am–4pm • Donation

Parakramabahu is popularly credited with having created Dedigama's major sight, the huge **Suthighara Cetiya**, just past the Kota Vihara, whose impressive remains – comprising the huge base and lower portion of a dagoba on a high, three-tiered base – seem totally out of scale with the tiny modern-day village.

Next to the dagoba, the **Dedigama Museum** contains a cache of objects recovered from the dagoba's relic chamber, and that of a second, but now vanished, dagoba, including a fine sequence of tiny and delicately carved gold-plated Buddhas and an unusual elephant-topped oil lamp. There are also full-size models of the dagoba's upper and lower relic chambers, and a model of the *yantragala* (relic tray) which was once filled with the semi-precious stones and crystal reliquaries.

Dambadeniya

A detour can be made by heading north from Warakapola to a former seat of Sinhalese power, some 10km north of the highway at the village of **DAMBADENIYA**, the first of the short-lived Sinhalese capitals that were established following the fall of Polonnaruwa. The new capital was founded by **Vijayabahu III** (1232–36) and also served as the seat of his son, **Parakramabahu II** (1236–70), whose long reign saw a brief renaissance in Sinhalese political power. Parakramabahu II succeeded in expelling the Indian invader Magha with Pandyan help, and his forces reoccupied the shattered cities of Anuradhapura and Polonnaruwa, though this purely symbolic victory was followed by further turmoil, and his son, Vijayabahu IV (1270–72), lasted only two years before being assassinated by Bhuvanekabahu, who moved the capital to Yapahuwa.

Vijayasundara Vihara

The main attraction in Dambadeniya is the rambling **Vijayasundara Vihara** ("Beautiful Vijaya Temple", named in honour of Vijayabahu III, who founded it), a rough-and-ready structure supported by rudimentary stone columns covered in spots of moss. The attractively rustic central shrine formerly housed the island's famous Tooth Relic, which was kept in a room on the upper storey, its exterior walls decorated with faded paintings under sections of cut-away plaster.

Inside, Kandyan-era strip paintings show various scenes including the Tooth Relic procession and a vivid depiction of the Jataka story of King Dhamsonda, in which the Buddha, in a previous incarnation, can be seen jumping into the mouth of a hungry demon to assuage its hunger. Fragments of very ancient stone carvings, probably dating back to the thirteenth century, are scattered around the temple, including some old guardstones. A statue, said to be of Parakramabahu II, stands on the far side of the complex.

The Royal Palace

A couple of minutes' drive from the Vijayasundara Vihara, the remains of Dambadeniya's **Royal Palace** sit atop a large granite outcrop dotted with rock-cut pools and approached

3

by a fine stone staircase. Not much remains of the palace itself, bar some simple brick foundations, although the setting, surrounded by bird-filled jungle, is atmospheric.

Panavitiya

A few kilometres north of Dambadeniya, the village of **PANAVITIYA** is home to an interesting little **ambalama** (rest house), built to provide shelter for travellers along the road (this was the old highway to Anuradhapura). The tiny but intricately carved rosewood structure is richly decorated with assorted Kandyan-style carvings, similar to those found at the Embekke Devale and Padeniya Raja Mahavihara, including a mahout with elephant and stick, wrestlers, dancers and drummers, demons, coiled snakes, peacocks and many other human and animal figures, framed in decorative bands of lotus rosettes and coiled rope motifs. Unfortunately, termites have gobbled up significant chunks of the original wood, which accounts for the clumsy lumps of filler which hold parts of the structure together.

The turn-off to Panavitiya is in the village of **Metiyagane**: from here, turn north along Panavitiya Danggolla Road for around 2km, then turn left at the black archeological department sign to Panavitiya. The *ambalama* is a few hundred metres further along.

West from Kegalle to Kandy

The main highway from Colombo to Kandy climbs steeply to reach the bustling town of **KEGALLE**, crammed into a single hectic main street along the side of an elevated ridge – the top of the town's cute yellow clocktower is said to be modelled on the hat of a British governor.

Just beyond Kegalle, and some 40km west of Kandy, a turn-off heads to the **Pinnewala Elephant Orphanage** (see opposite) and the **Millennium Elephant Foundation** (see p.204) beyond which are immediate views of the dramatically steep and densely forested mountain of **Utuwankanda** (also known by its British name of Castle Rock), the former stronghold of the infamous robber **Saradiel** (see box below). The road then climbs steeply again, giving increasingly grand views of craggy, densely wooded hills, including the prominent, flat-topped **Bible Rock** to the right, which acquired its pious name thanks to dutiful local Victorians on account of its alleged resemblance to a lectern.

Past Bible Rock the road enters **Mawanella**, beyond which are more spice gardens and another steep climb as the road hairpins ever upwards, with increasingly spectacular views, to the top at the famous viewpoint at **Kadugannawa Pass**, the most dramatic point along the highway, with spectacular views of Bible Rock and surrounding peaks – a

---

SARADIEL: SRI LANKA'S ROBIN HOOD

The spectacular rock-topped peak of Utuwankanda is famous in local legend as the hideout of the Sri Lankan folk hero, **Deekirikevage Saradiel** (or Sardiel), who terrorized traffic on the main Kandy to Colombo highway throughout the 1850s and early 1860s, and whose exploits in fleecing the rich while succouring the poor have provoked inevitable comparisons with Robin Hood, whose flowing locks and predilection for remote forest hideouts Saradiel shared.

Based in the impenetrable jungle around Utuwankanda, Saradiel's gang waylaid carriages, regularly disrupting traffic on the Kandy road and forcing the British authorities into a massive manhunt to track down the elusive bandit. Saradiel was eventually lured to Mawanella and captured by a detachment of the Ceylon Rifles following a shoot-out, during which his companion, Mammalay Marikkar, had shot dead a certain Constable Shaban, the first Sri Lankan police officer to die in action – an event still commemorated annually by the island's police. Saradiel and Marikkar were taken to Kandy, sentenced to death, and hanged on May 7, 1864. Thousands thronged the streets of the city to catch a glimpse of the notorious criminal, but were surprised to see a slim and pleasant-looking figure rather than the ferocious-looking highwayman they had expected – a police statement described him as just 5ft 3in tall, with long hair and hazel eyes.

panorama which brings home the ruggedness and scale of the hill country terrain and makes you realize why the Kingdom of Kandy was able to hold out against European invaders for so long. The road up cuts through a short rock-hewn tunnel before reaching the top of the pass, where there's an imposing monument to British engineer **W.F. Dawson** (d.1829), who oversaw the construction of the Kandy road. A bit further on you'll pass the **Highway State Museum**, a rather grand name for a collection of five old colonial-era steamrollers, plus a replica of the Bogoda Bridge, laid out along the side of the road.

Beyond Kadugannawa town the long urban sprawl leading into Kandy begins – a tediously slow journey, especially during the morning and evening rush hours. The fantastically crowded little town of Pilimatalawa follows soon after, merging also seamlessly into Kiribathgoda and then Peradeniya, home to Kandy's university and famous botanical gardens (see p.227), on the outskirts of Kandy proper.

Pinnewala Elephant Orphanage

Daily 8.30am–6pm; feeding sessions 9.15am, 1.15pm & 5pm; bath times 10am–noon & 2–5pm • Rs.2000

Due west of Kandy, situated in the rolling hills around the Ma Oya river, the **Pinnewala Elephant Orphanage** remains one of Sri Lanka's most popular tourist attractions – despite increasing concerns about the treatment of the animals kept here (see box below). First set up in 1975 to look after five orphaned baby elephants, Pinnewala's population has now grown to almost a hundred, making it home to the world's largest group of captive elephants. The animals here range in age from newborns to elderly matriarchs, and include orphaned and abandoned elephants, as well as those injured in the wild (often in conflicts with farmers); famous residents include the three-legged Sama, who stood on a land mine, and the blind Raja (the orphanage's oldest elephant, aged almost seventy). In addition, the orphanage's population is constantly augmented by new arrivals born in captivity: one or two elephants are born here every year, and the babies here are without doubt the tiniest and cutest you're ever likely to see.

It's best to time your visit to coincide with one of the three daily **feeding sessions**, an entertaining sight as the older elephants stuff their faces with trunkloads of palm leaves, while youngsters guzzle enormous quantities of milk out of oversized baby bottles (for Rs.250, you can feed an elephant one bottle of milk yourself). Twice a day the elephants are driven across the road to the Ma Oya river for a leisurely bath – you can observe their antics from the riverbank or, in greater comfort and for the price of an expensive drink, from the terraces of the *Pinnalanda* or *Elephant Park Hotel* restaurants above the river.

ARRIVAL AND DEPARTURE   **PINNEWALA**

Pinnewala is on a side road a few kilometres north of the road between Colombo and Kandy, just to the east of Kegalle, near the 82km post. With your own vehicle the journey should take around an hour, or perhaps slightly less depending on

---

ANIMAL RIGHTS AND WRONGS

Sadly, despite its original, and very laudable, aims, increasing concerns have been raised over the past few years about the treatment of Pinnewala's resident elephants, including repeated allegations of systematic **animal cruelty** – many visitors feel that Pinnewala is now not so much an orphanage as a zoo (or circus) in which the money-grubbing antics of the resident mahouts completely overshadow the welfare of the increasingly malnourished and mistreated elephants they are supposed to be caring for. Various malpractices have been described, including the inappropriate chaining of elephants and excessive use of the elephant goad (*ankus*), the hooked metal tool used to train and control elephants – in 2011 one of the orphanage's largest male elephants died after apparently being repeatedly stabbed with an *ankus*. Serious concerns have also been raised about the practice of donating elephants from the orphanage to various temples and other organizations or individuals, with a large proportion of donated elephants, it is alleged, being abused, and sometimes dying, after their transfer into private ownership.

traffic. The orphanage can also be visited from **Colombo**: take one of the regular buses from the Bastian Mawatha terminal to Kegalle, or a train from Fort Railway Station to Rambukkana (around 5 daily from Colombo; 2hr 30min). From **Negombo**, a day-trip to the orphanage by taxi will cost around $50.

By taxi/tuktuk The return trip by taxi from Kandy costs around $25–30. It's also possible to get a tuktuk from Kandy (around $20), though it's a smelly and uncomfortable ride, and not worth the small saving.

By bus Take a service from the Goods Shed terminal towards Kegalle (every 15min; 1hr) and get off at Udamulla, a few kilometres before Kegalle. From here, catch a bus for Rambukkana and get off at Pinnewala (every 20min; 10min) or catch a tuktuk (around Rs.250, but make sure they don't take you to the Millennium Elephant Foundation instead.

By train Catch a service to Rambukkana (served by slow trains from Kandy to Colombo, approximately 5 daily; 1hr 40min), 3km from the orphanage, from where you can either hop on a bus or take a tuktuk.

ACCOMMODATION

Elephant Bay ☎035 226 5731, ⓦhotelelephantbay .com. Large modern hotel close to the main elephant bathing spot, with comfortable and well-equipped (if rather bland) modern rooms, most with river views. B&B **$59**

Elephant Park ☎035 226 6171, ⓦpinnalanda.com. The nicest option in the village, in an unbeatable riverside location. Rooms (all a/c and with hot water) are comfortable and modern, and some also have beautiful river views right above the elephant bathing spot. **Rs.4600**

Greenland Guest House ☎035 226 5668, ⓔpinnawala@msn.com. The cheapest place in the village, tucked away on the side road leading to the elephant bathing spot, and with a range of slightly spartan fan rooms and fancier a/c rooms with wi-fi and TV. **Rs.1800**; a/c **Rs.3200**

Ralidiya Hotel ☎035 226 5321, ⓦhotelralidiya.com. On the main road through the village, this place is aimed mainly at local wedding parties, but also has a handful of comfortable, river-facing a/c rooms. **Rs.4500**

SHOPPING

Numerous **handicraft shops** are found around the village (especially along the road leading from the orphanage to the river), with a wide range of stock, including leather goods and elephant paper (which is also sold at the orphanage) – see box below. There are also heaps of **spice gardens** en route to Pinnewala.

DIRECTORY

Bank The ATM at the Hatton National Bank in the village accepts foreign Visa and MasterCards.

The Millennium Elephant Foundation

Daily 7.30am–5.30pm • Rs.600 • ⓦ millenniumelephantfoundation.com

A few kilometres down the road from Pinnewala towards Kandy, the **Millennium Elephant Foundation** (also known as the "Elephant Bath"); has a rather more didactic aim than Pinnewala – indeed the two places complement one another rather neatly. With the exception of the young Pooja, who was born at the foundation in 1986 (the only birth here to date), the eight or so elephants here are all former working animals

---

SHIT HAPPENS: PACHYDERM PAPER

One of the most novel wildlife initiatives in Sri Lanka in recent years has been the invention of **pachyderm paper**: paper made from elephant dung. As well as their many remarkable abilities, elephants are also a kind of paper factory on legs. During feeding, they ingest a huge amount of fibre which is then pulped in the stomach and delivered in fresh dollops of dung, ready prepared for the manufacture of paper. The dung is dried in the sun and boiled, and the resultant pulp used to make high-quality stationery. The texture and colour vary according to the elephants' diet, while other ingredients including tea, flowers, paddy husks and onion peel are also added according to the required finish. More than just a novelty stationery item, pachyderm paper could prove an important source of income to locals – and thus a significant help in conservation measures.

You can see the paper being made and buy a range of pachyderm paper products at the **Pinnewala Elephant Dung Paper Products** factory, on the side road to the elephant bathing spot near *Greenland Guesthouse*. Elephant paper is also available at the small shop by the elephant bathing spot, at the Millennium Elephant Foundation (see above) or online at ⓦpaperhigh.com.

given to the foundation either because of ill health, injury or because their owners could no longer afford to look after them. The foundation's guides will tell you everything you need to know about elephants and demonstrate how they are trained to work, and there's also a range of packages (from Rs.2000 for 30min) allowing you to feed, clean and ride the elephants. You can also sign up to do voluntary work with the foundation's mobile veterinary unit – see the website for details. The foundation was also instrumental in introducing pachyderm paper (see opposite) to the Sri Lankan market.

The small **museum** here is full of elephant skulls and (remarkably heavy) bones, along with a few poster displays.

Kandy

Hidden away amid precipitous green hills at the heart of the island, **KANDY** is Sri Lanka's second city and undisputed cultural capital of the island, home to the **Temple of the Tooth**, the country's most important religious shrine, and the **Esala Perahera,** its most exuberant festival. The last independent bastion of the Sinhalese, the Kingdom of Kandy clung onto its freedom long after the rest of the island had fallen to the Portuguese and Dutch, preserving its own unique customs and culture which live on today in the city's unique music, dance and architecture. The city maintains a somewhat aristocratic air, with its graceful old Kandyan and colonial buildings, scenic highland setting and pleasantly temperate climate. And although modern Kandy has begun to sprawl considerably, the twisted topography of the surrounding hills and the lake at its centre ensure that the city hasn't yet overwhelmed its scenic setting, and preserves at its heart a modest grid of narrow, low-rise streets which, despite the crowds of people and traffic, retains a surprisingly small-town atmosphere.

Brief history

Kandy owes its existence to its remote and easily defensible location amid the steep, jungle-swathed hills at the centre of the island. The origins of the city date back to the early thirteenth century, during the period following the collapse of Polonnaruwa, when the Sinhalese people drifted gradually southwards (see p.400). During this migration, a short-lived capital was established at Gampola, just south of Kandy, before the ruling dynasty moved on to Kotte, near present-day Colombo.

A few nobles left behind in Gampola soon asserted their independence, and subsequently moved their base to the still more remote and easily defensible town of **Senkadagala** during the reign of Wickramabahu III of Gampola (1357–74). Senkadagala subsequently became known by the sweet-sounding name of **Kandy**, after Kanda Uda Pasrata, the Sinhalese name for the mountainous district in which it lay (although from the eighteenth century, the Sinhalese often referred to the city as Maha Nuwara, the "Great City", a name by which it's still sometimes known today).

The rise of the Kandyan kingdom

By the time the Portuguese arrived in Sri Lanka in 1505, Kandy had established itself as the capital of one of the island's three main kingdoms (along with Kotte and Jaffna) under the rule of Sena Sammatha Wickramabahu (1473–1511), a member of the Kotte royal family who ruled Kandy as a semi-independent state. The Portuguese swiftly turned their attentions to Kandy, though their first expedition against the city ended in failure when the puppet ruler they placed on the throne was ousted by the formidable **Vimala Dharma Suriya**, the first of many Kandyan rulers who tenaciously resisted the European invaders. As the remainder of the island fell to the Portuguese (and subsequently the Dutch), the Kandyan kingdom clung stubbornly to its independence, remaining a secretive and inward-looking place, protected by its own inaccessibility – Kandyan kings repeatedly issued orders prohibiting the construction of bridges or the

3

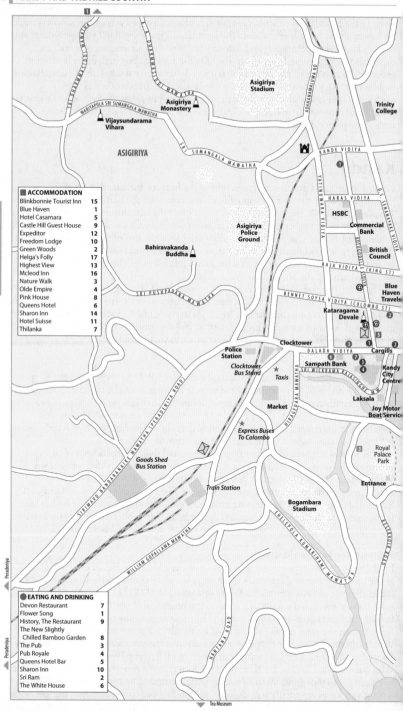

Asigiriya Stadium

Trinity College

Asigiriya Monastery

Vijaysundarama Vihara

ASIGIRIYA

KANDE VIDIYA

HARAS VIDIYA

HSBC

Commercial Bank

Asigiriya Police Ground

British Council

RAJA VIDIYA (KING ST)

Bahiravakanda Buddha

Blue Haven Travels

BENNET SOYSA VIDIYA (COLOMBO ST)

SRI PUSHPADANA MAWATHA

Kataragama Devale

Clocktower

Cargills

Police Station

DALADA VIDIYA

Clocktower Bus Stand

Sampath Bank

★ **Taxis**

Kandy City Centre

Market

Laksala

Joy Motor Boat Service

★ **Express Buses To Colombo**

Royal Palace Park

Goods Shed Bus Station

Entrance

Train Station

Bogambara Stadium

■ ACCOMMODATION	
Blinkbonnie Tourist Inn	15
Blue Haven	1
Hotel Casamara	5
Castle Hill Guest House	9
Expeditor	12
Freedom Lodge	10
Green Woods	2
Helga's Folly	17
Highest View	13
Mcleod Inn	16
Nature Walk	3
Olde Empire	4
Pink House	8
Queens Hotel	6
Sharon Inn	14
Hotel Suisse	11
Thilanka	7

● EATING AND DRINKING	
Devon Restaurant	7
Flower Song	1
History, The Restaurant	9
The New Slightly Chilled Bamboo Garden	8
The Pub	3
Pub Royale	4
Queens Hotel Bar	5
Sharon Inn	10
Sri Ram	2
The White House	6

Peradeniya

Peradeniya

Tea Museum

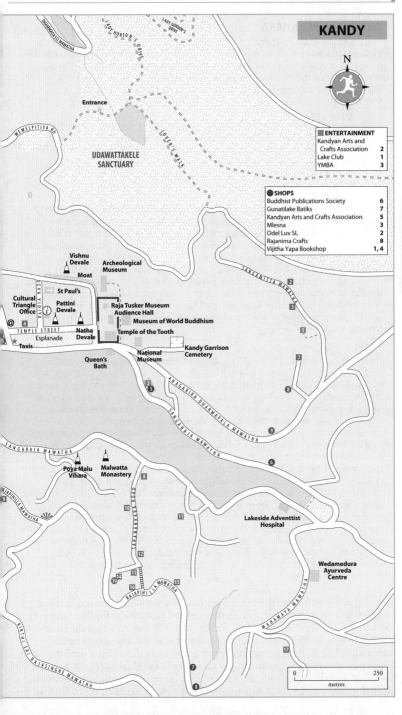

KANDY

N

■ ENTERTAINMENT
Kandyan Arts and	
Crafts Association	2
Lake Club	1
YMBA	3

● SHOPS
Buddhist Publications Society	6
Gunatilake Batiks	7
Kandyan Arts and Crafts Association	5
Mlesna	3
Odel Luv SL	2
Rajanima Crafts	8
Vijitha Yapa Bookshop	1, 4

3

LADY HORTON'S DRIVE

DHAMMASSI MAWATHA

LADY GORDON'S DRIVE

Entrance

WEWELPITIYA RD

LOVER'S WALK

UDAWATTAKELE SANCTUARY

Vishnu Devale

Archeological Museum

Moat

St Paul's

DEVA VIDIYA

Cultural Triangle Office

Pattini Devale

Raja Tusker Museum
Audience Hall

Museum of World Buddhism

SANGAMITTA MAWATHA

TEMPLE STREET

Esplanade

Natha Devale

Temple of the Tooth

@

Taxis

Queen's Bath

National Museum

Kandy Garrison Cemetery

ANAGARIKA DHARMAPALA MAWATHA

SANGARAJA MAWATHA

SANGARAJA MAWATHA

Poya Malu Vihara

Malwatta Monastery

Lakeside Adventtist Hospital

YAPINILLA MAWATHA

Wedamedura Ayurveda Centre

RAJAPIHILLA MAWATHA

MAHAMAYA MAWATHA

KIRTHI SRI RAJASINGHE MAWATHA

0   250
metres

3

THE ESALA PERAHERA

Kandy's ten-day **Esala Perahera** is the most spectacular of Sri Lanka's festivals, and one of the most colourful religious pageants in Asia. Its origins date back to the arrival of the **Tooth Relic** (see p.212) in Sri Lanka in the fourth century AD, during the reign of Kirti Siri Meghawanna, who decreed that the relic be carried in procession through the city once a year. This quickly developed into a major religious event – the famous Chinese Buddhist Fa-Hsien, visiting Anuradhapura in 399 AD, described what had already become a splendid festival, with processions of jewel-encrusted elephants.

Occasional literary and artistic references suggest that these celebrations continued in some form throughout the thousand years of upheaval which followed the collapse of Anuradhapura and the Tooth Relic's peripatetic journey around the island. Esala processions continued into the Kandyan era in the seventeenth century, though the Tooth Relic lost its place in the procession, which evolved into a series of lavish parades in honour of the city's four principal deities: Vishnu, Kataragama, Natha and Pattini, each of whom had (and still has) a temple in the city.

The festival took shape in 1775, during the reign of **Kirti Sri Rajasinha**, when a group of visiting Thai clerics expressed their displeasure at the lack of reverence accorded to the Buddha during the parades. To propitiate them, the king ordered the Tooth Relic to be carried through the city at the head of the four temple processions: a pattern that endures to this day. Sri Rajasinha's own enthusiastic participation in the festivities, and that of his successors, also added a political dimension – the Nayyakar kings of Kandy (who were from South India) probably encouraged the festival in the belief that by associating themselves with one of Buddhism's most sacred relics, they would reinforce their dynasty's shaky legitimacy in the eyes of their Sinhalese subjects. The Tooth Relic itself was last carried in procession in 1848, since when it's been considered unpropitious for it to leave the temple sanctuary – its place is now taken by a replica.

THE FESTIVAL

The ten days of the festival begin with the **Kap Tree Planting Ceremony**, during which cuttings from a tree – traditionally an Esala tree, though nowadays a Jak or Rukkattana are more usually employed – are planted in the four *devales* (see p.217), representing a vow (*kap*) that the festival will be held. The procession (perahera) through the streets of Kandy is held nightly throughout the festival: the first five nights, the so-called **Kumbal Perahera**, are relatively low-key; during the final five nights, the **Randoli Perahera**, things become progressively more spectacular, building up to the last night (the Maha Perahera, or "Great Parade"), featuring a massive cast of participants including as many as a hundred brilliantly caparisoned elephants and thousands of drummers, dancers and acrobats walking on stilts, cracking whips, swinging fire pots and carrying banners, while the replica casket of the Tooth Relic itself is carried on the back of the **Maligawa Tusker** elephant (see p.215).

Following the last perahera, the **water-cutting ceremony** is held before the dawn of the next day at a venue near Kandy, during which a priest wades out into the Mahaweli Ganga and "cuts" the waters with a sword. This ceremony symbolically releases a supply of water for the coming year (the Tooth Relic is traditionally believed to protect against drought) and divides the pure from the impure – it might also relate to the exploits of the early Sri Lankan king, **Gajabahu** (reigned 114–136 AD), who is credited with the Moses-like feat of dividing the waters between Sri Lanka and India in order to march his army across during his campaign against the Cholas.

widening of footpaths into the city, fearing that they would become conduits for foreign attack. The city was repeatedly besieged and captured by the Portuguese (in 1594, 1611, 1629 and 1638) and the Dutch (in 1765), but each time the Kandyans foiled their attackers by burning the city to the ground and retreating into the surrounding forests, from where they continued to harry the invaders until they were forced to withdraw to the coast. Despite its isolation, the kingdom's prestige as the final bastion of Sinhalese independence was further enhanced during the seventeenth and eighteenth centuries by the presence of the **Tooth Relic** (see p.212), the traditional

After the water-cutting ceremony, at 3pm on the same day, there's a final **"day" perahera**, a slightly scaled-down version of the full perahera. It's not as spectacular as the real thing, though it does offer excellent photo opportunities.

THE PROCESSION

The perahera is a carefully orchestrated, quasi-theatrical event – there is no spectator participation here, although the astonishing number of performers during later nights give the impression that most of Kandy's citizens are involved. The perahera actually comprises five separate processions, which follow one another around the city streets: one from the Temple of the Tooth, and one from each of the four *devales* – a kind of giant religious conga, with elephants. The exact route changes from day to day, although the procession from the Temple of the Tooth always leads the way, followed (in unchanging order) by the processions from the Natha, Vishnu, Kataragama and Pattini *devales* (Natha, as a Buddha-to-be, takes precedence over the other divinities). As its centrepiece, each procession has an elephant carrying the insignia of the relevant temple – or, in the case of the Temple of the Tooth, the replica Tooth Relic. Each is accompanied by other elephants, various dignitaries dressed in traditional Kandyan costume and myriad dancers and drummers, who fill the streets with an extraordinary barrage of noise. The processions each follow a broadly similar pattern, although there are slight differences. The Kataragama procession – as befits that rather unruly god – tends to be the wildest and most freeform, with jazzy trumpet playing and dozens of whirling dancers carrying *kavadis*, the hooped wooden contrivances, studded with peacock feathers, which are one of that god's symbols. The Pattini procession, the only one devoted to a female deity, attracts mainly female dancers. The beginning and end of each perahera is signalled by a deafening cannon shot.

PERAHERA PRACTICALITIES

The perahera is traditionally held over the last nine days of the lunar month of Esala, finishing on Nikini poya day – this usually falls during late July and early August, though exact **dates** vary according to the vagaries of the lunar calendar. Dates can be checked on ⓦ sridaladamaligawa.lk and ⓦ daladamaligawa.org.

Accommodation during the Esala Perahera can get booked up months in advance, and prices in most places double or triple. If you get stuck for somewhere to stay, the tourist counter in the Kandy City Centre mall should be able to help you out; in addition, many locals rent out rooms during the festival.

The perahera itself begins between 8pm and 9pm. You can see the parade for free by grabbing a spot on the **pavement** next to the route. During the early days of the perahera it's relatively easy to find pavement space; during the last few nights, however, you'll have to arrive four or five hours in advance and then sit in your place without budging – even if you leave for just a minute to go to the toilet, you probably won't get your spot back. Not surprisingly, most foreigners opt to pay to reserve one of the thousands of **seats** which are set out in the windows and balconies of buildings all along the route of the perahera. On the last three or four nights seats start at $15–25 for the cheapest spots (usually on the upper floors of streetside buildings and with restricted views) and go for $50 or more for good street-level positions with unrestricted views – while the very best seats can go for considerably more than this; on earlier nights a good seat will cost $25–30. If possible, check exactly which seat you're being offered before handing over any cash, and beware of unscrupulous touts who might simply disappear with your money – it's safest to book a seat through your guesthouse or hotel.

---

symbol of Sinhalese sovereignty, while an imposing temple, the Temple of the Tooth, was constructed to house the relic.

The Nayakkar dynasty

It had long been the tradition for the kings of Kandy to take South Indian brides descended from the great Vijayanagaran dynasty, and when the last Sinhalese king of Kandy, Narendrasinha, died in 1739 without an heir, the crown passed to his Indian wife's brother, Sri Viyjaya Rajasinha (1739–47), so ending the Kandyan dynasty established by Vimala Dharma Suriya and ushering in a new Indian **Nayakkar** dynasty. The Nayakkar embraced Buddhism and cleverly played on the rivalries of the local Sinhalese nobles who, despite their dislike of the foreign rulers, failed to unite behind a single local leader. In a characteristically Kandyan paradox, it was under the foreign Nayakkar that the city enjoyed its great Buddhist revival. **Kirti Sri Rajasinha** came to the throne in 1747 and began to devote himself – whether for political or spiritual reasons – to his adopted religion, reviving religious education, restoring and building temples and overseeing the reinvention of the **Esala Perahera** (see box, p.208) as a Buddhist rather than a Hindu festival. These years saw the development of a distinctively Kandyan style of architecture and dance, a unique synthesis of local Sinhalese traditions and southern Indian styles.

Kandy under the British

Having gained control of the island in 1798, the **British** quickly attempted to rid themselves of this final remnant of Sinhalese independence, although their first expedition against the kingdom, in 1803, resulted in a humiliating defeat. Despite this initial reverse, the kingdom survived little more than a decade, though it eventually fell not through military conquest but thanks to internal opposition to the excesses and cruelties of the last king of Kandy, **Sri Wickrama Rajasinha** (ruled 1798–1815). As internal opposition to Sri Wickrama grew, the remarkable **Sir John D'Oyly** (see p.217), a British government servant with a talent for languages and intrigue, succeeded in uniting the various factions opposed to the king. In 1815, the British were able to despatch another army which, thanks to D'Oyly's machinations, was able to march on Kandy unopposed. Sri Wickrama fled, and when the British arrived, the king's long-suffering subjects simply stood to one side and let them in. On **March 2, 1815**, a convention of Kandyan chiefs signed a document handing over sovereignty of the kingdom to the British, who in return promised to preserve its laws, customs and institutions.

The colonial era and after

Within two years, however, the Kandyans had decided they had had enough of their new rulers and **rebelled**, an uprising which soon spread across the entire hill country. The British were obliged to call for troops from India and exert their full military might in order to put down the uprising. Fears of resurgent Kandyan nationalism continued to haunt the British during the following decades – it was partly the desire to be able to move troops quickly to Kandy which prompted the construction of the first road to the city in the 1820s, one of the marvels of Victorian engineering in Sri Lanka. Despite the uncertain political climate, Kandy soon developed into an important centre of British rule and trade, with the usual hotels, courthouses and churches servicing a burgeoning community of planters and traders. In 1867, the **railway** from Colombo was completed, finally transforming the once perilous trek from the coast into a comfortable four-hour journey, and so linking Kandy once and for all with the outside world.

Post-colonial Kandy has continued to expand, preserving its status as the island's second city despite remaining a modest little place compared to Colombo. It has also managed largely to avoid the Civil War conflicts which traumatized the capital, suffering only one major LTTE attack, in 1998, when a **truck bomb** was detonated outside the front of the Temple of the Tooth, killing over twenty people and reducing the front of the building to rubble.

Kiri Muhuda

Kandy's centrepiece is its large artificial **lake**, created in 1807 by Sri Wickrama Rajasinha in an area of the town previously used for paddy fields. Although nowadays considered one of Kandy's defining landmarks, at the time of its construction the lake was regarded by the city's put-upon inhabitants as a huge white elephant, and proof of their king's unbridled delusions of grandeur – a number of his subjects who objected to labouring on this apparently useless project were impaled on stakes on the bed of the lake. Rajasinha named the lake the **Kiri Muhuda**, or Milk Sea, and established a royal pleasure house on the island in the centre; the more practically minded British subsequently converted it into an ammunition store, but also added the attractive walkway and parapet that encircles the lake. Despite the traffic which blights the southern shore (especially during Kandy's anarchic rush hour), the walk round the perimeter offers memorable views of the city, with the long white lakeside parapet framing perfect reflections of the Temple of the Tooth and old colonial buildings around the *Queen's Hotel*. If you want to get out onto the water, the **Joy Motor Boat Service**, at the western end of the lake, offers fifteen-minute spins around the lake (daily 9am–6pm, Rs.1500/boat seating up to fifteen people).

The south side of the lake is dotted with assorted religious buildings. These include the **Malwatta Monastery**, with its distinctive octagonal tower, built in imitation of the Pittirippuva at the Temple of the Tooth on the opposite side of the lake. The temple is reached from the lakeside through an impressive stone arch decorated with creatures both real (lions, geese, birds) and imaginary (toranas, centaurs). A tiny circular monks' bathing house stands right by the lakeside pavement, close to the gate.

A hundred metres along the lakeside road back towards town (go up the broad steps to the building signed Sri Sangharaja Maha Pirivena) is another cluster of monastic buildings belonging to the **Poya Malu Vihara**, including an interesting square colonnaded **image house**, with a colourfully painted upper storey and a finely carved stone doorway very similar to one in the Temple of the Tooth's main shrine.

Royal Palace Park

Daily 9am–4.30pm • Rs.100

From the southwestern corner of the lake, steps ascend to the entrance to Rajapihilla Mawatha and the entrance to the modest **Royal Palace Park**, also known as Wace Park, another of Sri Wickrama Rajasinha's creations. The small ornamental gardens at the top of the park provide an unlikely setting for a Japanese howitzer, captured in Burma during World War II and presented to the city by Lord Mountbatten (who had his wartime headquarters here in the *Hotel Suisse*). Beyond the ornamental gardens, a series of terraced footpaths wind down a bluff above the lake, offering fine views of the water and Temple of the Tooth – usually chock-full of snogging couples hiding in every available corner.

There are better views over the lake and into the green ridges of hills beyond from **Rajapihilla Mawatha**, the road above the park – the classic viewpoint is from the junction of Rajapahilla Mawatha and Kirthi Sri Rajasinghe Mawatha, from where one can look down over the entire town below, laid out at one's feet as neatly as a map.

The Temple of the Tooth

Daily 5.30am–8pm • Rs.1000 (including free audioguide if you leave passport or other ID); video camera Rs.300 • Ⓦ sridaladamaligawa .lk and Ⓦ daladamaligawa.org

Posed artistically against the steep wooded hills of the Udawattekele Sanctuary, Sri Lanka's most important Buddhist shrine, the **Temple of the Tooth**, or Dalada Maligawa, sits on the lakeshore just east of the city centre. The temple houses the legendary **Buddha's Tooth** (see box, p.212), which arrived here in the sixteenth century after various peregrinations around India and Sri Lanka, although nothing remains of the original temple, built around 1600. The main shrine of the current temple was originally constructed during the reign of Vimala Dharma Suriya II (1687–1739) and was rebuilt and modified at various times afterwards, principally during the reign of Kirti Sri Rajasinha (1747–81).

It was further embellished during the reign of Sri Wickrama Rajasinha, who added the moat, gateway and Pittirippuva; the eye-catching golden roof over the relic chamber was donated by President Premadasa in 1987.

The temple was badly damaged in 1998 when the LTTE detonated a massive **truck bomb** outside the entrance, killing over twenty people and reducing the facade to rubble. Restoration work was swift and thorough, however, and there's little visible evidence left of the attack, although crash barriers now prevent vehicular access to the temple, and all visitors have to pass through stringent security checks.

Guides of varying standards hang around at the entrance; count on around Rs.500 for a thirty-minute tour; some are very informative, but check how good their English is first and always agree a price before starting. **Pujas** (lasting around 1hr) are held at 5.30am, 9.30am and 6.30pm, although the temple can get absolutely swamped with tourists during the 9am and 6.30pm pujas. The main attraction of the three pujas is the noisy drumming which precedes and accompanies the ceremony. Most of the actual ceremony is performed behind closed doors, although at the end of each puja the upstairs room housing the Tooth Relic is opened to the public gaze. You're not actually allowed into the Tooth Relic chamber, but you are permitted to file past the entrance and look inside for a cursory glance at the big gold casket containing the relic.

The Pittirippuva

The temple's exterior is classically plain: a rather austere collection of unadorned white buildings whose hipped roofs rise in tiers against the luxuriant green backcloth of the Udawattakele Sanctuary. The most eye-catching exterior feature is the octagonal tower, the **Pittirippuva**, projecting into the moat that surrounds the temple; strictly speaking, it's not part of the temple at all. Sri Wickrama Rajasinha used the upper part as a platform from which to address his people, and it's now where all new Sri Lankan heads of state give their first speech to the nation.

THE BUDDHA'S TOOTH

Legend has it that when the Buddha was cremated in 543 BC at Kushinagar in North India, various parts of his remains were rescued from the fire, including one of his **teeth**. In the fourth century AD, as Buddhism was declining in India in the face of a Hindu revival, the Tooth was smuggled into Sri Lanka, hidden (according to legend) in the hair of an Orissan princess. It was first taken to Anuradhapura, then to Polonnaruwa, Dambadeniya and Yapahuwa. In 1284, an invading Pandyan army from South India captured the Tooth and took it briefly back to India, until it was reclaimed by Parakramabahu III some four years later.

During these turbulent years the Tooth came to assume increasing political importance, being regarded not only as a unique religious relic but also as a symbol of Sri Lankan sovereignty – it was always housed by the Sinhalese kings in their capital of the moment, which explains its rather peripatetic existence. After being reclaimed by Parakramabahu III, it subsequently travelled to Kurunegala, Gampola and Kotte. In the early sixteenth century, the Portuguese captured what they claimed was the Tooth, taking it back to Goa, where it was pounded to dust, then burnt and cast into the sea (Buddhists claim either that this destroyed Tooth was simply a replica, or that the ashes of the Tooth magically reassembled themselves and flew back to Sri Lanka). The Tooth finally arrived in Kandy in 1592 and was installed in a specially constructed temple next to the palace, later becoming the focus for the mammoth Esala Perahera.

The exact nature and authenticity of the Tooth remains unclear. Bella Sidney Woolf, writing in 1914 when the Tooth was still regularly displayed to the public, described it as "a tooth of discoloured ivory at least three inches long – unlike any human tooth ever known," unconsciously echoing the sentiments of an earlier Portuguese visitor, a certain de Quezroy, who in 1597 claimed that the Tooth had actually come from a buffalo. Whatever the truth, the Tooth remains an object of supreme devotion for many Sri Lankans. Security concerns mean that it is no longer taken out on parade during the Esala Perahera, though it is put on display in the Temple of the Tooth for a couple of weeks once or twice every decade.

The Maha Vahalkada

The entrance to the temple proper is through the **Maha Vahalkada** (Great Gate), which was formerly the main entrance to the royal palace as well as the temple. Once through the gateway, further steps covered by a canopy painted with lotuses and pictures of the perahera lead up to the entrance to the temple proper, via a gorgeously carved stone door adorned complete with moonstone, guardstones and topped by a *makara torana* archway – although modern tourists are pointed to the left, through a side entrance.

The shrine

The interior of the temple is relatively modest in size, and something of an architectural hotchpotch. In front of you lies the **Drummers' Courtyard** (Hewisi Mandapaya), into which is squeezed the two-storey **main shrine** itself. The exterior of the shrine has a strangely ad hoc appearance: some portions have been lavishly embellished (the three doors, for instance), but many of the painted roundels on the walls have been left unfinished, giving the whole thing the effect in places of a job only half done – although the overall effect is still undeniably impressive.

Three doors lead into the ground floor of the shrine: the main doors are flanked by elephant tusks and made out of gorgeously decorated silver (though they're usually hidden behind a curtain except during pujas), with two intricately carved stone doors on either side. The walls are decorated with an intricate confusion of lotuses, vines and lions, and dotted with painted medallions of the **sun and moon**, a symbol of the kings of Kandy – the image of the twinned heavenly orbs representing the light-giving and the eternal nature of their rule. A quirky touch is supplied by numerous paintings of **hares** curled up inside some of the moons (see box, p.214), while the overhanging eaves are also embellished with a fine sequence of paintings. What's perhaps strangest about all this decoration, however, is its largely royal and secular content: Buddha images, in this holiest of Sri Lankan temples, are notable largely by their absence.

The Pirit Mandapa and Tooth Relic Chamber

A set of stairs to the left (as you face the main shrine) from the drummers' courtyard leads to the upper level; halfway up you'll pass the casket in which a replica of the Tooth Relic is paraded during the Esala Perahera, along with golden "flags" and umbrellas which are also used during the procession. At the top of the steps is the **Pirit Mandapa** (Recitation Hall), a rather plain space whose unusual latticed wooden walls lend it a faintly Japanese air. This leads to the entrance of the **Tooth Relic Chamber** itself, on the upper level of the main shrine. You can't actually go into the relic chamber, and the entrance is railed off (except during pujas), although you can make out some of the details of the fantastically ornate brass doorway into the shrine, framed in silver and decorated in a riot of embossed ornament, with auspicious symbols including dwarfs, some holding urns of plenty, plus entwined geese, peacocks, suns, moons and dagobas. Paintings to either side of the door show guardstone figures bearing bowls of lotuses, surmounted by *makara toranas*.

The **interior** of the Tooth Relic chamber is divided by golden arches into three sections, though the chamber is kept shut except during pujas, and even then you'll only be able to get a brief glimpse as you're hurried past the door amid the throngs of visitors. The Tooth Relic is kept in the furthest section, the **Vedahitina Maligawa** (Shrine of Abode), concealed from the public gaze in a dagoba-shaped gold casket which is said to contain a series of six further caskets, the smallest of which contains the Tooth itself.

On the far side of the Pirit Mandapa, another flight of stairs leads back down to the courtyard. Halfway down, a door leads into the diminutive interior of the **Pittirippuva** (whose exterior you will have seen on the way in) crammed with assorted Buddhist artefacts and lined with cabinets stuffed full of antique ola-leaf books including the huge, 1600-page Pansiya Panas Jathakaya containing the 550 Jataka

HARES IN THE MOON

The paintings of hares in the moon shown on the exterior of the Tooth Relic shrine refer to one of the most famous of the **Jataka** stories, describing the previous lives of the Buddha before his final incarnation and enlightenment. According to the Jataka story of the Hare in the Moon, the future Buddha was once born as a hare. One day the hare was greeted by an emaciated holy man, who begged him – along with a fox and a monkey, who also happened to be passing – for food. The fox brought a fish, the monkey some fruit, but the hare was unable to find anything for the holy man to eat apart from grass. Having no other way of assuaging the ascetic's hunger, the hare asked him to light a fire and then leapt into the flames, offering his own body as food. At this moment the holy man revealed himself as the god Indra, placing an image of the hare in the moon to commemorate its self-sacrifice, where it remains to this day.

The Jataka fable may itself be simply a local version of a still more ancient Hindu or Vedic myth – traditions referring to a hare in the moon can be found as far away as China, Central Asia and even Europe, while the story also appears, in slightly modified form, in one of the Brothers Grimm fairy tales.

3

stories narrating the past lives of the Buddha, which a sign claims to be the oldest ola-leaf book in existence.

Alut Maligawa

At the back of the Drummers' Courtyard, the **Alut Maligawa** (New Shrine Room) is a large and undistinguished building completed in 1956 to celebrate the 2500th anniversary of the Buddha's death. The interior, as if to compensate for the lack of Buddhist imagery in the main section of the temple, is filled with a glut of Buddha statues, many donated by foreign countries, which offer an opportunity to compare different Asian versions of traditional Buddhist iconography, with images from Thailand (in the middle), China, Sri Lanka, Japan, Korea and Taiwan. Beneath the central Thai image is a holographic Buddha face from France, set in a minute dagoba, which turns its head to follow you as you move around the room.

A sequence of 21 **paintings** hung around the chamber's upper walls depict the story of the Tooth Relic from the Buddha's death to the present day. The Buddhas below were a gift from Thailand to commemorate the fiftieth anniversary of Sri Lanka's independence.

Sri Dalada Museum (Tooth Relic Museum)

Entrance included in main temple ticket

On the first and second floors of the Alut Maligawa building, the **Sri Dalada Museum** (reached via the rear exit from the ground-floor shrine room) contains a medley of objects connected with the Tooth Relic and temple. The **first floor** is dominated by a sequence of large and solemn busts of all the *diyawardene nilambe* (temple chiefs) from 1814 to 1985. Other exhibits include photos of the damage caused by the 1998 bombing, fragments of murals destroyed in the blast, and a few old fabrics, including a selection of the enormous ceremonial handkerchiefs designed for the royal noses of the kings of Kandy.

The more interesting **second floor** is largely occupied by the bewildering assortment of objects offered to the Tooth Relic at various times, including several donated by former Sri Lankan presidents. The highlight is the gorgeous silk Buddha footprint which is said to have been offered to the temple in the reign of Kirti Sri Rajasinha by a visiting Thai monk on behalf of the king of Siam.

The Royal Palace and around

The Temple of the Tooth originally lay at the heart of the sprawling **Royal Palace**, a self-contained complex of buildings immediately surrounding the temple and housing various royal residences, audience chambers and associated structures. Significant sections of the original palace complex survive, although it's difficult to get a very clear sense of how it would originally have looked, thanks to the many additions and alterations made to the area since 1815.

The layout of the surviving palace buildings is rather confusing. Two of its buildings – the **Audience Hall** and **Raja Tusker Museum** – can only be reached by going through (and buying a ticket for) the Temple of the Tooth. The others, including the **National** and **Archeological museums**, are reached by walking around the outside of the temple along the lakeside (or alternatively by walking around from the Vishnu Devale).

The Audience Hall

Immediately north of the temple (and reached via a side exit from it, or from the exit from the Sri Dalada Museum) lies the imposing **Audience Hall**, an impressively complete Kandyan pavilion set on a raised stone plinth, open on all sides and sporting characteristic wooden pillars, corbels and roof, all intricately carved. The hall originally dated from 1784, though it was set on fire by the Kandyans during the British attack of 1803 – the conservation-minded British invaders obligingly put out the fire and subsequently restored the building. It was here that the Kandyan chiefs signed the treaty that handed over power to the British on March 2, 1815.

3

Raja Tusker Museum

Daily 8.30am–4.30pm • Free entrance with Temple of the Tooth ticket

Just north of the Audience Hall stands the **Raja Tusker Museum**, devoted to the memory of Sri Lanka's most famous elephant, **Raja**. The main attraction is the stuffed remains of Raja himself, now standing proudly in state in a glass cabinet. Raja died in 1988 after fifty years' loyal service as Kandy's **Maligawa Tusker** – the elephant which carries the Tooth Relic casket during the Esala Perahera. Such was the veneration in which he was held that his death prompted the government to order a day of national mourning, while the animal's remains are now an object of devotion to many Sinhalese, who come to pray at Raja's glass case. The museum also has photos of Raja in various peraheras, plus sad snaps of him surrounded by anxious vets during his last illness in 1988.

The National Museum and around

Tues–Sat 9am–5pm • Rs.500 (camera Rs.250, video camera Rs.1500)

Beyond the Queen's Bath (and immediately behind the Temple of the Tooth, though not directly accessible from it) lies the Kandy branch of the **National Museum**, set in a low white building which was formerly the Queen's Palace (or "King's Harem", as it's also described). The museum provides a rather dusty setting for a treasure trove of Kandyan traditional artefacts, with exhibits attesting to the high levels of skill achieved by local craftsmen – jewellery, fabrics, musical instruments, lacquerware and so on, plus a fine display of minutely detailed ivory objects (look for the cute figurines of various Kandyan bigwigs).

MALIGAWA TUSKERS

No single elephant has yet proved itself able to fill Raja's considerable boots, and at present the role of **Maligawa Tusker** is shared between various different elephants. All Maligawa Tuskers must fulfil certain physical requirements. Only male elephants are permitted to carry the relic and, most importantly, they must be **Sathdantha** elephants, meaning that all seven parts of their body – the four legs, trunk, penis and tail – must touch the ground when they stand upright. In addition, the elephant's tusks must be formed in the curved shape of a traditional winnow, and it must have a flat back and reach a height of around twelve feet. It has proved increasingly difficult to find such "high-caste" elephants locally, although the temple already owns several suitable beasts, including ones donated by notables including various prime ministers of Sri Lanka and India, as well as the king of Thailand.

Notable exhibits include the superb golden crown of Rajasingha II (1635–87) along with more homely objects including the riding whip used by Sir John D'Oyly (see opposite) and an unusual gunpowder flask made from the testicles of an elk. Look out too for the intriguing selection of **water clocks**: small copper bowls with a tiny pinhole in the bottom: floated on water, they sink after precisely 24 minutes, the equivalent to one Sinhalese hour, or *paya* (in a neat but coincidental reversal of Western time-keeping, the Sinhalese divided each day into sixty hours of 24 minutes).

Next door to the National Museum is the modest **Queen's Chamber**, a discreet low white structure with tiny balustraded windows and stone pool inside. Close by, just southwest of the museum on the edge of the lake, sits the **Queen's Bath** (Ulpenge), a grand but rather dilapidated structure, rather like a boathouse; the upper storey was added by the British.

Museum of World Buddhism

Daily 8am–7pm • Rs.500

A short walk past the National Museum behind the Temple of the Tooth leads to the imposing British-era Neoclassical building (formerly the city's High Court) which now provides a grand setting for the entertainingly strange new **Museum of World Buddhism**, showcasing Buddhist beliefs and artefacts from a range of Asian countries. The museum begins soberly enough with assorted displays on Sri Lankan Buddhism, while subsequent galleries feature a colourful recreation of a Bhutanese shrine, displays on Gandharan-era Buddhism from Pakistan, a couple of random rooms devoted to Nepal and Bangladesh, and a large room, entirely empty, pledged to displays from India, which had yet to arrive at the time of writing.

Things really fire into life in the **upstairs galleries**, stuffed full of a weird, occasionally wonderful and unquestionably random selection of displays and artefacts focusing on the religious heritage of countries ranging from Indonesia to Japan. Many of the displays appear to have been donated as PR exercises by the various countries involved, and the general impression is not so much of a curated museum as an international travel fair, with assorted promotional videos looping endlessly in the background. It's not without a certain bizarre appeal, and some of the exhibits are undeniably impressive, including a room full of dazzling gilded Buddhas from Myanmar and a fine array of Chinese and Tibetan artefacts. Elsewhere, things become decidedly haphazard, such as the huge photos of Mahinda Rajapakse in the Thailand gallery (including one in which he appears to be receiving treatment for lice) and the entire Vietnamese room, which bears an uncanny resemblance to a Hong Kong seafood restaurant.

Archeological Museum

Daily except Tues 8am–5pm • Reached via the path between the Museum of World Buddhism and the back of the Vishnu Devale • Donation

Occupying the former **palace** of King Vimala Dharma Suriya (1591–1604), Kandy's dusty **Archeological Museum** comprises a modest collection of assorted pots, bits of masonry, fragments of carved stones and old wooden pillars. It's all fairly humdrum, although the former palace building is impressive: a long, low, barn-like structure sporting an ornate gateway and doors decorated with the sun and moon symbol of the kings of Kandy, along with other auspicious symbols.

The Kandy Garrison Cemetery

Garrison Cemetery Rd (signposted from beside the National Museum) • Mon–Sat 8am–1pm & 2–6pm • Donation

The evocative **Kandy Garrison Cemetery** was established in 1817, shortly after the British seized control of Kandy, to provide a final resting place for expired British colonists. Having fallen into complete dereliction, the cemetery has recently been painstakingly restored and now offers a moving memorial to Ceylon's former colonial master. Shockingly few of the people buried here made it to the age of 30, and even those who avoided the usual hazards of tropical diseases and hostile natives found unusual ways to meet their maker, such as John Spottiswood Robertson (died 1856), trampled to death by a wild elephant; David Findlay (died 1861), killed when his house collapsed on top of him; and William Watson Mackwood (died 1867), who somehow managed to impale himself on a stake while dismounting from his horse.

The most notable burial, however, is **Sir John D'Oyly**, the remarkable colonial official who brokered the surrender of the city to the British in 1815. D'Oyly was one of the most fascinating figures in the history of colonial Ceylon – at once a supreme diplomat who manipulated the Kandyan nobility with almost Machiavellian genius, and also a kind of proto-hippy who became a strict vegetarian, avoided European society and devoted himself to the study of Sinhala and Buddhism. As an observer remarked in 1810: "He lives on plantain, invites nobody to his house, and does not dine abroad above once a year. When I saw him… I was struck with the change of a Cambridge boy into a Cingalese hermit." Despite his brilliant orchestration of the bloodless coup at Kandy, D'Oyly's subsequent attempts to protect the Kandyans from British interference and Christian missionaries were little appreciated, and by the time of his death from cholera in 1824, he had become a lonely and marginalized figure – not that you'd realize it, judging by the size of his memorial, the largest in the cemetery, topped by a broken Greek pillar. It's on your left as you come in, quite close to the entrance.

3

The devales

Kandy traditionally lies under the protection of four gods, each of whom is honoured with a temple (*devale*) in the city. Three of these temples, the **Pattini**, **Natha** and **Vishnu** *devales*, sit next to one another just in front of the Temple of the Tooth – a fascinating and picturesque jumble of shrines, dagobas and bo trees. The fourth *devale*, dedicated to **Kataragama**, lies a couple of blocks west in the city itself. Besides their obvious artistic merits, the *devales* offer a fascinating lesson in the way in which Hindu and Buddhist beliefs shaded into one another in Kandy, as throughout Sri Lankan history: two of the four *devales* are dedicated to adopted Hindu gods, while the principal shrine of the Natha *devale* is housed in a building that wouldn't look out of place in South India.

Pattini Devale

The **Pattini Devale** is the simplest of the four temples. The cult of the goddess **Pattini** (see box, p.218) was introduced from South India in the second century AD by King Gajabahu (reigned 114–136 AD); she remains a popular deity among poorer Sri Lankans, thanks to her lowly origins. Her golden ankle bracelet, brought back from India by Gajabahu, is said to be kept here (though you can't see it). Entering from Deva Vidiya, you're confronted by the **Wel-Bodhiya**, a huge bo tree, perched on an enormous, three-tiered platform; it's believed to have been planted by **Narendrasingha**, the last Sinhalese king of Kandy, in the early eighteenth century. The actual shrine to Pattini is off to the right, set in a modest little enclosure entered through gorgeous embossed brass doors decorated with the usual sun and moon symbols, *makara toranas* and guardstone figures. The shrine itself is set in a small but beautiful Kandyan wooden pavilion, and is usually the most popular of all the *devales* among visiting worshippers. To either side stand subsidiary shrines to the Hindu deities Kali and Mariamman – the latter, like Pattini, is a female deity of humble South Indian origins who is believed to protect against disease. You may be approached by a temple flunkey at this point asking for a donation; he'll most likely show you a book in which previous donations are listed, many of which appear to have been wildly inflated by the addition of surplus zeros.

Natha Devale

A gate leads from the Pattini Devale directly through to the **Natha Devale**. **Natha** is the most purely Buddhist of the gods of the four *devales*, and thus the most important in the city, being considered a form of the Mahayana Bodhisattva **Avalokitesvara**, who is

3

PATTINI

Pattini (originally named Kannaki) was a humble Indian girl from the city of Madurai who married a certain **Kovalan**, an errant spouse with a weakness for dancing girls. Despite Pattini's considerable charms, the feckless Kovalan abandoned his wife and bankrupted himself in pursuit of one particular amour until, ashamed and penniless, he returned to Pattini to beg forgiveness. The pliable Pattini welcomed him back without even a word of reproach and handed over her last possession, a golden ankle bracelet, for him to sell. The unfortunate Kovalan did so, but was promptly accused of stealing the bracelet by the king's goldsmith and executed. The distraught Pattini, legend states, descended upon the royal palace, tore off one of her breasts, caused the king to drop dead and then reduced his palace to ashes before being taken up into the heavens as a goddess.

Pattini's cult was originally introduced to Sri Lanka by King Gajabahu in the second century BC, but enjoyed its heyday during the Kandyan era, when the kingdom's Hindu rulers revived her cult and built her Kandy temple. Pattini is now revered as the ideal of the chaste and devoted wife: pregnant women come here to pray for a safe delivery (rather inexplicably, since Pattini was childless), while she is also thought to protect against infectious diseases such as chicken-pox, smallpox and measles.

still widely worshipped in Nepal, Tibet, China and Japan. Natha was thought to have influence over political events in the kingdom – new kings of Kandy were obliged to present themselves at the shrine on attaining the throne – although the god's exalted status means that his shrine is far less popular with the hoi polloi than that of humble Pattini next door.

Away to your right at the end of the enclosure is the **Natha Shrine** itself, built by Vikramabahu III in the fourteenth century, and thus the oldest building in Kandy. This low gedige (South Indian-style stone shrine), topped with a small *shikhara* dome, is very reminiscent in style of similar temples at Polonnaruwa, and shows strong Indian influence (the fact that the city's most Buddhist deity sits in its most Hindu-style temple is entirely characteristic of the syncretic nature of Kandyan culture). The shrine is fronted by a much later pavilion sporting beautifully carved wooden pillars. In the middle of the enclosure stands a **Buddha shrine**, with two elaborately railed bo trees to the rear. Exit the temple through the archway to the north, its exterior wall richly carved and painted with *makara torana* and guardstone figures.

Vishnu Devale

From the back of the Natha Devale, steps lead up through a wooden pavilion into the third of the *devales*, the **Vishnu Devale** (also known as the Maha Devale, or "Great Temple"). The first building you come to is an open-sided **digge** pavilion, in which drummers and dancers would formerly have performed in honour of the deity – you can still occasionally see trainee dancers being put through their paces here. Past the *digge*, further steps leads up to the main **Vishnu shrine**. The Vishnu image here is thought to come from Dondra on the south coast, though it's usually hidden behind a curtain; ceremonial objects used in Esala Perahera line the sides of the shrine. Behind and to the left of the Vishnu shrine stands a subsidiary shrine to **Dedimunda** (a local god of obscure origins), his image framed by a gorgeously embossed gilded arch featuring the ubiquitous sun and moon motif.

The rest of the city

Away from the Temple of the Tooth, Royal Palace and *devales*, most of Kandy has a largely modern appearance, although a fair number of crusty old colonial-era buildings also survive. The centre of the modern city spreads out around **Dalada Vidiya**, confined, thanks to the hilliness of the surrounding terrain, to a compact and crowded grid of streets lined with small shops and honeycombed in places with tiny alleyways. The most interesting area is along the eastern end of Bennet Soysa Vidiya (generally known by its old name of Colombo Street), where fruit and veg sellers sell their wares from the narrow and congested pavements. At the far end of Dalada Vidiya stands Kandy's unusually ornate **clocktower**, with golden elephant friezes and a cute, hat-like top.

St Paul's Church

Immediately north of the Pattini Devale, the quaint neo-Gothic **St Paul's Church** (1843) offers a homesick and thoroughly incongruous memento of rustic English nostalgia amid the surrounding Buddhist monuments – indeed the irreverent insertion of such a large Christian building into such a sacred Buddhist precinct says much about British religious sympathies, or lack of. The **interior** is a piece of pure English Victoriana, with beautiful wooden pews, floor tiles decorated with floral and fleur de lys patterns, wooden rood-screen and choir stalls, naff stained glass, brass eagle lectern and a grand piano, all tenderly preserved. The various monuments date back to the 1840s, recording deaths in parts of the empire as far flung as Bombay, Port Said, Wei-Hai-Wei and South Africa. Opposite here, the walls of the buildings are all but buried underneath a surfeit of **signs** in English and Sinhala advertising the services of local lawyers, whose offices stand along the street, occupying a former Victorian-era army stables and barracks.

Kataragama Devale

The fourth of the city's principal *devales*, the **Kataragama Devale**, sits buried away in the city centre, somewhat separate from the other *devales*, entered through a lurid blue gateway on Kotugodelle Vidiya (though it's surprisingly easy to miss amid the packed shopfronts). This is the most Hindu-influenced of Kandy's temples, right down to the pair of resident Brahmin priests. The attractive central Kataragama shrine is topped by a broad wooden roof and protected by two intricately gilded doors, with a pair of Buddha shrines behind and to the left. The right-hand side of the enclosure has a very Indian flavour, with a line of shrines housing images of Durga, Krishna, Radha, Ganesh and Vishnu – those at the back have ornate gold doors with tiny bells on them which devotees ring to attract the gods' attention.

The Bahiravakanda Buddha
Daily 6am–8pm • Rs.200

West of the city centre, the immense white **Bahiravakanda Buddha** stares impassively over central Kandy from its hilltop perch. The statue was constructed at the behest of the religiously minded **President Premadasa**, who also contributed the striking golden roof of the principal shrine of the Temple of the Tooth, as well as various other religious edifices around the island – though these many pious acts didn't save him from being blown to smithereens by an LTTE suicide bomber in 1993.

You can walk up to the statue – a stiff 15–20min hike – although in truth it's hardly worth the effort and the views, although extensive, aren't as attractive as those from Rajapahila Mawatha, which is much less of a climb, and also free.

Udawattakele Sanctuary
Daily 6am–6pm • Rs.644

On the opposite (north) side of the lake, providing a dense green backdrop to the Temple of the Tooth, **Udawattakele Sanctuary** was formerly a royal reserve, subsequently preserved and protected by the British. The sanctuary sprawls over two square kilometres of densely forested hillside, with imposing trees, plenty of birdlife, snakes, and a few mammals including monkeys, porcupines and pigs – as well as lots of leeches if it's been raining. Two main paths, Lady Horton's Drive and Lady Gordon's Road (both named after the wives of British governors) wind through the reserve, with a few smaller paths and nature trails branching off them. The entrance to the park is a steep hike from town:

go up past the post office along Kandy Vidiya and then Wewelpitiya Road; the easy-to-miss entrance is next to the Sri Dalada Thapowanaya temple.

ARRIVAL AND DEPARTURE KANDY

Thanks to its position roughly in the centre of the island, Kandy is within fairly easy striking distance of pretty much everywhere in the country, although if you're heading to the south coast, it's normally easiest to go back to Colombo and start from there. Heading south into the hill country, the **train** connects Kandy with most places you're likely to want to go, while to the north, all the sites of the Cultural Triangle are no more than two to three hours away by road. For details of **tours and taxis** from Kandy, see p.226. Note that the city's **tuktuk** drivers are possibly the most rapacious in Sri Lanka and you may have to pay well over the odds to reach your hotel. If you're heading to the **airport**, all buses to Negombo pass the turn-off to the airport, about 2km from the terminal itself; alternatively, take a (non-inter-city) Colombo train to Veyangoda, then catch a bus or tuktuk for the thirty-minute trip to the airport.

By bus Most long-distance bus services depart from Kandy's main bus station, the disorienting Goods Shed Bus Terminal opposite the train station (the Clocktower Bus Stand, south of the clocktower at the west end of the city centre, is used for local departures only). If you can't find the bus you're looking for, ask at one of the two wire-mesh information kiosks in the middle of the terminal. For Ella, you'll probably have to travel via Badulla, and for Haputale via Nuwara Eliya and/or Bandarawela; in both instances it's far easier to take the train. All buses to Polonnaruwa travel via Habarana and Giritale.

Destinations Anuradhapura (every 30min; 3hr 30min); Badulla (hourly; 4hr); Colombo (express services every 10–15min; 3hr; these leave from the roadside on Station Rd about halfway between the Goods Shed terminal and the clocktower); Dambulla (every 20min; 2hr); Negombo (hourly; 3hr 30min); Jaffna (4 daily, leaving either early morning or overnight; 9hr); Kegalle (for Pinnewala; every 15min; 1hr); Kurunegala (every 15min; 1hr 30min); Nuwara Eliya (every 30min; 2hr 30min); Polonnaruwa (every 30min; 3hr 45min); Ratnapura (5 daily; 3hr 30min); Sigiriya (1 daily at 7.15am; 2hr 30min; otherwise change at Dambulla); Trincomalee (every 45min; 6hr).

By train Kandy's train station sits close to Goods Shed bus station on the southwest edge of the city centre; timetables for the principal train services from Kandy are given at the beginning of the chapter (see p.200). The ride through the hills up to Nanu Oya (for Nuwara Eliya), Haputale, Ella and Badulla is slow but unforgettable, though note that these trains travel via Peradeniya station, 5km outside Kandy, rather than Kandy itself; it's well worth trying to bag a seat in the observation car (see p.30). Travelling to Colombo, sit on the south side of the train (the left-hand side, as you face the front) for the best views.

Destinations Badulla (from Peradeniya; 3 daily; 7–8hr); Colombo (6 daily; 2hr 30min–3hr 30min); Ella (from Peradeniya; 3 daily; 6–7hr); Haputale (from Peradeniya; 3 daily; 5–6hr); Hatton (from Peradeniya; 3 daily; 2–3hr); Nanu Oya (from Peradeniya, for Nuwara Eliya; 3 daily; 3hr 20min–4hr).

ACCOMMODATION

There's a huge selection of **accommodation** in all price ranges in and around Kandy, although guesthouses in the city are no longer the bargain they once were. Note that the **temperature** in Kandy is markedly cooler than along the coast – you probably won't need air-conditioning, but you probably will want hot water (all the following places have this unless stated otherwise). In general, the better the view, the further from town – and the more taxing the walk from the centre. Most of the following places can also arrange tours (see p.226). If you're staying on Rajapihilla Mawatha note that there's a useful **shortcut** up to the road from the top of Sarankara Rd (starting next to *Highest View* guesthouse).

HASSLES IN KANDY

Kandy formerly had a well-deserved reputation for **hassle**, **touts** and **con artists**. The situation has now improved markedly, although it still pays to be aware of potential set-ups. Touts traditionally hang out along the south side of the lake en route to Saranankara Road, where you may still potentially be approached by opportunistic scroungers. Some con artists may attempt to embroil you in conversation by pointing out the splashes made by "water-snakes" in the lake (the splashes actually being created by a hidden accomplice chucking stones into the water) as a way of getting into conversation with you and gaining your confidence before setting you up for one of various wallet-emptying schemes. Popular local scams include offering tourists the chance to meet a "dancing teacher" or the "head priest" at the Temple of Tooth, as well as all the old islandwide favourites (see p.51).

CITY CENTRE

Hotel Casamara 12 Kotugodelle Vidiya ☎ 081 222 4688, ⊛ www.casamarahotel.com. The most centrally located hotel in Kandy, and much nicer than its drab exterior would suggest, offering dated but well-maintained rooms with a/c, satellite TV and minibar, plus pool (non-guests Rs.500), restaurant and rooftop bar. **$65**

Olde Empire 21 Temple St ☎ 081 222 4284. This venerable establishment is the only reliable cheapie in the city centre, with a charmingly antiquated wood-panelled interior, a picturesque streetside veranda, and six basic white rooms (three with shared bath; cold water only), all clean and very good value. Shared bath **Rs.1100**; en-suite **Rs.2200**

Queens Hotel Dalada Vidiya ☎ 081 222 2813, ⊛ queenshotel.lk. Dating back to the 1860s, this venerable hotel is one of central Kandy's most famous landmarks, and still has a certain olde-worlde style. The spacious rooms (most with a/c) have plenty of colonial character, although all but nine of them overlook busy roads and so are rather noisy. It's excellent value nonetheless, and there's also a pool (non-guests Rs.250) plus endearingly old-fashioned in-house bar and restaurant. **$73**

SOUTH OF THE LAKE

Blinkbonnie Tourist Inn 69 Rajapihilla Mw ☎ 081 222 2007, ⊛ blinkinn.com. Perched high above town, with fine views from its terrace restaurant. Rooms (some with a/c) are looking a bit past their best, although all have balconies with some sort of view, and there's also free wi-fi, free pick-up from bus or train stations and motorbike rental (guests only). **Rs.3100**; a/c **Rs.4400**

Castle Hill Guest House 22 Rajapihilla Mw ☎ 081 222 4376, ✉ ayoni@sltnet.lk. Characterful colonial villa set in gorgeous gardens high above the lake and town, offering one of the best of Kandy's many memorable views. There are just four rooms: the two at the front are a bit bare, but with lovely views and big enough to swing a sackful of cats; the two at the back are smaller and rather gloomy. Excellent value at current rates. **Rs.3600**

★ **Expeditor** 41 Saranankara Rd ☎ 081 223 8316, ⊛ expeditorkandy.com. Smart modern guesthouse, owned by Kandy's leading tour guide (see p.226) and with a wide range of rooms, from a couple of downstairs cheapies with shared bathroom for as little as Rs.1000 to smart upstairs en-suite rooms with high wooden ceilings and fine lake views – all are nicely furnished, very comfortable and scrupulously maintained. Good home-cooking, too. Shared bath **Rs.1000**; en suite **Rs.2000**

★ **Freedom Lodge** 30 Saranankara Rd ☎ 081 222 3506, ✉ freedomomega@yahoo.com. Excellent and professionally run family guesthouse offering a very friendly welcome and accommodation in smart and comfortable modern rooms. There's also free wi-fi, and a

new restaurant, roof terrace and kitchen for guests' use should have been finished by the time you read this. **Rs.3500**

★ **Helga's Folly** Off Mahamaya Mw ☎ 081 223 4571, ⊛ helgasfolly.com. Utterly maverick and magical place, set high above Kandy in a rambling old house whose former house guests have included Gandhi, Nehru and Laurence Olivier – not to mention Stereophonics frontman Kelly Jones, who penned a song in honour of the place. The extraordinary interior is a riot of colourful invention, with each room decorated in a different theme and colour, from the eye-popping yellow lounge, with petrified dripping candles, deer heads, Indonesian puppets and colonial photos, to the individual bedrooms (all a/c), each with a unique design featuring any combination of wacky murals, colonial furniture and unusual objets d'art. Facilities include a small cinema and a (very shallow) pool. **$190**

Highest View 129/3 Saranankara Rd ☎ 081 223 3778, ⊛ highestview.com. At the very top of Saranankara Rd (although the view from the nearby Mcleod Inn is even higher). Rooms are bright and modern, albeit rather small and beginning to look slightly past it, although all come with private balconies from which to enjoy the sweeping lake views. **Rs.360**

★ **Mcleod Inn** 65A Rajapihilla Mw ☎ 081 222 2832, ✉ mcleod@sltnet.lk. Kandy's best bargain, perched in a peerless location high above town. The ten rooms are clean, modern, spacious and excellent value; two (Rs.500 extra) have views to dream of through enormous French windows, as does the dining room. Free internet and wi-fi. **Rs.2000**

Pink House 15 Saranankara Rd ☎ 0779 018 552. Long-established, popular and sociable cheapie in a quaint if rather battered old house with six basic but clean rooms sharing two communal bathrooms (plus one en-suite room for Rs.1500). It's all pretty down at heel, but OK at current rates, which are among the cheapest in the island. **Rs.900**

★ **Sharon Inn** 59 Saranankara Rd ☎ 081 222 2416 or 2446, ⊛ hotelsharoninn.com. The smartest and best set up of the Saranankara Rd guesthouses, slightly more expensive but well worth the extra rupees. It's set right at the top of the road, with modern, nicely furnished rooms in a bright, white and scrupulously clean building; all rooms have marvellous bird's-eye views over the town from private balconies, plus satellite TV. There's also free internet access and wi-fi, and the best rice and curry in town (see p.223). B&B **Rs.5000**

Hotel Suisse Sangaraja Mw ☎ 081 223 3024, ⊛ hotelsuisse.lk. This gracious old hotel served as Mountbatten's Southeast Asian headquarters during World War II and retains much of its time-warped colonial charm. Rates are surprisingly inexpensive, and rooms (some lake-facing; all with a/c, satellite TV and minibar) are spacious and neatly furnished. The attractive public

3

areas include a cosy bar, a billiards room, wi-fi and a pool (guests only). **$100**

NORTH OF THE LAKE

Blue Haven 30/2 Poorna Lane, Asigiriya ☎081 222 9617, Ⓦbluehaventours.com. In a pleasantly semi-rural setting on the edge of the centre, with bright, clean tiled rooms (some with optional a/c for Rs.600), an attractive upstairs veranda and a terrace restaurant looking out over the tree tops. Rough Guide readers are promised a ten percent discount. B&B **$30**

Green Woods 34A Sangamitta Mw ☎081 223 2970. A real rural retreat, with simple but comfortable rooms in a beautifully secluded setting overlooking Udawattakele Sanctuary, whose birdlife can be ogled for free from the veranda. B&B **Rs.2500**

Nature Walk 9 Sangamitta Mw ☎0777 717 482, Ⓦnaturewalkhr.net. Well-run guesthouse with comfy and good-value modern tiled rooms. Those at the front are bright and spacious and come with a/c, balcony and mountain views through big French windows; cheaper fan rooms at the back are a smaller and viewless, but still decent value at the price. **Rs.2500**; a/c **Rs.3000**

Thilanka 3 Sangamitta Mw ☎081 223 2429, Ⓦthilankahotel.com. Set high above the lake (and topped by a large neon sign which disfigures the Kandyan skyline on a nightly basis), this is one of the most attractive mid-range options in the area, with outstanding views and stylish modern rooms. Activities and facilities include yoga classes, a rustic and reasonably priced Ayurveda centre and the most spectacularly situated swimming pool in town (non-guests Rs.200). Good value. **$115**

AROUND KANDY

The following places are shown on the "Around Kandy" map (p.228).

Amaya Hills 7km southwest of Kandy ☎081 447 4022, Ⓦamayaresorts.com. The highest hotel in the immediate vicinity of the city, this large pink edifice offers superlative views out over the hills, comfortable rooms with Kandyan-themed decor, a large pool (though it's quite cool up here), spa and wi-fi throughout. **$135**

Chaaya Citadel 2km west of Kandy ☎081 223 4365, Ⓦchaayahotels.com. Occupying an attractive perch above the Mahaweli Ganga, this low-rise four-star is the best value – and perhaps also the best looking – of the big hotels around Kandy, with spacious and stylish rooms (all with minibar, safe, satellite TV and balcony) and a large pool. **$130**

Earl's Regency 4km east of Kandy ☎081 242 2122, Ⓦwww.aitkenspencehotels.com. Large, plush and well run – if somewhat characterless – five-star in a fine position overlooking the Mahaweli Ganga. All rooms are attractive and well appointed, and the more expensive ones boast sweeping hill or river views. There's also a large U-shaped pool, a spa and a gym. **$210**

★**Kandy House** Gunnepana, 5km west of Kandy ☎081 492 1394, Ⓦthekandyhouse.com. Magical boutique guesthouse, 20min drive from central Kandy, set in a wonderfully atmospheric old traditional Kandyan walauwe (manor house) amid thick jungle full of wild spices. Rooms are furnished with antique-style furniture, four-poster beds, Victorian bathtubs and colourful contemporary silk and cotton fabrics, and are surrounded

---

MEDITATION

Kandy is the best place in Sri Lanka to study **meditation**, with numerous centres dotted around the surrounding countryside (though none right in the city itself). The Buddhist Publications Society (see p.227) has a full list of all the various centres in the area.

Dhamma Kuta Vippassana Meditation Centre Hindagala, 7km from Peradeniya ☎081 238 5774, Ⓦwww.beyondthenet.net /dhammakuta. Caters to experienced meditators only, with courses lasting between three and 45 days.

International Buddhist Meditation Centre Hondiyadeniya, Wegirikanda, 10km from Kandy on the road to Nuwara Eliya ☎081 380 1871, Ⓦwww.rockhillsrilanka.com. Runs challenging courses in Vipassana meditation during which students are required to adopt the ascetic lifestyle of a Buddhist monk.

Nilambe Meditation Centre Near Galaha, around 22km from Kandy ☎0777 804 555 or ☎0777 811 653, ✉upulnilambe@yahoo .com. This long-running centre is the place

most used to dealing with – and most popular among – foreign visitors, set in a beautifully tranquil spot in the hills. Potential visitors are advised to contact the centre at least two weeks in advance; there's no minimum length of stay. The cost is Rs.800/day, including basic vegetarian food and lodging. All levels are welcome, from novices to experienced meditators. To reach the centre, take the Deltota bus from Kandy's Goods Shed bus station and ask the conductor to put you off at Nilambe Office Junction, from where it's a 45-minute walk (or catch a tuktuk). Bring a torch (there's no electricity), umbrella, alarm clock and warm clothing.

by gorgeous landscaped gardens running down to a beautiful little infinity swimming pool. $\overline{S}330$

Mahaweli Reach 4km north of Kandy ☎ 081 247 2727, ⓦ mahaweli.com. Large, long-established hotel in a fine riverside setting by the Mahaweli Ganga. The whole place is pleasantly old-fashioned, with vaguely colonial-style architecture and extensive gardens full of flowering shrubs, while the wood-floored rooms are spacious and plush, and come with all the facilities you'd expect, given that it's one of only two five-stars in Kandy – although rates are surprisingly steep. $\overline{S}270$

★ **The Mansion** Aladeniya, 11km from Kandy ☎ 081 246 3166, ⓦ mansionkandy.com. One of Kandy's most engaging accommodation options, in a marvellous old 1920s walauwe (traditional country mansion) – former guests have included Mahatma Gandhi and Gregory Peck. The house and rooms are full of character, with a huge Rangoon teak staircase and creaky old floorboards, swastika-encrusted pillars and ceilings, Italian marble floors and a quaint stained-glass dome. Rooms (all a/c) are a mite musty, but similarly atmospheric, with antique furniture and period touches. Facilities include a good-size pool, attractive gardens, massage treatments and free wi-fi. An absolute steal at current rates. B&B $\overline{S}50$

Richmond House Heerassagala, 5km from Kandy ☎ 081 221 8495, ⓦ therichmondhousekandy.com. Midway between Kandy and Peradeniya, this attractive guesthouse offers bright and well-equipped modern tiled rooms (all with bathtub, a/c, satellite TV, minibar and free wi-fi) with a hint of slightly chintzy old-world charm, including colonial repro furniture, four-poster beds and a Hollywood staircase. Best not try to drive up the short but horribly steep access road, however. B&B $\overline{S}60$

★ **Stone House Lodge** 42 Nittawella Rd, 2.5km north of Kandy ☎ 081 223 2769, ⓦ stonehouselodge.lk. Small, upmarket guesthouse in a laid-back semi-rural setting, with an intimate and welcoming atmosphere and wonderful views of the hills from the immaculate garden. The four rooms are beautifully furnished in colonial style – and the master bedroom is a real work of art. $\overline{S}180$

Theva Hantana Rd, 3km from Kandy ☎ 081 738 8296, ⓦ theva.lk. Perched in a fine position high above town, this striking modern hotel sports stylish – if very minimalist – arctic-white rooms (more expensive deluxe rooms with fine views). There's also a small pool, if it's warm enough to swim, and an attractive dining room, although overall it's a bit pricey for what you get. $\overline{S}200$

★ **Villa Rosa** Asigiriya, 2km west of Kandy ☎ 081 221 5556, ⓦ villarosa-kandy.com. Beautiful boutique hotel in a stunning location high above the Mahaweli Ganga a couple of kilometres west of town, with spacious and stylish rooms. The attractively soothing orangey-pink decor complements the very serene atmosphere, while facilities include meditation and yoga platforms and an attractive Ayurveda centre. B&B $\overline{S}150$

EATING

Devon Restaurant 11 Dalada Vidiya. No-frills modern local restaurant constantly packed with locals thanks to its good selection of Sri Lankan staples, including hoppers, string hoppers, burianis, *lamprais* and devilled dishes (mains Rs.200-400), plus western and Sri Lankan breakfasts. Portions are large, though the food can be devilishly hot. Daily 7.30am–8.30pm.

Flower Song 137 Kotugodelle Vidiya ☎ 081 222 9191. Neat modern Chinese restaurant, serving up a big menu of Cantonese meat, fish and veg classics (mains Rs.500–750), all nicely cooked and a bit more authentic than most Sri Lankan Chinese chow. Tues–Sun 11am–10.30pm.

History, The Restaurant 27A Anagarika Dharmapala Mw ☎ 081 220 2109. "Kandy's only themed restaurant" occupies a pleasant modern dining room plastered with fascinating colonial-era photos of Sri Lanka, with a slide-show of further old photos projected continuously onto a wall. Food comprises the usual mix of Sri Lankan and Chinese standards plus a further smattering of South Asian, pasta and European-style meat dishes, generally well-prepared, and at honest prices. Most mains Rs.400–600. Daily 9am–10pm.

The New Slightly Chilled Bamboo Garden 29A Anagarika Dharmapala Mw ☎ 0771 887 255. Kandy's coolest nightspot (see p.224), *Slightly Chilled* is best for a drink but also does a passable range of Sri Lankan-style Chinese food, covering all the usual meat, veg and seafood Cantonese bases, plus assorted salads, sandwiches and pasta and chicken dishes. Most mains Rs.450–650. Daily 11am–11pm.

The Pub 36 Dalada Vidiya ☎ 081 223 4868. Touristy place with dim lighting and MTV plus international sports on the big-screen TV. The pub-style menu features an eclectic selection of reasonably prepared if slightly pricey international standards including pastas, fish, pork chops and steak (though hardly any vegetarian options). Also a good spot for a drink (see p.224). Most mains Rs.700–900. Daily 11am–1am.

★ **Sharon Inn** 59 Sarankara Rd ☎ 081 222 2416. The best rice and curry in town (Rs.990), served buffet-style daily at 7.30pm and comprising a sumptuous spread of fifteen or so dishes usually featuring a gourmet array of unusual Sri Lankan vegetables, plus chicken. Non-guests should reserve in advance by 4pm latest.

Sri Ram 87 Bennet Soysa Vidiya (Colombo St). Cosy little restaurant with a big menu of inexpensive South Indian standards including thalis, dosas and *idlis*, as well as a few North Indian offerings plus more unusual Chettinad (Tamil Nadu-style) veg and meat curries. Mains from around Rs.300. No alcohol. Daily 9.30am–9.30pm.

3

3

ROBERT KNOX AND SEVENTEENTH-CENTURY KANDY

In 1660, a party of English sailors who had gone ashore near the mouth of the Mahaweli Ganga were taken prisoner by soldiers of the king of Kandy, Rajasinha II. Among them was a 19-year-old Londoner named **Robert Knox**. Knox's subsequent account of his nineteen years as a hostage of the king was eventually published as *An Historical Relation of Ceylon*, a unique record which offers a fascinating snapshot of everyday life in the seventeenth-century Kingdom of Kandy. The book later served as one of the major sources of Daniel Defoe's *Robinson Crusoe*, and something of Knox's own industrious (if rather dour) character may have crept into Defoe's self-sufficient hero.

Upon arriving in Kandy, Knox was surprised to discover that he and his shipmates were not the only European "guests" being detained at Rajasinha's pleasure – also in Kandy were prisoners of war, shipwrecked sailors, army deserters and assorted diplomats. Knox seems to have admired many of the qualities of his hosts, though he did object (as have so many subsequent Western travellers to Asia) that "They make no account nor conscience of lying, neither is it any shame or disgrace to them, if they be catched in telling lies; it is so customary." He also recorded (with puritan disapproval) the kingdom's liberal attitude to sex: "Both women and men do commonly wed four or five times before they can settle themselves." Married women appeared free to have affairs with whoever took their fancy, so long as they were of an equal social rank, sometimes even leaving their husbands at home to look after the children. When important visitors called, husbands would offer them the services of their wives and daughters "to bear them company in their chamber". Men were allowed to have affairs with lower-caste women, but not to sit or eat with them. Polyandry, in which a wife was shared between two or more brothers, or in which one man married two or more sisters, was also accepted, while incest was reputedly common among beggars. If nothing else, the kingdom's sex drive was impressive. As Knox observed of the Kandyan women: "when their Husbands are dead, all their care is where to get others, which they cannot long be without."

In terms of material possessions, the life which Knox recorded was simple. Most Kandyans contented themselves with the bare necessities of life, encouraged in a life of indolence by the fact that the moment they acquired anything it was taken away by the king's mob of tax collectors. Justice was meted out by a court of local chiefs, but appeared to favour whoever was able to present the largest bribe – those convicted of capital offences were trampled to death by an elephant.

The White House 21 Dalada Vidiya ☎081 223 2765. Long-running old city-centre stalwart recently given a thorough upgrade. Downstairs there's a modern and very white bakery with assorted cakes and short eats, plus rice and curry buffets at lunchtime. The sedate upstairs dining room serves up a mix of Sri Lankan, Indian and Chinese mains, well prepared and quite moderately priced (Rs.400–500), plus a few more expensive pasta, seafood and steaks. Unlicensed. Daily noon–10pm.

DRINKING

The New Slightly Chilled Bamboo Garden 29A Anagarika Dharmapala Mw. Very chilled out bar-cum-restaurant (it's where the enormous red neon "PUB" sign is, visible from anywhere within about ten miles) set high above the lake, with an above-average drinks list including a smattering of cocktails and a decent selection of beers, washed down with a smooth soundtrack. Also does so-so food (see p.223). Daily 11am–2pm & 5–11pm.

The Pub 36 Dalada Vidiya. The outdoor terrace overlooking Dalada Vidiya here is one of the nicest spots in town for a drink, and there's a decent (though relatively pricey) list of draught, local and imported beers and spirits.
Daily 11am–2pm & 5–11pm.

Pub Royale Dalada Vidiya. Tourist-friendly pub in a corner of the *Queens Hotel* building still sporting some of its original colonial fittings including a fancy mirrored wooden bar and old plaster ceiling. Decent choice of beers and other drinks. Daily 10am–10pm.

Queens Hotel Bar Queens Hotel, Dalada Vidiya. Atmospheric, colonial-style drinking hole under a huge veranda at the back of the stately *Queens Hotel*, with an old wooden bar, armchair seating and long rows of fans whirling gently overhead. Daily 9am–10pm.

ENTERTAINMENT

Three places in town put on nightly shows of Kandyan **dancing and drumming** (all at 5.30pm and lasting around 1hr; Rs.500). All are touristy but fun, with a fairly standard range of dances, generally including snippets of both southern as well as Kandyan dances and usually culminating in a spot of firewalking.

KANDYAN DANCING AND DRUMMING

Kandyan dancing and drumming is Sri Lanka's iconic performing art, and you're unlikely to spend long in the city without seeing a troupe of performers going about their (rather noisy) business, clad in elaborate traditional costumes, with dancers twirling, stamping and gyrating to a pulsating accompaniment of massed drumming. The art form originated as part of an all-night ceremony in honour of the god Kohomba, an elaborate ritual featuring some fifty dancers and ten drummers. This ceremony flourished under the patronage of the kings of Kandy and reached such heights of sophistication that it was eventually adopted into local religious ceremonies, becoming a key element in the great Esala Perahera festival. Many temples in the Kandyan area even have a special columned pavilion, or **digge**, designed specifically for performances and rehearsals by resident dancers and drummers.

3

KANDYAN DANCING

There are five main **types of Kandyan dance**. The four principal genres are the *ves*, *pantheru*, *udekki* and *naiyandi*, all featuring troupes of flamboyantly attired male dancers clad in sumptuous chest plates, waistbands and various other neck, arm and leg ornaments which jangle as the dancers move about. The most famous is the **ves** dance, which is considered sacred to the god Kohomba. It's at once highly mannered and hugely athletic, combining carefully stylized hand and head gestures with acrobatic manoeuvres including spectacular backflips, huge high-kicking leaps and dervish-like whirling pirouettes. In the more sedate **pantheru** dance, the turbaned performers play small tambourines, while during the **udekki** dance they beat tiny hourglass-shaped drums.

The fifth and final style of Kandyan classical dance is the **vannam**. This began life as songs, before evolving into stylized dances, each of which describes a certain emotion or object from nature, history or legend – the most popular are the various animal-derived *vannams*, including those inspired by the movements of the peacock (*mayura*), elephant (*gajaga*), lion (*sinharaja*) and cobra (*naga*). *Vannams* are usually performed by just one or two dancers (and sometimes by women), unlike other Kandyan dances, which are ensemble dances featuring four or five performers, always men.

As well as the traditional Kandyan dances, the city's cultural shows usually include examples of a few characteristic **southern dances** such as the *kulu* (harvest dance) and the ever-popular *raban* dance – for more on which, see p.130.

KANDYAN DRUMMING

All genres of dance are accompanied by **drumming**, which can reach extraordinary heights of virtuosity – even if the finer points pass you by, the headlong onslaught of a Kandyan drum ensemble in full flight leaves few people unmoved,. The archetypal Sri Lankan drum is the *geta bera* (literally "boss drum"), a double-headed instrument carried on a strap around the drummer's waist and played with the hands. *Geta bera* are made to a fixed length of 67cm, with different types of skins (monkey and cow, for example) at either end of the drum to produce contrasting sounds. The double-headed *daule* drum is shorter but thicker, and is played with a stick in one hand and the palm of the other. The *tammettana bera* is a pair of tiny drums (a bit like bongos) which are tied together and played with a pair of sticks. A *horanava* (a kind of Sri Lankan oboe) is sometimes added to the ensemble, providing a simple melodic accompaniment.

Like the dancers they accompany, Kandyan drummers perform in **traditional costume**, dressed in a large sarong, a huge red cummerbund and a white tasselled turban – significant musical points are marked by a toss of the head, sending the tassel flying through the air in a delicate accompanying flourish.

Kandyan Arts Association Sangaraja Mw, north side of the lake, just east of the Temple of the Tooth. The biggest, ritziest and most touristy of the three dance shows, with flashy but fun performances drawing coach parties galore.
Lake Club Sangamitta Mawatha. Midway in scale between the YMBA and Kandyan Arts Association shows.

Usually a bit lacking in atmosphere, although convenient if you're staying at one of the nearby hotels.
YMBA Rajapihilla Mawatha. A similar programme to that offered by the Kandyan Arts Association, but in a much smaller auditorium and with contrastingly intimate atmosphere.

SHOPPING

Kandy is one of Sri Lanka's main artesanal centres: many local villages still specialize in particular **crafts** (metalware, lacquerware, leatherwork and so on) and the city is perhaps the best place in the island to pick up traditional souvenirs, even if some traditional arts are being increasingly adulterated to suit the tourist market. As well as the places listed below there are also several big crafts shops (and many jewellers) along Peradeniya Rd en route to the Botanical Gardens. More modern shopping opportunities are provided by the **Kandy City Centre** (entered from Dalada Vidiya near *Devons* restaurant), a shiny new a/c complex bang in the heart of the city, although not all the shops in the centre had opened at the time of writing.

ARTS, CRAFTS AND SOUVENIRS

Gunatilake Batiks 173A Rajapahilla Mw. A big shop stuffed full of batiks, ranging from cheesy Sri Lankan designs through to more traditional (and attractive) Indonesian-style pieces adorned with birds and flowers. Batiks cost from $20 and up (bargaining recommended) and there are also clothes and tableware. You can also visit the factory downstairs to see them being made. Daily 8am–5.30pm.

Kandyan Arts and Crafts Association Sangaraja Mw. Showcases the full range of Kandy arts and crafts – metalwork, lacquerware, wood carvings, drums and so on – all relatively inexpensive, although not the greatest quality. Local artisans can often be seen at work around the veranda, plying looms, brushes and needles. Daily 9am–6pm.

Odel Luv SL Dalada Vidiya, next to Pub Royale. Kandy offshoot of the leading Colombo department store offering funky clothes plus assorted souvenirs, ranging from traditional masks and teas to toiletries, Ayurvedic products and bric-a-brac. There's a branch of Odel proper (mainly clothes) on the first floor of Kandy City Centre. Daily 10am–8pm.

Rajanima Crafts 173 Rajapahilla Mw. Good-quality selection of local crafts including *kolam* masks (painted in either chemical or – more expensive – natural dyes), Buddha and elephant carvings in sandalwood, teak and mahogany, drums, chess sets and carrom boards and so on (bargaining possible). You can also watch craftsmen at work in the factory next door. Daily 8am–5.30pm.

TOURS FROM KANDY

The main **taxi stand** (minivans and cars) is opposite the Clocktower Bus Stand at the west end of the centre. Drivers charge around $25–30 to Pinnewala, $25–30 for the three-temples circuit; and around $35–40 for the two combined.

Almost all the city's guesthouses can arrange **tours**; count on $50–60 per day for the hire of a car and driver. Alternatively, contact the reliable and inexpensive Blue Haven Tours and Travels, 25 D.S. Senanayake Mw (☎081 222 0572, mobile ☎0777 372 066, ◍bluehaventours .com) who can arrange inexpensive local and islandwide tours. They also run a handy six-day package tour (◍best6daytourinsrilanka.com) taking in some major sights around the hill country and Cultural Triangle for just $190 per person (all-inclusive except for entrance tickets) in a couple or larger group, or you can customize individual sections of the tour to suit.

The vastly experienced **Sumane Bandara Illangantilake** (c/o *Expeditor guesthouse*, Saranankara Rd ☎081 490 1628 or ☎223 8316, ◍srilankatrekkingexpeditor.com) and his team of guides offer islandwide tours, plus trips and hikes around Kandy including an unusual off-road version of the three-temples walk (see p.230); all walks can be customized to suit different levels of physical fitness. Sumane is also the island's leading guide to the Knuckles Range, an authority on the Veddhas, and can arrange visits to pretty much anywhere you might fancy going. For tours, count on around $65–75 per person per day (in a group of 2–4), excluding entrance fees; a proportion of profits is returned to local communities. **Ravi Desappriya** (☎071 499 7666, ◍srilankatrekking.com) is another good local guide, organizing a similar range of trips including good Knuckles treks and Wasogamuwa excursions, plus night safaris, wilderness camping (including "canoe camping" on the water) and mountain biking.

BOOKSHOPS

Buddhist Publications Society Sangaraja Mw. Enormous selection of Buddhist titles and books on Sri Lankan history. Mon–Sat 9am–4.30pm.

Vijitha Yapa Bookshop Ground floor, Kandy City Centre. Reasonable selection of English-language and Sri Lankan titles (Sarasavi Bookshop next door has a few more English-language books but isn't as good). There's another branch of Vijitha Yapa nearby on Kotugodelle Vidiya. Daily 9am–7pm.

TEA AND SUPERMARKETS

There's a handy (but often hectic) Cargills supermarket on Dalada Vidiya, and a much more peaceful Keells supermarket in the basement of Kandy City Centre (both open daily 8am–9pm); both have good selections of local tea and spices.

Mlesna Ground floor, Kandy City Centre. This posh tea shop offers a good range of gift tea sets, fancy teapots and other upmarket tea-making kit. Mon–Thurs & Sun 8am–6pm, Fri & Sat 9am–7pm.

DIRECTORY

Ayurveda A number of hotels in and around Kandy have Ayurveda centres: those at the *Earl's Regency*, *Amaya Hills*, *Thilanka* and *Villa Rosa* (see listings on pp.220–223) are all reputable and well run. Alternatively, the well-set-up Wedamedura Ayurveda Centre at 7 Mahamaya Mw (☎081 447 9484, ⓦ ayurvedawedamedura.com) offers an inexpensive range of treatments including steam and herbal baths, massages, reflexology, pedicures and aromatherapy, plus full panchakarma treatments. A resident Ayurveda doctor offers consultations and treatment plans, and you can arrange complete courses including accommodation and meals.

Banks There are heaps of banks in the city centre (see map, p.206), the majority on Dalada Vidiya, most with ATMs that accept foreign cards.

Cricket Kandy is one of the island's three test-match venues (along with Colombo and Galle). Matches are now held at the custom-built Muttiah Muralitharan International Cricket Stadium (or Pallekele International Cricket Stadium), 15km outside the city, which was opened in 2009. Aficionados might also enjoy a visit to the city's former test-match arena, the Asigiriya Stadium, shoe-horned into the hills just west of the centre and often described as one of the most beautiful cricket grounds in the world.

Golf The magnificent eighteen-hole, par-73 course at the

Victoria Golf Club (☎081 237 6376, ⓦ www.golfsrilanka .com) is around 20km east of Kandy at Rajawella, tucked into a scenic spot between the Knuckles Range and the Victoria Reservoir. Green fees are Rs.5000/day on weekdays, Rs.6500 at weekends.

Hospital Lakeside Adventist Hospital, 40 Sangaraja Mw (☎081 222 3466), on the lakeshore 100m beyond the *Hotel Suisse*; there's also a dental clinic here.

Internet The best option to get online is the cheap and well-equipped Sumathi Information Technologies (daily 8am–8pm; Rs.70/hr), on Kotugodelle Vidiya. Failing this, there are two other places further south along Kotugodelle Vidiya (the Sivaram Internet Café and Digital Teleprints, either side of the road just south of the Kataragama Devale) and a couple of others a block east next to the DHL office near the southern end of D.S. Senanayake Vidiya.

Pharmacy Two convenient pharmacies are Raj Medicals (daily 8am–9pm), at the back of Keells supermarket in the basement of Kandy City Centre; and Sri Lanka Pharmacy, 39 D.S. Senanayake Vidiya (Mon–Sat 8.30am–7.30pm).

Post office The main post office is opposite the train station (Mon–Sat 7am–9pm). In the city centre, try the Seetha Agency Post Office (daily 7am–10pm), 29 Kotugodelle Vidiya, a couple of doors south of the Kataragama Devale.

3

Around Kandy

The countryside around Kandy is full of attractions, comprising an interesting blend of the cultural and the natural – elephants, historic temples, hill walking and more. Top of most visitors' lists is the famous **Pinnewala Elephant Orphanage**, usually followed by the idyllic **Peradeniya Botanical Gardens**. There's also a fascinating collection of Kandyan-era **temples** scattered around the countryside, while the dramatic but little-visited **Knuckles Range** boasts some of the island's finest wilderness trekking.

Peradeniya Botanical Gardens

Daily 7.30am–5.45pm • Rs.600 • A tuktuk to the gardens will cost around Rs.800–1000 return from Kandy, including waiting time; alternatively, frequent buses leave the Clocktower Bus Stand for Peradeniya

Set 6km southwest of Kandy in a loop in the Mahaweli Ganga the **Peradeniya Botanical Gardens** are the largest and finest gardens in Sri Lanka, covering almost 150 acres and stuffed with a bewildering variety of local and foreign tree and plant species. The history of the site dates right back to the fourteenth century, when Wickramabahu III established a royal residence here. The park itself was created during the eighteenth century by King Kirti Sri Rajasinha to serve as a pleasure garden for the Kandyan nobility. It was

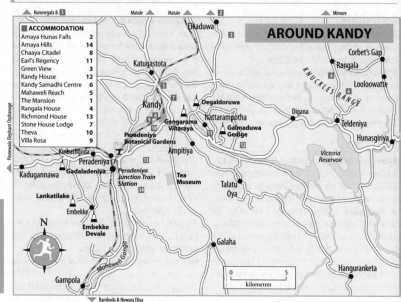

transformed into a botanical garden by the British in 1821 during the enterprising governorship of Edward Barnes, who had Sri Lanka's first tea trees planted here in 1824, though their full commercial potential wasn't to be realized for another half-century.

Of the ten thousand or so trees in the gardens, a fair proportion are labelled, though unfortunately many of the signs have weathered away to illegibility, while others show only the tree's Latin name – not much help unless you're an expert botanist. The area around the entrance is largely given over to small-scale flora, including an **orchid house**, a **flower garden** and a tiny and rather unimpressive **Japanese garden**, where the most interesting sight is a bizarre-looking snake creeper, whose tangled aerial roots look just like a writhing knot of vipers.

Royal Palm Avenue

Running from the entrance, the principal thoroughfare, stately **Royal Palm Avenue**, bisects the gardens, heading in an arrow-straight line from the entrance to the Mahaweli Ganga at the far northern end, via the **Great Circle** at the centre. The eastern side of the Great Circle is dotted with a sequence of **memorial trees** planted at various times by assorted international bigwigs including two of princes of Wales (1875 and 1922) and the Czar of Russia (1891 – the tree has lasted rather longer than the czar) through to Joseph Tito (1959) and various post-independence Sri Lankan prime ministers and presidents.

The Great Lawn

To the west of the avenue stretches the **Great Lawn**, home to Peradeniya's most majestic sight: a huge Javan fig whose sprawling roots and branches create a remarkable natural pavilion. (There's also an overpriced **restaurant** near here, and cheaper drinks in a kiosk next door.) Running along the southern side of the Great Lawn, **Double Coconut Palm Avenue** is flanked with coco de mer trees, rather stumpy and unimpressive-looking things, though their massively swollen coconuts – which can weigh up to 20kg – are the world's largest and heaviest fruit. There are also a few stunning kauri pines here from Queensland (they're actually broadleaved trees, not pines), while a long line of strangely twisted Cook's pines flank the east side of the lawn.

The northern gardens

The northern half of the gardens has an altogether wilder quality, and is home to vast populations of **fruit bats**, which hang in spooky clusters from the branches overhead. At its northern end, Royal Palm Avenue curves around to the right, following the bank of the Mahaweli Ganga; you'll often see troupes of **macaque monkeys** here amid the spectacularly large clumps of riverside bamboo. A pleasant circuit leads right round the edge of the park, following the river through some of the gardens' most peaceful and shady areas to reach **Cabbage Palm Avenue**, lined with West Indian cabbage palms with their unusual, greenish trunks. **Palmyra Palm Avenue** leads off to the left, lined with very tall and slender Palmyra palms with their distinctively spiky tops, a familiar sight to anyone who has visited the Jaffna peninsula, where they are the dominant palm species, though they're much less common elsewhere in the island.

South of here is a marvellous group of **Java almonds**, whose huge buttressed roots line the side of the path. Returning to Cabbage Palm Avenue and continuing south brings you to **Cannon Ball Avenue**, lined with beautiful cannon ball trees, wreathed in creepers from which hang the characteristically large, round fruits, after which the militaristic

3

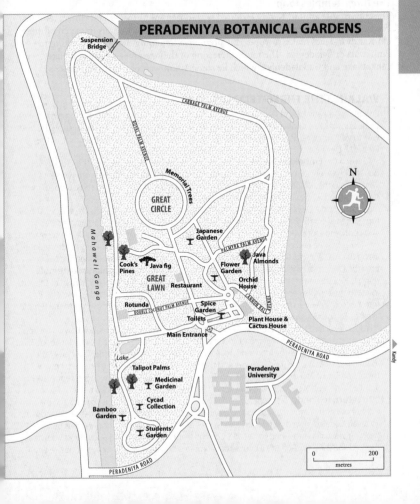

British named the tree. The Sinhalese (who call them *sal* trees) hold their beautiful flowers sacred, since they appear to comprise a tiny dagoba, shaded by a cobra's hood and surrounded by tiny florettes, which are thought to represent a crowd of worshippers. Beyond here, the avenue curves around away from the river, before returning you to the Orchid House and entrance.

The southern gardens

South of the Great Lawn lies a small but picturesque **lake**, covered in waterlilies and overlooked by a classical rotunda and an enormous clump of giant bamboo. Continuing south brings you to a didactic but dull little area of carefully laid out medicinal and aquatic plants, plus various types of grass. Next to these is a line of far more striking **talipot palms**, identifiable by the unusual criss-cross bark pattern at the foot of the trunk (the remains of old leaves) and by their enormous leaves – the trees as a whole look rather like enormous toilet brushes. Beyond here, at the southernmost edge of the gardens, is the pretty little **Students' Garden**, surrounded by weird cycads and ferns.

The three-temples loop

The countryside around Kandy is dotted with dozens of historic Kandyan-era **temples**. Few see any foreign visitors, and setting off into the local backwaters in search of these old Kandyan relics makes a wonderful alternative to joining the hordes flocking to Pinnewala or Peradeniya. The most interesting of these temples are the **Embekke**, **Lankatilake** and **Gadaladeniya**, which lie some 10km west of Kandy and make a

---

WALKING THE THREE-TEMPLES LOOP

Embekke, Lankatilake and Gadaladeniya temples can all be visited (albeit with some difficulty) by bus or, far more conveniently, by taxi (count on around $25–30 for the round-trip). The best way to visit, however, is to **walk** at least part of the way between the three, starting at the Embekke Devale and finishing at the Gadaladeniya (or vice versa).

To reach the **Embekke Devale** and the start of the walk, take a bus from the Clocktower bus station (every 20min; 1hr). You'll be dropped off in **Embekke village**, from where it's a 1km walk to the temple: turn right onto the tiny road opposite the red postbox, then follow it straight ahead as it switchbacks up over a steep hill.

From Embekke Devale, retrace your steps back up the road towards Embekke village. At the top of the hill, about 200m from the temple, the road forks. Go left here, climbing a steep hill and continuing for 500m through the edge of the village. At the end of the village you reach a gorgeous bo tree and paddy fields, with a huge rock outcrop to your right. Continue straight along the road for a further 500m until the road forks. Keep right here and continue over the brow of a hill, from where you'll catch your first, magical sight of the **Lankatilake temple** rising out of the tea plantations ahead. Continue ahead, ignoring another side-road to the left, to reach the temple's access road, which leads off on the left. This leads to the base of the temple, from where a magnificent flight of rock-cut steps leads precipitously up to the temple itself, giving glorious views of the surrounding hills.

From Lankatilake temple, return to the road by the pylon then continue left, following the road as it hairpins up to reach a larger road and another village. Turn here and continue for about 3km, keeping right whenever the road forks, to reach the **Gadaladeniya temple**. This part of the route is less special – the road is bigger and there's more traffic, although there are plenty of tuktuks around if you get bored with walking. The area is also a major metalworking centre, and you'll pass dozens of shops selling traditional oil lamps, looking a bit like overblown cake stands.

To return to Kandy, carry on down the road for a further ten minutes to reach the main Colombo–Kandy highway. Buses back to Kandy pass every minute or so – just flag one down. To reach Gadaladeniya directly from Kandy, take any of the numerous non-express buses heading west along the road to Kegalle, Colombo or Kaduganawa and ask to be set down at the Gadaladeniya turn-off (it's a couple of kilometres beyond Kiribathgoda, and before you reach Kadugannawa).

rewarding day-trip – they are often combined into a round-trip by vehicle or on foot, known as the **three-temples loop** (a further trio of temples is described on p.232); for details of the walking route between the three (see box opposite). All three temples were constructed during the fourteenth century, in the early days of the nascent Kandyan kingdom, when the region was ruled from Gampola and Tamil influence was strong.

Embekke Devale

Daily 8am–6pm • Rs.200 • Buses to Embekke depart from the Clocktower bus station (every 20min; 1hr)

Dating from the fourteenth century, the rustic little Embekke Devale, dedicated to Kataragama, is famous principally for the fine pavilion, the **digge** (drummer's pavilion), fronting the main shrine. The *digge*'s intricately decorated wooden pillars were apparently brought here from another temple at Gampola; each bears a different design, with an entertaining jumble of peacocks, entwined swans, wrestlers, dragons, dancers, horsemen, soldiers and Bodhisattvas (shown as composite figures: part man, part fish, part bird). One of the most famous panels depicts an elephant and lion fighting; another shows what looks curiously like a Habsburg double-headed eagle.

Two quaint lions flank the entrance to the **main shrine** behind, which is topped by a delicate pagoda-tower. To the left of the main building stands a rustic **granary**, raised on stones above the ground to protect its contents from wild animals; to the right, a subsidiary shrine with sumptuously carved wooden doors houses a Buddha and a fine (but difficult to see) wooden statue of a peacock, a bird traditionally associated with Kataragama.

Lankatilake

Daily 8am–6pm • Rs.200 • Buses to Lankatilake depart from the Goods Shed bus station (every 30min; 1hr)

Perhaps the finest temple in the district, **Lankatilake temple** is an imposingly solid-looking structure built on a huge rock outcrop and painted a faint blue rather than the usual white. It was founded in 1344, and its architecture is reminiscent of the solid, gedige-style stone temples of Polonnaruwa rather than the later and more decorative Kandyan-style wooden temples. The building was formerly four storeys tall, though the uppermost storeys collapsed in the nineteenth century and were replaced by the present, badly fitting wooden roof. The gloomy central **shrine**, with eighteenth-century Kandyan paintings, is magically atmospheric: narrow but tall, and filled with a great seated Buddha under a huge *makara torana*, above which rise tiers of decidedly Hindu-looking gods. The massive exterior walls contain a sequence of small shrines containing statues of Saman, Kataragama, Vishnu and Vibhishana, punctuated by majestic low-relief carvings of elephants. To the left of the temple, a large rock inscription in Pali records the details of the temple's construction.

Gadaladeniya

Daily 8am–6pm • Rs.200

Gadaladeniya dates from the same year – 1344 – as Lankatilake. The principal **shrine** is built on a rock outcrop at the top end of the site, and the style of the corbelled roof and carvings of dancers and drummers have a pronounced South Indian flavour, having been designed by a Tamil architect, a certain Ganesvarachari. The interior houses a fine gold Buddha (with oddly close-set eyes) under a marvellous *makara torana*. The whimsical subsidiary shrine, in the middle of the compound, consists of a cruciform building, each wing housing a tiny Buddha shrine and topped by a minuscule dagoba, with the entire structure being surmounted by a larger dagoba – one of the island's most unusual religious buildings.

Temples east of Kandy

Just east of the city there's another rewarding trio of temples dating from the Buddhist renaissance experienced under Kirti Sri Rajasinha (see p.210), who built all three.

Gangarama Viharaya

Daily 8am–6pm • Donation

About 2km east of Kandy (head east along the Mahiyangana road, then turn north towards Madawela) on the banks of the Mahaweli Ganga, lies the **Gangarama Viharaya**. This small monastery is notable mainly for its fine two-storey **image house**, decorated with Kandyan-era paintings and home to an 8m-tall standing Buddha statue, carved out of the natural rock outcrop around which the shrine is built. (You can see the rock outcrop poking out of the back of the image house, carved with an extensive rock inscription in Sinhala recording details of the temple's construction.) The walls inside are decorated with hundreds of tessellated sitting Buddhas, while the lower sections of the wall show Jataka stories and scenes from the Buddha's life, delicately painted in characteristic Kandyan style in narrow panels using a predominantly red palette. A small **digge** stands opposite the entrance to the image house.

Degaldoruwa

Daily 8am–6pm • Donation

The most interesting of this group of temples, **Degaldoruwa** is built in and around a large rock outcrop about 2km northeast of the Gangarama Viharaya. The temple consists of three small connected chambers: the first two – the *digge* and antechamber – are built outside the rock and topped by crumbling old wooden roofs, while the third, the main shrine, is hollowed out of the rock itself, and invisible from the outside. The **digge** has a few old wooden pillars and a couple of drums hanging from the rafters; it's unusual in being directly attached to the rest of the temple, rather than occupying a separate pavilion, as is usually the case. Old wooden doors lead into the **antechamber**, which preserves a fine moonstone and a sequence of murals showing scenes from the Jataka stories, painted in five vivid red panels.

From here, doors (whose metal fittings were formerly studded with jewels) lead into the **main shrine**. The main image inside is a large reclining Buddha, his head resting on a pillow inlaid with a glass copy of a huge amethyst – according to tradition, the painters who decorated the shrine worked by the light generated by this enormous jewel. The murals here are some of Sri Lanka's finest, though they're rather dark and difficult to make out, having until recently been covered in a thick layer of soot from fires lit inside the shrine – a tiny square of black wall has been left just next to one of the doors to show what the walls looked like before restoration. The wall opposite the reclining Buddha is painted with Jataka scenes and pictures of dagobas at Sri Lanka's principal pilgrimage sites, but the finest painting is on the ceiling, a magnificent depiction of the **Buddha's battle with Mara**, dating from the 1770s and rivalling the far better-known example at Dambulla.

Outside stands a belfry, apparently built in imitation of a Christian church tower. Steps to the left of the temple lead up to a large platform, where a stupa and bo tree stand facing one another above the temple.

Galmaduwa Gedige

The extremely unusual **Galmaduwa Gedige** is the main attraction at the village of Kalapura (signposted north off the Mahiyangana road about 5km east of the turn-off to the Gangarama and Degaldoruwa temples). The bizarre shrine here is enclosed in a cloister-like stone structure (the gedige) and topped by a stone pyramid – an odd but endearing Kandyan version of a traditional South Indian temple. Apparently, the gedige was left unfinished, and its exact purpose remains unclear (the image house at the back was only added during a restoration in 1967). Old ola-leaf manuscripts suggest that the innermost section was originally built as a jail to contain a single prisoner of noble birth who had offended the king, and that the surrounding ambulatory was added later.

Tea Museum

Daily except Mon and Sun afternoon 8.30am–3.30pm • Rs.500

South of Kandy, the small Hantana Road climbs steeply up into the hills through run-down tea estates, with sweeping views back to Kandy. Four kilometres along the road is the mildly interesting **Tea Museum**, housed in an attractively converted tea factory. The ground and first floors hold various imposing pieces of colonial-era machinery collected from defunct factories around the hill country, including assorted rollers, sifters, drying furnaces, withering trays and even a tractor, plus a cute little working model of a tea factory. The second floor has displays on two of Sri Lankan tea's great pioneers, with a small collection of the frugal personal effects (pipe, plate and walking stick) of James Taylor, who established the island's first commercial tea estate, and a display on the much more flamboyant career of Thomas Lipton (see p.440), who did so much to publicize Sri Lankan tea. There are also exhibits of other tea-related colonial-era bits and pieces, including Sri Lanka's oldest packet of tea, dating from 1944 and "Guaranteed by the Ceylon Tea Propaganda Board". The top floor has a small café, plus assorted tea and handicraft shops.

East of Kandy

The hill country **east of Kandy** remains largely off the tourist map and far less developed than the area to the west of the city – a refreshingly untamed area of rugged uplands which still preserves much of its forest cover. Two main highways run east from Kandy to Mahiyangana. The more circuitous but smoother **southern road** meanders around the south side of the **Victoria Reservoir and Dam**, opened in 1989 as part of the huge Mahaweli Ganga Project and one of the island's major sources of electricity. A **visitor centre**, just off the highway, offers fine views of the spectacular dam itself. Much of the densely forested area around the reservoir is protected as part of the Victoria-Randenigala Sanctuary (no entrance), and you might even spot the occasional elephant sticking its trunk out of the forest while you're travelling down the road.

Hanguranketa

Around 8km south of the southern road around Victoria Reservoir, and roughly 40km from Kandy, the sleepy little town of **HANGURANKETA** formerly served as a refuge for the kings of Kandy, who built a large palace here to which they would retreat during times of internal rebellion or external threat. The original palace was destroyed by the British in 1818 (or 1803, according to some sources) and its remains used to construct the **Potgul Maliga Vihara** ("Temple Library"), now home to an important collection of ola-leaf manuscripts, protected in their sumptuous original copper and silver covers. The temple as a whole is a good example of the high Kandyan style, with a fine central image house surrounded by smaller shrines and an unusual, mural-covered dagoba.

The Knuckles Range

The second of the two main roads east from Kandy, the rougher but dramatic **A26** twists and turns through the hills, skirting the northern edge of the Victoria Reservoir and running around the southern outliers of the **Knuckles Range**, the hill country's last great unspoilt wilderness, though its tourist potential remains largely untapped. The rugged peaks of the Knuckles (Dumbara Hills) – named by the British for their resemblance to the knuckles of a clenched fist – cover a rugged and still largely untouched area of great natural beauty and biodiversity. The steeply shelving mountain terrain reaches 1863m at the summit of the main Knuckles peak itself (the sixth highest in Sri Lanka) and includes stands of rare dwarf cloudforest. The area is home to leopard, various species of deer (sambhur, barking and mouse), monkeys (purple-faced langur and macaque), giant squirrels, rare species of lizard such as the horned black-lipped lizard, and an exceptionally fine collection of endemic bird species.

Exploring the Knuckles

The most straightforward approach to the Knuckles is from the main Kandy to Mahiyangana road. Some 27km east of Kandy, at **Hunasgiriya**, a left turn leads via **Rangala** into the range, hairpinning up via the village of Looloowatte (1065m) to **Corbet's Gap**, from where there are magnificent views of the main Knuckles directly ahead. The central parts of the range – described as a "super biodiversity hotspot" – are protected as a conservation forest and in 2010 were added to the list of World Heritage Sites along with Horton Plains National Park (the eighth place in Sri Lanka to achieve World Heritage status). An **entrance fee** of Rs.675 per person per day (which may rise to Rs.1000 in the near future) is charged to enter the conservation area. There are all sorts of intriguing **trekking** possibilities in the Knuckles, although you'll really need to go with a guide (see p.226) if you plan on doing any extended walks.

3

ACCOMMODATION	KNUCKLES RANGE
★ **Amaya Hunas Falls** (formerly Jetwing Hunas Falls) Elkaduwa, 27km north of Kandy ☎ 081 494 0320, ⊕ www.amayaresorts.com; map p.228. One of the most spectacularly located hotels in Sri Lanka, perched way up in the hills on the western edge of the Knuckles Ranges, a bumpy 1hr drive from Kandy. It's all surprisingly luxurious, despite the remote setting, with good food and plush rooms at a very reasonable price, while facilities include an Ayurveda centre and small golf course. <u>$110</u>	**Kandy Samadhi Centre** Kukul Oya Rd, 25km west of the city ☎ 081 447 0925, ⊕ thekandysamadhicentre .com; map p.228. Beautiful and serene retreat, a 50min drive west of the city in an unspoilt area of mountainous jungle. The emphasis is on simplicity and tranquillity, with elegantly simple rustic decor and rooms scattered among thirteen individual pavilions. Ayurveda treatments are available, and all food is home-grown and organic (no meat or alcohol). B&B <u>$100</u>
Green View Elkaduwa ☎ 081 567 1437 ⊕ greenview holidayresort.com; map p.228. Shangri-La guesthouse set in a very peaceful spot way up in the hills some 22km from Kandy (a 45min drive). The eight rooms are simple but comfy enough, with superb views through big picture windows out over the mountains. B&B <u>Rs.3300</u>	**Rangala House** Teldeniya, 25km west of Kandy ☎ 081 240 0294, ⊕ rangalahouse.com; map p.228. Cosy and very homely modern boutique guesthouse – more like staying in a friend's country house than in paying accommodation. The location up in the Knuckles Range, a 50min drive from Kandy, is beautiful, and it's also very convenient for the nearby Victoria Golf Club. <u>$136</u>

East to Mahiyangana

East of Hunasgiriya, the A26 gives increasingly fine views of the Knuckles Range to the north, with sheer rockfaces towering above the road and further craggy peaks rising beyond – Sri Lanka at its most alpine. Another thirty minutes' drive brings you to the dramatic escarpment at the eastern edge of the hill country, from where there are marvellous views of the dry-zone plains almost a kilometre below. The highway descends through a precipitous sequence of seventeen numbered hairpins – this stretch of the A26 is popularly known as Sri Lanka's most dangerous road, and although it's fairly small beer compared to Himalayan or Andean highways, the local bus drivers do their best to keep the adrenaline flowing. At the bottom of the hills, the village of **Hasalaka** is the starting point for the 45km road north to the little-visited Wasgomuwa National Park.

Mahiyangana

Lying spread out across the plains at the foot of the dramatic Knuckles Range, the small town of **MAHIYANGANA** (pronounced "my-*yan*-gana") is famous in Buddhist legend as the first of the three places in Sri Lanka which the Buddha himself is said to have visited (the others are Kelaniya and Nainativu). The large **Rajamaha Dagoba**, a kilometre or so south of town, is held to mark the exact spot at which the Buddha preached, and is also believed to enshrine a lock of his hair. The dagoba's origins are lost in antiquity; it's said to have been rebuilt by King Dutugemunu, and has been restored many times since. The present bell-shaped structure, picturesquely backdropped by the hill country escarpment, sits atop a large platform studded with elephant heads and approached by an impressively long walkway. The town's other eye-catching building is the striking replica of the famous **Mahabodhi Stupa** at Bodhgaya in India, erected at the behest of the late President Premadasa, which sits next to the main road on the west side of town.

Northeast of Mahiyangana lies the huge **Maduru Oya National Park** (see p.361).

ARRIVAL AND DEPARTURE   MAHIYANGANA

By bus Mahiyangana is something of a crossroads town between Polonnaruwa, Kandy, Badulla, Monaragala and Ampara, with reasonably frequent bus connections to all these places. The town itself is rather spread out, sprawling west from the Mahaweli Ganga.

ACCOMMODATION

There's a basic range of places to stay, including a cluster of budget places on Rest House Rd, next to the river, and a couple of more upmarket places further out.

The Nest About 2km east of town on Padiyathalawa Rd ☏ 0776 199 511, ⊛ nest-srilanka.com. Smaller and more characterful than Mahiyangana's other accommodation options, with four comfortable rooms (all with hot water, plus optional a/c for Rs.750) and good Sri Lankan food. The owner can organize trips to local Veddha villages and other local excursions. Rs.2750

New Rest House Rest House Rd, next to the river around 750m west of the bus station ☏ 055 225 7304. Perhaps the best of the town's cheaper places, this old-fashioned rest house has spacious if slightly shabby rooms, plus good food. The (old) *Rest House* and *Venjinn Guest House*, to the north and south of the *New Rest House* respectively, are other cheap options hereabouts. Rs.1848; a/c Rs.2464

Sorabora Gedara Hotel Sorabora Wewa Rd ☏ 055 225 8307, ⊛ soraboragedara.com. Neat, modern hotel in spacious grounds with comfy a/c doubles, a swimming pool, plus bar and restaurant. Rs.4000

Kotabakina

The country east of Mahiyangana is one of the last strongholds of Sri Lanka's ever-diminishing number of **Veddhas** (see box opposite), who live in the area around the village of **Dambana**, some 25km further along the A26. From Dambana, a rough track leads north a couple of kilometres to the principal Veddha village of **KOTABAKINA** ("King's Village"; also often but erroneously referred to as Dambana, though properly speaking this name refers to the Sinhalese village on the main highway). The village itself is a beautifully sylvan spot, with picturesque little bamboo-framed, mud-walled huts hemmed in by lush paddy fields. Men will be welcomed to the village with the traditional double-handed handshake, after which you can have a look round and talk to the village chief and other male villagers – instantly recognizable with their wispy uncut beards, shoulder-length hair and brightly polished little axes, which they carry over their shoulders. You won't meet any women, however, since all females retreat to their huts so as not to be seen by outsiders, and will stay there for the duration of your visit. You'll need to pick up an **interpreter** en route to the village, however (there are usually lots of volunteers offering their services for a consideration), since the Veddhas cannot – or perhaps will not – speak either English or standard Sinhalese, but stick doggedly to their own "Veddha language" (although whether it's a proper language or merely a strange sub-dialect of Sinhalese remains a moot point; native Sinhalese speakers can usually understand around a third of it).

Although undeniably interesting, visits to Kotabakina can also, sadly, be gratingly false. The Veddhas are used to entertaining passing coach parties with displays of dancing, singing, fire-making and bow-and-arrow shooting, and have become adept at extracting large sums of money for their services. Visits can be rather demeaning for

THE VEDDHAS

The **Wanniyala-aetto** ("People of the forest"), more usually known by the name of **Veddhas** (meaning "hunter"), were the original inhabitants of Sri Lanka, and are ethnically related to the aborigines of India, Sumatra and Australia. The Veddhas may have arrived in the island as far back as 16,000 BC, and developed a sophisticated matrilineal hunter-gatherer culture based on ancestor worship and an intimate knowledge of their forest surroundings, the latter allowing them to coexist in perfect harmony with their environment until the arrival of the Sinhalese in the fourth century BC. Veddhas feature extensively in early Sinhalese legend, where they are described as *yakkas*, or demons, and this common perception of them as demonic savages has persisted through the centuries. One memorably smug Victorian colonial official described them as a:

strange and primitive race [whose] members are but a degree removed from wild beasts. They know nothing of history, religion or any art whatever. They cannot count, know of no amusement save dancing, and are popularly supposed not to laugh. During the Prince of Wales's visit, however, one of those brought before him managed to grin when presented with a threepenny piece. The Veddhas have, however, of late years shown some signs of becoming civilised under British influence.

Faced by successive waves of colonizers, the Veddhas were forced either to assimilate with the majority Sinhalese or Tamils, or retreat ever further into their dwindling forests. Despite the best attempts of successive British and Sri Lankan governments to "civilize" them, however, an ever-diminishing population of Veddhas still cling obstinately to their traditions – about 350 pure Veddhas are now left in seven villages, mainly in the area east of Mahiyangana, and a small number have attempted to continue their traditional hunter-gatherer existence (even if they now use guns rather than bows and arrows), and also farm rice and other crops to supplement their diet and income. The creation of national parks, alongside government development and resettlement schemes and agricultural projects, have further encroached on traditional Veddha lands – in recent years they have campaigned vigorously for recognition and for the right to continue hunting on land now protected by the Maduru Oya National Park. Some "reserved" areas have now been set aside for their use, though their struggle for proper recognition continues.

For more on the Veddhas, see ⓦ www.vedda.org.

all concerned, and may well end in unedifying disputes over money. If you do agree to watch some dancing or whatever, make sure you agree a sum in advance, and don't expect to pay less than about $30 for the pleasure, or perhaps significantly more. Even if you don't, expect to hand over $10 or so to look around the village (plus a few dollars for your interpreter). Alternatively, you might be able to find some cut-price Veddhas along the main A26 at **Mavaragalpota**, a few kilometres back toward Mahiyangana, who offer similar displays at about a quarter of the price. Fake Veddhas have also been known to offer their services to unwary tourists along the road and around the temple in Mahiyangana. Having said which, you might consider that the whole experience is already sufficiently ersatz, and that a few imposter Veddhas more or less won't make much difference. If you have a genuine interest in the Veddhas, Sumane Bandara Illangantilake (see p.226) can arrange visits to Kotabakina on a more rewarding and equitable footing.

The southern hill country

The **southern hill country** is the highest, wildest and in many ways the most beautiful part of Sri Lanka. Although the area was an integral part of the Kandyan Kingdom, little physical or cultural evidence survives from that period, and most of what you now see is the creation of the British colonial period, when the introduction of **tea** here changed the economic face of Sri Lanka forever. The region's attractions are self-explanatory: a whimsical mixture of ruggedly beautiful scenery and olde-worlde colonial style, with sheer green mountainsides, plunging waterfalls and mist-shrouded tea plantations enlivened by quaint British memorabilia – clunking railways, half-timbered guesthouses, Gothic churches and English vegetables – while a further, unexpected twist is added by the colourful Hindu temples and saris of the so-called "Plantation Tamils", who have been working the tea estates since colonial times.

South from Kandy to Nuwara Eliya

The journey south from Kandy to Nuwara Eliya is spectacular both by train and by bus. The **bus** is far more direct and significantly quicker, cutting up through the hills and swinging round endless hairpins, passing the magnificent waterfalls at the village of **RAMBODA** en route, which plunge over the cliffs in two adjacent 100m cataracts. From Ramboda, it's a short drive on to Labookelie Tea Factory (see p.245) and Nuwara Eliya.

The **train** is significantly slower, but makes for a quintessentially Sri Lankan experience, as the carriages bump and grind their way painfully up the interminable gradients towards Nuwara Eliya (and occasionally lose traction and slither a yard or so back downhill again). The track climbs slowly through pine and eucalyptus forest into a stylized landscape of immaculately manicured tea plantations which periodically open up to reveal heart-stopping views through the hills, nowhere more so than above the village of **Dimbula**, at the centre of a famous tea-growing area, where the line passes high above a grand, canyon-like valley between towering cliffs.

ACCOMMODATION
RAMBODA

Lavender House Pussellawa ☎ 052 225 9928, ⊕ thelavenderhouseceylon.com. Occupying a fine old tea planter's villa of 1890, enclosed in idyllic gardens (with pool) and with five rooms beautifully furnished in traditional colonial style. Very appealing, but seriously expensive. **$325**

Ramboda Falls Hotel Ramboda ☎ 052 225 9582, ⊕ rambodafall.com. Functional but comfortable and good-value hotel close to – and offering a good view of – the Ramboda Falls, as well as of a second, smaller set of falls right next to the hotel. **$75**

Nuwara Eliya

Sri Lanka's highest town, **NUWARA ELIYA** lies at the heart of the southern hill country, set amid a bowl of green mountains beneath the protective gaze of Pidurutalagala, Sri Lanka's tallest peak. Nuwara Eliya (pronounced, as one word, something like "Nyur-*rel*-iya") was established by the British in the nineteenth century, and the town is often touted as Sri Lanka's "Little England", a quaint Victorian relic complete with municipal park, golf course, boating lake, a trio of fine old colonial hotels and frequent, very British, showers of rain.

Parts of Nuwara Eliya still live up to the hype, with a medley of doughty British-era landmarks whose misplaced architecture – from jaunty seaside kitsch to solemn faux-Tudor – lend some corners of the town an oddly English (or perhaps Scottish) air, like a crazily transplanted fragment of Brighton or Balmoral. Much of modern Nuwara Eliya, however, is far less of a period piece than the publicity would have you believe, while the unpredictable weather can add a further dampener. That said, if you take it with a pinch of salt, Nuwara Eliya still has a certain charm, especially if you can afford to stay in one of the town's nicer hotels, and it also makes an excellent base for **excursions** into the spectacular surrounding countryside and tea estates.

Brief history

Although there's evidence of Kandyan involvement in the region, Nuwara Eliya is essentially a British creation. The Nuwara Eliya region was "discovered" by the colonial administrator John Davy in 1819, and a decade later Governor **Edward Barnes** recognized its potential, founding a sanatorium and overseeing the creation of a road from Kandy, which he hoped would encourage settlement of the area. Barnes's

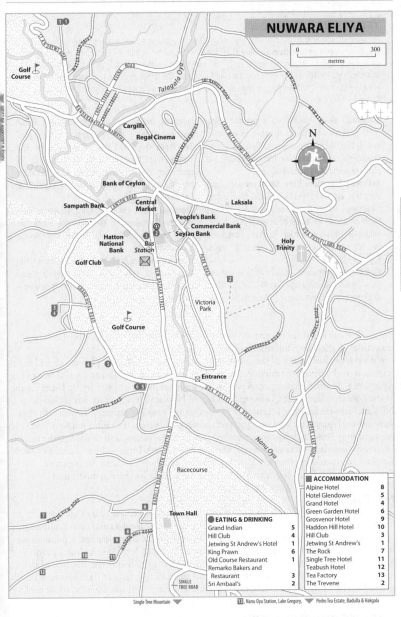

NUWARA ELIYA

3

plans slowly bore fruit, and during the 1830s the town gradually developed into a commercial and coffee-planting centre, with a largely British population. In 1847, **Samuel Baker** (who later distinguished himself by discovering Lake Albert in Africa and helping to identify the sources of the Nile) had the idea of introducing English-style agriculture to the area, laying the foundations for the town's market-gardening industry: vegetables grown here are still exported all over the island, while many of

3

TEA ESTATE BUNGALOWS

For a true taste of the colonial lifestyle of old Ceylon, you can't beat a stay in one of the sumptuous **tea estate bungalows** that dot the southern highlands. Originally built for British estate managers in the nineteenth and early twentieth centuries, many offer beautiful and atmospheric lodgings, often in spectacular locations. The following are just a small selection of what's available – further properties can be found at ⓦwww.boutiquesrilanka.com and ⓦwww.reddottours.com.

Cranford Villa Diyatalawa, around 15km south of Bandarawela, off the road to Haputale ☎011 281 9457, ⓦcranfordvilladiyatalawa.com. Characterful colonial bungalow with neat gardens and plenty of period atmosphere. B&B $91
Kelburne Mountain View Cottages 1km from Haputale ☎011 257 3382, ⓦkelburnemountain view.com. Three pretty colonial-style cottages (each with two or three bedrooms) in a breezy hillside location just outside Haputale, surrounded by tea gardens and with sweeping views. Rs.1600–18,200
Kirchhayn Bungalow Aislaby Estate, around 3km from Bandarawela ☎057 492 0556, ⓦkirchhaynbungalow.com. Characterful old

bungalow owned by the last remaining British planting family in Sri Lanka. B&B $307
Tea Trails ☎011 230 3888, ⓦteatrails.com. Four superb (but horribly expensive) bungalows of contrasting characters, all in working tea estates in the beautiful Bogawantalawa valley, close to Adam's Peak. Full-board from $580
Taprospa ☎011 438 0707, ⓦtaprospa.com. Three attractive bungalows on the Labookelie estate (see p.245) near Nuwara Eliya, plus another near Kalutara. From around $180
Warwick Gardens Ambewella, about 20km south of Nuwara Eliya ☎060 253 2284, ⓦjetwinghotels .com. Plush bungalow in its own six-acre estate deep in the heart of the southern hill country. $345

---

the area's local Tamil tea plantation workers supplement their incomes by growing vegetables in their own allotments.

With the gradual failure of the coffee crop during the 1870s, local planters turned their attention to the beverage which would radically change the physical and social face of the region: **tea**. The first experimental plantation was established in 1867 by Sir James Taylor at the Loolecondera Estate, between Kandy and Nuwara Eliya, and its success led to Nuwara Eliya becoming the centre of Sri Lanka's tea-growing industry. British influence went beyond quaint architecture and golf, however. Whereas the coffee industry had required only seasonal labour, tea required year-round workers, and this led to the arrival of massive numbers of Tamil migrant workers from South India – the so-called **Plantation Tamils** – who settled permanently in the area and decisively changed the region's demographic make-up; about sixty percent of the population here is now Tamil.

New Bazaar Street

There's nothing very historic about the centre of modern Nuwara Eliya, with its featureless procession of concrete shops strung out along **New Bazaar Street**, although it's worth sticking your nose into the determinedly local **Central Market**, a picturesque little covered alleyway of fruit and veg stalls stuffed full of local horticultural produce. Small-scale market-gardening (introduced during the British era) remains one of the mainstays of the modern town's economy and the odd spectacle of dark-skinned Tamils dressed up like English farm labourers in padded jackets and woolly hats, while carting

---

SPRING IN NUWARA ELIYA

A popular resort among Sri Lankans, Nuwara Eliya is at its busiest during the Sinhalese–Tamil **new year** in April, when spring comes to the hill country, the flowers bloom and the Colombo smart set descends. For ten days the town gets overrun and accommodation prices go through the roof, while visitors are entertained by a succession of events, including horse racing, golf tournaments, motor-cross (motorcycles), clay-pigeon shooting and a mini-carnival.

around great bundles of turnips, swedes, marrows, radishes and cabbages, is one of Nuwara Eliya's characteristic sights, adding a pleasantly surreal touch to the town's out-of-focus English nostalgia.

Victoria Park

Entrance on Uda Pussellawa Rd • Daily 7am–6.30pm • Rs.200

South of the Central Market, the workaday **Victoria Park** boasts a few neatly maintained trees and shrubs, and some of the tallest eucalyptuses you'll ever see. The park also has an unusual ornithological distinction: despite its proximity to the polluted town centre, it's something of an ornithological hotspot, being visited by a number of rare Himalayan migrant **birds**, including the Kashmir flycatcher, Indian blue robin and the pied thrush, as well as Sri Lankan endemics such as the Sri Lanka white-eye, yellow-eared bulbul and the dull-blue flycatcher. Unfortunately, the rip-off entry price imposed on foreigners may persuade you to take your money elsewhere.

Around Victoria Park

Opposite Victoria Park, Nuwara Eliya's sylvan **golf course** (see p.238) adds a further welcome splash of green, while to the south lies the town's scrubby **racecourse**, the scene of Sri Lanka's only horse-racing meetings, held here in April, August and December; each meeting lasts for a day, with ten to fifteen races. Beyond the racecourse, shabby **Lake Gregory** marks the town's southern end; you can follow footpaths around the banks, but it's not a particularly inspiring walk.

Single Tree Mountain

If you want to get a bird's-eye view out over the surrounding hills, there's a pleasant short walk, starting near the racecourse, to **Single Tree Mountain**. Go straight up the road immediately before the *Clifton Inn*, and walk up through tea plantations to the electricity station at the top, from where (in clear weather) there are marvellous views out to Hakgala and beyond.

Pidurutalagala

At the opposite, northern end of town rises the thickly forested mountain of **Pidurutalagala** (whose tongue-twisting name was transformed by the linguistically challenged British into the cod-Spanish Mount Pedro). At 2555m this is the highest peak in Sri Lanka, although sadly the summit now houses a major air-traffic control centre and so is out of bounds. Guided nature walks can sometimes be arranged through the nearby *St Andrew's* hotel (see p.242) to explore the wonderful patches of dense cloudforest skirting its base.

ARRIVAL AND DEPARTURE   NUWARA ELIYA

By train Nuwara Eliya doesn't have its own train station; the nearest stop is at Nanu Oya, about 5km down the road, with regular connections (see p.200) east to Haputale, Ella and Badulla, and west to Kandy and Colombo. Buses to Nuwara Eliya meet all arriving trains (despite what waiting touts and tuktuks driver might tell you); alternatively, a tuktuk will cost around Rs.500.

By bus The bus station is right in the middle of town. There are also occasional services to Bandarawela and Ella, though if heading towards either of these places, or Haputale, it's far easier to take the train (see timetables on p.200).

Destinations Badulla (every 30–45min; 3hr); Bandarawela (4 daily; 1hr 30min, or change at Welimada); Colombo (5 daily; 4hr 30min); Ella (4 daily; 2hr); Galle (1 daily; 8hr); Hatton (7 daily; 2hr); Kandy (every 30min; 2hr 30min–3hr); Matara (1 daily; 8–9hr); Nanu Oya (every 30min; 15min).

ACCOMMODATION

Although accommodation in Nuwara Eliya is plentiful, most places are poor value for money and are aimed more at Sri Lankan than foreign visitors – come the weekend or holiday periods, many cheaper places get overrun by parties of hormonal teenage boys or pissed-up locals. There's a particular shortage of good budget accommodation, and if money is tight you might prefer to head to Haputale or Ella. Wherever you stay, make sure you've got reliable hot water and blankets

– Nuwara Eliya can get surprisingly cold at night. Many places hike rates at weekends, especially over "long" weekends when the Friday or Monday is a poya day. Rates also rise steeply during December and Christmas, and over the "mini-season" during the school vacations in August, while rates in most places can triple or quadruple during the April new year period (see box, p.240).

Alpine Hotel 4 Haddon Hill Rd ☎052 222 3500, ⓦalpineecotravels.com. Well-run mid-range hotel in an extensively refurbished century-old colonial building in seaside Tudor style. Standard rooms are plush, if characterless; those in the "Colonial Wing" are brighter and more traditionally furnished. All come with satellite TV and heater, and there's also free wi-fi and a good range of tours (see p.245). $90

Hotel Glendower 5 Grand Hotel Rd ☎052 222 2501, ⓔhotelglendower@sltnet.lk. The most appealing mid-range option in town, this atmospheric half-timbered establishment makes a decent halfway alternative to the town's posh hotels – albeit a bit pricey for what you get. The whole place retains oodles of period character, including a cosy pub-style bar, a pleasant lounge and billiards table, and cosy rooms, plus the added bonus of the good in-house *King Prawn* Chinese restaurant (see p.244). B&B Rs.10,500

Grand Hotel Grand Hotel Rd ☎052 222 2881, ⓦwww.tangerinehotels.com. Doughty half-timbered pile, over a century old, which appears to have been lifted wholesale from a golf course in Surrey. The gorgeous public areas are painfully redolent of Blighty, with gracious old wooden decor and creaking furniture. As a period piece it's difficult to beat, although unfortunately current rack rates for the small and relatively undistinguished rooms are ludicrously overpriced. $249

Green Garden Hotel 16A Unique View Rd ☎052 223 4166, ⓔgreengarden.hotel@yahoo.com. Friendly little family-run guesthouse with smallish but cosy rooms (including some with satellite TV and balconies) and a homely little restaurant. Rs.2750

★ **Grosvenor Hotel** 6 Haddon Hill Rd ☎052 222 2307. Atmospheric small hotel in an old colonial building with a rather English-country-house feel. Rooms are large and quite smart, with reproduction colonial furniture; some also have fireplaces – staff will kindle a warming blaze for you on request. The attractive public areas include a cosy lounge with lots of big leather armchairs and a nice old-fashioned restaurant and bar. Superb value at current rates. B&B Rs.3300

Haddon Hill Hotel 24/3 Haddon Hill Rd ☎052 222 2087. Bland but comfortable modern hotel, with smart tiled rooms and efficient service. Not to be confused with the less appealing *Haddon Hill Inn* and *Haddon Hill Bungalow* further down the same road. Rs.3850

★ **Hill Club** Off Grand Hotel Rd ☎052 222 2653, ⓔhillclub@sltnet.lk. Founded in 1876, this baronial-looking stone and half-timbered structure is Sri Lanka's most famous exercise in nostalgia, with one of the island's best-preserved colonial interiors, complete with a cosy lounge, billiards room, a pair of bars and a fine old dining room. Rooms are homely, with creaky wooden floors, dark wood furniture and bathtubs; superior ones have (rather incongruous-looking) satellite TV and minibar. Even if you're not staying it's worth coming for dinner or a drink (see p.244). $150

★ **Jetwing St Andrew's** 10 St Andrew's Drive ☎052 222 2445, ⓦjetwinghotels.com. In a late Victorian former country club overlooking a swathe of immaculate lawn and the golf course, this serene colonial-style hotel is the smartest place in town. Rooms are spacious, well-equipped and pleasantly old-fashioned, while public areas – including an oak-panelled restaurant (see p.244), billiards room and cosy lounge – retain a delightful Edwardian ambience. Also offers a good range of walks and tours with the resident naturalist. $150

The Rock 60 Unique View Rd ☎052 567 9002, ⓦtherock.lk. Small, mid-range guesthouse, a steep 10min walk up the hill from town, though compensated for by fine views. Rooms are comfortably furnished in British B&B style; an extra $5 gets you a more spacious and plusher deluxe room with DVD, fridge and hairdryer. $47

Single Tree Hotel 1/8 Haddon Hill Rd ☎052 222 3009, ⓔkrishanthagamage@ymail.com. Comfortable and reasonably priced guesthouse with cosy wood-panelled rooms (some with satellite TV) in the main building or slightly less appealing ones in the house next door. Also has internet access (Rs.4/min) and free wi-fi, and is a good place to arrange tours (see p.245). Free pick-up from train or bus station. Rs.2750

Teabush Hotel 29 Haddon Hill Rd ☎052 222 2345, ⓦteabush-hotel.com. Small hotel set in a gracious colonial bungalow with a range of comfortable rooms of various standards and prices – more expensive ones attractively kitted out with old wooden furniture. There's a comfortable lounge to crash out in and a nice restaurant and bar with panoramic views. $65

The Trevene 17 Park Rd ☎072 230 4220, ⓦwww.hoteltrevenenuwaraeliya.com. Attractive guesthouse set in an atmospheric 200-year-old colonial bungalow complete with cosy old lounge and sunny veranda. The attractively time-warped rooms at the front have old wooden floors and period furniture; those at the back are simpler and cheaper. Free pick up from bus or train stations. Good value generally, although rates fluctuate. Rs.2000

AROUND NUWARA ELIYA

★ **The Tea Factory** Kandapola, 14km east of Nuwara Eliya ☎ 052 222 9526, ⬤ heritancehotels.com. Set on a hilltop surrounded by rolling tea estates, this spectacular five-star hotel was created out of the old Hethersett Estate Tea Factory, which closed in the 1970s. The factory's original exterior has been completely preserved, with corrugated-iron walls and green windows, and it's not until you step inside the stunning interior atrium that you realize the place isn't a working factory at all, although there's still plenty of old machinery lying around, giving the place a look which is at once industrial and futuristic. Rooms are stylish and extremely comfortable, with stunning views to all sides, and there are loads of facilities, including a plush spa. **$210**

EATING AND DRINKING

Several decent **restaurants** in the larger hotels offer good food and heaps of colonial charm. Many guesthouses and hotels also have convivial little **bars** – those at the *Hill Club* and *St Andrew's Hotel* are particularly good.

Grand Indian Grand Hotel, Grand Hotel Drive. Set at the foot of the hotel's driveway, this pleasant little café dishes up passable North and South Indian standards (mains around Rs.500–700) at lunch and dinner, and snacks at other times. The attached pastry shop is a decent place for a cup of tea and a cake. Daily 8am–8pm.

★ **Hill Club** Off Grand Hotel Drive ☎ 052 222 2653. Dining at this atmospheric old hotel offers a heady taste of the colonial lifestyle of yesteryear, complete with discreetly shuffling, white-gloved waiters. You must wear a jacket and tie to eat in the main dining room (or drink in the mixed bar) – if you don't have your own you can borrow the requisite clobber from the club wardrobe; ladies are expected to don "formal dress". Food is either a five-course set dinner ($25) or a selection of à la carte international dishes (mains $8–16); there's also a set lunch ($16), or just come for a drink in one of the two cosy bars. Confirmed misogynists should note that the erstwhile men-only bar has now been transformed into a "casual bar" and thrown open to the fairer sex. Daily noon–2.30pm, 7–10.30pm; temporary club membership fee (Rs.100) must be paid.

King Prawn Hotel Glendower, 5 Grand Hotel Rd ☎ 052 222 2501. One of the island's better Chinese restaurants, with an extensive menu of well-prepared chicken, beef, pork, fish and vegetarian Cantonese-style dishes prepared with a hint of Sri Lankan spice, plus a few Thai offerings. Most mains Rs.550–700. Daily noon–3pm & 7–10pm.

★ **Old Course Restaurant** St Andrew's Hotel, 10 St Andrew's Drive ☎ 052 222 2445. Set in the oak-panelled dining room of Nuwara Eliya's smartest hotel, the *Old Course* serves up a well-prepared and beautifully presented choice of local and international dishes, including a good vegetarian selection. You can watch your dinner being prepared in the open-plan kitchen and choose wine from Sri Lanka's only walk-in wine cellar. Mains $10–15. Daily 12.30–3pm & 7.30–10.30pm.

Remarko Bakers and Restaurant New Bazaar St. Cheap and cheerful little bakery-cum-restaurant with evening and lunchtime rice and curry and buriani buffets, short eats, rolls and cakes, along with a small selection of à la carte curries, seafood and Western dishes (Rs.250–350). Daily 5.30am–10pm.

Sri Ambaal's New Bazaar St. Cheery little South Indian-style café serving up cheap and tasty dosas (Rs.100–170) and short eats, plus sweets at the entrance counter. *Ambaal's* restaurant, diagonally opposite, is very similar. Daily 6am–8pm.

DIRECTORY

Banks The ATMs at the Commercial, Sampath, Bank of Ceylon and Hatton banks accept foreign Visa and MasterCards; those at the Seylan and People's banks accept Visa only.

Golf The gorgeous, 120-year-old Nuwara Eliya Golf Club course (☎ 052 222 2835, ⬤ negolf@sltnet.lk) winds through the town centre, beautifully landscaped with magnificent old cypresses, pines and eucalyptus. A round (including green fees, club hire, caddy and balls) costs around $70 on weekdays and $80 at weekends.

Internet Naveen Internet on Main St (daily 8am–6.30pm; Rs.60/hr).

Post office In the pink half-timbered eyesore on New Bazaar St, just south of the town centre (Mon–Sat 7am–8pm).

Taxis Can be found lined up along New Bazaar St.

Around Nuwara Eliya

The main reason for visiting Nuwara Eliya is to get out into the surrounding countryside, which boasts some of the island's highest and most dramatic scenery. The most popular and rewarding trip is to **Horton Plains National Park** and **World's End**, while you could also, at a push, use Nuwara Eliya as a base for visiting **Adam's Peak** – you'll need to leave at 10pm to arrive at Dalhousie at around 12.30am, then start climbing at 2am in order to reach the summit for dawn.

The Pedro tea estate

Daily 8.30am–6pm • Rs.200 • Bus #715 to Kandapola (every 30min) goes past the factory, or catch a tuktuk

If you're interested in finding out more about the local tea industry, the **Pedro Tea Estate**, set beneath a flank of Mount Pedro about 3km east of Nuwara Eliya, offers a convenient introduction. The factory building and tea fields are less picturesque than others in the highlands (there's rather too much suburban clutter, and pylons straggle impertinently across the views), but the easy accessibility and informative resident guide make it a worthwhile short excursion. Established in 1885, the estate remained under British ownership until being nationalized in 1975 (it was reprivatized in 1985); its factory is still home to a few impressive pieces of old British machinery, some still in operation.

Labookelie tea estate

Kandy–Nuwara Eliya highway • Daily 8am–5pm • Free

Around 20km north of Nuwara Eliya lies the expansive **Labookelie Tea Estate**, set in gorgeous rolling countryside at an elevation of around 2000m. The estate is part of the Mackwoods conglomerate, a famous old mercantile firm founded by William Mackwood in 1841. The Labookelie tea gardens are much more photogenic, and the countryside much more unspoilt, than at the Pedro estate, and the whole place is well set up for visitors, with free **tours** of the busy factory and a swish café in which to sup a cup of the resultant brew while nibbling a cake. Labookelie is also easy to reach, since all buses from Nuwara Eliya to Kandy pass right by the entrance.

Hakgala Botanical Gardens

Daily 8am–5pm • Rs.600 • Take any bus heading to Welimada or Badulla (every 15min; 20min)

Some 10km southeast of Nuwara Eliya, **Hakgala Botanical Gardens** lie beneath the towering **Hakgala Rock**, with majestic views across the hills of Uva Province receding in tiers into the distance. The rock is allegedly one of the various pieces of mountain scattered by Hanuman on his return from the Himalayas (see p.157) – Hanuman apparently carried this bit of mountain in his mouth, hence its name, meaning "Jaw Rock". The gardens were first established in 1861 to grow **cinchona**, a source of the anti-malarial drug quinine, and were later expanded to include a wide range of foreign species. They're also well known for their **roses** (in bloom from April to August).

The gardens sprawl up the steep hillside, ranging from the anodyne ornamental areas around the entrance to the far wilder and more interesting patches of forest up the hill where you'll find many majestic Monterey cypresses from California, plus fine old

TOURS FROM NUWARA ELIYA

The best and cheapest place to organize **local tours** is *Single Tree Hotel* (see p.242); the nearby *Alpine Hotel* is another possibility, although trips booked here tend to be more expensive. Both these places lay on a range of activities including tea factory visits, guided mountain-biking, horseriding, fishing, canoeing and an interesting full-day waterfall tour, visiting no fewer than sixteen cascades – a good way to get to see some of the hidden corners of the surrounding hill country. As a very rough rule of thumb, count on around $35 for a half-day tour, or $60 for a full day, including guiding and vehicle. The return trip to Horton Plains costs around $35 per vehicle; the journey to Horton Plains and then on to Haputale or Ella will cost around $55–60, while the trip to Adam's Peak goes for around $65.

There are also several good **walking guides** attached to *Single Tree*, including the excellent Raja (Neil Rajanayake, ⓦ srilankatrekkingraja.com), who leads various one-day walks throughout the area for around $50 per day inclusive of guiding and transport and is also working to establish a network of village homestays in the area – see his website for details. These include the fine hike up to Shantipura and Uda Radella (15km); an exhilarating downhill walk from Ohiya to Haputale (15km); another one-day walk from Bomburuwela (4km from Nuwara Eliya) to Welimada (17km); and a 20km hike up Great Western mountain, near Nanu Oya.

cedars, a section of huge tree ferns, stands of Japanese camphor, and pines and eucalyptus, including a shaggy cluster of bark-shedding Australian melaleucas. You might also glimpse of one of the gardens' elusive **bear monkeys**, while this is also an excellent place to spot endemic montane **bird** species, including the dull-blue flycatcher, Sri Lanka whistling thrush and Sri Lanka bush warbler.

The Sita Amman Temple
About 1.5km along the main road from Hakgala Botanical Gardens towards Nuwara Eliya, the **Sita Amman Temple** is said to be built at the spot where Rawana held Sita captive, as related in the Ramayana – although the same claim is also made for the Rawana Cave in Ella (see p.252) – the strange circular depressions in the rock by the adjacent stream are supposed to be the footprints of Rawana's elephant. The small temple – the only one in Sri Lanka dedicated to Sita – boasts the usual gaudy collection of statues, including a couple of gruesome Kali images, though there's not really much to see.

Waterfalls west of Nuwara Eliya
The area west of Nuwara Eliya around the tiny village of **DIMBULA** is one of the most scenically spectacular parts of the island, though its tourist potential remains almost totally unexploited. The easiest way to get a taste of the area is to go on one of the "waterfall tours" run by the *Single Tree Hotel* in Nuwara Eliya (see box, p.245), which usually include the Ramboda falls (see p.238) along with several picturesque cascades in the Dimbula area – notably the broad, two-tiered **St Clair Falls** and the taller and more precipitous **Devon Falls**, which lie less than 2km apart just north of – and clearly visible from – the A7 highway (although sadly the St Clair Falls are gradually drying up as a result of water being diverted into the nearby Kotmale Hydropower Project).

Horton Plains National Park and World's End
Daily 6am–4pm • $20 per person, plus additional service charge and taxes (see p.45)
Perched on the very edge of the hill country midway between Nuwara Eliya and Haputale, **Horton Plains National Park** covers a wild stretch of bleak, high-altitude grassland bounded at its southern edge by the dramatically plunging cliffs that mark the edge of the hill country, including the famous **World's End**, where the escarpment falls sheer for the best part of a kilometre to the lowlands below. Set at an elevation of over two thousand metres, Horton Plains are a world apart from the rest of Sri Lanka, a misty and rainswept landscape whose cool, wet climate has fostered the growth of a unique but fragile ecosystem. Large parts of the Plains are still covered in beautiful and pristine stands of **cloudforest**, with their distinctive umbrella-shaped keena trees, covered in a fine cobweb of old man's beard, whose leaves turn from green to red to orange as the seasons progress. The Plains are also one of the island's most important watersheds and the source of the Mahaweli, Kelani and Walawe rivers, three of the island's largest.

Wildlife
The park's **wildlife** attractions are relatively modest. The herds of elephants which formerly roamed the Plains were all despatched long ago by colonial hunters, while you'll have to be incredibly lucky to spot one of the 45-odd leopards which are thought to still live in the area. The park's most visible residents are its herds of sambar deer, while you might see rare bear-faced (also known as purple-faced) monkeys. The park is also one of the best places in the island for **birdwatching**, and an excellent place to see montane endemics such as the dull-blue flycatcher, Sri Lanka bush warbler, Sri Lanka whistling thrush and the pretty yellow-eared bulbul. You'll probably also see beautiful lizards, some of them boasting outlandishly fluorescent green scales, though their numbers are declining as the result of depredations by crows, attracted to the park

(as to so many other parts of the island) by the piles of litter dumped by less environmentally aware visitors.

Exploring the park

The best way of seeing Horton Plains is to follow the 9km **circular trail** around the park, starting from the visitor centre by the entrance and walkable at a gentle pace in two to three hours. There's also a much longer (22km return) trek to the top of **Kirigalpota** from here, as well as an easy shorter trail (6km return) to the summit of **Totapolakanda**, which starts a few kilometres back down the main road to Nuwara Eliya. If you haven't come with a guide, it's fairly easy to find your own way around – you may be able to pick up a guide at the entrance, but don't count on it. Wherever you go, remember that the Plains can get very cold and wet: take a thick sweater, stout shoes and something waterproof.

From the visitor centre, the main circular trail around the park leads for 500m through rolling plains covered in patana grass and dotted with rhododendron bushes; the altitude here is over 2000m and the air quite thin – fortunately, most of the main trail is more or less flat. This opening section of the trail gives a good view of the park's strange patchwork flora, with alternating stretches of bare patana grassland interspersed with densely wooded cloudforest. According to legend, the grasslands were created by Hanuman during the events described by the Ramayana. Tradition states that Hanuman, to avenge the kidnapping of Sita, tied a burning torch to his tail and swept it across the plains, creating the areas of treeless grassland which can still be seen today, although the prosaic explanation is that they're the result of forest clearances by prehistoric farmers – these areas were still being used to grow potatoes as recently as the 1960s. Beyond the grasslands, the path leads for 2km through a superb stretch of cloudforest: a tangle of moss-covered keena trees and nellu shrubs, along with many medicinal herbs and wild spices such as pepper, cardamom and cinnamon. From here, it's another couple of kilometres to reach the cliffs which bound the southern edge of the park and the first viewpoint, **Small World's End**.

World's End

Beyond Small World's End the path continues through another 1.5km of cloudforest, dotted with numerous clumps of dwarf bamboo, before reaching **World's End** proper (2140m). From here, the cliffs plunge almost vertically for 825m, revealing enormous views across much of the southern island; the large lake in the near distance is at Uda Walawe National Park, while on a clear day you can see all the way down to the coast. There are also marvellous views along the craggy mountains which line the escarpment, including Sri Lanka's second and third highest peaks, Kirigalpota (2395m) and Totapolakanda (2359m), which stand at the edge of the park (and which are reachable by the trails mentioned above). Another 200m beyond World's End, the path turns inland towards Baker's Falls. If you ignore this turning for a moment and continue along the cliff edge for a further 100m you'll reach another viewpoint from the overhanging rock ledge – it's said that no fewer than ten star-crossed couples have leapt to their deaths from here over the years.

From here, retrace your steps back to the main track and follow it as it loops back towards the visitor centre, through open patana grassland with cloudforest set back on both sides.

Baker's Falls

A couple of kilometres from World's End you pass **Baker's Falls**, named after the pioneering Samuel Baker (see p.239). It's a steep and slippery scramble down to the beautiful little falls themselves, after which you'll have to scramble back up again – if the altitude hasn't already got to you, it probably will here. The final couple of kilometres are relatively humdrum, crossing open patana grassland back to the entrance, enlivened during the early morning by the resonant croaking of thousands of frogs in the surrounding grasses and trees.

Poor Man's World's End

Just outside the entrance to the park on the Ohiya side, a track leads off the road to **Poor Man's World's End**, named back in the days when it was possible to come here to enjoy the view without having to pay the national park entry fee. The viewpoint is reachable along the plantation road which divides the national park itself from the Forestry Department land on the other side; look for the DWC stone post roughly 1km before the Ohiya-side ticket office. It's a five-minute walk to the viewpoint, although you can carry on along the plantation road for several kilometres, a superb little hike through tea plantations strung out along the edge of the ridge. It's a fine panorama, offering an interestingly different perspective of the dramatically plunging escarpment, and there are further sensational views of World's End from the road beyond as it plunges down towards Ohiya.

One other way of getting into Horton Plains was formerly to do the extremely taxing walk up from **Belihul Oya**, at the foot of the escarpment – a very steep 11km trek. Unfortunately, at the time of writing the path had been closed, though it may reopen at some point in the future.

ARRIVAL AND DEPARTURE   HORTON PLAINS NATIONAL PARK

Note that the view from World's End is generally obscured by mist from around 10am onwards, especially during the rainy months from May to July, so you'll have to arrive early to stand a realistic chance of seeing anything – most drivers will suggest you leave around 5.30am to reach the park entrance by 7am, and World's End by 8.30am.

By car You can reach Horton Plains from either Nuwara Eliya or Haputale; the return trip from either takes around ninety minutes and currently costs around $35–45/vehicle, including waiting time. The plains are bisected by a single road running between Pattipola (on the park's Nuwara Eliya side) and Ohiya (Haputale side); entrance fees (see p.246) are collected at ticket offices next to this road on either side of the plains. (Note that although the road is publicly owned and maintained, both locals and tourists now have to pay the national park entrance fee just to drive along it, even if you've no intention of going walking in the

Plains themselves – the latest and most spectacular in the Department of Wildlife Conservation's long list of dubious money-making rackets.) It's a 3km drive from either ticket office up to the main entrance into the park.

By train It's also possible – with considerable difficulty – to reach the park by public transport. The easiest place to start is Haputale; catch a train to Ohiya station, from where it's an 11km walk (around 3hr uphill, and 3hr back down) up the road to the national park entrance, a pleasant hike with fine views. Make sure you check latest train times before starting out to make sure you don't get stranded.

INFORMATION

Accommodation There are a few places to stay dotted around the edge of the park, including a couple of remote options around Bambarakanda Falls (see p.262).

Information The smart visitor centre at the park entrance has some interesting displays on the Plains' history, flora and fauna.

Badulla and around

Set on the eastern edge of the hill country, the bustling modern town of **BADULLA** is capital of Uva Province and its most important transport hub – you might pass through en route between the hill country and the east coast, and if you do get stuck here overnight, there are a couple of modest attractions to while away a few hours. Thought to be one of the oldest towns on the island, Badulla became a major centre on the road between Polonnaruwa and the south, though the old town has vanished without trace. Badulla thrived under the British, developing into a vibrant social centre complete with racecourse and cricket club, though there's almost nothing left to show from those days now. Nearby **Dunhinda Falls** (see p.250) and the unusual **Bogoda Bridge** (see p.250) are also both worth a look.

Kataragama Devale

Entrance from Devale St

Easily the most striking building in town is the eighteenth-century **Kataragama Devale**. Centrepiece of the temple is the quaint Kandyan-style **main shrine**, a rustic little structure with tiled wooden tower and the extensive remains of murals on the exterior walls showing scenes from a perahera. The shrine is entered via a colonnaded walkway leading to a cluster of finely carved columns and an elaborate door topped by a carving of buxom figure in a tiara, flanked by two elephants – possibly a bodhisattva. Inside, the principal image of Kataragama is, as usual, hidden behind a curtain except during pujas, flanked by statues of a pink Saman, holding an axe and flag, and Vishnu, bearing a conch shell and bell.

There's a smaller subsidiary shrine to **Pattini** (see p.218) to the right of the main shrine, with another finely carved wooden door, pillars and the slight remains of old murals.

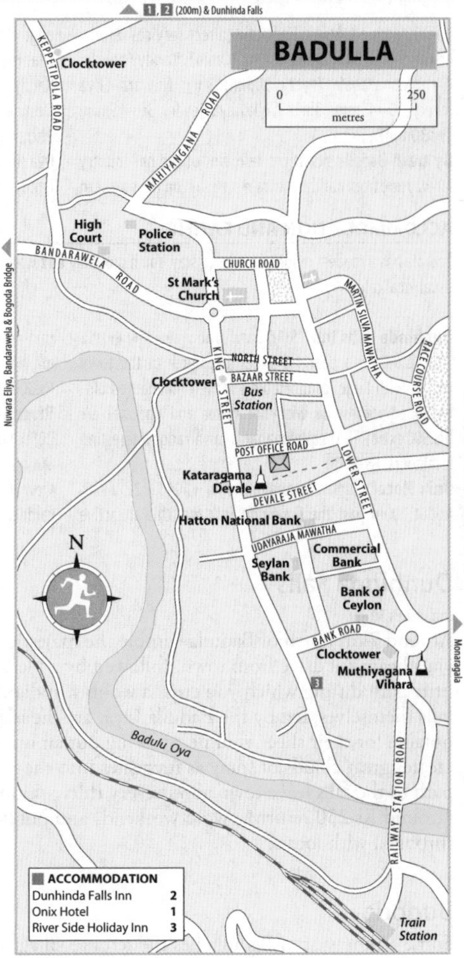

The rest of town

At the southern end of town stands the **Muthiyagana Vihara**, whose origins are believed to date back two thousand years to the reign of Sri Lanka's first Buddhist king, Devanampiya Tissa. It's a tranquil, if unremarkable, spot, occasionally enlivened by the presence of a rambling temple elephant.

Elephants are unlikely to be seen in the vicinity of the modest little **St Mark's Church**, one of the few mementos of Badulla's colonial-era past, flanking the roundabout at the northern end of King Street. Inside, a prominent tablet memorializes the infamous soldier and sportsman **Major Thomas William Rogers**, who is said to have shot well over a thousand elephants before being torched by a timely bolt of lightning at Haputale in 1845. The memorial concludes, appropriately enough, with the traditional biblical homily, "In the midst of life we are in death" – a sentiment with which Major Rogers, who alone despatched so many of island's most majestic creatures, would no doubt have agreed.

BADULLA

ACCOMMODATION

Dunhinda Falls Inn	2
Onix Hotel	1
River Side Holiday Inn	3

ARRIVAL AND DEPARTURE

BADULLA

By bus The bus station is bang in the middle of Badulla on King St, with regular services to all nearby towns and further afield.

Destinations Bandarawela (every 15min; 1hr); Colombo (hourly; 7hr); Ella (every 30min; 45min; or catch a Bandarawela bus to Kumbalwela Junction, 3km from Ella, where the Ella road branches off the main Bandarawela–Badulla road, and either wait for another bus or catch a tuktuk); Haputale (direct services hourly, or change at Bandarawela; 1hr 30min); Kandy (hourly; 4hr); Monaragala (every 30min; 3hr); Nuwara Eliya (every 30–45min; 3hr); Wellawaya (every 30–45min; 1hr 30min).

By train Badulla sits at the terminus of the hill country railway line from Kandy. The train station is on the southern edge of the centre, with regular services (see p.200) west to Ella, Haputale, Nuwara Eliya (Nanu Oya), Peradeniya (for Kandy) and Colombo.

Destinations Colombo (3 daily; 10–11hr); Ella (3 daily; 1hr); Haputale (3 daily; 2hr); Hatton (3 daily; 5hr); Nanu Oya (for Nuwara Eliya; 3 daily; 3hr 45min); Peradeniya (for Kandy; 3 daily; 7–8hr).

ACCOMMODATION AND EATING

Badulla has a modest range of places to stay. You'll probably **eat** where you're staying; the only other possibilities are the usual local cafés.

Dunhinda Falls Inn 35/10 Bandaranayake Mw ☏ 055 222 3028. On a peaceful street just north of the town centre, with large, comfortable and well maintained old-fashioned rooms; all with hot water and optional a/c (Rs.500 extra). The helpful manager can arrange interesting local tours. **Rs.2500**

Onix Hotel 69 Bandaranayake Mw ☏ 055 222 2426. About 100m past the *Dunhinda Falls Inn*, this attractive mid-range hotel has bright, nicely furnished rooms with a/c, hot water and cable TV (plus one cheaper fan room for Rs.3000); there's also a small pool. **Rs.3850**

River Side Holiday Inn 27 Lower King St ☏ 055 222 2090. Close to the centre, with pleasant modern rooms with optional a/c and a passable rooftop restaurant, though the view of the massed pylons next door probably isn't what you came to Sri Lanka to see. **Rs.2200**; a/c **Rs.2750**

Dunhinda Falls

Entrance Rs.50

Around 7km north of Badulla tumble the majestic, 63m-high **Dunhinda Falls**, reached via a beautiful drive from town, followed by a pleasant 1.5km scramble along a rocky little path during which you cross a wobbly, Indiana Jones-style suspension bridge. The falls themselves, fed by the Badulla Oya, are the island's seventh highest, but are most notable for their sheer volume, spewing out an impressive quantity of water which creates great clouds of spray as it crashes into the pool below. **Buses** running past the path to the falls leave town about every thirty minutes; alternatively, hire a tuktuk (around Rs.250 return). Avoid weekends and public holidays, when the falls are thronged with locals.

Bogoda

Some 15km west of Badulla lies the remote village of **BOGODA**, squirrelled away in a deeply rural setting on the banks of the small Galanda Oya amid the undulating fringes of the hill country. Steep steps lead from the village down to an unusual **roofed bridge**, a quaint little toy-like structure, with delicately balustraded sides and tiled roof elegantly balanced on a single wooden pier plunged into the rocky rapids below. The bridge lies on a pilgrimage route that connects with Mahiyangana and the Dowa Temple near Ella – there's thought to have been a bridge here since the twelfth century, though the present structure dates from around 1700. Next to the bridge is the **Raja Maha Vihara** temple, an attractive little whitewashed structure built into a large rock outcrop. The temple dates back to the eighteenth century and houses a large reclining Buddha, but not much else.

ARRIVAL AND DEPARTURE   BOGODA

By bus It's slightly tricky to reach Bogoda by public transport from Badulla. First, catch a Bandarawela-bound bus to Hali-Ela. In Hali-Ela, buses leave from outside the post office (on the side road on your right as you enter the village) to Katawela, from where it's a 4km walk or tuktuk ride (around Rs.400 return) to the bridge. A few buses go all the way from Hali-Ela to Bogoda. Alternatively, bus #312 goes directly to Katawela from Badulla. You could also visit the bridge from Bandarawela or Ella.

Ella

Set on the southeastern edge of Uva Province, **ELLA** is one of the hill country's most appealing destinations. This is the closest thing to an English country village you'll find in Sri Lanka, enjoying a pleasantly temperate climate and surrounded by idyllic green hills blanketed in tea plantations and offering some good walking, as well as one of the finest views in Sri Lanka.

There's not much to **Ella village** itself. An attractive scatter of cottages and bungalows enclosed in neat, flower-filled gardens, it preserves (for the time being at least) a pleasantly low-key atmosphere despite the number of foreign tourists passing through – although increasingly rapid and uncontrolled development around the edges of the village is increasingly beginning to threaten its peaceful rural charm. The single street meanders gently downhill, past assorted guesthouses and a scatter of cafés, before reaching the edge of the escarpment, just below the *Grand Ella Motel*, from where there's the classic view past the towering bulk of **Ella Rock** on the right and through a cleft in the hills – the so-called **Ella Gap** – to the plains far below. There's also a small Buddhist temple on the road here, where passing motorists stop and donate a coin for good luck before negotiating the treacherously twisting highway to Wellawaya, which descends into the sheer-sided valley below.

Little Adam's Peak

One of the best ways to spend a morning in Ella is to tackle the beautiful short walk up to the top of **Little Adam's Peak**, a pyramid-shaped rock which stands opposite the far larger Ella Rock and offers marvellous views out over the hills. The walk makes a very pleasant morning's excursion, and is fairly gentle and largely flat, apart from a small amount of climbing near the end. Count on around two hours return, and go early before the clouds set in. To begin the walk, head down the **Passara Road** for 1km, passing pine woods to your left. Just past the 1km marker the road turns sharp left by a garden centre; take the path that goes off the right-hand side of the road, straight ahead through beautiful tea plantations. Follow this path for 500m, ignoring the branch on your right which descends to a ramshackle tea pickers' village below. Keep left, following the path, with increasingly fine views to **Ella Rock** opposite and the **Newbourg Tea Factory** in the other direction. After

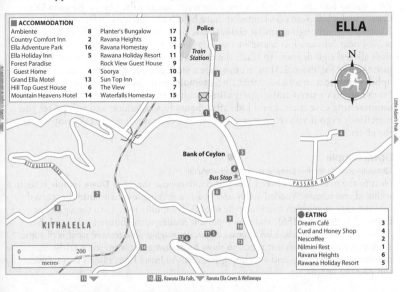

ACCOMMODATION

Ambiente	8	Planter's Bungalow	17
Country Comfort Inn	2	Ravana Heights	12
Ella Adventure Park	16	Ravana Homestay	1
Ella Holiday Inn	5	Rawana Holiday Resort	11
Forest Paradise		Rock View Guest House	9
Guest Home	4	Soorya	10
Grand Ella Motel	13	Sun Top Inn	3
Hill Top Guest House	6	The View	7
Mountain Heavens Hotel	14	Waterfalls Homestay	15

ELLA

N

Police

Train Station

Little Adam's Peak

KITHALELLA ROAD

Bank of Ceylon

Bus Stop

PASSARA ROAD

KITHALELLA

0   200
metres

Rawana Ella Falls,   Ravana Ella Caves & Wellawaya

EATING

Dream Café	3
Curd and Honey Shop	4
Nescoffee	2
Nilmini Rest	1
Ravana Heights	6
Rawana Holiday Resort	5

3

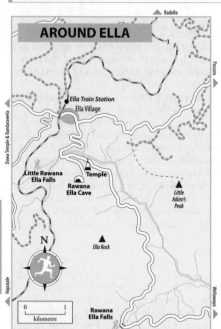

another 500m you reach a point where two tracks go off on the right close to one another. Take the second track (past the gate), and follow it for the final kilometre up to the top of Little Adam's Peak – the path weaves around the back of the peak and zigzags up to the summit, from where there are marvellous views of Ella Rock, Ella Gap and the very top of the Rawana Ella Falls.

Rawana Ella Falls

Ella is famous in Sri Lankan folklore for its Ramayana connections: according to one tradition, the demon king Rawana brought the captive Sita here and hid her away in a cave a couple of kilometres outside the present-day village. Rawana's name is now memorialized in the names of various village guesthouses, as well as in the dramatic **Rawana Ella Falls** (also known as the Bambaragama Falls), which plunge magnificently for some 90m over a series of rock faces 6km below Ella down the Wellawaya Road. It's an impressive sight, and you can clamber some way up the rocks to one side of the falls – locals may offer to show you the way for a consideration. To reach the falls, catch any bus heading down towards Wellawaya.

Rawana Ella Cave

En route to Rawana Ella Falls, a few kilometres out of Ella, lies the **Rawana Ella Cave**, in which Rawana is claimed to have held Sita captive, as related in the Ramayana – although a similar claim is made for the Sita Amman Temple (see p.246) near Nuwara Eliya, and in any case there's remarkably little to see, given the site's alleged significance. To reach the cave, head down the road from the village into the gap for about 1.5km, from where a side road on the right makes a stiff 1km uphill climb to a small and rather rustic **temple**, built underneath a rock outcrop. From here, it's a steep and slippery climb – often treacherous after rain – up to the uninteresting cave itself. Local kids offer themselves as guides, and will pester you mercilessly even if you've no interest in visiting the cave, but it's really not worth the effort.

Dowa Temple

10km southwest of Ella, 6km from Bandarawela • No set hours • Donation

Next to the main road between Ella and Bandarawela, the small **Dowa Temple** is set in a secluded and narrow wooded valley and boasts a striking low-relief Buddha, carved into the rock face which overlooks the temple. It's similar in style to the figures at Buduruwagala (see p.256), and may represent Maitreya, the future Buddha of the Mahayana pantheon who also appears at Buduruwagala. The temple itself is of some antiquity, though there's not much to show for it now apart from some fairly uninteresting paintings and a reclining Buddha. All buses from Ella to Bandarawela run past the temple.

WALKING UP ELLA ROCK

The most rewarding, and most taxing, hike around Ella is the ascent of the majestic **Ella Rock**, which looms over the village. It's around a four-hour hike in total, with an interesting mix of rail track, tea plantation, and some steep stuff near the summit. Carry food, water and good footwear, and take care in wet weather, when tracks can get slippery – and be aware, too, that mist and rain can descend quickly at the top. There are several different possible **routes**; most begin by following the rail line south out of the village, then following one of the various paths which strike off up the rock. Different people recommend different routes, but the following is perhaps the most direct and easy to follow.

Follow the rail line south out of Ella village for about 1.5km until the tracks cross a rickety bridge near the top of **Little Rawana Ella Falls**. A couple of metres before the bridge, a tiny path heads steeply down to the left. Scramble down this, then veer right, under the bridge, and follow the small irrigation channel back under the bridge again until you reach a small metal footbridge across top of Little Rawana Ella Falls.

Cross the footbridge and continue straight ahead. After 100m the path forks; bear right and follow the path as it climbs steeply for 300m. At the top of the hill (just before a large boulder) a narrow path cuts back on the right. Follow this path uphill, into a tea plantation. Keep left at the fork 200m further on and continue 150m until you reach a T-junction. Turn left here, aiming for the house on a low hill more or less directly ahead of you, keeping left at the next two forks to reach the house.

Directly in front of the house, a well-defined path branches off on the left. Ignore this and instead follow the very faint path straight ahead (it runs along the left-hand side of the small tea garden in front of the house). This path is very overgrown for the first 50m, but then becomes clearer. Follow this path as it climbs steadily for about 45 minutes until it reaches the edge of the ridge, keeping left wherever there's a choice of tracks. From here the path continues, very steep and stony now, to the summit of the rock – another thirty minutes or so of hard hiking.

ARRIVAL AND DEPARTURE ELLA

By bus Buses drop passengers off at the road junction outside the *Curd and Honey Shop* in the centre of the village, close to most of the guesthouses. No buses originate in Ella, so finding a seat when leaving can sometimes be tricky. Heading towards Bandarawela or (especially) Badulla, it's easiest to catch any bus heading to the main Badulla–Bandarwela road, about 3km from the village, and pick up a bus there. Both Haputale or Nuwara Eliya are easier to reach by train; heading to Haputale by bus, you'll have to change at Bandarawela. Ella is a convenient jumping-off point for the south coast, with regular services to Matara via Pamegamuwa Junction (for Tissa), Tangalla and Hambantota. There are a couple of direct buses daily to Kataragama and Tissamaharama; alternatively, take a Matara bus to Pamegamuwa and change there, or go to Wellawaya and catch an onward connection from there.

Destinations Badulla (every 30min; 45min); Bandarawela (every 10min; 30min); Hambantota (8 daily; 3hr); Kandy (2 daily; 7–8hr; or more regular services via Badulla); Kataragama (2 daily; 2hr 30min); Nuwara Eliya (5 daily; 3hr 30min); Matara (8 daily; 5hr); Tangalla (8 daily; 4hr); Tissamaharama (2 daily; 2hr 30min); Wellawaya (every 15min; 45min).

By train It's generally more comfortable and convenient to leave Ella by train where possible, especially if you're heading to Haputale or Nuwara Eliya – and railway buffs will also enjoy the famous loop which the train tracks make just east of Ella to gain height. The train station is on the north side of the village, a 5–10min walk from most accommodation. For timetable details, see p.200.

Destinations Badulla (3 daily; 1hr); Colombo (3 daily; 9–10hr); Haputale (3 daily; 1hr); Hatton (3 daily; 4hr); Nanu Oya (for Nuwara Eliya; 3 daily; 2hr 45min); Peradeniya (for Kandy; 3 daily; 6–7hr).

INFORMATION AND TOURS

Information Staff at the *Dream Café* are a good source of local information, including bus times.

Tours Most of the village's guesthouses can arrange taxis and tours. Alternatively, the *Dream Café* (☎ 057 222 8950) runs various excursions including day-trips to Horton Plains (Rs.6000 for vehicle only) and a useful one-day tour

combining Buduruwagala, Ravana Falls, Haputale, Diyaluma Falls, Dowa Temple and the nearby Uva Halpewatte Tea Factory (Rs.5000 for a minivan seating up to five). They also have 90cc scooters for rent (Rs.1300/day). Suresh Rodrigo (c/o the *Ella Holiday Inn*) also runs a range of tours including day-walks (around $30 for two people); camping trips to Yala; a useful day-trip combining the Diyaluma and Rawana Ella waterfalls along with

Buduruwagala ($55 for up to four people); and cooking lessons (Rs.2200 for half a day).

ACCOMMODATION

Ella has a huge range of accommodation for such a small place, although prices have soared in recent years and most guesthouses (with a few honourable exceptions) are poor value for money – and you'll pay a premium for anywhere with a view. All of the following have hot water, although heating isn't provided – Ella doesn't generally get too cold.

Ambiente Kithalella Rd ☎057 222 8867, ⓦambiente .lk. Attractive guesthouse set high above the village, with sublime views over Ella Gap and modern, tiled rooms (all with hot water, though cheaper ones are a bit small and bare). There's also good food, free internet and a pair of cute resident dogs who take guests for walks in the surrounding hills. **Rs.2640**

Country Comfort Inn 32 Police Station Rd ☎057 222 8532, ⓦhotelcountrycomfort.lk. A good and slightly smarter alternative to Ella's standard family-run guesthouses, in a quiet (but viewless) spot on the north side of the village. The new block has sparklingly clean, modern tiled rooms with ugly wooden furniture; the smaller and more attractive old wing occupies a pretty little colonial villa with a few neat and comfortable (though rather overpriced) rooms. Hot water and free wi-fi throughout. Old wing **$30**; new wing **$40**

Ella Holiday Inn Main Rd ☎072 465 6292, ⓦella holidayinn.com. Biggish modern mid-range guesthouse bang in the middle of the village, with a wide range of attractive tiled rooms (some with satellite TV) of various standards, ranging from simple budget rooms up to more plushly furnished rooms with wooden floors and high ceilings. Free internet and wi-fi. Rates may be susceptible to bargaining in slow periods, and Rough Guide readers are promised a ten percent discount on top of the already very competitive rates. **Rs.1600**

Forest Paradise Guest Home Off Passara Rd ☎057 222 8797, ⓦforestparadiseella.com. Low-key guesthouse with just five nicely furnished but slightly small rooms (with hot water) set next to pine forest on the outskirts of the village – very peaceful, though it's a bit of an uphill hike out of town. The owner arranges interesting activities including catamaran trips at Handapanagala (see p.256), mountaintop barbecues at Namunukula and free trekking. **Rs.1600**

Grand Ella Motel Wellawaya Rd ☎057 222 8655, ⓦceylonhotels.lk. This attractively upgraded old rest house boasts one of the best views of Ella Gap from its garden, plus spacious and comfortable rooms with minibar, satellite TV and (paid) wi-fi. **Rs.5000**

Hill Top Guest House Off Main Rd ☎057 222 8780, ⓔhilltopella@hotmail.com. Perched at the top of a very steep hill, with fine views of Ella Gap from the upper storey and veranda. The larger upstairs rooms are nice but overpriced; those downstairs are simpler but significantly cheaper. Free wi-fi and internet. **Rs.2200**

Mountain Heavens Hotel Kithalella ☎057 492 5757, ⓦmountainheavensella.com. Small modern hotel set out in the countryside a 15min walk from the village and with a jaw-dropping view right down the middle of Ella Gap. Standard rooms are a bit pokey; deluxe rooms (at over twice the price) are much more spacious, with big French windows through which to enjoy the scenery. **$50**

★ **Ravana Heights** ☎057 222 8888, ⓦravana heights.com. One of the nicest places to stay in Ella, occupying a modern one-storey house with just three bright, spacious and competitively priced rooms (with hot water decorated with colourful Thai fabrics and offering picture-perfect views of Ella Rock and the Gap. The owner can also arrange enjoyable hiking excursions (around $15), and there's also superior Thai food (see opposite). **$50**

Ravana Homestay Off Police Station Rd ☎077 695 4243. Tucked away in a very peaceful woodland setting, a 5min walk from the village; just two rooms (with hot water) – both neat, clean, comfy and at a very fair price. **Rs.1500**

Rawana Holiday Resort ☎057 222 8794, ⓔnalan kumara@yahoo.com. Decent selection of reasonably clean and comfortable rooms, plus good home-cooking (see opposite) in the large restaurant, which has fine views of Ella Gap. Also offers cookery classes plus free wi-fi and internet. **Rs.2200**

Rock View Guest House ☎057 222 8561, ⓔrockviewh@gmail.com. One of the longest-established places in the village, with marvellous view of Ella Rock and a mix of accommodation – choose between the spacious older rooms (currently being refurbished and upgraded) in the main house or the three smaller but newer ones with balcony in the annexe outside. **Rs.2000**

Sooriya ☎057 222 8906. Five clean, no-frills doubles (all with hot water) plus one family room at a (for Ella) sensible price – although rather near the main road, downstairs rooms especially, so traffic noise can intrude. **Rs.1750**

Sun Top Inn 18 Police Station Rd ☎057 222 8673, ⓔsuntopinn@yahoo.com. Welcoming family guesthouse with neat modern tiled rooms (all with extra-long beds); those downstairs are the cheapest and best value; those upstairs are a bit more expensive. There's also free wi-fi and bikes, plus cooking lessons on request. **Rs.2000**

The View ☎057 567 8050, ⓦellaholidayinn.com. A steep 10–15min walk up from the village, this recently opened guesthouse offers the loftiest accommodation currently available in Ella, with superlative views and accommodation in four neat rooms with attractive teak furnishings and French windows. Rs.4500

★ **Waterfalls Homestay** Kithalella ☎ 057 567 6933, ⓦ waterfalls-guesthouse-ella.com. Beautiful Australian-owned hideaway in a wonderfully peaceful location opposite Little Rawana Ella Falls. The place feels is more like a homestay than a conventional guesthouse, with just three colourful and very comfortable rooms (including one triple/family room). Communal meals are served in the spacious kitchen-cum-dining room (or you can cook your own) and there's a lovely terrace from which to watch the falls, plus a small Ayurvedic massage parlour downstairs. Excellent value. B&B Rs.4400

AROUND ELLA

Ella Adventure Park Wellawaya Rd, 10km south of Ella ☎ 055 355 5038, ⓦ ellaadventurepark.com. Rustic

eco-resort in a stunning forest setting with accommodation scattered amid the trees in a series of picturesque wooden structures (including one fun tree house) – albeit stronger on jungle atmosphere than creature comforts. Mountain-biking, trekking, kayaking and rock-climbing trips can be arranged, though the main appeal of the place is the chance to get very close to nature. $56

★ **The Planter's Bungalow** Wellawaya Rd, 10km south of Ella ☎ 057 492 5902, ⓦ plantersbungalow .com. Gorgeous new colonial-style boutique guesthouse in a superbly restored tea planter's bungalow of 1889 surrounded by lush wooded gardens. Accommodation is in three stylish rooms in the bungalow itself plus one cottage in the garden outside, and there's also excellent and authentic hill country-style Sri Lankan food – the breakfasts alone will keep you going for the next week. A real bargain at current rates. $66

EATING AND DRINKING

Ella is well stocked with places to eat, mainly strung out along Main St (though there's often good home-cooking in the various guesthouses as well, including plenty of rice and curry).

Curd and Honey Shop Main St. Long-established little backpacker café, handy for breakfast (with a big range of both Western and Sri Lankan offerings, including lots of curd) and daytime snacks, though it's right next to where the buses stop, so can be a bit noisy and smelly. Unlicensed. Daily 6.30am–9.30pm or later.

★ **Dream Café** Main St ☎ 057 222 8950. Easily the best of the cafés lining Main St, this suave modern place wouldn't look out of place in one of Colombo's smarter suburbs, with food and service to match. The menu features a big selection of well-prepared local and international dishes (mains mostly Rs.550–660), ranging from rice and curry through pasta, burgers, wraps and salads to some of the best pizza in the island. Good for breakfast, too, either Western or Sri Lankan. Free wi-fi and internet. Daily 8am until around 10pm.

Nescoffe Main St ☎ 077 180 4020. This funky, rather louche little café feels more beachside chill-out zone than hill country café, and is usually the last place to close in the village at nights. It's a nice spot for a drink (alcoholic or otherwise), although you'll have to be feeling very mellow to put up with the excrutiatingly

slow and erratic service. There's also assorted food on offer (most mains around Rs.550) – Sri Lankan and western breakfasts, sandwiches, pizzas, and so on – although you might die of hunger by the time it arrives. Daily 8am until late.

Nilmini Rest Main St. Old-style Ella café, wedged into a tiny terrace fronting a family house and offering a good selection of Western and Sri Lankan breakfasts and light snacks, although no real meals to speak of. Daily 8am–9pm.

Ravana Heights ☎ 057 222 8888. Above-average Thai or Sri Lankan dinners ($15) in this attractive guesthouse Book by 4pm.

Rawana Holiday Resort ☎ 057 222 8794. The main reason for coming here is to try the special garlic curry (Rs.450) – that's a plateful of curried whole garlic cloves, rather than garlic-flavoured curry (the cloves are first fried with onions and fenugreek, then boiled with coconut milk and tamarind to remove the after-smell). Pre-order by lunchtime. You can even come and watch it being prepared. Daily 7/8am–9/10pm.

DIRECTORY

Banks There's a small Bank of Ceylon opposite the *Ella Holiday Inn* with a single, temperamental ATM (Visa only).

Internet Numerous places up and down Main St offer internet access (and sometimes wi-fi). There's also free wi-fi at the *Dream Café*.

Wellawaya and around

Standing in the dry-zone plains at the foot of the hills of Uva Province, **WELLAWAYA** is, strictly speaking, not part of the hill country at all, though it's an important transport hub and provides regular connections to Ella, Haputale and beyond. The town itself is eminently forgettable, though there are a few worthwhile sights nearby – although it's also perfectly possible to visit these from Ella or Haputale. There are also a couple of excellent eco-lodges in the area around the town of **Buttala**, about 15km east of Wellawaya (see p.369).

Buduruwagala rock carvings

Head 5km south of Wellawaya along the main road towards Tissa, then turn right onto a signed side road for another 5km • Rs.200 • Open access 24hr • A tuktuk from Wellawaya will cost around Rs.400 return

Just south of Wellawaya lie the magical rock carvings of **Buduruwagala**, in a patch of beautifully unspoilt dry-zone forest populated by abundant birds and butterflies. The site features a series of seven figures carved in low relief into the face of a large rock outcrop (whose outline is sometimes fancifully compared to that of an elephant lying down). The figures are some of the largest in the island (the biggest is 16m tall), and are thought to date from the tenth century – they're unusual in displaying Mahayana Buddhist influence, which enjoyed a brief vogue in the island around this time. The large central standing **Buddha** in the *abhaya* ("have no fear") pose still bears traces of the stucco which would originally have covered his robes, as well as faint splashes of his original paint.

On the left-hand side of the rock stand a group of three figures. The central one, which retains its white paint and red halo, is generally thought to represent **Avalokitesvara**, one of the most important Mahayana divinities. To the left stands an unidentified attendant, while the female figure to his right in the "thrice-bent" pose is **Tara**, a Mahayana goddess. The three figures on the right-hand side of the rock are much more Hindu in style. The figure on the right is generally thought to represent the Tibetan Bodhisattva **Vajrapani**, holding a thunderbolt symbol (a *dorje* – a rare instance of Tantric influence in Sri Lankan Buddhist art); the central figure is **Maitreya**, the future Buddha, while the third figure is **Vishnu**. The presence of square-cut holes in the rock above some figures – particularly the central Buddha – suggests that they would originally have been canopied.

Handapanagala Tank

Head 8km south of Wellawaya along the main road towards Tissa (3km past the Buduruwagala turn-off), then 1.5km along a track on the left

Just beyond Buduruwagala lies the beautiful **Handapanagala Tank**. You get gorgeous views from here, especially if you scramble up the rock at the far end of the path that runs along the south side of the tank, with the great wall of Uva mountains spread out on one side and the arid dry-zone plains towards Tissa on the other. Although the tank is worth visiting just for the views, there's the possible added bonus of spotting wild **elephants**, who sometimes come to the tank to drink (late afternoon is usually the best time). It might also be possible to arrange a **catamaran trip** on the lake with local boatmen; count on around Rs.1000–1500.

Diyaluma Falls

Reached by any bus running between Wellawaya and Beragala/Haputale

Around 12km west of Wellawaya and 30km from Haputale, the **Diyaluma Falls** are the second-highest in Sri Lanka, tumbling for 220m over a sheer cliff-face in a single slender cascade. A circuitous walk (allow 1hr each way) to the top of the falls starts from the main road a few hundred metres east of the falls next to the km 207/5 marker. Follow the track here uphill for around twenty minutes until you reach a small rubber factory, where you'll need to stop and ask someone to point out the very faint and rough path up the steep and rocky hillside behind – if in doubt just keep on heading straight up. It's a steep and tiring hike (and you can't actually see the falls properly from the top), although you can cool off with a dip in one of the large natural rock pools near the summit of the falls.

The pleasant *Diyaluma Falls Inn*, on the main road below the falls, has fine views of the cascades and is a pleasant spot for lunch or a drink.

ARRIVAL AND INFORMATION — WELLAWAYA

By bus The bus stand is in the middle of town. Wellawaya is a major transport hub between the south coast and hill country, with good services in all directions, although if travelling to Kandy or Nuwara Eliya you might prefer to take a bus to Ella and then catch the train (see p.200) from there. For Tissamaharama, take a bus to Pannegamuwa Junction and change there; for Kataragama, change at Buttala.

Destinations Bandarawela (every 30min; 1hr); Badulla (every 30–45min; 1hr 30min); Buttala (every 15min; 40min); Colombo (every 45min; 6hr); Ella (every 15min; 45min); Embilipitiya (4 daily; 3hr); Hambantota (every 30min; 2hr); Haputale (hourly; 1hr); Kandy (2 daily; 6hr); Matara (every 30min; 4hr); Monaragala (every 15min; 1hr 15min); Nuwara Eliya (5 daily; 5hr); Pannegamuwa Junction (every 30min; 1hr 45min); Tangalla (every 30min; 3hr).

Banks The Commercial, Hatton National and People's banks all have ATMs which accept foreign cards.

ACCOMMODATION

Little Rose Inn 1km south of town on the Tissa road ⓣ077 657 3647, ⓦlittlerosewellawaya.com. The nicest of Wellawaya's scant accommodation options, this family-run guesthouse has clean, bright and spacious doubles and triples in the modern garden annexe plus a few slightly older but well-kept rooms inside the house itself. There's also organic food, bike rental and internet access, and the owners can arrange local excursions. **Rs.1200**

3

Bandarawela

Midway between Ella and Haputale, the scruffy little town of **BANDARAWELA** lacks either the rural charm of the first or the dramatic setting of the latter. The only real reason to stay here is to spend a night at the time-warped *Bandarawela Hotel*, although you might well find yourself changing buses (or money) here en route to somewhere else.

ARRIVAL AND DEPARTURE — BANDARAWELA

By bus Buses for Haputale, Ratnapura and Colombo leave from the stop near the main roundabout just south of Cargills. The stands opposite Hatton Bank on the east side of town are where you'll find buses to Ella, Wellawaya and Badulla. All other services leave from the main bus stand.

Destinations Badulla (every 15min; 1hr); Colombo (every 30min; 6hr); Ella (every 10min; 30min); Haputale (every 20–30min; 30min); Kandy (4 daily; 4–5hr); Matara (3 daily; 7hr); Nuwara Eliya (4 daily; 1hr 30min; or change at Welimada); Ratnapura (every 30min; 3hr 30min); Welimada (every 30min; 45min); Wellawaya (every 30min; 1hr).

By train Bandarawela is on the main hill country train line. For full details, see the timetables (p.200).

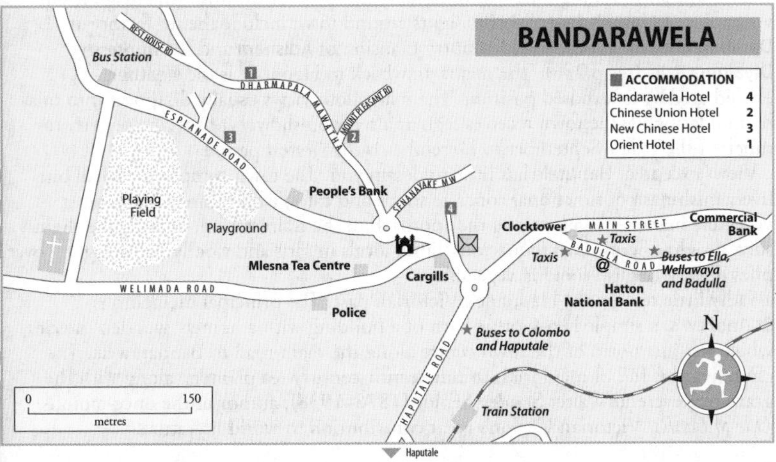

INFORMATION

Ayurveda About 3km east of Bandarawela on the Badulla road, the popular Suwamadhu Ayurveda centre (☎057 222 2504, ⚭www.ayurvedasuwamadhu.com) offers a standard selection of massages and herbal/steam baths at moderate prices.

Banks There are several banks scattered around town. The ATM at the Commercial Bank, near the Ella bus stand, accepts foreign Visa and MasterCards; that at the People's Bank on Esplanade Road accepts Visa.

ACCOMMODATION AND EATING

Bandarawela is largely a locals' resort, and although there's plenty of accommodation around town, none of it is especially appealing. Food is available at all the following places; the old-school restaurant at the *Bandarawela Hotel* is the nicest place for a meal.

★ **Bandarawela Hotel** 14 Welimada Rd ☎057 222 2501, ⚭www.aitkenspencehotels.com. Easily the best place to stay in Bandarawela, occupying a lovely old planters' clubhouse of 1893. The personable, rambling old wooden building is brimful of charm (albeit stronger on colonial atmosphere than modern creature comforts), with polished wooden floorboards, colonial fittings, bathtubs and quaint old metal bedsteads. A bargain at current rates – although the lack of visitors can sometimes make the place feel a bit moribund. $88
Chinese Union Hotel 8 Mount Pleasant Rd ☎057 222 2502. Characterful little place in an old colonial villa with

old-fashioned but well-maintained rooms and a pleasant little (alcohol-free) dining room. Rs.1650
New Chinese Hotel Esplanade Rd ☎057 223 1767. Characterless but spotless modern rooms (all with hot water), plus a decent range of Chinese food in the restaurant downstairs. Rs.1400
Orient Hotel 12 Dharmapala Mw ☎057 222 2377, ⚭orienthotelsl.com. Dated but comfortable hotel, popular with package tours and offering good-value accommodation in large, bright and attractively furnished rooms with cable TV. Staff here can also arrange tours around the hill country, including trekking and mountain-biking. $75

Haputale and around

One of the most spectacularly situated of all Sri Lankan towns, **HAPUTALE** (pronounced "ha-*poo*-tah-lay") is perched dramatically on the crest of a ridge at the southern edge of the hill country with bird's-eye views in both directions – south to the plains and coast, and inland across the jagged lines of peaks receding away to the north. The town itself is a busy but fairly humdrum little commercial centre with a mainly Tamil population, though the mist that frequently blankets the place adds a pleasingly mysterious touch to the workaday shops that fill the centre.

As with Ella, the principal pleasure of a stay in Haputale is the chance to get out and walk in the surrounding hills – most notably up to (or down from) the magnificent viewpoint at **Lipton's Seat**. Specific sights around town include the tea factory at **Dambatenne**, the evocative old country mansion of **Adisham** and the impressive **Diyaluma Falls** (see p.256). The major drawback to Haputale is the **weather**, exacerbated by its exposed position. The marvellous views usually disappear into mist by midday, while the town receives regular afternoon showers of varying severity for much of the year – September to December is the wettest period.

Views excepted, **Haputale** has little to detain you. The town comprises a small but lively mishmash of functional concrete shops and cafés, while a small fruit and vegetable market straggles along the approach to the train station, offering the slightly surreal sight of crowds of loquacious Tamil locals in saris and woolly hats haggling over piles of very English-looking vegetables.

Sadly little remains of Haputale's Victorian past. The principal memento is **St Andrew's**, a simple neo-Gothic barn of a building with a homely wooden interior which lies just north of the town centre along the main road to Bandarawela. The churchyard is full of memorials to nineteenth-century tea planters, along with the grave of Reverend Walter Stanley Senior (1876–1938), author of the once-famous *Ode to Lanka*, Victorian Ceylon's great contribution to world literature.

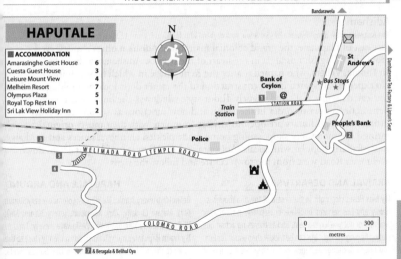

HAPUTALE

■ ACCOMMODATION	
Amarasinghe Guest House	6
Cuesta Guest House	3
Leisure Mount View	4
Melheim Resort	7
Olympus Plaza	5
Royal Top Rest Inn	1
Sri Lak View Holiday Inn	2

Dambatenne Tea Factory

Daily 8am to 6pm · Tours Rs.250 · Buses from south side of the bus stop in the centre of Haputale; a **taxi** will cost around $10 return, a tuktuk slightly less

East of Haputale, a scenic road leads 10km along the edge of the escarpment through beautiful tea estates to the rambling **Dambatenne Tea Factory**, built in 1890 by the famous tea magnate **Sir Thomas Lipton** (see box, p.440). The long white factory building is one of the most impressive in the highlands and preserves some of its original colonial-era equipment demonstrating the extent to which the tea-making process (and often the actual machinery as well) has remained unchanged for a hundred years or more. Informative factory tours explain the tea-making process from leaf to packet, although disappointingly, there's no tea for sale, either to take home or drink on the premises. Note that you've got more chance of seeing the entire factory in operation if you visit before noon, after which things slow down.

Lipton's Seat

Rs.50 · Buses from south side of the bus stop in the centre of Haputale; a **taxi** will cost around $15 return, a tuktuk slightly less

From Dambatenne, a marvellous walk leads up to **Lipton's Seat**, one of the finest viewpoints in the country – the equal of World's End, but minus the hefty entrance fee. The road offers increasingly expansive views the higher you go, leading steeply up through a perfect landscape of immaculately manicured tea plantations with scarcely a leaf out of place, connected by flights of stone steps and enclosed in fine old drystone walls. It's quite a strenuous hike to the seat – about 7km by road, though you can avoid the lengthy hairpins made by the tarmac and so reduce the overall distance by taking short-cuts up the stone steps. Lipton's Seat itself – named after Sir Thomas Lipton (see p.440), who often came here to admire the view – sits perched at the edge of a cliff, offering an almost 360-degree overview of the surrounding countryside; you can see all the way to the coast on a clear day. Taking a taxi up to Lipton's Seat then walking back down (either to Dambatenne Tea Factory or all the way back to Haputale) is one of Sri Lanka's finest, but most effortless, short hikes. As with World's End, the viewpoint clouds over most days from about 10am, so it's best to arrive early. The walk from here down to Dambatenne takes around two hours.

Adisham

3km east of Haputale along Welimada Rd · Sat & Sun, poya days and school holidays 9.30am–12.30pm & 1.30–4pm · Rs.50

Just east of Haputale, the grand colonial mansion of **Adisham** offers a misty-eyed moment of English nostalgia in the heart of the tropics. Adisham was built by **Sir Thomas Villiers**, who named it after the Kent village in which he was born. No expense was spared in the construction of the rather dour-looking building, with its rusticated granite walls and vaguely Tudor-style windows. The house was bought by the Benedictine monastic order in the 1960s and now functions as a monastery. Only the sitting room and library are open to visitors, complete with their musty original fittings; the monastery shop, selling home-made pickles, chutneys, sauces and cordials, is particularly popular with locals. Adisham is about 3km east of Haputale: go down Welimada Road west from the town centre and follow the signs.

ARRIVAL AND DEPARTURE   HAPUTALE AND AROUND

By bus Buses stop right in the centre of town, although as hardly any bus services originate in Haputale it's pot luck whether or not you'll get a seat, and as there's no actual bus station finding the right bus can be trickier than usual. For Ella, you'll need to change at Bandarawela. There are a couple of direct buses daily to Nuwara Eliya, or take a bus to Welimada and change there, although it's easier to catch the train.

Destinations Bandarawela (every 20–30min; 30min); Badulla (hourly; 1hr 30min; or change at Bandarawela);

Belihul Oya (every 30min; 1hr 30min); Colombo (every 30min; 6hr); Matara (3 daily; 7hr); Ratnapura (every 30min; 3hr); Welimada (every 20min; 90min); Wellawaya (hourly; 1hr).

By train Haputale's train station is conveniently close to the town centre, with direct connections to Ella, Bandarawela, Badulla, Nanu Oya (for Nuwara Eliya), Kandy and Colombo. See the timetable (p.200) for latest schedules, although services are sporadic, and for short journeys it's often quicker, if less atmospheric, to take the bus.

GETTING AROUND

Buses for Dambatenne and Lipton's Seat leave from the south side of the bus stop in the centre of town. Alternatively, a taxi will cost around $10 return to

Dambatenne, or $15 one-way to Lipton's Seat, a tuktuk slightly less (most guesthouses in town should be able to arrange this).

ACCOMMODATION AND EATING

Accommodation in Haputale is extremely good value, especially compared with Ella. All the following places have hot water and serve food. Note that if you're staying at one of the guesthouses west of town the quickest way of reaching the centre is to walk along the railway tracks – significantly more direct than following the twistier Welimada Rd; steps lead down to the tracks opposite where the path comes up onto Welimada Rd from the *Amarasinghe* guesthouse.

THE WALK TO IDALGASHINA

A fine walk leads west from Adisham along the ridgetop towards the village of **Idalgashina** through the **Tangamalai** (or Tangmale) nature reserve (open access; free), home to plentiful birdlife and wildlife including lots of monkeys. The path starts just to the left of the Adisham gates and runs for 3km through patches of dense subtropical jungle full of grey-barked, moss-covered *weera* trees alternating with airy stands of eucalyptus. The track is reasonably easy to follow at first, though it becomes indistinct in places further on (the directions below should suffice, though). After about 1km, the path comes out to the edge of the ridge with panoramic hill views stretching from Pidurutalagala and Hakgala near Nuwara Eliya to the left, Bandarawela below, and right towards the distinctive triangular-shaped peak of Namunakula, south of Badulla. Below you can see Glenanore Tea Factory and (a little later) the rail tracks far below (they will gradually rise to meet you).

From here on, the path sometimes sticks to the edge of the ridge, sometimes turns away from it, undulating slightly but always keeping roughly to the same height. After a further 1.5km you'll see the rail tracks again, now much closer. Over the next 500m the path winds down the edge of the ridge to meet the ascending rail line, at which point there's a wonderful view south, with impressive sheer cliffs to the left framing views of the lines of hills descending to the south, and the flat, hot plains beyond. From here you can either continue along the tracks to Idalgashina (about 6km) and catch a train back, or return to Haputale along the tracks (about 4km).

★ **Amarasinghe Guest House** ☎ 057 226 8175, ✉ agh777@sltnet.lk. Well-run family guesthouse with large – if slightly bare – rooms (although no views) and a very cosy lounge-cum-restaurant with internet, satellite TV and a good rice and curry served nightly. The guesthouse can be reached on foot by following the tiny footpath (signed) from the road by the rail tracks, just east of the *Olympus Plaza* hotel; alternatively you can drive up from the Colombo Rd, although the access road is nerve-janglingly narrow and twisty. Rs.2000

Cuesta Guest House ☎ 057 226 8110, ✉ kacp@sltnet.lk. Perched right on the edge of the ridge, this rather moribund place has small and slightly shabby rooms, although compensated for by dreamy views northwards (and small private balconies to enjoy them from). Rs.1430

Leisure Mount View Off Welimada Rd (signed on left about 500m past the Cuesta Guest House) ☎ 057 226 8327. Friendly little family guesthouse with four simple but cosy rooms (all with hot water) at rock-bottom prices. Slightly out of town in a very peaceful location, with superb views south. Rs.850

Olympus Plaza 75 Welimada Rd ☎ 057 226 8544, ⊕ olympusplazahotel.com. This ugly but comfortable new mid-range hotel is Haputale's only non-budget option. Rooms are spacious and nicely furnished, with private balconies and fine views over the hills below, plus hot water and satellite TV. There's also a so-so restaurant, a surprisingly chic little bar, gym, kids' play area, and internet and wi-fi. Rs.4500

Royal Top Rest Inn Station Rd ☎ 057 226 8178. Conveniently close to the train station, this place has well-maintained rooms, with or without views (all with hot water; a couple have shared bathrooms). Good value and comfortable, though not quite as nice as the nearby *Sri Lak View Holiday Inn*. Rs.1050

★ **Sri Lak View Holiday Inn** Sherwood Rd ☎ 057 226 8125, ⊕ srilakviewholidayinn.com. The best option in the town centre, with spotless, modern, tiled rooms (all with hot water), some with marvellous views south, at bargain rates. Free wi-fi. Rs.1650

3

AROUND HAPUTALE

Melheim Resort Lower Blackwood, Beragala–Diyaluma Rd, 6km from Haputale, 2km from Beragala ☎ 057 567 5969, ⊕ melheimresort.com. Recently opened boutique hotel marvellously situated on the edge of the hill country, with sweeping views south and the lights of Hambantota on the coast visible after dark. Rooms (all with satellite TV, DVD players and minibar) are bright and spacious, with attractive wooden furnishings, private balconies and big picture windows. Terraced gardens run down to a pool and kids' play area, and there are free bikes. $150

DIRECTORY

Banks There are ATMs accepting foreign cards at the Hatton National Bank, Bank of Ceylon and People's Bank (the last accepts Visa only).

Internet access At the *Amarasinghe* guesthouse (see above) and in town at Website Link on Station Rd (Mon–Fri roughly 8am–7pm, though may be open at weekends too; Rs.60/hr), a few doors along from the Bank of Ceylon.

Tours Haputale is a good place from which to visit Horton Plains – the *Cuesta* and *Amarasinghe* guesthouses and *Royal Top Rest Inn* can all arrange transport for around $35, as well as vehicles to visit local attractions such as Lipton's Seat (around $15 by car or $10 by tuktuk one way). *Cuesta* also have four 250cc motorbikes for hire (Rs.1500/day).

Belihul Oya and around

Around 30km west of Haputale, the little town of **BELIHUL OYA** lies in prettily wooded scenery at the foot of the hill country. There's not much to the town itself, but there's a reasonable spread of **accommodation**, so you might find yourself overnighting here. Sadly, the challenging 11km trek from Belihul Oya up to World's End is currently closed, although it is possible to walk up to World's End from nearby Bambarakanda Falls – see below.

Belihul Oya is also the nearest jumping-off point for the **Bambarakanda Falls**, which tumble out of the dramatic hills below the towering escarpment of World's End. The long, slender cascade has a total drop of 241m, making it the highest in Sri Lanka and five times taller than Niagara – although it can be slightly underwhelming during periods of low rainfall. The falls are 5km north of the main A4 highway between Haputale and Belihul Oya at the village of **Kalupahana**; lots of buses pass through Kalupahana, from where you should be able to pick up a tuktuk to take you up the tiny, hairpinning road to the falls. Bambarakanda is also the starting point for a 17km hike up to Horton Plains – a longer but less strenuous route than the old path up from Belihul Oya.

| ACCOMMODATION | BELIHUL OYA AND AROUND |

The places in **Belihul Oya** below are all situated close to one another along the main A4 highway, around 4km west of town (we list them in the order you reach them heading west). The three places listed under **Bambarakanda Falls** are among the most remote and dramatically situated in Sri Lanka – though you'll have to brave steep, twisting and nerve-racking roads to reach them.

BELIHUL OYA

Pearl Tourist Inn ☎ 045 228 0157. The cheapest place in town, though no bargain, with large, musty rooms and a flyblown restaurant. **Rs.1760**

Rest House ☎ 045 228 0156, ⓦ ceylonhotels.lk. This attractively old-fashioned place is easily the nicest place to stay in Belihul Oya, with a breezy setting next to the foaming waters of the Kudu Oya, a picturesque terrace restaurant and comfortable, reasonably priced rooms (some with a/c for $5 extra). B&B **$51**

Water Garden ☎ 045 228 0254. Attractive little modern hotel with neat modern rooms equipped with a/c, hot water and lots of rather minimalist pine furniture, plus a lovely garden terrace overlooking paddy fields. **Rs.6000**

AROUND BAMBARAKANDA FALLS

Hill Safari Eco-Lodge Off the road between Bambarakanda and Ohiya ☎ 0712 772 451 or ☎ 011 264 7582. Set in the middle of a tea estate in a dramatic location below the towering escarpment of World's End with simple but comfortable rooms, although the access road is hair-raisingly steep. Half-board **Rs.4000**

World's End Lodge ☎ 057 567 6977, ⓦ lankahotel .com. Perhaps the most spectacularly situated place to stay in Sri Lanka; look for the turn-off from the A4 highway between Haldumulla and Kalupahana, just east of the Bambarakanda Falls turning. From here, it's 4km up a very steep and rough hairpinning road – passable, but only just, in a normal car. Rooms are simple and slightly bare, with verandas from which to enjoy the wild and beautiful views, when not blanketed by mist. You can walk from here up to Horton Plains in around four hours. **Rs.5000**

Adam's Peak

Poking up from the southwestern edge of the hill country, the soaring summit of **ADAM'S PEAK (Sri Pada)** is simultaneously one of Sri Lanka's most striking natural landmarks and one of its most celebrated places of pilgrimage – a miniature Matterhorn which stands head and shoulders above the surrounding hills, giving a wonderful impression of sheer altitude (even though, at 2243m, it's actually only Sri Lanka's fifth-highest peak). The mountain has accumulated a mass of legends centred around the curious depression at its summit, the **Sri Pada** or Sacred Footprint. The original Buddhist story claims that this is the footprint of the Buddha himself, made at the request of the local god **Saman** (see box below); different faiths subsequently modified this to suit their own contrasting theologies. Sometime around the eighth century, Muslims began to claim the footprint to be that of **Adam**, who is said to have first set foot on earth here after being cast out of heaven, and who stood on the mountain's summit on one leg in penitence until his sins were forgiven – Hindu tradition, meanwhile, claimed that the footprint was created by **Shiva**. Many centuries later, the colonial Portuguese attempted to rescue the footprint for

---

SAMAN

Saman is one of the four great protective divinities of Sri Lanka, and the one who boasts the most modest and purely Sri Lankan origins. He is believed originally to have been a pious Indian trader (or possibly a king) who, thanks to the merit he had acquired, was reborn as a god residing at Sumanakuta (as Adam's Peak was originally called). According to the quasi-mythological chronicle of Sri Lankan history, the *Mahavamsa*, Saman was among the audience of gods to whom the Buddha preached during his visit to Mahiyangana, and upon hearing the Buddha, he immediately entered on the path of Enlightenment. When the Buddha returned to Sri Lanka on his final visit, Saman begged him to leave a footprint atop Sumanakuta to serve as a focus for worship; the Buddha duly obliged. Saman is still believed to reside on the mountain, and to protect pilgrims who climb it. He is usually shown in pictures with a white elephant, holding a red lotus, with Adam's Peak rising behind.

the Christian faith, claiming that it belonged to **St Thomas**, the founder of the religion in India, though no one seems to have ever taken this random assertion very seriously.

Despite all these rival claims, Adam's Peak remains an essentially Buddhist place of worship (unlike, say, the genuinely multi-faith pilgrimage town of Kataragama). The mountain has been an object of pilgrimage for over a thousand years, at least since the Polonnaruwan period, when Parakramabahu and Vijayabahu constructed shelters here for visiting pilgrims. In the twelfth century, Nissanka Malla became the first king to climb the mountain, while later foreign travellers including Fa-Hsien, Ibn Battuta, Marco Polo and Robert Knox all described the peak and its associated traditions with varying degrees of fanciful inaccuracy.

When to go

The ascent of Adam's Peak is traditionally made **by night**, allowing you to reach the top in time for dawn, which offers the best odds of seeing the extraordinary views free from cloud as well as a chance a glimpsing the peak's enigmatic **shadow** (see p.264).

Most visitors climb the mountain during the **pilgrimage season**, which starts on the Duruthu poya day in December or January and continues until the Vesak poya in May. During the season the weather on the mountain is at its best, and the chances of a clear dawn at the summit highest; the steps up the mountainside are also illuminated and little stalls and teashops open through the night to cater to the throngs of weary pilgrims dragging themselves up. It's perfectly possible, if less interesting, to climb the mountain **out of season**, though none of the teashops is open and the lights are turned off, so you'll need to bring a decent torch. Although most people climb by night, you can also go up the mountain **by day**, but the summit is often obscured by cloud and, even if it's clear, you won't see the famous shadow, or (assuming you're visiting during the pilgrimage season) be able to enjoy the spectacle of the night-time illuminations and all-night teashops on the way up.

Finally, don't despair if you arrive in Dalhousie and it's **pouring with rain**. The daily deluge which usually descends on the village out of season often stops at around midnight, allowing you a clear run at the summit during the night, although the path will be wet and the leeches will be out in force.

Routes up the Peak

The easiest ascent, described below, is from **Dalhousie**. An alternative, much longer route (15km; around 7hr), ascends from the **Ratnapura** side of the mountain via **Palabaddale** (see p.267). An interesting walk, if you could arrange the logistics, would be to ascend from Dalhousie and then walk down to Palabaddale. Another possibility is to take a tour from **Nuwara Eliya** (see p.245), climbing the peak from Dalhousie, although this makes for a long night.

Guides offer their services all round Dalhousie (Rs.1500–2000), though you'll only really need one if you're a solo woman or are attempting the climb out of season at night, when the mountain can be a very cold and lonely place. A (free) alternative is to borrow a dog – all the local mutts know the track well, and will be happy to accompany you– "Bonzo" at the *Green House* in Dalhousie is particularly companionable (although their famous three-legged dog known as "Tuktuk" is sadly no more).

However fit you are, the Adam's Peak climb is **exhausting** – a taxing 7km up a mainly stepped footpath (there are around 5500 steps) which can reduce even seasoned hill walkers to quivering wrecks. Allow around four hours to get up the mountain, including time for tea stops (although at particularly busy times, such as poya days, the crowds can make the ascent slower still). Dawn is at around 6–6.30am, so a 2am start should get you to the top in time, and there are plenty of tea houses to stop at on the way if it looks like you're going to arrive early (there's not much point in sitting around at the summit in the darkness for any longer than you have to). It can get bitterly cold at the summit: take warm clothing.

The climb

The track up the mountain starts at the far end of Dalhousie village, passing a large standing Buddha, crossing a bridge and looping around the back of the large pilgrim's rest hostel (if you reach the *Green House* guesthouse you've gone wrong). For the first thirty minutes the path winds gently through tea estates, past Buddha shrines and through the big *makara torana* arch which marks the boundary of the sacred area. Beyond here the path continues to run gently uphill to the large **Peace Pagoda**, built with Japanese aid during the 1970s. In wet weather the cliff-face opposite is spectacularly scored with myriad waterfalls.

Beyond the Peace Pagoda, the climb – and the steps – start in earnest; not too bad at first, but they become increasingly short and steep as you progress. By the time you reach the leg-wrenchingly near-vertical section equipped with handrails you're within about 1500 steps of the summit, although by then it's a real physical struggle. The path is very secure and enclosed, however, so unless you suffer from unusually bad vertigo, this shouldn't be a problem (unlike at Sigiriya, for example) – and obviously at night you won't be able to see anything on the way up in any case. The upper slopes of the mountain are swathed in dense and largely undisturbed stands of cloudforest which are home to various species of colourful montane birdlife such as the Sri Lanka white-eye and Eurasian blackbird, the sight of which might offer some welcome distraction during the slog up or down.

The summit

The **summit** is covered in a huddle of buildings. The **footprint** itself is surprisingly unimpressive: a small, irregular depression, sheltered under a tiny pavilion and painted in gold – although tradition claims that this is actually only an impression of the true footprint, which lies underground. Upon reaching the summit, pilgrims ring one of the two bells (tradition stipulates that pilgrims ring a bell once for every successful ascent of the mountain they have made). The views are as spectacular as you would expect, while as dawn breaks you may also see the mysterious **shadow** of the peak – a spooky, almost supernatural apparition which seems to hang magically suspended in mid-air in front of the mountain for around twenty minutes, given a clear sunrise. One of the mysteries of Adam's Peak is the shadow's perfectly triangular outline, which doesn't correspond to the actual – and far more irregular – shape of the summit itself. The Buddhist explanation is that it's not actually the shadow of the peak at all, but a miraculous physical representation of the "Triple Gem" (a kind of Buddhist equivalent to the Holy Trinity, comprising the Buddha, his teachings and the community of Buddhist monks). Locals reckon you've got an eighty percent chance of seeing the shadow during the pilgrimage season, falling to around forty percent (or less) at other times of year.

The **descent** is much quicker (count on around 2hr 30min) though no less painful, since by now your legs will have turned to jelly.

ARRIVAL AND DEPARTURE

ADAM'S PEAK

The main base for the ascent of Adam's Peak is the modest village of **Dalhousie** (pronounced "Del-house"; also increasingly known by its Tamil name of Nallatanniya). It's usually busy with visitors during the pilgrimage season, but can seem rather desolate at other times. Dalhousie lies just over 30km southwest of the busy town of **Hatton**, which is on the main rail line through the hill country.

By bus During the pilgrimage season once-daily buses run to Dalhousie from Nuwara Eliya and Colombo. Alternatively, take a bus or train (see p.200) to Hatton, from where there are regular buses (every 30min; 90min) to Dalhousie. Outside the pilgrimage season you'll first have to reach Hatton, then take a bus from there to Maskeliya, and then pick up one of the battered old minibuses which ply between Maskeliya and Dalhousie (every 30min; 45min). A taxi from Hatton to Dalhousie will cost around Rs.2500; a tuktuk costs around Rs.2000.

ACCOMMODATION

There's not much **accommodation** in Dalhousie; you might want to ring in advance, and you should definitely reserve if staying over a poya day. In addition to the places listed below, there are also the four superb Tea Trail bungalows (see p.240) dotted around the countryside nearby.

DALHOUSIE

The Green House Far end of the village, by the start of the track up Adam's Peak ☎051 351 9478. Friendly and long-established little place, occupying a small house surrounded by various rickety-looking wooden gazebo-type structures (and, yes, it *is* green). Accommodation is either in basic but adequate rooms with shared bathrooms (hot water on request) or more modern en-suites. Pickups from Hatton on request. Half-board Rs.2800; en suite Rs.3500

Punsisi Rest Middle of village ☎051 492 0313, ✉punsisirest@yahoo.com. Modern hotel with comfortable and good-value rooms which get nicer (and more expensive) the higher up the building you go: those on the ground floor are dark and poky; those at the top are bright and spacious. Don't be put off by the unusually ugly exterior, or by the gloomy restaurant downstairs. Rs.2000

Slightly Chilled Guest House (formerly the Yellow House). On the main road by the entrance to the village, just past Wathsala Inn ☎051 351 9430, ⒲slightlychilled.tv. The smartest place in the village, with spacious and attractive modern rooms in an attractive riverside setting, plus internet, mountain bikes and information about local hikes. B&B $50

Wathsala Inn On the main road by the entrance to the village ☎051 351 9606, ⒲adamspeakhotels.com. Simple, slightly musty but OK rooms (plus a couple of smarter ones upstairs), all with beautiful river views, plus the only bar in Dalhousie. Cheap pickups from Hatton on request, and they also arrange rafting trips to Kitulgala, canoeing and other excursions. Discounts out of season. Rs.3000

White House On the main road by the entrance to the village, just past Slightly Chilled Guest House ☎0777 912 009. The cheapest place in the village, with simple but clean rooms and very basic log cabins, set in a pretty little garden. The friendly owner can arrange local walks and tours. Rs.1000

DICKOYA

Upper Glencairn Bungalow 4km from Dickoya (and 7km from Hatton) on the road to Dalhousie ☎011 748 8288. Fine old colonial-era tea planter's house set high above Castlereagh Reservoir in a working estate, with atmospheric, time-warped rooms (almost all have hot water and bathtubs to soothe aching post-peak limbs). Good value, though if you don't have your own transport you'll have to shell out for a taxi to Dalhousie. $45

Kitulgala

The village of **KITULGALA** is set about halfway along the spectacular road that descends from Hatton down to the lowlands at Avissawella. The scenery is particularly dramatic hereabouts, with sheer-sided, forest-covered hills plunging down to the wild waters of the Kelani Ganga. The stretch of this river around Kitulgala provides the site for the best **whitewater rafting** in Sri Lanka, with grade two and three rapids some 5km upriver from the village. You can organize trips through the two hotels listed below (around $30/person for 1hr 30min–2hr), or in advance through local tour companies (see p.27).

Kitulgala's other claim to fame is that it provided the location for David Lean's classic 1957 film *Bridge on the River Kwai*. If you know the film you'll probably recognize some of the locations down along the river. About 1.5km east of the *Plantation Hotel*, a very big sign ("Bridge of the River Kwai" [sic]) points to a very small track leading down to the river. Step onto the path and a guide or two will magically materialize to show you along the slightly confusing route to the river and point out a few locations associated with the film, including the slight remains of the bridge's concrete foundations.

ACCOMMODATION

KITULGALA

Borderlands ☎011 441 0110, ⒲discoverborderlands .com. Half eco-resort and half adventure sports centre, with accommodation in nine well-appointed tents on quaint thatched stilt platforms in a gorgeous riverside setting, surrounded by lush jungle. Activities include rafting, canyoning, waterfall abseiling, kayaking (flatwater and whitewater), guided hikes and mountain biking ($50/day for two activities on top of the basic accommodation price). $90

Kitulgala Rest House ☎036 228 7528, ⒲ceylonhotels .lk. Attractive old rest house, with plenty of period charm and a mix of comfortable, slightly chintzy fan rooms and

more modern ones with a/c, a scenic position facing the river and a gracious old restaurant. B&B: $70; a/c $82
Plantation Hotel ☎ 036 228 7575, ⓦplantation grouphotels.com. In a restored colonial villa about 1.5km east of the *Rest House*, this place caters mainly to tour groups and has comfortable a/c rooms and a pleasant riverside restaurant, though it gets absolutely overrun with passing coach parties at lunchtime, when it has all the charm of a motorway service station. Rs.8095

Ratnapura

Nestled among verdant hills at the southwestern corner of the hill country, **RATNAPURA** (literally "City of Gems") is famous for its **precious stones**, which have been mined here in extraordinary quantities since antiquity. Naturally, the town makes a big deal of this, with plenty of touts offering trips to gem mines and stones for sale, though unless you have a specialist interest in gemology, this alone isn't really a sufficient reason to visit the place. If you are interested in learning more, your guesthouse or touts in town may be able to arrange a visit to a working mine. *Ratna Gems Halt* (see p.268) also run a convenient trip combining a visit to a gem mine, gem museum and Saviya Street (Rs.2000 for the vehicle), and even run a ten-day gem-cutting course if the subject really grabs your imagination.

Ratnapura does have other attractions, however. The town makes a possible base for visits to **Sinharaja** and **Uda Walawe national parks**; trips to both involve a long (4hr+) return drive, making for a big day, but this does avoid the considerable bother of getting to Deniyaya, Kudawa or Embilipitiya. Several guesthouses in town can arrange trips: the going rate for a minivan or jeep is around $50–60 to Sinharaja and $60–70 to Uda Walawe – try *Travellers Halt* guesthouse or *Ratna Gems Halt* (see pp.268–269). Ratnapura is also the starting point for an alternative ascent of

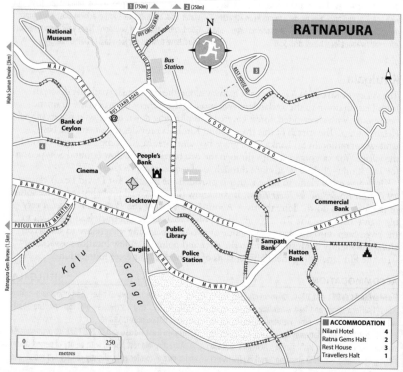

■ ACCOMMODATION	
Nilani Hotel	4
Ratna Gems Halt	2
Rest House	3
Travellers Halt	1

Adam's Peak, though it's significantly longer and tougher than the route up from Dalhousie. The path starts from the village of **Palabaddale**, from where it's a climb of five to seven hours to the summit. Buses run to Palabaddale via Gilimale during the pilgrimage season.

Ratnapura also has the distinction of being one of the **wettest places** in Sri Lanka, with an annual rainfall sometimes exceeding four metres – and even when it's not raining, the climate is usually humid and sticky.

Saviya Mawatha and around

A major regional commercial centre, Ratnapura is a busy and rather exhausting place, even before you've dealt with the attentions of touts trying to flog you gems or get you on visits to local mines. The heart of the town's gem trade is **Saviya Mawatha** (also spelt Zavier, Zaviya and Zavia), about 150m east of the clocktower, which presents an entertaining scene of crowds of locals haggling over handfuls of uncut stones; the shops of a few small dealers line the street (the town's traditional jewellers' shops are mainly located at the clocktower end of Main St). Trading takes place on weekdays until around 3pm. You're likely to be offered stones to buy – it should go without saying that unless you're an expert, steer well clear.

Ratnapura Gem Bureau

Potgul Vihara Mawatha • Daily 9.30am–4pm • Free (although a small donation may be requested)

If you want a detailed look at the area's mineral riches, head out to the **Ratnapura Gem Bureau**, usually simply referred to as the "Gem Museum", a couple of kilometres west of town on Potgul Vihara Mawatha. The museum is the brainchild of local gemmologist Purandara Sri Bhadra Marapana, and is intended as an altruistic and educational venture (although they might make a gentle attempt to flog you a few stones). The centrepiece is a colourful display of minerals and precious stones from around the world, including interesting Sri Lankan gems in both cut and uncut states. There are also displays of other handicrafts – stone carvings, metalwork and so on – designed by the versatile Mr Marapana.

National Museum

Main St • Tues–Sat 9am–5pm • Rs.300

There's surprisingly little coverage of the town's gem-mining heritage at the lacklustre **National Museum**, off Main Street on the northwest side of the town centre. Exhibits here run through the predictable gamut of Sri Lankan arts and crafts, including the inevitable Kandyan fabrics, jewellery, ivory carvings, a few entertaining *kolam* masks and a handful of beautiful Buddha statuettes. You'll also find the usual depressing collection of pickled and stuffed wildlife, plus large and unquestionably dull quantities of assorted rocks, uncut minerals, fossilized bones, the fossilized shells of snails on which prehistoric Ratnapura man presumably feasted and a few lion and pig teeth (also fossilized).

Maha Saman Devale

Horana Rd • Free

The most interesting sight hereabouts is the **Maha Saman Devale**, 3km west of town, the most important temple in the island dedicated to Saman (see box, p.262), who is said to reside on nearby Adam's Peak. There has been a temple here since the thirteenth century. It was rebuilt by the kings of Kandy during the seventeenth century, destroyed by the Portuguese, then rebuilt again during the Dutch era (a carving to the right of the entrance steps, showing a Portuguese invader killing a Sinhalese soldier, recalls European attacks against the town and temple). The present-day structure is impressively large, and although the overall effect is not of any especial antiquity, the entire complex has a pleasantly harmonious appearance, with rising tiers of tiled roofs

GEMS OF SRI LANKA

Sri Lanka is one of the world's most important sources of precious stones, and its gems have long been famous – indeed one of the island's early names was **Ratnadipa**, "Island of Gems". According to legend, it was a Sri Lankan ruby which was given by King Solomon to the Queen of Sheba, while Marco Polo described a fabulous ruby – "about a palm in length and of the thickness of a man's arm" – set in the spire of the Ruvenveliseya dagoba at Anuradhapura. The island also provided the "Blue Belle" sapphire which now adorns the crown of the British queen, while in 2003 a 478-carat Sri Lankan sapphire – larger than a hen's egg – fetched $1.5m at auction.

Gems are actually found in many parts of Sri Lanka, but the **Ratnapura** district is the island's richest source. The origin of these gems is the geological rubble eroded from the central highlands, which is washed down from the hills along the valleys which crisscross the area – a gravelly mixture of eroded rock, mineral deposits, precious stones and muddy alluvial deposits known as *illam*. Gem mining is still a low-tech, labour-intensive affair. Pits are dug down into riverbeds and among paddy fields, and piles of *illam* are fished out, which are then washed and sieved by experts who separate the precious stones from the mud. The mining and sorting is traditionally carried out by the Sinhalese, though gem cutters and dealers tend to be Muslim.

TYPES OF GEM

The most valuable precious stones found in Sri Lanka are corundums, a mineral family which includes sapphires and rubies. **Sapphires** range in colour from blue to as clear as a diamond. Sri Lankan **rubies** are "pink rubies" (also known as pink sapphires); the better-known red rubies are not found in the island. **Garnets**, popularly known as the "poor man's ruby", and ranging in colour from red to brown, are also found. **Cat's eyes** (green to brown) and **alexandrite** (whose colour changes under different light) are the best known of the chrysoberyl group of stones. **Tourmalines** are sometimes passed off as the far more valuable cat's eyes. Other common stones, found in varying hues, are **quartz**, **spinel** and **zircon**. The greyish **moonstone** (a type of feldspar) is a particular Sri Lankan speciality, though these are not mined in the Ratnapura area. Diamonds and emeralds are not found in Sri Lanka, though **aquamarine** (like emerald, a member of the beryl family) is.

and white walls leading up from the entrance to the main shrine, the whole structure enclosed by a large white balustraded wall, scored with tiny triangular niches to hold oil lamps. The main shrine to Saman is flanked by subsidiary shrines to the Buddha and Pattini (see box, p.218) – the latter is popular with local ladies, though her presence here is rather ironic: during the Kandyan era, the rise in her cult meant that she replaced Saman as one of the island's guardian deities. A big **Esala Perahera** takes place here during July or August. Numerous local **buses** run past the entrance to the temple, or you can catch a tuktuk.

ARRIVAL AND DEPARTURE
RATNAPURA

By bus Good roads head east and west from Ratnapura, served by regular buses. Heading north into the central hill country or south to the coast is significantly more time-consuming however, given the lack of good direct roads.

Destinations Akuressa (for Galle; 3 daily; 4hr 30min); Avissawella (for Hatton and Nuwara Eliya; every 10min; 1hr); Bandarawela (every 30min; 3hr 30min); Colombo (every 20min; 3hr; a/c express buses hourly); Deniyaya (for Sinharaja; 3 daily; 2hr 30min); Embilipitiya (every 15min; 2hr 30min); Haputale (every 30min; 3hr); Kalawana (for Sinharaja; every 15min; 1hr); Kandy (every 30min; 3hr 30min); Matara (3 daily via Deniyaya, or change at Embilipitiya; 5hr); Wellawaya (every 30min; 4hr).

ACCOMMODATION AND EATING

Nilani Hotel Dharmapala Mw ☎045 222 2170, ✉ nilanihotel@yahoo.com. Functional building – it looks like a gigantic air-conditioning unit – in a quiet road close to the town centre. Rooms (all with hot water) are comfy enough, although they've seen better days and are slightly pricey for what you get. **Rs.2400**; a/c **Rs.2950**

Ratna Gems Halt 153/5 Outer Circular Rd ☎045 222 3745, 🌐 ratnapura-online.com. Varied collection of modern and extremely good-value rooms, getting nicer (and more expensive) as you go up the building, from the rather poky, but also very cheap, ground-floor offerings to the bright, modern and spacious rooms on the top floor at slightly over double the price. **Rs.850**

Rest House Rest House Rd ☎045 222 2299, ⓦ resthousechain.info. Imposing old colonial rest house in a wonderful position on a hilltop above town with fine views. Rooms (a mix of fan and a/c, some with hot water) are clean, comfortable and reasonable value, if a bit bare,

and the in-house restaurant (mains from Rs.500) is the nicest in town; wi-fi. **Rs.2750**

Travellers Halt 30 Outer Circular Rd ☎045 222 3092, ⓔ no30_fernando@yahoo.com. In a quiet location just outside town, with a mix of older rooms (a few with a/c) in the main house plus a handful of larger and more modern rooms with hot water in an adjacent building. Comfortable enough, although a bit overpriced, and with only a limited choice of food. Also a good place to arrange trips to Sinharaja and Uda Walawe. **Rs.2400**; a/c **Rs.3400**

DIRECTORY

Banks A number of banks around the centre have ATMs which accept foreign Visa and MasterCards – the Hatton National Bank and Commercial Bank are generally the most reliable.

Internet Sara Net Café on Main St by the junction with Bus Stand Rd (daily 7am–10pm; Rs.40/hr); there's also wi-fi at the *Rest House*.

Sinharaja and around

The largest surviving tract of undisturbed lowland rainforest in Sri Lanka, **Sinharaja** is one of the island's outstanding natural wonders and a biodiverse treasure box of global significance (recognized by its listing as a UNESCO World Heritage Site in 1989). This is the archetypal rainforest as you've always imagined it: the air thick with humidity (approaching ninety percent in places) and alive with the incessant noise of birds, cicadas and other invisible creatures; the ground choked with a dense understorey of exotic ferns and snaking lianas wrapped around the base of towering tropical hardwoods, rising towards the forest canopy high overhead.

According to tradition, Sinharaja was formerly a royal reserve (as suggested by its name, meaning "Lion King"). The first attempts to conserve it were made as far back as 1840, when it became property of the British Crown. Logging began in 1971, until being banned in the face of national protests in 1977, when the area was declared a national reserve. Sinharaja is now safely protected under UNESCO auspices, using a system whereby inhabitants of the twenty-odd villages which surround the reserve have the right to limited use of the forest's resources, including tapping kitul palms for jaggery and collecting rattan for building.

Sinharaja stretches for almost 30km across the wet zone at the southern edges of the hill country, enveloping a series of switchback hills and valleys ranging in altitude from just 300m up to 1170m. To the north and south, the reserve is bounded by two sizeable rivers, the Kalu Ganga and the Gin Ganga, which cut picturesque, waterfall-studded courses through the trees.

Sinharaja's wildlife

A staggering 830 of Sri Lanka's endemic species of flora and fauna are found in Sinharaja, including myriad birds, reptiles and insects, while no less than sixty percent of the reserve's trees are endemic too. The reserve's most common **mammal** is the purple-faced langur monkey, while you might also encounter three species of squirrel – the dusky-striped jungle squirrel, flame-striped jungle squirrel and western giant squirrel – along with mongooses. Less common, and very rarely sighted, are leopards, rusty spotted cats, fishing-cats and civets. There's also a rich **reptile** population, including 21 of Sri Lanka's 45 endemic species, among them rare snakes and frogs. Many of the reserve's bountiful population of **insects** are yet to be classified, although you're likely to see various colourful spiders and enormous butterflies, while giant millipedes are also common.

Sinharaja has one of Sri Lanka's richest **bird** populations: 21 of the country's 26 endemic species have been recorded here (although some can only be seen in the

BIRDS OF DIFFERENT FEATHERS

Sinharaja is home to one of the world's finest examples of a "mixed-species feeding flock", as it's technically known, or **bird wave**, as it's popularly described: a memorably colourful and noisy rainforest spectacle during which myriad different species can be seen flying and foraging together, "scouring the forest from top to bottom like a giant vacuum cleaner, devouring animals and plant matter in their path" (as Sri Lankan wildlife expert Gehan de Silva Wijeyeratne puts it). From an evolutionary point of view, such collective feeding has clear practical advantages. Safety-in-numbers is one benefit, with members of the bird wave sometimes flocking together to beat off larger predators, while increased feeding efficiency is another.

Different species fly at different levels (ground, rainforest under-storey, canopy, and so on) with mutual benefits – a species feeding in the under-storey, for instance, may disturb insects which fly up and become easy prey for birds in the canopy above, while fruit and seeds dislodged by birds in the canopy may fall to species foraging on the ground.

Bird waves in Sinharaja may consist of over a hundred birds from dozens of different species. The crested drongo is the accepted leader of the pack, calling to other species to begin flocking and also taking responsibility for collective security, sounding an alarm call when danger threatens – at which point the whole flock will suddenly, silently freeze until the drongos give the all-clear. Other species also commonly join in with the wave as it passes through their territory, sometimes offering the remarkable sight of half-a-dozen rare endemics flocking together, while other animals including giant squirrels and mouse deer are also often seen following along.

reserve's difficult-to-reach eastern fringes). The density of the forest and the fact that its birds largely inhabit the topmost part of the canopy means that actually seeing them can be tricky, especially if entering via the Mederipitiya entrance, where the forest is particularly thick – as ever, a good guide (see below) is of the essence.

INFORMATION   SINHARAJA

Visiting the reserve The closest starting points for visits to Sinharaja are Deniyaya, on the eastern side of the reserve, and Kudawa, on its northern edge. It's also possible to arrange visits from guesthouses in Ratnapura or with a couple of tour operators in Unawatuna, though it will be a long day by the time you've driven to and from the reserve.

Entry points There are two entrances to the reserve. The most popular approach is via the northern entrance at Kudawa. The less frequently used eastern entrance to the reserve is at Mederipitiya, about 11km east of Deniyaya; the rainforest here is more dramatic than on the Kudawa side, though it makes bird- and wildlife-spotting correspondingly more difficult. The road from Deniyaya ends just short of the reserve, from where it's a pleasant 1.5km walk through tea plantations. The path isn't signposted (go right at the fork by the gravestones near the beginning).

Opening hours and entry fees The reserve is open daily 7am–6pm. Entry costs Rs.660, plus Rs.400/group for an obligatory guide (unless you bring your own), who will lead you on walking tours of up to 3hr.

Walking There are no driveable roads in the reserve, so you have to walk (which is, indeed, one of the pleasures of a visit). Waterproofs are advisable: Sinharaja receives up to 5m of rain annually. Leeches (see p.56) are abundant after rain.

Guides What you get out of a visit to Sinharaja relies on having a good guide – the rainforest is dense and difficult to decipher. Many of the reserve's guides speak very little English, although some may be able to turn up some interesting birdlife even so. A fail-safe option is to sign up for a tour with Bandula or Palitha Ratnayake, based at the *Sinharaja Rest* in Deniyaya (see p.272).

Kudawa

The village of **KUDAWA** is the most popular base for visiting Sinharaja. There's a better range of accommodation in the area on this side of the reserve, including a couple of top-end options, but it's more difficult to reach by public transport, so is likely to be of interest mainly to those with their own vehicle.

Note that Sinharaja and the area immediately around the reserve is one of the few places in Sri Lanka which doesn't have **mobile phone** coverage.

ARRIVAL AND DEPARTURE

KUDAWA

By car It's a slow and bumpy drive to Sinharaja from Ratnapura. With your own vehicle it's likely to take the best part of 2hr to reach Kudawa, or slightly over an hour to reach Kalawana and Koswatte.

By bus There are frequent buses from Ratnapura to Kalawana (15km north of Kudawa), from where there are infrequent (around four daily) buses to Kudawa itself.

ACCOMMODATION

There's not much choice of **accommodation** in Sinharaja, and prices are high. Accommodation on the Kudawa side of the reserve can be found in Kudawa itself and in the nearby villages of Weddagala, about 6km from the reserve entrance, and Koswatta, a further 10km back up the road, and about 2km from the town of Kalawana. In addition to the places listed below, Martin Wijesinghe (of *Forest View* – see below) is also building a new guesthouse near the ticket office which might have opened by the time you read this; rates are likely to be around $40/night.

KOSWATTA

Boulder Garden Koswatta ☎045 225 5812, ⓦ bouldergarden.com. Small eco-resort in a captivating natural setting some 16km from Sinharaja (a 45min drive), nestled between huge boulders and patches of rainforest. It's a lovely concept, although rooms, with their expanses of slate-grey stone, are a touch sombre, bathrooms are basic and the property really should be better looked after given the massively inflated rates. Facilities include a striking open-air restaurant underneath a huge rock overhang and a (very shallow) swimming pool. B&B $273

Singraj Rest Koswatta ☎045 225 5201. Quiet – verging on moribund – guesthouse, with a selection of modern rooms of various sizes and standards (including a couple with a/c for a hefty $20 supplement). Uninspiring, but the cheapest place in the area. $30

KUDAWA

Blue Magpie Lodge Kudawa ☎011 243 1872, ⓔ bluemagpielodge@gmail.com. In a perfect location close to the ticket office in Kudawa, with nicely furnished modern rooms grouped around a patch of lawn and a nice natural swimming area in the river below. Reasonable value by Sinharaja standards, particularly if you go for half- or full-board. $65

Forest View (Martin Wijesinghe's Guest House) Kudawa ☎045 568 1864. Long-established guesthouse run by a knowledgeable former Sinharaja ranger and on the edge of the reserve; staying here is the closest you can get to spending a night in the forest itself, and the after-dark cacophony of cicadas and other nocturnal creatures is extraordinary. Accommodation is in a handful of very basic but clean rooms, with simple meals (bring your own booze). It's around 3km by road from the ticket office – walkable in 15–20min via a tricky-to-find off-road shortcut; or arrange a jeep (around 20min drive, or longer during rainy months; $35 return). A memorable experience, although very expensive given the basic accommodation on offer, especially if you pay for a jeep to get there. B&B Rs.4200

WEDDAGALA

Rainforest Edge Rakwana Rd (about 6km from Sinharaja) ☎045 225 5912, ⓦ www.rainforestedge .com. Perched atop a hill, with sweeping views, this striking eco-lodge looks vaguely like a dislocated African bush village, with accommodation in a string of low thatched, ochre-coloured buildings – although the whole place is beginning to look disappointingly shabby given the hefty price tag. Rooms have a bright, ethnic look and open-air bathrooms with solar-powered hot water (but no TVs or a/c), and there's also a restaurant (Sri Lankan food only), Ayurveda centre and murky-looking rainwater pool. B&B $244

Rock View Motel Rakwana Rd, Weddagala, 8km from Sinharaja (signed 2km off road on left, 6km before you reach Sinharaja, past Rainforest Edge) ☎045 567 7990. One of the best deals at present in the Kudawa area, with attractively furnished, high-ceilinged modern rooms with hot water and private balconies offering fine views over the wooded hills opposite (plus a few cheaper but less appealing ones in the basement). Note that there's a reception hall downstairs, however, so can be noisy if there's a function in progress. Rs.4400

Deniyaya

The small town of **DENIYAYA** offers an alternative base for visiting Sinharaja if you haven't got your own vehicle; it can be reached either from Galle or Matara on the south coast or from Ratnapura to the north (although bus services are surprisingly skimpy).

ARRIVAL AND DEPARTURE DENIYAYA

By bus The bus station is right in the middle of town. Moving on from Deniyaya, there are irregular direct buses to Matara and Galle (roughly every 2hr). Otherwise change at Akuressa (every 30min; 1hr 30min), from where there are frequent onward connections to both these places. Transport northwards is much more infrequent, with about four buses to Pelmadulla and Ratnapura daily.

ACCOMMODATION

Rest House 500m south of the bus station ☎ 041 227 3600. Battered old rest house with large, bare and rather dimly lit rooms – all fairly shabby and basic, though fine views of hills from the veranda partly compensate, and rates are cheap. **Rs.1500**

Sinharaja Rest 500m north of the bus station ☎ 041 227 3368. Six simple but comfortable rooms, plus organic food. It's owned and managed by local guides Bandula and Palitha Ratnayake, who run day-trips to Sinharaja for Rs.3500/person (including entrance fees), entering the reserve through Mederipitiya and walking 12–14km. Shorter trips can also be arranged, as can longer excursions, such as the seven-hour hike over to Kudawa or the two-day (27km) trek across the entire reserve to Lion Rock. **Rs.2000**

DIRECTORY

Banks There are a couple of banks with ATMs in town, including the Commercial Bank (Visa and MasterCard) and People's Bank (Visa only).

Uda Walawe National Park and around

Entrance on the Embilipitiya–Tanamal road at km-post 7 • $15 per person, plus the usual additional charges and taxes (see p.45)

Sprawling across the lowlands due south of the towering cliff faces of Horton Plains, **Uda Walawe** has developed into one of Sri Lanka's most popular national parks mainly thanks to its large and easily spotted population of elephants – it's the best place in the island to see pachyderms in the wild, although in other respects it doesn't have the range of fauna and habitats of Yala or Bundala. The park is beautifully situated just south of the hill country, whose grand escarpment provides a memorable backdrop, while at its centre lies the **Uda Walawe Reservoir**, whose catchment area it was originally established to protect. Most of Uda Walawe lies within the dry zone, and its terrain is flat and denuded, with extensive areas of grassland and low scrub (the result of earlier slash-and-burn farming) dotted with the skeletal outlines of expired trees, scratched to death by the resident elephants. The actual landscape of the park is rather monotonous during dry periods, although the lack of forest cover makes it easier to spot wildlife than in any other Sri Lankan park and the whole place transforms magically after rain, when temporary lagoons form around the reservoir, drowning trees and turning the floodplains an intense, fecund green.

The principal attraction is, of course, **elephants**, of which there are usually around six hundred in the park; animals are free to migrate along an elephant corridor between here and Lunugamvehera National Park, though most stay here. There are also hundreds of **buffaloes**, plus macaque and langur monkeys, spotted and sambhur deer and crocodiles, while other rarely sighted residents include leopards, giant flying squirrels, jungle cats, sloth bears and porcupines. Uda Walawe is also good for **birds**, including a number of endemics and some birds of prey, while the reservoir also attracts a wide range of aquatic birds including the unmistakable Lesser Adjutant, Sri Lanka's largest – and ugliest – bird, standing at well over a metre tall.

Elephant transit home

Daily feeding sessions at 9am, noon, 3pm and 6pm • Free (but a donation may be requested)

About 5km west of the park entrance on the main road is the engaging **Elephant Transit Home** – usually referred to as the "Elephant Orphanage". Founded in 1995, the orphanage is home to around 25 baby elephants rescued from the wild after the loss of their parents. As at the better-known orphanage at Pinnewala, elephants here are bottlefed milk until the age of 3½, after which they're given a diet of grass. At the age of 5, most are released into the national park (around thirty so far); a few have been donated to important temples. You can't get quite as close to the elephants as at Pinnewala; outside feeding times the elephants are allowed to wander, so there's usually nothing to see.

ARRIVAL AND DEPARTURE — UDA WALAWE

On a Tour Uda Walawe's central location makes it accessible from a number of different places, and you can arrange tours here from as far afield as Ratnapura, Hambantota, Tissa and even Unawatuna (see the relevant town accounts for more details), although all these involve long drives to reach the park. The closest starting point is Embilipitiya, 20km distant.

By public transport Half-hourly buses from Embilipitiya to Tamanalwila go right past the entrance, where you can hire a jeep (seating 6–8) for around Rs.3000 for a few hours' drive.

ACCOMMODATION

If you want to stay inside the park itself, upmarket tented safaris are run by Kulu Safaris and Mahoora (see p.27), while you can also camp close to the park entrance at the rustic *Governor's Camp* (☎0773 829 123, ✆governorscampssrilanka.com).

Kalu's Hideaway Walawegama, 15min from park entrance ☎011 574 6338, ✆www.kalushideaway .com. Run by World Cup-winning former cricketer Romesh Kaluwitharana, with five attractive modern a/c rooms plus two chalets, all with cheery rustic touches and set in five acres of grounds (with small pool). Jeep transport to the park available for $40. B&B **$130**

Walawa Safari Village Right Bank Canal Rd, 12km from the park entrance (and clearly signed off the Embilipitiya–Uda Walawe road) ☎047 223 3201. The best option close to the park, with an attractively rustic atmosphere and neat and cosy little cabanas dotted around rambling gardens. You can arrange transport to and around the park from here for around Rs.3000. B&B **$50**

Embilipitiya

Halfway between Ratnapura and the coast, the medium-size town of **EMBILIPITIYA** is the closest base for visits to Uda Walawe, 20km distant, although there's not much to the town itself.

ARRIVAL AND DEPARTURE — EMBILIPITIYA

By bus Buses arrive at the station about 100m south of the clocktower at the centre of town. If you're heading towards the southeastern hill country, catch a bus to Tamanalwila, from where you can pick up a bus to Wellawaya, which has frequent connections with Ella, Haputale, Bandarawela and Badulla. To reach Deniyaya (for Sinharaja) you'll need to catch one of the early-morning buses from Embilipitiya to Suriyakanda (a two-hour journey; check latest times the night before), from where infrequent buses head south (or take a tuktuk for around Rs.2000). For Tissa, change at Hambantota.

Destinations Hambantota (every 15min; 1hr 30min); Matara (every 20min; 2hr 30min); Ratnapura (every 15min; 2hr 30min); Tamanalwila (every 30min; 1hr); Tangalla (every 20min; 1hr 30min).

ACCOMMODATION AND EATING

There's not really anywhere **to eat** apart from the two hotels listed below, both of which can also arrange half-day trips to Uda Walawe for around Rs.3500.

Centauria Tourist Hotel About 1.5km south of town ☎047 223 0104. Surprisingly well-appointed place for dusty little Embilipitiya. Accommodation is either in comfortable modern a/c rooms or in more stylish and spacious two-person villas overlooking Chandrika Wewa, and there's also a decent restaurant, pool and Ayurveda centre. **$83**

Sarathchandra Rest On the main road 100m south of the bus station ☎047 223 0044. Well-run hotel with comfortable modern rooms, all spacious and attractively furnished. There's also a good little restaurant downstairs, plus a rather rowdy local bar.. **Rs.2000**; a/c **Rs.3000**

DIRECTORY

Banks There are several banks close to the clocktower: the ATMs at the Commercial and Sampath banks both accept foreign Visa and MasterCards; those at the Seylan and People's Bank take Visa only.

Internet Vanik IT Center, next to *Sarathchandra Rest*.

The Cultural Triangle

280 Kurunegala

282 Around Kurunegala

286 North from Kandy to Dambulla

289 Dambulla and around

295 Northwest of Dambulla

297 Sigiriya and around

303 Habarana and around

307 Polonnaruwa and around

319 Anuradhapura

336 Mihintale

SCHOOLGIRLS, COUNCIL CHAMBER, POLONNARUWA

The Cultural Triangle

North of Kandy, the tangled green hills of the central highlands tumble down into the plains of the dry zone, a hot and denuded region covered in thorny scrub and jungle and punctuated by isolated mountainous outcrops that tower dramatically over the surrounding flatlands. Despite the unpromising natural environment, these northern plains – traditionally referred to as Rajarata, or "The King's Land", although now more popularly known as the Cultural Triangle – served as the crucible of early Sinhalese civilization, centred on the great cities of Anuradhapura and Polonnaruwa, whose grandiose monuments still serve as potent reminders of the golden age of Sinhalese civilization.

At the spiritual heart of the Triangle lies the great ruined city of **Anuradhapura**, capital of the island from the third century BC to 993 AD and one of medieval Asia's great metropolises, dotted with vast monasteries, elaborate palaces, enormous tanks and a trio of monumental dagobas, excelled in scale in the ancient world only by the Egyptian pyramids. The remains of **Polonnaruwa**, the island's second capital, are more compact but equally absorbing, while few visitors miss the chance to climb the spectacular rock citadel of **Sigiriya**, perhaps Sri Lanka's single most extraordinary sight. Other leading attractions include the marvellous cave temples of **Dambulla**, a magical treasure box of Buddhist sculpture and painting, and the religious centre of **Mihintale**, scene of the introduction of Buddhism to the island.

Major attractions aside, the Cultural Triangle is peppered with other intriguing but relatively little-visited ancient monuments, including the abandoned cities of **Yapahuwa** and **Panduwas Nuwara**; the great Buddha statues of **Aukana** and **Sasseruwa**; the absorbing temples of **Aluvihara** and **Ridi Vihara**; and the haunting forest monasteries of **Arankele** and **Ritigala**. And there is no shortage of natural attractions, either, at the national parks of **Minneriya**, **Kaudulla** and **Wasgomuwa**.

GETTING AROUND   THE CULTURAL TRIANGLE

Planning an itinerary The major Cultural Triangle sites are all relatively close to one another, and offer many different permutations in terms of where to stay and how to plan an itinerary. One possibility is to base yourself at one of the many hotels or guesthouses in or around Dambulla, Sigiriya or Habarana, whose central location makes it possible to visit all the major sights on day-trips.

Public transport Almost everywhere can be reached by public transport, but doing so is often a time-consuming business – you'll be able to see far more with your own transport. However, regular buses connect Kandy, Dambulla, Sigiriya, Anuradhapura and Polonnaruwa, while occasional trains run from Colombo, via Kurunegala, to both Anuradhapura and Polonnaruwa.

Triangular vision p.280
Unmadachitra p.284
A tale of two Buddhas p.296
Best bee-haviour p.301
Polonnaruwa or Anuradhapura? p.307
Parakramabahu the Great p.309
Nissankamalla the Vainglorious p.312

Anuradhapura orientation p.321
Water world: irrigation in early Sri Lanka p.322
Dutugemunu the Disobedient p.324
Yasalalakatissa and Subha p.328
The restoration of Anuradhapura p.330

SIGIRIYA WATER GARDENS

Highlights

❶ Dambulla The rock temples of Dambulla are a veritable Aladdin's cave of Buddhist art, packed with hundreds of statues and decorated with the finest murals in the country. **See p.289**

❷ Sigiriya The spectacular rock outcrop of Sigiriya was the site of Sri Lanka's most remarkable royal capital and palace, complete with water gardens, paintings of celestial nymphs, 1300-year-old graffiti and the paws of a giant lion statue. **See p.297**

❸ "The Gathering", Minneriya National Park Asia's largest gathering of wild elephants, as three hundred or more pachyderms congregate at the retreating waters of the Minneriya Tank during the northern dry season. **See p.306**

❹ Polonnaruwa This ruined city preserves an outstanding collection of ancient monuments, testifying to its brief but brilliant period as the island's capital. **See p.307**

❺ Anuradhapura The ruins of the ancient city of Anuradhapura remain one of the island's most compelling historical sites, as well as a major place of Buddhist pilgrimage. **See p.319**

❻ Mihintale Revered as the place where Buddhism was introduced to the island, Mihintale boasts an interesting collection of religious monuments scattered across a beautiful hilltop location. **See p.336**

HIGHLIGHTS ARE MARKED ON THE MAP ON PP.278–279

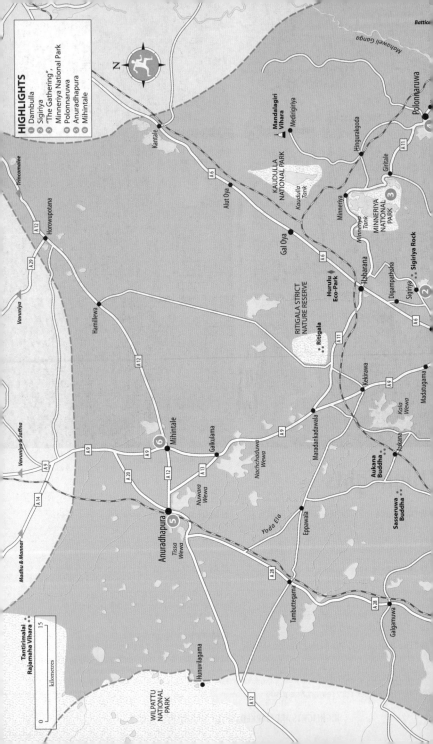

HIGHLIGHTS
1 Dambulla
2 Sigiriya
3 "The Gathering", Minneriya National Park
4 Polonnaruwa
5 Anuradhapura
6 Mihintale

N

Battice

Mahaweli Ganga

Trincomalee

Kantale

A6

Horowupotana

A12

A29

Vavuniya

A6

Alut Oya

KAUDULLA NATIONAL PARK

Kaudulla Tank

Mandalagiri Vihara

Medirigiriya

Hingurakgoda

A11

Giritale

Polonnaruwa

4

Gal Oya

A6

Minneriya

Minneriya Tank

3

MINNERIYA NATIONAL PARK

Sigiriya Rock

Habarana

Digampathaha

Sigiriya

2

A6

Hamillewa

A12

Hurulu Eco-Park

RITIGALA STRICT NATURE RESERVE

Ritigala

A11

Kekirawa

A9

Madatugama

Kala Wewa

Maradankadawala

A9

Galkulama

A33

Mihintale

6

A9

Askana

Aukana Buddha

Sasseruwa Buddha

A9

A12

Vavuniya & Jaffna

A20

A14

Anuradhapura

5

Tissa Wewa

Nuwara Wewa

Nachchaduwa Wewa

Epawala

Yoda Ela

A28

Tambuttegama

Galgamuwa

A28

Madhu & Mannar

Hunuwilagama

WILPATTU NATIONAL PARK

A12

Tantrimalai
Rajamaha Vihara

0   kilometres   15

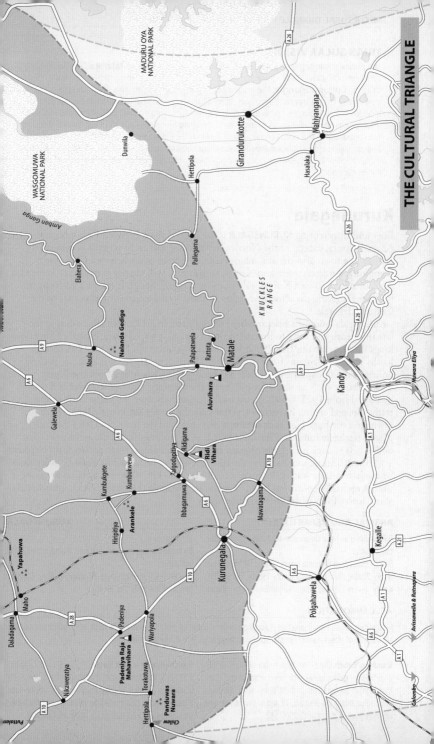

THE CULTURAL TRIANGLE

TRIANGULAR VISION

The plains of northern Sri Lanka have been known for millennia as **Rajarata**, "The King's Land", although nowadays the traditional name has largely lapsed and the region is generally referred to as the **Cultural Triangle**. The origins of the name date back to the 1970s and the government's attempt to restore and promote the region's great ruined monuments for the modern tourist industry – perhaps inspired by the "golden triangles" of Thailand and India. The three points of this imaginary triangle lie at the great Sinhalese capitals of Kandy in the south, Anuradhapura in the north and Polonnaruwa in the east, although in fact, this tourist-oriented invention presents a rather warped sense of the region's past, given that the history of Kandy is quite different and separate – both chronologically and geographically – from that of the earlier capitals.

Kurunegala

Busy and disorienting **KURUNEGALA** is the biggest town between Colombo and Anuradhapura, capital of the Northwest Province and an important commercial centre. The town also sits at a major junction on the roads between Colombo, Dambulla, Anuradhapura and Kandy, so you may well change buses here. There's no great incentive to visit Kurunegala in its own right, though it makes a convenient base for exploring the cluster of sights situated in the southwestern corner of the Cultural Triangle.

Kurunegala enjoyed a brief moment of eminence in Sri Lankan affairs during the late thirteenth and early fourteenth centuries when it served as the capital of Sinhalese kings Bhuvanekabahu II (1293–1302) and Parakramabahu IV (1302–26), though hardly anything remains from this period. The present-day town is a tightly packed honeycomb of busy streets – a rude awakening if you're coming from the sleepy backwaters of the Cultural Triangle. Apart from a pretty stone **clocktower** and war memorial from 1922, which stands watch impassively over the hurly-burly of the traffic-clogged centre, its main attractions are the breezy **Kurunegala Tank**, north of town, and the huge bare **rock outcrops** that surround the town, and lend the entire place a strangely lunar air. The inevitable legend professes that these are the petrified bodies of a strange menagerie of giant animals – including an eel, tortoise and elephant – who were threatening to drink the lake dry, only to be turned to stone by a demoness who inhabited the waters. If you've an hour or so to kill, it's worth walking or taking a tuktuk up to the enormous Buddha statue atop **Etagala** (Elephant Rock), immediately above town, from where there are fine views.

ARRIVAL AND DEPARTURE   KURUNEGALA

By bus Buses arrive at the overcrowded station bang in the town centre.
Destinations Anuradhapura (every 20min; 3hr); Colombo: (every 20min; 2hr); Dambulla (every 15min; 1hr 30min); Kandy (every 15min; 1hr); Negombo (every 30min;

1hr 30min).
By train The train station is just over 1km southeast of the bus station.
Destinations Anuradhapura (7 daily; 2–3hr); Colombo (8 daily; 1hr 40min–2hr 30min).

ACCOMMODATION

Most of Kurunegala's small selection of accommodation is clustered around **Kurunegala Tank**, north of the town centre, although most places are more used to local wedding parties than to foreign tourists.

Kandyan Reach Kandy Rd, 1km south of town ☎037 222 9510, ⓦkandyan-reach-hotel.athgirihotel.com. Kurunegala's biggest and poshest hotel, with spacious, good-value rooms (all with a/c, TV and hot water) ranged around a pool (non-guests Rs.200). $42

Ranthaliya New Rest House 11 South Lake Rd ☎037 222 2298. The closest accommodation to the town centre, attractively located on the southern side of the lake, although rooms (some with lake views, a/c and hot water) are spartan and a bit shabby. Rs.1800; a/c Rs.2500

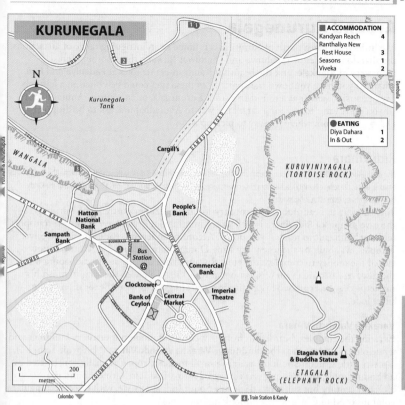

KURUNEGALA

N

Kurunegala Tank

WANGALA

Puttalam & Kurunegala

Negombo

NORTH ROAD

SOUTH LAKE ROAD

PUTTALAM ROAD

NEGOMBO ROAD

WILGODAPITTIYA MW

BUDHIKA MW

COLOMBO ROAD

MADUREDDY MW

KANDY ROAD

SURIYASHILA ROAD

PATHERIHILS ROAD

DAMBULLA ROAD

DAMBULLA ROAD

Dambulla

■ ACCOMMODATION	
Kandyan Reach	4
Ranthaliya New Rest House	3
Seasons	1
Viveka	2

● EATING	
Diya Dahara	1
In & Out	2

KURUVINIYAGALA (TORTOISE ROCK)

Cargill's

People's Bank

Hatton National Bank

Sampath Bank

Bus Station @

Commercial Bank

Clocktower

Bank of Ceylon

Central Market

Imperial Theatre

Etagala Vihara & Buddha Statue

ETAGALA (ELEPHANT ROCK)

0   200
metres

Colombo ▼   ⬛ Train Station & Kandy

4

Seasons 7 North Lake Rd ☎037 222 3452, ✉diya dahara@sltnet.lk. An overblown place, used mainly as a venue for weddings and functions, with four spacious modern rooms (with twelve more planned) with a/c and TV. They can be noisy if there's an event on, and are relatively expensive. The now virtually defunct *Diya Dihara* hotel opposite is where you'll find the hotel's reception and attractive lakeside restaurant (see below). Rs.4300

Viveka 64 North Lake Rd ☎037 222 2897, ✉viveka hotel64@sltnet.lk. Occupying an attractive old villa next to the lake, this low-key local drinking hole also offers decent accommodation, with four cosy rooms with chunky old wooden furniture, TV and optional a/c (Rs.500 extra). The spacious veranda is a nice place for a beer, and they also serve an above-average rice and curry. Rs.2500; a/c Rs.3000

EATING

Diya Dahara 7 North Lake Rd. Kurunegala's nicest place to eat, occupying a garden terrace overlooking the lake and serving up a competently prepared range of Sri Lankan standards, along with a few rather more hit-and-miss Chinese and Continental dishes, plus salads and sandwiches. Mains Rs.400–600. Daily 6am–10pm.

In & Out Puttalam Rd. Close to the bus station, this modern café-cum-Sri Lankan-style fast-food joint serves up a wide variety of snacks and meals ranging from cakes and sandwiches through to more substantial local and international mains (Rs.200–400) – anything from rice and curry to chop suey. Daily 6am–10pm.

DIRECTORY

Banks There are numerous banks in town with ATMs accepting foreign cards. The Commercial Bank is usually the most reliable for both Visa and MasterCard.

Internet Puttalam Road has several options, in the row of computer shops above the bus station.

Around Kurunegala

The little-visited area north of Kurunegala is home to an intriguing range of attractions: the abandoned cities of **Yapahuwa** and **Panduwas Nuwara**; the absorbing forest monastery of **Arankele**; and the beautiful Kandyan-era temples at **Padeniya** and **Ridi Vihara**. If you have your own transport, all of these sites could be visited in a leisurely day's excursion, either as a round-trip from Kurunegala, or en route to Anuradhapura. (If you don't want to pay for a car all the way to Anuradhapura, ask to be dropped at Daladagama, from where it's easy to pick up a bus.)

Ridi Vihara

2km outside Ridigama village • No set hours • Donation • Take a bus from Kurunegala to Ridigama (hourly; 45min) then either walk or take a tuktuk; by car, the temple is easily reached from either the Kurunegala–Dambulla highway (turn off at Talgodapitiya) or the Kandy–Dambulla highway (turn off at Palapatwela)

Tucked away in beautiful rolling countryside around 20km northeast of Kurunegala, the cave temple of **Ridi Vihara** is well worth hunting out if you have your own transport (although difficult to reach if you don't). According to legend, Ridi Vihara, or "Silver Temple", was built by the legendary King Dutugemunu (see p.324). Dutugemunu lacked the money to complete the great Ruvanvalisaya dagoba at Anuradhapura until the discovery of a rich vein of silver ore at Ridi Vihara allowed the king to finish his masterpiece – he expressed his gratitude by creating a temple at the location of the silver lode.

Varakha Valandu Vihara

Entering the complex, bear left in front of a cluster of modern monastery buildings and a fine old bo tree to reach the diminutive **Varakha Valandu Vihara** ("Jackfruit Temple"), a pretty little structure built up against a small rock outcrop. Originally constructed as a Hindu temple, the building was converted into a Buddhist shrine around the eleventh century but still looks decidedly South Indian in style, with heavy rectangular columns overhung by a very solid-looking stone roof.

Pahala Vihara

Beyond the Varakha Valandu Vihara lies the main temple, built beneath a huge rock outcrop said to resemble the shape of a cobra's hood. The temple is in two parts. The older **Pahala Vihara** (Lower Temple) is built into a cave beneath the rock. An exquisite ivory carving of five ladies stands next to the entrance door, while inside a series of huge statues pose solemnly in the semi-darkness. A huge sleeping Buddha occupies the left-hand side of the cave, in front of which is a platform inset with blue-and-white Flemish tiles, donated (it's said) by a Dutch ambassador to the Kandyan court and showing pictures of village life in the Netherlands along with a few biblical scenes – a sneaky bit of Christian proselytizing in this venerable Buddhist shrine. The weatherbeaten statues at the far end of the temple include an eroded image said to be of Dutugemunu himself.

Uda Vihara

To the right of the Pahala Vihara, steps lead up to the eighteenth-century Upper Temple, or **Uda Vihara** – the work of Kandyan king Kirti Sri Rajasinha (see p.210). The main chamber has an impressive seated Buddha set against a densely peopled background (the black figures are Vishnus), while the entrance steps outside boast a fine moonstone flanked by elephant-shaped balustrades. Note, too, the door to the small shrine behind, topped with an unusual painting of nine women arranged in the shape of an elephant. Outside, a dagoba sits almost completely covered under another part of the overhanging rock.

Back at the entrance to the monastery, more than a hundred steps, some cut into bare rock, lead up to a small restored **dagoba**, from which there are fine views across the surrounding countryside.

Arankele

Between Hiripitiya and Kumbukwewa, a couple of kilometres down the small back road connecting the two • Daily 6am–6pm • Free (although an entrance fee may be introduced soon) • Driving (there's no public transport to Arankele), the back road to the site is unsurfaced on the Hiripitiya side, although passable in a 2WD, and signage is minimal, so you may have to ask for directions; approaching from Kurunegala and Kumbukwewa, the road passes the rear entrance to the site (where the modern monastery is) first, before reaching the main entrance around 1km further down the road

Hidden away on a jungle-covered hillside some 25km north of Kurunegala, the ruined forest hermitage of **Arankele** is one of the Cultural Triangle's least-visited but most intriguing sites. Arankele was occupied as far back as the third century BC, although most of what you see today dates from the sixth to eighth centuries AD, while extensive parts of the site have yet to be excavated. A community of *pamsukulika* monks (see p.306) who have devoted themselves to a reclusive, meditative life still live at the monastery at the back of the site.

The monastery ruins

Just before you reach the entrance to the site, note the fine **Jantaghara** (literally "hot water bath" – perhaps some kind of monastic hospital similar to the one in Mihintale), with a fine old stone bathing tank enclosed in stout rectangular walls.

The main monastery

Immediately beyond the entrance lie the extensive ruins of the **main monastery**, distinguished by their fine craftsmanship and the staggeringly large chunks of stone used in their construction – the fact that early Sinhalese engineers and craftsmen were able to transport and work such huge rocks slightly beggars belief. Major structures here include the impressive chapter house, surrounded by a large moat to help cool the air, and, beside it, a large step-sided pond. Nearby you'll find the monastery's main reception hall, floored with just four enormous slabs of granite; an elaborate stone toilet; and, next to it, a small meditation walkway, originally roofed – the only one of its kind in Sri Lanka (the roof has long since gone, although the footings that supported the columns which formerly held it up can still be seen).

Meditation walkway

Beyond the main monastery begins Arankele's remarkable main **meditation walkway**: a long, perfectly straight stone walkway, punctuated by small flights of steps, its geometrical neatness making a strange contrast with the wild dry tropical forest through which it runs. After some 250m you reach a miniature "roundabout" on the path, popularly believed to have been built to allow meditating monks to avoid walking into one another, although it probably served as a rest area, covered with a (long since vanished) roof. Close by stand the remains of the principal monk's residence, with the base of a large hall, the inevitable toilet and (below) a jumble of pillars, partly collapsed, which would have supported an open-air meditation platform.

The meditation walkway continues a further 250m or so, ending at a small **cave-shrine** built beneath a rock outcrop. This is the oldest part of the ruins, dating back to the third century BC – the original drip-ledge and the holes where a projecting canopy was once fixed can still be seen. Inside, a small Buddha shrine sits flanked by two tiny meditation cells.

Beyond here the path continues to the **modern monastery**, with a long covered walkway leading to the rear entrance to the site.

Padeniya Raja Mahavihara

Some 25km northwest of Kurunegala, right in the centre of the village of **PADENIYA**, the **Padeniya Raja Mahavihara** is one of Sri Lanka's most attractive Kandyan-era temples, and well worth a halt. The unusual **main shrine** is set on a small rock outcrop and enclosed by fine walls, topped with cute lion statues. Inside, the fine old wooden roof is supported by around thirty beautifully carved wooden **pillars** showing various figures including a double-headed swan, a lion, an elephant, a man smoking a pipe, a Kandyan drummer and (rather strangely for a Buddhist temple) a dancing girl.

Next to the shrine sits a beautiful pond and a fine old **bo tree** growing out of an imposing three-tiered platform – the roots of the tree have worked their way down through the bricks, with marvellously photogenic results.

Panduwas Nuwara

Around 35km from Kurunegala • Unrestricted access • Free • Buses run approximately every hour from Kurunegala to Chilaw, passing through Panduwas Nuwara village, from where it's a 1km walk to the site

Buried away in the little-visited countryside roughly midway between Kurunegala and Chilaw lie the ruins of the ancient city of **Panduwas Nuwara**, one of the oldest in the country. The city is popularly believed to date back to the very earliest days of Sinhalese civilization, taking its name – "Town of Panduwas" – from the legendary Panduvasudeva (see p.397), and said to be the location of the mythical Ektem Maligaya (see box below), although as with much early Sinhalese history, the line between fact and fiction is somewhat blurred, if not totally smudged.

Most of the surviving ruins date from the reign of **Parakramabahu I** (see p.309), the royal adventurer who established his first capital here before finally seizing Polonnaruwa. The city that Parakramabahu created at Panduwas Nuwara is often seen as a trial run for his spectacular achievements at Polonnaruwa, and although the individual remains are relatively low-key in comparison, the overall scale of the place is undeniably impressive, and exudes an Ozymandias-like aura of vanished splendour.

The citadel

The ruined city sprawls over an area of several square kilometres. At its centre lies the **citadel**, surrounded by sturdy walls, protected by a (now dried-up) moat and pierced by just a single, east-facing entrance. Inside the citadel, facing the entrance, the main ruin is the two-tiered **royal palace**, reminiscent in layout of Parakramabahu's royal palace at Polonnaruwa – far less of it survives, although you can still see the footings for pillars which would have supported the long-since vanished wooden palace building. At the top of the steps on the left stands a table inscription recording a visit by the bumptious Nissankamalla (see box, p.312) to watch a dancing display. At the rear right-hand side of

---

UNMADACHITRA

Daughter of the legendary King Panduvasudeva (see p.397), **Unmadachitra** (which loosely translates as "she whose beauty drives men mad") was one of the great *femmes fatales* of early Sri Lankan history. When she was still a girl, a prophecy foretold that her future son would kill his uncles and usurp the throne. Panduvasudeva, anxious to prevent such an occurrence, had Unmadachitra shut up in a windowless circular tower, the **Ektem Maligaya**. As is generally the case with young princesses locked up in tall towers, however, Unmadachitra rapidly contrived to fall in love with an eligible young prince, a certain Digha-Gamini. The young couple were soon married and had a son, named **Pandukabhaya**, who was then spirited away into hiding. Coming of age, Pandukabhaya revealed himself and went into battle against his uncles, all of whom were duly killed with the exception of a certain **Anuradha**, the only one who desisted from taking up arms against the upstart nephew, and in whose honour Pandukabhaya subsequently named his new city: Anuradhapura.

this terrace are the remains of an ingenious medieval latrine: a water channel leading into a well-like cesspit. The slight remains of a few further buildings around the palace have been neatly restored, but the rest of the citadel remains unexcavated, with the mounds of numerous old buildings still buried under established woodland.

The monasteries
South of the citadel are the extensive remains of a trio of **monasteries**. The first is some 200m south, with a ruined brick dagoba, bo tree enclosure (*bodhigara*) and the ruins of a pillared image house (only the Buddha's feet survive). Immediately south lies a second monastery, with a Tamil pillar inscription at its entrance, plus two more ruined dagobas and further monastic buildings.

Some 250m further south lies the third, and perhaps most impressive of the trio, with the remains of an imposing stupa on a huge raised square base facing a smaller vatadage (on a round base), a high-walled *bodhigara* and the remains of a *tampita* (a shrine raised on pillars).

Further south lies a fourth, much more modern monastery, still very much in use. The core of the monastery dates back to the Kandyan period, with a rustic *tampita* fronted by an old wooden pavilion, surrounded by a cluster of colourful modern buildings.

Ektem Maligaya
Just a few metres from the modern monastery lies Panduwas Nuwara's most enigmatic and intriguing site, comprising the foundations of a small round building at the exact centre of a large, partially walled and perfectly circular depression – a structure completely unlike anything else on the island. According to popular legend, this is nothing less than the remains of the legendary **Ektem Maligaya** (see box opposite), although the more plausible historical explanation is it served as a place where Parakramabahu received oaths of loyalty, the circular space symbolizing the universe, with the king at its centre.

Panduwas Nuwara Museum
Daily except Tues 8am–4.30pm • Free

On your way out of the complex it's worth spending ten minutes at the modest **Panduwas Nuwara Museum**, displaying finds from the site. Highlights include an unusual polished-stone mirror and a tiny metal figurine of Parakramabahu posed in a very similar style to that of the famous statue of the king at the Potgul Vihara (see p.317) in Polonnaruwa.

Yapahuwa
Daily 8am–6pm • Rs.500

Around 45km north of Kurunegala, just off the road to Anuradhapura, lies the magnificent citadel of **Yapahuwa**, built around a huge granite rock rising almost 100m above the surrounding lowlands. Yapahuwa was one of the shortlived capitals established during the collapse of Sinhalese power in the thirteenth century founded by **Bhuvanekabahu I** (ruled 1272–84), who transferred the capital here from the less easily defensible Polonnaruwa in the face of recurrent attacks from South India, bringing the Tooth Relic (see p.212) with him. The move proved to be of no avail, however. In 1284, Yapahuwa was captured by the army of the South Indian Pandyan dynasty, who carried off the Tooth Relic to Madurai in Tamil Nadu. Following its capture, Yapahuwa was largely abandoned and taken over by monks and hermits, and the capital was moved to Kurunegala.

The palace stairway
Yapahuwa's outstanding feature is the marvellous **stone stairway**, which climbs with Maya-like steepness up to the palace – its neck-cricking gradient apparently designed

to protect the Tooth Relic at the top from potential attackers. Its top flight is a positive riot of decoration. Statues of elephants, *makara toranas*, dwarfs, goddesses and a pair of goggle-eyed stone lions flank the stairs, which are topped by a finely carved doorway and windows. Panels around the base and sides of each window are embellished with reliefs of dancers and musicians, one playing a Kandyan drum, the oldest pictorial record of Sri Lanka's most famous musical instrument. The quality of the craftsmanship and materials (solid stone, rather than plebeian brick) is strikingly high, and doesn't suggest the residence of a king on the run – although the decidedly Indian style pays unintentional tribute to the invaders who had driven Bhuvanekabahu here in the first place.

The Lion Terrace

At the top of the palace stairway, the so-called **Lion Terrace** is deeply anticlimactic after the grandiose approach. This was the site of the Temple of the Tooth itself, though there's not much to see now. At the rear left-hand side of the terrace, a rough path, crisscrossed with trailing tree roots, leads to the **summit** of the rock – a breathless ten-minute scramble offering panoramic views.

Around the rock

The extremely modest remains of the **rest of the city** lie scattered around the base of the rock, including the foundations of various buildings dotted round the area at the bottom of the palace stairway, bounded by a limestone wall and surrounded by a dried-up moat.

Close to the site entrance and ticket office is a gorgeous old Kandyan-style wooden barn (on the right as you come in) with a quaint belltower attached. Behind this is a **cave temple**, its entrance projecting from the rock outcrop, inside which are some extremely faded Kandyan-era frescoes plus assorted old plaster, wood and bronze Buddha images. The temple is usually locked, though someone from the ticket office may offer to open it for you.

ARRIVAL AND DEPARTURE   YAPAHUWA

By bus Catch any bus travelling between Anuradhapura and Kurunegala and get off at Daladagama, 8km west of the site. A round-trip in a tuktuk from either village will cost around Rs.500, including waiting time.
By train Yapahuwa is 5km from Maho train station, which is served by fairly regular local trains from Kurunegala and by fast trains between Colombo and Anuradhapura.
Destinations Anuradhapura (7 daily; 1hr 15min–2hr); Colombo (10 daily; 3–4hr).

ACCOMMODATION

Yapahuwa Paradise Resort 1.5km west of the site ☏ 037 397 5055, ⓦ hotelyapahuwaparadise.com. This cheery place, complete with obligatory stone lions – makes a more luxurious base than any of the guesthouses in Kurunegala for exploring the local area. Accommodation is in attractive white cottages dotted around the garden, with bright and comfortable rooms (all with a/c, satellite TV and minibar) and an inviting pool. B&B $80

North from Kandy to Dambulla

From Kandy, most visitors heading for the Cultural Triangle plough straight up the main road north to Dambulla, Sigiriya and beyond. If you have your own transport, however, there are several interesting sites en route. Two of these – the famous monastery of **Aluvihara** and the wonderful little temple at **Nalanda** – are right on the main highway.

The main road between Kandy and Dambulla is also littered with innumerable **spice gardens**. The temperate climate of the region – halfway in altitude between the coastal plains and the hill country – offers ideal horticultural conditions, and if you're interested in seeing where the ingredients of Sri Lankan cuisine come from, now is your chance. Entrance is generally free, but you'll be expected to buy some spices at inflated prices in return for a look at the various plants and shrubs.

Matale

Around 25km north from Kandy, the bustling town of **MATALE** (pronounced Mah-ta-lay) and surrounding area is an important centre for the production of traditional Sri Lankan **arts and crafts** (Matale itself is famous for its lacquerware) – and also a major traffic bottleneck when travelling to or from Kandy.

Sri Muthumariamman Thevasthanam

Main St • Daily 6.15–11.45am & 4.45–7.45pm (although you can still see exterior of temple outside these hours) • Rs.200

Modern Matale is unremarkable apart from the huge **Sri Muthumariamman Thevasthanam**, right next to the main road through town. This is one of the biggest Hindu temples in Sri Lanka outside the north, east and Colombo, dedicated to the goddess Mariamman (Mari meaning *shakti*, or female energy and power, and Amman meaning "mother"), an important female deity in South Indian and Sri Lankan Hinduism. The temple itself is characteristically cavernous and colourful, while a couple of rickety corrugated-iron garages in the surrounding courtyard are used to store the towering chariots used in temple's annual festival. The entrance fee helps support local social projects, including the little pre-school around the back of the temple.

Aluvihara

2km north of Matale • Daily 7.30am–7.30pm; no photography • Any bus heading north from Kandy to Dambulla goes right past the entrance • Rs.200

The monastery of **Aluvihara** sits right next to the main Kandy–Dambulla highway. Despite its modest size, Aluvihara is of great significance in the global history of Buddhism, since it was here that the most important set of Theravada Buddhist scriptures, the *Tripitaka*, or "Three Baskets", were first committed to writing. During the first five centuries of the religion's existence, the vast corpus of the Buddha's teachings had simply been memorized and passed orally from generation to generation. Around 80 BC, however, fears that the *Tripitaka* would be lost during the upheaval caused by repeated South Indian invasions prompted the industrious King Vattagamani Abhaya (who also created the Dambulla cave temples and founded the great Abhayagiri monastery in Anuradhapura) to establish Aluvihara, staffing it with five hundred monks who laboured for years to transcribe the Pali-language Buddhist scriptures onto ola-leaf manuscripts. Tragically, having survived almost two thousand years, this historic library was largely destroyed by British troops when they attacked the temple in 1848 to put down a local uprising.

Cave temples

The heart of the complex consists of a sequence of **cave temples**, tucked away in a picturesque jumble of huge rock outcrops and linked by flights of steps and narrow paths between the boulders. From the first temple (home to a ten-metre-long sleeping Buddha), steps lead up to the main level, where a second cave temple conceals another large sleeping Buddha and various pictures and sculptures demonstrating the lurid punishments awaiting wrongdoers in the Buddhist hell – a subject which seems to exert a ghoulish fascination on the ostensibly peace-loving Sinhalese. Opposite, another cave houses a similarly gruesome tableau vivant showing bloodthirsty punishments meted out by Sri Wickrama Rajasinha (see p.210), the last king of Kandy.

From here, steps lead up past the side of the second temple to another cave temple behind, devoted to the great Indian Buddhist scholar **Buddhaghosa**, who worked at

Anuradhapura during the fifth century AD (though there's no evidence that he ever visited Aluvihara) and produced a definitive set of commentaries on the *Tripitaka*. A statue of Vattagamani Abhaya stands in the corner of the cave, offering the scholar an ola-leaf manuscript, while a brilliant golden Buddhaghosa image from Thailand stands sentry outside. From here, a final flight of steps leads up past a bo tree (apparently growing out of solid rock) to the very top of the complex, where a dagoba and terrace offer fine views across the hills and over to a huge new golden Buddha (also donated by Thailand) that surveys the entire complex from a hillside far above.

Just up the hill to the left of the temple complex, the **International Buddhist Library and Museum** houses a few random objects including a vast antique ola-leaf copy of the *Tripitaka* in many volumes. A resident monk may also be on hand to demonstrate the ancient and dying art of writing upon ola-leaf parchment: the words are first scratched out with a metal stylus, after which ink is rubbed into the leaf, causing the invisible words to magically appear.

Nalanda Gedige

Daily 7.30am–5.30pm • Rs.500 • Any bus from Kandy to Dambulla will drop you at the turn-off to the temple on the main road, from where it's a 10min walk

Some 25km north of Matale, and 1km east of the main highway to Dambulla, stands the **Nalanda Gedige**, a little gem of a building and one of the most unusual monuments in the Cultural Triangle. The gedige (Buddhist image house) occupies a scenic location overlooking a tank, with fine views of the steep green surrounding hills – it originally stood nearby at a lower level amongst paddy fields, but was meticulously dismantled and reconstructed in its present location in 1980, when the Mahaweli Ganga hydro-electricity project led to its original site being flooded. The building is named after the great Buddhist university at Nalanda in northern India, though its origins remain mostly obscure – different sources date it anywhere between the seventh and twelfth centuries. According to tradition, it's claimed that Nalanda is located at the exact centre of Sri Lanka, although a glance at any map shows that it's actually rather closer to the west coast than the east.

The gedige

The **gedige** is pure South Indian in style, and looks quite unlike anything else in Sri Lanka. Constructed entirely of stone, it's laid out like a Hindu temple, with a pillared antechamber, or *mandapa* (originally roofed), leading to an inner shrine that is encircled by an ambulatory. There's no sign of Hindu gods, however, and it appears that the temple was only ever used as a Buddhist shrine. The **main shrine** is entered through a fine square stone door topped by an architrave comprising a line of miniature buildings. To the side, the southern tympanum of the unusual horseshoe-shaped roof features a carving of Kubera, the god of wealth, and the other walls are also richly carved, with many small faces in roundels. The carvings are now much eroded, although if you look carefully you may be able to find the erotic Tantric carving which adorns the southern face of the base plinth on which the entire gedige stands – the only example in Sri Lanka of a typically Indian sculptural motif. The brick base of a ruined (but much more modern) dagoba stands close by.

A tiny attached **museum** houses a few more heavily eroded pillars and a pillar inscription recovered from the site.

Wasgomuwa National Park

Wasgomuwa National Park is one of the most unspoilt of all Sri Lanka's reserves, enjoying an isolated position and being largely enclosed – and offered a measure of protection – by two large rivers, the Amban Ganga and Mahaweli Ganga, which bound it to the east and west. The park straddles the northeastern edge of the hill country, and ranges in elevation from over 500m to just 76m along the Mahaweli Ganga; it comprises mainly dry-zone evergreen forest along the main rivers and on the hills, and open plains in the southeastern and eastern sections. The park features the usual cast of Sri Lankan fauna, including up to 150 **elephants**, best seen from November to May (and especially from Feb–April); at other times they tend to migrate to Minneriya and Kaudulla national parks. Other wildlife includes sambar and spotted deer, buffalo and rarely sighted leopards and sloth bears, plus around 150 species of bird, including a number of endemics.

ARRIVAL AND DEPARTURE · WASGOMUWA NATIONAL PARK

Getting to Wasgomuwa is half the fun, with a range of scenic **approach routes** to the park providing views of pristine countryside and wildlife-spotting opportunities.

Kandy to Dambulla road Most people get to Hettipola via the Kandy to Dambulla road, turning off either at Naula, passing through Elahera (which can also be reached from Giritale to the north) and skirting the park's western side, or at Matale, from where the road climbs over the northern part of the Knuckles Range and through the villages of Rattota and Pallegama.

From Kandy via Mahiyangana An alternative approach to the park from Kandy is to take either of the two main highways that run east of the city to Mahiyangana. From Mahiyangana, head up north through Girandurukotte, and over the Japan Bridge to Hettipola. Alternatively, a more direct (though no quicker) alternative is to follow the northern road (the A26) from Kandy to Mahiyangana and turn off at Hasalaka, from where it's a beautifully rural 45km drive, via Hettipola, to the park entrance.

INFORMATION

Entrance The park's entrance is along its southern flank, about 20km north of the village of Hettipola, where all the roads converge.
Opening hours Daily 6am–6pm.
Admission fee $10, plus the usual additional fees and taxes (see p.45).
Guides Sumane Bandara Illangantilake (☎081 490 1628, ⓦsrilankatrekkingexpeditor.com) and Ravi Desappriya (☎071 499 7666, ⓦsrilankatrekking.com) in Kandy are both excellent guides to the park.

ACCOMMODATION

There are a couple of places to stay overlooking **Dunvila Lake**, a popular spot with local elephants, about 5km from the main gate in the park's southeastern corner.

Wasgamuwa Safari Village Dunvila Lake ☎066 366 9816 or ☎072 465 5085. Rustic place with a dozen thatched cabanas overlooking the lake. Half-board $40
Willys Safari Hotel Dunvila Lake ☎066 366 9268, ⓦwillyssafari.com. The most upmarket option hereabouts, with comfortable a/c rooms in a low-slung modern building. Pleasant enough, albeit seriously overpriced. Half-board $100

Dambulla and around

More or less at the heart of the Cultural Triangle, the dusty little town of **DAMBULLA** is famous for its remarkable **cave temples**: five magical, dimly lit grottoes crammed with statues and decorated with some of the finest murals in the country, offering a picture-perfect snapshot of Sinhalese Buddhist art at its finest.

Dambulla stands at an important junction of the Colombo–Trincomalee and Kandy–Anuradhapura roads, and is a convenient base for exploring the area. The **town** itself is one of the least attractive in the region, however, strung out along a single long, dusty and traffic-plagued main road. The centre is marked by the usual clocktower, north of which stretches the main run of shops, housed in a dispiriting string of ugly modern concrete buildings; to the south of the clocktower lies the town's bus stand, an anarchic wholesale **market** and, further south, most of its guesthouses.

Dambulla cave temples

About 2km south of Dambulla centre • Daily 7am–7pm; ticket office 7.30am–12.30pm & 1–6pm • Rs.1200; buy your ticket from the booth at the back of the Rangiri Dambulla Development Foundation building, straight ahead as you enter the complex

Dambulla's **cave temples** are cut out of an enormous granite outcrop that rises more than 160m above the surrounding countryside and offers majestic views across the plains of the dry zone as far as Sigiriya, over 20km distant.

Note that it's best to visit the caves in **reverse order**, starting at the end (cave 5) and working backwards – this way you get to see the caves in gradually increasing degrees of magnificence, culminating in the wonderful cave 2.

Brief history

The cave temples date back to the days of **Vattagamini Abhaya** (also known as Valagambahu or Valagamba; reigned 103 BC and 89–77 BC). Vattagamini lost his throne to a group of Tamil invaders and was forced into hiding for fourteen years, during which time he found refuge in these caves. Having reclaimed his throne at Anuradhapura, Vattagamini had temples constructed here in gratitude for the hiding place the rock had offered him – the individual caves which now house the temples were created by building partition walls into the space beneath what was originally a single huge rock overhang. The cave temples were further embellished by Nissankamalla (see box, p.312) – while comprehensive restorations and remodellings were carried out by the **Kandyan kings** Senerath (1604–35) and Kirti Sri Rajasinha (1747–82) – the latter also created the magnificent Cave 3 and commissioned many of the vast number of **murals** that now adorn the interiors. Most of what you now see dates from the reigns of these last two kings, although precise dating of individual paintings is made difficult, since these are traditionally repainted on a regular basis once their paintwork fades, and further changes and embellishments were added right through to the twentieth century.

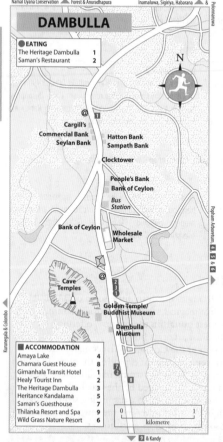

DAMBULLA

Namal Uyana Conservation ▲ Forest & Anuradhapura   Inamaluwa, Sigiriya, Habarana ▲ & Polonnaruwa

4

◉ EATING
The Heritage Dambulla	1
Saman's Restaurant	2

Cargill's
Commercial Bank
Seylan Bank

Hatton Bank
Sampath Bank

Clocktower

People's Bank
Bank of Ceylon

Bus
Station

Bank of Ceylon

Wholesale
Market

Popham Arboretum ▲ 3 & 6

Cave
Temples

Golden Temple/
Buddhist Museum

Dambulla
Museum

▮ ACCOMMODATION
Amaya Lake	4
Chamara Guest House	8
Gimanhala Transit Hotel	1
Healy Tourist Inn	2
The Heritage Dambulla	3
Heritance Kandalama	5
Saman's Guesthouse	7
Thilanka Resort and Spa	9
Wild Grass Nature Resort	6

Kurunegala & Colombo

0   1
kilometre

▼ 9 & Kandy

Cave 5

The small and atmospheric cave 5, the **Devana Alut Viharaya** ("Second New Temple"), is the most modern of the temples, and unlike most of the site's other statues, which are fashioned from solid rock, the images here are made of brick and plaster. The main figure is a 10m reclining Buddha. On the wall behind his feet are paintings of a dark Vishnu flanked by Kataragama with his peacock to the right and Bandara (a local deity) to the left. To the right of the door (as you exit) is a mural of a noble carrying lotus flowers, perhaps the man who endowed the temple.

Cave 4

Cave 4, the **Paccima Viharaya** ("Western Temple" – although cave 5, constructed later, is actually further west), is relatively small. Multiple identical figures of seated Buddhas in the meditation posture sit around the walls, along with a few larger seated figures, one (curtained) under an elaborate *makara torana* arch. A small dagoba stands in the middle; the crack in the side is the work of thieves who broke in, believing the dagoba to contain the jewellery of Vattagamini Abhaya's wife, Queen Somawathie. As in cave 5, the walls are covered with pictures of Buddhas and floral and chequered decorative patterns, most of which were heavily repainted in the early twentieth century.

Cave 3

Cave 3, the **Maha Alut Viharaya** ("Great New Temple") was constructed by Kirti Sri Rajasinha, and is on a far grander scale – the sloping ceiling reaches a height of up to 10m and gives the cave the appearance of an enormous tent, lined with over fifty standing and seated Buddhas. To the right of the entrance stands a statue of **Kirti Sri Rajasinha**, with four attendants painted onto the wall behind him. The meditating Buddha, seated in the middle of the cave, and the sleeping Buddha by the left wall, are both carved out of solid rock – an extraordinary feat in an age when every piece of stone had to be hacked off using rudimentary chisels.

The murals

Cave 3 has several interesting **murals**. Two ceiling paintings show the future Buddha, Maitreya, preaching in a Kandyan-looking pavilion. In the first (look up as you enter the cave), he preaches to a group of ascetic disciples; in the second (to the right of the entrance) he addresses a gathering of splendidly adorned gods in the Tusita heaven, where he is believed to currently reside pending his arrival on earth roughly five billion years from now. To the left of the door as you exit (behind a pair of seated Buddhas) is another interesting mural showing a picture of an idealized garden with square ponds, trees, elephants, cobras and Buddhas – a rather folksy, nineteenth-century addition to the original Kandyan-era murals.

Cave 2

Cave 2, the **Maharaja Vihara** ("Temple of the Great Kings"), is the biggest and most spectacular at Dambulla, an enormous, sepulchral space measuring over 50m long and reaching a height of 7m. Vattagamini Abhaya is credited with its creation, though it was altered several times subsequently and completely restored in the eighteenth century. The cave is named after the statues of two kings it contains. The first is a painted wooden image of **Vattagamini Abhaya** himself (just left of the door furthest away from the main entrance); the second is of **Nissankamalla** (see box, p.312), hidden away at the far right-hand end of the cave and almost completely concealed behind a large reclining Buddha – a rather obscure fate for this most vainglorious of Sinhalese kings.

The sides and back of the cave are lined with a huge array of Buddha statues. The main Buddha statue on the left of the cave, set under a *makara torana* in the *abhaya* ("Have No Fear") *mudra*, was formerly covered in gold leaf, traces of which can still be seen. To either side stand wooden statues of Maitreya (left) and Avalokitesvara or Natha (right). Against the wall behind the main Buddha are statues of Saman and Vishnu, while images of Kataragama and Ganesh are painted onto the wall behind, an unusually varied contingent of Theravada, Mahayana and Hindu gods within such a small space.

The murals

The ceiling and walls of Cave 2 are covered in a fabulous display of **murals** – the finest in Sri Lanka. On the ceiling at the western end of the cave (to the left as you enter), Kandyan-style strip panels show pictures of dagobas at Sri Lanka's holy places and scenes from the Buddha's life (you can just make out the small white elephant which appeared in a dream to the Buddha's mother during her pregnancy, symbolizing the rare qualities of her future child). These murals pale in comparison, however, with the three adjacent ceiling panels showing the **Mara Parajaya** ("Defeat of Mara"), which depict the temptations meted out to the Buddha during his struggle for enlightenment at Bodhgaya. In the first he is shown seated under a beautifully stylized bo tree whilst crowds of hairy grey demons attack him with arrows (one technologically advanced devil even carries a musket), supervised by a magnificent Mara riding on an elephant. This attempt to break the Buddha's concentration having failed, the next panel, the **Daughters of Mara**, shows him being tempted by bevies of seductive maidens. The Buddha's triumph over these stupendous feminine wiles is celebrated in the next panel, the **Isipatana**, which shows him delivering his first sermon to a vast assembly of splendidly attired gods.

Across the cave, sitting in a wire-mesh enclosure in the right-hand corner, is a pot that is constantly fed by drips from the ceiling; it's said never to run dry, even in the worst drought.

Cave 1

Cave 1, the **Devaraja Viharaya** ("Temple of the Lord of the Gods") is named after Vishnu, who is credited with having created the caves; a Brahmi inscription outside the temple to the right commemorates the temples' foundation. Inside, the narrow space is almost completely filled by a 14m-long sleeping **Buddha**, carved out of solid rock, which preserves fine traces of beautiful gold gilding on his elbow (often covered). By the Buddha's head, images of Vishnu and other figures are hidden behind a brightly painted wooden screen, while a statue of the Buddha's most faithful disciple, Ananda, stands at his feet. The cave's unusual **murals** are quite badly eroded in places; some are said to be the oldest at the site, though constant repainting over the centuries has dulled any clear sense of their antiquity; the bright frescoes behind Ananda's head (including a weird tree sporting an Italian-style cherub) are clumsy twentieth-century additions.

Outside, next door, is a small, blue **chapel** dedicated to Kataragama; a bo tree stands opposite.

Golden Temple

At the bottom of the steps up to the cave temples stands the bizarre **Golden Temple**, a shamelessly kitsch building topped by a 30m seated **golden Buddha**. A nearby sign claims this to be the largest Buddha statue in the world – although in fact it's not even the biggest in Sri Lanka (the actual largest Buddha statue in the world, at Leshan in China, stands over twice as tall at 71m).

Golden Temple Buddhist Museum

Daily 7am–9pm • Entrance included in cave temples ticket

At the foot of the golden Buddha statue sits the **Golden Temple Buddhist Museum**, entered through the golden mouth of an enormous lion-like beast. The museum itself is large but rather lacking in exhibits apart from some dull copies of the cave temple paintings, a few Buddhas donated from around the world and a sprinkling of other artefacts, none of which is labelled.

Dambulla Museum

Some 100m south of the Golden Temple • Daily except Tues 7am–5pm • $2

The excellent **Dambulla Museum** offers a comprehensive chronological overview of the fascinating but little-known art of Sri Lankan painting, showing the development of the island's rock and wall paintings from the stick-figure scribbles of the Veddhas, through the frescoes of Sigiriya and on to the genre's golden era during the Kandyan period (from which era most of Dambulla's murals date), before ending with the

European-influenced work of colonial-era artists such as George Keyt. The seven absorbing rooms consist of an expertly executed series of copies (on canvas) of paintings from cave temples, shrines and other locations around the island, gathering together under a single roof a compendium of Sri Lankan art from widely scattered and often remote and inaccessible locations; the copies manage to superbly mimic the cracked and flaking plaster effects of the older murals, and in many cases you get a much better view of the paintings here than in their original settings.

Popham Arboretum

Around 3km east of the cave temples, along the road to Kandalama • Daily 6am–6pm • Donation (minimum Rs.250); call to book day or evening guided walks • ☎ 077 726 7951 • Occasional buses (every 20–30min) run past the entrance; alternatively, a tuktuk from Dambulla will cost around Rs.150 each way

The **Popham Arboretum** was the creation of British tea planter and keen dendrologist, Sam Popham. Dismayed by the destruction of Sri Lanka's dry-zone forests, Popham established the arboretum in the 1960s as an experiment in reforesting an area of scrub jungle with minimal human interference, and the arboretum now preserves more than 225 tree species, including seven endemics, in a 36-acre stretch of woodland crisscrossed by a network of paths.

Visitors can explore the arboretum's colour-coded walking trails on their own or alternatively call to book a **guided walk**; these start from the arboretum's rustic **visitor centre**, a modest bungalow originally designed as Popham's quarters by his friend Geoffrey Bawa. Evening guided walks can also be arranged, offering an excellent chance of spotting some of the arboretum's elusive wildlife, including loris, spotted and mouse deer, and the rare pangolin.

ARRIVAL AND DEPARTURE

By bus The bus station is towards the southern end of town, a Rs.100–150 tuktuk ride from the various guesthouses. Leaving Dambulla, you can also flag down buses along the main road through Dambulla if you know where to stand and which bus to look out for (your guesthouse may be able to advise you), though it's probably easier just to head to the station.

Destinations Anuradhapura (every 30min; 2hr); Colombo (every 20min; 4hr); Habarana (every 20min; 45min); Inamaluwa Junction (every 15min; 20min); Kandy (every 20min; 2hr); Kurunegala (every 20min; 1hr 30min); Polonnaruwa (every 30min; 2hr); Sigiriya (every 30min; 40min).

ACCOMMODATION

There's no great choice of accommodation in Dambulla itself, and as all the town's options are strung out along the main road, traffic noise can be a problem – always try to get a room as far from the road as possible. The area immediately **around Dambulla** is home to a few enticing top-end places, while there are also accommodation options along the road to Sigiriya (see p.302) and Habarana (see p.304), neither of which is much more than a 30min drive from the cave temples. All the guesthouses reviewed here do meals.

DAMBULLA

Chamara Guest House Kandy Rd ☎ 066 228 4488. Simple guesthouse offering smallish rooms inside the main house or (for Rs.300 extra) two rather more spacious and modern rooms out the back. Rs.1650

★ **Gimanhala Transit Hotel** Anuradhapura Rd ☎ 066 228 4864, ⓦ gimanhala.com. The smartest place in town, set in an attractive modern building with pleasantly large and cool rooms, all with a/c, hot water and satellite TV. There's also a decent-sized pool (non-guests Rs.400), internet access and an attractive pavilion restaurant. Rs.7000

Healy Tourist Inn 172 Kandy Rd ☎ 066 228 4940. The best-value cheapie in Dambulla, with small, neat, clean and comfortable rooms – but get one away from the road. Rs.1200

The Heritage Dambulla Kandy Rd ☎ 011 558 5858, ⓦ ceylonhotels.lk. Dambulla's former rest house, now given a thorough makeover and offering four smart rooms, plus a nice attached cafe (see opposite) – although noise from the nearby road can intrude. Rs.3850

Saman's Guesthouse Kandy Rd ☎ 066 228 4412, ⓦ samans-guesthouse-dambulla.info. Long-established guesthouse currently undergoing a much-needed facelift.

4

The two attractive modern tiled a/c rooms upstairs have already been refurbished, while the simpler downstairs rooms (fan only, but with hot water) should have been upgraded to a similar standard by the time you read this. Also has free wi-fi and a good in-house restaurant (see below). Rs.1320; a/c Rs.3000

AROUND DAMBULLA

★ **Amaya Lake** 9km east of Dambulla on Kandalama Lake ⓣ066 446 8100, ⓦamayaresorts.com. Fun and colourful hotel, set in tranquil countryside east of town. The main building occupies two huge interlocking wooden pavilions, while the split-level rooms are set in stylishly decorated chalets dotted around the extensive grounds; alternatively, stay in one of the lakeside clay and palm-thatch huts in the "traditional" village complex (complete with very inauthentic flat-screen TV, minibar and bathtub). Facilities include a huge pool and a luxuriantly thatched Ayurveda centre. $140

★ **Heritance Kandalama** 9km east of Dambulla on Kandalama Lake ⓣ066 555 5000, ⓦheritancehotels.com. On the beautiful Kandalama Lake, this celebrated hotel is one of the finest works of Sri Lankan architect Geoffrey Bawa (see p.126). The whole place manages to be simultaneously huge but almost invisible, being built into a hillside and concealed under a lush jungle canopy, so that nature is never far away (bats fly up and down the corridors after dark). Rooms are stylishly furnished, with all mod cons, big picture windows and marvellous views, while facilities include three excellent restaurants, one of the most spectacular swimming pools on the island and a gorgeous spa. $240

Thilanka Resort and Spa Around 4km south of Dambulla on the Kandy road ⓣ066 446 8001, ⓦthilankaresortandspa.lk. This boldly simple luxury hotel and spa – all clean lines and right angles – is dominated by its dazzling pool, which flows almost into reception, and magnificent expanse of paddy. Bright and stylish rooms, in well-proportioned villas, feature eye-catching oversized prints and mod cons including TV and DVD players. $150

Wild Grass Nature Resort Kumbukkadanwala, 2km past the Amaya Lake hotel ⓣ066 567 0680, ⓦwildgrass.lk. Smooth boutique eco-retreat set in thirty acres of unfenced jungle – you may find yourself sharing the resort with elephants, deer or wild boar, plus a wide variety of birds. Accommodation is in five villas (each with private lounge and terrace) spread out around the grounds, with chic modern design and big picture windows through which to enjoy the stunning views. B&B $260

EATING

The Heritage Dambulla Kandy Rd ⓣ011 558 5858, ⓦceylonhotels.lk. A surprisingly chic little café for dusty Dambulla, and a convenient stop before or after a visit to the cave temples. Well-presented cafe food includes breakfasts, sandwiches, soups and salads plus more substantial Sri Lankan and European-style mains (Rs.500–600). Daily 8am–10pm.

Saman's Restaurant Saman's Guesthouse, Kandy Rd ⓣ066 228 4412, ⓦsamans-guesthouse-dambulla.info. This established restaurant is best known for its fine rice and curry spreads, featuring as many as twelve dishes (Rs.425); the new owner-cum-chef, however, recently arrived from Italy, has added a range of Italian dishes to the menu. Daily 11.30am–3pm & 8–11.30pm.

DIRECTORY

Banks The northern end of town has plenty of banks with ATMs accepting foreign cards.

Internet @Excellence, opposite the post office (daily 8am–6pm; Rs.100/hr), and Kopi Kade (daily 9am–8pm; Rs.60/hr), at the northern end of town near the *Gimanhala* hotel.

Northwest of Dambulla

The area **northwest of Dambulla**, en route to Anuradhapura, conceals the little-visited **Namal Uyana Conservation Forest** plus two of the island's finest ancient Buddhas, at **Aukana** and **Sasseruwa**, all three of which can be easily combined into a rewarding short day-trip if you have your own vehicle.

Namal Uyana Conservation Forest

Some 8km off the Dambulla to Anuradhapura road • Daily 6am–6.30pm • Rs.500

North of town, around 15km from the cave temples, the Jathika Namal Uyana, or **Namal Uyana Conservation Forest** is a remarkable natural phenomenon, preserving not just the largest extant forest of the indigenous **na tree**, or ironwood, in Sri Lanka but also a 550-million-year-old range of **rose quartz** hills, the biggest such deposit in South Asia, which rises lunar-like from the verdant woodland. The *na* is Sri Lanka's national tree, often planted close to Buddhist temples where its fragrant, four-petalled white flowers are a popular offering during puja. The forest, legend states, was planted by Devanampiya Tissa (see p.396), and later became a monastic retreat – various monastic remains are dotted around the site.

Exploring the forest

From the entrance, a path leads for about 1km though the forest, at its prettiest from April to June when the *na* trees are in bloom, to a ranger's hut, the ruins of a moss-covered **dagoba**, surrounded by a low wall decorated with pink-quartz stones, and a few other hard-to-decipher ruins. From here another trail climbs gently up the hillside (ask a ranger the way), the forest increasingly giving way to quartz outcrops. It's about a ten-minute hike across the pinky-grey rockface above the tree canopy to the pleasantly breezy **summit** of the first low mountain, surmounted by a small pink fibreglass Buddha, from where there are magnificent views across to Dambulla.

Aukana

30km northwest of Dambulla • Daily 7.30am–7.30pm • Rs.500 • Aukana is difficult to reach by public transport; the best option is to catch one of the buses that run from Dambulla to Anuradhapura, get off at Kekirawa, then catch a local bus or tuktuk to Aukana

The village of **AUKANA** is home to a magnificent 12m-high standing **Buddha**, one of the defining images of Sri Lankan art and religion. The statue stands close to the vast **Kala Wewa** tank, created by the unfortunate King Dhatusena (see p.298) in the fifth century, though the Buddha itself is likely to date from some three or four centuries later, contemporaneous with the images at Buduruwagala, Maligawila and Polonnaruwa's Gal Vihara and Lankatilaka. The brief craze for such monumental devotional statues may have been the result of Indian Mahayana influence, with its emphasis on the Buddha's superhuman, transcendental powers.

Aukana means "sun-eating", and dawn, when the low light brings out the fine detail of the east-facing statue, is the best time to visit (if you can organize a car and driver for such an early hour). The statue is in the unusual (for Sri Lanka) *asisa mudra*, the blessing position, with the right hand turned sideways to the viewer, as though on the point of delivering a swift karate chop. The figure is carved in the round, just connected at the back to the rock from which it's cut, though the lotus plinth it stands on is made from a separate piece of rock. The walls at the foot of the statue would originally have enclosed a vaulted image chamber.

A TALE OF TWO BUDDHAS

Two legends connect the **Sasseruwa and Aukana Buddhas**. The first, and more prosaic, says that cracks (which can be seen in the torso) started appearing during construction of the Sasseruwa Buddha, and that it was therefore abandoned, with a new statue being created at Aukana. A second and more poetic legend relates that the two Buddhas were carved at the same time in competition between a master and his student. The master's Aukana Buddha was finished first and the frustrated student, realizing his own limitations, abandoned the Sasseruwa image in disappointment. A third, and perhaps more convincing, theory has it that the two statues were created at completely separate times, with the Sasseruwa image dating from the third century AD and reflecting the Greek-influenced Gandharan style of sculpture, which originated in present-day Afghanistan and provided a model for Buddha images across South Asia – certainly the Sasseruwa Buddha's ungainly square head and rather heavy features are in striking contrast to the chiselled elegance of the Aukana image.

Sasseruwa

11km west of Aukana • Daily 7am–7pm •Donation • Sasseruwa is difficult enough to find even with your own transport (follow the signs to Reswehera), and all but impossible by public transport

The remote and little-visited **Sasseruwa Buddha** (also known as the Reswehera Buddha) is a standing Buddha almost as high as the one in Aukana, though apparently uncompleted. The figure is in the *abhaya mudra* ("Have No Fear" pose) and, as at Aukana, originally stood inside its own image house, as shown by the holes for beams cut into the rock around it. The statue was once part of a **monastery** which tradition claims was established by Vattagamini Abhaya, who found refuge here during his period in hiding from Tamil invaders (see p.290). Remains of the monastic complex surround the statue, including a pair of cave temples, one with a large reclining Buddha and another with Kandyan-era paintings and further Buddha images.

Sigiriya and around

Around 15km northeast of Dambulla, the spectacular citadel of **SIGIRIYA** rises sheer and impregnable out of the denuded plains of the dry zone, sitting atop a huge outcrop of gneiss rock towering 200m above the surrounding countryside. The shortest-lived but the most extraordinary of all Sri Lanka's medieval capitals, Sigiriya ("Lion Rock") was declared a World Heritage Site in 1982 and is the country's most memorable single attraction – a remarkable archeological site made unforgettable by its dramatic setting.

4

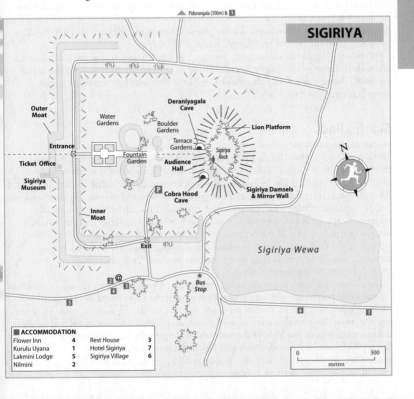

Brief history

Inscriptions found in the caves that honeycomb the base of the rock indicate that Sigiriya served as a place of religious retreat as far back as the third century BC, when Buddhist monks established refuges here. It wasn't until the fifth century AD, however, that Sigiriya rose briefly to pre-eminence in Sri Lankan affairs, following the power struggle that succeeded the reign of **Dhatusena** (455–473) of Anuradhapura. Dhatusena had two sons, **Mogallana**, by the most pre-eminent of his various queens, and **Kassapa**, his son by a lesser consort. Upon hearing that Mogallana had been declared heir to the throne, Kassapa rebelled, driving Mogallana into exile in India and imprisoning his father. Threatened with death if he refused to reveal the whereabouts of the state treasure, Dhatusena agreed to show his errant son its location if he was permitted to bathe one final time in the great Kalawewa Tank, whose creation he had overseen. Standing in the tank, Dhatusena poured its water through his hands and told Kassapa that the water, and the water alone, was all the treasure he possessed. Kassapa, none too impressed, had his father walled up in a chamber and left him to die.

Mogallana, meanwhile, vowed to return from India and reclaim his inheritance. Kassapa, preparing for the expected invasion, constructed a new residence on top of the 200m-high Sigiriya Rock – a combination of pleasure palace and impregnable fortress, which he intended would emulate the legendary abode of Kubera, the god of wealth, while a new city was established around its base. According to tradition, the entire extraordinary structure was built in just seven years, from 477 to 485.

The long-awaited **invasion** finally materialized in 491, Mogallana having raised an army of Tamil mercenaries to fight his cause. Despite the benefits of his impregnable fortress, Kassapa, in an act of fatalistic bravado, descended from his rocky eminence and rode boldly out on an elephant at the head of his troops to meet the attackers on the plains below. Unfortunately for Kassapa, his elephant took fright and bolted at the height of the battle. His troops, thinking he was retreating, fell back and left him cut off. Facing certain capture and defeat, Kassapa killed himself.

Following Mogallana's reconquest, Sigiriya was handed over to the Buddhist monks, after which its caves once again became home to religious ascetics seeking peace and solitude. The site was finally abandoned in 1155, after which it remained largely forgotten until modern times.

Sigiriya Rock

Daily 7am–6pm (last entrance 5pm) • $30

You'll need two or three hours to explore **Sigiriya Rock**; it's best to visit in the early morning or late afternoon, when the crowds are less dense and the temperature is cooler – late afternoon also brings out the rock's extraordinary ochre colouration, like a kind of Asian Ayers Rock. The site is best avoided at weekends (especially Sun) and on public holidays, when its narrow staircases and walkways can become unbearably congested. The ascent of the rock is a stiff climb but less gruelling than you might imagine when standing at the bottom of the towering cliff-face, and sufferers from vertigo might find some sections unpleasant. **Guides** can usually be hired at the entrance, though it pays to ask a few questions to check their knowledge and level of English before committing to anyone.

The site divides into two sections: the **rock** itself, on whose summit Kassapa established his principal palace; and the area **around the base** of the rock, home to elaborate royal pleasure gardens as well as various monastic remains pre-dating Kassapa's era. The entire site is a compelling combination of wild nature and high artifice – exemplified by the delicate paintings of the Sigiriya damsels which cling to the rock's rugged flanks. Interestingly, unlike Anuradhapura and Polonnaruwa, there's no sign here of large-scale monasteries or religious structures – Kassapa's Sigiriya appears to have been an almost entirely secular affair, perhaps a reflection of its unhallowed origins.

The Sigiriya Museum
Ⓦ sigiriyamuseum.com

The new **Sigiriya Museum**, close to the site entrance, showcases assorted prehistoric archeological finds alongside various artefacts discovered at the site; there's also a bird's-eye scale model of the rock and recreations of the frescoes and a section of Mirror Wall.

The Water Gardens

From the entrance, a wide, straight path arrows towards the rock, following the line of an imaginary east–west axis around which the whole site is laid out. This entire side of the rock is protected by a pair of broad moats, though the Outer Moat is now largely dried out. Crossing the Inner Moat, enclosed within two-tiered walls, you enter the **Water Gardens**. The **first section** comprises four pools set in a square which create a small island at their centre when full, connected by pathways to the surrounding gardens. The remains of pavilions can be seen in the rectangular areas to the north and south of the pools.

Beyond here is the small but elaborate **Fountain Garden**. Features include a serpentine miniature "river" and limestone-bottomed channels and ponds, two of which preserve their ancient fountain sprinklers. These work on a simple pressure-and-gravity principle and still spurt out modest plumes of water after heavy rain – after almost 1500 years of disuse, all that was needed to restore the fountains to working order was to clear the water channels that feed them.

The Boulder Gardens

Beyond the Water Gardens the main path begins to climb up through the **Boulder Gardens**, constructed out of the huge boulders that lie tumbled around the foot of the rock. Many of the boulders are notched with lines of holes – they look rather like rock-cut steps, but in fact they were used as footings to support the brick walls or timber frames of the numerous buildings which were built against or on top of the boulders.

The gardens were also the centre of Sigiriya's monastic activity before and after Kassapa: there are around twenty rock shelters hereabouts which were used by monks, some containing inscriptions dating from between the third century BC and the first century AD. The caves would originally have been plastered and painted, and traces of this decoration can still be seen in a few places; you'll also notice the dripstone ledges that were carved around the entrances to many of the caves to prevent water from running into them. The **Deraniyagala Cave**, just to the left of the path shortly after it begins to climb up through the gardens (no sign), has a well-preserved dripstone ledge and traces of old paintings including the faded remains of various *apsara* figures (celestial nymphs) very similar to the famous Sigiriya Damsels further up the rock. On the opposite side of the main path up the rock, a side path leads to the **Cobra Hood Cave**, named for its uncanny resemblance to that snake's head. The cave preserves traces of lime plaster, floral decoration and a very faint inscription on the ledge in archaic Brahmi script dating from the second century BC.

Follow the path up the hill behind the Cobra Hood Cave and up through "Boulder Arch no. 2" (as it's signed), then turn left to reach the so-called **Audience Hall**. The wooden walls and roof have long since disappeared, but the impressively smooth floor, created by chiselling the top off a single enormous boulder, remains, along with a 5m-wide "throne", also cut out of the solid rock. The hall is popularly claimed to have been Kassapa's audience hall, though it's more likely to have served a purely religious function, with the empty throne representing the Buddha. The small **Asana Cave** on the path en route to the Audience Hall retains colourful splashes of various paintings on its ceiling (though now almost obliterated by idiotic contemporary graffiti) and is home to another throne, while a couple more thrones can be found carved into nearby rocks.

Terrace Gardens

From the Asana Cave, you can carry on back to the main path, then head on up through "Boulder Arch no. 1". The path – now a sequence of walled-in steps – begins to climb steeply through the **Terrace Gardens**, a series of rubble-retaining brick and limestone terraces that stretch to the base of the rock itself, from where you get the first of an increasingly majestic sequence of views back down below.

The Sigiriya Damsels

Shortly after reaching the base of the rock, two incongruous nineteenth-century metal spiral staircases lead to and from a sheltered cave in the sheer rock face that holds Sri Lanka's most famous sequence of frescoes, popularly referred to as the **Sigiriya Damsels** (no flash photography). These busty beauties were painted in the fifth century and are the only non-religious paintings to have survived from ancient Sri Lanka; they're now one of the island's most iconic – and most relentlessly reproduced – images. It's thought that these frescoes would originally have covered an area some 140m long by 40m high, though only 21 damsels now survive out of an original total of some five hundred (a number of paintings were destroyed by a vandal in 1967, while a few of the surviving pictures are roped off out of sight). The exact significance of the paintings is unclear: they were originally thought to depict Kassapa's consorts, though according to modern art historians the most convincing theory is that they are portraits of *apsaras* (celestial nymphs), which would explain why they are shown from the waist up only, rising out of a cocoon of clouds. The portrayal of the damsels is strikingly naturalistic, showing them scattering petals and offering flowers and trays of fruit – similar in a style to the famous murals at the Ajanta Caves in India, and a world away from the much later and more stylized murals at nearby Dambulla. An endearingly human touch is added by the slips of the brush visible here and there: one damsel has three hands, while another sports an extra nipple.

The Mirror Wall

Just beyond the damsels, the pathway runs along the face of the rock, bounded on one side by the **Mirror Wall**. This was originally coated in highly polished plaster made from lime, egg white, beeswax and wild honey; sections of the original plaster survive and still retain a marvellously lustrous sheen. The wall is covered in **graffiti**, the oldest dating from the seventh century, in which early visitors recorded their impressions of Sigiriya and, especially, the nearby damsels – even after the city was abandoned, Sigiriya continued to draw a steady stream of tourists curious to see the remains of Kassapa's fabulous pleasure-dome. Taken together, the graffiti form a kind of early medieval visitors' book, and the 1500 or so decipherable comments give important insights into the development of the Sinhalese language and script.

Beyond the Mirror Wall, the path runs along a perilous-looking iron walkway bolted onto the sheer rock-face. From here you can see a huge **boulder** below, propped up on stone slabs. The popular explanation is that, in the event of attack, the slabs would have been knocked away, causing the boulder to fall onto the attackers below, though it's more likely that the slabs were designed to *stop* the boulder inadvertently falling down over the cliff.

The Lion Platform

Continuing up the rock, a flight of limestone steps climbs steeply up to the **Lion Platform**, a large spur projecting from the north side of the rock, just below the summit. From here, a final staircase, its base flanked by two enormous paws carved out of the rock, leads up across all that remains of a gigantic **lion statue** – the final path to the summit apparently led directly into its mouth. Visitors to Kassapa were, one imagines, suitably impressed both by the gigantic conceit of the thing and also by the heavy symbolism – lions were the most important emblem of Sinhalese royalty, and the

> ## BEST BEE-HAVIOUR
>
> The small wire-mesh cages you can see standing on Sigiriya's Lion Platform were built as a refuge in the event of **bee attacks** – several of which have occurred in recent years despite efforts (using a mixture of chemicals and exorcism rituals) to evict the offending insects from their nests, which can be seen clinging to the underside of the rock overhang above, to the left of the stairs. Local Buddhist monks claim that such attacks are divine retribution resulting from the impious behaviour of visiting tourists.

beast's size was presumably meant to reflect Kassapa's prestige and buttress his questionable legitimacy to the throne.

The whole section of rock-face above is scored with countless notches and grooves which once supported steps up to the summit: in a supreme irony, it appears that Kassapa was afraid of heights, and it's thought that these original steps would have been enclosed by a high wall – though this isn't much comfort for latter-day sufferers from vertigo, who have to make the final ascent to the summit up a narrow iron staircase attached to the bare rock-face.

The summit

After the tortuous path up, the **summit** seems huge. This was the site of Kassapa's palace, and almost the entire area was originally covered with buildings. Only the foundations now remain, though, and it's difficult to make much sense of it all – the main attraction is the fabulous views down to the Water Gardens and out over the surrounding countryside. The **Royal Palace** itself is now just a plain, square brick platform at the very highest point of the rock. The upper section is enclosed by steep terraced walls, below which is a large tank cut out of the solid rock; it's thought that water channelled to the summit using an ingenious hydraulic system powered by windmills. Below here a series of four further terraces, perhaps originally gardens, tumble down to the lower edge of the summit above Sigiriya Wewa.

The path down takes you along a slightly different route – you should end up going right past the Cobra Hood Cave, if you missed it earlier, before exiting the site to the south.

Pidurangala Royal Cave Temple

Some 2km north of Sigiriya

A couple of kilometres north of Sigiriya, another large rock outcrop is home to the **Pidurangala Royal Cave Temple**. According to tradition, the monastery here dates from the arrival of Kassapa, when the monks who were then living at Sigiriya were relocated to make room for the king's palace; Kassapa constructed new dwellings and a temple here to recompense them. It's a pleasant short bike or tuktuk ride to the foot of Pidurangala rock: head down the road north of Sigiriya and continue for about 750m until you reach a modern white temple, the **Pidurangala Sigiri Rajamaha Viharaya** (about 100m further on along this road on the left you'll also find the interesting remains of some old monastic buildings, including the ruins of a sizeable brick dagoba). Steps lead steeply up the hillside behind the Pidurangala Viharaya to a terrace just below the summit of the rock (a stiff 15min climb), where you'll find the Royal Cave Temple itself, although despite the rather grand name there's not much to see apart from a long reclining Buddha under a large rock overhang, its upper half restored in brick. The statue is accompanied by figures of Vishnu and Saman and decorated with very faded murals.

From here you may be able to find the rough path up to the **summit** of the rock (a 5min scramble), but you'll need to be fit and agile, and take care not to lose your way when coming back down, which is surprisingly easy to do. The reward for your efforts will be the best view of Sigiriya you can get short of chartering a balloon, showing the far more irregular and interestingly shaped northern side of the rock which you don't get to see when climbing up it, with the ant-like figures of those making the final ascent to the summit (which you're almost level with) just visible against the huge slab of red rock.

ARRIVAL AND DEPARTURE
SIGIRIYA AND AROUND

BY BUS
From Dambulla Regular buses (every 30min; 30min) connect Sigiriya with Dambulla.
From Polonnaruwa Take any bus heading to Dambulla and get off at Inamaluwa Junction, 10km west of Sigiriya on the main Dambulla–Trincomalee highway, from where you can pick up a tuktuk (around Rs.600) or wait for the half-hourly bus from Dambulla.
From Anuradhapura It's probably easiest to take a bus to Dambulla, then pick up the Sigiriya bus from there. Alternatively, take a bus to Habarana, then another bus to Inamaluwa Junction (see above).

Leaving Sigiriya It's probably worth going all the way back to Dambulla, even if you're heading up to Anuradhapura or Polonnaruwa, rather than trying to flag something down on the main road at Inamaluwa Junction. There's also one bus daily direct to Kandy (2hr 30min).

TOURS
Sigiriya is a convenient base for trips to Minneriya and Kaudulla national parks; most of the accommodation options (see below) can arrange jeeps (around $40–50/ half-day) for visits to either park.

ACCOMMODATION AND EATING
There's only a small choice of accommodation in Sigiriya itself – government restrictions have kept development in the village mercifully in check. Additional cheap accommodation, as well as a pair of top-end establishments, can be found along the road to **Inamaluwa Junction**, plus a couple of good mid-range alternatives hidden away in the countryside north of Sigiriya en route to Habarana. It's likely that you'll **eat** where you're staying – if you do want to venture out, *Sigiriya Village* or the *Hotel Sigiriya* are the places to head for.

SIGIRIYA
Flower Inn ☎066 567 2197. Appealing family guesthouse in a flower-filled garden, with quirky rooms stuffed full of artificial bouquets and assorted teddy bears. Eccentric furnishings apart, the modern tiled rooms are clean, bright, spacious and very good value, and there's also tasty home-cooking and a very friendly welcome. Rs.1200
Lakmini Lodge Sigiriya village, in front of the Post Office ☎066 492 3891, ⚑sigiriyalakminilodge .blogspot.co.uk. This peaceful, friendly family guesthouse offers fine views towards the rock from the garden tree house and a range of simple but comfortable rooms. Good home-cooked food on request. Rs.1500
Nilmini ☎066 567 0469, ✉nilmini_lodge@yahoo .com. A neat little family-run guesthouse with friendly owners and a choice of accommodation including basic but adequate fan rooms plus one a/c double with hot water. Reasonable home-cooking available, plus internet access (Rs.100/hr), wi-fi (Rs.300/day) and free bikes. Rs.1000; a/c Rs.2000
Rest House ☎066 228 6299, ⚑ceylonhotels.lk. This pleasant rest house has the village's finest view of the rock, with attractively old-fashioned rooms (all with a/c and hot water) set around a square of lawn – a nice place, although pricey for what you get. B&B Rs.6400
★ **Hotel Sigiriya** ☎066 223 1940, ⚑serendibleisure .com. Appealing and good-value resort-style hotel, set in a

rambling collection of low-slung, vaguely Kandyan-style buildings topped with red-tiled roofs. The stylish a/c rooms come with TV and minibar, while amenities include an Ayurveda centre and swimming pool (non-guests Rs.250) with fine views of the rock. There's also a fascinating range of nature walks with the resident naturalist. B&B $109
Sigiriya Village ☎066 228 6803, ✉sigiriyavillage @sltnet.lk. Similar country-resort concept to the *Hotel Sigiriya*, but rather less characterful. Rooms (all a/c, some with TV and minibar) are comfortable and quite stylish, though poor value compared to the *Sigiriya*. There's also a pool (non-guests Rs.250/hr), bike (Rs.300/hr), birdwatching trips (Rs.1000) and Ayurveda centre. B&B $130

AROUND SIGIRIYA
Ancient Villa 2km east of Inamaluwa Junction ☎0773 971 921, ⚑ancientvillasigiriya.com. Appealingly rustic place with accommodation either in a trio of unusual hexagonal cabanas (currently undergoing renovation) or a pair of bright modern rooms (all with hot water; a/c $10 extra). There's also free internet and wi-fi, inexpensive jeep trips ($35) to Minneriya and Kaudulla, and daily cookery classes on demand. $30; a/c $40
Elephant Corridor 4km east of Inamaluwa Junction, about 1.5km from the Sigiriya road ☎066 228 6950, ⚑elephantcorridor.com. Set in 200 acres of dry-zone scrub with stunning views of Sigiriya, this exclusive

boutique hotel boasts plenty of rather gimmicky opulence, with lavish suite-style rooms, all with private plunge pool, plus a fancy spa – although for overall appeal the whole place comes a rather distant second to *Vil Uyana* down the road. Rs365

Globetrotter Tourist Inn 1km east of Inamaluwa Junction ☎0777 801 818, ⓦone-two-srilanka.com. Laid-back guesthouse with clean modern rooms (with hot water and optional a/c for Rs.500), albeit rather lacking in furniture, and a bit expensive for what you get. Rs.2500

Grand Regent Tourist Holiday Resort 3km east of Inamaluwa Junction, at the beginning of the access road to Elephant Corridor ☎066 567 0136, ⓦgrandregenthotel.com. Despite the highfalutin name, this is an attractively low-key little resort, with modern tiled rooms (all with hot water; some with a/c and TV for Rs.500 extra) in chalets dotted around the extensive gardens. There's also a modest Ayurveda centre and attractive terrace restaurant. Rs.2750; a/c Rs.3250

Holiday Cottage 1km east of Inamaluwa Junction ☎072 764 5477. Newly opened place with two neat and nicely furnished rooms (a/c Rs.500 extra) in a little "cottage" set in attractive gardens. B&B Rs.3000; a/c Rs.3500

★ **Jetwing Vil Uyana** 3.5km east of Inamaluwa Junction, 1km from the Sigiriya road ☎066 228 6000, ⓦjetwinghotels.com. The island's most audacious hotel project, born from an ambitious scheme to create an artificial wetland out of abandoned agricultural land, using ancient Sri Lankan irrigation techniques combined with modern know-how. It's a fascinating, and very peaceful, environment, with its four habitats – marsh, paddy, forest and lake – attracting plenty of wildlife.

Accommodation is in a scatter of luxuriantly thatched villas, modelled on traditional Sinhalese dwellings, combining state-of-the-art mod-cons with the homeliness of an über-luxurious Japanese ryokan. Some have plunge pools, others are built on stilts over the lake, and all have private viewing decks. Other highlights include a magnificent infinity pool (non-guests Rs.1000), outstanding restaurant and a serene spa. $345

Kassapa Lions Rock Digampathaha (8km from Sigiriya, 7km from Habarana) ☎066 567 7440, ⓦkassapalionsrock.com. Very low-key resort hotel with good-value, attractively furnished rooms (all with TV, a/c and open-air showers) in bungalows dotted across a well-manicured lawn. There's a pool, restaurant and bar but not much else to do except sit and admire the gorgeous views across the plains to Sigiriya. $75

Kurulu Uyana Pidurangala ☎077 395 1527, ⓦbackofbeyond.lk. Idyllic eco-retreat set in four acres of bird-rich jungle at the base of the Pidurangala. Accommodation is in three colourful little cottages and one larger three-bed bungalow, all comfortably appointed with hot water and fan, while staff rustle up good Sri Lankan food and serve as ad hoc nature guides. $106

Sigiri Holiday Inn 500m east of Inamaluwa Junction ☎060 228 6330, ⓔsholidayinn@yahoo.com. Inamaluwa's best budget option, with a mix of simple older rooms inside the house and larger, more modern accommodation with hot water in a block in the shady garden outside (plus a couple of further attractive modern tiled rooms in the same family's *Rock View Resort* next door). Also has internet access and can arrange inexpensive jeep trips ($35) to Minneriya and Kaudulla. Rs.800

DIRECTORY

Banks There are no banks in Sigiriya, so bring whatever money you need with you.

Internet Sigiri Internet Cafe, next to *Nilmini* guesthouse (daily 8am–8pm; Rs.100/hr).

Habarana and around

Sitting on a major road junction almost equidistant between Polonnaruwa, Anuradhapura and Dambulla (and close to Sigiriya and Ritigala), the large village of **HABARANA** is of little interest in itself but has a decent spread of relatively upmarket accommodation, making it a convenient base from which to visit any of the Cultural Triangle's major sights. It's also the handiest point of departure for trips to **Minneriya and Kaudulla national parks**, which offer some of the island's best elephant-spotting.

The main attraction in Habarana is the fine **Habarana Lake**, encircled by a small footpath around which it's possible to walk in 90min or so. Alternatively, a number of hotels and tour operators offer **elephant rides** by the lake and elsewhere (around $25 for 1hr), although the sight of these mighty animals trudging lugubriously through town beneath a surfeit of chains may leave you feeling almost as uncomfortable as the elephants themselves.

By bus Habarana is located on a major road junction at the crossroads of the Dambulla, Anuradhapura, Polonnaruwa, and Trincomalee roads, and therefore sees a lot of passing buses, although not many originate here, so you may struggle to get a seat. Buses stop at (or close to) the junction itself, at the northern end of the town centre. Destinations Anuradhapura (every 45min; 2hr 30min); Dambulla (every 20min; 45min); Giritale (every 20min; 30min); Kandy (every 20min; 2hr 45min); Polonnaruwa (every 20min; 1hr); Trincomalee (every 30min; 2hr).

Banks There's a branch of the People's Bank with an ATM accepting foreign Visa cards next to the junction at the centre of the town.

Jeep tours Most local hotels and guesthouses (along with several outfits on the main road south of Habarana Junction) arrange jeep tours of the national parks; count on around $35 for a 3hr jeep trip to either park (transport only); some places also offer inclusive ticket-and-transport deals starting from around $50/person depending on group size.

ACCOMMODATION

Chaaya Village Dambulla Rd, 400m south of Habarana Junction (behind Cinnamon Lodge) ☎066 227 0047, ⊛chaayahotels.com. Traditional resort-style hotel close to the lake, with large, comfortable rooms in chalets dotted around sylvan grounds and an unusual fan-shaped pool. All rooms have a/c, TV and minibar; deluxe ones have bathtubs, DVD players and lake views. There's also the stylish Indonesian Asmara spa, though overall it lacks the class of its sister establishment, *Cinnamon Lodge*, next door. $152

★ **Cinnamon Lodge** Dambulla Rd, 400m south of Habarana Junction ☎066 227 0012, ⊛cinnamon hotels.com. One of the Cultural Triangle's most appealing places to stay, this stylish five-star occupies an idyllic setting spread out across superb grounds running down to the beautiful Habarana lake and with plenty of resident birds and wildlife, including troupes of monkeys cavorting in the trees overhead. Accommodation is in spacious and good-looking rooms in a string of attractive two-storey cottages scattered around the grounds, while facilities include a large pool, open-air pavilion restaurant and the stylish Indonesian

Asmara spa. B&B $214

Eagles Wings Guest House 2km west of Habarana Junction ☎0777 518 750, ⊛eagleswings.ontash.net. Friendly family guesthouse in a very rustic setting on the edge of the jungle, with two spotless rooms in the main house (including a family room), plus a pair of simple stilted wooden cabanas and a pair of cottages in the garden behind. Rs3000; a/c Rs3500

Heritage Habarana Habarana Junction ☎066 227 0003, ⊛ceylonhotels.lk. Habarana's former rest house, stylishly renovated with chic, nicely furnished rooms (with a/c and hot water) arranged around a neat veranda and with a smart little cafe, although road noise may intrude. $45

Sorowwa Resort and Spa Anuradhapura Rd, about 200m from Habarana Junction ☎066 227 0332, ⊛sorowwa.com. Attractive new hotel overlooking Habarana Lake (most rooms with lake-facing balconies) plus a small pool and functional Ayurveda spa – although the lack of grounds makes it feel rather hemmed in by the surrounding ramshackle buildings, and rates are steep. $200

EATING

Acme Transit Hotel About 500m from the junction down Polonnaruwa Rd. The one good option if you want to venture out of your hotel for food, this huge green eyesore has a surprisingly cosy interior, where you

can eat big portions of Sri Lankan classics (mains Rs.500–800), including vast lunchtime rice and curry spreads. Daily 8am–8pm.

Hurulu Eco-Park

3km north of Habarana along the Trincomalee Road • Daily 2–6.30pm • Rs.750

When the season is not right for wildlife-spotting at Minneriya and Kaudulla, jeep operators often run trips to **Hurulu Eco-Park**, on the edge of the vast Huluru Biosphere Reserve that stretches west of the Habarana–Trincomalee road. There's no lake here, and the park's terrain is more reminiscent of Uda Walawe, dominated by long grass that makes elephant viewing easy: from January to March you stand a chance of spotting herds of thirty or more of the beasts, though you're unlikely to see much other wildlife.

Ritigala

On a dirt track 8km north of the main Habarana–Anuradhapura highway, signposted 11km west of Habarana • Daily 7.30am–6pm • Rs.500; guides can be hired at the visitor centre by the entrance

Secreted away north of Habarana, on the slopes of a densely wooded mountainside protected by the Ritigala Strict Nature Reserve, lie the mysterious remains of the forest monastery of **Ritigala**. The mountainside on which the monastery sits is thought to be the *Ramayana*'s Aristha, the place from which Hanuman leapt from Lanka back to India, having discovered where Sita was being held captive. According to popular belief, Hanuman later passed by Ritigala again, carelessly dropping one of the chunks of Himalayan mountain which he was carrying back from India for its medicinal herbs (other fragments fell to earth at Unawatuna and Hakgala); this is held to account for the unusually wide range of plants and herbs found at Ritigala, although the mundane explanation is that the area, being higher and wetter than the surrounding plains, supports a correspondingly wider range of plant species.

Ritigala's remoteness appealed to solitude-seeking **hermits**, who began to settle here as far back as the third century BC. In the ninth century, Ritigala became home to an order of reclusive and ascetic monks known as *pamsukulikas*, who devoted themselves to a life of extreme austerity – *pamsukulika*, meaning "rag robes", refers to the vow taken by these monks to wear only clothes made from rags either thrown away or recovered from corpses. The order seems to have started as an attempt to return to traditional Buddhist values in reaction against the self-indulgent living conditions enjoyed by the island's clergy. So impressed was Sena I (831–851 AD) with the spirit of renunciation shown by the order that he built them a fine new monastery at Ritigala, endowing it with lands and servants – most of the remains you see today date from this era.

The ruins

Ritigala is magical but enigmatic, while the setting deep in a totally undisturbed tract of thick forest (not to mention the lack of tourists) lends an additional sense of mystery. Parts of the complex have been carefully restored, while others remain buried in the forest, but despite the considerable archeological work which has been done here, the original purpose of virtually everything you now see remains largely unknown. One striking feature is the site's complete lack of residential quarters – the monks themselves appear to have lived entirely in caves scattered around the forest.

Beyond the entrance, the path runs around the edge of the tumbled limestone bricks that once enclosed the **Banda Pokuna** tank – this possibly served a ritual purpose, with visitors bathing here before entering the monastery. At the far end of the tank, steep steps lead up to the beginning of a beautifully constructed **walkway** (similar to the meditation walkway at Arankele) which runs through the forest and links all the monastery's major buildings. After around 200m the walkway reaches the first of several sunken courtyards, bounded by a retaining wall and housing three raised terraces. The one nearest is one of the **double-platform** structures which are a characteristic feature of Ritigala. These generally consist of two raised platforms oriented east–west, linked by a stone "bridge" and surrounded by a miniature "moat"; one of the platforms usually bears the remains of pillars, while the other is bare. Various theories have been advanced as to the original functions of these structures. One holds that the "moat" around the platforms would have been filled with water, providing a natural form of air-conditioning, while the platforms themselves were used for meditation – communal meditation on the open platform and individual meditation in the building on the linked platform opposite. A few metres to the right-hand (east) end of this enclosure is a second sunken courtyard, usually described as the **hospital**, although it may have been an alms-house or a bathhouse.

Beyond here, the pavement continues straight ahead to reach one of the "**roundabouts**" that punctuate its length – perhaps formerly a covered rest area, like the similar roundabout at Arankele. About 20m before reaching the roundabout, a path heads off to the right, leading through enormous tree roots to the so-called "**Fort**", reached by a stone bridge high above a stream, and offering fine views over the forests below.

As you continue past the roundabout, a couple of **unexcavated platforms** can be seen off the path in the woods to the left, looking exactly as they must have appeared to British archeologist H.C.P. Bell when he first began exploring the site in 1893. After another 500m you reach two further sunken courtyards. The **first courtyard** contains a substantial double-platform structure, one of the largest buildings in the entire monastery. The left-hand side of the courtyard is bounded by two **stele**; according to one theory, monks would have paced between these whilst practising walking meditation. A few metres beyond lies the **second courtyard** and another large double platform.

Kaudulla National Park

6km off the main Habarana–Trincomalee road • Daily 6am–6pm • $10, plus the usual additional fees and taxes (see p.45); ask at the visitor centre at the entrance to arrange paddle-boats for birdwatching on the tank • Jeep tours to Kadulla can be arranged through guesthouses and hotels in Habarana, Polonnaruwa and Sigiriya (usually $35–50/half-day)

Some 22km north of Habarana, **Kaudulla National Park** was established in 2002 to provide another link in the migratory corridor for **elephants**, connecting with Minneriya and Wasgomuwa national parks to the south, and Somawathiya National Park to the north and east. As at Minneriya, the centrepiece is a lake, the **Kaudulla Tank**, where elephants collect when water dries up elsewhere. The best time to visit is between August and December, with elephant numbers peaking in September/October (slightly later than Minneriya's "Gathering") when up to two hundred congregate at the tank. Outside the dry season much of the park is under water, and elephants can be more difficult to spot. Other **wildlife** inhabiting the park's mix of grasslands and scrubby forest includes sambar deer, monkeys and the inevitable (but very rarely seen) leopards and sloth bears, plus a characteristically wide array of bird life.

Minneriya National Park

6km east of Habarana on the Polonnaruwa road • Daily 6am–6pm • $15, plus the usual additional fees and taxes (see p.45) • Most hotels in Polonnaruwa, Giritale, Sigiriya and Inamaluwa can arrange trips (around $35–50/half-day), or it can be marginally cheaper to pick up a jeep in Habarana

Just a ten-minute drive east of Habarana, **Minneriya National Park** offers something of a change of scenery for anyone suffering ruin fatigue. Its centrepiece is the large **Minneriya Tank**, created by the famous tank-builder and monk-baiter Mahasena (see p.325), and despite its relatively small size, the park also boasts an unusually wide range of habitat types, from dry tropical forest to wetlands, grasslands and terrain previously used for slash-and-burn (*chena*) agriculture. Much of the area around the entrance is covered in superb dry-zone evergreen forest dotted with beautiful satinwood, *palu* (rosewood), *halmilla* and *weera* trees – though the thickness of the forest cover means that it's relatively difficult to spot wildlife.

The principal attraction here is **elephants**. Minneriya forms part of the elephant corridor that joins up with Kaudulla and Wasgomuwa national parks, and large numbers of the beasts can be found here at certain times of year during their migrations between the various parks – local guides should know where the greatest concentrations of elephants are at any given time. They are most numerous from July to October, peaking in August and September when water elsewhere dries up and as many as three hundred or more come to the tank's ever-receding shores from as far away as Trincomalee to drink, bathe and feed on the fresh grass that grows up from the lake bed as the waters retreat – as well as to socialize and search for mates. This annual event has been popularly dubbed "**The Gathering**", the largest meeting of Asian elephants anywhere in the world. At other times, you may spot only a few elephants, which in fact are often more easily seen from the main Habarana–Polonnaruwa road that runs along the park's northern edge. Other **mammals** found in the park include sambar, spotted deer, macaque and purple-faced langur monkeys, sloth bears and around twenty leopards (although these last two are very rarely sighted), plus an enormous number of **birds**.

Polonnaruwa and around

The great ruined capital of **POLONNARUWA** is one of the undisputed highlights of the Cultural Triangle – and indeed the whole island. The heyday of the city, in the twelfth century, represented one of the high watermarks of early Sri Lankan civilization. The Chola invaders from South India had been repulsed by Vijayabahu and the Sinhalese kingdom he established at Polonnaruwa enjoyed a brief century of magnificence under his successors Parakramabahu and Nissankamalla, who planned the city as a grand statement of imperial pomp, transforming it briefly into one of the great urban centres of South Asia before their own hubris and excess virtually bankrupted the state. Within a century, their enfeebled successors had been driven south by new waves of invaders from southern India, and Polonnaruwa had been abandoned to the jungle, where it remained, unreclaimed and virtually unknown, for seven centuries.

Polonnaruwa's extensive and well-preserved remains offer a fascinating snapshot of medieval Sri Lanka and are compact enough to be thoroughly explored in a single (albeit busy) day. Remains aside, Polonnaruwa is also a good jumping-off point for the national parks at **Minneriya** and **Kaudulla** (see opposite).

Brief history

The **history** of Polonnaruwa stretches far back into the Anuradhapuran period. The region first came to prominence in the third century AD, when the creation of the Minneriya Tank boosted the district's agricultural importance, while the emergence of Gokana (modern Trincomalee) as the island's major port for overseas trade later helped Polonnaruwa develop into an important local commercial centre. As Anuradhapura fell victim to interminable invasions from India, Polonnaruwa's strategic advantages became increasingly apparent. Its greater distance from India made it less vulnerable to attack and gave it easier access to the important southern provinces of Ruhunu, while it also controlled several crossings of the Mahaweli Ganga, Sri Lanka's longest and most important river. Such were the town's advantages that four rather obscure kings actually chose to reign from Polonnaruwa rather than Anuradhapura, starting with Aggabodhi IV (667–683).

Throughout the anarchic later Anuradhapuran era, Polonnaruwa held out against both Indian and rebel Sinhalese attacks until it was finally captured by **Rajaraja**, king of the Tamil Cholas, following the final sack of Anuradhapura in 993. Rajaraja made it the capital of his short-lived Hindu kingdom, but in 1056 the city was recaptured

4

POLONNARUWA OR ANURADHAPURA?

Many visitors to Sri Lanka only have the time or the archeological enthusiasm to visit one of the island's two great ruined cities, but as the two are significantly different it's difficult to call decisively in favour of either. The ruins at **Polonnaruwa** cover a smaller area, are better preserved and offer a more digestible and satisfying bite of ancient Sinhalese culture – and there's nowhere at Anuradhapura to match the artistry of the Quadrangle and Gal Vihara. Having said that, **Anuradhapura** has its own distinct magic. The sheer scale of the site and the number of remains means that, although much harder to get to grips with, it preserves a mystery that much of Polonnaruwa has lost – and it's far easier to escape the coach parties. In addition, the city's status as a major pilgrimage centre lends it a vibrancy lacking at Polonnaruwa.

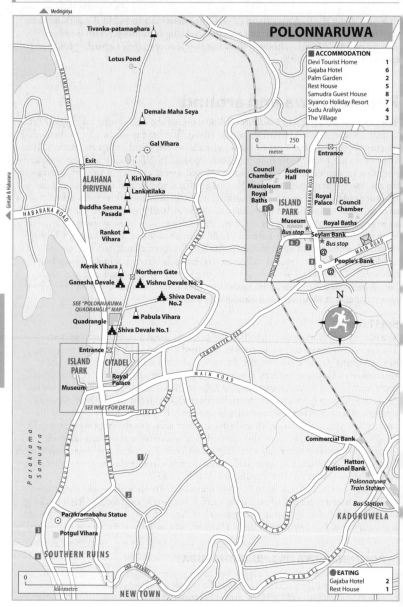

POLONNARUWA

■ ACCOMMODATION

Devi Tourist Home	1
Gajaba Hotel	6
Palm Garden	2
Rest House	5
Samudra Guest House	8
Siyanco Holiday Resort	7
Sudu Araliya	4
The Village	3

● EATING

Gajaba Hotel	2
Rest House	1

by the Sinhalese king **Vijayabahu** (1055–1110), who retained it as the new Sinhalese capital in preference to Anuradhapura, which had been largely destroyed in the earlier fighting. Vijayabahu's accession to the throne ushered in Polonnaruwa's golden age, although most of the buildings date from the reign of Vijayabahu's successor **Parakramabahu**, reigned 1153–86 (see box, p.309). Parakramabahu developed the city on a lavish scale, importing architects and engineers from India whose influence can be seen in Polonnaruwa's many Hindu shrines. Indian influence continued with Parakramabahu's successor, **Nissankamalla**, reigned 1187–96 (see box, p.312), a Tamil from the Kalinga dynasty and the last king of Polonnaruwa to enjoy any measure of islandwide power.

Nissankamalla's death ushered in a period of chaos. Opposing Tamil and Sinhalese factions battled for control of the city – the next eighteen years saw twelve changes of ruler – while at least four invasions from India threatened the stability of the island at large. This era of anarchy culminated with the seizure of the increasingly enfeebled kingdom by the notorious Tamil mercenary **Magha** (1215–55). Under Magha the monasteries were pillaged and onerous taxes imposed, while his soldiers roamed the kingdom unchecked and the region's great irrigation works fell into disrepair, leading to a decline in agricultural produce and a rise in malaria. Although Magha was finally driven out of Polonnaruwa in 1255, the damage he had inflicted proved irreversible, and Polonnaruwa was finally abandoned in 1293, when Bhuvanekabahu II moved the capital to Kurunegala. The city was left to be swallowed up by the jungle, until restoration work began in the mid-twentieth century.

The ancient city of Polonnaruwa

Daily 7.30am–6pm • $25; note that tickets have to be bought at the museum (see p.310) in the village – they can't be bought at the entrance itself • The site is rather too large to cover by foot; the best idea is to rent a bike (available from most of the town's guesthouses, or from Sachira Communications on the main street, for Rs.200–300/day)

The **ruins of Polonnaruwa** are scattered over an extensive area of gently undulating woodland about 4km from north to south. You can see everything at Polonnaruwa in a single long day, but you'll have to start early to do the city justice.

Polonnaruwa was originally enclosed by three concentric walls and filled with parks and gardens. At the heart of the city lies the **royal palace** complex, while immediately to the north are the city's most important cluster of religious buildings, the so-called **Quadrangle**, containing the finest group of remains in the city – and, indeed, Sri Lanka. Polonnaruwa's largest monuments are found in the northern part of the city,

4

PARAKRAMABAHU THE GREAT

The Sri Lankan monarch most closely associated with Polonnaruwa is Parakramabahu I (reigned 1153–86), or **Parakramabahu the Great**, as he's often styled, the last in the sequence of famous Sinhalese warrior kings, stretching back to the legendary Dutugemunu (see p.324), who succeeded in uniting the entire island under the rule of a single native monarch.

Parakramabahu (a grandson of Vijayabahu) was born at **Dedigama** (see p.200), capital of the minor kingdom of Dakkinadesa, which was ruled by his father. Upon becoming ruler of Dakkinadesa, Parakramabahu established a new capital at **Panduwas Nuwara** (see p.284) before launching a campaign against the king of Polonnaruwa, his cousin **Gajabahu**. After an extended series of military and political manoeuvrings, Parakramabahu finally triumphed and was crowned king of Polonnaruwa in 1153, although it took a brutal and protracted series of military campaigns before the entire island was finally subdued.

Even while Parakramabahu was mopping up the last pockets of resistance in the south, he began to embark on the gargantuan programme of building works and administrative reforms which transformed Polonnaruwa into one of the great cities of its age, as well as finding the time to launch a couple of rare military offensives overseas, first in Burma and then India. According to the *Culavamsa*, the new king built or restored over six thousand tanks and canals, including the vast new **Parakrama Samudra** in Polonnaruwa, as well as restoring the three great dagobas at Anuradhapura and rebuilding the monastery at Mihintale. It was at his new capital, however, that Parakramabahu lavished his greatest efforts, supervising the construction of a spate of imposing new edifices including the Royal Palace complex, the majestic Lankatilake, and the beautiful Vatadage, the crowning achievement of medieval Sinhalese architecture.

comprising the buildings of the **Menik Vihara**, **Rankot Vihara**, **Alahana Pirivena** and **Jetavana** monasteries, including the famous Buddha statues of the **Gal Vihara** and the soaring **Lankatilaka** shrine.

To the west of the city lies the great artificial lake, the **Parakrama Samudra** ("Sea of Parakramabahu"), providing a beautiful backdrop to the town – an evening stroll along the waterside Potgul Mawatha makes a scenic way to end a day. The lake was created by the eponymous king, Parakramabahu, though sections of the irrigation system date right back to the third century AD. Covering some 26 square kilometres, the lake provided the medieval city with water, cooling breezes and an additional line of defence, and also irrigated over ninety square kilometres of paddy fields. After a breach in the walls in the late thirteenth century, the tank fell into disrepair, and was restored to its original size only in the 1950s.

Although Polonnaruwa doesn't have the huge religious significance of Anuradhapura, the city's religious remains are still held sacred and signs outside many of the ruins ask you to **remove your shoes** as a token of respect – quite painful, unless you're accustomed to walking barefoot over sharp gravel, while the ruins' stone floors can often reach oven-like temperatures in the midday sun. Wimps wear socks.

The Polonnaruwa Museum

Museum Daily 9am–5.30pm **Ticket office** Daily 7.30am–5.30pm • Museum entrance with site ticket only

Close to the lakeshore on the northern edge of Polonnaruwa town is the modern **Polonnaruwa Museum**, one of the best in the country and well worth a look before setting off around the site. Exhibits include some fascinating **scale models** showing how the city's buildings might have looked in their prime, notably a fine mock-up of the Vatadage and a rather more conjectural model of Parakramabahu's Royal Palace. There's also a fine collection of **bronzes** and **sculptures** recovered from the site – many are elaborately carved images of Hindu deities, testifying to the overwhelming Indian influence in the city's culture. Copious background descriptions (in English) of every part of ancient Polonnaruwa add interesting details and insights and help flesh out the exhibits.

The Citadel

At the heart of the ancient city lie the buildings of the **Citadel**, surrounded by a (heavily restored) circuit of walls. At the centre of the complex lie the remains of Parakramabahu's **Royal Palace** (Vijayanta Prasada). According to the *Culavamsa* (see p.396), the palace originally stood seven storeys high and boasted a thousand rooms, although this was probably an exaggeration (a model in the museum shows a speculative impression of how this seven-storey palace might have looked). The remains of three brick storeys have survived (any further levels would have been built of wood and have long since disappeared), although they don't give much idea of how the building would originally have appeared – the ruin now looks more like a medieval European castle than a Sinhalese royal palace. The holes in the walls were for floor beams, while the vertical grooves up to the first floor would have held wooden pillars; numerous patches of original plaster also survive.

Just east of the Royal Palace stand the remains of Parakramabahu's **Council Chamber** (Raja Vaishyabhuganga) where the king would have granted audiences to his ministers and officials. The wooden roof has vanished, but the imposing base survives, banded with friezes of dwarfs, lions and galumphing elephants. The sumptuous steps are embellished with *makara* balustrades, a pair of fine moonstones and topped with two of the rather Chinese-looking lions associated with Sinhalese royalty during this period – other examples can be seen at Nissankamalla's Audience Chamber (see p.317) and at Yapahuwa.

Just east of here are the **Royal Baths** (Kumara Pokuna), designed in an unusual geometric shape (a square superimposed on a cross) and fed by two spouts carved with eroded *makaras*. Next to here stands the impressive two-tiered base of what is thought to have been the royal changing room, decorated with the usual lions and moonstone.

Shiva Devale no. 1

About 300m north of the Citadel lies the quaint little **Shiva Devale no. 1**, one of many temples at Polonnaruwa dedicated to either Vishnu or Shiva. The shrine dates from the Pandyan occupation of the early thirteenth century, following the collapse of Sinhalese power; the fact that the Indian invaders saw fit to construct an unabashedly Hindu shrine so close to the city's most sacred Buddhist precinct says much about their religious sympathies, or lack of.

The temple is made of finely cut, slate-grey stone, fitted together without the use of mortar. The bottom halves of two rudely truncated guardian figures stand by the doorway into the inner shrine, inside which stands a rather battered lingam – the extraordinary treasure trove of **bronze images** found here is now in the National Museum in Colombo (see p.83). Along the southern (left-hand) side of the temple stand cute little carvings showing a pair of heavily bearded figures, possibly representing Agni, the pre-Aryan Indian god of fire, accompanied by two even smaller attendants.

The Quadrangle

Just north of the Shiva Devale no. 1 stands the **Quadrangle** – originally, and more properly, known as the Dalada Maluwa ("Terrace of the Tooth Relic"), since the famous relic (see p.212) was housed in various shrines here during its stay in the city. This rectangular walled enclosure, built on a raised terrace, was the religious heart of the city, conveniently close to the royal palace of Parakramabahu – the king would

4

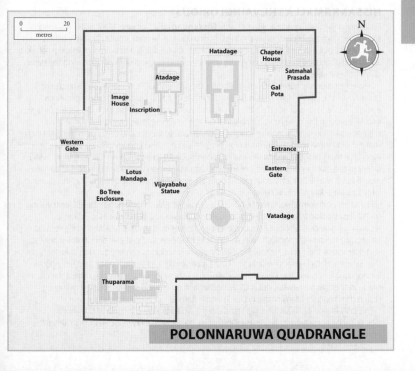

POLONNARUWA QUADRANGLE

probably have come here to listen to readings from the Buddhist scriptures – and is now home to the finest and most varied collection of ancient buildings anywhere on the island.

The Vatadage

The Quadrangle is dominated by the flamboyant **Vatadage** (circular relic house), arguably the most beautiful building in Sri Lanka. Built by Parakramabahu, it was later renovated and embellished by the crafty Nissankamalla (see p.312), who claimed credit for the whole building himself in the vast Gal Pota inscription (see opposite).

The structure consists of a central shrine plus miniature dagoba (originally covered with a wooden roof) enclosed in a high brick wall set on a raised terrace. Four sets of steps, aligned to the cardinal points, lead up to the terrace, each one a little sculptural masterpiece, decorated with dwarfs, lions and *makaras*, as well as magnificently carved *nagaraja* guardstones and some of the finest moonstones in the city. The remains of further pillars and carved capitals that would once have supported the now vanished roof lie scattered about the terrace.

From the terrace, further steps, aligned with those below, lead up into the central shrine through four entrances, each presided over by a seated Buddha, to the eroded remains of the central brick dagoba in which the **Tooth Relic** may have been enshrined – strangely enough, the inner sanctum is virtually unadorned, in striking contrast to the remainder of the building.

The Hatadage

Opposite the Vatadage stand the rather plain remains of the **Hatadage**, said to have been named after the fact that it was built in just sixty (*hata*) hours – which seems

---

NISSANKAMALLA THE VAINGLORIOUS

Following Vijayabahu and Parakramabahu, **Nissankamalla** (reigned 1187–96) is the third of the famous trinity of Polonnaruwan kings. A Tamil prince, Nissankamalla originally hailed from South India, but married into the Sinhalese nobility by wedding a daughter of Parakramabahu, and then succeeded in attaining the throne after a brief political skirmish following the death of his father-in-law.

Nissankamalla was notable chiefly for being the last king of Polonnaruwa to exercise real power over the whole island, even feeling secure enough to launch military expeditions against the Pandyans of South India. Perhaps conscious of his foreign birth, he seems to have endeavoured to become more Sinhalese than the Sinhalese, making a great show of his religious orthodoxy, purging the Sangha of disreputable monks and becoming the first king to make the pilgrimage to the summit of Adam's Peak. He is also known to have embarked on extensive tours of the island to discover the conditions under which his subjects were living, rather in the manner of a contemporary politician at election time – not that Nissankamalla would have worried much about public opinion, since he considered himself (as did many later Sinhalese kings) a living god.

For all his genuine achievements, however, Nissankamalla is best remembered for the long trail of **inscriptions** he left dotted around Polonnaruwa and other places in Sri Lanka, recording his valour, wisdom, religious merit and other outstanding qualities – he seems to have been the sort of monarch who wasn't able to sneeze without erecting a monument to commemorate the event. Nissankamalla's bombastic scribbles can be found in Polonnaruwa at the Gal Pota, Hatadage and Vatadage in the Quadrangle, and at the Rankot and Kiri viharas (plus a couple more in the Polonnaruwa Museum), though some historians regard the claims made in them as somewhat dubious, while Nissankamalla also stands accused of having stolen the credit for many of the building works carried out by Parakramabahu.

The only image of Nissankamalla stands in the Maharaja cave temple at Dambulla (see p.291). Ironically for this great self-publicist, it's tucked away in a corner, and almost completely hidden from sight.

highly unlikely. Commissioned by Nissankamalla (who placed a long inscription just inside the main entrance on the right claiming credit for the building), the Hatadage may originally have been constructed to house the Tooth Relic and was originally two storeys high, though the upper storey has long since crumbled away. It now houses three Buddha statues, possibly intended to represent the Buddhas of the past, present and future; the central one is positioned to line up through the shrine's doorway with the Buddha directly opposite in the Vatadage.

The Gal Pota

Immediately east of the Hatadage stands the **Gal Pota** ("Book of Stone"), an enormous slab of granite, some 9m long, covered in an densely inscribed panegyric praising the works of the bumptious Nissankamalla (see opposite) – an astonishing display of self-publicity that would put even a modern politician to shame. The stone itself, according to the inscription, weighs 25 tons and was brought over 90km from Mihintale, though exactly why this particular slab was considered so remarkable that it had to be dragged all the way here over such a distance remains unclear. On the end of the stone facing the Vatadage a carving shows the Hindu goddess Lakshmi being given a shower by two elephants, a traditional symbol of wealth.

The Satmahal Prasada

Next to the Gal Pota stands the strange **Satmahal Prasada** (the name means "seven-storey temple", though only six storeys survive). The ziggurat-like structure is unique in Sri Lanka and its original function remains unclear, although it may have been an unusual kind of step-sided stupa similar to those found in Southeast Asia – it's been hypothesized that Khmer (Cambodian) craftsmen may have been involved in the construction of the building, although no one really knows. The heavily eroded figures of a few deities and fragments of original white plaster can still be seen on its walls.

Just to the west of the Satmahal Prasada are the slight remains of a seventh-century **Chapter House** – just a tiny brick outline and a few pillars, including one in the unusual "thrice-bent" style of the Lotus Mandapa (see below).

The Atadage

On the other side of the Hatadage, the **Atadage** is one of the oldest structures in the city, having been constructed by Vijayabahu to house the Tooth Relic, although all that now remains are a few finely carved pillars and a delicate Buddha, standing contemplatively atop a lotus plinth in the middle of the now derelict structure. A **tablet inscription** immediately to the west records details of the building's construction and the arrival of monks from Burma, on the far side of which are the remains of an **image house** – the brick plinth inside would have supported a now-vanished reclining Buddha.

The Lotus Mandapa

As you continue anti-clockwise, the next building is the small but exquisite **Lotus Mandapa** (also known as the Latha Mandapaya or Nissankalata), a small open-air pavilion for religious rituals built by Nissankamalla. The *mandapa* features an unusual latticed stone fence, reminiscent of the Buddhist Railing at the Jetavana monastery in Anuradhapura, and a small platform surmounted by stone pillars shaped as thrice-bent lotus buds on stalks, a beautiful and very unusual design whose sinuous organic lines look positively Art Nouveau. In the centre of the platform are the remains of a tiny dagoba which was, according to different interpretations, either used to hold holy relics or which served as a seat for Nissankamalla during religious ceremonies (though not, presumably, both). In front of the Lotus Mandapa stands an armless **statue**, popularly thought to represent Vijayabahu, though it might be a bodhisattva.

The Thuparama

In the southwest corner of the Quadrangle stands one of its oldest but also one of its most intact structures, the **Thuparama**, an exceptionally large and well-preserved structure thought to date back to the reign of Vijayabahu. The building's original name is unknown; it was confusingly christened the Thuparama ("The Stupa") by the pioneering British archeologist H.C.P. Bell, though it isn't actually a stupa at all but a gedige, a type of rectangular image house with a vaulted brick roof.

The exterior walls are decorated with elaborately carved *vimanas* (miniature representations of the dwellings of the gods). Inside, the shrine preserves part of its sturdy vaulted roof and traces of its original plasterwork, as well as exceptionally thick brick walls whose massive dimensions keep the interior pleasantly cool – the walls are so thick that the architects were actually able to construct a staircase inside them (you can see the doorway set in a recess on the left). At the back of the shrine are eight beautiful old standing and seated crystalline limestone Buddhas, which sparkle magically when illuminated.

North of the Quadrangle

The road north from the Quadrangle runs through attractive light woodland and past a scatter of minor monuments. The most interesting is the diminutive **Shiva Devale no. 2**, the oldest surviving structure in Polonnaruwa. The temple dates back to the original Chola occupation during the early eleventh century; an inscription states that it was built by the great Chola emperor Rajaraja, whose army destroyed Anuradhapura in 993, in memory of one of his queens. This pretty little domed building is pure Indian in style, boasting the same distinctive rounded capitals and niche windows which adorn the Shiva Devale no. 1; four headless Nandis (Shiva's bull) stand guard around the shrine.

Just to the southwest stands the **Pabula Vihara** ("Red Coral Shrine"), named by H.C.P. Bell for the red corals he discovered during excavations here. Said to have been built by a certain Rupavati, one of Parakramabahu's wives, the vihara's main structure is a large brick dagoba, the third largest in Polonnaruwa, though restorations have reduced it to strange two-tier stump which gives no clue as to its original form. The remains of various brick image houses and Buddha statues lie scattered around the base.

Continuing north along the main track brings you to the remains of the **Northern Gate**, which marked the limits of the central walled city. The **Vishnu Devale no. 2** and **Ganesha Devale** stand on the main track opposite one another on the south side of the gate. The former has a fine Vishnu image and the remains of stone (rather than brick) walls, though little remains of the latter. Immediately south of the Ganesha Devale are the equally slight ruins of another **Shiva Devale**, comprising the base of a tiny one-room shrine enclosing a battered lingam.

Menik Vihara

The city's monastic areas begin immediately north of the northern gate with the rather uninteresting scattered remains of the **Menik Vihara**. Little survives other than heavily restored foundations of assorted monastic buildings, a few armless (and sometimes also headless) Buddhas, and the remains of a small brick dagoba whose top has crumbled away, exposing the relic chamber within.

Rankot Vihara

North of the Menik Vihara stands Nissankamalla's monumental **Rankot Vihara**, an immense red-brick dagoba rising to a height of some 55m. The fourth largest such structure in Sri Lanka, it's surpassed in size only by the three great dagobas at Anuradhapura, in imitation of which it was built, although its unusually steep sides and flattened top (it looks as though someone very large has sat on it) are less graceful than its Anuradhapuran antecedents. An inscription to the left of the entrance pathway describes how Nissankamalla oversaw work here, testifying to his religious devotion and the spiritual merit he presumably expected to gain from the stupa's construction – whether the forced labourers who were obliged to raise this gargantuan edifice shared the king's sense of religious idealism is not recorded.

Alahana Pirivena

A few hundred metres beyond the Rankot Vihara stretch the extensive remains of the **Alahana Pirivena** ("Monastery of the Cremation Grounds"), named after the royal cremation grounds which were established in this part of the city by Parakramabahu – the many minor stupas scattered about the area would have contained the relics of royalty or prominent monks. The monastery was one of the most impressive in the ancient city, and the remains here are some of the finest at the site.

Lankatilaka

At the heart of the Alahana Pirivena stands the majestic **Lankatilaka** ("Ornament of Lanka"), one of the city's finest monuments, with towering brick walls enclosing a huge – though now sadly headless – standing Buddha. The shrine as a whole emphasizes the change in Buddhist architecture and thought from the abstract symbolic form of the dagoba to a much more personalized and devotional approach, in which attention is focused on the giant figure of the Buddha (more than 14m high) which fills up the entire space within.

Built by Parakramabahu, the Lankatilaka is one of the biggest, and certainly the tallest, building to survive from ancient Sri Lanka (dagobas excepted) and still an imposing sight, despite the loss of its roof and much of its original decoration. The entrance is approached by two sets of steps; the outside face of the upper left-hand balustrade sports an unusually fine lion carving. More unusual are the intriguing low-relief **carvings** on the exterior walls showing a series of elaborate multistorey buildings, probably intended to represent the celestial dwellings (*vimanas*) of the gods.

Kiri Vihara

Next to the Lankatilaka is the so-called **Kiri Vihara**, the best preserved of Polonnaruwa's dagobas, believed to have been constructed at the behest of one of Parakramabahu's wives, a certain Queen Subhadra. *Kiri* means "milk", referring to the white lime plaster that covers the building and which was almost perfectly preserved when the dagoba was rescued from the jungle after seven hundred years – and which recent restoration has now returned to something approaching its original milkyness. As at the Rankot Vihara, Kiri Vihara boasts four *vahalkadas* and an unusual number of brick shrines around its base, while on the south side of the dagoba an inscription on a raised stone plinth records the location at which Nissankamalla worshipped.

Buddha Seema Pasada

South of the Lankatilaka, the **Buddha Seema Pasada** was the monastery's chapter house, a substantial building which might originally – judging by the thickness of its outer walls – have supported several upper storeys of brick or wood. In the middle of the building is a square pillared hall with a raised dais at its centre, surrounded by monks' cells and connected to the surrounding courtyard by four entrances, each with its own exquisite moonstone. Urns on pillars (symbolizing plenty) stand in the outer courtyard.

Gal Vihara

A short distance north of the Buddha Seema Pasada lies the magnificent **Gal Vihara** ("Stone Shrine"; also known as the Kalugal Vihara, or Black Stone Shrine), the undisputed pinnacle of Sri Lankan rock carving. The four Buddhas here, all chiselled from the same massive granite outcrop, originally formed part of the Alahana Pirivena monastic complex, with each statue formerly housed in its own enclosure – you still can see the sockets cut into the rock behind the standing image into which wooden beams would have been inserted (sadly, the modern answer to protecting the carvings from the elements is a pair of huge metal shelters which keep the statues in a permanent twilight).

The massive **reclining Buddha**, 14m long, is the most famous of the statues, a huge but supremely graceful figure which manages to combine the serenely transcendental with the touchingly human; the face, delicately flecked with traces of natural black sediment, is especially beautiful. The 7m-tall **standing Buddha** next to it is the most unusual of the set: its downcast eyes and the unusual position of its arms led some to consider it an image of Ananda, the Buddha's disciple, grieving for his departed master, though it's now thought to represent the Buddha himself in the weeks following his enlightenment – similar images are found in Kandyan-era murals.

Two splendid **seated Buddhas** complete the group, though they lack the iconic simplicity of the reclining figure, being posed against backdrops whose elaborate detail is rather unusual by the austere standards of Sri Lankan Buddhist art. The smaller seated Buddha, unfortunately now kept behind a metal grille and fibreglass shield, is placed in a slight cave-like recess (the other three would have been housed in brick shrines), seated in the *dhyani mudra* (meditation posture); other deities stand in the background, along with a distinctive arch modelled after the one at the great Buddhist shrine at Sanchi in India. Tiny strips of the beautifully detailed murals that once covered the interior of the cave can be seen hidden away in each corner.

The larger seated Buddha is also posed in *dhyani mudra* and entirely framed by another Sanchi-style arch, with tiny Buddhas looking down on him from their celestial dwellings – perhaps showing a touch of Mahayana Buddhist influence, with its belief in multiple buddhas and bodhisattvas.

North to the Tivanka-patamaghara

A kilometre north of the Gal Vihara, a rough side track leads to the **Demala Maha Seya** (or Damilathupa), an unfinished attempt by Parakramabahu to build the world's largest stupa using labour supplied by Tamil (*damala*, hence the dagoba's name) prisoners of war captured during fighting against the Pandyans. The dagoba is actually constructed on top of a natural hill: a retaining wall was built around the hill and the gap between filled with rubble, though it seems the dagoba was never finished. The remains of the structure have now been completely buried under dense forest, though a short section of the massive three-tiered base has been excavated and restored (around the back of the dagoba, about five minutes' walk from the main track) – not terribly interesting in itself, though it brings home the enormous scale of the restoration works carried out to rescue similarly jungle-covered stupas at both Polonnaruwa and Anuradhapura.

The Tivanka-patamaghara

Another 500m further north, just to the west of the main track, is an unusual **lotus pond**, formed from five concentric rings of stone finely carved in the shape of stylized lotus petals. The pond may have been used as a ritual bath for those entering the **Tivanka-patamaghara** image house, an exceptionally large and sturdy gedige-style brick structure a further 400m on at the far northern end of the site. Along with the lotus pond, the Tivanka-patamaghara is one of the few surviving structures of the **Jetavana monastery**. *Tivanka* means "thrice-bent", referring to the graceful but headless Buddha image inside which is in a position (bent at the shoulder, waist and knee) usually employed only for female images.

The interior is also home to a sequence of outstanding (but rather difficult to see) **frescoes**, depicting scenes from the Buddhist Jatakas and lines of very finely painted Hindu-looking deities in sumptuous tiaras. The **exterior** shows the influence of

South Indian architecture perhaps more clearly than any other Buddhist building in Sri Lanka, with densely pillared and niched walls decorated with the usual friezes of lions, dwarfs and *vimanas*. The overall effect is richly exuberant, and a world away from the chaste Buddhist architecture of Anuradhapura. Restoration work continues inside and out.

Ruins beyond the main site

Two further complexes of ruins lie outside the main site: the **Island Park**, on a promontory jutting out into the lake a little north of the museum, and the **southern ruins**, 1.5km south along the lakeshore. Although of lesser interest, they're still worth a visit and, as entry to them is free, you don't have to try and cram seeing them and the rest of the site into a single day.

Island Park

Open 24hr • Free

Reachable from behind either the museum or the *Rest House* (see p.318), the modest ruins of the **Island Park** (Dipanyana) complex comprise Parakramabahu's former pleasure gardens along with a string of later buildings constructed during the reign of Nissankamalla. The most interesting structure here is Nissankamalla's **Council Chamber**, similar to that of Parakramabahu (see p.310). The roof has vanished, but the raised base survives, studded with four rows of sturdy columns, some inscribed with the titles of the dignitaries who would have sat next to them during meetings with the king. A marvellous stone **lion** stands at the end of the plinth marking the position of Nissankamalla's throne.

Another of Nissankamalla's interminable **inscriptions** sits on the south side of the Council Chamber, while close by, the overgrown remains of a many-pillared **summer house** jut out into the lake. On the other side of the Council Chamber lie the slight remains of a large building, possibly Nissakamalla's **Audience Hall** (as it's signed), although it may have been his royal palace.

Just south of the Council Chamber are the remains of a small, square brick-built structure (signed "White Edifice"), possibly some kind of royal **mausoleum**, and sometimes said to mark the site of Nissankamalla's cremation. The surviving walls reach heights of around 5m and retain traces of red and white paint on their exterior – surprisingly bright and well preserved in places, considering that it's more than 800 years old. Nearby lie the remains of the extensive sunken **Royal Baths**.

The southern ruins

Open 24hr • Free

A scenic fifteen-minute walk along the raised bank of the lake brings you to Polonnaruwa's final group of remains, the modest **southern ruins**. The best-preserved building here is the **Potgul Vihara**, a circular image house surrounded by four small dagobas and the pillared ruins of monastic living quarters. The central room is thought to have housed a monastic library where the city's most sacred texts would have been stored, protected by massive walls that reach a thickness of around 2m at ground level.

The principal attraction, however, lies about 100m to the north: an imposing 3.5m-high **statue** of a bearded figure, thought to date from the ninth century, which has become one of Polonnaruwa's most emblematic images. It's usually claimed that the statue is a likeness of **Parakramabahu** himself, holding an object thought to be either a palm-leaf manuscript, representing the "Book of Law", or a yoke, representing the burden of royalty (the less reverent claim it's a slice of papaya). Another theory holds that the statue could be the sage named Pulasti, a hypothesis lent credence by its position near the monastic library.

ARRIVAL AND DEPARTURE

By bus The main bus station is in the town of Kaduruwela, 4km east along the road to Batticaloa. Arriving by bus, ask to be put off at Polonnaruwa "Old Town"; buses stop close to the Seylan Bank, within spitting distance of most of the guesthouses. Leaving Polonnaruwa you can hop on a bus at the stop on the main road, but to be sure of a seat it's easiest to take a tuktuk to the station at Kaduruwela and catch a bus there.

Destinations Anuradhapura (hourly; 3hr 30min); Batticaloa (every 30min; 3hr); Colombo (every 30min; 6hr); Dambulla (every 30min; 1hr 45min); Giritale (every 15min; 30min); Habarana (every 20min; 1hr); Kandy (every 30min;

POLONNARUWA AND AROUND

3hr 45min).

By train The train station is in the nearby town of Kaduruwela (see opposite).

Destinations Batticaloa (2 daily; 2hr 30min); Colombo (2 daily; 6hr).

TOURS

Polonnaruwa is a convenient starting point for trips to Minneriya and Kaudulla national parks; most guesthouses and hotels can arrange a jeep to either park from around $40–50; try the *Gajaba* hotel for good-value inclusive transport-and-ticket deals.

ACCOMMODATION

Polonnaruwa's **accommodation** is no great shakes, and given the paucity of mid- and top-end places, many people opt to stay at the village of **Giritale**, 15km down the road, which boasts three pleasant hotels, all perched on the edge of the beautiful Giritale lake. There are frequent buses to Polonnaruwa (every 15min) – or tuktuks for around Rs.800 – making Giritale a possible base even if you don't have your own transport.

POLONNARUWA

★ **Devi Tourist Home** 31 New Town Rd ☎ 027 222 3181. The nicest and best-run guesthouse in Polonnaruwa, set in a peaceful location 1km south of town with five comfy rooms (two with a/c and hot water), good home-cooking and very friendly service. **Rs.1200**; a/c **Rs.2500**

Gajaba Hotel 1st Canal Rd ☎ 027 222 2394, ⓦ hotelgajaba.com. This Polonnaruwa stalwart houses a wide range of rooms (some with a/c for Rs.500 extra) of varying sizes and standards either in the main house or in the quieter garden "cottage" – all are reasonably clean and well maintained, although showing their age. There are also reasonably priced jeeps, bikes, internet and a nice garden restaurant (see opposite). More luxurious rooms overlooking the tank and a new restaurant are under construction. **Rs.1200**; a/c **Rs.1700**

Palm Garden 2nd Canal Colony, 1km from town ☎ 027 222 2622, ✉ a_mahavitana@hotmail.com. Well-run guesthouse with four modern, very clean and very bare rooms (two with a/c and hot water), though the main attraction is the idyllic rural setting. There are free bikes for trips to town (or Rs.200 to visit the ancient city), and they can also arrange catamaran trips on the lake. **Rs.1500**

★ **Rest House** Rest House Rd ☎ 027 222 2299, ⓦ ceylonhotels.lk. In a peerless setting overlooking the lake, this venerable place retains plenty of period character. Rooms (all with a/c and TV) are extremely spacious, if a little bare; choose between standard and superior categories – the latter come with lake views and slightly more furniture – best is room #1, which accommodated Queen Elizabeth II for a night during her 1954 state visit to Ceylon. **$67**

Samudra Guest House Habarana Rd ☎ 027 222 2817. Simple little guesthouse with a selection of basic but clean rooms (some with hot water, one with a/c), all at bargain

rates. There's also a neat little garden and terrace restaurant, plus cheap bikes (Rs.200). **Rs.700**

Siyanco Holiday Resort 1st Canal Rd ☎ 027 222 6868, ⓦ siyancoholidayresort.com. The most upmarket option close to the central ruins, this bright if rather characterless modern hotel comes with spotless tiled rooms and a smart restaurant, plus small pool (non-guests Rs.600), bikes and internet. **Rs.3800**

★ **Sudu Araliya** New Town ☎ 027 222 5406, ⓦ hotelsuduaraliya.com. The smartest place in Polonnaruwa, with large, comfy a/c rooms equipped with chintzy neo-colonial furniture, minibar and TV. Facilities include a very large pool (non-guests free if you take a meal), a cute, cave-like Ayurveda centre and a poolside beer garden. Excellent value at current rates. **$77**

The Village New Town ☎ 027 222 3366, ⓦ vilapol.com. Very low-key hotel arranged around attractive gardens, with comfortable, pleasantly old-fashioned and good-value rooms (all with a/c, hot water and satellite TV). There's also a decent-size pool (non-guests Rs.300, or free if you have a drink at the poolside bar), and bikes to rent. **$50**

GIRITALE

The Deer Park Giritale ☎ 027 224 6272, ⓦ deerparksrilanka.com. Giritale's most appealing address, with accommodation in a string of cute little buildings scattered around beautiful wooded grounds. Choose between the spacious rooms and even larger two-storey cottages, all with lime-green decor and nice open-air showers. Facilities include a good-sized pool and Ayurveda centre. B&B **$157**

Giritale Hotel Giritale ☎ 027 224 6311, ⓦ giritalehotel.com. The oldest of the Giritale hotels, in a commanding location high above Giritale Tank. Looking a bit dated in places, but rooms (most with lake views) are cosy and well

maintained. Also has a pool and herbal massages. $85
The Royal Lotus Giritale ☏ 027 224 6316, ⊛ royallotus
.com. Comfortable two-star overlooking the tank, with
accommodation (with TV and a/c) either in lake-facing
rooms in the main building or in one of the self-contained
cottages in the gardens behind. There's also a pool and
modest Ayurveda centre. $100

EATING

All hotels and guesthouses in Polonnaruwa (see opposite) do meals – they're a pretty uninspiring bunch, however. The
following two are the best options.

Gajaba Hotel 1st Canal Rd ☏ 027 222 2394,
⊛ hotelgajaba.com. Attractive little terrace restaurant at
the back of this popular hotel, serving up mainstream Sri
Lankan food at slightly inflated prices – although both
food and service can be hit-or-miss. Daily 8am–10pm.
Rest House Rest House Rd ☏ 027 222 2299,
⊛ ceylonhotels.lk. Pleasantly time-warped (if slightly
gloomy) restaurant serving up a limited selection of
generally well-prepared Sri Lankan standards and a few
more European-style meat and fish dishes, plus a fine rice
and curry spread (lunchtime only; Rs.750). There's also a
nice outdoor terrace overlooking the lake, though it tends
to get plagued with mosqitoes after dark. Most mains
Rs.500–700. Daily 7am–10pm.

DIRECTORY

Bank The Seylan and People's banks both have ATMs
accepting foreign cards.
Internet There's unreliable internet access at several places
along the main road including Sachira Communications
(daily 8am–8pm; Rs.60/hr) and Aloka Communications,
near the People's Bank (daily 8am–7pm; Rs.100/hr).

Mandalagiri Vihara

4

Some 33km north of Polonnaruwa, and 3km north of the town of Medirigiriya • Daily 7.30am–6pm • Rs.500 • Buses run every 15min from
Polonnaruwa to the bustling village of Hingurakgoda, 13km north, where you can change onto a second bus, or take a tuktuk, for the
bumpy 30min ride to Medirigiriya; hiring a vehicle from Polonnaruwa should cost around $30, or $45 if you combine a trip to Medirigiya
with a visit to Ritigala

The remains of **Mandalagiri Vihara,** which was built and flourished during the
heyday of Polonnaruwa, are interesting, but the remoteness of the site and the
difficulty (or expense, if you hire transport) of reaching it mean that unless you have
an unusual interest in Sinhalese Buddhist architecture, you probably won't find it
worth the effort.

The main attraction here is the fine eighth-century **vatadage**, similar in size and
design to the vatadage at Polonnaruwa, though the quality of the workmanship is of a
far lower level. The vatadage sits atop an unusually high terrace and is approached by a
long flight of stone steps, with *punkalas* (stone urns, signifying plenty) at the top. The
remains of other **monastic buildings** lie around the vatadage, including the base of a
sizeable brick dagoba, a couple of tanks and assorted shrines and Buddha statues, many
of them now headless.

Anuradhapura

For well over a thousand years, the history of Sri Lanka was essentially the history of
ANURADHAPURA. Situated almost at the centre of the island's northern plains, the
city rose to prominence very early in the development of Sri Lanka, and maintained
its pre-eminent position for more than a millennium until being finally laid waste by
Indian invaders in 993. Today, Anuradhapura remains a magical place. The sheer
scale of the ruined **ancient city** – and the thousand-plus years of history buried here
– is overwhelming, and you could spend days or even weeks ferreting around
amongst the ruins.

At its height, Anuradhapura was one of the greatest cities of its age, functioning as the
island's centre of both temporal and spiritual power, dotted with dozens of **monasteries**

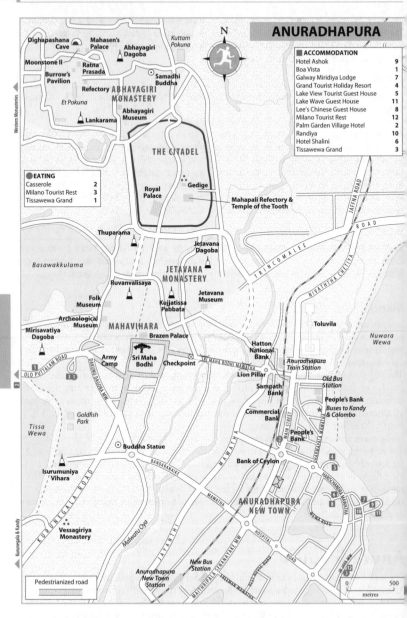

ANURADHAPURA

Dighapashana Cave
Mahasen's Palace
Abhayagiri Dagoba
Kuttam Pokuna
Moonstone II
Burrow's Pavilion
Ratna Prasada
Samadhi Buddha
Refectory ABHAYAGIRI MONASTERY
Et Pokuna
Abhayagiri Museum
Lankarama

Western Monasteries

THE CITADEL

Royal Palace
Gedige
Mahapali Refectory & Temple of the Tooth

JAFFNA ROAD

TRINCOMALEE ROAD

NIVATHTHA CHETIYA

EATING
Casserole   2
Milano Tourist Rest   3
Tissawewa Grand   1

Thuparama

Jetavana Dagoba

Basawakkulama

Ruvanvalisaya

JETAVANA MONASTERY

Folk Museum
Jetavana Museum
Kujjatissa Pabbata

Archeological Museum
Mirisavatiya Dagoba
MAHAVIHARA
Brazen Palace

Toluvila

Nuwara Wewa

Army Camp
Sri Maha Bodhi
Checkpoint
SRI MAHA BODHI MAWATHA
Hatton National Bank
Anuradhapura Train Station
OLD PUTTALAM ROAD
DAKUNU DAGOBA MW.
Lion Pillar
Old Bus Station
Sampath Bank
People's Bank
Buses to Kandy & Colombo
Goldfish Park
Tissa Wewa
Commercial Bank
People's Bank
Buddha Statue
Bank of Ceylon
BANDARANAIKE MAWATHA

MAIN STREET
TISSAWEWA MAWATHA
MAWALHA MAWATHA
HARISCHANDRA MAWATHA
WEWA ROAD

Isurumuniya Vihara
KURUNEGALA ROAD

Kurunegala & Kandy

ANURADHAPURA NEW TOWN

Vessagiriya Monastery

Malwatu Oya

New Bus Station

Anuradhapura New Town Station

JAYANTHI MAWATHA
HOSPITAL ROAD
MAITHRIPALA SENANAYAKE MW.
FREEMAN MAWATHA

Pedestrianized road

0   500
metres

populated by as many as ten thousand monks – one of the greatest monastic cities the world has ever seen. The **kings** of Anuradhapura oversaw the golden age of Sinhalese culture, and the temples and the enormous dagobas they erected were amongst the greatest architectural feats of their time, surpassed in scale only by the great pyramids at Giza. The city's fame spread to Greece and Rome and, judging by the number of Roman coins found here, appears to have enjoyed a lively trade with the latter.

ANURADHAPURA ORIENTATION

Anuradhapura divides into two distinct areas: **Anuradhapura New Town**, which is home to almost all the town's accommodation and practical services, and the **Sacred Precinct** to the west, site of the ancient city. The town is hemmed in by three great artificial **lakes**, or tanks: Nuwara Wewa to the east, and Tissa Wewa and Basawakkulama Tank to the west. The New Town is bisected by Main Street, where you'll find the post office, banks and other services. Most of Anuradhapura's accommodation is just east of here on or near Harischandra Mawatha.

THE SACRED PRECINCT

Anuradhapura's scatter of monuments and remains is vast and potentially confusing. The easiest way to get a mental handle on the Sacred Precinct is to think of it in terms of its three great monasteries: the **Mahavihara**, **Jetavana** and **Abhayagiri** – about two-thirds of the main sites belong to one of these complexes.

The most obvious place to start is the Mahavihara, at the physical and historical centre of the ancient city, beginning at the Ruvanvalisaya dagoba and walking south to Sri Maha Bodhi, before doubling back towards the Thuparama. From here you can either head east to the Jetavana Monastery or north to the Abhayagiri complex.

There are further important clusters of sights at the Citadel, between the Mahavihara and Abhayagiri monasteries; and south of the Mahavihara, between the Mirisavetiya dagoba and Isurumuniya Temple. The major **dagobas** provide useful landmarks if you get disoriented, though beware confusing the Ruvanvalisaya and Mirisavetiya dagobas, which can look very similar when seen from a distance.

The tanks

4

Anuradhapura lies nestled between a trio of **tanks** (see box, p.322) that provided the lifeblood of the ancient city – although from the fifth century onwards their waters were supplemented by those from larger and more distant tanks such as the Kalawewa. West of the Sri Maha Bodhi is the city's oldest tank, the **Basawakkulama**, created by Pandukabhaya around the fourth century BC. South of the city is the **Tissa Wewa**, built by Devanampiya Tissa, while on the east side of the city lies the largest of the three, the **Nuwara Wewa**, completed in around 20 BC and significantly expanded by later kings to reach its present imposing dimensions. The raised bunds (lakeside embankments) on the west and south sides of Nuwara Wewa are close to many of the town's guesthouses and perfect for an evening stroll and some birdwatching, while there are wonderful views of the city's dagobas from the north shore of the Basawakkulama.

The Mahavihara

The centre of ancient Anuradhapura was the **Mahavihara**, the oldest of the city's monasteries and for many centuries its most important. The monastery was founded around the **Sri Maha Bodhi** by Devanampiya Tissa, who also built Sri Lanka's first dagoba, the **Thuparama**, here, although this is now dwarfed by the great **Ruvanvalisaya**. The Mahavihara is still a living place of pilgrimage rather than an archeological site, with pilgrims flocking to the Ruvanvalisaya and Sri Maha Bodhi – the latter is still considered one of the world's most important Buddhist relics, rivalled in popularity in Sri Lanka only by the Tooth Relic in Kandy.

Sri Maha Bodhi

Not included in the Cultural Triangle ticket; you may be asked for a donation

At the spiritual and physical heart of Anuradhapura stands the **Sri Maha Bodhi**, or Sacred Bo Tree. According to popular belief, this immensely venerable tree was grown from a cutting taken from the original bo tree in Bodhgaya, India, under which the Buddha attained enlightenment, and brought to Sri Lanka by Princess Sangamitta, the sister of Mahinda (see p.336). The original bo tree in India was destroyed not long

WATER WORLD: IRRIGATION IN EARLY SRI LANKA

The map of Sri Lanka is studded with literally thousands of man-made lakes, commonly known as **tanks**, or *wewas* (pronounced, and occasionally spelt, "*vavas*"). The civilization of early Sri Lanka was essentially agricultural, and the need to ensure a regular supply of water for rice cultivation posed a crucial problem given the location of the island's early capitals in the dry plains of the north. The climate in these parts – a harsh contrast of famine and plenty, with brief monsoonal deluges separated by long periods of drought – made the use of irrigation, based on the storage of water for the regular cultivation of wet fields, a vital element in early Sinhalese civilization – one which, once mastered, succeeded in transforming the island's arid northern plains into an enormous rice bowl capable of supporting a burgeoning population.

The first, modest examples of hydraulic engineering date back to the earliest days of Sinhalese settlement in the third century BC, when farmers began to dam rivers and store water in small village reservoirs. With the later increase in royal power, Sri Lanka's kings began to take an active role in irrigation schemes, while Sinhalese engineers mastered the technology which allowed water in tanks to be stored until needed, then released through sluice gates and channelled through canals to distant fields.

The first giant reservoirs were constructed in the reign of **Mahasena** (274–301), who oversaw the construction of some sixteen major tanks, including the Minneriya tank, and **Dhatusena** (455–473), who constructed the remarkable Jaya Ganga canal, almost 90km long and maintaining a subtle gradient of six inches to the mile, which delivered water to Anuradhapura from the huge Kalawewa – whose waters ultimately hastened that unfortunate king's demise (see p.298). Further tanks and canals were built during to the reigns of **Mogallana II** (531–551), whose Padaviya tank, in the northern Vavuniya district, was the largest ever constructed in ancient Sri Lanka, and **Aggabodhi II** (604–614), who was responsible for the tank at Giritale, amongst other works.

The construction of large-scale irrigation works became a defining feature of early Sinhalese civilization, while the maintenance of such massive hydraulic feats required skilled engineering and a highly evolved bureaucracy. The captured waters allowed a second rice crop to be grown each year, as well as additional vegetables and pulses, all of which supported much higher population densities than would otherwise have been possible. The surplus agricultural produce created by large-scale irrigation and the taxes raised from the system were major sources of royal revenue, allowing expansive building works at home and military campaigns overseas culminating in the reign of the Polonnaruwan king, **Parakramabahu I**, who famously declared that "not one drop of water must flow into the ocean without serving the purposes of man", and who oversaw the creation of the vast Parakrama Samudra at Polonnaruwa, one of the last but finest monuments of ancient Sinhalese irrigation.

afterwards, but the Sri Maha Bodhi survived. Cuttings from it have been grown all over the island (and indeed throughout the Buddhist countries of Southeast Asia).

The Sri Maha Bodhi sits at the centre of a large and elaborate enclosure, dotted with numerous younger bo trees and festooned with prayer flags. A series of elaborate terraces decorated with gold railings have been built up around the trunk, although the tree itself is disappointingly unimpressive, appearing neither particularly large nor old (despite one trailing branch propped up on iron supports). Far more interesting is the general scene in the enclosure, which is usually full of rapt pilgrims (the women dressed neatly in white saris) contemplating the tree and praying. During poya days, huge crowds of devotees flock here to make offerings.

The Brazen Palace

Just north of the Sacred Bo Tree stand the remains of the **Brazen Palace** ("Loha Pasada"), named on account of the copper roof which once covered it. The "palace" was built by Dutugemunu, though despite its name it only ever served as a monastic, rather than a royal, residence – the *Mahavamsa* describes a nine-storeyed structure with a thousand rooms (though the second part of this claim is doubtless hyperbole, and perhaps the first as well). Unfortunately, since most of the palace was made of wood, it burnt down just fifteen years after its construction and on a number of occasions thereafter, and had to be repeatedly rebuilt, most recently by Parakramabahu the Great in the twelfth century.

Little remains of the palace now apart from a dense forest of plain, closely spaced columns – some 1600 in total – which would have supported the first floor. Confusingly, many of these did not belong to the original structure but were salvaged from other buildings at Anuradhapura. The only hint of decoration is on the fallen capitals, carved with dwarfs, which lie scattered around the ground in the southeast corner of the palace. The entire palace is closed to visitors, although the modern brick pavilion surrounded by slender wooden pillars at the centre is popular with grey langur monkeys.

Ruvanvalisaya dagoba and around

North of the Brazen Palace stands the huge white **Ruvanvalisaya**, also known as the Maha Thupa, or "Great Stupa", though it's actually only the third largest in the city. Unlike the massive stupas at the Jetavana and Abhayagiri monasteries, the Ruvanvalisaya dagoba is fully restored, painted white and busy with pilgrims throughout the day. The dagoba was the crowning achievement of **Dutugemunu** (see p.324), built to commemorate his victory over Elara; it is popularly believed to enshrine various remains of the Buddha, and is thus the most revered in the city.

The dagoba now stands 55m high, rather less than its original height, with the entire base encircled by a strip of coloured ribbon almost 300m long. According to tradition, the dagoba's original shape was inspired by the form of a bubble – a perfect hemisphere – though the effects of subsequent renovations have flattened its outline slightly. It stands on a terrace whose outer face is decorated with life-sized elephant heads (most are modern replacements). Symbolically, the elephants support the platform on which the dagoba is built, just as, in Buddhist cosmology, they hold up the earth itself (at a more prosaic level, elephants also helped in the construction of the stupa, being used to stamp down the dagoba's foundations). Four subsidiary dagobas stand in each corner of the terrace – considerable structures in their own right, but completely dwarfed by the main stupa.

From the entrance, steps lead up to the huge terrace on which the dagoba stands. Four **vahalkadas** mark the cardinal points around the base of the dagoba: tall, rectangular structures decorated with bands of elephant heads and, above, friezes of lions, bulls and elephants carved in low relief – the one on the western side is the oldest and yet to be restored. Walking clockwise around the dagoba you immediately reach a modern **shrine** holding five standing Buddha statues. The four identical limestone figures date back to the eighth century and are thought to represent three previous Buddhas and the historical Buddha; the fifth (modern) statue is of the future Buddha, Maitreya, wearing a tiara and holding a lotus. Continuing clockwise brings you to an extremely eroded limestone **statue** in a small glass pavilion, facing the dagoba's south side and popularly believed to represent Dutugemunu contemplating his masterpiece.

A couple of hundred metres east of the Ruvanvalisaya is the **Kujjatissa Pabbata**, the remains of a small dagoba on a stone base with well-preserved guardstones. The structure dates from around the eighth century, but probably occupies the site of an earlier building – it's been suggested that this was the place, just outside what was once the south gate into the city, where Dutugemunu buried Elara and raised a memorial in his honour.

Thuparama and around

North of the Ruvanvalisaya, a broad walkway leads 300m to the **Thuparama**. This was the first dagoba to be built in Sri Lanka (its name means simply "The Stupa"), though by later Anuradhapuran standards it's a modest affair, standing less than 20m high. It

DUTUGEMUNU THE DISOBEDIENT

Of all the two hundred or so kings who have ruled Sri Lanka over the past millennia, none is as revered as the semi-legendary **Dutugemunu** (reigned 161–137 BC), the great warrior prince turned Buddhist king whose personality – a compelling mixture of religious piety and anti-Tamil nationalism – continues to provide inspiration for many Sinhalese today.

Dutugemunu grew up during the reign of the Tamil general **Elara**, who seized control of Anuradhapura in around 205 BC and reigned there for 44 years. Much of the island remained outside the control of Anuradhapura, however, being ruled by various minor kings and chiefs who enjoyed virtual autonomy, although they may have professed some kind of token loyalty to Elara. The most important of these subsidiary kings was **Kavan Tissa**, husband of the legendary Queen Viharamahadevi (see p.185). From his base in the city of Mahagama (modern Tissamaharama), Kavan Tissa gradually established control over the whole of the south. Despite his growing power, the naturally cautious Kavan Tissa demanded that his eldest son and heir, Gemunu, swear allegiance to Elara. On being asked to make this oath, the 12-year-old Gemunu threw his rice bowl from the table in a fury, saying he would prefer to starve rather than declare loyalty to a foreign overlord, and subsequently demonstrated his contempt for his father by sending him items of women's clothing – all of which unfilial behaviour earned him the name of Dutugemunu, or "Gemunu the Disobedient".

On the death of his father, Dutugemunu acceded to the throne. Having fought off an insurrection by his brother Saddhatissa (a clash marked by the great dagoba at Yudaganawa), Dutugemunu raised an army and set off to do battle armed with a spear with a Buddhist relic set into its shaft and accompanied by a large contingent of Buddhist monks, thus casting himself not only as a military leader, but also as the religious liberator of his island – the leader of a kind of Buddhist jihad. Dutugemunu's campaign was a laborious affair. For some fifteen years he fought his way north, conquering the succession of minor kingdoms which lay between Mahagama and Anuradhapura, until he was finally able to engage Elara himself at Anuradhapura. After various preliminary skirmishes, Elara and Dutugemunu faced one another in single combat, each mounted on their elephants. A mighty tussle ensued, at the end of which Dutugemunu succeeded in spearing Elara, who fell lifeless to the ground.

Dutugemunu buried Elara with full honours, decreeing that anyone passing the defeated general's tomb should dismount as a sign of respect – this decree was still apparently being obeyed in the early eighteenth century, some two thousand years later, though curiously enough, no one now knows where Elara's tomb is located. His conquest complete, the new king began an orgy of building works at Anuradhapura, including the mighty **Ruvanvalisaya** dagoba, which Dutugemunu himself did not live to see finished. He is supposed to have looked on the unfinished structure from his deathbed and said, "In times past…I engaged in battles; now, singlehanded, I commence my last conflict – with death, and it is not permitted to me to overcome my enemy."

As the leader who evicted the Tamils and united the island under Sinhalese rule for the first time, Dutugemunu is regarded as one of Sri Lanka's great heroes (at least by the Sinhalese). Despite his exploits, however, the fragile unity he left at his death quickly collapsed under subsequent, less able rulers, and within 35 years, northern Sri Lanka had once again fallen to invaders from South India.

was constructed by Devanampiya Tissa shortly after his conversion to Buddhism at the behest of Mahinda (see p.336), who suggested that the new Sinhalese faith be provided with a suitable focus for worship. A monk was despatched to Ashoka, the Buddhist emperor of India, who obligingly provided Devanampiya Tissa with two of his religion's most sacred relics: the Buddha's right collarbone and alms bowl. The bowl was sent to Mihintale (and subsequently disappeared), whilst the bone was enshrined in the Thuparama, which remains a popular pilgrimage site to this day.

By the seventh century, the original structure had fallen into ruins; Aggabodhi II had it restored and converted into a **vatadage** (circular relic house), a uniquely Sri Lankan form of Buddhist architecture, with the original dagoba being enclosed in a new roof, supported by four concentric circles of pillars of diminishing height – an excellent model in the Archeological Museum (see below) shows how it would all have looked. The roof has long since disappeared and the surviving pillars now topple unsteadily in all directions, though you can still make out the very eroded carvings of geese (*hamsas*, a protective bird) which adorn their capitals. The dagoba itself is actually a reconstruction of 1862, when it was restored in a conventional bell shape – the original structure was built in the slightly slope-shouldered "heap of paddy" form.

The area just south of the Thuparama is littered with the remains of buildings from the Mahavihara monastery, including numerous living units arranged in the quincunx pattern (like the five dots on the face of a die) which is characteristic of so many of the city's monastic dwellings. About 100m south of the Thuparama is a pillared shrine set on an imposing brick platform, with one of the most magnificent **moonstones** at Anuradhapura, though sadly it's protected – as are most of the city's best moonstones – by an ugly metal railing. The outer faces of the **balustrades** flanking the entrance steps are decorated with unusual carvings showing canopied panels filled with deer, hermits, monkeys, delicately sculpted trees and a pair of large lions. Their meaning remains unclear, though they may be intended to depict an ideal Buddhist realm in which creatures of all persuasions live harmoniously together.

The Archeological Museum
Daily 8.30am–4.30pm • Entrance only with site ticket

West of the Ruvanvalisaya dagoba lie a pair of museums, although they can't be reached directly from the dagoba; you have to follow the road which runs north of Ruvanvalisaya and west to Basawakkulama, and then turn south along the lakeside road. The **Archeological Museum** has numerous sculptures from Anuradhapura and beyond displayed in the rooms and garden of a creaking old colonial British administrative building, though it's looking increasingly denuded as exhibits are carted away to fill newer museums around the Cultural Triangle. Items on show include a number of simple standing and seated Buddhas plus an interesting cut-away model of the Thuparama (see p.323) along with a reconstruction of the relic chamber from a dagoba at Mihintale and (in the same room) colourful fragments of ancient murals recovered from inside the relic chamber of the great dagoba at Mahiyangana.

Outside, the museum's garden is home to further sculptures including assorted *nagarajas*, dwarfs, a selection of finely carved urinal stones and "squatting plates", and lots of pillar inscriptions recording grants of land and other administrative details.

Folk museum
Tues–Sat 9am–5pm • Rs.300

A little further down the same road as the Archeological Museum, west of the Ruvanvalisaya dagoba, the less interesting **Folk Museum** explores rural life in the North Central Province, with forgettable displays of cooking vessels, handicrafts and the like. Save your money.

Jetavana monastery

The last of the three great monasteries built in Anuradhapura, the **Jetavana monastery** was raised on the site of the Nandana Grove – or *Jotivana* – where Mahinda (see p.336) once preached, and where his body was later cremated. The monastery was founded during the reign of the great tank-building king, **Mahasena** (274–301), following one of the religious controversies that periodically convulsed the ancient city. Relations between Mahasena and the Mahavihara monastery had been strained ever since the king had disciplined some of its monks. They retaliated by refusing to accept alms from the king, who responded by pulling down some of the Mahavihara's buildings and then establishing the new Jetavana monastery on land owned by the Mahavihara. The king gave the monastery to a monk called Tissa – who was then promptly expelled from the Sangha for breaking the rule that individual monks should not own any private property. Despite this, the new monastery continued under a new leader, becoming an important rival source of Theravada doctrine within the city.

The Jetavana dagoba

The centrepiece of Jetavana is its monumental red-brick **dagoba**. Descriptions of this massive edifice tend to attract a string of statistical superlatives: in its original form the dagoba stood 120m high and was at the time of its construction the third tallest structure in the world, surpassed only by the two great pyramids at Giza in Egypt. It was also the world's biggest stupa and is still the tallest and largest structure made entirely of brick anywhere on earth, having taken a quarter of a century to build and containing more than ninety million bricks – enough, as the excitable Victorian archeologist Emerson Tennant calculated, to build a 3m-high wall from London to Edinburgh (though why anyone would wish to erect such a pointless construction at this exact height and between these two particular cities has never been satisfactorily explained). The dagoba has now lost its topmost portion, but still reaches a neck-wrenching height of 70m – similar to the Abhayagiri dagoba.

UNESCO-sponsored restoration began in 1981 and is slowly grinding towards completion, though there's plenty of rubble lying around, and sections on the north side remain to be excavated. All of the dagoba's four **vahalkadas** have now been restored, however, with gaps in the masonry filled by brick; the one facing the entrance on the southern side is particularly fine, studded with eroded elephant heads, with *naga* stones to either side and two figures to the right – the top is a *nagaraja*, the lower one an unidentified goddess.

The rest of the monastery

The area south of the dagoba is littered with the extensive remains of the **Jetavana monastery**, all carefully excavated and landscaped. The monastery would once have housed some three thousand monks, and the scale of the remains is impressive, although except in a few places only the bases of the various structures survive. The first monastery buildings were constructed in the area north of the dagoba (which remains largely unexcavated) and gradually spread south and east as the monastery expanded over the next six centuries – most of what you see today dates from the ninth and tenth centuries.

Immediately behind the Jetavana Museum (see p.328) lies a deep and beautifully preserved **bathing pool** and the unusual latticed **Buddhist Railing**, which formerly enclosed either a bo tree shrine or an image house; the three tiers of the fence are claimed to represent Buddhism's "three jewels" (see p.424). Slightly east of here stands the **Uposathagara** (chapter house), with dozens of roughly hewn and very closely spaced pillars; these probably supported upper storeys, since a room with this many pillars crowded into it would have been of little practical use.

To the west of the dagoba is the **Patimaghara** (image house), the largest surviving building at Jetavana: a tall, slender door leads between eight-metre-high walls into a narrow image chamber, at the end of which is a lotus base which once supported a standing Buddha. Below this is a latticed stone "**relic tray**" consisting of 25 holes in which relics or statues of various deities would have been placed; further examples are on show in the Jetavana Museum. Around the image house are more extensive remains of monastic residences – many are laid out in the characteristic quincunx (five-of-dice) pattern, with a large central building, in which the more senior monks

would have lived, surrounded by four smaller structures, the whole enclosed by a square brick wall.

Jetavana Museum

Daily 8.30am–5.30pm • Entrance with site ticket only

The interesting **Jetavana Museum** holds a striking collection of objects recovered during excavations around the monastery. The first of the three rooms contains fine fragments of decorative friezes and carvings from the site, including assorted Buddhas, a fine guardstone and an unusually large relic tray. The second room is the most absorbing, filled with an assortment of finely crafted personal items that give a rare glimpse into the secular life of Anuradhapura, with displays of necklaces, beads, bangles, ear ornaments and gold jewellery, as well as precious stones such as amethysts and garnets. Next door is a less engaging collection of pottery, though look out for the ingenious three-tiered urinal pot. A pavilion outside has more stone sculptures: friezes, elephants and guardstones.

The Citadel

The area north of the Thuparama, between the Mahavihara and Abhayagiri monasteries, is occupied by the **Citadel**, or royal palace area. This was the secular heart of the city, enclosed by a moat and thick walls, which perhaps reached a height of 5m.

Royal Palace

At the southern end of the complex lie the remains of the **Royal Palace**, one of the newest buildings in the Sacred Precinct, having been built by Vijayabahu I after his victory over the Cholas in 1070, although by this time power had shifted to Polonnaruwa and the palace here was no more than a secondary residence. Little now remains of it apart from the terrace on which it stood and a few bits of wall, although two fine **guardstones** survive, flanking the main steps up to the terrace and featuring a couple of unusually obese dwarfs (a similar pair guard the steps on the far side). A wall on the terrace, protected by a corrugated-iron shelter, bears a few splashes of paint, all that remains of the frescoes that once decorated the palace.

Mahapali Refectory

About 100m east of the Royal Palace, on the opposite side of the road, are the remains of the **Mahapali Refectory**, or **Royal Alms Hall**. The huge stone trough here would have been filled with rice for the monks by the city's lay followers and could have fed as many as five thousand – any monk could find food here, even during periods of famine. Next to the refectory is an impressively deep stepped **well**.

YASALALAKATISSA AND SUBHA

The kings of ancient Anuradhapura set great store by their shows of piety and beneficence – though in reality they often fell somewhat short of the ideals that they claimed to embody. The true murkiness of the Anuradhapuran royal character is famously encapsulated by the story of **King Yasalalakatissa** (reigned 52–60), who had seized the throne by murdering his brother. Yasalalakatissa had a weakness for practical jokes. Upon discovering an uncanny resemblance between himself and a palace gatekeeper called **Subha**, he swapped clothes with Subha in order to enjoy the spectacle of the island's nobles paying homage to a lowly servant. So greatly did this amuse Yasalalakatissa that he had the prank repeated several times, until one day Subha, playing the role of king, ordered the execution of his "gatekeeper" for impertinence. Yasalalakatissa's claims to be the real king were met with disbelief, and he was promptly murdered. It says something about the debased standards of the Anuradhapuran monarchy that even when Subha's deception was unmasked, he was allowed to rule for a further six years before being assassinated in turn.

Temple of the Tooth

Immediately north of the Mahapali Refectory are the remains of a building studded with a cluster of columns reaching up to 4m high; this is thought to be the very first **Temple of the Tooth**, constructed to house the Tooth Relic (see p.212) when it was originally brought to the island in 313. The columns may have supported a second storey, and it's been suggested that the Tooth Relic was kept on the upper floor, thus setting the pattern for all the shrines that subsequently housed it. The Tooth Relic was taken annually in procession from here to the Abhayagiri in a ceremony which was the ancestor of today's great Esala Perahera at Kandy. Just east of here are the partially reconstructed remains, reaching up to 8m high, of a brick **gedige**, with several original stone doorways and some of its window frames intact.

Abhayagiri monastery

The third of Anuradhapura's great monasteries, **Abhayagiri** lies on the northern side of the city, and was founded by King Vattagamini Abhaya (89–77 BC), the creator of the Dambulla cave temples (see p.290), in 88 BC. According to the *Mahavamsa*, Vattagamini had earlier lost his throne to a group of invading Tamils, but subsequently returned with an army and drove them out. Upon returning to Anuradhapura he quickly established a new Buddhist monastery in the place of the existing one, naming it after the second part of his own name (meaning "fearless" – as in the *abhaya*, or "Have No Fear", Buddhist *mudra*).

Abhayagiri rapidly surpassed the older Mahavihara as the largest and most influential monastery in the country. By the fifth century it was home to five thousand monks and had become an important source of new Buddhist doctrine, and a flourishing centre of artistic activity and philosophical speculation. Although it remained within the Theravada tradition, elements of Mahayana and Tantric Buddhism were taught here (much to the disgust of the ultra-conservative clergy of the Mahavihara, who labelled the monks of Abhayagiri heretics), and the monastery established wide-ranging contacts with India, China, Burma and even Java.

Abhayagiri is in many ways the most interesting and atmospheric quarter of the city. One of the great pleasures here is simply in throwing away the guidebook and wandering off at random amongst the innumerable ruins that litter the area – getting lost is half the fun. The sheer scale of the monastic remains is prodigious, while their setting, scattered amid beautiful light woodland, is magical – and particularly memorable early in the morning or at dusk.

Abhayagiri Museum and around

Daily 7.30am–4.30pm • Entrance with site ticket only

At the centre of the complex, the small but informative **Abhayagiri Museum** gives a detailed account of the monastery's history backed by a small but interesting selection of well-preserved artefacts recovered here. These include a fine (though armless) Buddha and an unusually large *nagaraja*, both very eroded, along with assorted coins, jewellery and other artefacts. Further stone sculptures are displayed on the veranda outside, including an impressive collection of guardstones and urinal stones.

Just south of here on the main road are the remains of the first-century BC **Lankarama** vatadage, thought to have originally formed part of the Abhayagiri nunnery. The vatadage's unusually square central dagoba has been thoroughly rebuilt in modern times, though many of the original pillars which formerly supported the vatadage's wooden roof have survived around it, some retaining their finely carved capitals.

Abhayagiri dagoba

As at Mahavihara and Jetavana, Abhayagiri's most striking feature is its great **dagoba**, said to mark the spot where the Buddha left a footprint on one of his three visits to

THE RESTORATION OF ANURADHAPURA

Following the collapse of the great northern Sinhalese civilization, Anuradhapura was reclaimed by the jungle, and largely forgotten by the outside world, except by the communities of reclusive monks and guardians of the sacred bo tree who continued to live here. The British "rediscovered" the city in the nineteenth century, making it a provincial capital in 1833, after which Anuradhapura slowly began to rise from the ashes. Since the 1950s, the considerable Anuradhapura New Town has sprung up to the east of the Sacred Precinct, while in 1980 a huge UNESCO programme began with the goal of effecting a complete **restoration** of the ancient city. The programme continues to this day, and has assumed enormous national significance for the Buddhist Sinhalese, who see the reclamation of Anuradhapura's great dagobas and other monuments from the jungle after over a millennium as a powerful symbol of national identity and resurgence.

Sri Lanka, standing with one foot here and the other on top of Adam's Peak. The dagoba was originally built by Vattagamini Abhaya and enlarged during the reign of Gajabahu I (114–136); it formerly stood around 115m tall, only slightly smaller than the Jetavana dagoba, making it the second tallest in the ancient world – though the loss of its pinnacle has now reduced its height to around 70m. Ongoing restoration of the dagoba continues apace, with the entire structure currently encased in an enormous cage of scaffolding.

Flanking the main entrance stand two guardian statues of **Padmanidhi** and **Samkanidhi**, two fat and dwarfish attendants of Kubera, the god of wealth. The statues have become objects of devotion in their own right, with pilgrims tying prayer ribbons to the grilles of the ugly little concrete sheds in which they are ignominiously confined. At the top of the steps stand a pair of the incongruously Grecian-looking urns, symbolizing prosperity, which can be found at several points around the monastery, while just beyond is a modern temple with a large reclining Buddha.

The dagoba's four **vahalkadas** are similar in design to those at the Ruvanvalisaya. Most interesting is the eastern *vahalkada*, flanked by unusual low-relief carvings showing Classical-looking elephants, bulls and lions, all jumping up on their hind legs, plus two winged figures looking like a pair of angels who've flown straight out of the Italian Renaissance.

The Samadhi Buddha

Around 250m east of the dagoba lies the so-called **Samadhi Buddha**, one of Anuradhapura's most celebrated images. A classic early example of Sinhalese sculpture, the figure was carved from limestone in the fourth century AD and shows the Buddha in the meditation (*samadhi*) posture – though the artistry of the figure is somewhat compromised by the ugly modern concrete shelter in which it's now enclosed. The Buddha was originally one of a group of four statues (the base and seated legs of another figure can be seen opposite it); it's thought that all four were originally painted, and sported gems for eyes.

Kuttam Pokuna

Northeast of the Buddha lie the superbly preserved **Kuttam Pokuna** ("Twin Baths"), constructed in the eighth century for monks' ritual ablutions, with stepped sides leading down into the baths. One of the two is significantly bigger than the other. Standing at the far end of the smaller pond and looking to your right you can see a small stone pool at ground level. Water would have been fed into this and the sediment left to settle, after which the cleaned water would have been released into the smaller bath through the conduit with the eroded lion's head on one side. The superb *naga* (snake) stone next to this conduit was a symbol of good fortune, while the urns at the top of the stairs down into the bath symbolize plenty. Water passed from the smaller to the larger bath through small holes that connect the two.

West to Et Pokuna

The area **west of the Abhayagiri dagoba** is particularly rich in small monuments, while copious new signs help make some sense of the bewildering profusion of remains that litter the forest hereabouts. West of the dagoba, a side road (signed "Elephant Pool and Refectory") leads past a second *samadhi* Buddha statue (similar to but less finely carved than the main Samadhi Buddha, and now missing its arms) to reach the Abhayagiri's **refectory**, complete with the usual huge stone trough – more than big enough to hold food for the monastery's five thousand-odd monks.

A short distance further along stands the so-called **Burrows Pavilion**, a neat little stone structure named in honour of S. M. Burrows (archeological surveyor of Sri Lanka from 1884 to 1886 and author of the *Buried Cities of Ceylon*), a leading figure in the nineteenth-century "discovery" of Anuradhapura. Nearby stand two impressive tenth-century pillar **inscriptions** recording various monastic rules and administrative details. The pavilion forms a kind of entrance to an extensive bo tree enclosure, signed **Bodhi Tree Shrine III**. The original tree has vanished but the enclosing walls and a cluster of stone-slab seats survive largely intact along with another *samadhi* Budda, numerous *sri pada* carvings and a stone floor studded with lotus-shaped pillar bases.

From here it's a short walk south to the colossal **Et Pokuna** ("Elephant Pool"). Dug out of the bedrock, this is the largest bathing pool in the ancient city and quite big enough to hold a whole herd of elephants, should the need arise.

Ratna Prasada

Northeast of the Burrows Pavilion rise the slender pillars of the ruined **Ratna Prasada** ("Gem Palace"; signed as "Guardstone"), built in the eighth century to serve as the main chapter house of the Abhayagiri monastery, and originally standing five storeys tall.

The main attraction here is the magnificent **guardstone** by the building's entrance showing the usual *nagaraja* standing on a dwarf, shaded by a seven-headed cobra and carrying various symbols of prosperity: lotus flowers, a flowering branch and an urn. The **arch** that frames this figure shows an extraordinary chain of joined images, with four *makaras* swallowing two tiny human couples and two equally microscopic lions, separated by four flying dwarfs; an unimpressed elephant stands to one side. Not surprisingly, the symbolism of this strange piece of sculpture remains obscure.

Mahasen's Palace and around

A short distance north of Ratna Prasada, on the other side of the main track through this part of the monastery, lies **Mahasen's Palace** (signed as "Moonstone I"), though it's not actually a royal residence at all, but an image house dating from the eighth or ninth century. It's famous principally for its delicately carved **moonstone**, sadly enclosed within a metal railing. Behind this rises a flight of finely carved steps supported by the inevitable dwarfs, squatting like tiny sumo wrestlers.

About 100m west of here is another magnificent (and unfenced) **moonstone** (signed as "Moonstone II"), almost the equal of the one at Mahasen's Palace, and with further portly dwarves supporting the steps behind.

Dighapashana Cave

Northeast of Moonstone II lies the recently excavated **Dighapashana Cave** (signed "Sudassana Padhanaghara"), comprising the remains of a rudimentary brick structure nestled beneath a giant boulder. On the right-hand side of the cave, steps lead up to a long Pali inscription, carved into the rock, although the site is currently fenced off, so it's difficult to see much.

The southern city

If you have the energy after seeing the rest of the site, make for the cluster of interesting remains that lie west and south of the Sri Maha Bodhi along the banks of the **Tissa Wewa**.

Mirisavatiya dagoba

Around 1km west of the Sri Maha Bodhi lies the **Mirisavatiya dagoba**, a huge structure that was the first thing to be built by Dutugemunu after he captured the city, very similar to – and only slightly smaller than – the Ruvanvalisaya dagoba. The obligatory legend recounts how the new king went to bathe in the nearby Tissa Wewa, leaving his famous spear (in which was enshrined a Buddhist relic) stuck in the ground by the side of the tank. Having finished bathing, he discovered that he was unable to pull his spear out of the ground – an unmistakable message from the heavens. At the dagoba's consecration, Dutugemunu dedicated the monument to the Sangha, offering it in compensation, the great king declared, for his once having eaten a bowl of chillies without offering any to the city's monks, a small incident which says much about both the island's culinary and religious traditions.

The dagoba was completely rebuilt by Kassapa V in the tenth century and is surrounded by various largely unexcavated monastic ruins. Northeast of the dagoba you may be able to find the remains of a monks' **refectory**, furnished with the usual enormous stone rice troughs.

Goldfish Park

South of Mirisavatiya dagoba, on the banks of the Tissa Wewa, lie the royal pleasure gardens, known as the **Goldfish Park** after the fish that were kept in the two **pools** here. The pools were created in the sixth century and used water channelled from the adjacent Tissa Wewa; the northern one has low-relief carvings of bathing elephants very similar to those at the nearby Isurumuniya temple, cleverly squeezed into the space between the pool and the adjacent rock outcrop.

Isurumuniya Vihara

Daily 7.30am–6pm • Rs.250

Continuing south of Goldfish Park for 500m brings you to the **Isurumuniya Vihara**. This venerable rock temple dates right back to the reign of Devanampiya Tissa, and though it's a bit of a hotchpotch architecturally, it's worth a visit for its interesting stone **carvings**.

The main shrine and around

The steps leading up to the **main shrine** are embellished with the usual fine, though eroded, guardstones and moonstone, while to the right, just above the water line of the adjacent pool, are low-relief carvings of elephants in the rock, designed so that they appear to be bathing in the waters. To the right of the shrine door is an unusual carving showing a man with a horse looking over his shoulder, while inside the shrine a gold Buddha sits in a niche carved directly into the rock, framed by a finely carved and brightly painted *makara* arch.

To the left of the main shrine is a modern shrine with an ugly reclining Buddha and a small **cave** inhabited by an extraordinary number of bats.

The Isurumuniya Vihara museum

Daily 8am–6pm

The temple's **museum** is home to a number of its most famous carvings, all rather Indian in style. Perhaps the most famous is the fifth-century sculpture known as **The Lovers**, probably representing either a bodhisattva and his consort or a pair of Hindu deities, though the figures are popularly thought to represent Prince Saliya, the son of Dutugemunu, and Asokamala, the low-caste girl he fell in love with and married, thereby giving up his right to the throne. Another carving (labelled "King's Family") depicts a palace scene showing five figures, said to include Saliya, Asokamala and Dutugemunu.

The viewing platforms

Next to the temple museum steps lead up to the rock above the temple, passing two beautiful *sri padas* on the way up; very steep rock-cut steps go up to one of two **platforms** at the top. Climb the steps up to the top of the temple for a sweeping **view** east over the forest to the Jetavana dagoba, and west over Tissa Wewa, best at sunset.

Vessagiriya Monastery

South of Isurumuniya Vihara lie the large, scattered rock outcrops that formed the core of the **Vessagiriya Monastery**, once home to five hundred monks. The monastery was first established in the third century BC by King Tissa, but it was the infamous Kassapa of Sigiriya (see p.298) who rebuilt and expanded it, constructing an extensive monastery here, though most of the stone was later carted off for use elsewhere. It's a picturesque spot, with huge boulders and rock outcrops offering views out over the Sacred Precinct from the top, though there's not much to see apart from a few rock-cut steps, the stumps of pillars and occasional fragments of carved stone. An intriguing archeological footnote is provided (if you can find them) by the extremely ancient **inscriptions** written in a proto-Brahmi script similar to that found at the Kantaka Chetiya in Mihintale (it looks rather like cuneiform) – they're on the road-facing side of a few of the rocks.

4

ARRIVAL AND DEPARTURE
ANURADHAPURA

By bus There are two bus stations in Anuradhapura: the New Bus Station, at the southern end of Main St is where most services arrive and depart, while the Old Bus Station, off the northern end of Main St, is the terminus for express buses from Kandy via Dambulla and from Colombo via Kurunegala (although many buses call at both stations). When leaving, check at your guesthouse to make sure you're going to the right bus station. For Sigiriya, take a Kandy bus to Dambulla and pick up a Sigiriya bus from there.

Destinations Colombo (every 30min; 5hr); Dambulla (every 30min; 2hr); Habarana (every 45min; 2hr 30min); Jaffna (every 2hr; 5hr); Kandy (every 30min; 3hr 30min); Kurunegala (every 20min; 3hr); Polonnaruwa (hourly until 3.45pm; 3hr 30min); Trincomalee (2 daily; 4hr); Vavuniya (every 30min; 3hr).

By train The principal train station is on Main St just north of the centre of the New Town, a short tuktuk ride from the Harischandra Mawatha guesthouses. The subsidiary Anuradhapura New Town Station lies at the southern end of Main Street, though not all services stop here.

Destinations Colombo (6 daily; 3hr 15min–6hr); Kurunegala (7 daily; 2–3hr); Vavuniya (6 daily; 1hr).

GETTING AROUND

By bike The Sacred Precinct is much too big to cover on foot, and it's far easier to explore by bicycle; these can be hired from virtually all the town's guesthouses for Rs.200–300/day, though note that bikes (and indeed any other type of vehicle) aren't allowed anywhere near the Sri Maha Bodhi.

INFORMATION

Sacred Precinct tickets Most (but not all) of the sites at Anuradhapura are covered by a single ticket ($25), which can be bought at the Jetavana, Abhayagiri and Archeological museums, and at the ticket office at the northern entrance to the Jetavana dagoba. At the time of writing it was possible to use the ticket for up to three consecutive days (although this might change); make it clear when you buy the ticket if you want to use it for more than one day and it will be stamped with the relevant endorsement. Most visitors in any case tend to cram it all into a day, although this isn't really long enough to get the full flavour of the place. The site is actually open access and ticket checks are rare except at the museums and the Samadhi Buddha. The Isurumuniya and Folk Museum aren't covered by the main ticket, while you may also be asked for a donation when visiting the Sri Maha Bodhi.

Guides Guides hang out mainly at the Jetavana Museum (see p.328). If you go with a guide, you might like to check their accreditation (they should be in possession of a

Sri Lanka Tourism site guide's licence for Anuradhapura) to make sure you're getting someone genuine. Expect to pay around $15 for half a day, though you may be able to bargain.

Festivals The ancient city is crowded with pilgrims at weekends and, especially, on poya days, and is also the focus of several festivals. The largest, held on Poson poya

day (June), commemorates the introduction of Buddhism to Sri Lanka with enormous processions.

Tours Anuradhapura also makes a convenient base for a trip to Wilpattu National Park (see p.111); tours can be arranged through some of the local guesthouses, including *Milano Tourist Rest* and *Shalini*, for around $80.

ACCOMMODATION

Anuradhapura has a good spread of budget accommodation, plus a few mid-range places, though a relative paucity of upper-range options. Most places are located in the residential enclave east of the New Town on or near **Harischandra Mawatha**; those on Harischandra Mawatha itself aren't as peaceful as those closer to the lake.

Hotel Ashok Off Harischandra Mawatha, near Nuwara Wewa ☎025 222 2753, ⓦashokhotel.lk. Functional-looking place, totally lacking in atmosphere, but offering decent accommodation at a reasonable price, with a selection of pleasantly old-fashioned, well-maintained rooms (optional a/c Rs.880), some with lake views. **Rs.3300**; a/c **Rs.4180**

Boa Vista 142 Old Puttalam Rd ☎025 223 5052, ⓦsrilankaboavista.com. Large guesthouse-cum-hotel in a superb position in the heart of the Sacred Precinct. The upstairs a/c rooms are spacious and come with fine lake views, TV and hot water (although not much furniture); the much more basic non-a/c rooms in the basement are grubby and overpriced. There's an in-house restaurant (no alcohol served) plus pricey internet access and wi-fi. **Rs.2000**; a/c **Rs.4000**

Galway Miridiya Lodge Wasaladantha Mawatha ☎025 222 2112, ⓦgalway.lk. The poshest New Town option, comprising a plain and rather dated resort-style hotel arranged around attractive gardens running down to Nuwara Wewa. Rooms (all with a/c; some with TV) are bright and cheery, and there's a good-sized pool (non-guests Rs.400). **$65**

Grand Tourist Holiday Resort Mihindu Mawatha ☎025 223 5173, ⓔthegranddami@yahoo.com. Despite the overblown name, this is a modest hotel in an attractive location overlooking Nuwara Wewa, with views of Mihintale in the distance. The huge, high-ceilinged rooms in the main house (with a/c and hot water) have a certain amount of (slightly threadbare) period atmosphere; cheaper rooms in the adjacent annexe are more modern but rather stuffy. There's also a nice terrace restaurant, though the food is nothing special. **Rs.2650**; a/c **Rs.3300**

Lake View Tourist Guest House Mihindu Mawatha ☎025 222 1593. Modern house in a peaceful location near Nuwara Wewa with a range of fan and a/c rooms – some with hot water) of varying standards and prices – all good value, if slightly uninspiring. **Rs.1100**; a/c **Rs.2300**

Lake Wave Guest House Off Harischandra Mawatha, near Nuwara Wewa ☎077 5627 669, ⓔupalikalu bowila@yahoo.com. Right on the edge of Nuwara Wewa, this low-key guesthouse has five rooms of varying

standards (more expensive ones with a/c and hot water) in a peaceful waterside location. The owner is also opening a second lakeside guesthouse south of the new bus station with bright modern rooms in a similarly peaceful setting. **Rs.1500**; a/c **Rs.2200**

Lee's Chinese Guest House Off Harischandra Mawatha ☎025 223 5476. Three large and well looked after modern rooms with particularly good single rates (Rs.1000) and a passable Chinese restaurant (bring your own booze) attached. **Rs.2000**

★ **Milano Tourist Rest** J.R. Jaya Mawatha ☎025 222 2364, ⓦmilanotouristrest.com. The new town's standout accommodation option, with a big selection of bright, modern and attractively furnished rooms spread across two buildings (all with hot water, satellite TV and optional a/c) at very competitive rates. There's also a good restaurant (see opposite), free pick-up from the bus/train stations, plus bike hire, internet access and free wi-fi. **Rs.2000**; a/c **Rs.2800**

★ **Palm Garden Village Hotel** Puttalam Rd, Pandulagama, 6km west of town ☎025 222 3961, ⓦpalmgardenvillage.com. Anuradhapura's only upmarket option, occupying a scatter of elegant colonial-style buildings set within extensive and idyllic tree-studded gardens. Accommodation is in a range of attractively furnished rooms (or fancier suites) kitted out with teak and mahogany furnishings, and there's also good food, an attractive bar, huge pool and Ayurveda and spa centre. **$138**

Randiya Muditha Mawatha, off Harischandra Mawatha ☎025 222 2868, ⓦhotelrandiya.com. Small, well-run hotel with old-fashioned but cosy standard rooms and larger and fancier superior rooms (all with a/c and satellite TV), although the whole place feels a bit institutional, and rates aren't the best value in town. Bike hire and internet access also available. **Rs.5200**

Hotel Shalini 41/388 Harischandra Mawatha ☎025 222 2425, ⓦhotelshalini.lk. Well-run, slightly upmarket guesthouse with a big selection of comfortable, if rather expensive, rooms (a/c Rs.500 extra), all with hot water and satellite TV (get one away from the road). There's also a nice in-house restaurant, internet access, bike hire and free pick up/drop-off from bus or train stations. **Rs.3500**; a/c **Rs.4000**

★ **Tissawewa Grand** Sacred Precinct, near the Mirisavatiya dagoba ⓣ025 222 2299, ⓦquickshaws.com. Anuradhapura's most memorable place to stay, this famous old rest house is set in a rambling and gorgeously atmospheric nineteenth-century mansion (built for a former British governor) in the heart of the Sacred Precinct. The attractively refurbished ground-floor a/c rooms combine comfort and character; the less appealing unrenovated rooms upstairs retain their original colonial atmosphere but are beginning to look decidedly shabby. Rates are steep and service haphazard, but for location and atmosphere it can't be beaten. $50; a/c $93

EATING

As usual, all the hotels and guesthouses have restaurants, though few of them offer particularly memorable food. One speciality is **lake fish** from the local tanks – these rather undernourished creatures are fresh but decidedly bony, and are best when fried.

Casserole Main St. This cavernous modern restaurant has all the atmosphere of a large cupboard but makes a change from yet more rice and curry, with a big menu of Chinese meat, fish and veg standards spiced up for its Sri Lankan clientele – far from authentic, but surprisingly tasty. Mains mostly Rs.300–400. Unlicensed. Daily 11am–10pm.

Milano Tourist Rest J.R. Jaya Mawatha ⓣ025 222 2364, ⓦmilanotouristrest.com. The restaurant at this excellent hotel (see opposite) is one of the best in town, with exceptionally friendly and professional service and a usually convivial atmosphere. The menu covers all bases, from rice and curry through to seafood and assorted Chinese and Continental dishes – prices are slightly above average (most mains Rs.550–750) but generally worth it. Daily 6am–11.30pm.

Tissawewa Grand Sacred Precinct. A lovely old colonial hotel (see above) with a splendid terrace that makes an excellent lunch stop while exploring the Sacred Precinct, serving up assorted salads, sandwiches and soups (Rs.250–400) plus more substantial Sri Lankan mains (Rs.400–600). No alcohol is served, due to the restaurant's location in the Sacred Precinct. Daily 11.30am–2pm & 7.30–9pm.

DIRECTORY

Banks There are branches of all the major banks strung out along Main Street, most with ATMs accepting foreign cards.

Internet *Milano* or *Shalini* guesthouses are your best bet, and there's also wi-fi in the *Milano* restaurant (see above).

4

Tantirimalai

50km northwest of Anuradhapura • Open access 24hr • Free (although there are rumours of an entrance charge being introduced) • The most direct approach is from Anuradhapura (car and driver will cost around $50–60, perhaps more), heading northwest along the back road to the village of Nikawewa and then north along an unsurfaced track to Tantirimalai; an alternative approach is from A14 to Mannar, where a track (also unsurfaced) leads to the site from around 5km west of Neriyakulam on the main road

On the border of Wilpattu National Park some 50km northwest of Anuradhapura, **Tantirimalai** (or Tantirimale) is one of the Cultural Triangle's most remote and least-visited destinations – which for many is a major part of its appeal. The ruins here, of the original Tantirimalai Rajamaha Vihara (royal temple), are said to date back to the third century BC, marking one of the places at which Princess Sangamitta (see p.321) rested while travelling to Anuradhapura to deliver a cutting from the legendary bo tree under which the Buddha gained enlightenment to the newly converted Devanampiya Tissa.

The ruins are widely scattered over a strikingly lunar landscape of bare, undulating rock, dotted with the occasional stunted tree. A modern dagoba marks the highest point of the site, while the nearby bo tree is said to have been grown from a cutting from the original cutting brought to the island by Sangamitta. Below this, a striking image of a meditating Buddha has been cut out of the side of a rock outcrop while on the northern side of the dagoba is an even larger reclining Buddha, again chiselled painstakingly from solid rock. Numerous other monastic ruins can be found dotted around the site, including the remains of the former monastic library, built into a cave, and a bathing pond that is said never to run dry.

You'll need the best part of a day to reach and fully explore the site.

Mihintale

MIHINTALE, 12km east of Anuradhapura, is famous as the place where Buddhism was introduced to Sri Lanka. In 247 BC (the story goes) the Sinhalese king of Anuradhapura, **Devanampiya Tissa** (reigned 250–210 BC), was hunting in the hills of Mihintale. Pursuing a stag to the top of a hill, he found himself confronted by **Mahinda**, the son (or possibly brother) of the great Buddhist emperor of India, Ashoka, who had been despatched to convert the people of Sri Lanka to his chosen faith. Wishing first to test the king's intelligence to judge his fitness to receive the Buddha's teaching, Mahinda proposed his celebrated **riddle of the mangoes**:

"What name does this tree bear, O king?"
"This tree is called a mango."
"Is there yet another mango besides this?"
"There are many mango-trees."
"And are there yet other trees besides this mango and the other mangoes?"
"There are many trees, sir; but those are trees that are not mangoes."
"And are there, beside the other mangoes and those trees which are not mangoes, yet other trees?"
"There is this mango-tree, sir."

Having established the king's shrewdness by means of this laborious display of arboreal logic, Mahinda proceeded to expound the Buddha's teachings, promptly converting (according to the *Mahavamsa*) the king and his entire entourage of forty thousand attendants. The grateful king gave Mahinda and his followers a royal park in Anuradhapura, which became the core of the Mahavihara (see p.321), while Mihintale (the name is a contraction of *Mahinda tale*, or "Mahinda's hill") also developed into an important Buddhist centre. Although modern Mihintale is little more than a large village, it remains an important pilgrimage site, especially during **Poson Poya** (June), which commemorates the introduction of Buddhism to

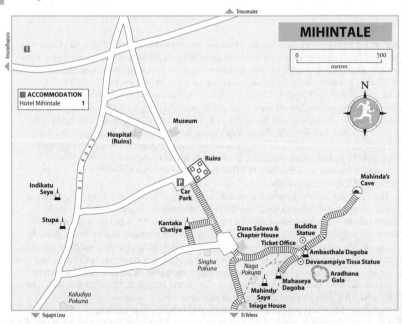

Sri Lanka by Mahinda, during which thousands of white-robed pilgrims descend on the place.

The ruins and dagobas at Mihintale are relatively ordinary compared to those at Anuradhapura, but the setting – with rocky hills linked by beautiful old flights of stone steps shaded by frangipani trees – is gorgeous. Mihintale can be tiring, however: there are **1850 steps**, and if you want to see all the sights you'll have to climb almost every single one of them (although you can avoid the first flight by driving up the Old Road to the Dana Salawa level). It's a good idea to visit in the early morning or late afternoon to avoid having to tackle the steps in the heat of the day.

The site

Open 24hr (no photography) • Rs.500

At the bottom of the site, near the car park, lie the remains of a **hospital**, including fragments of treatment rooms and a large stone bath in which patients would have been washed in healing oils and herbs. Most of the island's larger religious complexes had similar infirmaries, where doctors used a highly developed system of Ayurvedic medicines and treatments that were perhaps not so far from those used in today's hotels and clinics. On the other side of the road stand the remains of a monastic structure, its buildings arranged in a characteristically Anuradhapuran quincunx pattern.

Just north of the hospital is the site **museum**, currently closed for renovations.

The Kantaka Chetiya

The broad first flight of steps heads up directly from the car park. At the first small terrace, steep steps lead off on the right to the remains of the **Kantaka Chetiya** dagoba. Not much remains of the body of this dagoba, which originally stood over 30m high, but the four Anuradhapura-style *vahalkadas*, decorated with elephants, dwarves and other creatures, are extremely well preserved.

Just south of the dagoba, on a huge boulder perched precariously on its side, is an unusual inscription in a very early, proto-Brahmi script, similar to that found in inscriptions at the Vessagiriya monastery in Anuradhapura.

The Medamaluwa monastery

Returning to the main steps from the Kantaka Chetiya and continuing up brings you to a large terrace and the remains of the **Medamaluwa** monastery, the most important at Mihintale. The first building on your left is the **Dana Salawa** ("Alms Hall"), home to an enormous stone trough (plus a somewhat smaller one next to it at a right angle) that would have been filled with food for the monastery's monks by lay followers.

The terrace immediately above, built on enormous slabs of stone, was the site of the former **chapter house**, its doorway flanked with two large stone **tablets** in Sinhala. Erected during the tenth century, these stelae lay down the rules and responsibilities pertaining to the various monks and lay staff at the monastery – a kind of medieval Sinhalese job description. The brick bases of vanished dagobas lie all around, along with the remains of further monastic buildings, including the **Conversation Hall**, which preserves a few of its original 64 pillars.

On the opposite side of the terrace, near the top of Old Road, is the small **Singha Pokuna** ("Lion Pool"), named after the unusual, though very eroded, sculpture of a lion rampant, through whose mouth water was fed into a now vanished pool. The small frieze above is decorated with a well-preserved strip of carvings showing lions and dancers.

The upper terrace

To the right of the Conversation Hall, a long flight of steps leads up to the heart of Mihintale, located (it's claimed) at the very spot at which Devanampiya Tissa met

Mahinda. You have to buy a **ticket** at the top of the stairs before entering the terrace, and hand over your shoes to an attendant (who will expect a small tip).

At the centre of the terrace is the **Ambasthala dagoba**, a surprisingly small and simple structure for such an important site – the name means "Mango Tree Dagoba", referring to Mahinda's convoluted conundrum. The dagoba was subsequently roofed over, vatadage-style, as testified by the two rows of pillars around it. Immediately next to it is a single simple **sri pada** surrounded by two sets of gold and silver railings; people throw coins in here for luck. Nearby is an extremely ancient **statue**, claimed to be of Devanampiya Tissa, though it might just be of a bodhisattva. Its arms have long since vanished, while its head has fallen off and now sits Yorick-like on a brick plinth in front. According to tradition, the Ambasthala dagoba covers the spot where Mahinda stood during the famous meeting, while the statue marks the position of Devanampiya Tissa, though given how far apart they are, this seems unlikely, unless their conversation – and the mango riddle – was conducted as a kind of shouting match.

Aradhana Gala

Various pathways lead from the upper terrace to a number of further sights. Close to the ancient statue, irregular rock-cut steps lead very steeply up the bare rock outcrop of **Aradhana Gala** ("Invitation Rock"), from which Mahinda preached his first sermon. On the other side, a shorter flight of steps lead up to a large, modern white **seated Buddha**, posed in an unusual composite posture: the left hand is in the meditation posture, while the right is in the "explanation" (*vitarka*) pose.

Mahinda's Cave

A long path from the upper terrace leads to **Mahinda's Cave** (Mahindu Guhawa), a bit of a hike down a rough woodland path (particularly challenging without shoes). The "cave" is actually an opening beneath a huge boulder poised precariously on the edge of the hillside at the edge of a large drop. On the floor is a simple rectangular outline cut out of the rock, popularly believed to be Mahinda's bed.

Mahaseya dagoba

Once you've seen all the sights around the upper terrace, collect your shoes (but don't put them on) and head up one final set of steps to the white **Mahaseya dagoba**, claimed to enshrine some ashes and a single hair of the Buddha. The dagoba (which can be seen quite clearly all the way from Anuradhapura) is the largest and the second highest at Mihintale, in a breezy hilltop location and with wonderful 360-degree views over the surrounding countryside – you can usually just make out the great dagobas of Anuradhapura in the distance. Immediately next to it are the substantial remains of the lower portion of a large brick dagoba, the **Mahindu Saya**, which is thought to enshrine relics associated with Mahinda.

Et Vehera

If you walk past the Mahindu Saya (you can put your shoes on now) down a path cut into the rock, you will come to the ruins of an **image house** atop the usual stone base with flights of stairs and remains of pillars. From here, a tough ten-minute slog up steep steps (and lots of them) leads to **Et Vehera**, located at what is easily the highest point at Mihintale. There's nothing much to see apart from the remains of a small brick dagoba – despite the great sense of altitude, the views aren't really any better than those from the Mahaseya dagoba.

Naga Pokuna

From Et Vehera you can retrace your steps to the image house and head back downhill via the **Naga Pokuna**, or "Snake Pool", a rock-cut pool guarded by a carving of a five-headed cobra (though it's sometimes submerged by water). Romantic legends associate this with the queen of Devanampiya Tissa, though the prosaic truth is that it was simply part of the monastery's water-supply system.

Outlying remains

West of the main site on the Old Road are the remains of another monastery and two dagobas, the larger known as **Indikatu Seya**. South of here lies the hill of **Rajagiri Lena**. Brahmi inscriptions found here suggest that the caves on the hillside might have been home to Sri Lanka's first-ever Buddhist monks. The tranquil **Kaludiya Pokuna** pool nearby looks natural but is actually man-made. Beside it are the remains of a small tenth-century monastery, including a well-preserved cave-building with windows and a door – either a bathhouse or a monk's dwelling.

ARRIVAL AND DEPARTURE   **MIHINTALE**

By tuktuk A tuktuk to Mihintale from Anuradhapura costs around Rs.2000 return including waiting time.

By bus Buses leave for Mihintale from Anuradhapura's New Bus Station roughly every 15min.

ACCOMMODATION

Hotel Mihintale Trincomalee Rd ☎025 226 6599, ⓦceylonhotels.lk. Attractive, good-value hotel, arranged around a lovely colonial-style colonnaded courtyard and with spacious modern rooms (all with a/c and hot water). <u>Rs.3080</u>

4

The east

345 Trincomalee

349 North of Trincomalee

353 South of Trincomalee

361 Arugam Bay and around

367 Monaragala and around

KALI TEMPLE, TRINCOMALEE

5

The east

Sri Lanka's east coast is a mirror image of its west. When it's monsoon season in the west, the sun is shining in the east; where the west coast is predominantly Sinhalese, the east is largely Tamil and Muslim; and where parts of the west coast are crowded with tourists and almost buried under a surfeit of hotels, the east remains largely untouched and tourist-free – for the time being, at any rate.

Much of the east's beautifully pristine coastal scenery derives, ironically, from its often tragic wartime past, during which the region splintered into a fluid patchwork of territories controlled variously by government and LTTE forces. Two decades of fighting took a devastating toll on the region's already struggling economy: villages were abandoned, commerce collapsed and the coast's few hotels were simply blown up and allowed to fall into the sea. Meaningful reconstruction and economic development became possible only after the LTTE were finally driven out of the area in 2007, and although the lingering effects of war can still be seen in places, the east's fortunes appear finally to be turning, with ambitious plans to tap into the coast's massive tourist potential, exemplified by the extraordinary glut of new resorts under construction around the formerly war-torn and deserted **Passekudah Bay**.

Much of the region's population is concentrated in the long string of mainly Tamil and Muslim towns and villages that line the coast, backed by fine sandy beaches and labyrinthine lagoons; the vast swathes of predominantly Sinhalese country inland – whose arid climate has always discouraged settled agriculture – remain sparsely populated and largely undeveloped. Capital of the east is the vibrant town of **Trincomalee**, with its appealing blend of faded colonial charm, colourful Hindu temples and beautiful coastal scenery. Few tourists venture this way, however, except to press onto the extremely low-key beachside villages of **Uppuveli** and **Nilaveli**, just up the coast. South from here, the formerly unspoilt beaches at **Passekudah** and **Kalkudah** are currently in the throes of major tourist development, while continuing south brings you to the personable town of **Batticaloa**, strung out around its enormous lagoon. Further south, the laid-back surfing hotspot of **Arugam Bay** is currently the only place in the east to see significant numbers of foreign visitors and also makes a convenient starting point for trips to the national parks of **Lahugala** and **Yala East**, and the remote forest hermitage at **Kudimbigala**.

Brief history

Although now something of a backwater, the east was for many centuries the most outward-looking and cosmopolitan part of the island, a fact borne out by its (for Sri Lanka) unusually heterogeneous **ethnic make-up** – with roughly equal numbers of Sinhalese, Tamils and Muslims, the region is the most culturally diverse in Sri Lanka. Much of the area's early history revolved around **Gokana** (modern Trincomalee), the island's principal trading port during the Anuradhapuran and

Koneswaram above and below the waves p.347
Whale-watching around Trincomalee p.350
Diving and watersports around Uppuveli and Nilaveli p.352
Pigeon Island p.352
The singing fish of Batticaloa p.358
Surfing at Arugam Bay p.361
Tours from Arugam Bay p.362
The 1883 tsunami p.366

Highlights

❶ Trincomalee Founded around one of the world's finest deep-water harbours, bustling Trinco boasts a lovely coastal setting, fine colonial fort and an absorbing mixture of Hindu, Muslim and Christian traditions. **See p.345**

❷ Arugam Bay The east coast's most appealing beach hangout, with quirky cabanas, mangrove-fringed lagoons and world-class surfing. **See p.361**

❸ Lahugala National Park Small but beautiful national park, home to the east's largest

elephant population and conveniently close to Arugam Bay. **See p.365**

❹ Kudimbigala Remote forest hermitage, with shrines and stupas scattered amidst beautiful, rock-strewn jungle. **See p.366**

❺ Maligawila This remote village is home to two superb large-scale Buddha statues, hidden away in an atmospheric forest setting. **See p.368**

HIGHLIGHTS ARE MARKED ON THE MAP ON P.344

HIGHLIGHTS
1. Trincomalee
2. Arugam Bay
3. Lahugala National Park
4. Kudimbigala
5. Maligawila

Pankulam Aru

Pigeon Island

Velgam Vihara

Nilaveli

Commonwealth War Cemetery

Uppuveli

A 12

Kanniyai Hot Springs

Anuradhapura & Vavuniya

Mora Wewa

1 Trincomalee

NAVAL HEADWORKS SANCTUARY

Koddiyar Bay

Foul Point

Vendarasan Kulam

Per Aru

Mutur

A 15

Kantale Tank

A 6

KAUDULLA NATIONAL PARK

Kaudulla Oya

Upaar Lagoon

Vakarai

I N D I A N

O C E A N

MINNERIYA NATIONAL PARK

A 15

Anuradhapura

Polonnaruwa

A 11

Parakrama Samudra

Mannampitiya

Maduru Oya

Valaichchenai

Passekudah Bay

Kalkudah

N

Mahaweli Ganga

Kalkudah Bay

A 15

Eravur

WASGOMUWA NATIONAL PARK

Batticaloa

A 5

Batticaloa Lagoon

Maduru Oya Reservoir

MADURU OYA NATIONAL PARK

A 4

A 27

Koddaikallar

Dambana

A 5

Kalmunai

A 26

Karativu

Kandy

Mahiyangana

A 5

Inginiyagala

Ampara

Randenigala Reservoir

Senanayake Samudra

A 25

Akkaraipattu

GAL OYA NATIONAL PARK

Kandy

Pannela Oya

A 4

Badulla

A 5

A 25

LAHUGALA NATIONAL PARK

Karanda Oya

Ella

Siyambalanduwa

Heda Oya

3

Pottuvil

Ratnapura

Bandarawela

Monaragala

Peacock Rock

Magul Maha Vihara

2

Arugam Bay

A 4

A 4

Yudaganawa

Buttala

5

Maligawila

Wila Oya

Panama

A 2

Wellawaya

Detamahal Vihara

Kudimbigala

4

B 35

Menik Ganga

YALA (RUHUNA) NATIONAL PARK

Kumbukkan Oya

YALA EAST NATIONAL PARK

Okanda

Tissamaharama

Kataragama & Tissamaharama

Kumana Wewa

0   20

kilometres

Polonnaruwan eras, and the harbours of the east continued to serve as an important conduit for foreign influences in subsequent centuries. Islam spread widely along the coast thanks to visiting Arab, Malay and Indian traders, while the European powers also took a healthy interest in the region. The Dutch first established a secure presence on the island at the town of **Batticaloa**, while it was the lure of Trincomalee's superb deep-water harbour more than anything else that drew the British to the island.

With the rise of the new ports at Galle and later Colombo, the east gradually fell into decline, while its fortunes nosedived during the **civil war**, which turned Tamils, Muslims and Sinhalese against one another in a frenzy of communal violence. LTTE attacks against unprotected Sinhalese and Muslim villagers were a recurring feature of the war years, including one particularly gruesome massacre of around 150 men and boys at Kattankudi mosque in 1990. The LTTE also seized pockets of territory throughout the area (including, for a time, Batticaloa itself), and was only finally driven from its last eastern strongholds in 2007. Today, former LTTE leader Colonel Karuna (see p.413) remains a major figure in the region's politics.

GETTING AROUND   THE EAST

Arrival For most travellers, getting to the east remains a bit of a slog, at least until flights from Colombo to Trincomalee resume, although the opening of the new airport in Hambantota (see p.181) will make Arugam Bay and the southern part of the region more easily accessible.
Getting around It is becoming easier to get around the east following extensive improvements to major roads: the coastal road from Valaichchenai (near Passekudah) via Batticaloa to Arugam Bay has been comprehensively upgraded, although that between Trinco and Batticaloa is still in poor condition – most traffic takes the long inland detour via Habarana and Polonnaruwa.

Trincomalee

Eastern Sri Lanka's major town, **TRINCOMALEE** (or "Trinco") has been celebrated since antiquity for its superlative deep-water **harbour**, one of the finest in Asia – the legendary Panduvasudeva (see p.397) is said to have sailed into Trincomalee (or Gokana, as it was originally known) with his followers, while the town served as the major conduit for the island's seaborne trade during the Anuradhapuran and Polonnaruwan periods. The harbour was later fought over repeatedly during the colonial period and even attracted the hostile attentions of the Japanese air force during World War II.

Trincomalee suffered massively following the onset of the **civil war** in 1983. Although Trinco avoided the massive bomb damage inflicted on Jaffna, the town's position close to the front line made it the island's major collecting point for war-displaced refugees, while tensions between the town's Tamil, Muslim and Sinhalese communities regularly erupted into communal rioting. Things have been a lot quieter following the expulsion of the LTTE from the east in 2007, and Trinco is now once again looking to the future with renewed, if cautious, optimism.

Although most visitors are drawn to this part of the island by the beaches at nearby Nilaveli and Uppuveli, a day in Trincomalee offers an interesting change of scenery. The setting is beautiful, straddling a narrow peninsula between the Indian Ocean and the Inner Harbour, rising up to the imposing **Swami Rock**, the dominant feature on the coast hereabouts. The town itself possesses an understated but distinct charm all of its own, with an interesting old **fort** and sleepy backstreets lined with pretty colonial villas dotted with mosques, churches and dozens of colourful little **Hindu temples**. Catering to the town's predominantly Tamil population, the temples give parts of the city a decidedly Indian flavour, especially at around 4pm when Trinco fills with the ringing of bells and the sound of music from myriad temples for the late-afternoon puja.

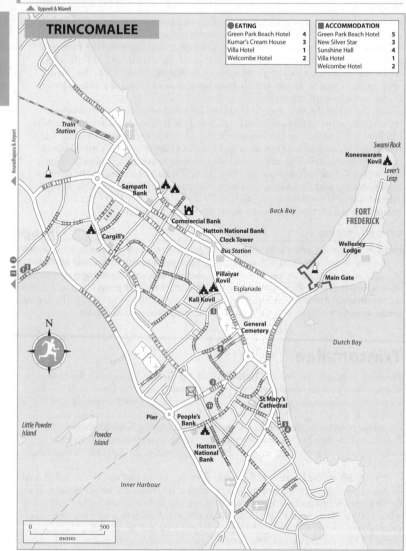

TRINCOMALEE

●EATING	
Green Park Beach Hotel	4
Kumar's Cream House	3
Villa Hotel	1
Welcombe Hotel	2

■ACCOMMODATION	
Green Park Beach Hotel	5
New Silver Star	3
Sunshine Hall	4
Villa Hotel	1
Welcombe Hotel	2

Fort Frederick

Open access 24hr • Free

The centrepiece of Trincomalee is **Fort Frederick**, whose buildings sprawl across the narrow peninsula that pokes out into the sea from the middle of town, dividing Back Bay from Dutch Bay. The fort was constructed by the Portuguese in 1623 and captured in 1639 by the Dutch. The Dutch held it until 1782, after which it was captured by the British and then the French, who ceded it back to the British, who returned it briefly to the Dutch before getting their hands on it for good in 1795. The British rechristened it Fort Frederick in 1803 after the then Duke of York and enjoyed undisputed possession of the place until Independence, troubled only by a solitary Japanese air raid on April 9, 1942.

The fort is still in military use, although visitors are free to walk through along the road up to Swami Rock. Entrance is through the attractive main gate, its outer face carved with the date 1675 and a British coat of arms bearing the legend "Dieu et Mon Droit".

Wellesley Lodge
Inside the fort, the pleasantly shady grounds are dotted with fine old trees and home to a small population of wandering deer. A few colonial buildings survive, including one known variously as **Wellesley Lodge** or Wellington House, named after Arthur Wellesley, later the Duke of Wellington, who stayed in here in 1800. A popular legend claims that the Iron Duke fell ill here and was thus unable to sail with his ship, which subsequently sank with the loss of all crew, although the story has got somewhat twisted in the telling. In fact, Wellesley made it as far as India before being struck down with a combination of fever and the "Malabar Itch". A course of lard and sulphur failed to shift the infection, and the future duke was forced to stay behind in Bombay while the doomed ship sailed off without him.

Swami Rock
The main road through the fort leads up to **Swami Rock**, a towering cliff-top vantage point offering sweeping views back to town, along the coast and down the sheer cliff-face to the deep-blue waters way below – blue whales can occasionally be seen from here.

At the highest point of Swami Rock sits the **Koneswaram Kovil** (see box below), one of the five most holy Shaivite temples on the island, although there's not much visible evidence of its former glory.

Lover's Leap
Just outside Koneswaram Kovil, close to the highest point of Swami Rock, a tree clings precariously to the edge of the rock, its branches adorned with prayer flags that supplicants have somehow managed to attach. This spot is popularly known as **Lover's Leap** in commemoration of a certain young Dutch woman, Francina van Rhede, who is said to have jumped from the cliff here in 1687. The details are confused: some say that the heartbroken van Rhede, who had been abandoned by her lover, leapt but survived the fall; others claim that she didn't even jump. Whatever the truth, government archives record her subsequent marriage eight years later, after which she (presumably) lived happily ever after.

KONESWARAM ABOVE AND BELOW THE WAVES
There's thought to have been a shrine on the site of the **Koneswaram Kovil** for at least 2500 years. According to legend, Indra, king of the gods, worshipped here, while Ravana is said to have brought the temple's venerated *swayambhu* lingam here from Mount Kailash in the Himalayas. Ravana subsequently tried to make off with the entire temple but was stopped by Shiva; the cleft in Swami Rock is said to have been created when Shiva forced him to drop his sword.

The medieval temple was patronized by the great Chola, Pandyan and Pallava dynasties of southern India, developing into Sri Lanka's pre-eminent Hindu shrine – the "Rome of the Orient", as it was described – with three separate temples spread across the headland, soaring gopurams and a magnificent "thousand-columned" hall. Unfortunately, the splendour of the complex attracted the attentions of the Portuguese, who destroyed the temple in 1624 during one of their iconoclastic rampages. Some stones from the various temples were reused in the construction of the neighbouring fort, while the rest of the complex was simply shoved over the edge of the cliff into the waters below, where it remained for 350 years before being rediscovered in the 1960s by author Arthur C. Clarke and photographer Mike Wilson. Wilson also recovered the famous *swayambhu* lingam, subsequently enshrined (along with other statues recovered from the waves) in the modest modern temple you see today.

5

The commercial centre
West of the fort, modern Trincomalee's **commercial centre** comprises an undistingui-shed and low-key trio of parallel streets lined by tiny one-storey shops and dotted with the occasional small mosque.

The beach
In the commercial centre, turn off N.C. Road, officially Ehamparam Road, down Pattana Road (there's a very faded road sign) to reach a magical little stretch of **beach**, with small pastel-painted Hindu temples on one side, colourful fishing boats drawn up at the water's edge on the other, and rabbit warrens of tiny shacks behind, their neat, brightly painted facades giving the beachfront a prettiness which belies the considerable poverty in which most of the people here live.

The Esplanade and around
At the southeastern end of the commercial centre lies the wide and grassy **Esplanade**. A couple of pretty Hindu temples enliven the western side of the green, the large **Kali Kovil** and the much smaller (though equally gaudy) **Pillaiyar Kovil**. Both burst into life with drumming, music and lines of supplicants during the late-afternoon puja (around 4–5pm).

General Cemetery
Just south of the Esplanade lies the decaying and utterly neglected old **General Cemetery**, the final resting place of Trinco's Christian population, with a few picturesquely dilapidated colonial tombs dating back to the 1820s alongside more modern graves. Jane Austen's brother, Charles, is supposed to be buried here – but it's all but impossible to find him. The cemetery is usually kept locked, but it's easy enough to hop over the low wall (although slightly more difficult to climb out again).

The Inner Harbour
A number of roads run southwest from the centre down towards the **Inner Harbour** – much of this quarter of town retains a pleasantly old-fashioned feel, with numerous colonial villas, some of them embellished with quirky, slightly Art Deco-looking decorative motifs. The expansive harbour itself is an attractively breezy spot, its choppy waters dotted with container ships and various port facilities, framed against a circle of rugged green hills that ring the bay – it's particularly lovely at night, when a thousand lights twinkle around its perimeter.

Dutch Bay
The oceanfront Fort Frederick Road along **Dutch Bay** offers fine sea views, while the beach that edges the road is a popular spot around dusk, when half the town seems to congregate here to promenade along the seafront and loll around on the sands. Beyond here lie further low-key but charming rows of colonial villas, most particularly along **Dyke Street**, lined with quaint pastel facades. Nearby, it's also worth hunting out the colonial-era **St Mary's Cathedral**, an imposing blue structure buried amid lush gardens.

ARRIVAL AND DEPARTURE
TRINCOMALEE

By plane The airport is at China Bay, a few kilometres out of town. Scheduled flights on SriLankan Airlines air taxi network (see p.30) may have restarted by the time you read this.

By bus Buses arrive at the bus station, right in the centre of Trinco at the bottom of Main Street.

Destinations Anuradhapura (2 daily; 3hr 30min);

Batticaloa via Habarana (3 daily; 8hr); Colombo (every 30min; 8hr); Habarana (every 30min; 2hr); Jaffna via Vavuniya (5 daily; 7hr); Kandy (hourly; 6hr); Polonnaruwa (3 daily; 4hr).

By train The train station is at the northwest end of town. There's currently just one, slow, overnight service to Colombo (daily; 8hr 30min).

ACCOMMODATION

There's not a great deal of choice of accommodation in Trinco, and costs are relatively high, though there's somewhere to stay in most price brackets.

Green Park Beach Hotel 312 Dyke St ☎ 026 222 2369, ✉ greenparktco@live.com. Well-run mid-range option in a picturesque setting on Dutch Bay. Rooms (all with a/c, hot water and TV) are modern, tiled and clean, albeit relatively pricey, and there's also a decent in-house Indian restaurant (see below). Rs.4375

New Silver Star 27 College St ☎ 026 222 2348. Trinco's most consistently reliable budget option, with a range of accommodation spread over three floors. The spotless modern rooms on the ground floor are the best value; the considerably pricier upstairs rooms with a/c less so. Rs.1500; a/c Rs.4000

Sunshine Hall 4–5 Green Rd ☎ 026 222 0288. Functional hotel-cum-wedding hall offering neat tiled modern rooms with fan at bargain rates – currently Trinco's best deal, although the slightly fancier a/c rooms (at almost four times the price) are decidedly expensive. Rs.1000; a/c Rs.3500

Villa Hotel 22A Lower Rd, Orr's Hill ☎ 026 222 2284. Smart modern hotel overlooking the bay, with gleaming a/c rooms done up with smooth pine furnishings and chic bathrooms – but don't bother with the grubby and overpriced non a/c rooms below. Also has a reasonable restaurant. Rs.2750; a/c Rs.4950

Welcombe Hotel 66 Lower Rd, Orr's Hill, 2km west of the centre ☎ 026 222 2373, ⊛ welcombehotel.com. Trinco's biggest and poshest hotel, occupying a lovely position high above the Inner Harbour in a striking modern building topped with recycled railway sleepers (or copies thereof). Standard rooms (all with a/c, TV and fridge) are spacious but disappointingly ordinary given the price, and even a bit grubby in places; the optimistically titled "super-luxury" rooms are better value and considerably nicer, with colonial-style wooden furniture. There's also a large pool (non-guests Rs.250), musty bar and decent restaurant (see below). $78; "super-luxury" rooms $88

EATING AND DRINKING

Green Park Beach Hotel 312 Dyke St ☎ 026 222 2369. Sedate hotel restaurant offering a huge menu of Indian food including meat, fish and veg standards – tandooris, kormas, *vadais*, *shorbas* and so on. Quality is average, but the setting is nice, and portions are huge. Evening meals are sometimes served up on the attractive first-floor waterfront terrace. Mains Rs.300–500. Unlicensed. Daily 7–9.30am, 11am–3.30pm & 6–9pm.

Kumar's Cream House Post Office Rd. Bright little modern bakery selling drinks, short eats (samosas, cutlets, *vadais*), plus Indian sweets, cakes and Elephant House ice cream. Daily 6.30am–1pm & 2.30–6.30pm.

Villa Hotel 22A Lower Rd, Orr's Hill ☎ 026 222 2284. Swish glassed-in hotel restaurant with big picture windows offering views over the bay below and a menu featuring a reasonably prepared mix of Sri Lankan standards alongside European-style fish, seafood and meat mains at very reasonable prices (around Rs.450). Daily 11am–11pm.

Welcombe Hotel 66 Lower Rd, Orr's Hill ☎ 026 222 2373. Trinco's smartest restaurant, with seating either on the beautiful outdoor terrace high above the Inner Harbour (although you can't see much after dark, when the midges and mozzies come out in force) or in the glassed-in dining room within. Food (most mains Rs.700–800) comprises a mix of the usual Sri Lankan standards plus a few generic European offerings, competently, if unexceptionally prepared. Daily 6am–10pm.

DIRECTORY

Banks There are plenty of banks with ATMs accepting foreign cards scattered around town.
Internet Available at a couple of places on Power House

Road near the junction with Post Office Road; try Google internet café (daily 8.30am–9pm; Rs.60/hr).

North of Trincomalee

North of Trincomalee the coast is lined with a fine strand of wide golden beach, beginning at the village of **Uppuveli** and continuing through to **Nilaveli** and beyond: a superb stretch of coast whose enormous tourist potential has as yet barely even been scratched – which is a large part of its appeal. Both Uppuveli and Nilaveli were saved from development during the civil war by their position close to the front line, and have little changed since – although a handful of courageous local entrepreneurs continue to plug away against the odds, sustained by a steady stream

5

WHALE-WATCHING AROUND TRINCOMALEE

Following the recent development of **whale-watching tours** in Mirissa (see p.168), Trincomalee is rapidly emerging as another internationally important whale-watching destination. **Blue whales** in particular (plus smaller numbers of sperm whales) can regularly be seen around six to eight nautical miles east of Trincomalee (about 30min by boat), and can even occasionally be spotted from the land – with Swami Rock (see p.347) offering the best vantage point. **Dolphins** (mainly Spinner) are also regularly seen. Most **sightings** occur between March/April and August/September, as whales continue their migrations around the island from the south coast (where they mainly congregate from December to April) – this means that Sri Lanka offers around ten months of continuous whale-watching annually at different points around the coast.

WHALE-WATCHING TOURS

Whale-watching in Trinco is still in its infancy, and the information here is particularly susceptible to change. The easiest place to arrange **trips** is likely to be through the *Chaaya Blu* (see opposite) hotel in Uppuveli, which will run tours in its own boat, while the *Pigeon Island Resort* (see p.353) and *Nilaveli Beach Hotel* (see p.353) should also be able to arrange trips, either through a local boatman or the Sri Lankan Navy (🌐whalewatching.navy.lk).

of NGOs on weekend jollies. Both places remain extremely low-key even during the season from May to September, and at other times of the year are usually more or less comatose.

Uppuveli

Just a few kilometres north of Trinco, the low-key village of **UPPUVELI** is little more than a modest cluster of guesthouses, a couple of hotels, a few fishing boats, and a great many palm trees. Uppuveli's guesthouses managed to eke out a tenuous existence during the war years, while the village was lucky enough to escape the widespread destruction wrought by the tsunami on nearby Nilaveli thanks to its sheltered position behind Trincomalee's Swami Rock. The long-anticipated postwar resurgence has yet to be felt here, however, and although the village has a little more life than Nilaveli further down the coast, the atmosphere remains deeply somnolent.

Commonwealth War Cemetery

On the main Nilaveli Road, 200m north of *Chaaya Blu* • Open access 24hr • Free

The **Commonwealth War Cemetery** holds 362 graves, mainly of Allied and other servicemen who died in Sri Lanka during World War II. Military personnel of many nationalities are buried together here, including Indians, Italians, Australians, Canadians, Dutch, Burmese and, of course, numerous British fighters, including the aircrews killed during the Japanese air raid of April 1942 and seamen who perished aboard various Royal Navy vessels sunk by the Japanese in the Indian Ocean. In striking contrast to the General Cemetery in Trinco, the War Cemetery is beautifully looked after, though the long lines of graves and the ages recorded on the headstones (few of those interred here were older than 25) makes a visit a rather sombre experience.

Kanniyai Hot Wells

Around 8km inland from Uppuveli and 1km south of the road to Anuradhapura

According to tradition, the **Kanniyai Hot Wells** were created by Vishnu himself, and these days are a popular bathing spot for local Tamils. You can't actually submerge yourself in the waters here – the springs are collected in small tiled tubs, and you use a bucket to pour the water over yourself – but they're fun for a quick splash.

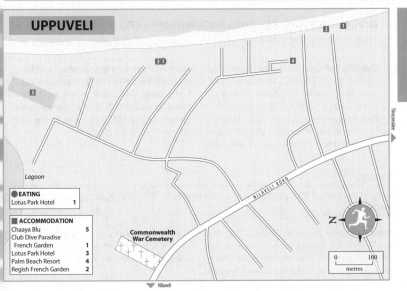

UPPUVELI

Lagoon

● **EATING**
Lotus Park Hotel   1

■ **ACCOMMODATION**
Chaaya Blu   5
Club Dive Paradise
  French Garden   1
Lotus Park Hotel   3
Palm Beach Resort   4
Regish French Garden   2

**Commonwealth
War Cemetery**

NILAVELI ROAD

Trincomalee

0   100
          metres

Nilaveli

Velgam Vihara

A few kilometres beyond Kanniyai Hot Wells towards Anuradhapura and 4km north of the main road • Donation requested

A trip to the Kanniyai Hot Wells can be combined with a visit to the remains of the **Velgam Vihara**. The temple is thought to date back to the era of King Devanampiya Tissa, who is said to have planted a bo tree here, and although subsequently abandoned to the jungle following the collapse of Polonnaruwa, extensive remains survive, including a stupa, image house and a well-preserved standing Buddha.

ARRIVAL AND DEPARTURE   UPPUVELI

By bus Buses run from Trinco to Uppuveli every 20–30min, although they tend to get nightmarishly packed; it's well worth catching a tuktuk instead (Rs.250–300).

ACCOMMODATION

Chaaya Blu Towards the northern end of the beach ☎ 026 222 1611, ⓦ chaayahotels.com. This pleasant if decidedly old-fashioned resort (formerly the *Club Oceanic*) scrubbed up its accommodation and doubled its prices in a burst of five-star delusion. Rooms are nicely furnished, if on the small side, while the concrete-heavy decor is vaguely reminiscent of an upmarket bomb shelter. There's also a pool (which non-guests can use if they buy a meal), dive school (see p.352) and whale-watching trips (see opposite), although unfortunately rates are currently so over-the-top it's almost funny – so long as someone else is paying. Much better to head to the *Lotus Park* or the *Nilaveli Beach Hotel* down the road (see p.353). **$250**

Club Dive Paradise French Garden 500m south of Chaaya Blu ☎ 077 772 8266, ⓔ cdp.french@yahoo.com. Similar to the neighbouring *Regish French Garden*, although rooms are slightly smarter (and more expensive) – the bathrooms could do with an upgrade. **Rs.1500**

Lotus Park Hotel Immediately south of Chaaya Blu ☎ 026 222 5327, ⓦ lotustrinco.com. Neat little resort hotel, popular with visiting NGOs and infinitely better value than the *Chaaya Blu* next door. Choose between the pleasantly furnished standard rooms in the old wing and fancier deluxe rooms (about $20 more) in the new building, plus a few unappealingly poky beachfront chalets. Also has a good restaurant (see p.352). **Rs.5775**

Palm Beach Resort 400m south of Chaaya Blu ☎ 026 222 1250. Cheerful Italian-run guesthouse set in lush gardens, with a sociable atmosphere, authentic Italian cooking and spotless, comfortable and well-maintained rooms. Closed mid-Oct to Dec. **Rs.2400**; a/c **Rs.4000**

Regish French Garden (formerly the *Pragash French Garden*) 500m south of Chaaya Blu ☎ 060 220 0397. The longest-established cheapie in Uppuveli scores highly for its attractive beachfront location, although the basic rooms could be cleaner. **Rs.1000**

5

DIVING AND WATERSPORTS AROUND UPPUVELI AND NILAVELI

There are several **dive schools** in the area, offering trips around Pigeon Island and Swami Rock.

Club Dive Padi Club Dive Paradise French Garden, Uppuveli T 077 772 8266, E cdp.french@yahoo.com. Basic range of dives during season around Pigeon Island and Swami Rock. Open March–Oct.

Dive centre Chaaya Blu hotel, Uppuveli T 0711 323 974. A range of dive trips, plus PADI courses, snorkelling trips at Pigeon Island, and various other watersports and excursions including waterskiing, kayaking and boat trips to Swami Rock. Open all year.

Scuba Lanka Dive School Nilaveli Beach Hotel, Nilaveli T 026 223 2295. Dives and watersports, plus sports-fishing trips (Rs.2500 first hour, then Rs.1250/hr). Open April–Sept/Oct.

EATING

All the local guesthouses do simple meals, usually with the emphasis on fish and seafood, although don't expect anything too fancy.

Lotus Park Hotel Immediately south of Chaaya Blu T 026 222 5327, W lotustrinco.com. Attractive hotel restaurant serving up a wide range of nearly everything – Sri Lankan, European, Chinese and Indian (most mains Rs.500–700), including a particularly big seafood selection, along with lighter meals including burgers, sandwiches and salads. Free wi-fi. Daily 6am–10pm.

Nilaveli

Some 10km north of Uppuveli, the straggling settlement of **NILAVELI** is home to another fine stretch of largely deserted beach, though the village has yet to recover from the twin effects of war and tsunami and the whole place still feels moribund, at least apart from the attractive *Nilaveli Beach Hotel*, the area's major – indeed only – landmark, and one of the east coast's most attractive boltholes.

PIGEON ISLAND

About 1km offshore from Nilaveli, tiny **Pigeon Island** is home to one of the east coast's finest patches of coral reef, now back to something approaching its best after being thoroughly trashed during the early noughties by indiscriminate blast-fishing, damage caused by careless day-trippers, and the destructive effects of the tsunami. The island has now been declared a national park, which is good news for the local environment. The high admission charges, however, are somewhat less good news for foreign tourists.

The main reason to visit is to enjoy the island's excellent **snorkelling** (best from May to September, when visibility is clearest). All the live coral lies on the sea-facing side of the island, some 40m off the beach in around 1.5m of water. The coral on the beach-facing side is unfortunately dead, although the waters here compensate with a remarkable range of tropical fish – well over a hundred species have been recorded.

VISITING THE ISLAND

You must buy **tickets** to visit Pigeon Island from the ticket office (daily 8am–5pm) on the beach immediately north of the *Nilaveli Beach Hotel*; they currently cost Rs.1100 plus additional charges and taxes, which add around another Rs.1000 per boat. **Boats** to reach the island can be hired on the beach next to the ticket office (Rs.1500/boat seating up to around 8 people) or, for a surcharge, via the *NBH*, *Pigeon Island Beach Resort* or *Chaaya Blue* in Uppuveli. Boatmen on the beach also have **snorkelling equipment** (Rs.600), or alternatively you might be able to hire this through the dive centre at the *NBH* (April–Sept only).

ARRIVAL AND DEPARTURE | **NILAVELI**

By bus Buses run from Trinco to Nilaveli every twenty to thirty minutes, although they tend to get absolutely jam-packed, and can be horrible if you've got luggage. In addition, the various hotels in Nilaveli are a further hike (up to 1km) from the main road, meaning that overall it's well worth catching a tuktuk (around Rs.800).

ACCOMMODATION AND EATING

All the hotels listed here offer food, although only at the *Nilaveli Beach Hotel* will you find anything more than simple tourist staples.

Coral Bay 4km south of the Nilaveli Beach Hotel ☏ 026 326 6196, ⌨ hotelcoralbay.com. Small and very low-key hotel in a single sea-facing block, with bright if rather expensive modern rooms (all a/c) in a coconut-palm garden, plus a pool right on the beach. **Rs.4500**

★ **Nilaveli Beach Hotel ("NBH")** ☏ 026 223 2295, ⌨ tangerinehotels.com. Long-established landmark, completely rebuilt and modernized following the tsunami, with attractive modern buildings set among idyllic tree-studded gardens running down to the beach. Standard rooms are a tad bare; deluxe rooms ($40 extra) are more stylishly equipped. There's also a big L-shaped pool and a smart restaurant. B&B **$110**

Pigeon Island Beach Resort 500m north of the Nilaveli Beach Hotel ☏ 026 492 0633, ⌨ pigeon islandresort.com. Small resort hotel (formerly the *Mauro Beach Hotel*) with nicely furnished tiled rooms overlooking a long thin garden and a decent-sized pool running down to the sea, although with rates equivalent to a deluxe room at the NBH it's decidedly overpriced. B&B **$150**

Surya Lagoon 11th Mile Post (on the inland side of the main road between the NBH and Pigeon Island Resort) ☏ 071 272 8504, ✉ suryalagoon@hotmail.com. Attractive new guesthouse in a colonial-style villa, with four attractively (if rather scantily) furnished rooms and extensive grounds running down to the adjacent lagoon. B&B **Rs.5500**

South of Trincomalee

The stretch of coastline between Trincomalee and Batticaloa remains one of the poorest and least-developed in Sri Lanka – until 2007 much of this area was controlled by the LTTE – although things are once again looking up, at least if the burgeoning development at **Passekudah** is anything to go by. The A15 highway runs the length of the coast, though it's in poor condition between Trinco and Mutur and is punctuated by several river crossings where vehicles are carried over by ferry – buses from Trincomalee to Batticaloa make the long detour inland via Habarana.

Passekudah and Kalkudah

Way back in the 1970s and early 1980s, the twin beaches of **Passekudah** and **Kalkudah** were the east coast's most developed tourist destinations, home to a modest cluster of resort hotels and drawing a steady string of European tourists to this far-flung corner of the island. All that ended following the outbreak of war. The hotels were first abandoned, and subsequently blown up by the LTTE to prevent them being used by the Sri Lankan Army – their ghostly skeletons remained, until quite recently, standing sentry over the deserted beaches.

Now the area is on the cusp of a second, and even more dramatic coming, earmarked as a special tourist development zone and already in the throes of enormous development. The formerly deserted arc of **PASSEKUDAH BAY** is now ringed with the concrete skeletons of no fewer than thirteen new hotels under construction (along with the already completed *Maalu Maalu* resort) which are likely to transform this sleepy village into the east coast's answer to Beruwala within just a couple of years. By contrast, neighbouring **KALKUDAH BAY** remains mercifully unchanged, so far at least, with a superb sweep of powder-fine golden sand – blissfully deserted and unspoilt, although a couple of plots of land have already been fenced off for future development, suggesting that Kalkudah's days as a sleepy backwater are also numbered. See it while you can.

5

By bus Buses run regularly from Batticaloa to Valaichchenai (and, less frequently, from Polonnaruwa). There are currently only three buses daily from Valaichchenai to Kalkudah village. A tuktuk costs around Rs.200.

By train Kalkudah has its own train station, though it's inconveniently located some 5km beyond the village; there are frequent connections with Batticaloa (4 daily; 50min). To reach Colombo, you'll have to change at Gal Oya Junction or Maho.

By car The turn-off to Kalkudah and Passekudah is signed off the main road at Valaichchenai, from where it's a rough 7km drive down a narrow, badly potholed road (although chances are it will be upgraded shortly). This road brings you first into Kalkudah village. Passekudah Bay lies beyond here, on the left (follow the signs to the *Maalu Maalu* resort). To reach Kalkudah Bay and beach, drive through Kalkudah village and then follow the side road which runs past the entrance to the army camp and then swings around, running parallel to the beach. Side roads lead off to beach itself.

ACCOMMODATION AND EATING

Only one hotel is currently open on **Passekudah Beach**, although many more will start coming into service over the next few years. Low-key **Kalkudah Village**, strung out along the approach road to Passekudah Beach, already boasts a surprising array of budget and mid-range options.

PASSEKUDAH BEACH

Maalu Maalu Coconut Board Rd ☎ 065 738 8388, ⓦ maalumaalu.com. Gorgeous new boutique beach resort, designed like a miniature (but very upmarket) fishing village, with two wings of palm-thatched wooden chalets framing views of a wonderful infinity pool and beach and a carpet-smooth and very shallow stretch of sea beyond, protected by a coral reef. Rooms are a bit humdrum in comparison (and at the price), with nursery-style fish-inspired decor – but lovely bathrooms. Facilities include Ayurveda and watersports centres, a jazz bar, karaoke and nightclubs, and a beach bar in a salvaged boat. Half-board $324

KALKUDAH VILLAGE

Nandawanam Guest House Main St ☎ 065 225 7258, ⓔ nandawanam@live.com. Inside a spacious family house surrounded by attractive gardens, with four large and attractively furnished a/c rooms (with more to come) – the whole place is kept so spotlessly clean you could probably eat your dinner off the floor. A bargain at current rates. Rs.3000

The New Land Main St ☎ 065 568 0440. Currently the area's best budget option, with four simple, neat and comfortable rooms (including one larger a/c room). The friendly and very helpful owner also has free bikes to get to Kalkudah beach and serves up inexpensive food. Rs.1000; a/c Rs.2500

Simla Inn Main St ☎ 077 926 5506, ⓔ simlainn @yahoo.com. This famous old place somehow kept going through the civil war years, surviving pitched battles between the LTTE and SLA, only to get flattened by the tsunami, although it's now back in business. Accommodation is in three clean tiled rooms – perfectly pleasant, although decidedly overpriced, especially if you take the optional a/c. Rs.3000; a/c Rs.4500

Victoria Guest House Main St ☎ 077 926 5506. Next door to the *Simla Inn* (and owned by the same family) this place offers five spacious and attractive modern rooms, some with a/c. Rs.2000; a/c Rs.3500

Batticaloa

The principal east-coast settlement south of Trincomalee, **BATTICALOA** (often shortened to "Batti") is one of Sri Lanka's most appealing but least-known larger towns, mainly thanks to its long years of isolation and turbulence during the civil war. Throughout the conflict, the town and surrounding area was a major flashpoint between LTTE and Sri Lankan Army forces, with the army controlling the town and the LTTE running their own parallel administration – complete with courts, police force and tax collectors – from the village of Kokkadicholai, a short drive south. As Indian journalist Nirupama Subramanian put it in *Sri Lanka: Voices from a War Zone*: "Technically, Batticaloa town came under the government … That was by day. By night, the town took orders from the Tigers."

The LTTE are now gone, although intriguing reminders of Batti's long colonial history can still be seen, while the mercantile hustle and bustle of the main commercial areas suggests a town now increasingly on the mend. The town's setting is also magical,

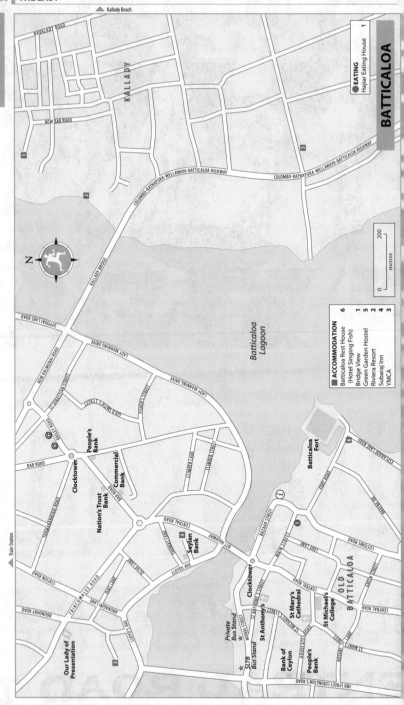

BATTICALOA

Kallady Beach

KALLADY

NAVALADY ROAD

NEW BAR ROAD

COLOMBO-RATNAPURA-WELLAWAYA-BATTICALOA HIGHWAY

COLOMBO-RATNAPURA-WELLAWAYA-BATTICALOA HIGHWAY

N

KALLADY BRIDGE

Batticaloa
Lagoon

UPPODAI LANE ROAD

LADY MANNING DRIVE

LADY MANNING DRIVE

NEW KALMUNAI WAY

GOLD SMITH'S STREET

OLD KALMUNAI STREET

FISHER'S STREET

COVINGTON STREET

BAILE ROAD

People's
Bank

Commercial
Bank

Clocktower

BAR ROAD

Nation's Trust
Bank

BAR ROAD

TRINCOMALEE ROAD

CUMBER LANE

CUMBER STREET

CENTRAL ROAD

BTI HIGHWAY

Seylan
Bank

THIRUMURUGAN ROAD

BAZAAR STREET

Train Station

STATION ROAD

FEINCOMALEE ROAD

ARUNAGIRI LANE

DICK LANE

PILLAI LANE

LLOYDS AVE

BOUNDARY ROAD

Our Lady of
Presentation

Private
Bus Stand

SLTB
Bus Stand

MUNAI STREET

St Anthony's

ST JOHN STREET

ST ANDREW'S STREET

St Mary's
Cathedral

MAIN STREET

LOVE LANE

Batticaloa
Fort

FORT ROAD

ESPLANADE LAKE ROAD

BAY ROAD

CUSTOMS ROAD

OLD BATTICALOA

LADY'S LANE

ADVOCATE'S LANE

ST MICHAEL'S LANE

CENTRAL ROAD

CENTRAL ROAD

MILLER'S ROAD

ST MARY'S LANE

3RD STREET (COVINGTON'S ROAD)

Clocktower

Bank of
Ceylon

People's
Bank

St Michael's
College

0   200
metres

● EATING
Hajiar Eating House   1

■ ACCOMMODATION
Batticaloa Rest House   6
(Hotel Singing Fish)
Bridge View   1
Green Garden Hostel   5
Riviera Resort   2
Subaraj Inn   4
YMCA   3

perched on a narrow sliver of land backed by the serpentine **Batticaloa Lagoon** and surrounded by water on three sides, with the constantly shifting views of land, lagoon and ocean lending Batticaloa an interesting – if disorienting – character.

Brief history

Historically, Batticaloa is best known as the site of the first landing (in 1602) by the **Dutch** in Sri Lanka, and as the place where they established their first lasting foothold on the island by seizing the local fort from the resident Portuguese in 1638 (colonial influence lives on in the town's name, which appears to be a Portuguese corruption of the Sinhalese Mudda Kalapuwa, meaning "muddy lagoon"). Many Muslims also settled in the area under the protection of the kings of Kandy during the same period to escape Portuguese persecution elsewhere, mixing with the region's largely Tamil population.

Batticaloa and the surrounding area was a major LTTE stronghold throughout the **civil war**, and perhaps one of the most dangerous places in the island, for civilians at least, over a thousand of whom were killed in or around Batti in the late 1980s and early 1990s. Two of the war's most gruesome events occurred close to the city. The first, in August 1990, when almost 150 Muslims were massacred by the LTTE in a mosque at Kattankudi (just south of town); the second, just a month later, when more than 180 Tamil civilians (including 47 children under the age of 10) were slaughtered by the Sri Lankan Army in three nearby villages. Towards the end of the war, the region was also wracked by clashes between rival factions of the LTTE, as Colonel Karuna (see p.413) launched his breakaway movement. Widespread disappearances of civilians by the Sri Lankan security services continued to be reported even after the end of fighting in the east in 2007.

The Fort

Batticaloa's solid-looking **Fort** was one of the last to be built by the Portuguese in Sri Lanka, constructed in 1628, although just ten years later it was seized by the Dutch – their first foothold on the island. The rugged exterior walls have withstood both civil war and tsunami and remain in surprisingly good shape; a moat encloses the fort on two sides, while the northern walls plunge directly into the lagoon.

The main **entrance** is on the east side of the fort, flanked by a pair of rusty cannon and topped with a very eroded carving of the VOC emblem. Inside, the **central courtyard** is now home to assorted municipal offices, with an incongruous little Hindu shrine standing in the centre. Most of the buildings are modern, although the original Dutch-era west wing survives, a marvellous period piece with huge wooden-shuttered windows and doors, shaded by a superb two-storey veranda supported on enormous Doric columns.

Main Street

Batticaloa has a largely Tamil population, and a distinctly Indian flavour in places. This is most obvious along the colourful **Main Street** and adjacent **Bazaar Street**, which run parallel to one another along the south side of the central lagoon west of the fort, offering a colourful medley of jewellers, clothes shops and fancy goods emporia.

Old Batticaloa

South of Main Street, roads climb up the hill into the heart of **old Batticaloa**, an atmospheric tangle of streets lined with tree-swathed villas and dotted with a sequence of imposing colonial-era churches. Immediately behind Main Street lies **St Anthony's**, a lovely old cream-coloured structure, topped with an enormous expanse of red-tiled roof and with a rustic, barn-like interior beneath a huge sloping wooden roof. Further up the hill sits the even larger **St Mary's Cathedral**, a sprawling, sky-blue Neoclassical edifice with soaring facade and, opposite, the venerable old **St Michael's College**, founded in 1872, and one of the largest and most prestigious schools in the east.

5

East to Kallady

On the opposite side of the lagoon it's worth having a look at the landmark **Our Lady of Presentation**, a huge, bizarre-looking blue structure topped by a strange octagonal tower and glass cupola – like a miniature lighthouse plonked on top of a pagoda.

From here, it's a twenty-minute walk through the modern town centre along Trinco, Bar and Bailey roads to reach the creaking old **Kallady Bridge**, dating from the 1930s (when it was known as Lady Manning Bridge) and formerly the longest in the country. It's also said to be the best place to here Batti's famous **singing fish** (see box below). The bridge is regularly jammed with vehicles, although the opening of a new bridge alongside should ease traffic.

Kallady

Over Kallady Bridge lies the sleepy beachside suburb of **Kallady**, home to several of the town's better accommodation options and with a pleasantly village-like atmosphere – quite different from the bustle of central Batti just over the lagoon. The far side of the district is bounded by a long sweep of fine golden **beach**, usually lined with boats and busy with fishermen sorting the day's catch or mending nets.

ARRIVAL AND DEPARTURE   BATTICALOA

By bus There are separate bus stands for SLTB and private buses, next to one another on the south side of the lagoon. Services to Colombo leave mainly either first thing in the morning or in the evening between 8pm and 10pm (with a couple more services in the afternoon). Heading down the coast to Arugam Bay, there's currently one direct service daily; alternatively, catch one of the frequent buses south to Kalmunai, then change at Kalmunai Pottuvil, then catch a bus or tuktuk from Pottuvil to Arugam Bay (which all

sounds rather laborious, but is actually reasonably straightforward).
Destinations Arugam Bay (1 daily; 3hr); Colombo (10 daily; 8hr); Kandy (2 daily; 5hr); Polonnaruwa (3 daily; 2hr 30min); Trincomalee (via Habarana; 3 daily; 5hr).
By train The train station is on the north side of the town centre.
Destinations Colombo (2 daily; 8–9hr); Polonnaruwa (2 daily; 2hr 10min).

INFORMATION

Tourist Information Centre Bazaar St. The opening of a dedicated tourist centre (daily 9am–5pm) in this formerly war-torn outpost says a lot about Batti's changing fortunes,

although don't expect much more than a few free photocopied handouts listing local information and attractions.

ACCOMMODATION

Accommodation in Batti is split between the town centre and the quieter beachside suburb of Kallady (see above), a Rs.200–250 tuktuk ride (or 20min walk) from the centre.

TOWN CENTRE

Batticaloa Rest House (Hotel Singing Fish) Brayne Drive ☎ 065 222 7882. Right next to the fort, this recently restored and reopened rest house in an old colonial villa has

three modern, tiled a/c doubles – all neat and clean, if a bit bare – plus six slightly older and gloomier triples. There's also a good-looking a/c restaurant, and the location can't be beaten, although overall it's pricey for what you get. <u>Rs.3300</u>

THE SINGING FISH OF BATTICALOA

Batti is famous in Sri Lankan folklore for its **singing fish**. According to tradition, between April and September a strange noise – described variously as resembling a plucked guitar or violin string, or the sound produced by rubbing a wet finger around the rim of a glass – can be heard issuing from the depths of the lagoon. The "singing" is allegedly strongest on full moon nights, though no one knows exactly what causes it. The most popular explanation is that it's produced by some form of marine life – anything from catfish to mussels – while another theory states that it's made by water flowing between boulders on the lagoon floor. The best way to listen to the singing is apparently to dip one end of an oar in the water and hold the other end to your ear. Kallady Bridge is traditionally held to be a good place to tune in.

Subaraj Inn 6/1 Lloyds Ave ☎065 222 5983. Long-running little hotel with a mix of old but well-maintained (if slightly cell-like) rooms with a/c and hot water in the main building, and rather more basic but cheap non-a/c rooms in the annexe outside, plus a nice little courtyard restaurant. Rs.990; a/c Rs.2200

YMCA 26 Boundary Rd South ☎065 222 2495. Functional modern YMCA in a good central location, if you don't mind the somewhat institutional atmosphere. Accommodation includes spacious and clean doubles and triples (with optional a/c), plus bargain singles (Rs.690) and accommodation in five-bed dorms. Friendly management, and profits go to fund a local school for deaf children. Dorms Rs.400; doubles Rs.1300; a/c Rs.1900

KALLADY

Bridge View Off New Dutch Bar Rd ☎065 222 3723, ⓦhotelbridgeview.com. Well-run hotel, lacking the nearby *Riviera*'s lagoon views and garden setting but with good accommodation in a range of old but spacious fan rooms or smart modern rooms with a/c and hot water in

the new annexe – the most upmarket lodgings in town at present, at a very reasonable price. There's also free internet and wi-fi, and a pleasant glassed-in restaurant. Rs.1300; a/c Rs.3150

Green Garden Hotel Off Kalmunai Rd ☎065 222 2155. Set in a long, verandaed block, with neat, clean and very green rooms (and bathrooms) – all cosy and good-value. Optional a/c for Rs.1000. To reach the hotel, go roughly 500m beyond the turn-off to the *Riviera Resort* then left down a small road off the roundabout with the (clock-less) clocktower. Rs.1520; a/c Rs.2520

Riviera Resort Off New Dutch Bar Rd ☎065 222 2164, ⓦriviera-online.com. With friendly and professional management, this is the most appealing of the various Kallady hotels, popular with NGOs. Accommodation is in a scatter of buildings dotted around attractive lagoonside gardens, ranging from good-value non-a/c rooms through to slightly smarter but relatively expensive rooms with a/c and hot water. There's also an attractive garden restaurant (mains need to be pre-ordered at least an hour in advance) and free wi-fi. Rs.1350; a/c Rs.3500

EATING

You're most likely to eat where you're staying. If not, you can choose from the usual simple places in town – head for the row of cafés along Main Street.

Hajiar Eating House East end of Main Street. The smartest of the cafés along this stretch of Main Street. They serve a few basic rice-and-curry and buriani-style dishes during the day (virtually everything under Rs.200), and

come alive at dusk with the clatter of machete-wielding *kottu rotty* makers. If this doesn't appeal, try the nearby *Ibrahim Eating House* or the *Hotel Thameeny*. Daily 8am–8pm.

DIRECTORY

Banks There are banks all over town. The ATMs at the Commercial and Seylan banks on Bar Road both accept foreign Visa and MasterCards.

Internet Wisdom internet café, 39/B Bailey Rd (daily 8am–8pm; Rs.40/hr), or Eastern Light, further down the road into town.

South of Batticaloa

Beyond Batticaloa, the fine new coastal highway sweeps traffic effortlessly south – although disappointingly it runs out of sight of the sea except around the expansive **Koddaikallar lagoon**, a memorable maze of palm-fringed water. Much of the road is lined with an endless succession of mainly Tamil and Muslim settlements, surprisingly built up in places, particularly along the stretch of coast between the twin towns of **Kalmunai** and **Karativu** with their entertaining clutter of mosques, temples and makeshift shops, plus the occasional cow wandering across the road.

From Karativu, the A31 highway turns inland towards **Ampara**, offering a striking contrast between the bustling commercial towns of the Tamil–Muslim coast and the largely unpopulated and undeveloped rural hinterlands behind, still predominantly Sinhalese, with little to interrupt the landscape apart from the occasional mud hut amidst endless paddy fields.

Ampara

Unassuming **AMPARA** is a typical one-horse rural Sri Lankan town, rarely visited by foreign tourists (although a fair number of expat NGO workers pass through).

5

Ampara's main draw is as a possible jumping-off point for the nearby **Gal Oya National Park** (see below), although there are also a couple of modest sights closer to hand.

Mandala Mahavihara

Follow the road running north of the main road near the Commercial Bank

In town, the **Mandala Mahavihara** temple is notable for its unusual dagoba. Sitting on a grass-covered terrace, this modest white structure looks perfectly ordinary from the outside. The real surprise lies within, with a small door leading into the hollow interior, its ceiling painted to resemble the sky, supported on a single giant pillar and boasting as impressive an echo as you could hope to hear.

Japanese Peace Pagoda

A few kilometres west of town • Head along Inginiyagala Road, then take the signed turn-off on the right just past the 3km post

The main local attraction hereabouts is the **Japanese Peace Pagoda** (Nipponzan Myohoji), set in peaceful countryside west of Ampara. The florid dagoba itself, surrounded by covered walkway, occupies a fine setting overlooking Ampara tank, while wild elephants can often be seen marching past on their way towards the tank, particularly in the hours before dusk.

ARRIVAL AND INFORMATION   AMPARA

By bus Regular buses connect Ampara and the coast; change at Karativu for Batticaloa, or head to Akkaraipattu for Pottuvil and Arugam Bay. Frequent services also run to Siyambalanduwa and Monaragala.

Banks There are a number of banks along the main street.

The ATMs at the Commercial and Seylan banks both accept foreign cards.

Tours Trips to Gal Oya National Park and other sites of local interest can be arranged through the *Monty Hotel* and *Chinese and Western Food Court*.

ACCOMMODATION AND EATING

Chinese and Western Food Court Just off Main St, down the side road diagonally opposite the Commercial Bank ☏ 063 222 2215. Attractive place offering a wide spread of accommodation ranging from simple but comfortable fan rooms through to smart and attractively furnished deluxe rooms with TV, hot water and free wi-fi. Rs.1500; deluxe rooms Rs.4750

Monty Hotel C32 First Ave (down the road past the Chinese and Western Food Court) ☏ 063 222 2169, ☏ montyhotel.com. Large and unexpectedly chic hotel for such a backwater town, and popular with expense-account

NGOs – which perhaps explains the prices. Rooms (all a/c) are spacious and cool; the more expensive "luxury" options come with hot water, TV and attractive furnishings, and there's also a pool and neat little gardens. Rs.4270; luxury rooms Rs.11,000

Nature Inginiyagala Rd (on road to Japanese Peace Pagoda, signed on left just before the 2km post) ☏ 063 222 3366. In a very peaceful rural location west of town with neat and simple (if slightly battered-looking) rooms (optional a/c). Elephants can sometimes be seen from here towards dusk. Rs.1000; a/c Rs.1600

Gal Oya National Park

Around 20km west from Ampara; entrance at Inginiyagala • Daily 6am–6pm • $10 per person, plus the usual additional charges and taxes (see p.45)

The enormous **Gal Oya National Park** lies some 50km inland from the coast in a little-visited corner of the island. Like the nearby Maduru Oya (see p.361), it was closed for much of the civil war and remains poorly set up for visitors at present. The centrepiece of the park is the vast **Senanayake Samudra**, one of the largest lakes in Sri Lanka, and the tours of the park are usually made – uniquely in Sri Lanka – by boat (you can hire a boat for a trip around the lake at the entrance). As usual, elephants are the main draw, with herds of up to 150 visiting during their annual peregrinations. Elephant-spotting is best from March to July.

Maduru Oya National Park

Some 40km west of Batticaloa • Daily 6am–6pm • $10 per person, plus the usual additional charges and taxes (see p.45) • The most common way to get to the park is to use the southern entrance, via Dambana (see p.236); you can also get there via the village of Mannampitiya – 14km east of Polonnaruwa on the main road to Batticaloa – from where a road leads 25km south to the entrance

Flanking the road inland from Batticaloa to Mahiyangana, the huge and remote **Maduru Oya National Park** was established in 1983 to protect the catchment area of the enormous **Maduru Oya Reservoir** and four smaller reservoirs (more than fifteen percent of the park area is made up of water). Much of Maduru Oya's predominantly low-lying terrain was previously used for slash-and-burn agriculture, and is now mostly covered by open grasslands and secondary vegetation, although there are a few rocky mountains in the southwest corner reaching elevations of 685m. The usual range of fauna can be seen here: elephants, various species of monkeys and deer, abundant birdlife, rare sloth bears and even rarer leopards. The park attracts very few visitors, and in truth it's probably the least interesting national park in the country.

Arugam Bay and around

Easygoing **Arugam Bay** is by far the most engaging of the east coast's resorts. A-Bay, as it's often known, has long been popular with the **surfing** fraternity, who come here to ride what are generally acknowledged to be the best waves in Sri Lanka. It's also a good launching-pad from which to explore the gorgeous surrounding countryside and its varied attractions, from the elephant-rich **Lahugala National Park** and the little-visited **Yala East National Park** to the atmospheric forest hermitage at **Kudimbigala**.

SURFING AT ARUGAM BAY

With waves fresh from Antarctica crashing up onto the beach, Arugam Bay is sometimes claimed to be one of the top ten **surf** points in the world, and periodically plays host to international tournaments. The **best time** for surfing is between April and Oct/Nov.

WHERE TO GO

There are several breaks close to Arugam Bay, plus others further afield. The biggest waves **in A-Bay** itself are at **The Point** (near *Mambo's* guesthouse), a long right-hand break which has (on a good day) 2m waves and a 400m ride. Another good break can be found straight off the beach by the *Siam View Hotel*. **Baby Point** (between *Mambo's* and *Siam View Hotel*) is ideal for beginners, with smaller waves and a sandy bottom (unlike The Point, which is coral-bottomed), while the beach break in front of the *Stardust Beach Hotel* is also good for beginners and body surfing.

South of Arugam Bay, the break near **Crocodile Rock** (3km south of Arugam Bay) is an excellent spot for beginner and intermediate surfers if there's sufficient swell. Some 5km further on, **Peanut Farm** has two surf points: a perfect tube for expert surfers and a smaller ride ideal for beginners; there are also good waves further south at **Okanda**.

A number of spots **north of Pottuvil** are also becoming popular among more experienced surfers (and are generally quieter than those in A-Bay). About 9km north of Arugam Bay, **Pottuvil Point** breaks off a long and deserted sandy beach; the ride can be as long as 800m, though the waves are a bit smaller than in A-Bay. Other nearby breaks include Whiskey Point and Lighthouse Point (aka "The Green Room").

INFORMATION AND RENTAL

The best places for general surfing **info and equipment hire** are A-Bay Surf Shop and the surf shop at the *Surf N Sun* guesthouse. These places and some of the village's guesthouses rent bodyboards and surfboards (from around Rs.600/day), as well as offering **surfing safaris** to various other spots along the coast.

5

Arugam Bay

There's not much to **ARUGAM BAY** village itself: just a single main road running parallel to the beach dotted with guesthouses, cafés and shops, including some of Arugam Bay's trademark quirky homespun architectural creations – rustic palm-thatch cabanas, teetering treehouses and other quaint structures (not to mention the distinctive wooden pavilion restaurant and red British telephone box of the landmark *Siam View Hotel*). The **beach** is now looking better than ever following recent clearances during which the authorities ordered the removal of all buildings within 20m of the waterline (albeit at considerable cost to local hoteliers and other residents, who were forced to watch as the government bulldozers rolled in and summarily razed significant slices of prized real estate).

A-Bay also marks the rough border between the Sinhalese-majority areas to the south and the mainly Tamil and Muslim areas further up the coast, and boasts an unusually eclectic but harmonious mix of all three ethnic groups – as well as a growing number of Western expats. Fears that the village's uniquely (for Sri Lanka) alternative and slightly off-the-wall character will be erased by larger and more mainstream tourism developments remain, however, especially given the forthcoming opening of the new **Hambantota airport**, which will make the village significantly easier to reach for international visitors. For the time being, however, Arugam Bay preserves its own enjoyably eccentric charm.

ARRIVAL AND DEPARTURE — ARUGAM BAY

By bus Heading west, there's currently a direct daily bus from Arugam Bay to Colombo via Monaragala at 6.30am, plus a very comfortable a/c private bus from Pottuvil to Colombo at 9am (tickets Rs.700). There are also around another three buses to Monaragala in the morning from A-Bay, plus further services west from Pottuvil. Alternatively take a bus from Pottuvil to Siyambalanduwa, from where there are more frequent onward services.

Heading north, there's a direct service at 11am to Batticaloa; alternatively, take one of the regular buses (every 30min) from Pottuvil to Kalmunai, from where there are frequent onward connections connections. For Ampara, take a Kalmunai bus from Pottuvil and change at Akkaraipattu.

By plane SriLankan Airlines runs scheduled air taxis (see p.30) from Colombo to Arugam Bay in high season.

INFORMATION

Tourist information The best sources of information are the *Arugambay Surf Resort* and the *Stardust* and *Siam View* hotels.

Websites The *Stardust* (ⓦ arugambay.com) and *Siam View* (ⓦ arugam.com) hotels have useful websites. Another very good source is ⓦ arugam.info.

TOURS FROM ARUGAM BAY

For a convenient whistle-stop tour of the area, the *Arugambay Surf Resort* run useful **day-tours by tuktuk** (Rs.4500/vehicle) taking in most of the major local attractions including Kudimbigala, Okana, Magul Maha Vihara and Lahugala. The **Pottuvil Lagoon Tour** (Rs.3500/two-person boat; bookings and info on ☎075 489 6583) consists of a gentle 2hr canoe trip during which a local fisherman will paddle you out into Pottuvil lagoon, 8km north of town, and through the beautiful mangrove swamps that fringe its shores, offering the chance to spot birds, monitor lizards and perhaps the occasional crocodile or elephant. They also arrange **sea safaris** (2hr; Rs.6000 for two people) in engine-powered boats, with a good chance of seeing dolphins, flying fish and other marine life. You can also **dive** from the boat if you have your own equipment or do some fishing.

In addition to the tours detailed above, the **Arugam Bay Tourism Assocation** can also arrange more unusual excursions; ask at the *Arugambay Surf Resort* (and book the day before). **Surfing tours** are also a good option (see box, p.361) as are trips to (the edges of) **Lahugala** (see p.365) and **Yala East** (see p.366) **national parks**.

ACCOMMODATION

Arugam Bay offers rustic and often quirky **accommodation** in palm-thatch cabanas, huts on stilts, treehouses and the like – fun, if fairly basic, and prices are often surprisingly high. There are a handful of conventional places to stay too, though you should avoid the bay's twin low-grade resort-style hotels, the cheerless and overpriced *Tri-Star* and *New Tri-Star*. The local tourism association can organize **homestays**; ask at the *Arugambay Surf Resort*. A-Bay is very quiet out of **season**, when you may find some of the places listed below (and many others) closed for repairs.

Aloha Cabanas Northern end of the beach ☎063 224 8379, ⓦaloha-arugambay.com. Crashed-out surfers' hangout set in a rambling garden leading down to the beach. The bright and roomy concrete cabanas (with attractive little upstairs terraces with hammocks) are reasonable value by A-Bay standards; the smaller and rather rickety palm-thatch ones less so. Concrete cabanas $30

★ **Arugambay Surf Resort** Middle of the village ☎063 224 8189, ⓦarugambay.lk. This long-time A-Bay stalwart was formerly known as the *Arugambay Hillton* until it was forced to change its name after legal proceedings by the US hotel chain – probably the most pointless piece of corporate litigation ever. Accommodation is in a mix of neat and comfortable (if smallish) rooms decorated in cheerful colours plus rustic cabanas set around a pleasant courtyard garden-restaurant (see p.364). There's also internet (Rs.50/hr), free wi-fi and 50cc scooters for rent (Rs.1000/day), and the very clued-up owner can arrange all sorts of local tours (see box opposite). Rs.2500

★ **Beach Hut** Northern end of the beach ☎0773 179 594, ⓔarugambaybeachhut@gmail .com. A quintessential slice of Arugam Bay, with a selection of rustic wooden cabanas in a quirky range of styles (including a couple on stilts, and a picturesque treehouse). It's rustic and fairly basic (the cheapest cabanas come with shared bathroom), but excellent value, and has bags of laid-back charm and character. Also a sociable choice for evening meals, with good, inexpensive Sri Lankan food served at a communal table (book in advance). Rs.500

The Danish Villa On the land side of the road, northern side of the village ☎077 695 7936, ⓦdanishvilla.com. One of the village's more upmarket options, in a low-slung white villa set amid pretty gardens with seven attractively furnished a/c rooms. Rs.4600

Galaxy Lounge Northern end of the beach ☎063 224 8415, ⓦgalaxysrilanka.com. Nice beachfront location with accommodation in a mix of large and attractive two-storey palm-thatch cabanas, plus a breezy open-air restaurant. Rs.2500

★ **Hideaway** On the land side of the main road, southern side of the village ☎063 224 8259, ⓦhideawayarugambay.com. One of the nicest places to stay in Arugam Bay, set in a characterful

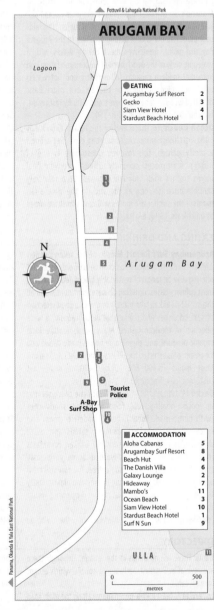

Pottuvil & Lahugala National Park

ARUGAM BAY

Lagoon

● **EATING**
Arugambay Surf Resort	2
Gecko	3
Siam View Hotel	4
Stardust Beach Hotel	1

N

Arugam Bay

Tourist Police

A-Bay Surf Shop

■ **ACCOMMODATION**
Aloha Cabanas	5
Arugambay Surf Resort	8
Beach Hut	4
The Danish Villa	6
Galaxy Lounge	2
Hideaway	7
Mambo's	11
Ocean Beach	3
Siam View Hotel	10
Stardust Beach Hotel	1
Surf N Sun	9

Panama, Okanda & Yala East National Park

ULLA

0 _____ 500
metres

5

two-storey house swathed in tropical greenery. The rooms in the main house are attractively furnished, with open latticework brick walls and slatted wooden fronts – pleasantly cool, if not terribly private. There are also two smart new a/c rooms in a separate annexe, plus a handful of upmarket whitewashed brick cabanas-cum-bungalows. Rs.5000; a/c Rs.8500; cabanas-cum-bungalows Rs.6500

Mambo's On the bay opposite the main beach ☎ 0777 822 524, ⊕ mambo.nu. Mainly aimed at surfers, this laid-back place has the closest accommodation to the Arugam Bay surf point, right over the breaking waves with a sweeping view of the beach opposite. Accommodation is in upmarket modern cabanas (all with a/c and hot water) with cool, tiled interiors, or cheaper but more basic thatched wooden cabanas. There's also a funky restaurant, bar, chill-out zone and free wi-fi. $50

Ocean Beach Northern end of the beach ☎ 063 224 8405, ⊕ theoceanbeacharugambay.com. Set around a pretty garden, this low-key guesthouse is one of A-Bay's few places currently offering conventional rooms (rather than wooden cabanas) at a relatively sensible price (so long as you stick to the simple fan rooms – the similar a/c rooms will cost you three times as much). Rs.1500; a/c Rs.4500

Siam View Hotel Middle of the village ☎ 077 320 0201, ⊕ arugam.com. Attached to the landmark A-Bay restaurant (see below), with spacious modern rooms, all with a/c, free wi-fi, satellite TV and fridge. Rs.4900

★ **Stardust Beach Hotel** Northern end of the beach ☎ 063 224 8191, ⊕ arugambay.com. Arugam Bay's smartest hotel, with bright and stylish rooms (those upstairs have great ocean views from the sea-facing balconies) including four in the new "Villa Wonne" next door and a selection of upmarket (if rather pricey) wooden cabanas. There's also a yoga pavilion (group and individual classes available), a canoe for lagoon trips and a good restaurant (see below) with free wi-fi. Rooms $70; cabanas $43

Surf N Sun Middle of the village ☎ 0776 065 099, ⊕ thesurfnsun.com. Party-atmosphere surfers' hangout, set in luxuriant, green gardens and with some of the village's most attractive cabanas – a mix of simpler wooden structures and larger concrete-walled affairs almost buried under vast palm-thatch roofs, with airy, spacious interiors. There's a lively restaurant and reggae bar (open till 3/4am in season), plus a surf shop, and it's also a good place to organize tours. $25

EATING AND DRINKING

Arugambay Surf Resort Middle of the village ☎ 063 224 8189, ⊕ arugambay.lk. Small beachfront restaurant offering a wide range of reasonably priced food covering most culinary bases including Chinese, continental and all the usual Sri Lankan favourites, along with a good selection of seafood dishes and (somewhat incongruously) a wide selection of Mexican dishes. Many meals feature local organic produce, and there's also home-made bread and ice cream, plus assorted breakfasts, sandwiches and salads. Most mains Rs.400–600. Daily 6.30am until last customer leaves at night.

Gecko Middle of the village. Neat little place serving up good, healthy café food including sandwiches (with home-made bread), home-made ice cream and cakes, all-day breakfasts, burgers, salads and pasta dishes, plus rice and curry and Sri Lankan breakfasts (most mains Rs.700–900), washed down with tasty sugar-free juices and fair-trade coffee. You can also refill used water bottles here, saving money and plastic. Daily 6.30am until late in season, reduced opening hours at other times.

★ **Siam View Hotel** Middle of the village ☎ 077 320 0201, ⊕ arugam.com. Easily the best place for a night out in the village, occupying an open-sided first-floor wooden pavilion with incongruous red British telephone box standing sentry outside. The food, authentic Thai (with perhaps some non-Thai dishes during season; mains around Rs.600–750), is excellent, while real-ale enthusiast owner Fred also usually has a superb range of home-brewed beers on tap from the downstairs micro-brewery – a blessed relief from yet more Lion Lager. Good cocktail list too, plus free wi-fi and A-Bay's best soundtrack, as well free movie screenings in a side room most evenings. Daily 6pm–late (up to 6am in season, when it may also be open during the day).

Stardust Beach Hotel Northern end of the beach ☎ 063 224 8191, ⊕ arugambay.com. Attractive pavilion restaurant with an appetizing selection of snacks and well-prepared meals (most mains around Rs.800–1000) including a good selection of breakfasts and sandwiches (with home-made bread) alongside international dishes ranging from pasta and goulash through to dosas and rice and curry. Free wi-fi. Daily 7.45am–10pm.

DIRECTORY

Bank There are no banks in the village, although there are several in Pottuvil, including a couple which accept foreign cards.

Internet At least half-a-dozen places along the main road offer internet (and sometimes wi-fi), and there's also free wi-fi at the *Stardust*, *Arugambay Surf Resort* and *Siam View Hotel* restaurants.

Lahugala National Park

15km inland from Arugam Bay • Free

A short way inland from Arugam Bay the main road west passes through the small but beautiful **Lahugala National Park**, comprising Lahugula Tank and a magnificent swathe of dry mixed evergreen forest, dotted with lofty rosewoods and satinwoods. The park is best known for its **elephants**: up to 150 congregate around the tank during July and August, when the rest of Lahugala's waters dry up, to drink and feed on the *beru* grass which grows prolifically around the water. The tank is also good for spotting a wide range of aquatic **birds**, including innumerable snowy white egrets that can often be seen hitching a ride on the backs of obliging elephants. When the rains come the elephants disperse, and large sections of the park turn a brilliant, post-monsoonal green.

Lahugala isn't officially open to the public, and no vehicles are allowed in, although you're free to walk into the park from the main road between Arugam Bay and Monaragala, which runs right through it. Be aware, however, that walking through jungle with a large elephant population carries a degree of risk, so it's best to stick to one of the recognized **viewpoints** close to the road. The easiest (and safest) option is to head to **Lahugala Hospital** (at the 306km post). Just west of here along the main road, several small paths run off to the right to the raised bund at the edge of Lahugala Tank, about 100m away, which offers a secure vantage point and good chances of spotting elephants.

Guesthouses in Arugam Bay can arrange **jeeps** to Lahugala, although given that you can't actually drive these into the park, you might as well save your money and catch a bus or tuktuk (around Rs.2000).

Magul Maha Vihara

Just east of Lahugala (and signposted from the main road just west of the 309km post) • No set hours • Donation

According to tradition, the evocative remains of the **Magul Maha Vihara** temple mark the site of the wedding of Kavan Tissa and Viharamahadevi (see p.185), one of ancient Sri Lanka's most famous celebrity couples – the resident monk will point out the *poruwa*, a special wedding platform decorated with a lion frieze, which was erected for the event. Following the ceremony, the land was walled and presented to the Sangha, who established a monastery here. The unexcavated remains of Kavan Tissa's palace lie in jungle to south; it was here that the couple's son, the legendary Dutugemunu (see p.324), was born and lived until his teens, when he and his parents moved to Tissa.

Stone inscriptions found at the site record that the current temple buildings were erected by King Dhatusena during the mid-fifth century, and later restored in the mid-fourteenth century. The extensive remains include a Buddha shrine, image house, dagoba, *poyage* and well-preserved moonstones, as well as the finely carved *poruwa*, all lent an additional layer of mystery by the thick jungle that surrounds them on every side.

South of Arugam Bay

The countryside and coastline **south of Arugam Bay** is beautifully unspoilt. Buses run three times daily along the good tarmac road which rolls through rice paddies and scrub jungle as far as the dusty little village of **PANAMA**, 12km south of Arugam Bay. There are miles of superb deserted beach along this stretch, and a pair of huge rock outcrops popularly known as **Elephant Rock** and **Crocodile Rock** for their alleged resemblance to these creatures, though you'll need a tuktuk (or 4WD) to reach them. Elephants are sometimes seen wandering in the vicinity. Panama itself has a fine, dune-backed beach, 1km south of town; to reach it, pass through the village and follow the road round to the left.

The road **south of Panama** is currently unsurfaced, although the dirt track is kept in reasonable condition and is usually passable in a 2WD (tuktuks make the journey with ease). The countryside here is almost completely uninhabited, and very similar in

5

THE 1883 TSUNAMI

Contrary to popular belief, the **tsunami** that devastated Sri Lanka in 2004 was not the first the island has experienced in modern times. As recently as August 1883, the massive eruption of **Krakatoa**, between Java and Sumatra in Indonesia, unleashed gigantic tidal waves that sped west across the Indian Ocean before reaching Sri Lanka. At Galle, a sequence of fourteen freak waves, each separated by a few minutes, was observed. The *Ceylon Observer* described the scene preceding the arrival of the waves, one eerily prescient of events 121 years later: "The sea receded as far as the landing stage on the jetty. The boats and canoes moored along the shore were left high and dry for about three minutes. A great number of prawns and fishes were taken up by the coolies and stragglers about the place before the water returned." Further around the coast, a 3.5m-high wave hit Hambantota, while at Panama on the east coast "ships suddenly sunk downwards and were then drawn backwards to be left stuck in the drying mud, their anchors exposed – and just as suddenly were borne up by an inrushing surge of water. The local streams, with hitherto sweet water, all promptly turned salty for at least a mile and a half upriver" (as Simon Winchester describes it in his vivid account of the eruption, *Krakatoa*). What the 1883 tsunami mercifully lacked, however, was the destructive force of its 2004 counterpart. Only a single casualty was recorded in the entire island, at Panama, where a woman was swept away from the harbour bar – probably the unluckiest victim of a volcanic eruption more than 3000km distant.

appearance to that of Yala (West) National Park, with extensive lagoons, scrub jungle and huge populations of aquatic birds, as well as occasional elephants and crocodiles.

Kudimbigala

Just beyond the 12km post on the road south of Panama

Around a 45min drive from Arugam Bay, a turning on the right leads for 500m to reach the beautiful forest hermitage of **KUDIMBIGALA**, whose hundreds of caves are thought to have been occupied by Buddhist monks as far back as the first century BC.

From the car park, follow the path ahead of you (keeping the modern rock-top dagoba to your right) into the surrounding woodland, following the track as it squeezes through the trees and between enormous rock outcrops to reach, after about ten minutes, the **Sudasharna Cave**, a small white shrine half-covered by an overhanging rock outcrop bearing the faint remains of ancient Brahmi script next to an unusual little carving symbolizing the Triple Gem.

Following the path to the left of the cave leads after another ten minutes up to the **Madhya Mandalaya** ("Plain of Ruins"), with a small dagoba and other monastic remains scattered over a rocky hilltop. Alternatively, heading right from the cave brings you to the huge **Belumgala**, a towering rock outcrop topped by yet another small dagoba. Rock-cut steps lead to the top, a breathless ten-to-fifteen-minute climb, at the end of which you'll be rewarded by one of the finest views anywhere in the east: a vast swathe of jungle dotted with huge rock outcrops running down to the sea, and with scarcely a single sign of human habitation in sight.

Okanda

30km south of Arugam Bay

Beyond Kudimbigala, the village of **OKANDA** has another popular surfing spot, and also boasts a major **Hindu temple**, marking the spot where Kataragama is said to have landed on the island and now an important staging point on the overland pilgrimage to Kataragama. The village is also the entrance point for **Yala East National Park**.

Yala East National Park

30km south of Arugam Bay • Daily 6am–6pm • $10 per person, plus the usual additional charges and taxes (see p.45) • Some guesthouses in Arugam Bay offer day-trips by jeep, seating four to six people, for around $100 (possibly including Okanda and Kudimbigala as well)

Yala East National Park (also known as the Kumana National Park) has recently reopened after extended closure during the war years, when it served as an LTTE hideout. The main attraction within the park is the Kumana Wewa tank and surrounding mangroves, home to an outstanding array of aquatic birds.

Monaragala and around

Just beyond the easternmost fringes of the hill country east of Wellawaya, the small town of **MONARAGALA** sits at the foot of the huge **Peacock Rock**, whose sheer sides loom dramatically over the countryside hereabouts. The town itself is principally of interest as the gateway to Arugam Bay, and also provides a convenient base for visiting the remote and magical Buddhist statues of **Maligawila** and the huge ruined stupa of **Yudaganawa**.

ARRIVAL AND DEPARTURE

MONARAGALA

By bus The bus station is bang in the centre of town. There are around seven buses daily from Monaragala to Arugam Bay; most leave in the morning (last bus currently at 3.30pm) and the journey takes around 2hr. Alternatively, take a bus to the town of Pottuvil, a 5km tuktuk ride from Arugam Bay, or catch a bus to Siyambalanduwa, from where there are more regular connections onto Pottuvil/Arugam Bay. Heading west, catch a bus to Wellawaya or Badulla, from where there are plentiful onward connections.

Destinations Ampara (hourly; 3hr); Arugam Bay (7 daily; 2hr); Badulla (every 30min; 3hr); Buttala (every 30min; 45min); Wellawaya (every 10min; 1hr 15min).

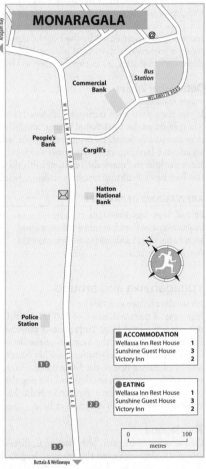

ACCOMMODATION AND EATING

Accommodation options in Monaragala are – not surprisingly – limited, as are places to eat, although all the following are fine for a night, and do reasonable food as well.

Sunshine Guest House Wellawaya Rd ☏ 055 227 6313. The nicest and (assuming it's not hosting a wedding) quietest option in town, in a bright modern orange block set slightly back from the road with neat modern tiled rooms and very cheap optional a/c. Rs.2750; a/c Rs.3000
Victory Inn Wellawaya Rd ☏ 055 227 6100. Decent modern rooms with fan, or smarter ones with a/c, although prices are a bit steep, and rooms overlooking the road are noisy – try to get one around the side. Rs.3000; a/c Rs.3550
Wellassa Inn Rest House Wellawaya Rd ☏ 055 227 6815. Characterful but shabby old rest house set behind a spacious garden, and with a pleasant terrace restaurant. Rooms have seen better days, although it's significantly cheaper than the local competition. Rs.1375

DIRECTORY

Bank Several banks with ATMs can be found along the main Wellawaya Road; the Commercial Bank is usually reliable for both Visa and MasterCard.
Internet Samudra Communications, by the bus station, has a couple of old machines (daily 8am–6pm; Rs.60/hr).

5

Maligawila and around

The remote village of **MALIGAWILA**, little more than a sandy clearing surrounded by a few makeshift shacks, is home to two giant standing Buddhist **statues**, fashioned out of crystalline limestone, which are thought to have once formed part of an extensive monastic complex. The images, which had collapsed and fallen to bits, were restored in 1991, when the various pieces were rescued from the jungle floor and painstakingly reassembled – though the Maitreya statue still looks rather patched up. The statues are impressive in themselves, but are made additionally mysterious by their setting, hidden away in a stretch of pristine lowland jungle.

The statues

From the car park, a path leads into the woods, reaching a T-junction after about 300m. Turn left to reach the first of the two statues, an 11m-high standing **Buddha** in the *abhaya mudra* ("Have No Fear") pose, freestanding apart from a discreet supporting brick arch at the back.

Return to the T-junction and follow the other path for 200m to reach the second statue, dating from the seventh century AD and thought to represent either the bodhisattvas **Maitreya** or **Avalokitesvara**. This is a more elaborate structure, with the remains of ornate entrance steps, a moonstone and two flanking guardstones, plus a pillar inscription in medieval Sinhala erected during the reign of Mahinda IV (956–972), recording acts performed by the king in support of the Buddhist order. The statue itself is set on a sequence of five raised plinths, like a ziggurat, and clothed in a richly ornamented dress; unfortunately, it's currently protected by an ugly concrete pavilion.

Detamahal Vihara

6km west of Maligawila

If you have your own transport, it's worth making the short detour about 6km west of Maligawila to the **Detamahal Vihara**, a mildly interesting temple with marvellous views over the paddy fields. Its origins date right back to the first or second century BC, and an ancient-looking, red-brick stupa survives, along with traces of Polonnaruwa-era stonework in the main shrine, itself built on an even older stone base. Next to here a modern brick building houses a striking, blackened twelfth-century Buddha image.

ARRIVAL AND DEPARTURE   **MALIGAWILA AND AROUND**

By bus Buses from Monaragala to Maligawila leave roughly every 45min and take around an hour, dropping you in the tiny village's dusty main square, from where it's a short walk to the statues.

By taxi or tuktuk A taxi from Monaragala will cost around Rs.2500. Taking a tuktuk is cheaper – around Rs.1500 – though it's a long journey, and you won't be able to appreciate the attractive countryside en route.

Yudaganawa and around

2km west of Buttala • Open access 24hr • Free

Just west of the small town of **BUTTALA** (and 20km southwest of Monaragala) lie the remains of the huge **Yudaganawa dagoba**, one of the biggest in the east. The stupa is said to mark the location of the decisive second battle (see p.324) between Dutugemunu and his younger brother Saddhatissa. Dutugemunu was victorious, and Saddhatissa fled to the Detamahal Vihara (see above), although the brothers were subsequently reconciled and the dagoba was commissioned by Saddhatissa to commemorate the peace. Parakramabahu (see p.309) is said to have subsequently enshrined the ashes of his mother here.

The dagoba

Of the original dagoba, only the huge, three-tiered **base** now survives (heavily restored), although even this gives an impressive sense of the enormity of the original structure, with a circumference of 310m, even bigger than the mighty Ruvanvalisaya dagoba in Anuradhapura.

A small Kandyan-era **shrine** stands in front of the stupa, richly decorated inside with intricate, though faded, murals and a painted wooden ceiling – the pictures flanking the door are particularly fine, showing a meditating Buddha shaded by a grinning cobra on one side and an unusually slim, black-headed Ganesh on the other. (Note that you'll probably be asked for a donation when entering the shrine, although you don't need to give any money to see the dagoba itself.)

On the way out you'll pass the slight remains of the **Culangani Vihara**, said to mark the site of a first clash between Dutugemunu and Saddhatissa, although little now remains of the original temple beyond a small mossy dagoba and fragments of two very bashed-up Buddhas – only the torsos survive, plus a single pair of feet.

ARRIVAL AND DEPARTURE YUDAGANAWA AND AROUND

By car To reach the stupa head 1km west of Buttala along the Wellawaya Road, then 1km down a side road signed on the right. If you don't have your own transport you'll have to walk from Buttala or catch a tuktuk.

ACCOMMODATION

Well off the beaten track, the remote countryside around the town of **Buttala**, 2km east of Yudaganawa, is an unlikely home to two of the island's most memorable – and idiosyncratic – **eco-retreats**.

Kumbuk River 9km east of Buttala ☎ 0773 632 182, ⓦ kumbukriver.com. This unique riverside retreat offers you probably the only chance you'll ever get to sleep *in* an elephant – an extraordinary 12m-long, thatch-roofed beast constructed from local *kumbuk* wood. There's also a second, and equally comfortable and spacious, non-pachyderm eco-chalet; both sleep up to ten. Full board, minimum stay two nights. $250

Tree Tops Jungle Lodge 9km southeast of Buttala ☎ 0777 036 554, ⓦ treetopsjunglelodge.com. This jungle lodge really is out in the wilds – visitors are advised to arrive no earlier than 9am and no later than 3pm to avoid wandering elephants – with accommodation in rustic tree huts in an unspoiled forest setting. There are no mod cons here (and no electricity) but it manages to be very comfortable even so, and the excellent and highly informative jungle walks, accompanied by a four-man local tracker team, are second to none. Advance booking required. Full board. $280

Jaffna and the north

374 The Vanni

379 Jaffna

386 The Jaffna Peninsula

391 The islands

COLONIAL ARCHITECTURE, JAFFNA

Jaffna and the north

The north is a world away from the rest of Sri Lanka. Closer to southern India than to Colombo, the region was settled early on by Tamil migrants from southern India and has retained a unique character and culture, one which owes as much to Hindu India as to Buddhist Sri Lanka. From 1983 to 2009 the entire region was engulfed in the civil war between the rebel guerrillas of the LTTE (Liberation Tigers of Tamil Eelam, or Tamil Tigers), and the Sri Lankan Army (SLA), and the decades of fighting have further reinforced the two-thousand-year history of difference that separates the Tamil north from the Sinhalese south.

For much of the past two decades, large areas of the north were controlled by the LTTE, who established their own de facto independent state stretching from just north of Vavuniya through to Elephant Pass (while for a period they also controlled Jaffna and the Jaffna Peninsula until it was recaptured by the SLA in 1995). The region is only gradually emerging from the long years of isolation and fighting, and the painfully slow process of rebuilding shattered towns and villages, de-mining fields, restoring roads and returning refugees to their former homes is likely to continue for some time to come.

For the traveller, the north is Sri Lanka's final frontier, and offers a fascinating opportunity to explore a region emerging from over twenty years of isolation and civil war. Reaching the area is now straightforward, and although it still entails a long road journey (or short flight), for those who make the effort there are rich rewards. Foremost of these is the fascinating town of **Jaffna**, with its absorbing mixture of colonial charm and vibrant Tamil culture, while the **Jaffna Peninsula** and surrounding **islands** offer a string of remote temples, beaches and more off-beat attractions. Further south, the vast swathe of sparsely populated countryside known as the **Vanni** is little visited, even by Sri Lankans, although the remote church at **Madhu** draws a steady stream of pilgrims of all faiths while the war-torn town of **Kilinochchi**, former capital of the LTTE, provides a stark reminder of the destructiveness of the war.

INFORMATION

Getting around Public transport throughout the region is sketchy: there are no trains north of Omantai, and far fewer buses than in other parts of the country. Obviously, the best plan is to take your own car and driver if you can manage it, though Sinhalese drivers may be a little wary about travelling to the north, while there are few cars for hire in the region itself.

Access Foreign visitors are currently allowed to travel freely up and down the main A9 highway from Vavuniya to Jaffna (and around the Jaffna Peninsula itself), and along the A14 to Mannar, although there are still restrictions on travelling in more remote parts of the region, including to the east coast town of Mullaitivu, close to the scene of the LTTE's final stand in 2009. On the A9 there are still police checkpoints at Omantai and Elephant Pass where you'll need to show a passport and perhaps fill in a form, although these are unlikely to detain you long.

Safety There are currently no major safety concerns or

The Liberation Tigers of Tamil Eelam p.376

The sieges of Jaffna p.382

The EPRLF headquarters p.384

The Nallur Festival p.384

Vanishing landmarks of the LTTE p.390

The Nilavarai Well p.391

NALLUR KANDASWAMY TEMPLE, JAFFNA

Highlights

❶ Our Lady of Madhu Pilgrims of all faiths flock to this remote church to pay homage to the miracle-working statue of Our Lady of Madhu, said to protect against snakebite and other dangers. **See p.375**

❷ Jaffna Quite unlike anywhere else in the island, the vibrant city of Jaffna offers a fascinating insight into Sri Lankan Tamil culture, as well as many intriguing reminders of its colonial and wartime past. **See p.379**

❸ Nallur Kandaswamy Temple and Festival Sri Lanka's finest Hindu temple, and home to the north's largest and longest festival – a 25-day

extravaganza of colour, ceremony and spectacle. **See p.384**

❹ Jaffna Peninsula The fertile peninsula is home to myriad contrasting sights, from sand dunes and sacred springs to abandoned villages and war-torn temples. **See p.386**

❺ The islands Splintering off the tip of the Jaffna Peninsula, the starkly beautiful islands of Kayts, Karaitivu, Nainativu and Delft are a world away from the rest of Sri Lanka, home to little-visited Hindu temples, colonial forts and remote beaches. **See p.391**

HIGHLIGHTS ARE MARKED ON THE MAP ON P.374

security threats when it comes to visiting the north. The only possible concern is the danger from landmines. An estimated half a million mines still lie buried around the north, and – in the unlikely event that you find yourself in areas of remote northern countryside it's a good idea to stick to roads or well-defined paths rather than wandering off into the jungle.

The Vanni

The huge area of northern Sri Lanka between **Vavuniya** and the Jaffna Peninsula – **the Vanni** – has been devastated by the civil war, and large areas now lie ruined, abandoned and heavily mined – the task of bringing life back to the region following the most recent round of fighting is likely to be a long and difficult one. This entire region was

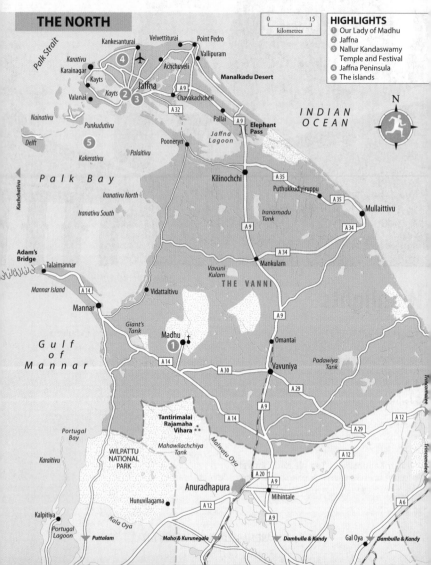

controlled by the LTTE until 2008–09 from their "capital" at **Kilinochchi**, on the northern edge of the Vanni.

Vavuniya

The gateway to the Vanni is the town of **VAVUNIYA** (pronounced "Vowvneeya"), the largest between Anuradhapura and Jaffna. Vavuniya sits roughly at the borderline between Sinhalese and Tamil Sri Lanka, and has frequently found itself on or close to the front line of the fighting, serving as an important staging post for the SLA from which to mount military operations to the north. There's a significant Tamil population here, and if you've travelled up from Anuradhapura, you'll start to notice subtle cultural changes in language, food and attire compared with places further south.

Vavuniya's only attraction, the modest **Archeological Museum** has a small collection of fifth- to tenth-century Buddhist statues, although it is only erratically open.

ARRIVAL AND INFORMATION   VAVUNIYA

By bus Vavuniya is a major transport hub and the starting point for buses west to Mannar.
Destinations Anuradhapura (every 30min; 2hr); Colombo (every 30min; 5–6hr); Kandy (every 30min; 4hr); Jaffna (hourly; 4hr); Madhu (every 2hr; 2hr); Mannar (hourly; 2hr); Trincomalee (3 daily; 3hr 30min).
By train Vavuniya stands close to the end of the train line

north (which has recently been reopened up to Omantai).
Destinations Anuradhapura (6 daily; 1hr); Colombo (5 daily; 4–6hr).
Banks A number of banks around town have ATMs accepting foreign cards; the Commercial Bank opposite the Archeological Museum is the most reliable.

ACCOMMODATION

The town has a few basic places to stay, although unless you're utterly stuck it's better to press on to Anuradhapura.

Hotel Nelly Star 84, 2nd Cross St ☎ 024 222 4477. Vavuniya's most upmarket option (not that that's saying much), professionally run and with a/c restaurant and bar, a decent-sized, although rather murky-looking, pool. Wi-fi and internet. To reach the hotel head south down the main road from the clock tower then left down Second Cross St; the hotel is about 300m down the road on your right.
Rs.2200; a/c Rs.3100

Hotel Swarkka 33 Soosaipillaiyarkulam Rd ☎ 024 222 1090. Friendly little place, with clean tiled rooms (albeit somewhat lacking in windows). To reach the hotel go east from the clocktower down Bazaar St/Kandaswamy Kovil Rd for around 400m then turn left. Rs.2250; a/c Rs.2750

Madhu

Northwest of Vavuniya lies the remote village of **MADHU**, the most important place of Christian pilgrimage in Sri Lanka. The large, nineteenth-century Portuguese-style church here is home to the allegedly miraculous statue of **Our Lady of Madhu**. The image was brought to Madhu in 1670 by Catholics fleeing Dutch persecution in the Mannar area, and subsequently became revered for its magical qualities, particularly its supposed ability to protect devotees against snakebite. The shrine is revered by both Sinhalese and Tamil Catholics and, in characteristic Sri Lankan fashion, has also become popular among non-Christians, offering a rare beacon of religious and racial harmony in the troubled north. A **festival** in honour of the statue held here annually in August draws huge crowds – an estimated 500,000 pilgrims visited in 2011.

ARRIVAL AND DEPARTURE   MADHU

By bus The village lies 45km from Vavuniya, north of the A14. Buses run from Mannar and Vavuniya to Madhu every

couple of hours, taking about two hours to make the journey.

6

THE LIBERATION TIGERS OF TAMIL EELAM

Terrorists in the eyes of some, freedom fighters to others, the **Liberation Tigers of Tamil Eelam** (LTTE), popularly known as the **Tamil Tigers**, were until their final defeat in 2009 one of the world's most committed, effective and ruthless militant organizations. The LTTE was founded in the early 1970s, one of a string of paramilitary groups established by young Tamils in response to the decades of official discrimination meted out by the Sinhalese governments of Colombo to the Tamils of the north and east. The failure of the older Tamil leaders to secure political justice for Tamils and the heavy-handed behaviour of the Sinhalese-dominated Sri Lankan Army and police in Tamil areas drove many young Tamils to espouse violence. All these groups of young militants called for the establishment of an independent Tamil state in the north and east of the island, to be called **Eelam** ("Precious Land"), and a number received training from special Indian government forces who were initially sympathetic to their cause.

PRABHAKARAN: ELUSIVE LEADER

The LTTE gradually rose to pre-eminence thanks to its ruthless suppression of all competing political groups and the assassination of rival politicians, and by the beginning of the civil war in 1983, the LTTE had become the leading player in Tamil affairs. At the heart of the LTTE's mystique lay their founder and leader, the enigmatic **Velupillai Prabhakaran** (born 1954). Legends about this reclusive figure abound. According to some, he was a shy and bookish student with a fascination for Napoleon and Alexander the Great, who turned militant when he saw an uncle burnt alive by Sinhalese mobs, and who later trained himself to endure pain by lying in sacks of chillies. Known as *Thambi*, or "Little Brother", Prabhakaran was held in quasi-religious veneration by many of his recruits, and proved a consummate political survivor who evaded capture for two decades until finally being ambushed and killed by the SLA in May 2009. He also proved a gifted military strategist, although reports suggest that much of the LTTE's earlier engagements were based on the study of *Rambo* and Arnold Schwarzenegger videos – a classic example of life imitating (bad) art.

GUERRILLA TACTICS

The LTTE began life as a classic **guerrilla operation**, harrying the (to begin with) far better-equipped and numerically superior forces of the Sri Lankan Army and later the Indian Peacekeeping Force (see p.410) with hit-and-run attacks, before retreating back into the countryside and mixing with local populations. These guerrilla tactics were combined with gruesome, attention-grabbing attacks such as that at Anuradhapura in 1985, when dozens of civilians and pilgrims were gunned down by LTTE soldiers in the symbolic centre of Sinhalese culture. The LTTE also pioneered the practice of **suicide bombing** (whose technology they are believed to have exported to militant Palestinian organizations such as Hamas), with

Mannar Island

Connected to the mainland by a 2km bridge, long, thin **Mannar Island** pokes out into the sea, like a finger pointing westwards towards India, barely 10km distant over the Palk Strait. Mannar was long famous for its **pearl banks**, which were exploited from antiquity until the colonial period: as late as 1905 some five thousand divers recovered a staggering eighty million oysters here in a single season – they also provided the inspiration for Bizet's *The Pearl Fishers*, the only opera ever to be set in Sri Lanka. Arab traders also flocked to Mannar, introducing donkeys (an animal virtually unknown elsewhere in Sri Lanka), and planting the baobab trees which remain another of the island's distinctive features. Mannar suffered greatly during the war, when its position close to India made it a major conduit for refugees fleeing the country. The island's large Muslim population, a legacy of its years of Arab trade, was driven out by the LTTE in 1990, though the local population still includes many Catholics – some forty percent, the highest proportion of anywhere in Sri Lanka.

notable attacks against Colombo, the international airport and the Temple of the Tooth in Kandy, amongst many others. Suicide bombers have also been used in a string of high-profile **political assassinations** – victims included former Indian Prime Minister Rajiv Gandhi in 1991, and Sri Lankan Prime Minister Ranasinghe Premadasa in 1993, making the LTTE the only militant organization to have assassinated two world leaders. As the war progressed and the LTTE acquired better armaments and military know-how, they gradually began to function more as a **conventional army** – exemplified by their seizure of Elephant Pass, at the southern end of the Jaffna Peninsula, from the heavily entrenched forces of the SLA in 2000.

6

THE TIGERS: PAST, PRESENT AND FUTURE

The LTTE's ability to take on and defeat the huge forces of the Indian and Sri Lankan armies reflected its legendary discipline and commitment to the cause, fostered by relentless **political indoctrination** and quasi-monastic **discipline**. In addition, hardly any LTTE fighters were ever captured alive, thanks to the phials of cyanide which all cadres wore around their necks. They also – by Asian standards at least – had impeccable **feminist** credentials. The shortage of men of fighting age led to many women – the so-called "Freedom Birds", memorably described by British writer William Dalrymple as "paramilitary feminist death squads" – being absorbed into the LTTE military apparatus and often pitched into its toughest fighting engagements.

Attitudes towards the LTTE have always been sharply divided. In the early years of the civil war they were often seen as heroes who were prepared to lay down their lives in the fight against Sinhalese oppression. As the conflict dragged on, however, opinions changed thanks to the LTTE's systematic assassination of rival Tamil politicians, their massacres of innocent Sinhalese civilians, Muslims and suspected "collaborators", their use of child soldiers and abduction of young Tamils to fight for the LTTE, the widespread extortion of money from Tamils at home and abroad, the ethnic cleansing of areas under their control and their indiscriminate use of suicide bombers – all of which led to their being proscribed as a **terrorist organization** by over thirty governments worldwide. In addition, their apparent use of thousands of Tamil civilians as human shields during the concluding stages of the war would most likely have seen their generals charged with war crimes, had any of them survived.

Virtually the entire leadership of the LTTE was killed by the end of the war (as well as a large proportion of its fighters). Rumours of surviving LTTE activists attempting to resurrect the organization regularly circulate, although it seems unlikely that the Tigers will rise again in any meaningful way, not least because of their widespread atrocities against their own people, which has effectively destroyed whatever popular support they once enjoyed. The fact that the LTTE are held responsible for the deaths of over eight thousand of their fellow Tamils proves that it was ultimately the Tigers, far worse than any Sinhalese government, which ended up oppressing and brutalizing the very people they had once claimed to protect.

Around the island

The island's principal settlement is the busy town of **Mannar**, at the island's eastern end, whose main sight is the imposing **Portuguese fort** (later strengthened by the Dutch), near the entrance to town. Around 1km north of town stands a famous **baobab**, said to be the largest tree in Asia, with a circumference of 20m; it's thought to have been planted in 1477.

At the far, western end of the island, the small town of **Talaimannar** was formerly the departure point for ferries to India, though it's now largely deserted in the wake of fighting during the war. West of here, a chain of islets and sandbanks known as **Adam's Bridge** stretch all the way to India, 30km distant. According to the Ramayana, these were the stepping stones used by the monkey god Hanuman to travel from India to Lanka, and also served as the causeway by which the earliest human settlers reached the island some 250,000 to 300,000 years ago. These sandbanks lie less than 2m under water in many places, and may have been submerged as recently as 1480.

ARRIVAL AND DEPARTURE   MANNAR

By bus Colombo (4 daily; 7hr); Talaimannar (hourly; 1hr); Vavuniya (hourly; 2hr).

ACCOMMODATION

Four Tees Rest Inn Station Rd, Thoddawelli, 8km northwest of Mannar town off the road to Talaimannar ☎023 323 0008, 🌐4teesrestinn.com. Neat modern guesthouse set amidst spacious gardens, with friendly service, decent food and large fan rooms. **Rs.2500**; a/c **Rs.3000**

Kilinochchi

North of Vavuniya the A9 runs through huge areas of eerily deserted land, a few ruins and the odd palm-thatch hut. Most of the villages marked on maps of the country along the A9 en route to Kilinochchi have largely disappeared, although life is now returning – very slowly – to the region.

About 80km north of Vavuniya, the small town of **KILINOCHCHI** served as the headquarters of the LTTE administration – effectively the Tamil Tiger capital –for many years. The town was finally recaptured by the SLA after an intense three-month battle between government troops and rebel cadres – the fall of Kilinochchi in January 2009 effectively marked the beginning of the end for the Tigers, and was greeted with wild celebrations around much of the island.

The town – which was more or less obliterated in the course of the 2008–09 siege – is now rising energetically from the ashes. A rash of shiny new shops, offices and government buildings have sprung up along the main road and much of the wartime devastation has now been patched up, although a huge **water tower**, blown up by the LTTE during the final stages of fighting, has been left where it fell next to the road, serving as a powerful reminder of the appalling physical devastation wrought by the war. Slightly further down the road stands a striking **war memorial** – an enormous grey stone cube, pierced by an artillery shell and with a lotus blooming out of the top.

Elephant Pass

Some 15km north of Kilinochchi along the A9, the **Elephant Pass** is where a narrow causeway connects the Jaffna Peninsula with the rest of the island – a rather bleak and featureless stretch of land divided by a narrow strip of water. The pass was named for the elephants which were once driven across to the peninsula here, though it's now best known as the location of two of the civil war's largest battles, fought here in 1991 and 2000; it was during the latter that the LTTE finally succeeded in dislodging the Sri Lankan Army from its heavily fortified position at the entrance to the Jaffna Peninsula – a crucial moment in the progress of the war, though the LTTE narrowly failed to follow up this victory with the capture of the Jaffna Peninsula itself. The tables were turned in 2009 following the fall of Kilinochchi when the SLA returned, driving the remnants of the LTTE out of their long-held positions.

War memorials

Another triumphalist **war memorial** now stands next to the police checkpoint on the main highway showing four hands holding up a map of Sri Lanka with a lotus blossoming from the Jaffna Peninsula. A sign at the base explains the monument's laborious symbolism accompanied by a large dose of self-congratulatory propaganda praising President Rajapakse's "determined, courageous political commandership … unshaken as a mountain, which brought an end to the era of terror". Another sad, if obvious, reminder that history is written by the victors.

Close by, on the other side of the main highway, the scorched remains of an **armoured bulldozer** provide another – altogether more realistic – memorial of the conflict. The bulldozer was used as an improvised tank by the LTTE during their unsuccessful attempt to capture the Elephant Pass in 1991. Seeing the damage machine-gun fire from the bulldozer was causing to government positions, young Sri Lankan Lance Corporal **Gamini Kularatne** jumped aboard the vehicle and denotated two grenades, instantly killing himself and everyone inside – an act of suicidal bravery for which he subsequently became the first recipient of the Parama Weera Vibhushanaya, Sri Lanka's highest military honour.

Jaffna

Remote and war-torn **JAFFNA** is far and away the largest town in northern Sri Lanka and the undisputed cultural capital of the Sri Lankan Tamils, who have controlled the area since the thirteenth century. The town was the focal point of many of the early civil war's fiercest battles, although having remained under government control since 1995 it at least avoided being caught up in the devastating fighting which enveloped the rest of northern Sri Lanka during 2008–09. Largely inaccessible for over two decades, Jaffna is now once again freely open to visitors, still unexpectedly vibrant, despite its many years of isolation, and, in places, strangely beautiful.

Jaffna is closer to India than to Colombo, and in many ways looks across the Palk Strait to the Indian state of Tamil Nadu rather than to Sinhalese Sri Lanka for its cultural and political inspiration. Arriving in Jaffna can come as something of a culture shock if you've spent much time in the rest of the island, and you can't fail to notice the profound **Indian influence** here, exemplified by the replacement of the Buddhist dagoba with the Hindu gopuram, and by the switch from the singsong cadences of Sinhala to the quickfire intonations of Tamil – as well as myriad other details like the sultry Indian pop music which blares out of shops and cafés, and the quasi-subcontinental hordes of kamikaze cyclists who rattle around the congested streets. Yet although there's a fair bit of India in Jaffna, the town has its own unique and complex identity shaped, in true Sri Lankan fashion, by a wide cross-section of influences, including Muslim, Portuguese, Dutch, British and Sinhalese. Although Hinduism remains the dominant religion, Christianity is also strong, and the town presents an intriguing mixture of Tamil and European elements, with colourful temples set next to huge churches, and streets of a beguiling, faded colonial charm dotted with old Dutch and British residences. Perhaps most striking of all, is the sense of cultural sophistication here, embodied by the remarkably cosmopolitan and highly educated populace who, despite battling for almost half a century against institutionalized racism and devastating civil war, retain a charm, curiosity and intelligence which is one of Jaffna's most unexpected but memorable attractions.

Brief history

The Jaffna Peninsula has always been a focus for **Tamil settlement** in Sri Lanka, thanks to its proximity to the Tamil heartlands of India, not much more than 50km away across the Palk Strait. The earliest settlers arrived as far back as the second or third century BC, and this population was constantly supplemented over successive centuries by migrants, mercenaries and assorted adventurers. Interestingly, some of these early settlers may have been Buddhist rather than Hindu, as borne out by the enigmatic cluster of dagobas at Kantharodai (see p.388).

There are few records of the Jaffna region's early history, but by the thirteenth century, as the great Sinhalese civilizations of Anuradhapura and Polonnaruwa had fallen into terminal decline, Jaffna had developed into the capital of a powerful Tamil kingdom known as **Jaffnapatam**. In 1284, a Pandyan general, Arya Chakravati, seized control of the north. Over the next fifty years, his successors extended their power gradually southwards, gaining control of Mannar and its valuable pearl industry and continuing to push south. For a brief period in the mid-fourteenth century they gained control of the whole of the west coast, almost as far as Colombo – the greatest expansion of Tamil power in the history of Sri Lanka. In the fifteenth century, Parakramabahu VI (1412–67), king of Kotte, turned the tables, gaining control of the whole of the north by 1450; the Tamil kingdom quickly re-established its independence, however.

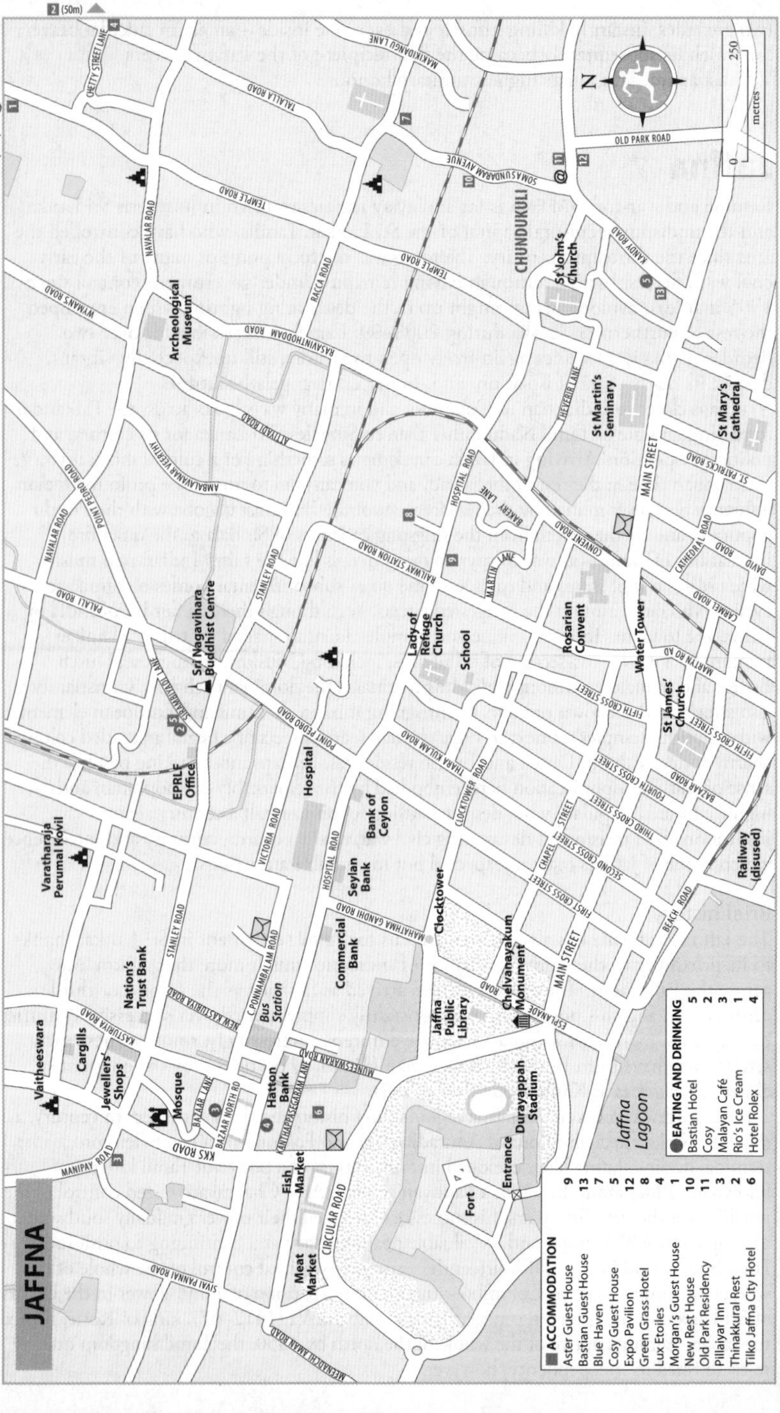

JAFFNA

Map labels (north arrow, scale)

N

0 — 250 metres

Roads and areas:
- Nallur Kandaswamy Temple & ②
- 2 (50m)
- CHETTY STREET LANE
- MAXIMINARD LANE
- TALAILA ROAD
- OLD PARK ROAD
- CHUNDUKULI
- SOMASUNDARAM AVENUE
- KANDY ROAD
- NAVALAR ROAD
- TEMPLE ROAD
- RACCA ROAD
- WYMANS ROAD
- Point Pedro
- POINT PEDRO ROAD
- PALALI ROAD
- NAVALAR ROAD
- AMBALAVANAR VEEDITY
- ATTIYADY ROAD
- BASAVITHODDAM ROAD
- St John's Church
- St Martin's Seminary
- St Mary's Cathedral
- THEVENI LANE
- ST PATRICK'S ROAD
- MAIN STREET
- CONVENT ROAD
- HOSPITAL ROAD
- BAKERY LANE
- MARTIN LANE
- RAILWAY STATION ROAD
- Archeological Museum
- Sri Nagavihara Buddhist Centre
- Lady of Refuge Church
- School
- Rosarian Convent
- Water Tower
- EPRLF Office
- Hospital
- POINT PEDRO ROAD
- STANLEY ROAD
- THABA VILLAM ROAD
- FIFTH CROSS STREET
- St James' Church
- AMMAN ROAD
- OLD MARTIN ROAD
- Varatharaja Perumal Kovil
- VICTORIA ROAD
- HOSPITAL ROAD
- Bank of Ceylon
- CLOCKTOWER ROAD
- FOURTH CROSS STREET
- THIRD CROSS STREET
- BAZAAR ROAD
- Railway (disused)
- Vaitheeswara
- KASTURIYA ROAD
- Cargills
- Jeweller's Shops
- Nation's Trust Bank
- Seylan Bank
- CHAPEL STREET
- SECOND CROSS STREET
- FIRST CROSS STREET
- BEACH ROAD
- MANIPAY ROAD
- KKS ROAD
- Mosque
- Hatton Bank
- ANTHONIPPILLAI ROAD
- Commercial Bank
- Clocktower
- Chelvanayakam Monument
- MAIN STREET
- Jaffna Public Library
- SIVAN PANNAI ROAD
- Fish Market
- Meat Market
- CIRCULAR ROAD
- Durayappah Stadium
- Entrance
- Fort
- Jaffna Lagoon
- MUNTHIRIKAI LANE
- POINNAMBALAM ROAD
- NEW KASTURIYA ROAD
- Bus Station
- BAZAAR NORTH RD
- BAZAAR LANE
- ESPLANADE
- TEMPLE ROAD

ACCOMMODATION

Aster Guest House	9
Bastian Guest House	13
Blue Haven	7
Cosy Guest House	5
Expo Pavilion	12
Green Grass Hotel	4
Lux Etoiles	1
Morgan's Guest House	8
New Rest House	10
Old Park Residency	11
Pillaiyar Inn	3
Thinakkural Rest	2
Tilko Jaffna City Hotel	6

● EATING AND DRINKING

Bastian Hotel	5
Cosy	2
Malayan Café	3
Rio's Ice Cream	1
Hotel Rolex	4

Portuguese invaders

In the early 16th century, Jaffna was faced with the **Portuguese**, who coveted the kingdom, since its strategic position next to the Palk Strait allowed it to control the sea route between east and west India, and also because its ruler had the revenues of the huge pearl banks at Mannar. The Portuguese were taxing the pearl industry as early as 1513, and they spent much of the sixteenth century harassing the rulers of Jaffna from their base in Mannar and converting large numbers of the local fishermen to Catholicism – though it wasn't until 1621 that they finally seized Jaffna itself. The Portuguese spent much of their time destroying Hindu temples and building churches in their place, though God appears not to have looked favourably upon their actions, since in 1658 they were evicted from Jaffna by the **Dutch**. The Dutch gave the town an imposing fort before the British took over in 1796. Jaffna became something of a backwater during the later colonial era, although the railway arrived in 1905 and the Jaffna Tamils continued to thrive under the British administration.

After independence

Following **independence**, Jaffna found itself increasingly at the centre of the island's growing ethnic storm, with regular clashes between young Tamil militants and Sinhalese soldiers and police culminating in the infamous destruction of the Jaffna library by government thugs in 1981. The burning of the library, however, was just a small foretaste of the destruction to come during the **civil war** itself, during which large parts of the centre were reduced to rubble by the various battles which raged in and around the town (see p.382).

Central Jaffna

Jaffna divides into the busy **commercial district** centred on the Hospital Road and the area around the bus station, and the much more sedate colonial-era suburbs **east of the centre**, with their enormous churches and atmospheric Dutch-era buildings.

Hospital Road itself forms the spine of the modern commercial district, a vibrant mercantile thoroughfare lined with shops and banks. Traces of old Jaffna can still be seen here and there, particularly in the old-fashioned shops around the *Hotel Rolex* (opposite the lurid yellow central market building) with their traditional hand-painted signs, wooden counters and glass-fronted display cabinets stacked high with merchandise. You may also see one or two of the lovingly preserved **vintage cars** – Morris Minors, Morris Oxfords, Austin Cambridges and the like – which were formerly a common sight in Jaffna, kept going through the long decades of the civil war when the import of new vehicles was banned, although these are becoming increasingly rare following the end of hostilities.

Vaitheeswara Temple

On the northwest side of the centre, up Kankesanthurai (KKS) Road, a tall grey-blue gopuram marks the **Vaitheeswara Temple**, the most interesting of central Jaffna's numerous Hindu temples. Dedicated to Shiva, it was built during the Dutch era by an influential local merchant. At its centre lies a richly decorated stone shrine, painted in orange hues and surrounded by a beautiful old wooden-roofed ambulatory, rather like a Dutch veranda, complete with Doric columns, with a small tank to one side.

Kasturiya Road and around

A short walk east of the Vaitheeswara Temple and north of the bus station is **Kasturiya Road**, the heart of Jaffna's jewellery industry, home to a long sequence of jewellers, mainly trading in gold.

Continue east along Stanley Road and then turn north to reach the **Varatharaja Perumal Kovil**, a large but decidedly kitsch temple, with a huge, polychromatic gopuram and brightly coloured buildings – the whole complex is entertainingly Disneyfied, although rather less atmospheric than the Vaitheeswara.

Jaffna Fort

Daily 6am–6pm • Free

The largest Dutch fort in Asia, the huge **Jaffna Fort** was built on the site of the former Portuguese stronghold in the characteristic star shape favoured by the Dutch (the pointed bastions offering greater protection against cannon fire). The inner defences were completed in 1680 and the outer ring of bastions in 1792, though just three years after it was completed the fort was surrendered to the British without a shot being fired. Sadly, having survived two hundred years without seeing action, the fort was finally pressed into military service during the civil war, when the outer defences were repeatedly bombarded by both sides and the old Dutch buildings inside, including the beautiful **Groote Kerk** ("Great Church"), destroyed.

The battered remains of the fort are currently undergoing comprehensive restoration, scheduled to finish by early 2013. Sections of the ramparts have already been renovated, although the appearance of the newly cut and polished stonework looks disconcertingly modern, given the restored sections the appearance (and appeal) of a concrete bomb shelter. An archway emblazoned "Anno 1680" on the east side of the

---

THE SIEGES OF JAFFNA

As the principal town of the north, Jaffna played a pivotal – and tragic – role in the early stages of the **civil war**. During the opening phase of the war, from 1983 to 1987, the LTTE gradually acquired control over much of the town and the surrounding peninsula, rendering SLA troops stationed in the area increasingly powerless. In the end, however, the first counterattack against the LTTE in Jaffna came not from the SLA but from the **Indian Peace Keeping Force**, or IPKF (see p.410), who had arrived to police a ceasefire between the two sides and ensure fair treatment for the embattled Tamils – though in the event, they ended up attacking the people they had allegedly come to protect. In October 1987 the IPKF attacked Jaffna in an offensive called **Operation Pawan** ("Wind"). This was expected to last just two days, though in the event the Indian advance became bogged down by the LTTE's determined resistance and a bloodbath ensued, with massive civilian casualties caused by indiscriminate IPKF shelling and bombing. IPKF forces were also widely accused of rape, looting and the random murder of civilians – most notoriously the storming of Jaffna hospital and the massacre of many of its patients. In the end it took three weeks of vicious street-by-street fighting before the IPKF could claim control of Jaffna.

The LTTE retreated into the countryside, from where they continued to harry the IPKF until the latter's **withdrawal** from Sri Lanka in March 1990, at which point the LTTE simply reoccupied Jaffna. A brief ceasefire followed, though hostilities swiftly resumed. In June 1990 the LTTE captured and massacred around eight hundred Sinhalese policemen stationed in the east of the island. In retaliation, the SLA went on the warpath once more, advancing across the Jaffna Peninsula and subjecting Jaffna to a **second siege**. This proved a far more protracted affair than the first. Once again, Jaffna suffered indiscriminate shelling, killing hundreds of civilians. At the same time, the Sinhalese troops and others who had been trapped in Jaffna at the sudden resumption of hostilities took refuge in the town's fort, where they were held by LTTE forces for three months – a bizarre siege within a siege – until a force of SLA commandos succeeded in rescuing them in a daring raid led by future Sri Lankan presidential candidate General (then Colonel) Sarath Fonseka (see p.417).

Jaffna finally fell to the SLA in December 1995. As they had done in 1987, LTTE forces disappeared back into the countryside and merged with the local population, while continuing to attack the SLA. The LTTE never came close to retaking Jaffna, which remained relatively peaceful (at least compared to other parts of the region) right through until the end of the civil war, being mercifully spared the devastation visited on other northern towns during the final phase of the war.

fort leads through into the largely empty interior courtyard, dotted with indecipherable fragments of ruins. It's also possible to walk around parts of the ramparts, with fine views over town.

The south side of the fort is bounded by the calm, shallow waters of the **Jaffna lagoon**, the ocean inlet that divides the Jaffna Peninsula from the rest of Sri Lanka. This is one of the few places in town where you can actually reach the lagoon, since most of the shoreline has been fenced off; the low-lying bridge-cum-causeway which connects Jaffna to Kayts can be seen disappearing into the waters close to the fort.

6

Jaffna Public Library
In an impressive Indo-Saracenic-style building immediately east of the fort lies the **Jaffna Public Library**. The original library was torched by pro-government Sinhalese mobs during election riots in 1981, an act of vandalism which reduced one of South Asia's greatest public collections (including many irreplaceable works of Tamil literature) to ashes – a key event in the build-up to the civil war. In a symbolic gesture, this was the first major public building to be rebuilt following the temporary ceasefire of 2002, and visitors are welcome to browse the library's extensive collection of Tamil and English volumes.

The area around here suffered particularly extensive damage during the war. Most of the former devastation has now been repaired, although a few collapsing buildings can still be southeast of the clocktower in the area between Main and Chapel streets.

The clocktower
Pointing skywards just northeast of the library is the town's unusually tall and slender **clocktower**, an endearing architectural mongrel mixing Islamic and Gothic styles. The tower – designed by British architect J.G. Smither (who was also responsible for Colombo's Old Town Hall and National Museum) – was built in 1875 to commemorate a visit by the Prince of Wales, although its four original clocks have now been replaced by ugly modern digital replacements, none of which works.

Chelvanayakum monument
Competing for air space close to the clocktower, the enormous Hindu-style column at the south end of Esplanade Road is a monument to the famous local politician **S.J.V. Chelvanayakum** (1898–1977), founder and first leader of the Tamil United Liberation Front. A leading figure in post-independence Sri Lanka, Chelvanayakum became increasingly frustrated with Sinhalese political oppression and was an early advocate of Tamil separatism, although his love of Gandhian-style *satyagraha* (non-violent protest) could hardly have been further removed from the tactics used by the rebels who subsequently adopted the cause of Tamil Eelam.

East of the centre
East of the commercial centre, Jaffna assumes a residential and colonial character, with quiet, tree-shaded streets lined by sedate Dutch villas and a string of imposing churches. The walk along **Main Street** (rather sleepy, despite its name) is particularly atmospheric, lined with crumbling old colonial houses and assorted churches and other religious foundations. The first is the **Rosarian Convent**, occupying a beautiful sequence of Dutch colonial buildings which are now home to the Rosarian Sisters, well known hereabouts for their home-made wine cordial and grape juice. A little further east along Main Street is the equally atmospheric **St Martin's Seminary**, an attractive Victorian neo-Gothic period piece dating from the 1880s, with verandaed buildings and a musty little chapel in the middle.

Just south of St Martin's Seminary stands the largest of Jaffna's outsize churches, the gigantic **St Mary's Cathedral**. It's quasi-Portuguese in style, although actually dating from the Dutch era, and is built on a positively industrial scale, with a pleasingly simple interior.

6

THE EPRLF HEADQUARTERS

Just around the corner from the Archeological Museum on Stanley Road you may notice the Jaffna headquarters of the **Eelam People's Revolutionary Liberation Front (EPRLF)**, an extraordinary-looking building resembling a heavily fortified military bunker rather than a political secretariat. The EPRLF were long-term opponents of the LTTE, who repeatedly attacked their offices and leaders, most notably EPRLF supremo Douglas Devananda, who survived over ten LTTE assassination attempts – although it's worth noting that Devananda (now member of parliament for Jaffna and part of Mahinda Rajapakse's ruling PA coalition) is himself wanted in India on charges of murder and abduction.

The Archeological Museum
Navalar Rd • Mon–Sat 9am–5pm • Donation

Jaffna's modest little **Archeological Museum** houses various Hindu artefacts from Jaffna and around, including a number of small and beautiful wooden *vahanams* ("vehicles"), the various animals – horse, bull, elephant, lion – on which Hindu gods rode from place to place. Other curiosities include a pile of whale bones, a seven-mouthed musical pot and a fetching wooden model of Harischandra – the legendary Indian king who never told a lie – and his wives. Look out, too, for the much-abused portrait of the young Queen Victoria recovered from the Fort – the tears in the canvas are apparently bullet holes.

Nallur Kandaswamy Temple

Jaffna's most notable sight is the large **Nallur Kandaswamy Temple**, about 2km northeast of the town centre. Dedicated to Murugam (known to the Buddhist Sinhalese as Kataragama), this is the most impressive Hindu temple in Sri Lanka, and the only one on the island to rival the great shrines of India. The original temple is thought to date back to the mid-fifteenth century, though it was destroyed in 1620 by the Portuguese. The present structure was begun in 1807 and has now developed into an enormous religious complex, surrounded by red-and-white striped walls. There are numerous shrines inside, richly decorated corridors framed in rows of golden arches and a beautiful courtyard with a large tank. Men must remove their shirts before entering. There are no fewer than six **pujas** daily, with three between 4pm and 5pm, the best time to visit.

THE NALLUR FESTIVAL

Nallur Kandaswamy Temple is a fascinating place to visit at any time, but becomes unforgettable during the latter stages of the annual **Nallur Festival**, which runs for 25 days, finishing on the poya day in August. The crowds of festival-goers rival those at the far better-known Kandy Esala Perahera, and many Jaffna expatriates return for the celebrations. Men dress in fresh white sarongs, while ladies don their best saris, transforming the entire temple complex into a vast a sea of intense blues, reds and greens. Held on the 24th of the 26 days, the **Ther** festival is the biggest night, when an enormous chariot is pulled around the town by huge crowds of sarong-clad men; on the following day, particularly enthusiastic devotees mortify themselves by driving skewers through their bodies in honour of the god and making their way to the shrine accompanied by drumming and piping, stopping periodically to dance en route. Even more extraordinary are the devotees who, using skewers driven through their backs, suspend themselves from poles. These poles are then attached to the front of trucks and tractors, and the devotees are driven through town to the temple, dangling in front of their vehicle like bait on a fishing line. Supplicants who perform these self-mortifications believe that the god will protect them from any sense of pain. Many also carry a **kavadi**, the distinctive symbol of Murugam (or Kataragama), a semicircular yoke, placed across the shoulders, with peacock feathers at either end.

ARRIVAL AND DEPARTURE

JAFFNA

It's possible to reach Jaffna either by bus or plane, but not by train (although there's talk of relaying the railway line which was ripped up during the civil war). It's possible to reach Jaffna direct from Colombo, but unless you're flying it makes more sense to break the journey up – Anuradhapura is the logical starting point, and only around five hours from Jaffna by bus.

By plane Flights to Jaffna from Colombo's Ratmalana airport are currently operated by Expo Aviation (www. expoavi.com); it's possible that SriLankan Airlines will also begin flights in the near future. Flights leave from Ratmalana airport, in southern Colombo (near Mount Lavinia) to Palali Airport, around 15km north of Jaffna (from where a free bus will be provided to take you into town). There are currently services twice daily in each direction; flights take around an hour and cost roughly $100 one way or $190 return. Tickets can be bought online at www.expoavi.com or at Expo's offices in Colombo (6 Joseph Lane, Colombo 4 ☎ 011 255 5156) or Jaffna (141F Palali Rd, Thirunelvely ☎ 021 222 3891).

By bus Buses arrive right in the middle of Jaffna at the bus station on Hospital Rd. Private minibuses to local destinations line up along the street (C. Ponnambalam Rd) on the north side of the bus station, although most are signed in Tamil only. From Colombo, Jaffna is served by SLTB services from Saunders Bus Station and more

comfortable private buses run by various companies along Galle Rd around Wellawatte Market; alternatively, travel agents elsewhere in the city may be able to arrange a ticket for you. In Jaffna, tickets for Colombo buses can be bought directly from the various private bus operators, all of whom have offices on Hospital Road, diagonally opposite the south side of the bus station. Buses to and from the capital (10–12hr, though the road is increasingly being improved) include a range of semi-luxury and luxury a/c services (Rs.850–Rs.1300); most run overnight, although there are also a couple of early-morning departures. Arriving in Colombo, buses run across the city, dropping off passengers en route before terminating in Wellawatte.

Destinations Anuradhapura (every 2hr; 5hr); Batti, via Polonnaruwa (6 daily; 11hr); Colombo (3 daily; 10–12hr); Kandy (5 daily; 8hr); Point Pedro (every 15min; 1hr); Trincomalee (5 daily; 7hr); Vavuniya (hourly; 3hr).

ACCOMMODATION

Jaffna has plenty of accommodation, although it's all much of a muchness and there are few bargains to be had, and not many places are used to dealing with foreign tourists.

Aster Guest House 744 Hospital Rd ☎ 021 320 7478. Small guesthouse with a handful of neat, clean tiled modern rooms, although no food. Rs.2000; a/c Rs.3000

Bastian Guest House (aka New Bastian Hotel) 11 Kandy Rd ☎ 021 222 7374. One of Jaffna's nicer and better-value places, occupying a low-slung villa with spotless a/c rooms with cable TV (some with hot water). There's no sign; it's in the building immediately south of the GIZ office. Rs.3500.

Blue Haven 70 Racca Rd ☎ 021 222 9958, ⓦ bluehavenjaffna.com. Comfortable if characterless modern guesthouse with spotless tiled rooms (all with a/c and hot water), plus a nice little pool. Rs.3850

Cosy Guest House 15 Sirambiyadi Lane ☎ 021 222 5899. A handful of simple but clean and quiet rooms behind the restaurant of the same name (see p.386). Singles are a particularly good deal, especially non a/c, which are about half the price of doubles. Rs.2200; a/c Rs.2750

Expo Pavilion 40 Kandy Rd ☎ 021 222 3790, ⓔ expopavilion@expoavi.com. Jaffna's most stylish place to stay, in an attractive colonial-style villa, with suave rooms with colourful fabric touches and smooth furnishings, plus a cool dining room. Surprisingly chic,

although mightily expensive for what you get. B&B Rs.9150

Green Grass Hotel 33 Aseervatham Lane, off Hospital Rd ☎ 021 222 4385, ⓦ jaffnagreengrass.com. One of Jaffna's few proper hotels with facilities, including a nice big pool, restaurant, bar and 24hr room service. Rooms (all with a/c and h/w) are clean but uninspiring, with random furniture and bashed-up decor, although rates are relatively low. The garden gets busy with local drinkers in the evenings, however, so it's not the most peaceful place in town. Rs.3300

Lux Etoiles 34 Chetty Street Lane ☎ 021 222 3966. Attractive and well-run hotel with a range of rooms (all a/c with hot water and satellite TV) – rather pricey (and cheaper rooms are on the small side) although the professional service and Jaffna's biggest swimming pool at least partly compensate. $68

Morgan's Guest House 215 Temple Rd ☎ 021 222 3666. Almost in the shadow of the Nallur Temple, this attractive old colonial villa has more character than most accommodation in Jaffna, with comfortable (if rather dark) rooms, all with a/c and hot water. The owner can also arrange tours of the city and peninsula in his own vehicle (Rs.6000/day). Rs.3500

6

New Rest House 19 Somasundaram Ave ☎021 222 7839. One of Jaffna's few real budget options, with spacious if slightly basic rooms, kept reasonably clean. Not much English spoken. Fan Rs.1000; a/c Rs.2000

Old Park Residency 75 Kandy Rd ☎021 790 2607, ⓔ oldparksothi@live.com. Spacious and spotless rooms (albeit a bit dark), all with a/c, although hot water, should you require it, comes in a bucket. B&B Rs.3500

Pillaiyar Inn 31 Manipay Rd ☎021 222 2829, ⓦ pillaiyarinn.com. Attractive little haven spread around a pleasant little garden right in the heart of Jaffna – usually surprisingly peaceful, assuming it's not hosting a wedding or other function. Rooms (all with a/c and hot water) are old but reasonably well maintained, although cheaper ones are a bit pokey. $25

Thinakkural Rest 45 Chetty Street Lane ☎021 222 6476. One of Jaffna's better-value options at present, with large and rather functional but good-value tiled rooms in a quiet Nallur side street. Rs.1650; a/c Rs.2750

Tilko Jaffna City Hotel 70/6 KKS Rd ☎021 222 5969, ⓦ tilkojaffna.com. The biggest hotel in town, spread over two large buildings around a swathe of lawn set back from the road. Accommodation is in spacious and rather plush rooms, and facilities are the best in town, with restaurant, bar, gym and a simple spa (but no pool). Rs.8855

EATING AND DRINKING

There aren't many culinary treats in Jaffna – and (ironically) you'll get better South Indian food in Colombo. Places for a drink are also in short supply compared to most places in Sri Lanka – the dining room of the *Bastian Hotel* and the garden of the *Green Grass Hotel* are two of the better places.

Bastian Hotel Kandy Rd. Ignore the noisy drinking den downstairs and head upstairs to the breezy first-floor dining room, popular with NGOs and other Western visitors. There's a long menu of the usual simple rice and noodle dishes (mains Rs.250–500), although only a few dishes are available most nights. Still, the beer's cheap and the atmosphere is friendly. Daily 11am–2pm & 5–9pm.

Cosy Restaurant 15 Sirambiyadi Lane. Huge array of competently prepared North Indian meat and veg dishes (plus assorted Chinese offerings). Tandoori meat dishes and breads are the speciality (evenings only), prepared in the restaurant's genuine tandoor oven. Mains Rs.300–600. Unlicensed. Daily 8am–10.30pm.

Malayan Café 36–38 Grand Bazaar, Bazaar North Rd Time-warped slice of traditional Jaffna, with a lovely old wood-panelled, incense-laden dining room constantly busy with locals filling up on bargain South Indian-style thalis served up on glossy banana leaves (once finished, deposit your leaf in the "Use Banana Leaf" chute by the washbasins). Daily 6.30am–8.30pm.

Rio's Ice Cream Behind the Nallur Temple. One of a line of colourful ice-cream parlours around the back of the Nallur Temple serving up big helpings of fluorescent ice cream (most under Rs.100) in unusual flavours. The nearby *Rajah Cream House*, *Lingam Cream House* and *Subhas Cream House* are all very similar. Daily 8am–10pm.

Hotel Rolex 340 Hospital Rd. Friendly little café near the bus station offering a range of tasty staples including buriani, string hoppers, *pittu*, curry, chicken and fish. Daily 6.30am–10pm.

DIRECTORY

Banks There are several banks along Hospital and Stanley roads with ATMs accepting foreign cards.

Internet Red Mo Net Café (daily 9am–4pm), in the Sri Lanka Red Cross Society building opposite *Expo Pavilion*, is convenient if you're staying in Chundukuli.

The Jaffna Peninsula

The agricultural hinterland of Jaffna town – and the source of much of its former prosperity – is the **Jaffna Peninsula**, a fertile arc of land criss-crossed with a lattice of small country roads and lined with endless walled gardens and smallholdings in which the peninsula's famed mangos are grown, along with a wide variety of other crops including chillies, onions, bananas, jackfruit and grapes. Physically and culturally the peninsula is virtually an island, almost completely detached from the rest of the country, and has always been far more densely populated than the more arid lands of the Vanni further south.

CLOCKWISE FROM TOP NAGA POOSHANI AMBAL KOVIL, NAINATIVU, JAFFNA PENINSULA (P.392); ST MARY'S CATHEDRAL, JAFFNA (P.383); TSUNAMI CEMETERY, MANALKADU, JAFFNA PENINSULA (P.390); THE VEGETABLE MARKET IN JAFFNA (P.381)

North of Jaffna

The 20km journey **north of Jaffna** across the peninsula to the opposite coast at Keerimalai offers a good taste of the peninsula's rural scenery as well as combining a number of attractions en route, including the fine temples of **Maviddapuram** and **Naguleswaram**, the enigmatic dagobas of **Kantharodai** and the hot springs at **Keerimalai** itself.

Kantharodai
Open access 24hr • Free

About 10km north of Jaffna, and 2km west of the village of Chunnakam on the main road to Kankesanturai (KKS), lies the curious archeological site of **Kantharodai** – an unusual huddle of around twenty miniature dagobas, ranging in height from one to three metres, crammed together in a small plot along with the unexcavated bases of many other dagobas. The site is quite unlike anything else in Sri Lanka, and is of great antiquity, dating back at least two thousand years, though no one can quite agree on its exact purpose – a popular theory is that the dagobas enshrine the remains of Buddhist monks; others claim that they are "votive" dagobas erected in fulfilment of answered prayers.

Tellipalai

A few kilometres north of Chunnakam, the small town of **Tellipalai** formerly lay at the heart of one of the Jaffna's controversial **high security zones** – a patchwork of military areas across the peninsula, occupied by the Sri Lankan Army, from which the civilian population had been driven out. The area has now been largely returned to its original inhabitants, although the battered remnants of the town itself remain eerily deserted.

Maviddapuram Kandaswamy Temple

About 5km north of Tellipalai, next to the turn-off to Keerimalai, stands the imposing **Maviddapuram Kandaswamy Temple**, said to have been commissioned by a grateful Pandyan princess, a certain Maruthapura Veeravalli, whose face it is said bore an unfortunate resemblance to a horse until a dip in the nearby Keerimalai springs (see below) restored her to her true beauty. The temple suffered significant bomb damage in 1990 but has now been largely rebuilt.

Naguleswaram Temple

Right on the coast some 2km north of Maviddapuram Kandaswamy Temple, and next to the Keerimalai hot springs, is the even grander **Naguleswaram Temple** (ⓦnaguleswaram.org), one of Sri Lanka's five holiest Shiva temples, the *pancha iswaram*. The original temple was destroyed by the Portuguese in 1620, rebuilt in the late nineteenth century, and then largely destroyed again by Sri Lankan Army shells in 1990. Reconstruction work continues apace, while the temple remains busy with visitors.

Keerimalai hot springs

A few metres beyond the Naguleswaram Temple on the peninsula's northern shore are the **Keerimalai hot springs**, whose therapeutic powers have been recognized since the time of the Mahabharata: Pandyan princess Maruthapura Veeravalli (see above) and a local Indian holy man, Nagula Muni, whose austerities had given his features the appearance of a mongoose (*keeri*) both found cures here, and a steady string of bathers now follow in their footsteps. Locals flock here to bathe in the neat little concrete pool overlooking the ocean in which the springs have been captured, while fine beaches stretch away on either side.

6

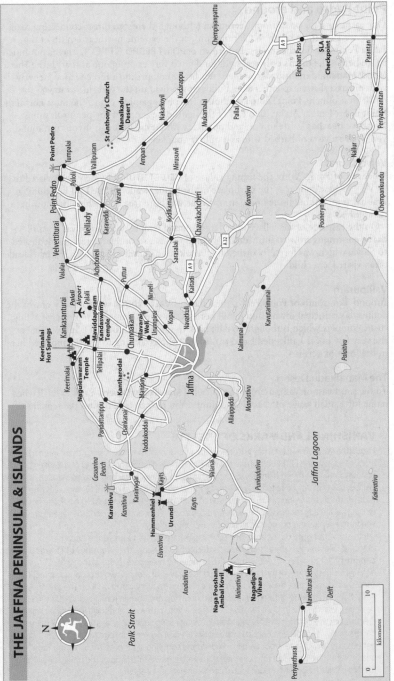

THE JAFFNA PENINSULA & ISLANDS

Palk Strait

Kadikatavu

Chempiyanpattu

A9

SLA
Checkpoint

Elephant Pass

Parantan

Periyaparantan

Kudarappu

Nakarkoyil

Manalkadu
Desert

Pallai

Mukamalai

Nallur

St Anthony's Church

Chempankundu

Point Pedro

Tumpalai

Vallipuram

Ampan

Minuswil

Pooneryn

Karativu

Pololi

Point Pedro

Varani

Kodikamam

Chavakachcheri

A32

Velvettiturai

Nelliady

Karaveddi

Achchuveli

Sarasalai

A9

Kautarimunai

Valalai

Puttur

Kaitadi

Kalmunai

Palali
Airport

Palali

Nirveli

Kopai

Navatkuli

Paladitivu

Keerimalai
Hot Springs

Kankasanturai

Mavidapuram
Kandaswamy
Temple

Chunnakam

Nilavarai
Well

Unumpai

Keerimalai

Nagueswaram
Temple

Tellipalai

Kantharodai

Manipay

Jaffna

Mandativu

Pandattaripu

Chankanai

Allaippiddi

Vaddukoddai

Casuarina
Beach

Karaitivu

Valanai

Punkudutivu

Jaffna Lagoon

Kakerativu

Karativu

Karainagar

Kayts

Eluvativu

Hammenhiel

Urundi

Kayts

Analaitivu

Naga Pooshani
Ambal Kovil

Nainativu

Nagadipa
Vihara

Mandativu

Delft

Mavelitturai Jetty

Periyanthurai

N

0   kilometres   10

Point Pedro and around

Due east along the coast from Keerimalai (although there's no direct connecting road; you'll need to return south to Chunnakam), at the extreme northeastern tip of the Jaffna Peninsula lies the modest little town of **POINT PEDRO** ("PPD"). There's not much to see here – the town's only real sight (and not a very exciting one at that) is the **Theru Moodi Madam**, a traditional travellers' rest house comprising a roofed stone archway, with pillared shelters to either side, built across a road on the east side of town.

Just west of here, **Point Pedro Lighthouse** (no photography) marks the most northerly point in Sri Lanka. About 2km east of the lighthouse is one of the peninsula's most attractive **beaches** – safe to visit and popular with locals, although if you turn round you'll have a vista of barbed wire and military bunkers.

Velvettiturai

Due west of Point Pedro, the fishing village of **VELVETTITURAI** (widely abbreviated to "VVT") is best known as the birthplace of the former leader of the LTTE, Velupillai Prabhakaran, although the house in which he was born (see box below) has now been demolished.

On the east side of the village lies a large **Amman Temple**, whose festival in April draws enormous crowds. Immediately behind this is a second large temple, dedicated to Shiva, which was formerly owned by Prabakharan's family and which the rebel leader often visited as a child.

Vallipuram

Around 5km south of Point Pedro, the village of **VALLIPURAM** was formerly one of the peninsula's principal towns, and is still home to its second largest temple: a sprawling, rustic complex which is thought to date back to the first century AD. It's also one of the very few in Sri Lanka dedicated to Vishnu, who according to legend appeared here in the form of a fish.

The Manalkadu Desert

To the southeast of Vallipuram is the so-called **Manalkadu Desert**, a rather far-fetched name for a small range of coastal sand dunes. You may be able to find the remains of

---

VANISHING LANDMARKS OF THE LTTE

The Jaffna Peninsula was formerly dotted with a number of memorials and other landmarks associated with the LTTE which have now been destroyed following the end of the war. Prabhakaran's childhood **home** was one such place, formerly attracting a steady stream of visitors, many of whom recorded panegyrics to the great leader in graffiti on the walls (the more enthusiastic visiting LTTE cadres used to write messages in their own blood). The house, which was already roofless, has now been razed completely, and a resident soldier will prevent you from even taking photographs of the now empty plot.

If the government's decision to destroy Prabhakaran's house to prevent it becoming an object of pilgrimage is understandable, its decision to bulldoze the enormous **LTTE war cemetery** at Kopai (along with other LTTE cemeteries elsewhere in the island) is less defensible. The cemetery formerly contained the graves of around two thousand fallen LTTE cadres, although these have now been destroyed and an army camp built on the site. The army claims that none of the graves actually contained any human remains and that the entire cemetery was in fact simply a massive LTTE propaganda exercise, although it's difficult not to feel, irrespective of the graves' actual contents, that razing such a place amounts to a pointless and barbaric act of desecration. The cemetery's alleged power to inspire future freedom fighters is in any case far from certain – indeed the sobering sight of so many young Tamil dead might have provided future generations with a powerful image of the futility of war, and therefore have helped to ensure such a conflict never arises again.

THE NILAVARAI WELL

About 8km from Jaffna, right next to the Jaffna–Point Pedro highway, is the **Nilavarai Well**. Despite its unexciting appearance, the well is traditionally believed to have been the work of Rama himself, who created it by sticking an arrow into the ground to assuage his thirst. Its waters are said to be bottomless and appear to be somehow connected directly to the sea: the water is fresh near the top, but becomes increasingly salty the deeper you go.

St Anthony's Church, built around 1900 and now picturesquely half-buried in the sand. From the church there's a clear view of the strange and melancholy seafront cemetery nearby, with dozens of crosses stuck into the top of the dunes marking the graves of locals, most of whom perished in the tsunami, with the fateful date 2004.12.26 written on cross after cross.

6

The islands

West of Jaffna, a string of **islands** straggle out into the waters of the Palk Strait towards India. Two of them – **Kayts** and **Karaitivu** – virtually join up with the mainland, to which they're connected by causeways, as is **Punkudutivu** further west. Punkudutivu is the starting point for ferries to **Nainativu**, home to two important religious shrines, and the remote island of **Delft**.

There are few specific sights. The point and pleasure of a trip here is in the journey, and in the subtle but memorable land- and seascapes, with the flat and largely uninhabited islands merging almost imperceptibly into the blue waters of the Jaffna lagoon and Palk Strait. There's also an undeniable pleasure in simply reaching such a remote and little-visited corner of Sri Lanka.

ARRIVAL AND DEPARTURE
THE ISLANDS

By bus Buses leave Jaffna's bus station roughly every hour to Kayts and Punkudutivu.

Kayts

Pronounced "Kites", **KAYTS** is the largest of the islands and the closest to Jaffna – its eastern tip lies just over the lagoon from Jaffna town and is reached via a causeway through very shallow water, beyond which you'll have to negotiate the inevitable checkpoint. Like the other islands, Kayts is only lightly inhabited and largely devoid of either people or buildings – a pancake-flat expanse studded with innumerable Palmyrah palms and a succession of imposing Hindu temples standing in proud isolation in the middle of empty countryside.

At the far (western) end of the island is **Kayts town** (actually little more than a sleepy village), where you'll find the beautiful shell of the nineteenth-century **St James** church (the facade bears the date 1716, but the building actually dates from 1815). The facade and exterior walls survive, but the roof has gone and there's nothing inside but wooden scaffolding, giving the entire structure the appearance of an elaborate film prop.

Just beyond the village lie the scant remains of **Urundi Fort**, also known as Fort Eyrie, now no more than a couple of picturesquely decaying coral-stone walls which are being gradually swallowed up by vegetation. Urundi and Hammenhiel (see p.392) forts were originally built by the Portuguese to control this entrance to the Jaffna lagoon, though the Dutch neglected Urundi, concentrating their defences in Hammenhiel – of which there's a beautiful view from here.

There's a decent **beach** at **Valanai**, near the eastern end of Kayts and just a few kilometres from Jaffna.

6

Karaitivu

The most northerly of the islands, **Karaitivu**, is reached by road some 12km north of Jaffna. En route to the island, 10km from Jaffna at the village of Vaddukoddai, you'll pass the barn-like **Portuguese Church**, in whose churchyard are 27 tombstones, moved here for safekeeping from the Groote Kerk in Jaffna fort. Most are Dutch colonial; the oldest dates back to 1666. A kilometre further down the road is the **Punnalai Varatharaja Perumal Kovil**, dedicated to Vishnu and one of the peninsula's two oldest temples. The shrine holds an ancient stone tortoise which was apparently fished ashore here.

On the north coast of Karaitivu itself is **Casuarina Beach**, the peninsula's most popular patch of sand, although it's not particularly clean. Swimming is safe (though the water is shallow), but there are no facilities. Just off the southern tip of the island, in the waters between Karaitivu and Kayts, is the old Dutch fort of **Hammenhiel** – its name, literally "Heel of Ham", refers to the prosaic old Dutch belief that Sri Lanka resembled a leg of ham. The fort is a fine sight, seemingly floating on the waters of the lagoon, though it's still in operational use so you can't visit. You also get a good view of it from Urundi Fort on Kayts (see p.391).

ARRIVAL AND DEPARTURE
KARAITIVU

By bus Buses run roughly every hour to Karainagar, the main village on Karaitivu, from Jaffna's bus station; Casuarina Beach is a short ride from here by tuktuk.

Punkudutivu

The island of **Punkudutivu** lies southeast of Kayts, to which it's connected by a 4km causeway through the very shallow waters of the Palk Strait – looking out of the windows of your vehicle while crossing the causeway will give you the bizarre illusion that you're driving across the top of the sea. The road across the island reveals constantly shifting vistas of sea and land, passing tiny country hamlets, bombed-out buildings and a succession of large Hindu temples, often the only buildings to be seen in this very rural landscape – as throughout the Jaffna region, the number and size of these shrines seems completely out of proportion with the island's very modest number of inhabitants. At the end of the road, a tiny jetty on the island's western side is the departure point for boats to Nainativu and Delft.

Nainativu

A couple of kilometres east of Punkudutivu is the small island of **Nainativu** just 10km from top to bottom and a few kilometres wide. Immediately in front of the ferry jetty is the ornate **Naga Pooshani Ambal Kovil**, a Hindu temple sacred to the goddess Ambal – newborn babies are brought here to receive the goddess's blessings. The original temple was, as usual, destroyed by the Portuguese, and the large and impressive complex you see today dates from 1788; the gopuram was added in 1935. Thousands of people attend a major festival here in June/July.

A ten-minute walk south of here leads to the **Nagadipa Vihara**, a rare place of Buddhist worship in the Hindu north. This marks the spot of the Buddha's second legendary visit to Sri Lanka, when he is said to have achieved the reconciliation of two warring naga kings. A rather modest little temple marks the spot; the building next to it houses a superb golden Buddha from Thailand. The temple sits within an area used by the Sri Lankan Navy, so you'll have to talk your way through a checkpoint to visit it.

ARRIVAL AND DEPARTURE
NAINATIVU

By bus There are buses roughly every hour from Jaffna to Punkudutivu, from where it's a fifteen-minute trip by ferry to Nainativu. Ferries run every hour or so until 6.30pm – the trip over to Nainativu in one of these colourful little wooden fishing boats is half the fun of visiting the island.

Delft

By the time you reach the island of **DELFT**, named after the famous Dutch town, you'll begin to feel you're a long way from anywhere – although, despite its remoteness, the island was occupied by all three colonial powers. It's a place of bleak, minimalist beauty, crisscrossed with coral-rock walls and boasting an unusual population of **wild ponies**, the descendants of those first introduced by the Portuguese – they're found mainly in the southern centre of the island.

Ferries from Kurikadduwan dock at the northeast corner of the island. A short distance west of the ferry dock lie the remains of the old Portuguese **fort** – better preserved than Urundi, though you'll still need a good imagination to make much sense of the remains. There's a nice **beach** just east of the fort. South of the ferry dock stands a stumpy **baobab tree**, one of Central Africa's most distinctive species but almost unknown in Sri Lanka apart from this specimen and a few around Mannar. It's presumed to have been planted by Arab seamen.

Some 30km southwest of Delft lies the tiny island of **Kachchativu**, used as a base by passing Sri Lankan and Indian fishermen, but otherwise uninhabited, inaccessible, and boasting just a single man-made structure, the church of **St Anthony** – Sri Lanka's most isolated building and almost as close to India as to Jaffna.

ARRIVAL AND DEPARTURE   DELFT

By ferry Delft is some 20km southwest of Punkudutivu island, an hour's journey by ferry from the town of Kurikadduwan, which is connected to Jaffna by five daily buses. There are around five ferries in each direction daily, though they all leave in the morning, with the last outbound ferry at around midday and the last return ferry at around 2.30pm. A single bus plies the island's main road.

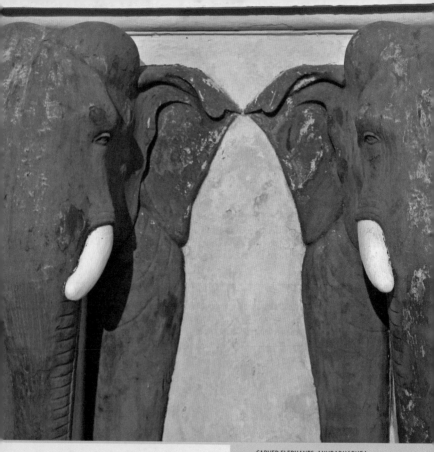

CARVED ELEPHANTS, ANURADHAPURA

Contexts

395 History

419 Sri Lankan Buddhism

426 Sri Lankan Buddhist art and architecture

432 Sri Lankan wildlife

438 Ceylon tea

441 Books

444 Language

History

Sri Lanka's past is sunk in an inextricable mixture of the historical and the mythological, exemplified by the curious story of Prince Vijaya (see box, p.397), from whom the Sinhalese people claim descent. Early hominids (Homo erectus) are thought to have reached the island by around 500,000 BC (perhaps much earlier), crossing the land-bridge that formerly connected India and Sri Lanka until as recently as 5000 BC, while vestiges of prehistoric settlements dating back to around 125,000 BC have been discovered – evidence of a Sri Lankan branch of Homo sapiens popularly known as "Balangoda Man" after archeological discoveries made in the vicinity of modern Balangoda, in the southern hill country. The only modern survivors of these prehistoric peoples are the Veddhas (see p.237), probably related to the aborigines of Australia, the Nicobar Islands and Malaysia. The Veddhas initially lived by hunting and gathering, and later developed knowledge of iron and agriculture, while quartz tools have been discovered at Bandarawela and simple pottery at Balangoda.

Most of the history of Sri Lanka, however, is concerned with two immigrant, rather than indigenous, peoples: the North Indian-descended **Sinhalese**, who form the majority of modern Sri Lanka's population; and the minority, South Indian-descended **Tamils**, found mainly in the north and east of the island – relations between these two ethnic groups have shaped much of the country's history, and continue to do so. Early Sri Lankan history thus remains a controversial subject, as both Sinhalese and Tamils continue to argue about who arrived first, their respective rights to the island, and exactly what it means to be Sri Lankan.

The argument continues to this day, given the lack of firm historical evidence. The early Sinhalese conveniently equipped themselves with a legendary historical pedigree, as recounted in the *Mahavamsa* and encapsulated in the legend of Prince Vijaya. The history of Tamil settlement in the island remains an altogether cloudier affair. According to the Sinhalese version of events there was no substantial Tamil presence in the island until the Chola invasions of the tenth century AD, although archeological discoveries, the fact that Tamil kings were ruling at Anuradhapura from as early as the second century BC, and plain common sense, given the island's proximity to the Tamil areas of South India, suggest that Tamil settlement of some kind dates back far earlier, whatever modern Sinhalese historians and politicians might claim.

The arrival of the Sinhalese

From around the fifth century BC, waves of Indo-Aryan immigrants began to arrive in Sri Lanka from northern India. Their exact origins remain obscure, though it's thought

125,000 BC	**c.500 BC**	**377 BC**	**246 BC**
Early homo sapiens – aka "Balangoda Man" – living in Sri Lanka.	First Sinhalese immigrants arrive in Sri Lanka.	Founding of Anuradhapura.	Arrival of Buddhism.

THE MAHAVAMSA AND CULAVAMSA

Much of our knowledge of early Sri Lankan history is owed to the **Mahavamsa** ("Great Chronicle") and its continuation, the **Culavamsa** ("Little Chronicle"). The *Mahavamsa* was compiled by Buddhist monks during the sixth century (the *Culavamsa* dates from the thirteenth century) and was intended to commemorate and legitimize the Sinhalese royal lineage and the island's impeccable Buddhist credentials. Their narration of actual historical events is therefore at best questionably biased, and at worst totally imaginary – a fact illustrated by the *Mahavamsa*'s meticulous descriptions of the three visits that the Buddha himself is claimed to have made to the island.

For more information on both books, visit ⓦmahavamsa.org.

that the first settlers came from present-day Gujarat, followed by second waves of colonists from Orissa and Bengal. These people, the ancestors of the present-day **Sinhalese**, first arrived on the western coast of the island. At first they were limited to river valleys, these being the only areas in which they were able to cultivate rice, but as their expertise in irrigation increased, they were able to strike inland towards the island's dry northern plains – during which expansion the indigenous Veddhas were either absorbed by intermarriage with the new arrivals or driven east and south.

The Anuradhapura period

The first major Sinhalese kingdom developed around the city of **Anuradhapura**, in the island's dry northern plains. The city's origins are shrouded in the semi-legendary depths of early Sinhalese history, though archeological evidence suggests that the city has been occupied for at least three thousand years. The first documented history comes from the *Mahavamsa*, which states that Anuradhapura was founded in 377 BC by the third king of the Vijaya dynasty, Pandukabhaya (reigned 380–367 BC), a rebellious noble of the Vijaya clan, who built a new capital on the site of the palace of his great-uncle, a certain Anuradha, after whom the new city was named.

The arrival of Buddhism

The fledgling city initially enjoyed only limited power over the surrounding region, though its status rose significantly during the reign of **Devanampiya Tissa** (c.300–260 BC), who oversaw the arrival of Buddhism in the island and established the city as a major centre of Buddhist pilgrimage and learning. According to the *Mahavamsa*, **Mahinda**, son of the great Indian Buddhist emperor Ashoka, arrived in Sri Lanka in 246 BC with a retinue of monks to proselytize on behalf of Buddhism, quickly converting the king of Anuradhapura, Devanampiya Tissa. Mahinda was soon followed by his sister, **Sangamitta**, who arrived with a valuable collection of relics including the Buddha's begging bowl, collarbone and a cutting from the sacred bo tree under which the Buddha attained enlightenment in Bodhgaya – the tree subsequently grown from this cutting still flourishes today.

Buddhism found a ready audience in Sri Lanka, and within half a century the island's Sinhalese had all converted to the new faith. Buddhism gave the Sinhalese a new-found sense of national identity and inspired the development of a distinctively Sri Lankan culture, exemplified by the religious architecture of Anuradhapura, whose enormous

161 BC	89 BC	67 AD	114–136
Dutugemunu defeats Elara at Anuradhapura and takes control of island.	Vattagmanini Abhaya expels Tamils and seizes throne.	Lambakanna dynasty begins.	Reign of Gajabahu; military campaigns against Cholas of South India.

PRINCE VIJAYA

According to Sinhalese tradition, recorded in the *Mahavamsa*, the Sinhalese people trace their origins back to the union between a lion ("sinha", hence Sinhalese) and a rather disreputable North Indian princess ("Very fair she was and very amorous, and for shame the king and queen could not suffer her"). The princess is said to have been travelling in a caravan when the lion attacked. The princess's companions fled, but, as the *Mahavamsa* touchingly relates:

… the lion beheld her [the princess] from afar. Love laid hold on him, and he came towards her with waving tail and ears laid back. Seeing him…without fear she caressed him, stroking his limbs. The lion, roused to fiercest passion by her touch, took her upon his back and bore her with all speed to his cave, and there he was united with her.

In due course the princess gave birth to twins, a boy and a girl, who subsequently married one another. The fruit of this incestuous union was sixteen sons, the eldest of whom was **Prince Vijaya**. Growing to manhood, Vijaya made such a nuisance of himself that there were calls for him and seven hundred of his male companions to be put to death. Instead, the king packed them all into a boat and sent them off into exile. Vijaya and his friends arrived on Sri Lanka sometime in the sixth century BC.

Landing on the island's west coast, they were confronted by a *yaksa*, or devil, who appeared to them in the form of a dog. Following the dog, they found another *yaksa*, this one in the shape of a woman hermit named **Kuveni**, who proceeded to magically ensnare all Vijaya's friends until the prince, protected by a magic thread conferred by the god Vishnu himself, seized her and threatened to cut off her head. Kuveni released the men, agreed to hand over the kingdom to Vijaya and, transforming herself into a young and desirable woman, retired with Vijaya to a splendidly appointed bed. They subsequently married and had two children, though Vijaya eventually came to feel the need for a more reputable consort, and drove Kuveni back into the forest. Their children escaped and married one another; it was their descendants who became, according to tradition, the **Veddhas**.

The lack of women on the island was finally relieved when Vijaya sent to the Pandyan court in India for wives for himself and his followers. Vijaya himself married a Pandyan princess, but failed to produce an heir, and towards the end of his reign sent for his younger brother to come and take his place as ruler. The brother, unwilling to leave his native land, instead sent his youngest son, **Panduvasudeva**. Having landed with 32 followers on the east coast at Gokana (present-day Trincomalee), Panduvasudeva was duly enthroned and continued the Vijaya dynasty.

To what extent these mythological events reflect actual history is a matter of considerable speculation. Vijaya himself was perhaps a symbolic rather than an actual historical figure – his name means "victory", perhaps representing the triumph of the North Indian immigrants over the native Veddhas. Equally, Vijaya's union with Kuveni would seem to commemorate the intermingling of the Sinhalese immigrants with the Veddhas, while his subsequent marriage to a Pandyan princess again probably has its roots in actual historic links between the early Sinhalese and the Tamils of South India – even Panduvasudeva may simply be another symbolic figure representing the second wave of settlement. The essentially symbolic nature of the tale is supported by fact that the Sinhalese themselves – and indeed the staunchly Buddhist writers of the *Mahavamsa* – feel no compunction in tracing their ancestry to a violent outcast whose immediate ancestry included both bestial and incestuous relations.

274–301	473	491
Reign of Mahasena; construction of numerous major tanks and the Jetavana monastery in Anuradhapura.	Dhatusena murdered by his son Kassapa, who establishes new capital at Sigiriya.	Mogallana defeats Kassapa at Sigiriya and returns capital to Anuradhapura.

stupas were amongst early Asia's greatest monuments. Sri Lanka's proximity to South India made it a constant target of invasions, however, while the reliance of the Sinhalese on Tamil mercenaries (given the traditional Buddhist regard for the sanctity of life, the Sinhalese have always had difficulties raising an effective army – at least until the past few decades) left them at the mercy of their own fighting forces. Tamils had already begun migrating to the island from the third century BC, and shortly after Devanampiya's death, two Tamil captains in the Anuradhapuran army – Sena and Guttika – staged a coup and ruled over the city for two decades. Following their murder, another Tamil soldier, **Elara**, seized power around 205 BC and ruled the city for a further 44 years. Elara's reign was finally ended in 161 BC by **Dutugemunu** (see box, p.324), the legendary Buddhist warrior-king who eventually defeated the old Tamil general after a protracted conflict and succeeded in uniting Sri Lanka under Sinhalese rule for the first time.

Dutugemunu's heady combination of military heroics and unimpeachable Buddhist piety proved an inspiration for all who followed him, even if none of the other 113 kings (and two queens) of Anuradhapura was able to emulate his achievements. Of the kings who followed, fifteen ruled for under a year, 22 were murdered, four committed suicide, thirteen were killed in battle and eleven were dethroned.

Soon after Dutugemunu's death, Anuradhapura was once again the target of South Indian attacks, and this constant external pressure, combined with incessant internal feuding, regularly succeeded in reducing the city to chaos. Tamil invaders seized Anuradhapura again in 103 BC, and despite being swiftly evicted by Vattagamini Abhaya (89–77 BC), founder of the Abhayagiri monastery and the cave temples at Dambulla, the kingdom soon descended once again into a period of chaos, exemplified by the reign of the notorious queen Anula (48–44 BC) who in five years is said to have married and then murdered 32 husbands.

The great tank builders

In 67 AD, the accession to the throne of Vasabha (67–111), the first of the **Lambakanna** dynasty, inaugurated Anuradhapura's greatest era of peace and prosperity. Vasabha initiated the first of the massive irrigation works that transformed the arid plains of the northern part of the island into fecund agricultural land capable of supporting a dense population and a highly developed civilization. Despite further struggles with invading Tamil forces – encapsulated in the legendary exploits of **Gajabahu**, who reigned from 114–136 (see p.208) – the following four centuries of Lambakanna rule were largely peaceful. Later kings contributed further to the city's magnificent Buddhist heritage and the northern island's irrigation system, most notably **Mahasena** (274–301), who is said to have constructed no fewer than sixteen major reservoirs, including the Minneriya and Kaudulla tanks, as well as the Jetavana, the last of the city's three great monasteries.

A new period of uncertainty began in 429 with yet another invasion from South India and the rule of seven Tamil generals who reigned in succession until being evicted by **Dhatusena** (455–473), who celebrated in the by now customary fashion by constructing (according to the *Mahavamsa*) no fewer than eighteen new temples and the enormous Kalawewa reservoir, near Aukana. Dhatusena met an unholy end at the hands of his own son, **Kassapa** (see p.298), who temporarily removed the capital to Sigiriya, before another of Dhatusena's sons, Mogallana, succeeded in wresting back control, albeit again with South Indian assistance.

853	993	1070
Anuradhapura sacked by South Indian Pandyans.	Final destruction of Anuradhapura by Chola king, Rajaraja, who establishes new capital at Polonnaruwa.	Vijayabahu drives Cholas from island and re-establishes Sinhalese rule.

This event signalled a renewal of Tamil influence: the island's kings again sought Tamil support in their own disputes, and South Indian mercenaries became both an important and unpredictable faction in the Sinhalese state and a powerful influence at court. **Tamil** influence in Sri Lankan affairs continued to grow during the fifth century AD, following the resurgence of Hinduism in southern India and the rise of three powerful new Tamil kingdoms there: the Cholas (based in Thanjavur), the Pandyas (Madurai) and the Pallavas (Kanchipuram), all of whom would at various times become entangled in Sri Lankan affairs.

Decline and fall

A final interlude of peace was enjoyed during the reigns of Aggabodhi I (571–604) and Aggabodhi II (604–14), who between them restored many of Anuradhapura's religious edifices and carried out further irrigation projects. The latter's death ushered in the most chaotic period in the history of the Anuradhapura kingdom, with incessant civil wars and the growing influence of South Indian mercenaries, who were recruited by disaffected Sinhalese nobles or rival claimants to the throne and frequently paid for by wealth plundered from Buddhist monasteries.

By the end of the seventh century, power had effectively passed to these Tamil mercenaries, who acted as kingmakers until the last of the great Anuradhapuran kings, **Manavamma** (684–718), was placed on the throne with the support of the Pallavas, establishing a second Lambakanna dynasty. Manavamma's reign ushered in a final century of relative peace before Anuradhapura's destruction. In 853, an invading Pandyan army sacked Anuradhapura before being bought off at great cost. Despite the best efforts of Sri Lankan diplomacy, the ever-present threat of South Indian invasion continued to hang over the kingdom, fuelled by the religious animosity that the Hindu kingdoms of South India bore towards their Buddhist neighbour. In 946–947, the Cholas sacked Anuradhapura, and the city's soldiers were obliged to flee to Ruhunu until the Cholas had returned home. By 992, the last king of Anuradhapura, Mahinda V (983–993), found he had no funds to pay the wages of his mercenaries and was forced to flee to Ruhunu. Anuradhapura and the northern areas of the island fell into chaos, with bands of soldiers pillaging at will. Attracted by the disorder, the Chola king **Rajaraja** despatched an army that sacked Anuradhapura for the very last time in the fateful year of **993**, reducing the once great city to ruins – the single greatest watershed in Sri Lankan history.

The Polonnaruwa period

Having destroyed Anuradhapura, the Cholas established themselves in the city of **Polonnaruwa**, from where they ruled for the next 75 years until **Vijayabahu I** ejected them from the island in 1070 AD. Although Vijayabahu had himself crowned for symbolic reasons amidst the ruins of Anuradhapura, he decided to move the capital to Polonnaruwa, which was further removed from India and situated in more easily defensible territory.

The relocation ushered in the beginning of a final Sinhalese golden age. Vijayabahu's successor **Parakramabahu I** (see box, p.309), who reigned from 1153–86, reformed the island's economy, transformed Polonnaruwa into one of the great cities of South Asia and even launched raids against the Pandyas and a naval expedition against Burma. After Parakramabahu, the throne passed to his Tamil brother-in-law, **Nissankamalla**

1153–86	1186–96	1215
Reign of Parakramabahu the Great; golden age of Polonnaruwa.	Reign of Nissankamalla.	South Indian mercenary Magha seizes control of Polonnaruwa; widespread disorder and collapse of Sinhalese civilization in Rajarata; Arya Chakaravarti founds new Tamil kingdom, Jaffnapatnam, in north.

(see p.312), who reigned from 1186–96, and the influence of South India increased once again. Nissankamalla was the last effective ruler of Polonnaruwa, though his zeal for lavish new building projects came close to bankrupting the state, which had already been labouring under the expense of Parakramabahu's wars overseas.

Nissankamalla's death without a designated heir resulted in the usual disorder. A series of weaker rulers followed until, in 1212, a new wave of Tamil invaders, the Pandyans, arrived in the island and seized power, only to be displaced three years later by another South Indian adventurer, the despotic **Magha** (1215–55), who instituted a chaotic reign of terror during which the kingdom's complex irrigation systems gradually fell into disrepair, and the population began to abandon Polonnaruwa and move steadily southwards.

The Sinhalese move south

The following period of Sri Lankan history presents a complex and disordered picture, as various Sinhalese and South Indian factions jockeyed for position amidst an increasingly politically fragmented island. As Polonnaruwa fell into chaos under Magha, so the Sinhalese aristocracy began to establish rival centres of power located in inaccessible terrain beyond his reach. Initially, the Sinhalese established a new capital at **Dambadeniya**, about seventy miles southwest of Polonnaruwa, under Vijayabahu III (1232–36). Vijayabahu III's successor, **Parakramabahu II** (1236–70), succeeded in expelling Magha with Pandyan help, though further political instability soon followed. Under Bhuvanekabahu I (1272–84) the Sinhalese capital was moved briefly northwards to the isolated rock fortress of **Yapahuwa**. After further skirmishes, Bhuvanekabahu II (1293–1302) moved the capital south again, to **Kurunegala**, although increasing political fragmentation meant that none of these kings enjoyed much real power. By around 1340, the monarchy itself had split, with rival Sinhalese kings established at **Gampola** and **Dedigama**.

The southwards drift of Sinhalese power had dramatic social and economic consequences. As the island's population moved quickly from one town to another, so the complex **irrigation systems** that had supported the advanced civilization of the dry zone fell into further disrepair. The carefully oiled machinery of Sinhalese society wound down: the great tanks and canals of the northern plains dried up, reducing the area of cultivable land (with a consequent decline in population and revenue), while a losing battle was fought against the encroaching jungle, which began to reclaim the abandoned cities and villages. The Sinhalese increasingly found themselves driven south into the central highlands. Capital cities were now selected mainly for their defensibility, and became military strongholds rather than economic centres, situated in difficult terrain and away from populous areas. As irrigation systems and large-scale agriculture broke down, so fewer taxes were paid to the state, further weakening centralized control.

These economic changes also had implications for the island's cherished Buddhist faith. As revenues – literally – dried up, so the funds available to the Buddhist establishment declined. Kings continued as patrons of Buddhism, but their own reduced circumstances meant that Buddhist institutions no longer enjoyed the wealth they once had. The great monasteries of Anuradhapura and Polonnaruwa were disbanded, while indiscipline and theological schisms spread throughout the **Buddhist Sangha** (clergy).

1232	1272	1293	c.1340
Vijayabahu III establishes new capital at Dambadeniya.	Bhuvanekabahu I moves capital to Yapahuwa.	Bhuvanekabahu II moves capital to Kurunegala.	Rival Sinhalese kings ruling from Gampola and Dedigama.

The influence of Hinduism once again rose, with Hindu gods assuming increasingly important roles in the island's Buddhist temples and festivals.

The Jaffna kingdom

The erosion of Sinhalese authority left a power vacuum in the north of the island. Following the invasion of Magha in 1215 a South Indian general, **Arya Chakaravarti**, seized power in the north, founding a Tamil kingdom, **Jaffnapatnam**, with its capital at Nallur in the Jaffna Peninsula. This kingdom soon expanded southwards, coming into conflict with the centres of Sinhalese power, until by the mid-fourteenth century the Tamil kingdom even attacked and defeated the rulers of Gampola (near present-day Colombo), establishing its own tax collectors in the kingdom.

As the Sinhalese migrated steadily south and the Tamils established an independent kingdom in the north, so the island became increasingly divided into two along the linguistic, cultural and religious lines that survive to this day. Previously, Tamil settlements had been interspersed among the Sinhalese. Now, for the first time, the island's northern and eastern areas became predominantly Tamil (compounded by fresh migrations from South India following the collapse of the Pandyan kingdom in the fourteenth century). Jaffna became a major seat of Tamil culture, its society organized along similar lines to the Tamil regions of South India, while the Tamil language became entrenched in the island, developing a literary culture that was nurtured by the kings of Jaffna and enriched by contact with South India.

The rise of Kotte

The Jaffna kingdom's mid-fourteenth-century attack against Gampola marked its high-water point. In the second half of the fourteenth century a new Sinhalese dynasty, the **Alagakkonaras** (or Alakesvaras) rose to power in Gampola. Establishing a fort at **Kotte**, near Colombo, they expelled the Tamil tax collectors and re-established their independence, though internal feuding fatally weakened them. In 1405, a Ming Chinese fleet under the legendary general **Cheng Ho** arrived in Sri Lanka on a mission to gain possession of the **Tooth Relic**. The Alagakkonaras, not surprisingly, refused to hand it over. A few years later, Cheng Ho returned and carried off the last of the Alagakkonara rulers, Vira Alekesvara, to China for five years in retaliation.

Vira Alekesvara was eventually returned unharmed to Sri Lanka, only to find that during his absence a minor member of the Gampola nobility had seized power and had himself crowned as **Parakramabahu VI** of Kotte (1412–67). The last of the great Sinhalese unifiers, Parakramabahu first subdued the independent kingdom of the highlands, then saw off an invasion of the Vijayanagarans (the dominant power in South India at that time), and finally, in 1450, succeeded in taking possession of the Jaffna kingdom and uniting the entire island, for the final time, under Sinhalese rule. As on so many previous occasions, however, the unity achieved by one strong ruler failed to survive his death, and within a few years the kingdoms of Jaffna, Rajarata and the central highlands had once more asserted their independence, so that the subsequent rulers of Kotte, although they continued to claim sovereignty over the whole of Sri Lanka, increasingly found themselves hemmed into a small area in the island's southwestern corner.

c.1350 onwards	1405	1412–67
Rise of Kotte kingdom, near modern Colombo.	Chinese admiral Cheng Ho visits Sri Lanka.	Reign of Parakramabahu VI of Kotte; island reunited under Sinhalese rule for final time.

The Portuguese

As agricultural revenues declined following the collapse of irrigation systems and the loss of territory, so **trade** became increasingly important. Spices were the most important exports: cinnamon, found in the southwestern forests, was first exported in the fourteenth century, and was soon followed by pepper and other spices – all of them subject to royal monopolies. Colombo, Galle and other coastal settlements in the island's southwest developed into important **ports**, attracting foreign merchants and establishing wide-ranging commercial contacts – as early as 1283 Bhuvanekabahu I had despatched a trade mission to the Mamluk sultan of Egypt. The most important of these traders were the **Arabs**, who began visiting Sri Lanka from around the tenth century and who established settlements around the coast – including the small town of Kolamba, the forerunner of modern Colombo. They also brought Islam to the island, while exporting cinnamon and other spices that had begun to fetch premium prices in Western markets.

The island's trading possibilities soon began to attract attention from even further afield. In 1497, the **Portuguese** navigator Vasco da Gama pioneered the sea route to India around the southern tip of Africa, opening the Indian Ocean to European mariners. In 1505, a Portuguese fleet, prospecting for spices, was blown off course into the mouth of the Kelani Ganga, near Colombo. The Portuguese received a friendly audience from the king of Kotte, Vira Parakramabahu, who was understandably fascinated by these exotic, armour-clad foreigners, described by one of the king's scouts as "a race of men, exceeding white and beautiful. They wear boots and hats of iron, and they are always in motion. They eat white stones [bread] and they drink blood [wine]."

Kotte and Sitawake

The Portuguese had noted the island's commercial and strategic value – in particular its vast supply of cinnamon – and soon returned, being granted trading concessions and permission to build a fort at Colombo. They found themselves rapidly overtaken by the imbroglio of Sri Lankan politics, however, and spent the next seventy years fighting to retain a foothold on the island. In 1521 three sons of the then king of Kotte, Vijayabahu, put their father to death and divided the kingdom between themselves. The oldest of the brothers, **Bhuvanekabahu**, ruled at Kotte, whilst the two others set up independent kingdoms at Sitawake and Rayigama. The ambitious king of Sitawake, **Mayadunne**, soon began the attempt to seize control of his brother's kingdom at Kotte; Bhuvanekabahu, in turn, sought Portuguese assistance, becoming increasingly reliant on their military support.

Mayadunne gradually succeeded in capturing a large part of the Kotte kingdom, while following his death, his son **Rajasinha** continued to prosecute the war against the Portuguese successfully on land, though he had no way of combating Portuguese sea power. Following Rajasinha's death in 1593, however, the Portuguese were able to take control of much of Kotte, while a series of northwards expeditions were also launched, culminating in the conquest of the kingdom of Jaffna in 1619. The Portuguese continued to expand their control, annexing the lower reaches of the central highlands, the east-coast ports of Trincomalee and Batticaloa, and eventually gaining control over the entire island except for the kingdom of Kandy in the central highlands.

Portuguese rule largely retained the traditional Sinhalese systems of caste and tribute, using local officials from the Sinhalese nobility who were loyal to the incomers; however, all tribute that had been due to the Sinhalese kings was now taken by the

1497	1505	1518	1521
Vasco da Gama discovers sea route to India.	Portuguese fleet arrives in Sri Lanka.	Portuguese build fort in Colombo.	Kingdom of Kotte splits into kingdoms of Kotte, Sitawake and Rayigama. Mayadunne, ruler of Sitawake, begins to launch attacks against Portuguese.

TAKING THE PORTUGUESE TO KOTTE

Following the arrival of the first Portuguese on the coast of Sri Lanka, they were invited to present themselves to the king of Kotte, who was understandably intrigued by these strange foreigners. A delegation was prepared and dispatched to meet the king. However, before they could do so, the king's messengers, in order to disguise the smallness of their kingdom and the fact that the royal capital lay a mere 13km inland, led the Portuguese on a convoluted three-day march around the coastal regions in a vain attempt to delude them into believing the kingdom of Kotte a much grander affair than it actually was. Sadly, the Portuguese saw straight through this attempted subterfuge, but despite the failure of the attempt, the expression "**Taking the Portuguese to Kotte**" remains to this day a Sri Lankan euphemism for double-dealing of all kinds.

Portuguese, including a monopoly in elephants and cinnamon, and control of the lucrative trade in pepper and betel nuts. Even so, the burdens they placed upon the island's inhabitants led to hardship and popular hostility.

Portuguese rule was also marked by intense Roman Catholic **missionary activity**. Missionary orders were lavishly endowed, often using funds appropriated from Buddhist and Hindu temples, while members of the landed aristocracy embraced Christianity and took Portuguese surnames – the ancestors of the thousands of de Silvas, de Zoysas, Fernandos and Pereiras who still fill the telephone directories of modern Sri Lanka. Many coastal communities underwent mass conversion, particularly around Jaffna, Mannar and along the coast north of Colombo. Surnames and religion apart, hardly any physical evidence remains of Portuguese rule – virtually all their modest houses, churches and forts were subsequently rebuilt or knocked down by the Dutch or the British.

The Kandyan kingdom and the arrival of the Dutch

The origins of the Kingdom of **Kandy**, situated in the remote and rugged hill country at the heart of the island, date back to the fourteenth century (see p.205). By the time the Portuguese arrived, it had developed into one of the island's three main kingdoms, along with Kotte and Jaffna. The Portuguese first turned their attention to Kandy in 1591, though their attempt to place a puppet ruler on the throne was thwarted by an ambitious Sinhalese nobleman sent to accompany the Portuguese nominee, who enthroned himself instead, proclaiming independence from the Portuguese and taking the name of **Vimala Dharma Suriya**. Using guerrilla tactics, Vimala Dharma Suriya routed a Portuguese attack in 1594, as well as subsequent attacks in 1611, 1629 and 1638.

Realizing he couldn't drive the Portuguese out of Sri Lanka without sea power, Dharma Suriya saw the arrival of the **Dutch**, who had had their eyes on the island for a number of years, as an opportunity to gain naval support against his adversaries. Dutch envoys met Dharma Suriya in 1602 and determined upon a joint attack against the Portuguese. At least that was the plan. The Dutch leader, Admiral Sebald de Weert, invited the king to come back to the coast and inspect his ships. Dharma Suriya demurred, replying that he was reluctant to leave his queen, Dona Caterina, alone. De Weert, who appears to have been somewhat the worse for drink, replied that from what he had heard the queen was unlikely to be alone for long, whereupon he and his companions were, perhaps not surprisingly, hacked to death.

1593–1638	1602	1630
Portuguese seize control of coastal areas as far as Jaffna, and launch unsuccessful attacks against Kingdom of Kandy.	First Dutch emissaries arrive in island, meeting with king of Kandy.	Kandyans attack Colombo and Galle but are eventually driven off.

Despite this unfortunate turn of events, Dharma Suriya's successor, **Senarat**, continued to seek Dutch support. The Dutch again promised military help, though in the event they were unable to provide it and the king turned instead to the Danes, who dispatched an expedition, though by the time it arrived Senarat had concluded a peace agreement with the Portuguese (the tardy Danes instead founded a colony on the Coromandel coast of India). The truce was short-lived, however, and in 1630 the Kandyans invaded Portuguese territory, laying siege to Colombo and Galle, though again their lack of sea power prevented them from dislodging the Portuguese permanently.

The Dutch seize control

In 1635, Senarat was succeeded by his son **Rajasinha II**. The new king once again sent emissaries to the Dutch, who arrived in Sri Lanka with a fleet of ships and began attacking Portuguese positions. Between 1638 and 1640 they drove the Portuguese out of a number of important coastal towns, but refused to hand over their conquests to Rajasinha, saying they had not been paid their expenses. The king of Kandy was still waiting when, in 1640, the offensive against the Portuguese was temporarily halted by a truce declared in Europe between the United Provinces of the Netherlands and Spain, which at that time ruled Portugal and its overseas possessions.

Fighting eventually resumed in 1652. The Kandyans launched attacks on Portuguese positions in the interior, pushing them back to their coastal strongholds despite fierce resistance. The Dutch, meanwhile, laid siege to Colombo by sea and land, and in May 1656 the Portuguese finally surrendered the city to the Dutch, who promptly shut the Kandyans out of its gates. Faced with this duplicity, Rajasinha torched the lands around Colombo and then withdrew back to the hills. Despite this loss of local support, the Dutch continued to drive the Portuguese from the island, attacking Portuguese strongholds in northern Sri Lanka until, with the conquest of Jaffna in 1658, they had replaced the Portuguese as masters of coastal Sri Lanka.

Compared with the Portuguese, the Dutch were less interested in saving souls than in making money. Even so, the early years of **Dutch rule** did see an enthusiastic effort to spread the Reformed Calvinist faith in Sri Lanka. Roman Catholicism was declared illegal, and its priests banned from the country; Catholic churches were given to the Reformed faith, and many Sinhalese and Tamil Catholics nominally embraced Protestantism. Meanwhile, the Dutch tried to promote trade with neighbouring countries, though these efforts were stifled by the strict monopolies that they maintained in the lucrative export markets of cinnamon, elephants, pearls and betel nuts.

Their most lasting contributions to Sri Lanka, however, can be seen in the nation's cuisine, culture and architecture. The Dutch are credited with the invention of the popular dish of *lamprais* (see p.36), while the classic Sri Lankan rice and curry spread may also have been inspired by the *rijsttafel* (literally "rice table"), an elaborate type of meal created by the Dutch in Indonesia and comprising numerous contrasting dishes accompanied by rice. They also brought several classic Southeast Asian fruits such as durian, mangosteen and rambutan from their colonies in the Dutch East Indies (modern-day Indonesia), from where they also imported the stitched sarong and the art of batik-making. In architecture they established the style of colonial villa – with shady interior courtyards and huge, pillared verandas – which is still widely employed to this day, and which can be seen at its finest in the magnificent old fort at **Galle**, the

1638–40	**1652**	**1656**
Dutch begin attacking and driving Portuguese out of their coastal strongholds.	Dutch resume attacks against Portuguese in alliance with Kandyans.	Dutch capture Colombo from Portuguese. Beginning of Dutch rule.

Sri Lankan Dutch colonial town par excellence. Dutch settlers stayed in Sri Lanka even after they had lost control of the island to the British (see below), and their descendants – the so-called **Burghers** (see box, p.146) – remain a small but significant element in the nation's life right up to the present day.

The arrival of the British

The French Revolution initiated a major shake-up in relations between the leading European powers. When the Netherlands fell to the French in 1794, the **British East India Company**'s forces occupied Sri Lanka, having already for some time coveted the magnificent natural harbour at Trincomalee. In theory, the British were meant to be protecting Dutch territory against the French, though the forgivably suspicious Dutch mounted a halfhearted resistance before surrendering the island to their British "protectors" in 1796. Despite the supposedly temporary nature of the British administration, the new colonists soon began to appreciate Sri Lanka's strategic and commercial value, and quickly moved to make their hold on the island permanent, and, in 1802, Sri Lanka was ceded to Britain under the Treaty of Amiens with France.

One of the priorities of the new colonizers was to subdue the Kandyan kingdom and finally unify the island under a single rule. The British launched a disastrous expedition against the kingdom in 1803, but it wasn't until 1815 that they finally achieved their end, when the Kandyans – enraged by the megalomaniac behaviour of their king, Sri Wickrama Rajasinha – simply stood to one side and allowed British soldiers to march in and occupy the city. After two centuries of spirited resistance, the last bastion of Sri Lankan independence had finally been extinguished.

Though reluctant to upset traditional Sinhalese institutions, the British abolished slavery, relieved native officials of judicial authority and relaxed the system of compulsory-service tenure. Agriculture was encouraged, and production of cinnamon, pepper, sugar cane, cotton and coffee flourished. Internal communications were extended, Christian missions dispatched and restrictions on European ownership of land lifted. English became the official language of government and the medium of instruction in schools. In addition, the British quickly opened up the island's economy, abolishing all state monopolies. Crown land was sold off cheaply to encourage the establishment of new plantations, and capital flowed in. The most notable result of these changes was the spectacular growth in the island's **coffee** production from around 1830 to 1870. As the area under cultivation for coffee expanded, so new roads, rail lines and port facilities were constructed to service the industry, while indentured labourers from southern India begin arriving in large numbers to make good the island's labour shortage – almost a million arrived between 1843 and 1859. In the 1870s, however, the island's coffee production was destroyed by a leaf disease. The void, however, was soon filled by the introduction of **tea** (see p.438), with plantations quickly spreading around the slopes of the central highlands, while rubber and coconuts also acquired increasing importance.

The rise of nationalism

Sri Lanka's traumatic encounters with European colonial powers led to a major re-evaluation of its own traditional culture. In the nineteenth century, revivalist

1658	1794	1802
Dutch take Jaffna from Portuguese and consolidate hold over much of island.	British East India Company forces occupy Dutch territory following fall of Netherlands to the French in Europe.	Sri Lanka ceded to British under Treaty of Amiens.

Buddhist and Hindu movements sprang up, with the aim both of modernizing native institutions in the face of the Western onslaught, and of defending the island's traditional culture against missionary Christianity. The major figure in this movement was the charismatic David Hewavitharane (1864–1933), who subsequently adopted the name **Anagarika Dharmapala** ("Protector of the Dharma") upon committing himself to a life of Buddhist activism – almost every town in Sri Lanka now has a road named after him. Dharmapala campaigned tirelessly for Buddhist rights and recognition, receiving unexpected support from the maverick American theosophist **Henry Steel Olcott** (see p.76). Gradually, this burgeoning **nationalist consciousness** acquired a political dimension. Grassroots organizations began to demand greater Sri Lankan participation in government, though the uncoordinated nature of these protests meant they were easily ignored by the government – even so, **constitutional reforms** passed in 1910 made the small concession of allowing a limited number of "educated" Sri Lankans to elect one member to the government's Legislative Council.

During World War I, the forces of nationalism gathered momentum. British arrests of prominent Sinhalese leaders after minor civil disturbances in 1915 provoked widespread opposition, leading in 1919 to the foundation of the **Ceylon National Congress**, which united both Sinhalese and Tamil organizations and drafted proposals for constitutional reforms. Concessions slowly followed, and in 1931 a new constitution gave the island's leaders the chance to exercise political power and gain legislative experience, with a view towards eventual self-government. In addition, the new constitution granted universal franchise, bringing all Sri Lankans into the political process for the first time, and making the country the first Asian colony to achieve universal suffrage.

During **World War II**, Sri Lankan nationalist leaders supported the British war effort while continuing to lobby for full independence. When Singapore, Indonesia and Burma fell to the Japanese, Sri Lanka suddenly found itself close to the front line of the war in the east, a fact brought home by Japanese bombing raids against Colombo and Trincomalee (during which a number of British warships were sunk). By the end of 1942, Sri Lanka had become the major base of British operations in Asia. Lord Mountbatten established his South East Asia Command headquarters at Kandy, while Trincomalee hosted a wing of the Special Operations Executive, which launched saboteurs and resistance coordinators behind Japanese lines.

Independence

Sri Lanka's long-awaited **independence** finally came on February 4, 1948, with power passing from the British to the **United National Party** (**UNP**), under the leadership of **D.S. Senanayake**. The essentially conservative UNP was dominated by the English-educated leaders of the colonial era, though it did include people from all the country's ethno-linguistic groups.

The first years of independence were kind to Sri Lanka: exports were doing well in world markets, there was a sizeable sterling balance earned during the war while the island even came close to eradicating malaria. There were, however, some basic weaknesses. The ruling parties largely represented the views of the island's English-educated, Westernized elite – an ideology that most of the population found incomprehensible or irrelevant. In addition, **economic difficulties** began gradually to

1815	1820s	1870s
Fall of Kandy, the last independent Sinhalese kingdom; British rule extended across entire island.	Construction of first road linking Kandy to the coast	Collapse of coffee industry and beginning of tea production; thousands of Tamil immigrants arrive to work on the new plantations.

emerge. Falling rubber and tea prices on the world markets, rises in the cost of imported food and a rapidly increasing population ate quickly into the country's foreign exchange, while the expanded school system produced large numbers of educated persons unable to find suitable employment. Meanwhile, Tamil plantation workers found themselves suddenly disenfranchised by the UNP (conveniently so, given that they largely voted for their own, sectarian, Tamil parties). The Senanayake government insisted on classifying the **Plantation Tamils** as "foreigners", even if they had been living on the island for generations, and attempted to repatriate them to India, an episode that tarnished relations between the two countries for years.

In 1952, D.S. Senanayake died after being thrown from his horse on Galle Face Green in Colombo and was briefly succeeded by his son, Dudley Senanayake, though he was forced to resign following disastrous attempts to cut rice subsidies, an act that provoked widespread strikes and rioting. In 1953, he was succeeded by his uncle, **John Kotelawala**, a bout of nepotism that earned the UNP the name of the "Uncle Nephew Party".

The Bandaranaikes

As the 1950s progressed, the UNP's Westernized and elitist political leaders proved increasingly out of touch with the views and aspirations of the majority of the island's population. In the elections of 1956, the UNP lost to the socialist-nationalist **Sri Lanka Freedom Party** (**SLFP**) under the leadership of the charismatic **S.W.R.D. Bandaranaike**, ushering in an extraordinary dynastic sequence in which power alternated between various members of the Senanayake clan (through the guise of the UNP), and assorted Bandaranaikes (through various incarnations of the SLFP).

The new government immediately set about changing the country's political landscape, instigating a huge programme of nationalization, making Sinhala the sole official language and instigating state support for the Buddhist faith and Sinhalese culture, largely in reaction to the Anglo-Christian values foisted upon the island by the British. Bandaranaike's new policies had the unfortunate side effect of stoking the fires of ethnic and religious tension. His language policy alienated the Tamils, his educational policies outraged the small but influential Christian community, while even factions amongst the Sinhalese communities were disturbed by his cultural and religious reforms. As passions grew, the island experienced its first major **ethnic riots**, in May 1958. Tamils were driven from Colombo and other places where they had traditionally lived alongside the Sinhalese, while Sinhalese in turn fled from Tamil areas in the north and east. In September 1959, Bandaranaike opened **talks with the Tamils** in an attempt to calm the situation, and was promptly assassinated by a militant Buddhist monk – not the first or last time the island's Buddhist clergy would play a role in stoking up religious intolerance on the island.

Bandaranaike was succeeded by his widow, Sirimavo – or **Mrs Bandaranaike**, as she is usually known – who thus became the world's first-ever female prime minister. Mrs Bandaranaike's government continued to implement the policies of Sinhalese nationalism: all private schools were nationalized in an attempt to neutralize the influence of Christian missions in the educational system, while important national industries were also taken over by the state; in addition, she had half a million Plantation Tamils deported to India. Despite her symbolic importance for women worldwide, Mrs Bandaranaike was less appreciated at home, and had to survive an

1880	1910	1919
Arrival of Henry Steel Olcott and Madame Blavatsky, who champion Buddhist causes as part of island-wide Buddhist revival.	Constitutional reforms allow election of one Sri Lankan member to government's Legislative Council.	First national political party, the Ceylon National Congress, founded.

attempted coup before being finally trounced at the polls in 1965 by the UNP, who returned to power under **Dudley Senanayake**, with the emphasis once again on private enterprise and economic stability.

The JVP and the road to civil war

The Sri Lankan electorate's habit of kicking out whichever party happened to be in power repeated itself in the **1970 elections**, when the UNP were defeated and the irrepressible Mrs Bandaranaike once again became prime minister at the head of a new SLFP-led coalition, the **United Front**. The interminable yo-yoing between parties and policies thus continued, with Mrs Bandaranaike reversing the policies of the UNP and resuming her old aims of restricting private enterprise and increasing nationalization of key industries, while introducing policies aimed at reducing social inequality via an ambitious programme of land reform. Her government also ditched a further memento of the island's colonial past by changing its **name** from Ceylon to Sri Lanka (see box opposite).

Though these measures appeased the island's underprivileged, they did nothing to address basic economic problems such as the mounting trade deficit. The country's youth, impatient for radical change, expressed their discontent through the extreme left-wing and anti-Tamil **JVP** (Janatha Vimukthi Peramuna, or People's Liberation Front). In 1971, the JVP launched an armed rebellion with the aim of overthrowing the government, but despite brief successes, the insurrection was easily and ruthlessly suppressed by the army, with thousands of the poorly organized rebels (mainly students) losing their lives. Meanwhile, Sri Lanka's **economic decline** continued, and the immense power held by the state provided the party in power with the opportunity for patronage, nepotism and corruption. Mrs Bandaranaike continued her nationalization programme, seizing hold of tea estates and private agricultural lands, two of the few areas of the economy that were still functioning successfully. By 1977, unemployment had risen to about fifteen percent.

The LTTE and civil war

In June 1977, the United Front was defeated by a reinvigorated UNP under the leadership of **J.R. Jayawardene**, who became the first non-Senanayake to control the UNP. Jayawardene immediately began to tamper with the democratic process, however, writing yet another new constitution in 1978 that gave the country's president (previously an essentially ceremonial role) new powers. In the same year, Jayawardene resigned as prime minister and was promptly elected the country's first president (and re-elected in 1982, after further tinkering with the constitution).

The Jayawardene government again tried to revitalize the private sector and attract back some of the foreign capital driven away by Mrs Bandaranaike. These policies enjoyed some success: by 1983, unemployment had been halved, while the island became self-sufficient in rice by 1985. Meanwhile tourism and expatriate Sri Lankans working in the Middle East brought in valuable foreign currency, though these gains were undercut by rampant inflation, unstable tea and rubber prices and, most seriously, by the country's descent into **civil war**.

The origins of this latest Sinhalese–Tamil conflict had first been sparked in the early 1970s via new legislation designed to cut the number of Tamil places at the country's

1931	1942	1948
New constitution devolves limited political power to local leaders and grants universal suffrage to all Sri Lankans.	Sri Lanka becomes major base of operations for British war effort in Southern Asia; Japanese air force attacks Trincomalee.	Sri Lanka attains independence; D.S. Senanayake becomes prime minister at head of United National Party (UNP).

SRI LANKA OR CEYLON?

The origins of Sri Lanka's colonial name, **Ceylon**, stretch back to the island's ancient Sanskrit name of Sinhaladvipa, meaning the land (*dvipa*) of the Sinhala tribe. In the classical Buddhist language of Pali, Sinhala is Sihalam, pronounced "Silam", which mutated over the centuries into the Portuguese Ceilão, and thence into the Dutch Zeylan and the British Ceylon. Arab traders, meanwhile, transformed Sihalam into Serendib (or Serendip), the root of the English word "serendipity" (or the making of fortuitous discoveries by accident), coined in the eighteenth century by the English man of letters Horace Walpole, inspired by a Persian fairy tale, "The Three Princes of Serendip".

Not that this was the only name by which the island was known overseas. The Greeks and Romans had previously called the island **Taprobane**, derived from another ancient Sanskrit name for the island, Tambapanni, after the copper-coloured beach on which Prince Vijaya and his followers (see p.397) are claimed to have first landed. The island's own inhabitants, however, have always known the island by a different name entirely: in Sinhalese, **Lanka**, and in Tamil as **Ilankai**. The reversion from the British colonial Ceylon to the indigenous **Sri Lanka** (or, to be precise, the Democratic Socialist Republic of Sri Lanka) was finally made in 1972 – the additional "Sri" is Sinhalese for "auspicious" or "resplendent".

universities, while the new constitution of 1972 further aggravated Tamil sensibilities by declaring Buddhism to hold the "foremost place" amongst the island's religions. These measures provoked growing unrest amongst Sri Lanka's Tamils, culminating in a **state of emergency** that was imposed on northern areas of the island for several years from 1971. Since the police and army who enforced this state of emergency included few Tamils (one result of the constitution's insistence that only Sinhala speakers be allowed to occupy official posts), and were often undisciplined and heavy-handed, they were increasingly seen by the Tamils as an occupying force.

The rise of the Tigers

By the mid-1970s some young Tamils had begun to resort to violence, calling for an independent Tamil state, **Eelam** ("Precious Land"). Tamil bases were established in jungle areas of northern and eastern Sri Lanka, as well as in the southern districts of the Indian state of Tamil Nadu, where Tamil groups received considerable support. A number of militant groups emerged, most notably the **LTTE**, or Liberation Tigers of Tamil Eelam, popularly known as the **Tamil Tigers** (see box, p.376). Founded in 1976, the LTTE rapidly established a reputation for violence and ruthlessness under their elusive leader, **Velupillai Prabhakaran**, consolidating themselves as the leaders of the resistance struggle thanks to their repeated attacks against Sinhalese government forces and also to their murderous suppression of rival Tamil groups.

Despite limited **reforms** – such as the promotion of Tamil to the status of a "national language" to be used in official business in Tamil areas – violence continued to escalate in the north. The point of no return arrived in 1983, following the ambush and massacre of an army patrol by a group of Tamil Tiger guerrillas near Jaffna. For several weeks afterwards – a period subsequently christened "**Black July**" – Sinhalese mobs rampaged across the south, indiscriminately killing Tamils and looting and destroying their shops and houses. As many as two thousand Tamils were murdered during these weeks, while some Tamil-majority areas, notably Colombo's Pettah district, were reduced to rubble.

1952	1953	1956	1958
D.S. Senanayake dies following riding accident and is succeeded by his son, Dudley Senanayake.	John Kotelawala becomes prime minister.	S.W.R.D. Bandaranaike becomes prime minister at head of new Sri Lanka Freedom Party.	Anti-Tamil riots convulse island.

The government, police and army, meanwhile, showed themselves singularly unable – or unwilling – to stop the violence. Tens of thousands of Tamils fled to the north of the island, while many others left the country altogether. Equally, Sinhalese started to move out of Jaffna and other Tamil areas. In the following years, violence continued to escalate, with several massacres, including a notorious attack at Anuradhapura in May 1985, when 150 mainly Sinhalese victims were gunned down by the LTTE at one of the symbolic centres of the island's Sinhalese and Buddhist culture. Both sides were routinely accused of torture, intimidation and disappearances.

The government's offer, in the mid-1980s, of **limited Tamil self-government** proved to be too little and too late. By the end of 1985, fighting between Sri Lankan government forces and the LTTE had spread across the north and down the east coast, while fighting between Tamils and the east coast's large Muslim population also flared up. War had a devastating effect on the economy. Tourism slumped, military spending rose and aid donors threatened to cut money as a result of human rights abuses. And, to add to the country's woes, tea prices collapsed.

The Indian Peace Keeping Force

In 1987, government forces succeeded in pushing the LTTE back to Jaffna, prompting a further exodus of Tamil refugees to India. The Indian government (for whom the fate of the Sri Lankan Tamils has always been a sensitive issue, given the massive number of Tamils in its own country) began supplying food by air and sea to the beleaguered Tamils, leading to clashes between the Indian and Sri Lankan navies. In the same year, President Jayawardene came to an arrangement with India whereby the government pledged that the Sri Lankan Army would hand its positions over to an **Indian Peace Keeping Force**, or **IPKF**, whose aim would be to disarm the Tamil rebels and maintain peace in the north and east.

The deal attracted opposition from all quarters, including Muslims and the LTTE, and provoked riots in Colombo amongst Sinhalese, who saw the Indian presence in the north as a threat to national sovereignty and a latter-day re-enactment of previous Indian invasions. In the event, the Indian army's hopes of simply keeping the peace proved to be purest fantasy. No sooner had they arrived than they became embroiled in clashes with the LTTE, which soon escalated into full-scale war, culminating in the bloody siege and capture of Jaffna itself (see p.382).

Then, in 1987–88, a second **JVP rebellion** broke out in the south of the island, launching a series of strikes and political assassinations that terrorized the inhabitants of the highlands and crippled the economy. At the end of 1988, President Jayawardene retired, and the new UNP leader, **Ranasinghe Premadasa**, defeated the indefatigable Mrs Bandaranaike in new presidential elections. Premadasa was a new thing in Sri Lankan politics: a low-caste boy made good, who had grown up in a shack in Colombo and who introduced a blast of fresh air into the insular world of island politics. Premadasa promised to end the fighting against both the JVP and the LTTE and succeeded at least in the first pledge. When the JVP refused to lay down its arms, Premadasa sent out paramilitary death squads, which went about the country assassinating suspected JVP activists. By the end of 1989, most JVP leaders were dead or in prison, while thousands of their sympathizers disappeared amidst an international human rights outcry. Some estimates put the number of those killed in the insurrection as high as seventeen thousand.

1959	1965	1970
S.W.R.D. Bandaranaike is assassinated by a Buddhist monk; his widow, Sirimavo Bandaranaike, succeeds him, becoming the world's first female prime minister.	UNP returns to power under Dudley Senanayake.	Sirimavo Bandaranaike returns to power.

The IPKF, meanwhile, remained in an impossible position. Despite the Indians' having managed to contain the LTTE, Sinhalese nationalists were vociferous in demanding that the IPKF leave the country. The LTTE themselves, who had suffered so greatly at their hands, agreed a ceasefire in the hope of seeing the back of them, and the IPKF finally pulled out in March 1990. At their height they had numbered some eighty thousand soldiers, a thousand of whom had died in the fighting.

The 1990s

The fact that a home-grown guerrilla organization like the LTTE had been able to survive a massive offensive by the world's second-largest army enormously enhanced its own sense of power and self-confidence, and no sooner had the IPKF withdrawn than it resumed hostilities against the Sri Lankan government – a new phase of the conflict often referred to as "**Eelam War II**". By the end of 1990, the LTTE had recaptured much of the north, though the east was back under government control. This new war reached a peak in mid-1991 with a series of battles around Jaffna, while the LTTE's influence also reached into India itself, where they assassinated India's former prime minister, Rajiv Gandhi, using a new and deadly weapon – the **suicide bomber**. In mid-1992, a major new assault against the LTTE was launched by the Sri Lankan Army, coupled with a long-overdue attempt to rebuild relations with terrorized Tamil civilians. By this time, tens of thousands had died in the conflict, while 700,000 people had been displaced, including 200,000 Sri Lankan Tamils who had fled to Tamil Nadu in India, about half of whom were living in refugee camps.

In 1993, President Premadasa became the first Sri Lankan head of state to be **assassinated**, blown up by another suicide bomber – the LTTE, though suspected, never claimed responsibility. At around the same time, **Chandrika Bandaranaike Kumaratunga**, the daughter of S.W.R.D. and Sirimavo Bandaranaike, gained leadership of the SLFP (it was around this time that people began referring to the SLFP as the "Sri Lanka Family Party"). Following her election victory in 1994 at the head of the SLFP-dominated **People's Alliance (PA)** coalition, Kumaratunga became Sri Lanka's first female president. One of her first acts was to appoint her mother prime minister, thus continuing the clannishness that had marked the country's politics since the early days of independence.

The new PA was largely unrecognizable as the old SLFP, having abandoned Sinhalese nationalism and pseudo-socialism in favour of national reconciliation and free-market economics. The PA's principal pledge was to end the civil war, but Kumaratunga's attempts to negotiate with the LTTE in 1995 soon broke down, leading to a new round of fighting – "**Eelam War III**" – involving renewed attacks against LTTE positions followed by retaliatory LTTE **bomb attacks**, most notably the devastating strikes against the Central Bank in Colombo in 1996 and the Temple of the Tooth in Kandy in 1998. Thousands of troops were dispatched to the Jaffna peninsula, while Jaffna itself was taken by the Sri Lankan Army in December 1995; further major offensives against the LTTE followed in 1997 and 1998. In December 1999, shortly before new presidential elections, Kumaratunga survived an assassination attempt, though she was blinded in one eye. A few days later, she was re-elected president for a second term.

Despite her electoral success, Kumaratunga was unable to make any steps towards a lasting peace. In addition, her policy of trying to negotiate from a position of military

1971	1972	1975 onwards
JVP insurrection, ruthlessly surpressed by government forces. State of emergency declared in Tamil areas in the north.	Name of country changed from Ceylon to Sri Lanka.	Emergence of Tamil militant groups in the north, most notably the LTTE (Tamil Tigers).

strength received a huge blow in April 2000 when the LTTE captured the strategic **Elephant Pass** – perhaps their greatest military success of the entire conflict. A year later, in July 2001, LTTE suicide bombers led a daring raid against the **international airport**, destroying half of SriLankan Airlines' fleet. The pictures of bombed-out planes and eyewitness accounts by hapless holidaymakers caught in the crossfire made headline news around the globe, and had a predictably disastrous effect on the country's already fragile tourist industry.

The ceasefire

In October 2001, Kumaratunga dissolved parliament just before a no-confidence vote which her PA coalition looked likely to lose. In the ensuing **elections of December 2001**, the UNP won a narrow victory under the leadership of **Ranil Wickramasinghe.** Despite her party's defeat, Kumaratunga remained president, the first time Sri Lanka's prime minister and president had come from different parties, a situation that would have disastrous political consequences. Wickramasinghe had made an end to the civil war central to his candidacy, and he quickly moved to open **negotiations with the LTTE**, mediated by diplomats from Norway – who had previously played a key role in securing the famous peace deal between Israel and the Palestinians in 1993. The timing for talks seemed propitious. Both the Tamil and Sinhalese people had become intensely war-weary, whilst the LTTE appeared to have increasingly lost the support of its own people. Wickramasinghe's conciliatory approach was also an important factor, while the events of September 11 and the subsequent US-led "War on Terror" threatened to cut off international funding for the LTTE, who had recently been proscribed as a terrorist organization by many countries, including the US and UK.

In December 2001, the LTTE declared a temporary **ceasefire**, which was made permanent in February 2002. Events thereafter moved with unexpected swiftness: decommissioning of weapons began; the road connecting Jaffna to the rest of the island was reopened; and in September 2002 the government lifted its ban on the LTTE. The initial stages of the peace process proved hugely positive, but despite early successes, the inevitable **problems** began to emerge during the latter part of 2002 and 2003. President Kumaratunga became an increasingly vociferous critic of the peace process, claiming that the government was making too many concessions to the Tamils, who were to have enjoyed a large degree of autonomy, with their own parliament, prime minister and even army, and accusing the Norwegian mediators of bias – including one famous outburst during which she labelled them "salmon-eating busy-bodies". Sporadic clashes between the LTTE and Sri Lankan Army, as well as serious civilian conflicts between Tamils and Muslims in the east of the country, were seen by Kumaratunga and her allies as evidence that the LTTE was simply using the peace process as a cover under which to regroup and rearm. In April 2003, against a background of increasing political uncertainty and arguments over the implementation of the peace process, the LTTE pulled out of talks.

Even with talks stalled, the ceasefire held, and attention increasingly turned to the growing **tension between Kumaratunga and Wickramasinghe**. Events came to a head in November 2003, when Kumaratunga invoked her presidential powers, sacking three of Wickramasinghe's ministers and taking personal charge of the key Defence Ministry. At the same time, the LTTE themselves faced a unprecedented crisis, as their commander

1977	1978	1983
UNP returns to power under leadership of J.R. Jayawardene who rewrites constitution to enhance presidential powers.	J.R. Jayawardene elected president.	Black July, during which thousands of Tamil civilians massacred and Tamil communities devastated in the south by Sinhalese mobs.

in the east, **Colonel Karuna**, broke away from the rest of the movement, taking several thousand troops with him and raising the spectre of a further battle for power amidst the protagonists in the increasingly precarious peace process.

With the peace process paralysed and the government rendered virtually powerless, fresh **elections** were called for April 2004. Kumaratunga's new coalition, the so-called **Freedom Alliance** (FA), won a narrow victory. After frantic political horse-trading, the FA managed to create an unlikely **coalition government**, their principal partners being the newly respectable JVP (Kumaratunga thus found herself sharing power with the people who had assassinated her husband, the popular actor-turned-politician Vijaya Kumaratunga, in 1988). The populist southern politician **Mahinda Rajapakse** was appointed prime minister, whilst reassuring noises were made about the coalition's commitment to the peace process. The LTTE leadership, meanwhile, regained control of its eastern wing after brief fighting, forcing Colonel Karuna to flee.

Not surprisingly, the peace process, which had already stumbled under Wickramasinghe, became completely stalled under Rajapakse. Although both sides paid lip service to the agreement, growing violence in the east between the Sri Lankan military, the LTTE and the remains of Colonel Karuna's forces suggested that a return to all-out war was simply a matter of time.

The tsunami

The country's deteriorating political situation, however, was suddenly and dramatically overshadowed by a far more immediate and tragic natural disaster. Early on the morning of December 26, 2004, a sub-oceanic earthquake off the coast of Indonesia generated a massive **tsunami** which, radiating outwards in all directions, caused havoc along the coastlines of countries around the Indian Ocean as far apart as Malaysia and Tanzania, and which wrought particular devastation in Sri Lanka, with three-quarters of the island's coastline reduced to a rubble of collapsed houses, smashed boats and wrecked vehicles. Over forty thousand people were killed and a million displaced from their homes, while thousands of buildings were destroyed, along with at least half the island's fishing boats and significant sections of road and rail line – the total damage was estimated at well over a billion dollars. The only good news was that, mercifully, Colombo itself was largely untouched.

The scale of the devastation was astonishing, although the massive **international response** to the event was heartening. Sadly, the Sri Lankan government itself appeared to contribute very little to the frantic global relief effort. Few Sri Lankans received anything more than token insurance payouts, while even fewer received direct government aid, despite the millions of dollars pouring into the country. The government's main contribution to the disaster relief was the enactment, in January 2006, of the infamous **100-metre rule**, which forbade those living within 100m of the coast from rebuilding their houses on their previous sites. Officially this was designed to protect those living around the coast from the possibility of a second tsunami, although many saw the ruling as a cynical attempt to steal valuable coastal land from impoverished villagers in order to hand it over to hotel developers at a later date. Meanwhile, hundreds of thousands of villagers who had lived close to the sea now found themselves deprived not only of their destroyed homes, but also of the land on

1985	1987	1987–89
LTTE massacre of 150 civilians at Anuradhapura; fighting between government forces and LTTE spreads across north and east.	Arrival of Indian Peace Keeping Force in the north amidst widespread opposition; Jaffna captured after intense fighting.	Second JVP insurrection brings chaos to the south; thousands die during ensuing fighting.

which they had previously stood, leaving them no alternative but to live in the temporary tents or wooden shelters provided by international aid agencies, while their own government debated their case with infinite slowness.

Post-tsunami reconstruction efforts were also considerably hindered by **worsening violence** in the east and north of the country. Periodic clashes between the Sri Lankan military, the LTTE and the Karuna faction continued throughout 2005, although the seriousness of the situation was brought home by a pair of events in Colombo itself. In July, the capital saw its first **suicide bomb attack** since the ceasefire when a female bomber attempted to gain access to the offices of the well-known anti-LTTE Tamil politician Douglas Devananda. This event was overshadowed, however, by the assassination in August of one of the country's most respected politicians, Foreign Minister **Lakshman Kadirgamar**, another Tamil who had consistently fought against the LTTE.

The presidency of **Chandrika Kumaratunga**, the woman who had dominated Sri Lankan politics for a decade, thus stumbled towards a messy and unsatisfactory conclusion. In July 2005, incumbent prime minister Mahinda Rajapakse was chosen as the SLFP's presidential candidate and successor to Kumaratunga in the forthcoming elections.

The Rajapakse era

The **presidential elections of November 2005** were widely seen as one of the most important in Sri Lankan history: effectively a head-to-head between the former prime minister **Ranil Wickramasinghe**, the business-minded and peace-oriented UNP leader who had brokered the original ceasefire in 2002 and the populist, nationalist SLFP prime minister **Mahinda Rajapakse**. The choice appeared clear: between a Westernized, liberal candidate committed to the ongoing peace process, and a populist Sinhalese demagogue who was likely to tip the island back into civil war. Shortly before the election, Rajapakse signed a controversial agreement with the JVP. In return for their backing, Rajapakse agreed to refuse the LTTE the right to share aid and promised to remove the Norwegians from their role as mediators in the peace process. He also committed himself to reviewing (and potentially revoking) the ceasefire agreement and, perhaps most importantly, to denying the possibility of self-rule under a federal system for the north and east – a stridently confrontational, anti-Tamil agenda that drew howls of protest even from members of his own party, including outgoing president Chandrika Kumaratunga.

In the event, Rajapakse triumphed over Wickramasinghe by the narrowest of margins, assisted by an **LTTE-imposed boycott** that ensured that none of the Tamils living in LTTE-controlled areas or the Jaffna peninsula was able to vote (the only person who did had his hand cut off). The loss of these votes – which would traditionally have gone to Wickramasinghe – almost certainly cost him the presidency, although the reasons for the LTTE boycott remain unclear. One theory is that they wished completely to dissociate themselves from the Sinhalese electoral process; another, and more sinister, explanation is that in helping Rajapakse to power, they increased the possibility of an early return to hostilities, which many people believe was their objective all along.

Rajapakse's election was followed, unsurprisingly, by a massive **upsurge in violence** in the north and east, with a spate of landmine and bomb attacks, mainly aimed at SLA personnel. Violence continued apace against both military and civilian targets, with massacres of non-combatants on both sides of the ethnic divide and repeated bomb attacks

1988	1990	1991	1993
Ranasinghe Premadasa of UNP elected president.	Indian Peace Keeping Force withdraws from Sri Lanka. LTTE retake Jaffna.	Continued fighting between government forces and LTTE; LTTE suicide bomber assassinates former Indian premier Rajiv Gandhi in Tamil Nadu.	President Premadasa assassinated by LTTE suicide bomber in Colombo.

against buses, markets and other unprotected targets claiming hundreds of lives. By early 2006, the general consensus was that although the ceasefire might still exist on paper, in reality, the north and east of the country had returned to a state of undeclared civil war.

Fighting in the east...

The two sides were finally tipped back into full-scale war in July 2006, when the Tigers closed the sluice gates of the **Mavil Oya reservoir**, in LTTE territory south of Trincomalee, cutting off the water supply to thousands of villages further down the river in government-held areas. Heavy fighting ensued, as government forces first captured the reservoir itself, and then beat off large-scale LTTE assaults around Trincomalee, Mutur and the Jaffna peninsula.

These sudden attacks heightened SLA fears about the vulnerability of Trincomalee harbour to attack from nearby LTTE posts, and SLA forces set about driving the Tigers from the town of **Sampur**, near Mutur – the Tigers' first significant loss of territory since the ceasefire was implemented. The LTTE launched inevitable retaliatory attacks, including a strike against Galle harbour, the furthest point south they had ever ventured. They also staged a notable coup in March 2007 when they launched their first-ever **air attack**, targeting the military airport adjoining the international airport at Katunayake, apparently using small Czech-made light aircraft which had been smuggled into the country piece by piece and then reassembled and fitted with home-made bomb racks.

Following the capture of Sampur, the government began to talk openly about its plan to drive the LTTE from the few remaining pockets of territory that they still held in the east. The SLA's next target was the town of **Vakarai**, about halfway between Batticaloa and Trincomalee – and the Tigers' last piece of eastern territory with direct access to the sea. Heavy fighting and the displacement of thousands of civilians, many of whom died in the clashes, ensued before the town was finally captured in January 2007. The SLA followed this up with successful attacks against LTTE-held areas first in Ampara district and finally in Thoppigala region, northwest of Batticaloa. By July 2007, the whole of eastern Sri Lanka was under government control for the first time in twenty years.

...and the north

Back **in the north**, clashes between the SLA and LTTE along the front lines dividing their respective territories had become an almost daily fact of life, with the SLA making some territorial gains during the later part of 2007.

The year **2008** began in ominous fashion: on January 2, the government officially pulled out of the by-now derisory official ceasefire as if symbolically to clear the decks for a final assault on the LTTE. The SLA was now larger, more disciplined and better equipped and financed than perhaps at any time in its previous history, as well as being backed by the implacable political will of Rajapakse and his hard-line allies in Colombo. At the same time, the LTTE's international reputation was becoming increasingly tarnished, while its sources of foreign funding and supply lines through India and eastern Sri Lanka were being increasingly squeezed, or cut off entirely.

Despite setbacks, during the first half of 2008 the SLA began to advance slowly but steadily northwards into LTTE territory. By the middle of the year the army had

1994	1995
Chandrika Bandaranaike Kumaratunga elected Sri Lanka's first female president at head of SLFP-led People's Alliance coalition.	Government–LTTE talks break down; renewed fighting in north leading to capture of Jaffna by Sri Lankan Army; Kumaratunga re-elected president after narrowly surviving attempted assassination.

recaptured the whole of the Mannar area. By October they had fought their way to within two kilometres of the hugely symbolic town of Kilinochchi, the de facto capital of the Tigers' independent northern regime. By November, a further wing of the SLA had succeeded in pushing up to Pooneryn, clearing the entire western coast of LTTE fighters and reopening a land route between the Jaffna peninsula and the rest of government-controlled Sri Lanka for the first time in decades.

The long-awaited **fall of Kilinochchi**, after months of intense fighting, finally occurred on January 2, 2009. Within a week the SLA had captured the strategically and symbolically important Elephant Pass, and by the end of the month had taken the east coast town of Mullaitivu, the last significant LTTE stronghold. Following the fall of Mullaitivu, the surviving LTTE fighters found themselves pinned by the SLA into a tiny strip of territory, just few kilometres long, to the north of Mullaitivu, along with thousands of trapped **civilians** who were unable to flee the conflict zone. The SLA alleged that the LTTE was using these trapped civilians as a human shield, while the LTTE countered that they were too afraid to leave, and that thousands were being killed by heavy artillery shells being fired by the SLA at civilian targets, including hospitals.

This last enclave of LTTE territory finally fell in late May 2009, at which point Rajapakse triumphantly announced victory for the SLA and an end to all hostilities, capped off with news of the **death of Prabhakaran**, shot dead whilst attempting to escape from advancing government forces – finally putting an end to the famously elusive rebel leader who had almost single-handedly driven the LTTE through its three decades of bloody resistance.

After the war: human-rights fallout

Not surprisingly, the enormous human and financial cost of bringing the civil war to a close was felt in virtually every corner of Sri Lankan society, and despite the mood of triumphalism that descended on large parts of the island following the final defeat of the LTTE, serious questions remained to be answered. Foremost amongst these were widespread allegations of **war crimes** by both LTTE and SLA forces during the closing stages of the war, during which perhaps more than forty thousand people are believed to have died (although given that the entire LTTE high command had been wiped out, attention inevitably focused on the Sri Lankan government's role in the alleged atrocities). Serious concerns were raised by a range of governmental departments and NGOs including the UN, EU, USA State Department, Amnesty International and Human Rights Watch, focusing particularly on the SLA's alleged shelling of civilian "safe zones" and the summary execution of surrendering LTTE cadres, as well as other civilians suspected of LTTE involvement.

The Sri Lankan government staunchly rejected all such accusations, promising a full enquiry, although the committee it set up to investigate the alleged war crimes – the **Lessons Learnt and Reconciliation Commission** (LLRC) – was widely seen as a whitewash. Delivered in late 2011, the LLRC's final report concluded, not surprisingly, that the military had given the "highest priority" to protecting Tamil civilians, although it did at least call the government to task for failing to disarm illegal pro-government militia and for its unsatisfactory response to the numerous reported "disappearances" (meaning extra-judicial execution) of former LTTE fighters following their surrender or capture.

2000	2001	2002
LTTE forces drive Sri Lankan army out of strategic Elephant Pass.	LTTE suicide bombers destroy half the SriLankan Airlines fleet during attack on international airport. UNP win parliamentary elections, and Ranil Wickramasinghe becomes prime minister. LTTE declare ceasefire.	LTTE ceasefire declared permanent; beginnings of Norwegian-sponsored peace process. Road to Jaffna reopene

At the same time that the LLRC submitted its report, the government announced that it was close to finalizing a **census** of all those who had died during the conclusion of the conflict, asserting that the number of people killed by SLA troops was "far too small" to constitute war crimes – although at least acknowledging that a small number of soldiers may have been guilty of certain abuses. Sadly, given the fact that many of those involved are now dead, and the fact that no independent monitors were in situ during the fighting, this means that the various allegations will now probably never be properly answered, and those guilty of war crimes are extremely unlikely ever to be brought to justice.

Rajapakse vs Fonseka

Allegations of war crimes aside, Rajapakse's first serious postwar challenge came from an entirely unexpected source. The **presidential elections of 2010** might have been considered a formality, given the recent successful conclusion to the war. Instead, Rajapakse found himself facing an unlikely opponent in the form of **General Sarath Fonseka**, the former supreme commander of the Sri Lankan Army – a legendary hardliner and national military hero who had played a crucial role in defeating the LTTE, and who had previously enjoyed a close relationship with Rajapakse. Fonseka's bid for the presidency was backed by a coalition of all the main opposition parties, including the UNP and JVP, although the general's own motives for entering the political fray appeared deeply suspect, appearing to revolve mainly around his personal pique at being sidelined following the war. And although many liberal Sri Lankans were not exactly overjoyed to see the opposition line up behind a man intimately connected with the excesses of the final phase of the conflict (and who himself stood accused of war crimes by some observers), Fonseka was at least seen as someone who could genuinely challenge the newly garlanded president.

In the event, **Rajapakse won** comfortably, with 57 percent of the vote versus forty percent for Fonseka, although the victory was tainted by serious allegations of electoral malpractice, including misuse of state resources and extensive media bias. Immediately after the results were announced, Fonseka and his entourage, who had retreated to the five-star *Cinnamon Lakeside* hotel in Colombo, found themselves surrounded by government troops. Following a brief stand-off, Fonseka was arrested, accused of assorted "military offences" and sentenced to three years in prison, where he currently languishes.

A fresh round of **parliamentary elections**, held in April 2010, led to further government gains and a consolidation of Rajapakse's position against an opposition once again led by the increasingly supine and toothless Ranil Wickramasinghe. Further constitutional amendments followed soon afterwards, allowing the country's president (previously restricted to two terms in office) to serve for an unlimited period – opening the possibility of Rajapakse becoming Sri Lanka's supreme ruler in perpetuity.

A new era

Even before the war was concluded, Rajapakse had launched into a major bout of development to transform the island's infrastructure and economy. Foremost amongst these new projects was the construction of a **new international airport** and Chinese-sponsored **deep-water port** at Rajapakse's hometown of Hambantota (the diversion of huge sums of government money to the Rajapakse family's traditional power-base

2003	2004	2005
Increasing setbacks to peace process; LTTE pull out of talks, while Colonel Karuna leads breakaway faction of eastern LTTE forces.	Asian tsunami devastates island's coast.	Worsening violence in north and east; Mahinda Rajapakse elected president.

being just the most striking of the various forms of seigneurial patronage that increasingly characterize present-day Sri Lanka). The island's creaking road network is also enjoying a long-overdue upgrade, headlined by the Southern Expressway motorway (see p.28) from Colombo to Galle.

Even so, the **economy** remains in a parlous condition. Thanks to wartime expenditure Sri Lanka now ranks as one of the world's twenty most-indebted countries (at around eighty percent of GDP), a problem compounded by the lack of hard-currency exports – tourism earnings and foreign-currency remittances from expat Sri Lankans (mainly working in the Gulf) continue to supply the country with most of its dollar earnings. Inflation remains endemic (although it has at least fallen from its wartime high of twenty percent), while the prices of essentials ranging from rice to petrol continue to soar, leaving many ordinary Sri Lankans mired in poverty. The good news is that the economy grew by eight percent in 2010, although whether even growth at this rate will enable the country to meet its vast debt repayments is a moot point.

Political concerns also loom large. Press censorship remains heavy-handed, with routine threats and violence against any journalists who speak out against the Rajapakse regime (the January 2009 murder of the hugely respected *Sunday Leader* editor Lasantha Wickramatunga being the most flagrant example). Despite a slight improvement following the end of the war, the island still ranks a lowly 158 out of 178 countries surveyed by the Index of Press Freedom in 2010 – below Saudi Arabia, Pakistan and Nigeria. Meanwhile, Tamil civilian activists continue to disappear, while the wider question of exactly how Rajapakse's government intends to rebuild the north and help relieve the interminable suffering of ordinary Tamil civilians – not to mention how (or if) it intends to meet Tamil political aspirations and calls for some form of regional autonomy and self-determination – has yet to be properly answered.

Rajapakse **family nepotism** offers another growing challenge to Sri Lanka's democratic credentials, with members of the extended clan now embedded in a wide range of senior government and other positions. Two of Mahinda's brothers continue to play a crucial role in the current administration. The vastly experienced political strategist **Basil Rajapakse**, current Minister of Economic Development, is widely regarded as the Machiavellian power behind Mahinda's throne, while **Gotabhaya Rajapakse**, current Minister of Defence and distinguished former SLA commander, is seen as the man, if any, most likely to replace his brother as president, in the (possibly unlikely) event that Mahinda decides to step aside. Both have distinguished themselves in recent years by their strident anti-Tamil rhetoric and violent rejection of any kind of international criticism or mediation. In addition, Mahinda's son **Namal** was elected member of parliament for Hambantota district in 2010 – and will doubtless be groomed for great things in the future. Other Rajapakse family members currently hold influential posts including Speaker of Parliament, Chief Minister of Uva Province, Director and Chairman of SriLankan Airlines, and ambassadors to the USA and Russia.

In short, the general consensus is that Sri Lanka has now effectively become a one-family dictatorship, with the various members of the Rajapakse clan exercising a suffocating influence on all aspects of state. This virtual loss of political freedom is a price many Sri Lankans appear willing to pay in return for continued stability, peace, and the promise of possible – if elusive – future prosperity, although what the long-term effects of the increasingly entrenched Rajapakse dynasty will have on the country at large, let alone the embattled Tamil populace in the north and east, remains anyone's guess.

2006	2007	2008	2009	2010
Resumption of full-scale fighting between LTTE and Sri Lankan Army.	LTTE defeated in the east.	Final Sri Lankan Army offensive against LTTE in the north.	Fall of Kilinochchi and final defeat of LTTE accompanied by mass civilian casualties; Prabhakaran killed.	Mahinda Rajapakse re-elected president.

Sri Lankan Buddhism

Buddhism runs deep in Sri Lankan life. The island was one of the first places to convert to the religion, in 247 BC, and has remained unswervingly faithful in the two thousand years since. As such, Sri Lanka is often claimed to be the world's oldest Buddhist country, and the religion's trappings are apparent everywhere, most obviously in the island's myriad temples, as well as in its vibrant festivals and large and highly visible population of monks.

The life of the Buddha

Siddhartha Gautama, the Buddha-to-be, was (according to tradition) born the son of the king in the small kingdom of Lumbini in what is now southern Nepal during the fourth or fifth century BC – 563 BC is often suggested as a possible date, though modern scholars have suggested that it might have been as much as a century later. Auspicious symbols accompanied the prince's conception and birth: his mother dreamt that a white elephant had entered her womb, and according to legend Siddhartha emerged from beneath his mother's right arm and immediately talked and walked, a lotus flower blossoming beneath his foot after each of his first seven steps.

Astrologers predicted that the young prince would become either a great king or a great ascetic. His father, keen to prevent the latter outcome, determined to protect his son from all knowledge of worldly suffering, ensuring that Siddhartha knew only the pampered upbringing of a closeted prince. Not until the age of 29 did he even venture out of his palace to ride through the city. Despite his father's attempts to clear all elderly, ugly and sick people from the streets, a frail elderly man wandered into the path of Siddhartha's chariot. The young prince, who had never seen an old person before, was, not surprisingly, deeply troubled by the sight, having previously been spared all knowledge of the inevitability of human mortality and physical decay.

On subsequent occasions the prince travelled from his palace three more times, seeing first a sick person, then a corpse, and finally an ascetic sitting meditating beneath a tree – an emblematic representation of the inevitability of age, sickness and death, and of the possibility of searching for a state that transcended such suffering. Determined to discover the path that led to this state, Siddhartha slipped away from the palace during the night, leaving his wife and young son asleep, exchanging his royal robes for the clothes of his servant, and set out to follow the life of an ascetic.

For six years Siddhartha wandered the countryside, studying with sages who taught him to achieve deep meditative trances. Siddhartha quickly equalled the attainments of his teachers, but soon realized that these accomplishments failed to release him from the root causes of human suffering. He then met up with five other ascetics who had dedicated themselves to the most extreme austerities. Siddhartha joined them and followed their lifestyle, living on a single grain of rice and a drop of water each day until he had wasted away virtually to nothing. At which point Siddhartha suddenly realized that practising pointless austerities was equally unhelpful in his spiritual quest. He therefore determined to follow the so-called **middle way**, a route that involved neither extreme austerities nor excessive self-indulgence.

Enlightenment

His five companions having contemptuously abandoned him on account of his apparent lack of willpower, Siddhartha sat down beneath a bo tree and vowed to remain there until he had found an answer to the riddle of existence and suffering. Siddhartha plunged himself into profound meditation. Mara, the god of desire, seeing that the prince was attempting to free himself from craving, and therefore from Mara's control, attempted to distract him with storms of rocks, coals, mud and darkness. When this failed, he sent his three beautiful daughters to tempt Siddhartha, but this attempt to distract the prince also proved fruitless. Finally, Mara attempted to dislodge the prince from the ground he was sitting on, shaking the very earth beneath him. Siddhartha extended his right hand and touched the earth, calling it to witness his unshakeable concentration, after which Mara withdrew.

Having conquered temptation, Siddhartha continued to meditate. As the night progressed he had a vision of all his millions of previous lives and gained an understanding of the workings of karma and of the way in which good and bad actions and desires bear fruit in subsequent lives, creating a potentially infinite and inescapable sequence of rebirths. During the final phase of his great meditation, Siddhartha realized that it was possible to pass beyond this cycle of karma and to reach a spiritual state – which he called **nirvana** – where desire, suffering and causality finally end. At this point he attained **enlightenment** and ceased being Prince Siddhartha Gautama, instead becoming **the Buddha**, "the Enlightened One".

Following his enlightenment, the Buddha at first felt reluctant to talk to others of his experience, doubting that it would be understood. According to tradition, it was only at the intervention of the god Brahma himself that the Buddha agreed to attempt to communicate his unique revelation and help others towards enlightenment. He preached his **first sermon** to his former ascetic companions, whom he found in the Deer Park in Sarnath, near present-day Varanasi in north India. In this sermon he outlined the **Four Noble Truths** (see p.422). The five companions quickly understood the Buddha's message and themselves became enlightened.

After this, the Buddha's teaching spread with remarkable rapidity. An order of monks, the **Sangha**, was established (as well as an order of nuns, or *bhikkuni*) and the Buddha appears to have travelled tirelessly around northeast India preaching. He continued to travel and teach right up until his death – or, to be precise, his passing into nirvana – at the age of around eighty at the town of Kusinagara.

The history of Buddhism in Sri Lanka

Over the centuries following the Buddha's death, Buddhism rapidly established itself across much of India, becoming the state religion under the great Indian emperor **Ashoka**. Ashoka despatched various Buddhist missions to neighbouring countries, one of which, under the leadership of his son Mahinda, arrived in Sri Lanka in 247 BC (see p.336). Mahinda's mission was spectacularly successful and Buddhism quickly became the dominant faith on the island, the religion giving the Sinhalese people a new-found sense of identity. Buddhism and Sinhalese nationalism have remained closely connected ever since, linked to a view of Sri Lanka as the chosen land of the faith – a kind of Buddhist Israel.

Buddhism gradually withered away in India over the following centuries, but continued to flourish in Sri Lanka despite repeated Tamil invasions and the attendant influx of Hindu ideas. It was the chaos caused by these invasions, and the fear that the principal Buddhist teachings, the so-called **Tripitaka** (which had hitherto been passed orally from generation to generation), would be lost that prompted King Vattagamini Abhaya to have them transcribed in the first century BC in the monastery at Aluvihara – the first time that the key Buddhist texts were committed to writing.

Although Buddhism in India had fallen into terminal decline by the fourth century AD, it continued to spread to new countries. From India it travelled north into Nepal, Tibet and China, developing in the process, a new type of Buddhism, **Mahayana** (see p.422). Sri Lanka, by contrast, preserved the **Theravada** tradition (see p.422), which it subsequently exported to Burma and Thailand, from where it spread to neighbouring countries – Buddhists in Southeast Asia still regard Sri Lanka as the guardian of the original Theravada tradition.

Buddhism continued to flourish throughout the Anuradhapuran and Polonnaruwan eras. For much of this period Sri Lanka was virtually a theocracy: huge monasteries were established and much of the island's agricultural surplus went to supporting a vast population of monks. The resources devoted to maintaining the clergy meant that the practice of begging for alms largely disappeared in Sri Lanka from an early date, while the Buddha's traditional requirement that monks lead a wandering life in order to spread the religion was similarly ignored.

Not until the abandonment of Polonnaruwa in the face of further Tamil assaults in the thirteenth century did Sri Lankan Buddhism begin to face serious difficulties. As Sinhalese power and civilization fragmented, so Buddhism lost its central role in the state. Monasteries were abandoned and the population of monks declined. Hinduism became entrenched in the north, where a new Tamil kingdom had been established in the Jaffna Peninsula, while further religious competition was provided by the traders who began to arrive from Arabia from around the eighth century, and who established sizeable Muslim enclaves around parts of the coast.

The colonial era

Buddhism reached its lowest point in Sri Lanka during the seventeenth and eighteenth centuries as the coast fell to Portuguese (and later Dutch) colonists. Portuguese missionaries set about winning over the natives for the Roman Catholic faith with a will, ordering the destruction of innumerable temples and converting considerable sections of the population. Meanwhile, the throne of the Kingdom of Kandy, the island's last independent region, passed into Tamil hands, and Hindu influence gradually spread.

By 1753, the situation had become so bad that there were not enough monks left to ordain any further Buddhist clergy. The king of Kandy, Kirti Sri Rajasinha, sent out for monks from Thailand, who performed the required ordination services, thus re-establishing the Sangha in the island and founding the so-called **Siyam Nikaya**, or "Siam Order". The revived order flourished, although it became increasingly exclusive, allowing only those belonging to the land-owning Goyigama caste to be ordained (a very un-Buddhist practice). A second sect, the **Amarapura Nikaya**, was established, again with Thai monks providing the initial ordinations. Further disputes over points of doctrine led to the foundation of the **Ramanna Nikaya** in the late nineteenth century. These three *nikayas* remain the principal orders right up to the present day, with each sect preserving its own ordination tradition.

Sri Lankan Buddhism was also threatened by Victorian missionary Christianity – and the influence of Western ideas generally – for much of the British colonial period. Faced with the Western onslaught, many local Buddhists reaffirmed their traditional beliefs and the later part of the nineteenth century saw something of a **Buddhist revival**. This was stimulated by the arrival of Madame Blavatsky and Colonel Olcott (see box, p.76), the founders of Theosophy, who arrived in Sri Lanka in 1880 declaring themselves to be Buddhist. Olcott returned many times to the island, playing a major role in the revival and establishing hundreds of Buddhist schools islandwide to counterbalance the influence of the increasingly dominant British Anglican educational system. One of Blavatsky and Olcott's young assistants, **Angarika Dharmapala** (1864–1933) subsequently became the movement's leading figure, travelling the world in order to promote the Buddhist cause – and also sparking a modest Buddhist revival in India in the process. He remains a revered figure in Sri Lanka to this day, with many streets renamed in his honour.

The Buddhist belief system

The Buddha's teachings, collectively known as the **dharma**, were codified after his death and passed on orally for several centuries until finally being written down at Aluvihara in Sri Lanka in the first century BC. The essence of Buddhist belief is encapsulated in the **Four Noble Truths**. Simply put, these are (1) life is suffering; (2) suffering is the result of craving; (3) there can be an end to suffering; (4) there is a path that leads to the end of suffering, the so-called **Noble Eightfold Path**, which consists of a set of simple rules to encourage good behaviour and morals.

All beings, Buddhism asserts, will experience a potentially infinite sequence of rebirths in various different forms: as a human, an animal, ghost or god, either on earth on in one of various heavens or hells. The engine that drives this permanent sequence of reincarnations is **karma**. Meritorious actions produce good karma, which enables creatures to be reborn higher up the spiritual food chain; bad actions have the opposite result. In this classically elegant system, good deeds really are their own reward. No amount of good karma, however, will allow one to escape the sequence of infinite rebirths – good behaviour and the acquiring of merit is simply a stage on the route to enlightenment and the achievement of nirvana. Every desire and action plants seeds of karma that create the impetus for further lives, and further actions and desires – and so on. Some schools of ancient Indian philosophy took this idea to its logical conclusion – the Jains, for example, decided that the best thing to do in life was nothing at all, and more extreme proponents of that religion were known to sit down and starve themselves to death in order to avoid involvement in worldly actions, for good or bad.

The exact route to enlightenment and nirvana is long and difficult – at least according to the older schools of Buddhism – requiring millions of lifetimes. Exactly what **nirvana** is meant to be remains famously vague. The Buddha himself was notoriously elusive on the subject. He compared a person entering nirvana to a flame being extinguished – the flame doesn't go anywhere, but the process of combustion ceases.

Theravada and Mahayana

Theravada Buddhism (the "Law of the Elders") is the dominant form of the religion in Sri Lanka, as well as in Southeast Asia. It is the older of the two main schools of Buddhism and claims to embody the Buddha's teachings in their original form. These teachings emphasize that all individuals are responsible for their own spiritual welfare, and that any person who wishes to achieve enlightenment must pursue the same path trodden by the Buddha himself, giving up worldly concerns and developing spiritual attainments through meditation and self-sacrifice. This path of renunciation is, of course, impossible for most members of the Theravada community to follow, which explains the importance of **monks** in Sri Lanka (and in other Theravada countries), since only members of the Sangha are considered fully committed to the Theravada path, and thus capable of achieving enlightenment – and even then only in rare instances. Lay worshippers do have a (limited) role in the Theravada tradition, though

---

THE BUDDHIST FLAG

One of Sri Lanka's most instantly recognizable Buddhist symbols is the multicoloured **Buddhist Flag**, which can be seen flying from temples and bo trees across the island, and many other places besides. The flag was designed in 1885 by a panel of local notables and first raised on Vesak poya day, 28 April 1885, the first time Vesak had been celebrated as a public holiday under British rule. The flag was subsequently adopted by Buddhist countries around the world (sometimes with minor variations in colour), serving as an international symbol of the religion.

The flag consists of six vertical strips, representing the six colours of the aura that is said to have shone out of the body of the Buddha following his enlightenment. The colours are: **blue** (*nila*; symbolizing universal compassion); **yellow** (*pita*; The Middle Way); **red** (*lohita*; the blessings arising from the practice of Buddhism); **white** (*odata*; the purity of the Buddha's teachings and the liberation they bring); and **orange** (*manjesta*; the Buddha's teachings – wisdom). The wider sixth strip shows all five colours superimposed, symbolizing the compound hue said to be formed by their combination, known as *pabbhassara*, or "essence of light".

this is mainly to earn merit by offering material support to monks. Otherwise they can hope for little except to lead a moral life and hope to be reborn as a monk themselves at some point in the future.

The rather elitist aspect of Theravada doctrine led to it being dubbed **Hinayana Buddhism**, or "Lesser Vehicle", a slightly pejorative term that compares it unfavourably with the **Mahayana**, or "Greater Vehicle", sect. Mahayana Buddhism developed as an offshoot of Theravada Buddhism, eventually becoming the dominant form of the religion in China, Tibet and Japan, although it has had only a slight influence on Sri Lankan Buddhism. As Theravada Buddhism developed, it came to be believed that the Buddha himself was only the latest of a series of Buddhas – Sri Lankan tradition claims that there have been either sixteen or 24 previous Buddhas, and holds that another Buddha, Maitreya, will appear at some point in the remote future when all the last Buddha's teachings have been forgotten. The Mahayana tradition expanded this aspect of Buddhist cosmology to create a grand array of supplementary deities, including various additional Buddhas and **bodhisattvas** – a Buddha-to-be who has chosen to defer entering nirvana in order to remain on earth (or in one of the various Buddhist heavens) to help others towards enlightenment. Instead of trying to emulate the Buddha, devotees simply worship one or more of the Mahayana deities and reap the spiritual rewards. Not surprisingly, this much more populist – and much less demanding – form of the religion became widely established in place of the Theravada tradition. Compared with the countless lifetimes of spiritual self-improvement that Theravada Buddhism requires its followers to endure, some schools of Mahayana claim that even a single prayer to the relevant bodhisattva can cause one to be reborn in one of the Buddhist heavens – hence its description of itself as the "Greater Vehicle", a form of the religion capable of carrying far greater numbers of devotees to enlightenment.

The Buddhist pantheon in Sri Lanka

While it's true that Buddhism in Sri Lanka hasn't experienced the byzantine transformations it has undergone in, say, China, Tibet or Japan, the religion in Sri Lanka has acquired its own particular flavour and local characteristics – mainly the result of the strong influence of Hinduism over many centuries. Buddhism evolved from the same roots as **Hinduism** and makes many of the same assumptions about the universe, so the inclusion of many Hindu deities within the Sri Lankan Buddhist pantheon isn't as inconsistent as it might initially appear. (The Buddha himself never denied the existence or powers of the myriad gods of ancient Indian cosmology, simply arguing that they were subject to the same laws of karma and rebirth as any other creature – indeed according to tradition the Buddha ascended to the various heavens to preach to the gods on several occasions.) Thus, although other gods may be unable to assist in helping one towards the ultimate goal of attaining nirvana, they still have power to assist in less exulted aims – the success of a new business, the birth of a child, the abundance of a harvest – and are therefore be worshipped alongside the Buddha.

Various Hindu gods have been appropriated by Sri Lankan Buddhism over the centuries, going in and out of fashion according to the prevailing religious or political climate. There are countless shrines across the island dedicated to these subsidiary gods, either as lesser shrines within Buddhist temples or as separate, self-contained temples – these shrines or temples are known as **devales** to differentiate them from purely Buddhist temples (viharas) and Hindu temples (kovils). Thus, the supreme Hindu deity, **Vishnu** (often known locally as **Upulvan**), is regarded in Sri Lanka as a protector of Buddhism and is worshipped by Buddhists, as is the god **Kataragama** (see p.191), another deity of mixed Hindu–Buddhist descent. Other popular gods in the Buddhist pantheon include **Saman** (see p.262) and **Pattini** (see p.218), while the elephant-headed Hindu god **Ganesh** is also widely worshipped. Recent decades have also seen a dramatic increase in the popularity of the fearsome Hindu goddesses **Durga** and **Kali**.

Daily Buddhist ritual and belief

Despite the Buddha's emphasis on the search for enlightenment and nirvana, for most Sri Lankans, daily religious life is focused on more modest goals. Theravada Buddhism traditionally states that only monks can achieve enlightenment, and even then only on very rare occasions: Sri Lanka's last *arhat* (enlightened monk) is supposed to have died in the first century BC. Thus, rather than trying to emulate the Buddha's own spiritual odyssey and attempt the near-impossible task of achieving enlightenment, the average Sri Lankan Buddhist will concentrate on leading a moral life and on acquiring religious merit in the hope of ensuring rebirth higher up the spiritual ladder.

To become a Buddhist, one simply announces the fact that one is "taking refuge" in the **Three Jewels**: the Buddha, the Dharma and the Sangha. There is no form of organized or congregational worship in Buddhism, as there is in Christianity or Islam – instead, devotees visit their local temple when they please, saying prayers at the dagoba or Buddha shrine (or that of another god), perhaps offering flowers, lighting a candle or reciting (or having monks recite) Buddhist scriptures, an act known as **pirith**. Although Theravada holds that the Buddha himself should not be worshipped, many Sinhalese effectively do so.

Buddhist places of pilgrimage and festivals play a vital role in sustaining the faith. The island's major **places of pilgrimage** – the Temple of the Tooth at Kandy (see p.211), the revered "footprint" of the Buddha at Adam's Peak (see p.262), and the Sri Maha Bodhi at Anuradhapura (see p.321) – attract thousands of pilgrims year-round. The timing of pilgrimages is often linked to significant dates in the Buddhist calendar, which is punctuated by a further round of Buddhist holidays and festivals. Full-moon – or **poya** – days are considered particularly important, particularly **Vesak Poya**, the day on which the Buddha is said to have been born, achieved enlightenment and passed into nirvana. Buddhist devotees traditionally visit their local temple on poya days to spend time in prayer or meditation; they might also practise certain abstinences, such as fasting or refraining from alcohol and sex. Some poya days are also celebrated with elaborate **festivals**, often taking the form of enormous **processions** (peraheras), when locals parade along the streets, sometimes accompanied by elaborately costumed elephants. Nowhere are these processions more extravagant than during the magnificent **Esala Perahera** in Kandy (see p.208), one of Sri Lanka's – indeed Asia's – most visually spectacular pageants.

The Sangha

Even if you don't go near a temple, you won't travel far in Sri Lanka without seeing a shaven-headed Buddhist monk clad in striking orange or red robes. Collectively known as **the Sangha**, the island's twenty thousand or so monks form one of the most visible and distinctive sections of Sri Lankan society, and serve as living proof of the island's commitment to the Buddhist cause. The monastic tradition is deeply embedded in the national culture, and the importance of the Buddhist clergy can been seen in myriad ways, from the monks who sit in the nation's parliament to the seats in every bus that are reserved for their use. The Sinhala language, meanwhile, features special forms of address only used when talking to a monk, even including a different word for "yes".

Young boys are traditionally chosen to be monks if they show a particular religious bent, or if their horoscope appears favourable – although many are given to the Sangha by poor Sinhalese families in order to provide them with a decent standard of living and an education. Boy monks are first initiated into the Sangha as novices around their tenth birthday, going to live and study in a monastery and largely severing their ties with home (there is no minimum age at which boys can be ordained – according to tradition, a boy can become a novice when he's old enough to chase away crows). Higher ordination occurs at the age of 20. At this point the monk becomes a full member of the **Sangha**. Monks are supposed to commit themselves to the Sangha for life – the custom, popular in Thailand and Burma, of laymen becoming monks for a short period then returning to normal life is not considered acceptable in Sri Lanka – although in practice significant numbers of monks fail to last the course and return to secular society, often once they've secured an education.

On entering the Sangha the new monk shaves his head and dons the characteristic robes of a Buddhist cleric (usually saffron, sometimes red or yellow – the precise colour has no significance, and monks wear whatever is given to them, apart from forest-dwelling monks, who tend to wear brown robes). He also takes a new name: the honorific *thero* or *thera* is often added after it, along with the name of the town or village in which the monk was born, while "The Venerable" (or "Ven.") is frequently added as a prefix. Monks commit themselves to a code of conduct that entails various prohibitions. These traditionally include: not to kill; not to steal; not to have sex; not to lie about spiritual attainments; not to drink alcohol; not to handle money; not to eat after midday; and not to own more than a bare minimum of personal possessions.

The great monastic foundations of ancient Sri Lanka have largely vanished, and most monks now live in local village temples. These temples are intimately connected to the life of the village they serve, which usually provides the resident monks with their only source of material support via regular offerings, in return for which the monks act as teachers and spiritual mentors to the local population. The actual functions required of a Buddhist monk are few. The only ceremonies they preside at are funerals, although they are sometimes asked to recite Buddhist scriptures (*pirith*). Monks traditionally act as spiritual advisers; some monks also gain reputations as healers or astrologers, and many teach.

A less savoury aspect of the Sri Lankan Buddhist clergy has been their involvement in **ultra-nationalistic politics** – the view that many monks hold of Sri Lanka as the "chosen land" of Buddhism has disturbing parallels with hard-line Jewish attitudes towards Israel. In 1959, Prime Minister S.W.R.D Bandaranaike was shot dead by a Buddhist monk, and the clergy have constantly involved themselves in politics ever since; some of the more right-wing monks reputedly formed a clandestine ultra-nationalist group called the Circle of Sinhalese Force, whose members used Nazi salutes and spouted wild propaganda about the perceived threat to their land, race and religion – a mixture of *Mahavamsa* and *Mein Kampf*. In earlier decades, monks had contented themselves with influencing politicians, though in recent years they have started entering politics on their own account, representing the monk-led **Jathika Hela Urumaya** party (National Heritage Party; JHU). A Buddhist monk was first elected to parliament in 2001, while in the elections of 2004 a total of seven JHU monks were voted into office, forming a crucial political grouping in a delicately balanced minority government; as of 2011 they continue to form a small but significant fraction of President Rajapakse's ruling coalition.

Throughout the later war years, leading monks consistently denounced any attempts by the government to cede autonomy to the Tamils of the north and campaigned vigorously for a military rather than a negotiated solution to the conflict, led by the vociferous Athurliye Rathana, dubbed the "War Monk" by the Sri Lankan press. Even following the end of the conflict certain monks appear determined to continue stoking up sectarian tensions. In late 2011, cleric Amatha Dhamma led a group of other monks and lay followers in destroying a Muslim shrine in Anuradhapura – a confrontational and inflammatory act with disturbing parallels to the notorious destruction of the Babri Mosque in India in 1992. Unfortunately, some at least of Sri Lanka's Sangha apparently see no contradiction between the Buddhist ideals in which they profess to believe and their frequently xenophobic, intolerant and rampantly sectarian rhetoric – all the more unfortunate, given that they continue to command widespread popular support and respect.

Sri Lankan Buddhist art and architecture

Sri Lanka's art and architecture – ranging from Dravidian temples to Portuguese Baroque churches – offer a fascinating visual legacy of the varied influences that have shaped the island's eclectic culture. Despite the number of races and religions that have contributed to the artistic melting pot, however, the influence of Buddhism remains central to the nation's cultural fabric, and it is in Buddhist art and architecture that Sri Lanka's greatest artistic achievements can been found.

Although the **Mahayana** doctrines (see p.422) that transformed Buddhist art in many other parts of Asia largely bypassed Sri Lanka, the island's religious art was significantly enriched from around the tenth century by the influence of **Hinduism**, introduced by the numerous Tamil dynasties that periodically overran parts of the north. This influence first showed itself in the art of **Polonnaruwa**, and later blended with Sinhalese traditions to create the uniquely syncretized style of **Kandyan** temple architecture, which reached its apogee during the fifteenth to eighteenth centuries.

Buddha images

Early Buddhist art was symbolic rather than figurative. The Buddha himself (according to some traditions) asked that no images be made of him after his death, and for the first few centuries he was represented symbolically by objects such as dagobas, bo trees, thrones, wheels, pillars, trees, animals or footprints.

Exactly why the first **Buddha images** were made remains unclear, though they seem initially to have appeared in India in around the first century BC. Buddha images are traditionally highly stylized: the intention of Buddhist art has always been to represent the Buddha's transcendental, superhuman nature rather than to describe a personality (unlike, say, Western representations of Jesus). The vast majority of Buddha figures are shown in one of the canonical poses, or **mudras** (see box opposite).

Many sculptural details of Buddha figures are enshrined in tradition and preserved in the *Sariputra*, a Sinhalese treatise in verse for the makers of Buddha images. Some of the most important features of traditional Buddha images include the **ushnisha**, the small protuberance on the top of the head, denoting superior mental powers; the **siraspata**, or flame of wisdom (the Buddhist equivalent of the Christian halo), growing out of the *ushnisha*; the elongated **earlobes**, denoting renunciation (the holes in the lobes would have contained jewels that the Buddha gave up when he abandoned his royal position); the shape of the **eyes**, modelled after the form of lotus petals; the **eyebrows**, whose curves are meant to resemble two bows; the **mouth**, usually closed and wearing the hint of a smile; and the **feet**, which traditionally bear 32 different auspicious markings.

The one area in which Mahayana Buddhism has had a lasting impact on Sri Lankan religious art is in the **gigantic Buddha statues**, some standing up to 30m high, which can be found all over the island, dating from both ancient (Aukana, Sasseruwa, Maligawila, Polonnaruwa) and modern (Dambulla, Weherehena, Wewurukannala) times. Such larger-than-life depictions reflect the change from Theravada's emphasis on the historical, human Buddha to Mahayana's view of the Buddha as a cosmic being who could only be truly represented in figures of superhuman dimensions.

BUDDHIST MUDRAS AND THEIR MEANINGS

The following are the *mudras* most commonly encountered in Sri Lankan art, though others are occasionally encountered, such as the *varada mudra* ("Gesture of Gift Giving"), and the *asisa mudra* ("Gesture of Blessing", a variant form of the *abhaya mudra*), employed in the famous Aukana Buddha.

Abhaya mudra The "Have No Fear" pose shows the Buddha standing with his right hand raised with the palm facing the viewer.

Dhyani or **samadhi mudra** Shows the Buddha in meditation, seated in the lotus or half-lotus position, with his hands placed together in his lap.

Bhumisparsha mudra The "Earth-Witness" pose shows the Buddha touching the ground with the tips of the fingers of his left hand, commemorating the moment in his enlightenment when the demon Mara, in attempting to break his concentration, caused the Earth to shake beneath him, and the Buddha stilled the ground by touching it.

Vitarka mudra and **dharmachakra mudra** In both positions ("Gesture of Explanation" and "Gesture of the Turning of the Wheel of the Law" respectively) the Buddha forms a circle with his thumb and one finger, representing the wheel of dharma. Used in both standing and sitting poses.

Reclining poses In Asian Buddhist art, the reclining pose is traditionally considered to represent the Buddha at the moment of his death and entrance into nirvana – the so-called Parinirvana pose. Reclining poses are particularly common in Sri Lanka, although the island's sculptors make a subtle distinction between two types of reclining image: the sleeping pose, and the true *parinirvana* pose. Sleeping and *parinirvana* Buddhas are distinguished by six marks (although the distinctions between the two are often quite subtle). In the sleeping pose: the eyes are open; the right hand is at least partially beneath the head; the stomach is a normal size; the robe is smooth beneath the left hand; the bottom of the hem of the robe is level; and the toes of the two feet are in a straight line. In the *parinirvana* pose, the hand is away from the head; the eyes are partially closed; the stomach is shrunken; the robe is bunched up under the left hand (the clenched hand and crumpled robe indicating the pain of the Buddha's final illness); the hem at the bottom of the robe is uneven; and the left knee is slightly flexed, so that the toes of the two feet are not in a straight line.

Dagobas (stupas)

The stupa, or **dagoba**, as they're known in Sri Lanka, is the world's most universal Buddhist architectural symbol, ranging from the classically simple hemispherical forms found in Sri Lanka and Nepal to the spire-like stupas of Thailand and Burma and the pagodas of China and Japan (the Sinhalese word "dagoba" has even been mooted as one possible source for the term "pagoda"). Dagobas originally developed from the Indian burial mounds that were raised to mark the graves of important personages, although popular legend traces their distinctive form back to the Buddha himself. Upon being asked by his followers what shape a memorial to him should take, the Buddha is said to have folded his robe into a square and placed his upturned begging bowl and umbrella on top of it, thus outlining the dagoba's basic form.

As Buddhist theology developed, so the elements of the dagoba acquired more elaborate symbolic meanings. At its simplest level, the dagoba's role as an enormous burial mound serves to recall the memory of the Buddha's passing into nirvana. A more elaborate explanation describes the dagoba in cosmological terms: the main dome (*anda*), built in the shape of a hill, is said to represent Mount Meru, the sacred peak that lies at the centre of the Buddhist universe, while the spire (*chattravali*) symbolizes the *axis mundi*, or cosmic pillar, connecting earth and heaven and leading upwards out of the world towards nirvana.

The earliest dagobas were built to enshrine important **relics** of the Buddha himself or of other revered religious figures (the Buddha's own ashes were, according to tradition, divided into forty thousand parts, providing the impetus for a huge spate of dagoba building, while many notable monks were also interred in dagobas). These relics were traditionally placed in or just below the harmika, the square relic chamber at the top of the dome. As Buddhism spread, the building of dagobas became seen as an act of religious merit, resulting in the construction of innumerable smaller, or "votive", dagobas, some no larger than a few feet high.

Dagobas still serve as important objects of pilgrimage and religious devotion: as in other Buddhist countries, devotees typically make clockwise circumambulations of the dagoba – an act known as *pradakshina* – which is meant to focus the mind in meditation, although this practice is less widespread in Sri Lanka than in other countries (similarly, the prohibition against walking around dagobas in an anticlockwise direction, which is frowned upon in some other countries, isn't much observed).

Structure and shape

It was in the great dagobas of Anuradhapura and Polonnaruwa, however, that early Sri Lankan architecture reached its highest point, both figuratively and literally. These massive construction feats were Asia's nearest equivalent to the Egyptian pyramids. The foundations were trampled down by elephants, then the main body of the dagobas filled with rubble and vast numbers of bricks (it's been estimated that the Jetavana dagoba at Anuradhapura uses almost one hundred million), after which the entire structures were plastered and painted with a coat of lime-wash.

Dagobas consist of four principal sections. The entire structure usually sits on a square terrace whose four sides are oriented towards the cardinal points. Many larger stupas have four small shrines, called **vahalkadas** (or *adimukas*), arranged around the base of the dagoba at the cardinal points – a uniquely Sri Lankan architectural element. The main hemispherical body of the stupa is known as the **anda**, surmounted by a cube-like structure, the **harmika** (relic chamber), from which rises the **chattravali**. In the earliest Indian stupas this was originally a pillar on which a series of umbrella-like structures were threaded, though in Sri Lankan-style dagobas the umbrellas have fused into a kind of spire. The interior of almost all dagobas consists of completely solid brick, although a few hollow dagobas can also be found, including those at Kalutara and Ampara.

Sri Lankan dagobas preserve the classic older **form and shape** of the stupa, following the pattern of the great stupa at Sanchi in central India erected in the third century BC by the emperor Ashoka – although constant repairs (and the fact that new outer shells were often constructed around old stupas) means that it's often difficult to determine the exact origins or original shape of some of the island's most famous dagobas. Despite the superficial similarities shared by all Sri Lankan dagobas, there are subtle variations, with six different basic shapes being recognized, ranging from the perfectly hemispherical "bubble-shape" favoured by the builders of ancient Anuradhapura and Polonnaruwa through to the narrower and more elongated "bell-shape" that became fashionable during the nineteenth century, as well as innumerable other small nuances in design.

Buddhist temples

Sri Lankan **Buddhist temples** (viharas or viharayas) come in a bewildering array of shapes and sizes, ranging from the intimate cave temples of Dambulla and Mulkirigala to the enormous monastic foundations of Anuradhapura and Polonnaruwa. As well as purely Buddhist temples, there are also numerous **devales**, independent shrines dedicated to other gods such as Vishnu, Kataragama, Pattini or Saman – nominally Buddhist, though often showing a strong dash of Hindu influence. These shouldn't be confused with **kovils**, however, which are purely Hindu temples, and have no connection with Buddhism at all.

Despite their enormous variety, most of the island's Buddhist temples comprise three basic elements: an image house, a dagoba (see above), and a bo tree enclosure. The

A BUDDHIST BESTIARY

Animals, both real and imaginary, form an important element in Buddhist iconography. The following are some of the most common.

Makaras The *makara* is a mythical beast of Indian origin, formed from parts of various different animals: the body of a fish; the foot of a lion; the eye of a monkey; the trunk and tusk of an elephant; the tail of a peacock; the ear of a pig; and the mouth of a crocodile. One of the most ubiquitous features of Sri Lankan Buddhist architecture is the *makara torana*, or "dragon arch", made up of two *makaras* connected to a dragon's mouth, which is designed to ward off evil spirits and used to frame entrances and Buddha images in virtually every temple in the island.

Nagarajas *Nagarajas* (snake kings) are represented as human figures canopied by cobra hoods. They apparently derive from pre-Hindu Indian beliefs and are regarded as symbols of fertility and masters of the underground world. Despite their apparently pagan origins, they derive some Buddhist legitimacy from the fact that the *nagaraja* Muchalinda is said to have sheltered the meditating Buddha as he achieved enlightenment – as a result of which cobras are held sacred. *Nagarajas* (plus attendant dwarfs) are often pictured on the

guardstones that flank the entrances to many ancient Sri Lanka buildings, and were intended, like *makara toranas*, to prevent evil influences from entering the building.

Dwarfs *Nagarajas* are often shown with dwarfs (*gana*), who can also often be seen supporting the base of steps or temple walls – these jolly-looking pot-bellied creatures are associated with Kubera, the god of wealth, though their exact significance and origins remain obscure.

Elephants Carved in low relief, elephants commonly adorn the walls enclosing religious complexes, their massive presence symbolically supporting the temple buildings.

Lions Though they possess no definite religious significance except to suggest the Buddha's royal origins, lions are also common features of Buddhist architecture. The animal is also an emblem of the Sinhalese people, who trace their ancestry back to – and indeed owe their name to – a lion.

Geese Considered a symbol of spiritual knowledge and purity, geese (*hamsa*) are often found on moonstones, and used decoratively elsewhere in temples.

image house (*pilimage* or *patimaghara*) houses the temple's Buddha image (or images) along with statues and/or paintings of other gods and attendants; it may be preceded by an antechamber or surrounded by an ambulatory, although there are countless variations in the exact form these shrines take and in the particular gods found inside them. Larger temples may have **additional shrines** to other gods considered important by Sri Lankan Buddhists – Vishnu (considered a protector of Buddhism in Sri Lanka) is the most frequently encountered, although other deities from the Hindu pantheon such as Ganesh and Pattini can also sometimes be seen, while the eternally popular Kataragama (see p.191) is also well represented.

During the late Polonnaruwan and early Kandyan period, image houses developed into the **gedige**, a type of Buddha shrine strongly influenced by South Indian Hindu temple architecture, being constructed entirely out of stone on a rectangular plan, with enormously thick walls and corbelled roofs. Important examples can be found at Polonnaruwa, Nalanda and at the Natha Devale in Kandy. Other variations on the standard image house include the **tampita**, a small shrine raised on pillars, and the distinctive **vatadage**, or circular image house. These have a small dagoba at their centre, usually flanked by four Buddha images at the cardinal points and surrounded by concentric rows of pillars that would originally have supported a wooden roof. There are notable examples at Medirigiya, at the Thuparama in Anuradhapura and in the Quadrangle at Polonnaruwa.

The **bo tree enclosure** (*bodhighara*) is a uniquely Sri Lankan feature. The Buddha achieved enlightenment while meditating beneath a bo (or bodhi) tree, and these trees serve as symbols of, and a living link with, that moment – many of the island's

MOONSTONES

Originally from India, the **moonstone** developed in Sri Lanka from a plain slab to the elaborate semicircular stones, carved in polished granite, which are found at Anuradhapura, Polonnaruwa and many other places across the island. Moonstones are placed at the entrances to shrines to concentrate the mind of the worshipper upon entering. Carved in concentric half-circles, they represent the spiritual journey from samsara, the endless succession of deaths and rebirth, to nirvana and the escape from endless reincarnations.

CLASSIC DESIGN ELEMENTS

The exact design of moonstones varies; not all contain every one of the following elements, and the different animals are sometimes combined in the same ring.

Flames Flames (often in the outermost ring) represent the flames of desire – though they also purify those who step across them.
The four Buddhist animals Representing the inevitability of birth, death and suffering, are the elephant (symbolizing birth), the horse (old age), the lion (illness) and the bull (death and decay) – the way in which the images in each ring chase one another around the moonstone symbolizes samsara's endless cycle of deaths and rebirths. The animals are sometimes shown in separate rings, but more usually combined into a single one.
Vines Vines (or, according to the interpretations of some art historians, snakes), represent desire and attachment to life.
Geese Purity (the goose is a Hindu symbol: as Hamsa it is the vehicle of Brahma, and a sign of wisdom).
Lotus At the centre of the design, the lotus is the symbol of the Buddha and nirvana, and of escape from the cycle of reincarnation.

EVOLVING DESIGN

The classic moonstone pattern as outlined above experienced two important modifications during the **Polonnaruwa period**. To begin with, the bull was omitted: as an important Hindu image (the bull Nandi is the vehicle, or chariot, of Shiva), this particular animal had become too sacred to be trodden on in the increasingly Hinduized city. In addition, the lion was also usually absent (although one can be seen in the moonstone at the Hatadage) due to its significance as a royal and national symbol of the Sinhalese.

Moonstone design continued to evolve right up until the **Kandyan period**, by which time it had evolved into the almost triangular designs found at the Temple of the Tooth and many other shrines in the central highlands. During this evolution, the moonstone also lost virtually all its symbolic meaning; the floral designs found on Kandyan-era moonstones are of purely decorative import, although the lotus survives at the heart.

specimens have been grown from cuttings taken from the great tree at Anuradhapura, which is itself believed to have been grown from a cutting taken from the very tree (long since vanished) under which the Buddha meditated in India. More important bo trees are often surrounded by gold railings, with tables set around them on which devotees place flower offerings; the trees themselves or the surrounding railings are often draped in colourful strings of prayer flags. Older and larger bo trees are sometimes enclosed by retaining brick terraces with conduits at each corner into which devotees pour water to feed the tree's hidden roots; these are gradually built up around the trunk as it grows, and can sometimes reach a surprising size and height, as at the massive Wel-Bodhiya in the Pattini Devale in Kandy.

Many temples old and new are also attached to monasteries boasting living quarters and refectories, as well as a **poyage** ("House of the Full Moon") in which monks assemble to recite Buddhist scriptures and confess breaches of the monastic code on poya (full-moon) days. Temples in the Kandy area also sometimes have a **digge**, or drummer's hall, usually an open-sided columned pavilion, where drummers and dancers would have performed during temple ceremonies – there's a good example at the Vishnu Devale in Kandy.

Buddhist temple iconography

Sri Lankan temples typically sport a wealth of symbolic decorative detail. The bases of stairways and other entrances into temples are often flanked by **guardstones** (*doratupalas* or *dvarapalas*), showing low-relief carvings of protective **nagarajas**, or snake kings (see box, p.429), who are believed to ward off malign influences. Another notable feature of Sri Lankan art found at the entrances to temples is the **moonstone** (see box opposite).

Many details of Buddhist iconography depict real or imaginary animals (see box, p.429). Another standard decorative element is the **lotus**, the sacred flower of Buddhism, often painted decoratively on ceilings and walls or carved at the bases of columns. The fact that these pure white flowers blossom directly out of muddy waters is considered symbolic of the potential for Buddhahood that everyone is believed to carry within them – seated Buddha figures are often shown sitting on lotus thrones. Other common symbolic devices include the **chakra**, or Buddhist wheel, symbolizing the Buddha's teaching – the eight spokes represent the Eightfold Path (see p.422). A common detail in the doors of Kandyan temples is the **sun and moon** motif, originally a symbol of the Buddha during the Anuradhapura period, though later appropriated by the kings of Kandy as a royal insignia.

Temples are often decorated with **murals** of varying degrees of sophistication, ranging from primitive daubs to the great narrative sequences found in the cave temples at Dambulla. Perhaps the most popular subject for murals, especially in the south of the island, are tales from the **Jatakas**, the moral fables describing the Buddha's 547 previous lives, while pictures of **pilgrimage sites** around the island are another common theme.

Sri Lankan wildlife

Sri Lanka boasts a variety of wildlife quite out of proportion to its modest size, including one of the world's largest populations of both wild and captive elephants plus an array of other fauna ranging from leopards, sloth bears and giant squirrels through to huge monitor lizards and crocodiles – not to mention a fascinating collection of endemic birdlife. This richness is partly a result of Sri Lanka's complex climate and topography, ranging from the denuded savannas of the dry zone to the lush montane forests of the hill country, and partly due to its geographical position, which makes it a favoured wintering spot for numerous birds, as well as a nesting site for five of the world's species of marine turtles.

Elephants

Intimately connected with the history and culture of Sri Lanka, the **elephant** has fulfilled many different social, religious and economic roles in the island over the centuries (see p.8). The Sri Lankan elephant (*Elephas maximus maximus*) is a subspecies of the Asian elephant (*Elephas maximus*), which is lighter and has smaller ears than the African elephant (*Loxodonta africana*), and also differs from its African cousins in that fewer than one in ten males – so-called **tuskers** – have tusks. This at least had the benefit of discouraging ivory poachers, although it failed to deter British colonial hunters, who saw the elephant as the ultimate big-game target – the notorious Major Rogers is said to have dispatched well over a thousand of the unfortunate creatures during a twelve-year stint around Badulla, before his murderous career was terminated by a well-aimed blast of lightning. By the beginning of the twentieth century there were only around twelve thousand elephants left in the wild in Sri Lanka, while towards the end of the civil war in 2007 that figure had fallen as low as an estimated three thousand, although numbers are believed to have recovered since.

Following the end of the civil war, the principal pressure on elephants nowadays is **habitat loss**, as more and more of the island's undeveloped areas are cleared for agriculture. This has led to conflicts between villagers and roaming elephants, with tragic consequences – it has been estimated that around two hundred elephants and a similar number of people are killed in clashes every year. Elephant herds still migrate across the island for considerable distances, sometimes gathering in large herds during the dry season around the shores of receding lakes and other water sources, most spectacularly at Minneriya National Park. Large sections of these well-established migratory routes – popularly known as "**elephant corridors**" – now fall within areas protected by various national parks, but despite this, there are still frequent conflicts between farmers and wandering herds, which trample crops and raid sugar plantations (elephants have a pronounced sweet tooth). Herds are periodically rounded up and chased back to the national parks, though these so-called "elephant drives" have frequently become a source of conflict between locals and conservationists.

Wild elephants usually live in close-knit family groupings of around fifteen under the leadership of an elderly female; each herd needs a large area to survive – around five square kilometres per adult – not surprising, given that a grown elephant drinks 150 litres of water and eats up to 200kg of vegetation daily. Elephants' gestation period averages 22 months and they can live up to 70 years. **Trained elephants** are still a major feature of Sri Lankan life, and can often be seen shambling along roads around the island. Captive elephants work under the guidance of skilled **mahouts**, who manipulate their charges using a system of 72 pressure points, plus various verbal commands – a measure of the animals' intelligence is given by the fact that elephants trained to recognize instructions in one language have been successfully re-educated to follow commands in a different one. The life of a trained elephant can be demanding, and it's likely that not all are treated as well as they should be – mahouts are occasionally injured or even killed by their disgruntled charges, proving the truth of the old adage about elephants never forgetting (one particular elephant who had killed two of his mahouts was even put on trial in a court of law – and subsequently acquitted after evidence was presented that he had been mistreated by his handlers). Having said that, elephants can also become objects of remarkable veneration, most famously in the case of the venerable Maligawa Tusker Raja (see p.215), whose death in 1998 prompted the government to declare a day of national mourning.

Leopards

The Sri Lankan **leopard** (*Panthera pardus*) is the island's most striking – and one of its most elusive – residents. These magnificent animals, which can grow to over two metres in length, are now endangered in Sri Lanka due to habitat destruction, although the island still has more of the creatures per square kilometre than anywhere else in the world. It's thought that there are around five hundred in the whole of the island, with some two hundred concentrated in **Yala National Park**. Each hunts within a set territory, preying on smaller or less mobile mammals, most commonly deer; most hunting is done at dawn or dusk, which is generally the best time to spot them. Leopards have a diverse diet and will eat anything from insects to deer, although some leopards develop a taste for certain types of meat – the notorious man-eating leopard of Punanai, whose story is recounted in Christopher Ondaatje's *The Man-Eater of Punanai* (see p.442), is said to have acquired a particular fondness for human flesh. They are also expert climbers, and can sometimes be seen sitting in trees, where they often store the remains of their kills; they are also commonly spotted basking in the sun on rocky outcrops.

Leopards can be found in various parts of the island, including many national parks. Easily the best place to spot one is Yala National Park; you'll have to be amazingly lucky to come across one anywhere else. Block 1 of Yala (the area that is open to the public) is thought to have a leopard density of as high as one animal per square kilometre, probably the highest in the world. Leopards here, particularly young males, have become remarkably habituated to human visitors, and often stroll fearlessly along the tracks through the park.

Monkeys and other mammals

Three species of **monkey** are native to Sri Lanka. The most distinctive and widely encountered is the graceful **grey langur** (*Semnopithecus priam* (*thersites*); also known as the common or Hanuman langur), a beautiful and delicate long-limbed creature with silver-grey hair, a small black face and an enormous tail. Grey langurs can be seen all over the island and are particularly numerous around the southeast, both in national parks and in areas of human habitation, ranging from Bundala National Park to the sacred precinct at Kataragama. They are naturally shy, though some troupes in places frequented by humans have become slightly less reclusive, albeit still engagingly skittish.

Also relatively common, though rather less attractive, is the endemic **toque macaque** (*Macaca sinica*; also known as the red-faced macaque), a medium-sized, reddish-brown creature with a rather baboon-like narrow pink face topped by a distinctive circular tuft of hair. Macaques are much bolder (and noisier) than langurs, and sometimes behave aggressively towards humans when searching for food; they also frequently raid gardens with destructive results. They can be found in most rural parts of the island, usually in troupes of twenty to thirty.

The third native species, also endemic to Sri Lanka, is the **purple-faced leaf monkey** (*Trachypithecus vitulus*; also known as the purple-faced langur). This is similar in build to the grey langur, with long, slender limbs, but with a blackish coat and a white rump and tail. They're found along the west coast, while a more shaggy-coated subspecies, known as the **bear monkey**, is found in the hill country, particularly in the area around Horton Plains.

Sri Lanka's most endearing mammal is the rare **sloth bear** (*Melursus ursinus*), an engagingly shaggy, shambling creature, about a metre in length, which is occasionally spotted in Yala and other national parks. You're far more likely to see the island's various types of **deer** – species include the spotted, sambar and muntjac (or "barking") deer. Wild **buffalo** are also common. Sri Lanka boasts several species of **squirrel**, ranging from the beautifully delicate little palm squirrels, instantly recognizable by their striped bodies and found everywhere (even on the beach), to the rare giant squirrels that can occasionally be seen in montane forests. **Flying foxes** – large, fruit-eating bats that can reach up to a metre in length – are a common sight islandwide, while **mongooses** are also often encountered in the island's national parks, as are rabbits. Less common is the **wild boar**, similar to the wild boars of Europe, and equally ugly. A number of local mammals are largely nocturnal, including the **porcupine** and **pangolin**, as well as the rare **fishing cat**, a large, greyish-brown creature that can grow up to almost 1m in length. They usually live near water, scooping prey out with their paws – hence the name.

Birds

Sri Lanka is a rewarding and well-established destination for dedicated birders: the island's range of habitats – from coastal wetlands to tropical rainforest and high-altitude cloudforest – supports a huge variety of birdlife, which is further enriched by migrants from the Indian Subcontinent and further afield. The island boasts 233 **resident species**, including 33 **endemics**, while another two hundred-odd **migratory** species have been recorded here. Most of the latter visit the island during the northern hemisphere's winter, holidaying in Sri Lanka from around August through to April. In addition, some pelagic birds visit Sri Lanka during the southern hemisphere's winter.

Some species are confined to particular **habitats**, and most of the island's endemics are found in the wet zone that covers the southwestern quarter of the country. For casual bird-spotters, any of Sri Lanka's national parks should yield a large range of species – Bundala, Yala and Uda Walawe are all excellent destinations, and a day's birdwatching in any of these could easily turn up as many as a hundred species. Dedicated birders generally head to more specialist sites, such as Sinharaja, which is home to no fewer than seventeen endemics (although they can be difficult to see), and Horton Plains and Hakgala in the hill country, both excellent for spotting montane species. With careful planning, dedicated birders might succeed in seeing all the island's endemics in a week or two.

Sri Lanka's 33 **endemic birds** range from the spectacular, multicoloured Sri Lanka blue magpie to relatively dowdy and elusive species such as the tiny Legge's flowerpecker, the Sri Lanka whistling thrush and the ashy-headed laughing thrush. Other attractive endemics include the dusky-blue flycatcher, yellow-eared bulbul, black-crested bulbul, yellow-fronted and crimson-fronted barbets, Layard's parakeet, Sri Lanka hanging parrot and the Sri Lanka white-eye, as well as the national bird, the Sri Lanka jungle fowl, which can often be seen rootling around the ground in the island's forests.

Even if you don't manage to catch any of the endemics, there are plenty of other eye-catching birds to watch out for. **Common species** include bee-eaters, scarlet minivets, orioles, parakeets, Indian rollers, Indian pittas, hoopoes, sunbirds and the various species of dazzling kingfisher – the latter is a frequent sight around water (or perched on cables) throughout the island. Other ubiquitous – albeit less colourful – species include the common myna, bulbul, spotted dove and the yellow-billed babbler, the last instantly recognizable thanks to its distinctive hopping gait. Another frequently encountered resident of the national parks is the peacock (or, more precisely, the Indian peafowl), a common but always memorable sight when perched in the trees of the dry-zone jungle. Other spectacular Sri Lankan birds include the Malabar pied hornbill, with its strange double beak, and the Asian paradise flycatcher, with its sweeping brown tail feathers.

The rich population of resident and migrant **water birds** includes various species of grebe, cormorant, pelican, bittern, heron, egret, stork, ibis, plover, lapwing, sandpiper, tern and stilt. Look out particularly for the colourful painted stork, the magnificent Indian darter and the huge (and impressively ugly) lesser adjutant, while Bundala National Park attracts huge flocks of migrant flamingoes. **Birds of prey** include the common Brahminy kite (frequently spotted even in the middle of Colombo), the majestic sea eagle and the huge black eagle and grey-headed fish eagle. The island's fine range of **owls** includes the extraordinary-looking spot-bellied eagle owl, oriental scops owl and the difficult-to-spot frogmouth.

Finally, one bird you can't avoid in Sri Lanka is the **crow** – indeed the rasping and cawing of flocks of the creatures is one of the distinctive sounds of the island. Burgeoning numbers of these avian pests can be found wherever there are heaps of rubbish, and infestations are now common not only in towns but also in formerly unspoilt areas such as Horton Plains National Park, where they have been responsible for eating many of the beautiful lizards that formerly lived there.

Reptiles

Sri Lanka boasts two species of **crocodile: mugger** (also known as marsh or swamp) crocodile (*Crocodilus palustrus*), and the **saltwater** (or estuarine) crocodile (*Crocodilus porosus*); both species live in burrows and feed on fish, birds and small mammals, killing their prey by drowning. Muggers can grow up to 4m in length and tend to frequent shallow freshwater areas around rivers, lakes and marshes; the larger and more aggressive saltwater crocs can reach lengths of up to 7m and prefer the brackish waters of river estuaries and lagoons near the sea. Crocodiles are commonly seen in Bundala and Yala – despite their fearsome appearance they aren't usually considered dangerous unless provoked, although attacks are not unknown.

Sri Lankan crocodiles are occasionally confused with **water monitors**, or *kabaragoya* (*Varanus bengalensis*), though these grow up to only 2m in length and have a quite different – and much more lizard-like – appearance, with a narrower, blue-black head and yellow markings on their back. Water monitors are just one of numerous impressive monitor species found here, including the similar land monitor, or *talagoya* (*Varanus salvator*). The island also boasts a wide and colourful range of smaller lizards, which can be seen islandwide, from coastal beaches to the high-altitude moorlands of Horton Plains National Park.

Sri Lanka is home to eighty-odd species of **snake**, including five poisonous varieties, all relatively common (especially in northern dry zones) and including the cobra and the extremely dangerous Russell's viper. The island has the dubious distinction of having the highest number of **snakebite** fatalities, per capita, of any country in the world.

Turtles

Five of the world's seven species of **marine turtle** visit Sri Lanka's beaches to nest, a rare ecological blessing that could potentially make the island one of the world's leading turtle-watching destinations; however official support for conservation efforts remains lukewarm, despite the number of privately run turtle hatcheries that have sprung up along the west coast.

Turtles are amongst the oldest reptiles on earth, and offer a living link with the dinosaur age, having first evolved around two hundred million years ago; they also have a longer lifespan than most creatures, with some of them living for more than 100 years. Tragically, despite having survived for so long, the world's turtle population is now on the point of being wiped out. All five of the species that visit Sri Lanka are now highly endangered, thanks to marine hazards such as fishing nets and rubbish thrown into the sea, as well as widespread poaching of eggs, hunting for meat and shells, and the disturbance or destruction of nesting sites.

Sea turtles occupy an unusual evolutionary niche. Originally land-dwelling reptiles like tortoises, their limbs evolved into flippers, transforming them into marathon swimmers, and they now generally only leave the water during the breeding season, when females emerge onto land to lay eggs in a hole scooped out of the sand (male turtles, by contrast, rarely leave the ocean). The eggs take six to eight weeks to hatch – if they escape the attentions of human poachers or avoid being dug up by dogs or other creatures. When the newborn turtles hatch, they head instinctively towards the sea – the first journey across the beach to the water is the most dangerous, since they're at the mercy of birds, crabs and other predators. Most females go back to lay their own eggs on the very same stretch of sand on which they were born – their so-called **natal beach** – proof of an extraordinary natural homing instinct, although the disturbance or destruction of such beaches is one of the crucial factors in declining turtle populations. This homing instinct is particularly remarkable given the immense distances sea turtles sometimes travel to return from their feeding grounds to their natal beaches: green turtles can travel up to 5000km, while tagged leatherbacks have swum across the Atlantic, though exactly how they navigate over such vast distances is imperfectly understood.

The most widespread marine turtle – and the one most commonly sighted in Sri Lanka – is the **green turtle** (*Chelonia mydas*), named for its greenish fat; green turtles are actually brown in colour, albeit with a greenish tinge. They grow to up to 1m in length and 140kg in weight and are found in warm coastal waters worldwide, feeding mainly on marine grasses. Female green turtles are the most prolific egg-producers of any sea turtle, laying six or seven hundred eggs every two weeks. The largest and more remarkable sea turtle is the **leatherback** (*Dermochelys coriacea*), which commonly grows to over 2m in length (indeed unconfirmed sightings of three-metre-long specimens have been reported) and weighs up to 800kg. One of the planet's greatest swimmers, the leatherback can be found in oceans worldwide, ranging from tropical waters almost to the Arctic Circle; they can also dive to depths of up to a kilometre and hold their breath for half an hour. The leatherback's name derives from its unique carapace – the "shell" is actually made up of separate bones buried in blackish skin; another unique evolutionary adaptation is their spiny throats, designed to help them swallow their favourite food, jellyfish.

The reddish-brown **loggerhead** (*Caretta caretta*) is another immense creature, reaching lengths of up to 2m; it's similar in appearance to the green turtle, but with a relatively larger head. The **hawksbill** (*Eretmochelys imbricata*) is one of the smaller sea turtles, reaching a length of around 0.5m and a weight of 40kg – it's named for its unusually hooked jaws, which give its head a rather birdlike appearance. Both the hawksbill and loggerhead are found in warm waters worldwide and feed on both plants and animals. The **olive ridley** (*Lepidochelys olivacea*) – one of the ridley turtles, named for its greenish colour – has a wide, rounded shell and reaches sizes of up to 1m. It inhabits the warm waters of the Indo-Pacific region and feeds on both animal and vegetable material.

Whales and dolphins

The recent discovery of whale migratory routes around southern (see p.168) and eastern (see p.350) coasts of Sri Lanka means that the island may turn out to be one of the top two or three places in the world for seeing blue whales, and perhaps the best place in the world for seeing them alongside sperm whales (although whale-watching in Sri Lanka is still in its relative infancy, and long-term data are not yet available).

Blue whales are the most commonly seen cetacean off the Sri Lankan coast. Believed to be the largest animal ever to have lived on the planet, the blue whale reaches over 30m in length and weighs almost two hundred tons. The blue whale is a "baleen whale", feeding mainly on huge quantities of small crustaceans, or krill, which they catch by sieving water through the three hundred or so metre-long baleen plates in their mouths (ingesting 40–60 tonnes of water in a single "mouthful", and consuming around forty million krill per day). If you're lucky, you may also catch sight of a **sperm whale** (named for the milky-white "spermaceti" oil found in tubes in the front of their heads), slightly smaller than the blue whale, though with the largest brain of any creature on the planet. The sperm whale is a "toothed whale" and hunts for fish, squid and other deep-water creatures; they can dive up to 3km and hold their breath for more than an hour. The easiest way to distinguish between the two while at sea is usually by comparing their "blows": that of the blue whale is tall (typically around 10m) and upright, while that of the sperm whale is smaller and more "bushy", and also typically slanted forwards and to the left. **Humpback** and **Bryde's whales** are also occasionally spotted.

In addition to whales, numerous pods of **spinner dolphins** can be found around the island, an extrovert creature well known for (and named after) its acrobatic spins out of the water. In parts of the island, as many as two thousand spinner dolphins have been sighted at one time, not just in whale-watching areas such as Mirissa but in other places around the coast, most notably Kalpitiya. **Risso's and bottlenose dolphins** are other species known to inhabit Sri Lanka's waters.

Ceylon tea

In the minds of many outsiders, Sri Lanka remains synonymous with one thing: tea. Tea cultivation underpinned much of the island's prosperity during the British colonial period, and also had major cultural and environmental side-effects, leading to the clearance of almost all the highland jungles and the arrival of large numbers of Tamil labourers, drafted in to work the plantations. The industry remains crucial to Sri Lanka's economy, and tea estates still dominate the hill country, with endless miles of neatly trimmed bushes carpeting the rolling uplands.

The first use of the leaves of the **tea** plant as a beverage is generally credited to the Chinese emperor Sheng-Nung, who – in truly serendipitous manner – discovered the plant's potable qualities around 2700 BC when a few leaves chanced to fall off a wild tea bush into a pot of boiling water. Tea developed into a staple drink of the Chinese, and later the Japanese, though it wasn't until the nineteenth century that it began to find a market outside Asia. The British began commercial production in India in the 1830s, establishing tea plantations in Assam and, later, Darjeeling, where it continues to flourish.

The success of Ceylon tea (as it's still usually described, rather than "Sri Lankan") was built on the collapse of the island's coffee trade. Throughout the early British colonial period, coffee was the principal plantation crop in the highlands, until the insidious leaf virus *hemileia vastatrix* – popularly know as "Devastating Emily" – laid waste to the industry during the 1870s. Tea bushes had been grown in Sri Lanka in Peradeniya Botanical Gardens as far back as 1824, but it wasn't until 1867 that the island's first commercial tea plantation was established by the Scottish planter **James Taylor**, a modest nineteen-acre affair at Loolecondera, southeast of Kandy. When the coffee industry finally collapsed, a decade later, interest in tea really took off. Bankrupt coffee estates were snapped up for a song and converted to tea production, while rapid fortunes were made from what soon became known as Sri Lanka's "green gold". Hundreds of colonial planters and speculators began descending on the island to clear new land and establish estates of their own, clearing vast swathes of hill country jungle to make way for new tea gardens in the process.

The introduction of tea also had a significant social byproduct. The coffee estates had already employed large numbers of migrant Tamil labourers, brought to Sri Lanka from South India due to a chronic shortage of local manpower in the hills. Work on the coffee plantations was seasonal, meaning that these labourers returned to South India for six months of the year. By contrast, tea production continued year-round, which led to the permanent settlement of thousands of expatriate labourers, Sri Lanka's so-called "**Plantation" Tamils**, whose descendants still work the island's tea gardens today, although they remain one of the island's poorest and most marginalized communities.

Tea remains vital to the **economy** of modern Sri Lanka – so much so that the entire industry was nationalized, with disastrous consequences, in 1975. The government's inept management of the estates over the following decade led to plummeting standards that came close to crippling the entire industry, after which estates were gradually restored to private ownership, where they remain to this day. Sri Lanka is currently one of the world's top three exporters, along with India and Kenya, and tea still makes up around a quarter of the country's export earnings. Almost half these exports now go to Middle Eastern countries, however, which has made the industry vulnerable to the effects of warfare and sanctions in that region, although significant quantities of low-grade tea particles find their way into the tea-bags of major international brands such as Tetley and Lipton's.

Tea production

The tea "bush" is actually an evergreen tree, *Camellia sinensis*, which grows to around ten metres in height in the wild. Cultivated tea bushes are constantly pruned, producing a repeated growth of fresh young buds and leaves throughout the year. Ceylon tea is divided into three types, depending on the altitude at which it is grown. The best-quality tea, so-called **high-grown**, only flourishes above 1200m in a warm climate and on sloping terrain, for which Sri Lanka's hill country provides the perfect location. Bushes at higher altitude grow more slowly but produce a more delicate flavour – among connoisseurs, premium high-grown Ceylon teas are rated as second only to the finest Indian Darjeelings in terms of subtlety. **Low-grown tea** (cultivated below 600m) is stronger and less subtle in taste; **mid-grown tea** is somewhere between the two – in practice, blends of the various types are usually mixed to produce the required flavour and colour.

The island's finest teas are grown in Uva province and around Nuwara Eliya, Dimbula and Dickoya; the flavours from these different regions are quite distinct, showing (at least to trained palates) how sensitive tea is to subtle variations in soil and climate. Low-grown teas are mainly produced in the Galle, Matara and Ratnapura regions. Most Ceylon tea is black (fermented), though a few estates have recently diversified into producing fine green (unfermented) and oolong (partially fermented) teas, the staple form of the drink in China and Japan.

Tea production remains a labour-intensive, resolutely low-tech industry, and the manufacturing process – indeed often the machinery itself – has remained pretty much unchanged since Victorian times. The entire tea production process, from plucking to packing, takes around 24 hours. The first stage – **plucking** the leaves – is still extremely labour-intensive, providing work for some 300,000 estate workers across the island (mainly but not exclusively female). Tea pickers select the youngest two leaves and bud from the end of every branch – bushes are plucked every seven days in the dry season, twice as often in the wet. Following plucking, leaves are **dried** (or "withered") by being spread out in huge troughs while hot air is blown through them to remove moisture, after which they are **crushed** for around thirty minutes, an action that releases juices and enzymes and triggers fermentation – the conditions and length of time under which the leaves ferment is one of the crucial elements in determining the quality of the tea. Once sufficient fermentation has taken place, the tea is **fired** in an oven, preventing further fermentation and producing the black tea that is the staple form of the drink consumed worldwide.

Types of tea

The resultant "bulk" tea is then filtered into different-sized particles and **graded**. Like wine, tea comes in an endless variety of forms and flavours, and a complex and colourful vocabulary has grown up over the centuries to describe the various styles and standards available. The finest teas – also described as "leaf" teas, since they consist of relatively large pieces of unbroken leaf – are known as **Orange Pekoe** (OP), signifying a tea made with young, whole leaves, and the slightly lower-quality **Broken Orange Pekoe** (BOP), which uses broken pieces of the same leaves. Finer grades of OP and BOP come with the added designations "Flowery", "Golden" or "Tippy", signifying teas which also include varying quantities and types of young buds mixed in with the leaves to give the tea a distinctively delicate flavour, such as the prized FTGFOP, or (to give it its full name) Finest Tippy Golden Flowery Orange Pekoe – also known amongst aficionados as Far Too Good For Ordinary People.

Lower grades are designated as **"fannings"** (BOPF) or as an even finer residue, unappetizingly described as **"dust"** (D). Despite the unprepossessing names, these grades are perhaps the two most important, since their tiny particles produce a rich, strong, instant brew that is perfect for the tea bags favoured in many parts of the world – Ceylon tea, blended with leaves from other countries, is used in many major international tea brands, including Lipton's and Tetley. The larger OP and BOP grades, which yield a much paler and more delicate liquor, are traditionally favoured in the Middle East.

Following production, tea is **sampled** by tea tasters – a highly specialist profession, as esteemed in Sri Lanka as wine tasting is in France – before being sent for auction, mostly in Colombo. The vast majority of Sri Lanka's tea is exported, although there's an increasingly good range of home-grown teas available in local shops and supermarkets (especially Cargills) including various blends by major Sri Lankan tea retailers Dilmah and Tea Tang, while unblended, single-origin estate teas are also increasingly available – Ceylon tea at its purest. When buying, look out for the Ceylon Tea Board lion logo, which guarantees that the stuff you're buying comprises only pure Ceylon tea.

SIR THOMAS LIPTON AND THE RISE OF CEYLON TEA

For all the pioneering efforts of Sir James Taylor, the father of Sri Lanka's tea industry, it was another Scot, **Sir Thomas Lipton**, who almost single-handedly put Ceylon tea on the global map. Born in 1850 in Glasgow, Lipton displayed his appetite for adventure young, stowing away at the age of 14 on a ship to the US, where he worked for five years as a farm labourer and grocery clerk. Returning to Glasgow, Lipton opened his first grocery store in 1871, using the sort of eye-catching **publicity stunts** he had seen employed to tremendous effect in America, including leading a parade of well-fed pigs through the streets of Glasgow, their backs hung with placards declaring "I'm going to Lipton's, the best shop in town for Irish bacon!" By 1880 he had twenty shops; by 1890, three hundred.

In 1889, Lipton moved into **tea** retailing, announcing his new wares with a parade of brass bands and bagpipers; by undercutting the then going price by two-thirds, he succeeded in selling ten million pounds of tea in just two years. The real birth of the Lipton's tea dynasty, however, began in 1890. En route to Australia, Lipton stopped off in Ceylon and – true to his "cut out the middleman" motto – bought up five bankrupt tea estates, including what would become his favourite, at Dambatenne, near Haputale. Trumpeting his new acquisitions with relentless advertising and a new slogan ("Direct from the Tea Gardens to the Teapot"), Lipton put Ceylon tea firmly on the world map and massively stimulated demand for it back in Britain. His was also the first company to sell tea in pre-packaged cartons, thus guaranteeing quantity and quality to hard-pressed housewives – while ensuring that the Lipton's brand received the widest possible exposure.

As a commercial expression of the might of the British Empire, Lipton's tea was unparalleled. Lipton succeeded not only in establishing his brand as the number one tea at home and throughout the colonies, but also largely killed off demand for the traditional and more delicate but unpredictable China teas that had previously formed the mainstay of the trade, fostering a taste for the black, full-bodied and reliably strong blends that remain the norm in the UK right up to the present day. The Lipton's tea phenomenon in turn paved the way for the commercial success of other brands established in the late nineteenth century, such as Typhoo (despite the compellingly oriental-sounding name, the tea itself was, again, sourced entirely from Sri Lanka) and Brooke Bond's PG Tips.

The fortunes of Lipton's own brand were mixed, however. It continued to be a major player in British markets well into the twentieth century, but gradually lost out to Brooke Bond, Typhoo and others, largely due to the fact that it was sold only through Lipton's own shops. With the rise of supermarkets such as Tesco (which itself had its roots in the tea trade – the name is an amalgam of the surname of another entrepreneurial grocer, Jack Cohen, with that of his tea dealer, T.E. Stockwell), sales slowly decreased and the Lipton's brand largely disappeared from Britain, leading to the final irony whereby Lipton's, which is still synonymous with tea throughout Asia and in many other parts of the world, is now virtually unknown in the land of its founder's birth.

Books

Contemporary Sri Lanka has a rich literary tradition, and the island has produced a string of fine novelists in recent years, including Booker Prize-winner Michael Ondaatje. Although virtually all of them now live abroad, the island, its culture and twentieth-century history continue to loom large in their work – all the novels of Shyam Selvadurai and Romesh Gunesekera, for instance, deal with Sri Lankan themes, even though Gunesekera now lives in London and Selvadurai in Canada.

In the selection of books below, only small-press publishers outside the US or UK are named. The ★ symbol marks titles that are particularly recommended.

FICTION

★ **Romesh Gunesekera** *Reef*. This deceptively simple but haunting story about a house boy, his master and their twin obsessions – cooking and marine science – beautifully captures the flavour of the island, as well as plumbing some surprising depths. Gunesekera's other three books, *Monkfish Moon*, *The Sandglass* and *Heaven's Edge*, are also partly or wholly set in Sri Lanka, though none is a patch on *Reef*.

★ **Michelle de Kretser** *The Hamilton Case*. Set in the years just before and after independence, this beautifully written and cunningly plotted novel – part period piece, part elegant whodunnit – chronicles the career of lawyer Sam Obeysekere, a loyal subject of the Empire, whose life and loyalties are blighted by his chance involvement in the mysterious murder of a British tea planter.

Carl Muller *The Jam Fruit Tree* trilogy. The prolific novelist and journalist Muller is something of a cultural institution in Sri Lanka. His most famous work, *The Jam Fruit Tree* trilogy (*The Jam Fruit Tree*, *Yakada Yaka* and *Once Upon a Tender Time*), is an intermittently entertaining account of the lives, loves and interminable misadventures of the von Bloss clan, a family of ruffianly, party-loving and permanently inebriated Burghers. Other books include the comic short stories of *A Funny Thing Happened on the Way to the Cemetery*; the chunky historical epics *The Children of the Lion* (based on the mythological history of early Sri Lanka) and *Colombo*; and a collection of essays, *Firing At Random*.

★ **Michael Ondaatje** *Running in the Family*. Perhaps the best book ever written about the island, this marvellous memoir of Ondaatje's Burgher family and his variously dipsomaniac and wildly eccentric relations is at once magically atmospheric and wonderfully comic. Ondaatje's other Sri Lankan book, the altogether more sombre *Anil's Ghost*, offers a very lightly fictionalized account of the civil war and JVP insurrection seen through the eyes of a young forensic pathologist attempting to expose government-sponsored killings.

Shyam Selvadurai *Funny Boy* and *Cinnamon Gardens*. *Funny Boy* presents a moving and disquieting picture of Sri Lanka seen through the eyes of a gay Tamil boy growing up in Colombo in the years leading up to the civil war. *Cinnamon Gardens* offers a similarly simple but eloquent account of those trapped by dint of their sex or sexuality in the stiflingly conservative society of 1930s Colombo.

A. Sivanandan *When Memory Dies*. Weighty historical epic describing the travails of three generations of a Sri Lankan family living through the end of the colonial period and the island's descent into civil war. The same author's *Where The Dance Is* (same publisher) comprises a sequence of inventive and acutely observed short stories set in Sri Lanka, India and England.

★ **Leonard Woolf** *The Village in the Jungle*. Future luminary of the Bloomsbury set, Leonard Woolf served for several years as a colonial administrator in the backwaters of Hambantota. First published in 1913, this gloomy little masterpiece tells a starkly depressing tale of love and murder in an isolated Sri Lankan village, stifled by the encroaching jungle and by its own poverty and backwardness.

HISTORY, RELIGION AND TRAVELOGUES

Adele Barker *Not Quite Paradise: An American Sojourn in Sri Lanka*. Intermittently engaging account of the author's year teaching at Peradeniya University, near Kandy, and subsequent travels around the island in the wake of the tsunami.

Juliet Coombe and Daisy Perry *Around the Fort in 80 Lives* (Sri Serendipity Publishing, Sri Lanka). Warm, evocative and beautifully illustrated portrait of today's Galle Fort, told in a series of affectionate sketches of its diverse cast of idiosyncratic characters, from street peddlers to millionaire expats.

Richard Gombrich *Theravada Buddhism: A Social History from Ancient Benares to Modern Colombo*. This academic but accessible guide to Theravada Buddhism gives an absorbing account of the religion from a social and cultural, rather than theological, angle, with extensive coverage of the faith's development in Sri Lanka. The same author's difficult-to-find *Precept and Practice: Traditional Buddhism in the Rural Highlands of Ceylon* offers a revealing insight into the idiosyncrasies of local Buddhist practice.

Yasmine and Brendan Gooneratne *This Inscrutable Englishman: Sir John D'Oyly (1774–1824)*. Detailed biography of the brilliant English diplomat who brokered the surrender of the Kandyan kingdom to the British in 1815 – the sheer drama of the events described makes it an interesting read, despite the authors' laboriously academic tone.

★ **John Clifford Holt (ed)** *The Sri Lanka Reader: history, culture, politics*. This weighty but fascinating volume offers an absorbing overview of the island's history and culture, anthologizing a vast selection of texts ranging from the *Mahavamsa* and Sigiriya graffiti through to colonial-era documents and contemporary newspaper articles (including the moving "And Then They Came for Me" by murdered journalist Lasantha Wickrematunga) – all expertly threaded together by the editor.

H.A.J. Hulugalle *Ceylon of the Early Travellers* (Arjuna Hulugalle, Sri Lanka). This tiny book offers a series of entertaining snapshots of Sri Lankan history seen through the eyes of foreign travellers, traders and soldiers, including accounts of some of the more bizarre incidents in the island's past, such as the British plan to capture Colombo using a giant cheese.

Robert Knox *An Historical Relation of Ceylon* (Tisara Prakasakayo, Sri Lanka). Knox's account of his twenty-year captivity in the Kandyan kingdom (see p.224). An interesting read, especially the autobiographical section, dealing with Knox's own Job-like trials and tribulations and culminating in the nail-biting story of his carefully planned escape.

Dennis B. McGilvray *Crucible of Conflict, Tamil and Muslim Society on the east coast of Sri Lanka*. Detailed ethnographic study – academic, but absorbing – of eastern Sri Lanka, centred on the town of Akkaraipattu and offering unrivalled insights into the region's cultural and religious complexities.

Roy Moxham *Tea: Addiction, Exploitation and Empire*. This detailed and very readable account of the development of the tea industry in the British colonies paints a compelling portrait of Victorian enterprise and greed – and of the terrible human price paid by Indian plantation workers. Includes extensive coverage of Sri Lanka.

Christopher Ondaatje *The Man-Eater of Punanai*. Famous Sri Lankan expatriate and entrepreneur Christopher Ondaatje (brother of Michael) returns to the island of his birth to go searching for leopards in the war-torn east, and for memories of his own youth – including the spectre of his maverick father, who also appears as one of the stars of *Running in the Family* (see p.441). Ondaatje's more recent *Woolf in Ceylon: An Imperial Journey in the Shadow of Leonard Woolf 1904–11* offers an interesting and beautifully illustrated account of Leonard Woolf's seven years in Ceylon (see p.182), mixed up with further bits and pieces of Sri Lankan history and personal reminiscence.

K.M. de Silva *A History of Sri Lanka* (Vikas, India). The definitive history of the island, offering a considered and intelligent overview of events from prehistory to the late twentieth century.

Rory Spowers *A Year in Green Tea and Tuk-Tuks*. Insightful account of a British environmental activist's attempts to create an ecologically sustainable farm in the hills near Galle, while dealing with natural hazards, disgruntled workers and the occasional death threat en route.

Nath Yogasundram *A Comprehensive History of Sri Lanka: From Prehistory to Tsunami* (Vijitha Yapa Publications, Sri Lanka). Less scholarly than de Silva's *History* (see above), though intelligently written, and also more up to date, with coverage up to 2006.

THE CIVIL WAR

★ **William McGowan** *Only Man Is Vile*. Written in the late 1980s, this classic account of the civil war and JVP insurrection combines war reportage, travelogue and social commentary to produce a stark, compelling and extremely depressing insight into the darker aspects of the Sinhalese psyche.

M.R. Narayan Swamy *Inside An Elusive Mind: Prabhakaran* (Vijitha Yapa, Sri Lanka). Detailed account of the career of the LTTE supremo, covering events up until the turn of the millennium, although many of the LTTE's less savoury activities – such as their numerous massacres of civilians, political assassinations, the use of child soldiers and the widespread terrorizing of their own people – are conveniently ignored or

white-washed. The same author's *Tigers of Lanka* covers very similar ground, although again only up to the turn of the millennium.

Anita Pratap *Island of Blood: Frontline Reports from Sri Lanka, Afghanistan and other South Asian Flashpoints* (Vijitha Yapa, Sri Lanka). Vivid, if sometime irritatingly self-congratulatory, eyewitness accounts of various Asian flashpoints by a well-known Indian journalist, including extended coverage of the Sri Lankan civil war.

K.M. de Silva *Reaping the Whirlwind: Ethnic Conflict, Ethnic Politics in Sri Lanka*. Definitive exploration of the social and political roots of the island's Tamil–Sinhalese conflict. Excellent on the decades preceding the war, although with relatively little coverage of the war itself.

★ **Nirupama Subramanian** *Sri Lanka: Voices from a War Zone* (Vijitha Yapa, Sri Lanka). Published in 2005, this eloquent collection of essays by an Indian Tamil journalist gives a powerful account of the later stages of the civil war, combining military and political analysis of the conflict with the personal stories of those affected by the fighting on both sides of the ethnic divide.

★ **Gordon Weiss** *The Cage: the fight for Sri Lanka and the last days of the Tamil Tigers.* Written by a former UN staffer in Colombo, this searing book offers a meticulously documented account of the last months of the civil war and its aftermath, serving up a grim indictment of both government and LTTE military as well as a scorching critique of Rajapakse family rule. The preliminary history expertly unravels the origins of the conflict, while the eyewitness accounts and reconstructions of battlefield events – and the horrific sufferings of Tamil civilians trapped in the fighting – are unlikely to be bettered.

ART, ARCHITECTURE AND CULTURE

Emma Boyle *Culture Smart! Sri Lanka: A Quick Guide to Customs and Culture.* Insightful look at Sri Lankan society, customs and cultural quirks by a seasoned UK expat.

Robert E. Fisher *Buddhist Art and Architecture.* Concise, well-illustrated overview of Buddhist architecture, sculpture and painting. There's little specific coverage of Sri Lanka, although the discussions of different national styles provide illuminating context.

★ **Ronald Lewcock, Barbara Sansoni and Laki Senanayake** *The Architecture of an Island: the Living Heritage of Sri Lanka.* This gorgeous book, a work of art in itself, offers revealing insights into the jumble of influences that have gone into creating Sri Lanka's distinctive architectural style. The text discusses 95 examples of traditional island architecture – from palm shacks and hen coops to Kandyan temples and colonial cathedrals, all beautifully illustrated with line drawings by Barbara Sansoni.

Meher McArthur *Reading Buddhist Art.* Absorbing, richly illustrated introduction to the myriad signs and symbols of Buddhist iconography, with clear explanations of everything from sacred footprints to mythical animals, as well as introductions to the main deities of Mahayana Buddhism.

★ **David Robson** *Geoffrey Bawa: The Complete Works.* Written by a long-term Bawa associate, this comprehensive volume offers the definitive overview of the work of Sri Lanka's outstanding modern architect, with copious beautiful photographs and fascinating text on Bawa's life and creations, plus many revealing insights into Sri Lankan culture and art.

FLORA AND FAUNA

Indraneil Das and Anslem de Silva *Snakes and Other Reptiles of Sri Lanka.* Excellent photographic pocket guide to Sri Lanka's fascinating but little-known population of lizards, snakes and other slithery creatures.

John Harrison and Tim Worfolk *A Field Guide to the Birds of Sri Lanka.* The definitive guide to Sri Lanka's avifauna.

Sriyanie Miththapala and P.A. Miththapala *What Tree is That?* (Ruk Rakaganno, Sri Lanka) Well-presented basic guide to the most common tree species of Sri Lanka, with good line drawings.

Gehan de Silva Wijeyeratne *Sri Lankan Wildlife: A Visitor's Guide.* Excellent introductory primer covering the full range of island wildlife, from elephants, leopards and birds through to dragonflies, lizards and whales.

★ **Gehan de Silva Wijeyeratne, Deepal Warakagoda and T.S.U. de Zylva** *A Photographic Guide to Birds of Sri Lanka.* Invaluable pocket-sized title, with excellent photos of all listed species and clear descriptions.

Language

Sri Lanka is a trilingual nation. The main language, Sinhala, is spoken by around 75 percent of the population; Tamil is spoken by around 25 percent (including not only the Tamils themselves, but many of the island's Muslims). English is also widely used by Westernized and urban sections of the population, and is the first language of most Sri Lankan Burghers – many people speak it more or less fluently, and even native Sinhala speakers (especially in Colombo) often employ English in conversation alongside their native tongue, switching between languages as the mood takes them. English sometimes serves as a link language between the island's communities, too – relatively few northern Tamils speak Sinhala, and even fewer Sinhalese speak Tamil.

Language is an emotive issue in Sri Lanka – the notorious "Sinhala Only" legislation of 1956, which downgraded Tamil from the status of an official language and effectively barred Tamils from most forms of government employment, was one of the most significant root causes behind the subsequent civil war, and although Tamil was restored to the status of an official language in 1988, the subject is still politically sensitive. All official signs, banknotes, government publications and the like are printed in all three languages, and (except in the north, where Sinhala is rarely seen or heard) many businesses and shops follow suit.

Sinhala

Sinhala (or Singhala; also referred to as Sinhalese/Singhalese, although properly speaking this is the name of the people themselves, rather than their language) is an Indo-Aryan language, related to other North Indian languages such as Hindi and

THE SINHALA ALPHABET

අ	ah	ආ	aah	ඇ	a	ඈ	aa
අං	ahng	ඉ	i	ඊ	ee	උ	u
ඌ	oo	එ	e	ඒ	eh	ඔ	o
ඖ	oh	ඖ	au	ක	kah	ඛ	khah
ග	gah	ඝ	ghah	ච	cha	ඡ	chah
ජ	jah	ට	tah	ඨ	tah	ඩ	dah
ණ	nah	ත	tah	ථ	thah	ද	dhah
ධ	dhah	න	nah	ප	pah	ඵ	phah
බ	bah	භ	bhah	ම	mah	ය	yah
ර	rah	ල	lah	ව	vah	ශ	shah
ෂ	shah	ස	sah	හ	hah	ළ	lah

Some vowel sounds are represented using the characters shown above. Others are shown by modifying a basic consonant character, either by adding small additional strokes to it or by placing vowel symbols on one or both sides of the basic character. Most characters follow the same basic pattern:

ප	pah (basic character)	පු	poo	පි	pi
පු	pu	පා	paah	පො	po
ප්	p (consonant only)	පෙ	pe	පී	pee

Bengali, as well as to Sanskrit, the classic ancient language of the Indian Subcontinent, and Pali, the sacred language of Buddhism. The language was first brought to Sri Lanka by the original Sinhalese settlers from North India around the fifth century BC, though it has developed since then in complete geographical isolation from other North Indian Indo-Aryan languages, being heavily influenced by Tamil, as well as acquiring numerous words from Dutch, Portuguese, Malay and English. Sinhala is found only in Sri Lanka; its closest relative is Dhivehi, spoken in the Maldives.

Sinhala **pronunciation** is relatively straightforward – most Sinhala words, despite their sometimes fearsome length, are generally built up out of chains of simple vowel sounds, typically a vowel plus a consonant, as in the expression for "please", *karuna karala*. There are a few awkward consonant clusters, but these are relatively uncommon.

Written Sinhala uses a beautifully elegant and highly distinctive system of 47 curvilinear characters. Most characters represent a consonant plus a vowel sound that is indicated by a subtle addition to the basic character (see box opposite).

There's little **printed material** available on Sinhala. The best resource is Lonely Planet's *Sinhala Phrasebook* by Swarna Pragnaratne. *Say it in Sinhala* by J.B. Dissanayake and the *Sri Lanka Words and Phrases* phrasebook published by Arjuna Hulugalle are both useful.

Tamil

Tamil is one the most important of the various Dravidian languages of South India, spoken by almost sixty million people in the southern Indian state of Tamil Nadu, as well as by Tamils in Sri Lanka, Singapore, Malaysia and elsewhere around the world. The language in Sri Lanka has developed in isolation from the Tamil spoken in South India, acquiring its own accent and vocabulary – the relationship between Indian and Sri Lankan Tamil is roughly similar to that between British and North American English.

Tamil has a long and distinguished history, and a literary tradition stretching back to the third century BC – surpassed amongst Indian languages only by Sanskrit. It's also a famously difficult language to master, thanks to its complex grammar, extended alphabet and repertoire of distinctive sounds (the so-called "reflexive consonants", common to all Dravidian languages, pronounced with the tongue curled against the back of the teeth) – these also make the language virtually impossible to transliterate into Roman script. The language is written in the beautiful **Vattelluttu** ("round script"), a combination of rectangular shapes and elegant curvilinear flourishes.

Sri Lankan English

As with Indian English, the version of the language spoken in Sri Lanka, sometimes referred to as "**Sringlish**" (not to be confused with "Singlish", or Singaporean English) is not without its own charming idiosyncrasies of grammar, spelling and punctuation, along with a few colourful local expressions. A "bake house" is of course a bakery, though you might not realize that a "cool spot" is a small café, or that a "colour house" is a paint shop. Remember too that "taxis" are most often just everyday tuktuks, while a "hotel" is frequently a cheap eating establishment rather than a place to stay. And if someone at your (real) hotel starts talking about their "backside", don't worry – they're referring to the rear of the building, not a part of their anatomy. You might also come across classic old-time Sri Lankan idioms such as "men" (which can be used to refer to anyone listening, men and women); the monosyllabic "Is it?" (meaning anything from "I'm sorry, I don't quite understand" to "Go jump off a cliff"); or the quintessentially Sri Lankan "What to do?" – a kind of verbal shrug of the shoulders, which can mean virtually anything from "What shall we do?" to "The situation's completely hopeless" or "Let's have another beer."

For more on the idiosyncrasies of Sringlish, get hold of a copy of Michael Meyler's comprehensive and entertaining *A Dictionary of Sri Lankan English*.

Useful Sinhala and Tamil words and expressions

BASICS

	SINHALA	TAMIL
hello/welcome	hello/ayubowan	*vanakkam*
goodbye	ayubowan	*varavaanga*
yes	oh-ooh	*aam*
no	nay	*illai*
please	karuna karala	*thayavu seithu*
thank you	es-toothee	*nandri*
OK	hari (or hari-hari)	*sari (or sari-sari)*
excuse me	sama venna	*enga*
sorry	kana gartui	*mannikkavum*
do you speak English?	Oh-ya Inghirisee kata karenavada?	*ningal angilam paysu virhala?*
I don't understand	matah obahvah thehrum	*enakku puriyavillaiye gahna baha*
what is your name?	nama mokada?	*ungaludaya peyr enna?*
my name is…	mahgay nama…	*ennudaya peyr…*
how are you?	kohomada?	*ningal eppadi irukkirigal?*
well, thanks	hondeen innava	*romba nallayirukkudhu*
not very well	vadiya honda nay	*paruvayillai*
this	mayka	*ithu*
that	ahraka	*athu*
when?	kawathatha?	*eppa?*
where?	kohedah?	*enge?*
when does it open/close?	ehika kiyatada ahrinnay/vahhannee	*e thirakkiruthu/moodukiradu*
I want	mata onay	*enakku venam*
is there any…?	…-da?	*vere ethavathu irikkirutha*
how much?	ahhekka keeyada?	*ahdu evvalah-vur?*
can you give me a discount?	karuna karala gana?	*ithil ethavathu salugai adukaranna irikkirutha?*
big	loku	*pareya (perisu)*
small	podi	*sarreya*
excellent	hari hondai	*miga nallathu*
hot (weather)	rasnai	*ushnamana*
open	erala	*thira*
closed	vahala	*moodu*
shop	kaday	*kadi (kadai)*
post office	teppa kantorua	*anja lagam*
bank	bankua	*vangi*
toilet	vesikili	*kahlippadem*
police	polisiya	*kavalar*
pharmacy	farmisiya/bayhet sapua	*marunthu kadai*
doctor	dostara	*maruthuvar (vaidyar)*
hospital	rohala	*aspathri*
ill	asaneepai	*viyathi*

GETTING AROUND

	SINHALA	TAMIL
boat	bohtua	*padadur*
bus	bus ekka	*bas*
bus station	bus stand	*baas nilayem*
train	kohchiya	*rayil*
train station	dumriya pala	*rayil nilayem*
car	car	*car*

bicycle	bicycle	*saikal*
road	para	*pathai*
left	vama	*idathu*
right	dakuna	*valathu*
straight on	kelin yanna	*naerakapogavum*
near	langa	*arukkil*
far	athah	*turam*
station	is-stashama	*nilayam*
ticket	tiket ekkah	*anumati situ*

ACCOMMODATION

	SINHALA	*TAMIL*
hotel	hotelaya	*hotel*
guesthouse	guesthouse ekka	*virun-dhinnar vidhudheh*
bathroom	nahnah kamarayak	*kulikkum arai*
clean	suda	*suththam*
cold	seethai	*kulir*
dirty	apirisidui	*alukku (azhukku)*
room	kamaraya	*arai*
do you have a room?	kamara teeyenavada?	*arekil kidehkkumah?*
may I see the room?	kamaraya karuna karala?	*koncham kanpikkireengala penvanna?*
is there an a/c room?	a/c kamaraya teeyenavada?	*kulir seithu arayai park mudiyama?*
is there hot water?	unuvatura teeyenavada?	*sudu thanir irukkuma?*
please give me the bill	karuna karala bila ganna	*bill tharavum*

NUMBERS

	SINHALA	*TAMIL*
1	ekka	*ontru*
2	dekka	*erantru*
3	toona	*moontru*
4	hatara	*nangu*
5	paha	*ainthu*
6	hiya	*aru*
7	hata	*aelu*
8	ahta	*ettu*
9	navighya	*onpathu*
10	dahhighya	*pattu*
20	vissai	*erpathu*
30	teehai	*mupathu*
40	hatalihai	*natpathu*
50	panahai	*ompathu*
100	seeya	*nooru*
200	dayseeya	*irunooru*
1000	daha	*aiyuram*
2000	daidaha	*iranda iuram*
100,000	lakshaya	*latcham*

TIME

	SINHALA	*TAMIL*
today	ada	*indru*
tomorrow	heta	*naalay*
yesterday	eeyai	*neh-truh*
morning	udai	*kaalai*
afternoon	havasa	*matiyam*

SINHALA PLACE-NAMES

Aluthgama	අලුත්ගම	Kataragama	කතරගම
Ambalangoda	අම්බලන්ගොඩ	Kitulgala	කිතුල්ගල
Anuradhapura	අනුරාධපුර	Kurunegala	කුරුණෑගල
Arugam Bay	ආරුගම්බේ	Matara	මාතර
Badulla	බදුල්ල	Mihintale	මිහින්තලේ
Bandarawela	බන්ඩාරවෙල	Mirissa	මිරිස්ස
Batticaloa	මඩකලපුව	Monaragala	මොණරාගල
Bentota	බෙන්තොට	Negombo	මීගමුව
Beruwala	බේරුවල	Nilvaveli	නිලාවේලි
Colombo	කොළඹ	Nuwara Eliya	නුවර එළිය
Dambulla	දඔුල්ල	Polonnaruwa	පොළොන්නරුව
Ella	ඇල්ල	Ratnapura	රත්නපුර
Galle	ගාල්ල	Sigiriya	සිගිරිය
Giritale	ගිරිතලේ	Tangalla	තංගල්ල
Habarana	හබරණ	Tissamaharama	තිස්සමහාරාමය
Hambantota	හම්බන්තොට	Trincomalee	ත්‍රිකුණාමලය
Haputale	හපුතලේ	Unawatuna	උනවටුන
Hikkaduwa	හික්කඩුව	Uppaveli	උප්පුවේලි
Jaffna	යාපනය	Weligama	වැලිගම
Kalutara	කළුතර	Wellawaya	වැල්ලවාය
Kandy	මහනුවර		

day	davasa	*pakal*
night	reh	*eravu*
last/next week	giya/ilanga sahtiya	*pona/adutha vaaram*

FOOD AND DRINK

USEFUL PHRASES

	SINHALA	*TAMIL*
food	kanda	*unavu*
restaurant	kamata	*unavu aalayam*
the menu, please	menu eka penvanna	*thayavu seithu thinpandangal patti tharavum*
I'm vegetarian	mama elavalu vitaray	*naan oru saivam kannay*
please give me the bill	karuna karala bila ganna	*bill tharavum*

BASICS

SINHALA	*TAMIL*	
paan	*rotti/paan*	bread
bittaraya	*muttai*	egg
ay-is	*ice*	ice
baht	*arisi*	rice (cooked)
vaturah	*thannir*	water
drink botalayak genna	*oru pottal soda panam*	mineral water (bottle)
tay	*teyneer*	tea
kopi	*kapi*	coffee
kiri	*paal*	milk
seeni	*seeni*	sugar
bahta	*butter/vennai*	butter
hakuru	*seeni/vellam*	jaggery

FRUIT AND VEGETABLES

SINHALA	TAMIL	
palaturu	palam	fruit
keselkan	valaipalam	banana
pol	thengali	coconut
amba	mangai	mango
papol	pappa palam	papaya
annasi	annasi	pineapple
elavelu	kai kari vagaigal	vegetables
luunu	venkayam	onion
ala	uruka kilangu	potato
thakkali	thakkali	tomato

MEAT AND FISH

SINHALA	TAMIL	
harak mas	mamism	meat
kukulmas	koli (kozhi)	chicken
uroomas	pantri	pork
harak mas	maattu mamism	beef
batalu mas	aattu mamism	lamb
kakuluvo	nandu	crab
isso	iraal	prawns
pokirissa	periya iraal	lobster
malu	min	fish

Glossary

abhaya mudra "Have No Fear" pose in traditional Buddhist iconography

adimuka Alternative name for a vahalkada (the small shrines placed at the four cardinal points of a stupa)

ambalama Traditional pilgrim's resthouse

anda The main, hemispherical section of a dagoba

apsara Heavenly nymph

arhat Enlightened monk

Avalokitesvara Mahayana bodhisattva who is worshipped as the lord of infinite compassion, able to save all beings from suffering

Ayurveda Ancient Indian system of holistic healthcare

-arama or **-rama** park, garden or monastic residence

betel Popular and mildly narcotic snack, combining leaves from the betel tree with flakes of areca nut, a pinch of lime and sometimes a piece of tobacco; produces the characteristic red spittle whose stains can be seen on pavements throughout the country

bhikku Buddhist monk

bo tree (*Ficus religiosa*; also known as the bodhi tree) Species of tree held sacred by Buddhism, since the Buddha is believed to have achieved enlightenment while meditating beneath one

bodhigara Bo tree enclosure

bodhisattva A Buddha-to-be who, rather than passing into nirvana, has chosen to stay in the world to improve the spiritual welfare of other, unenlightened beings

bund Bank of a reservoir or tank

Burghers Sri Lankans of European (usually Dutch) descent

cetiya/chaitya Alternative Sinhalese word for a stupa

chattravali Spire-like pinnacle at the top of a stupa

chena Slash-and-burn farming

Cholas (or **Colas**) The dominant power in South India from the tenth to the twelfth centuries, with their capital at Thanjavur in Tamil Nadu; overran Sri Lanka in the late tenth century, sacking Anuradhapura in 993, after which they established a new capital at Polonnaruwa

coir Fibre made out of coconut husks

Culavamsa The "Lesser Chronicle" and continuation of the *Mahavamsa*

dagoba Stupa, a type of hemispherical monument found throughout the Buddhist world, traditionally enshrining religious relics and symbolizing both the person of the Buddha himself and the route to enlightenment

devale Shrine or temple to a deity, either freestanding or part of a Buddhist temple; nominally Buddhist, but often showing strong Hindu influence

dhyani mudra Meditation pose

digge Drummers' hall; often a pillared hall or pavilion in a temple where drummers and dancers rehearse

Durga The most terrifying of female Hindu deities, the demon-slaying Durga is considered an aspect of Shiva's consort, Parvati

duwa Small island

dwarfs Attendants of Kubera, the god of wealth, and thus symbols of prosperity

-ela Stream

-gaha Tree

-gala Rock

-gama Village

Ganesh Popular elephant-headed Hindu god, the son of Shiva, remover of obstacles and bringer of success and prosperity

ganga River

-ge Hall or house

gedige South Indian-style shrine, rectangular in shape and built entirely of stone or brick

-giri Rock

gopuram Tower of a Hindu temple, usually richly decorated with multicoloured statues

guardstone Carved figure placed at the entrance to a temple to protect against malign influences; often shows a figure of a *nagaraja*

Hanuman Monkey god who assisted Rama in recovering Sita from the demon Rawana, as related in the *Ramayana*

harmika The box-shaped section of a dagoba that sits on top of the dome (*anda*) and supports the *chattravali*

Hinayana Alternative and pejorative name for Theravada Buddhism

hypostyle Building constructed using many columns

image house (pilimage) building in a Buddhist temple housing a statue of the Buddha

Jatakas Stories describing the 547 previous lives of the Buddha

JHU Jathika Hela Urumaya, or National Heritage Party, led by Buddhist monks; promotes a broadly right-wing, nationalist and anti-Tamil agenda

JVP Janatha Vimukthi Peramuna, or People's Liberation Front. Marxist party with an extreme nationalist, anti-Tamil agenda. Originally made up largely of rural poor and students, the JVP launched armed insurrections against the government in 1971 and 1987–89, both put down with considerable loss of life. Since the second insurrection has transformed itself into an important mainstream political party with a strong parliamentary presence

-kanda or -kande Hill/mountain

Kataragama One of the principal Sri Lankan deities, believed to reside in the town of Kataragama

kavadi The "peacock dance" performed by devotees of the god Kataragama

kolam Masked dance-drama

kovil Hindu temple

-kulam Tank, lake

Lakshmi Hindu goddess of wealth, Vishnu's consort

lingam Phallic symbol representing Shiva; often placed within a yoni, representing female sexuality

LTTE Liberation Tigers of Tamil Eelam, popularly known as the Tamil Tigers

maha Great

Mahavamsa The "Great Chronicle", the semi-mythical account of early Sri Lankan history as narrated by the island's Sinhalese Buddhist clergy

Mahayana Buddhism One of the two major schools of Buddhism, and the dominant form of the religion in China, Japan and Tibet, though it has had only superficial influence on Sri Lankan Buddhism

mahout Elephant handler

Maitreya The next Buddha. Mahayana Buddhists believe Maitreya will reintroduce Buddhism to the world when all knowledge of the religion has been lost

makara Imaginary composite animal derived from Indian bestiary

makara torana Arch formed from two linked *makaras*

mandapa Pillared hall or pavilion

mawatha (abbreviated to "Mw") Street

moonstone Carved semicircular stone placed in front of entrance to shrine. Also a type of gemstone mined in the island

Moors Sri Lankans of Arab or Indian-Arab descent

mudra Traditional pose in Buddhist iconography

naga stone Stone decorated with the image of a hooded cobra

nagaraja Serpent king

nikaya Order of Buddhist monks

nuwara Town

ola/ola leaf Parchment made from the talipot palm; used as a writing material in Sri Lanka up to the nineteenth century

oya or stream Small river

Pali The sacred language of Theravada Buddhism. This early Indo-European language, related to Sanskrit, is close to the language spoken by the Buddha himself. The scriptures of Theravada Buddhism were originally written in Pali and are still recited in this language in Buddhist ceremonies

Pallavas South Indian Tamil dynasty (fifth–ninth centuries), based in Kanchipuram, who, along with the Pandyans and Cholas, periodically interfered in Sri Lankan affairs

Pandyans Major Tamil dynasty (sixth–fourteenth centuries), based in Madurai, who vied for control of South India with the Cholas and Pallavas from the ninth to thirteenth centuries and periodically involved themselves in Sri Lankan affairs. Sacked Anuradhapura in the ninth century

parinirvana mudra Reclining pose showing the Buddha on the point of entering into nirvana. One of the most common *mudras* in Sri Lankan art

pasada/prasada Palace

Pattini Hindu goddess worshipped as paragon of marital fidelity

perahera Procession

Pillaiyar Ganesh (Tamil)

pirith Ceremonial chanting of Buddhist scriptures

-pitiya Field or park

poya Full-moon day

poyage Building in a monastery used for ceremonial gatherings of monks on poya days (hence the name); sometimes translated as "chapter house"

puja Hindu or Buddhist religious offering or ceremony

-pura/-puram Town

Rajarata Literally "The King's Land" – the traditional name for the area now more generally known as the Cultural Triangle

Rama The seventh incarnation of Vishnu and hero of the *Ramayana*

Rawana (or **Ravana**) Demon-king and arch villain of the *Ramayana*; responsible for kidnapping Rama's wife Sita and holding her captive in Sri Lanka

Ruhunu (or **Rohana**) Traditional name for southern Sri Lanka

samadhi (dhyani) mudra Pose showing Buddha in state of meditation, seated in the lotus or half-lotus position

Saman The god of Adam's Peak

samudra Large tank

Sangha The worldwide community of Buddhist monks

Shiva One of the two principal Hindu gods, worshipped in many forms, both creative and destructive

Shiva Nataraj Classic subject of Hindu sculpture, showing a four-armed dancing Shiva enclosed by a circle of fire

sinha Lion

Skanda Son of Shiva (also known as Murugam and Subramanian). His identity in Sri Lanka has merged with that of Kataragama

SLA Sri Lankan Army

SLFP One of the two main Sri Lankan political parties, led successively by S.W.R.D. Bandaranaike, his wife and his daughter. Policies have tended to be the opposite of the pro-Western, free-market UNP, leaning instead towards a brand of populist nationalism (often with an anti-Tamil bias) featuring extensive state control of the economy

sri pada Holy footprint

tank Large man-made lake constructed for irrigation – almost always much larger than the English word suggests

-tara/-tota Port

Theravada Buddhism The older of the two main schools of Buddhism, and the dominant form of the religion in Sri Lanka

tuktuk Motorized rickshaw; also known as a three-wheeler, trishaw or taxi

UNP United National Party; one of Sri Lanka's two main political parties and the first ruling party of independent Sri Lanka. Policies have traditionally tended to be pro-Western and free-market

Upulvan Sri Lankan name for Vishnu

vahalkadas Shrines placed at the four cardinal points of a stupa

vatadage Characteristic Sri Lankan style of building formed by adding a roof and ambulatory to a dagoba

Veddha Sri Lanka's original aboriginal inhabitants

ves Style of traditional costume and dancing employed by Kandyan dancers

Vibhishana The youngest brother of Rawana. Despite his demonic nature, Vibhishana is revered in Sri Lanka, since he pleaded the captive Sita's cause with Ravana and later fought with Rama against his brother, suggesting the potential for right action in even the lowest creature

vidiya Street (in Kandy)

vidyalaya School

vihara (sometimes spelt *vehera* or *wehera*) Buddhist temple or monastery

vimana Palace of a god or celestial being

Vishnu One of the two principal Hindu gods, considered a protector of Buddhism in Sri Lanka

VOC Vereenigde Oost-Indische Compagnie (Dutch East India Company)

-watte Garden

-wewa (pronounced "-vava") Man-made reservoir (tank)

-wila Pond

Small print and index

453 Small print

454 Map symbols

455 Index

ABOUT THE AUTHOR

Gavin Thomas has spent much of his life trying to be somewhere else. He first visited Sri Lanka in 2001 and has been returning regularly ever since, as well as visiting some fifty other countries around the world, from Argentina to New Zealand. He now works as a full-time travel writer, his enthusiasm for abroad undimmed despite various life-threatening on-the-road encounters that have so far included being chased by wild elephants, being shot by Mexican bandits and being forced to eat dangerously large quantities of airline catering. He is also the author of the *Rough Guide to Dubai* and the *Rough Guide to Oman*, co-author of the *Rough Guide to Rajasthan, Delhi & Agra*, and a regular contributor to the *Rough Guide to India*.

Acknowledgements

Particular thanks to the peerless Nimal de Silva of Destination Sri Lanka, who drove me with consummate skill and patience across much of the island, supplied me with endless information en route and proved the best travelling companion I could have wished for. Big thanks also to Mark Thamel (*Ocean View Guesthouse*, Negombo); Dallas & Rushika Martenstyn and everyone at Alankuda; Ashan (*McLeod Inn*, Kandy); Sue & Faeiz Samad (*Sharon Inn*, Kandy); Sumane Bandara Illangantilake (Expeditor Tours, Kandy); Ravi Dessapriya (Sri Lanka Trekking, Kandy); Linton Wanniarachchi (Blue Haven Tours & Travels, Kandy); John & Susanna Geoghegan (*Planters Bungalow*, Ella); Jith (*Ravana Heights*, Ella); Tyrone David (*Tangalla Bay Hotel*); Sabri Khalid (*Khalid's*, Galle); and Roland, for co-piloting duties, and sharing the long road to Jaffna. Massive thanks also to Emma Boyle for invaluable Unawatuna updates and much more besides; to Angie Samuel, Riaz Cader and everyone at Jetwing; and, as ever, Dominic Sansoni for insights, information and entertainment in Colombo.

At Rough Guides, thanks to all who babysat the project at various times and especially to my two very fine editors, Samantha Cook and Tim Locke. Thanks also to all those who have worked on previous editions, particularly my old Sri Lankan compadre Edward Aves, who updated large sections of the guide last time round, and much of whose work survives in the new edition. Also in the UK, thanks to Sanjika Perera and Nalin Perera at the Sri Lanka Tourist Board; Mark Ellingham, for information, encouragement and the long-running Burgher box; and Gehan de Silva Wijeyeratne, for continuing inspiration regarding all things to do with the island. And finally a huge hug for Allison, with whom I first discovered Sri Lanka, and for Laura and Jamie, who I hope will one day discover it for themselves. This book is dedicated to the three of them, with all my love.

A ROUGH GUIDE TO ROUGH GUIDES

Published in 1982, the first Rough Guide – to Greece – was a student scheme that became a publishing phenomenon. Mark Ellingham, a recent graduate in English from Bristol University, had been travelling in Greece the previous summer and couldn't find the right guidebook. With a small group of friends he wrote his own guide, combining a highly contemporary, journalistic style with a thoroughly practical approach to travellers' needs.

The immediate success of the book spawned a series that rapidly covered dozens of destinations. And, in addition to impecunious backpackers, Rough Guides soon acquired a much broader readership that relished the guides' wit and inquisitiveness as much as their enthusiastic, critical approach and value-for-money ethos.

These days, Rough Guides include recommendations from budget to luxury and cover more than 200 destinations around the globe, as well as producing an ever-growing range of eBooks and apps.

Visit **roughguides.com** to see our latest publications.

Rough Guide credits

Editors: Samantha Cook, Tim Locke
Layout: Jessica Subramanian
Cartography: Ashutosh Bharti
Picture editor: Tim Draper
Proofreader: Stewart Wild
Photographer: Gavin Thomas
Managing editor: Keith Drew
Assistant editor: Jalpreen Kaur Chhatwal
Production: Gemma Sharpe
Cover design: Nicole Newman, Jessica Subramanian

Editorial assistant: Eleanor Aldridge
Senior pre-press designer: Dan May
Design director: Scott Stickland
Travel publisher: Joanna Kirby
Digital travel publisher: Peter Buckley
Reference director: Andrew Lockett
Operations coordinator: Becky Doyle
Publishing director (Travel): Clare Currie
Commercial manager: Gino Magnotta
Managing director: John Duhigg

Publishing information

This fourth edition published November 2012 by
Rough Guides Ltd,
80 Strand, London WC2R 0RL
11, Community Centre, Panchsheel Park,
New Delhi 110017, India
Distributed by the Penguin Group
Penguin Books Ltd,
80 Strand, London WC2R 0RL
Penguin Group (USA)
375 Hudson Street, NY 10014, USA
Penguin Group (Australia)
250 Camberwell Road, Camberwell,
Victoria 3124, Australia
Penguin Group (NZ)
67 Apollo Drive, Mairangi Bay, Auckland 1310,
New Zealand
Penguin Group (South Africa)
Block D, Rosebank Office Park, 181 Jan Smuts Avenue,
Parktown North, Gauteng, South Africa 2193
Rough Guides is represented in Canada by Tourmaline
Editions Inc. 662 King Street West, Suite 304, Toronto,
Ontario M5V 1M7
Printed in Singapore by Toppan Security Printing Pte. Ltd.

Readers' letters

Many thanks to all the readers who took the time to write in with their comments, updates and suggestions.

Kerry Abbott; Trevor Alexander; Jeremy Askew; Helen Barnett; P. Behr; Emma Boyle; Peter Bruckmann; Jill Cox; Gerard Crowe; Steve Dellow; Brenda van Eeden; Mark Ellingham; Faye; Billie Goodman; Jonathan Gorvett; Paul & Eileen Hanson; Michaela Hinterholzer; Fred Lubin; Konrad Menne; Tim Pare; Lukas Probst; Graeme Proud; Julie Ryan; Brian Sandford; Dominic Sansoni; Nimal de Silva; Chantal Sucaud; Liz Stone; Peter Turner; J.D. Tyson; Paul Watson; Adam Williams; Johnannes Wischt.

Help us update

We've gone to a lot of effort to ensure that the fourth edition of **The Rough Guide to Sri Lanka** is accurate and up-to-date. However, things change – places get "discovered", opening hours change, restaurants and rooms raise prices or lower standards. If you feel we've got it wrong or left something out, we'd like to know, and if you can remember the address, the price, the hours, the phone number, so much the better.

Please send your comments with the subject line "**Rough Guide Sri Lanka Update**" to @ mail@uk .roughguides.com. We'll credit all contributions and send a copy of the next edition (or any other Rough Guide if you prefer) for the very best emails.

Find more travel information, connect with fellow travellers and book your trip on ⓦ roughguides.com

Photo credits

All photos © Rough Guides except the following:
(Key: t-top; c-centre; b-bottom; l-left; r-right)

p.1 Getty Images: Robert Harding
p.2 Getty Images: David Hiser
p.4 Getty Images: Andy Rouse
p.7 Getty Images: Jereme Thaxton (tl); Rob Francis (tr); Ian Trower (b)
p.9 Alamy Images: Hemis
p.11 Alamy Images: Nandana de Silva (t). Getty Images: Gavin Hellier (b)
p.12 Alamy Images: Caro
p.13 Alamy Images: David Cherepuschak (t); Hemis (b). Getty Images: Hugh Sitton (c)
p.14 Alamy Images: Finnbarr Webster (t); Papilio (b)
p.15 Alamy Images: CuboImages srl (tl); David Hosking (tr); Hemis (b)
p.16 Alamy Images: Robert Harding (b)
p.17 Alamy Images: Celia Mannings (t); Boaz Rottem (b)
p.18 Alamy Images: Gary Taylor (c). Getty Images: Keren Su (b)

p.19 Gavin Thomas (t); Getty Images: Tony French (b)
p.20 Alamy Images: AHowden (t)
p.21 Alamy Images: Hemis (t). Getty Images: Andrea Thompson Photography (b)
p.22 Alamy Images: Thilanka Perera (l); Jon Arnold Images Ltd (r)
p.141 Alamy Images: David South
p.147 Getty Images: Ian Trower
p.159 Getty Images: Paula Bronstein (b)
p.233 Alamy Images: Benjamin Balfour (tr)
p.343 Alamy Images: Tony French
p.387 Getty Images: Ishara S. Kodikara (bl)

Front cover Fishermen, Kogalla © Stuart Pearce/Superstock
Back cover Pinnewala Elephant Orphanage © Alamy/Jon Arnold Images Ltd (t); Geese on moonstone, Anuradhapura © Rough Guides: Gavin Thomas (bl); Tuktuk, Jaffna © Rough Guides: Gavin Thomas (br)

Map symbols

The symbols below are used on maps throughout the book

✈	Airport	⚑	Golf course	Waterfall		Church (regional maps)
★	Bus stop	♜	Fortress	Tree		Church (town maps)
P	Parking	⊠	Gate	Banyan tree		Market
‿	Bridge	▲	Peak	Viewpoint		Stadium
♦	Point of interest	Rock		Lighthouse		Building
@	Internet access	Reef		Mosque		Park/jungle/forest
ⓘ	Tourist office	/|\\	Hill	Stupa/Buddhist temple		Beach
✉	Post office	∧ /∧	Earthworks	Hindu temple		Christian cemetery
⊞	Hospital	⌂	Cave	— Wall		Muslim cemetery
⊙	Statue	∴	Ruins	— Ferry route		
⊤	Gardens	Swamp				

Listings key

- ■ Accommodation
- ● Eating
- ■ Drinking/nightlife
- ● Shop
- ● Diving and Watersports

Index

Maps are marked in grey

A

accommodation.................32–34
bargaining.................................33
online resources.........................34
room rates.................................33
taxes...34
tea estate bungalows................240
top eco-lodges and hotels............46
Adam's Bridge............................377
Adam's Peak..... 13, 23, 262–265
Adisham....................................260
Ahangama..................................164
AIDS..56
air taxi.......................................30
airlines.......................................25
airport, Hambantota 181, 417
Airport, Katunayake
International................................88
Alankuda...................................113
alphabet, Sinhala......................444
Aluthapola Temple.....................108
Aluthgama.................................120
Aluthgama 117
Aluvihara...................................287
Ambalangoda............... 129–131
Ampara......................................359
Anawilundawa Wetland
Sanctuary 111
Angarika Dharmapala...............406
Angurukaramulla Temple........108
animals, Buddhist........................429
antiques, exporting.....................48
ANURADHAPURA 17, 23,
319–335
Anuradhapura....................... 320
Abhayagiri dagoba.....................329
Abhayagiri Monastery.........329–331
Abhayagiri Museum....................329
accommodation..........................334
Archeological Museum...............325
arrival and departure 333
Basawakkulama...........................321
Brazen Palace 322
Buddhist railing........................326
Burrows Pavilion........................331
Citadel, the................................328
Digapashana Cave.....................331
eating.......................................335
Et Pokuna...................................331
Folk Museum.............................325
Goldfish Park.............................332
guides and tours........................333
history.................................396–399
Isurumuniya Vihara....................332
Jetavana dagoba........................326
Jetavana Monastery...........325–328
Jetavana Museum........................328

Kujjatissa Pabbata.....................323
Kuttam Pokuna..........................330
Mahapali Refectory...................328
Mahasen's Palace 331
Mahavihara.......................321–325
Mirisavatiya dagoba 332
Nuwara Wewa 321
Ratna Prasada...........................331
restoration of.............................330
Royal Palace 328
Ruvanvalisaya dagoba 323
Samadhi Buddha........................330
Sri Maha Bodhi...........................321
Temple of the Tooth...................329
Thuparama..................................323
tickets.......................................333
Tissa Wewa 321
Vessagiriya Monastery................333
Arankele....................................283
architecture, Buddhist
.....................................426–431
arrack...39
art, Buddhist.............. 426–431
Arugam Bay 19, 23, 361–364
Arugam Bay........................ 363
ATMs..61
Aukana......................................296
Ayurveda 19, 118
Ayurveda resorts, Beruwala and
Bentota......................................119

B

babies, travelling with 50
Badulla........................... 248–250
Badulla.............................. 249
Baker, Samuel............................239
Baker's Falls..............................247
Balapitiya..................................128
ballooning.................................44
Bambarakanda Falls.................261
bananas......................................38
Bandaraike family.....................407
Bandaranaike, Mrs.....................407
Bandaranaike, S.W.R.D............407
Bandarawela..............................257
Bandarawela 257
banks...60
bargaining...........................48, 57
Barnes, Edward.........................238
bars...39
batik..48
Batticaloa 23, 354–359
Batticaloa 356
Bawa, Bevis 120
Bawa, Geoffrey 17, 34, 82, 85,
88, 120, 124, 126, 146, 443

beaches
Ambalangoda 129
Bentota....................................122
Beruwala 116
Hikkaduwa..............................131
Induruwa.................................127
Kalutara...................................115
Kosgoda...................................127
Mirissa.....................................168
Mount Lavinia 86
Negombo.................................100
Passekudah.............................353
Polhena....................................172
Tangalla...................................176
Unawatuna..............................157
Uppaveli..................................350
Weligama.................................165
beer 39
Belihul Oya...............................261
Belummahara 200
Bentota 19, 122–127
Bentota............................... 117
Bentota River.............................123
Beruwala 116–120
Beruwala, Aluthgama, Bentota
and Induruwa 117
Bhuvanekabahu I 285
Bible Rock..................................202
bird wave, Sinharaja.................270
birds...................................14, 434
birdwatching...............................46
Black July 72, 409
Blavatsky, Madame 76
blowhole, Hoo-maniya...........175
bo trees....................................429
bodhisattvas.............................423
Bogoda......................................250
bookings, train 30
books about Sri Lanka
.....................................441–443
books, buying in Sri Lanka.......50
Brief Garden 120
British East India Company....405
British in Sri Lanka....................405
Buddhaghosa............................287
Buddhism............... 10, 419–431
animals, Buddhist........................429
belief system..............................421
bo trees.....................................429
bodhisattvas..............................423
Buddha, life of............................419
Buddha images..........................426
Buddhist art and architecture
....426–431
Buddhist ritual............................424
dagobas (stupas).......................427
Eightfold Path............................422
festivals.......................................41
Four Noble Truths......................422

gods..423
Hinayana Buddhism.....................423
history of Sri Lanka......................420
iconography..................................430
karma..422
Mahayana Buddhism....................422
monks...424
moonstones..................................430
mudras..427
nirvana..422
poya days......................................424
Sangha, the..................................424
temples..................................428–430
Theravada Buddhism....................423
Three Jewels.................................424
Buddhist Theosophical Society
....76
budgeting for your trip.............56
Buduruwagala..............................256
Bundala National Park......23, 183
Burghers..146
buriani...36
buses..28
Buttala.......................256, 368, 369

C

Cadjugama....................................200
cakes..38
camping....................................33, 46
car and driver, hiring................31
carrom...48
Casuarina Beach..........................392
cellphones..61
censorship, press.........................418
Ceylon National Congress......406
Chakaravarti, Arya......................401
chakra..431
Chelvanayakum, S.J.V.............383
Chikungunya fever.......................56
Chilaw...110
children, travelling with............50
Chinese food...................................37
cholera...55
Christians, Sri Lankan...............100
cinema..40
civil war.........345, 372, 408–416
climate......................................10, 58
clothes..49
coffee.....................................38, 405
COLOMBO.................22, 70–100
Central Colombo............. 80–81
Colombo and the west coast
....68–69
Colombo Fort and the Pettah
.... 74
Greater Colombo 71
Mount Lavinia 87
4th Cross Street..............................77
accommodation..................91–93
airlines...88
airport, transport from..............88
airport bus......................................88

All Saints Church...........................78
arrival and departure...................88
Ayurveda in......................................99
Bambalapitiya.................................85
Bank of Ceylon Tower.................75
banks and exchange.....................99
Barefoot...98
bars...96
Bastian Mawatha bus station...89
Beira Lake..79
bookshops.......................................98
British Council................................99
buses..89
car rental...90
Cargills...73
Central Bus Stand.........................90
cinema..99
Cinnamon Gardens...............83–85
city transport.................................90
clocktower-lighthouse.................73
con artists..79
consulates..99
couriers..99
cricket venues................................99
De Soysa Circus (Lipton Circus)....83
Dehiwela Zoo.................................86
Devatagaha Mosque.....................83
district area codes.........................72
diving...99
drinking..96
Dutch Hospital...............................75
Dutch Period Museum..................76
eating..93–96
embassies...99
Fort...73–76
Fort Railway Station...................119
Gabo's Lane......................................77
Galle Face Green............................79
Galle Road.......................................85
galleries...97
Gangaramaya..................................82
Geoffrey Bawa's House.................85
golf...99
Grand Mosque................................78
Grand Oriental Hotel....................75
Green Path Art Gallery.................84
health clinics...................................99
history of...70
hospitals..99
Hulftsdorp......................................78
Independence Commemoration
Hall..83
information......................................90
internet access...............................99
Jami ul-Aftar...................................77
Kayman's Gate................................77
Kelaniya Raja Maha Vihara..........87
Kollupitiya.......................................85
Kotahena...78
Kotte..88
Laksala..98
left luggage......................................99
Lionel Wendt Art Centre.............97
Main Street, Pettah.......................77
Maritime Museum.........................78
Mount Lavinia................................86
National Art Gallery.....................85
National Museum...........................83
National Railway Museum...........78

Natural History Museum.............84
Navam Perahera............................82
New Kathiresan kovil.....................77
nightclubs..97
Old Kathiresan kovil.....................77
Old Town Hall.................................77
orientation......................................70
Parliament Building.......................88
Pettah, the........................17, 76
pharmacies......................................99
photographic shops.......................99
port...75
post offices......................................99
pubs..99
Ratmalana airport.........................89
St Andrew's Scotskirk...................85
St Anthony's Church......................78
St Peter's Sambodhi Chaitya.......75
Santa Lucia......................................78
Saunders Place Bus Station.........90
Sea Street..77
Secretariat.......................................79
Seema Malaka.................................82
shopping...................................97–99
Sinhalese Sports Club...................83
Slave Island................................79–83
spas...99
Sri Jayawardenepura....................88
Sri Subramanian Kovil..................79
Church..75
street names....................................72
Superior Law Courts......................78
supermarkets..................................99
swimming..99
taxis..99
tea...98
Temple Trees...................................85
theatre..97
Town Hall...83
trains......................................89, 90
tuktuks..90
Viharamahadevi Park....................83
Wellawatta.......................................85
Wolfendhal Church........................78
World Trade Center........................75
York Street.......................................73
Commonwealth War Cemetery
....350
communications bureaux.......61
con artists...........................51, 52
consulates and embassies,
Sri Lankan, overseas............59
coral and marine products,
buying...48
Corbet's Gap.................................235
costs of travelling in Sri Lanka
....56–58
costs, food.......................................35
costs, national parks..................45
couriers..60
cricket.......................................13, 42
crime.......................................50–52
crocodiles......................................435
Culavamsa, the.............................396
Cultural Triangle, the... 276–339
Cultural Triangle, the...278–279

cultural values 46
currency 60
custard apples 38
customs regulations 58
cycling 44

D

D'Oyly, Sir John 210, 217, 442
dagobas (stupas) 427
Dakkinadesa 200
Dalawela 161
Dalhousie 264
Dambadeniya 201, 400
Dambana 236
Dambatenne Tea Factory 259
Dambulla 20, 22, 289–295
Dambulla 290
Dambulla cave temples
.... **290–292**
dancing 130
Dawson, W.F. 203
de Silva, Ena 146
Debera Wewa 185
Dedigama 200, 400
Deepavali 42
Degaldoruwa 232
Delft 393
dengue fever 54
Deniyaya 271
Department of Immigration 59
Department of Wildlife
   Conservation 45
desserts and sweets 37
Detamahal Vihara 368
devales 428
Devanampiya Tissa 336, 396
Devi Nuwara Perahera 174
devil dancing 130
devilled dishes 36
Devon Falls 246
Dhatusena 298, 322, 398
diarrhoea 53
Dickoya 265
Dickwella 175
Dickwella Lace 175
digge 430
Dimbula 238, 246
disabled travellers 62
diving 43, 114
   Bentota 124
   Hikkaduwa 133
   Negombo 102
   Tangalla 178
   Unawatuna 160
   Weligama 167
Diyaluma Falls 256
doctors 52
dolphins 437
dolphin-watching 17, 46, 113
Dondanduwa 134

Dondra 174
dosa 37
Dowa Temple 252
driver, hiring 31
driving in Sri Lanka 30
drowning 51
drums 48
Dunhinda Falls 250
durian 38
Duruthu Poya 41
Dutch canal (Hamilton Canal)
.... 102
Dutch in Sri Lanka 403
Dutugemunu 282, 324, 398
dysentery 53

E

eastern Sri Lanka 344
eating and drinking 34–39
eco-hotels 46
eco-lodges 46
eco-tourism 46
economy 418
Eelam 376, 409
Elara 398
electricity 58
Elephant Pass 378
Elephant Transit Home 272
elephants 8, 46, 432
Ella 17, 22, 251–255
Ella 251
Around Ella 252
Ella Rock 253
embassies and consulates,
   Sri Lankan, overseas 59
Embekke Devale 231
Embilipitiya 273
emergencies 59
English, Sri Lankan (language)
.... 445
entrance charges 57
entrance charges, national parks
.... 45
Esala Perahera, Kandy 19, 208
Esala Poya 42
exchange rates 60

F

faluda 38
ferry, India to Sri Lanka 26
festivals 40–42
   calendar 41
   Buddhist 41
   Galle 145
   Hindu 41
   Muslim 41
film 40
flights 25, 26

folk dancing 130
Fonseka, General Sarath 417
food and drink terms 448
food hygiene 53
food, Sri Lankan specialities 36
food, where to eat 35
Fort Frederick, Trincomalee ... 346
fruits 38

G

Gajabahu 208
Gal Oya National Park 360
Galadeniya 231
Galagoda Sailathalaramaya
   Temple 130
GALLE 13, 22, 143–155
Galle 144
   accommodation 151
   All Saints' Church 148
   Amangalla Hotel 145
   arrival and depature 150
   Court Square 148
   cricket ground 150
   drinking 154
   Dutch Reformed Church 146
   eating 153
   festivals 145
   Flag Rock 149
   Fort 145–150
   Fort jumpers 149
   Great Warehouse 148
   Historical Mansion Museum ... 149
   history 143
   information 151
   lighthouse 149
   Main Gate 145
   Meeran Jumma Mosque 149
   National Maritime Museum 148
   National Museum 145
   new town 150
   Old Gate 148
   Queen's House 148
   ramparts 149
   shopping 154
   Sun, Moon and Star bastions ... 145
   tours 151
Galmaduwa Gedige 232
Gampola 400
Gangarama Mahavihara 133
Gangarama Viharaya (Kandy)
.... 232
Gathering, Minneriya 306
gay travellers 59
gedige 429
gems 49, 268
getting around Sri Lanka
.... **27–32**
getting married in Sri Lanka 63
giardiasis 53
Giritale 318
glossary 449–451
gods, Buddhist 423

Gokana 342
golf.......................................45
government service tax 57
guardstones 431
guavas 38
gulsambillas 38
Gunesekera, Romesh 441

H

Habarana 303
Hakgala Botanical Gardens....245
Hambantota 181–183
Hammenhiel fort 392
Handapanagala Tank 256
handicrafts 48
Handunugoda Tea Estate 164
Hanguranketa....................234
Hanuman 157, 306
Haputale.................23, 258–261
Haputale............................. 259
Hasalaka.............................235
hassle 51, 52
Hatton................................264
health................................52–56
health resorts Beruwala and
    Bentota.........................119
heatstroke 55
Hendala...............................106
Henerathgoda Botanical
    Gardens..........................108
hepatitis 55
Highway State Museum.........203
hiking 44
HIKKADUWA 131–137
Hikkaduwa 132
    accommodation....................135
    arrival and depature 134
    diving 133
    eating................................136
    Hikkaduwa Beach Fest..............131
    Hikkaduwa Marine National Park
       131
    nightlife.............................137
    snorkelling..........................133
    surfing...............................133
    watersports.........................133
hill country 198–199
Hindu festivals 41
history of Sri Lanka 395–418
HIV......................................56
Hiyare Rainforest Park............155
Hoo-maniya blowhole............175
hoppers 36
horseriding 44
Horton Plains National Park
    ....22, 23, 246–248
hotels, Geoffrey Bawa 34
hotels, ten top Sri Lankan 33
Hunasgiriya........................235
Hurulu Eco-Park 304

I

ice cream 38
Idalgashina 260
idlis 37
image house........................429
independence.....................406
Indian Peace Keeping Force.... 410
Indonesian food....................37
Induruwa 127
Induruwa 117
insect bites, avoiding 54
insurance 59
internet access.....................60
irrigation in early Sri Lanka....322
itineraries...........................22

J

jackfruit 38
JAFFNA 379–386
Jaffna 380
    accommodation....................385
    Archeological Museum............384
    arrival and departure 385
    Chelvanayakum monument....383
    clocktower..........................383
    drinking.............................386
    eating...............................386
    EPRLF headquarters..............384
    Groote Kerk........................382
    history...............................379
    Hospital Road......................381
    Jaffna Fort..........................382
    Jaffna lagoon......................383
    Jaffna Public Library..............383
    Kasturiya Road.....................381
    kingdom of.........................401
    Main Street.........................383
    Nallur Kandaswamy Temple 384
    Rosarian Convent..................383
    St Martin's Seminary..............383
    St Mary's Cathedral...............383
    sieges of 382
    Vaitheeswara Temple..............381
    Vatharaja Perumal Kovil 381
Jaffna Peninsula........... 386–391
Jaffna Peninsula 389
Jaffnapatam.......................379
jaggery 37
Japanese encephalitis 54
Jatakas...............................431
Jayawardene, J.R.............88, 408
jewellery 49
JHU (Jathika Hela Urumaya) ...425
JVP............................. 408, 410

K

Kachchaitivu.......................393
Kachimalai Mosque, Beruwala
   118

Kaduganawa Pass.................202
Kaduruwela........................318
Kala Wewa Tank...................296
Kalametiya Bird Sanctuary.....181
Kalawana 271
Kalkudah............................353
Kallady...............................358
Kalpitiya peninsula 112–114
Kalpitiya town....................23, 112
Kalutara.............................115
Kande Vihara 120
KANDY 20, 22, 205–227
Kandy............................ 206–207
Around Kandy.................... 228
    accommodation.............220–223
    Archeological Museum............216
    arrival and departure 220
    Audience Hall......................215
    Ayurveda............................227
    Bahiravakanda Buddha 219
    cricket................................227
    cultural shows......................225
    Dalada Maligawa .... see Temple
        of the Tooth
    dancing and drumming 20, 225
    Degaldoruwa........................232
    drinking.............................224
    eating................................223
    Embekke Devale 231
    Esala Perahera......................208
    Galadeniya..........................231
    Galmaduwa Gedige 232
    Gangarama Viharaya 232
    hassle.................................220
    history 205–210, 403, 405
    Kandy Garrison Cemetery 216
    Kataragama Devale.................219
    lake, the (Kiri Muhuda)............210
    Lankatilake..........................231
    Malwatta Monastery...............211
    meditation..........................222
    Museum of World Buddhism......216
    Natha Devale 217
    National Museum 215
    Pattini Devale.......................217
    Peradeniya Botanical Gardens
       227–230
    Poya Malu Vihara...................211
    Queen's Bath........................216
    Queen's Chamber...................216
    Raja Tusker Museum................215
    Rajapihilla Mawatha 211
    Royal Palace.........................214
    Royal Palace Park...................211
    St Paul's Church....................219
    scams.................................220
    shopping.............................226
    Sri Dalada Museum 214
    Tea Museum.........................234
    Temple of the Tooth....211–214
    three-temples loop................230
    tours from...........................226
    touts.................................220
    Udawattakelle Sanctuary..........219
    Victoria Golf Club..................227
    Vishnu Devale.......................218
Kantharodai.......................388

Karaitivu.................................392
Karavas..................................101
Karuna, Colonel......................413
Kassapa.........................298, 398
Kataluwa Purvarama
   Mahavihara.........................164
Kataragama 14, 23, 189–193
Kataragama............................ 190
Kataragama (god)...................191
Kataragama festival...........42, 190
Katunayake International
   Airport...............................88
Kaudulla National Park...........306
Kaudulla Tank........................306
kavadi...................................192
Kayts....................................391
Keerimalai hot springs...........388
Kelaniya..........................70, 87
Keyt, George..........................146
Kilinochchi....................378, 416
kiribath..................................38
Kirigalpota............................247
Kirinda.................................187
Kirti Sri Rajasinha....... 208, 210,
   290, 291
kitesurfing.............................113
kitul......................................37
Kitulgala...............................265
Knox, Robert...................224, 442
Knuckles Range................22, 234
Koggala.................................163
Koggala lagoon......................164
kolam...................................130
kolam masks....................48, 129
Koneswaram Temple,
   Trincomalee.......................347
Kosgoda.................................127
Koswatta...............................271
Kotabakina.............................236
Kotelawala, John.....................407
Kottawa Rainforest and
   Arboretum..........................155
Kotte............. 72, 88, 401, 402, 403
kotthu rotty............................36
kovils...................................428
Kudawa.................................270
Kudimbigala...........................366
Kularatne, Gamini...................378
Kumarakanda Vihara...............134
Kumaratunga, Chandrika
   ....**411–413**
Kurunegala......................280, 400
Kurunegala...............................281
Kusta Raja.............................166

L

Labookelie Tea Estate.............245
lacquerware............................48
lager.....................................39

Lahugala National Park...........365
Laksala...................................48
lamprais..................................36
language 444–449
Lankatilake..............................231
laundry...................................60
leatherwork.............................48
leeches...................................56
leopards........................46, 433
lesbian travellers.....................59
Lessons Learnt and
   Reconciliation Commission
   (LLRC)...............................416
lewayas, Hambantota...............182
Lipton, Sir Thomas 259, 440
Lipton's Seat..........................259
liquor shops.............................39
Little Adam's Peak...................251
lotus....................................431
**LTTE 72, 201, 345, 372, 376,
   408–416**
LTTE cemetery, Kopai..............390
Lunama lagoon.......................181
lunar calendar.........................41
Lunuganga.............................124

M

Madampe................................110
Madhu...................................375
Madu Ganga...........................128
Maduru Oya National Park.......361
magazines................................40
Magha...........................309, 400
Magul Maha Vihara, Lahugala
  365
Magul Maha Vihara, Yala.........189
Maha Saman Devale, Ratnapura
  267
Mahagama..............................184
Mahavamsa, the 396
Mahawewa..............................110
Mahayana Buddhism...............422
Mahinda.........................336, 396
Mahinda Rajapakse..... 413–418
Mahiyangana..........................235
mail.......................................60
malaria...................................53
Malays in Sri Lanka.................182
Maligawa tusker......................215
Maligawila.............................368
mallung..................................36
Manalkadu Desert...................390
Manavamma............................399
Mandalagiri Vihara..................319
mangosteens..................38, 115
Mannar..................................377
Mannar Island........................375
manners and etiquette 46
maps......................................60

Marawila................................109
Martin Wickramasinghe
   Museum.............................163
masala dosa.............................37
masks..............................48, 129
Matale...................................287
Matara............................170–174
Matara..................................... 171
Mavaragalpota........................237
Maviddapuram Kandaswamy
   Temple..............................388
Mawanella.............................202
Medawatta..............................172
medical resources.....................56
Medirigiya.............................319
meditation........................44, 222
meningitis................................55
metalwork................................48
Midigama...............................164
Mihintale.................23, 336–339
Mihintale................................ 336
Millennium Elephant
   Foundation.........................204
Minneriya National Park 306
Minneriya Tank.......................306
Mirissa.............. 20, 22, 168–170
Mirissa and Weligama 166
mobile phones..........................61
Mogallana..............................298
Monaragala............................367
Monaragala......................... 367
money....................................60
monitors................................435
monkeys................................433
monks, Buddhist.....................424
moonstones............................430
Mount Lavinia..........................86
Mount Lavinia 87
mudras, Buddhist....................427
muggings................................50
Mulkirigala.............................179
Muller, Carl............................441
Munnesvaram Temple..............110
Muralitharan, Muttiah.............. 42
Muslim festivals.......................41
Muthurajawela........................108

N

nagarajas................................431
Naguleswaram Temple.............388
Nainativu................................392
Nalanda Gedige.......................288
Nallatanniya...........................264
Nallur Festival........................384
Namal Uyana Conservation
   Forest...............................295
names of Sri Lanka.................409
Narigama...............................135
national parks...................45, 46

nature reserves..........................45
Navam Poya.............................41
Nayakkar dynasty..................209
NEGOMBO............... 100–106
Negombo beach 104
Negombo town 101
  accommodation................103–105
  arrival and departure 102
  Ayurveda.............................106
  boat trips...........................102
  diving.................................102
  drinking..............................106
  Dutch canal.......................102
  Duwa..................................101
  eating................................105
  fish market.........................100
  fort....................................100
  history...............................100
  lagoon...............................101
  Main Street.........................102
  St Mary's............................102
  tour operators in.................103
  watersports........................102
new year, Nuwara Eliya 240
new year, Sinhalese and Tamil
....41
news, online 39
newspapers.............................39
Nikini Poya.............................42
Nilavarai well.........................391
Nilaveli..................................352
Nilwala Ganga........................170
Nissankamalla............. 291, 309,
  312, 399
Nittambuwa...........................200
northern Sri Lanka 374
NUWARA ELIYA.......23, 238–246
Nuwara Eliya 239
  accommodation...............241–244
  arrival and departure 241
  drinking..............................244
  eating................................244
  golf course.........................244
  Hakgala Botanical Gardens.....245
  history...............................238–240
  Labookelie Tea Estate 245
  New Bazaar Street 240
  new year in.........................240
  Pedro Tea Estate.................245
  Pidurutalagala.....................241
  Single Tree Mountain............241
  Sita Amman Temple..............246
  tours from..........................245
  Victoria Park.......................241

O

observation car train seats........ 30
Okanda..................................366
Olcott, Henry Steel.........76, 406
Ondaatje, Christopher 442
Ondaatje, Michael....114, 146, 441
online information.................. 62
online news............................39
online travel warnings.............. 52

opening hours...........................61
opening hours, banks...............60
oruwa boats 101
Our Lady of Madhu................375
outdoor activities 42–45
overcharging...........................57

P

pachyderm paper...................204
Pada Yatra.............................190
Padeniya Raja Mahavihara.....284
Palabaddale...............263, 267
pamsukulikas.........................306
Pamunugama.........................106
Panama.................................365
Panavitiya..............................202
Pandukabhaya.......................284
Panduvasudeva.......................397
Panduwas Nuwara..................284
papaya...................................38
Parakramabahu I....201, 284, 308,
  309, 322, 399
Parakramabahu VI..................401
Passekudah............................353
Pattini...................................218
payphones...............................61
Peace Pagoda, Unawatuna 157
peace process, 2001...............412
Pedro Tea Estate....................245
People's Alliance (PA)............411
Peradeniya Botanical Gardens
.... 227–230
Peradeniya Botanical Gardens
.... 229
peraheras................................41
pharmacies.............................52
phones...................................61
photography............................62
Pidurangala Royal Cave Temple
....301
Pigeon Island........................352
Pinnewala Elephant Orphanage
....203
pittu.......................................36
planes, domestic...................... 30
Plantation Tamils 240, 407, 438
Point Pedro...........................390
Polhena.................................172
police....................................51
POLONNARUWA.........19, 22, 23,
  307–319
Polonnaruwa......................... 308
Polonnaruwa Quadrangle
.... 311
  accommodation...................318
  Alahana Pirivena.................315
  arrival and departure...........318
  Buddha Seema Pasada..........315
  Council Chamber of
    Parakramabahu..................310

Demala Maha Seya.................316
  eating................................319
  Gal Pota.............................313
  Gal Vihara..........................315
  Hatadage............................312
  history.......................307, 399
  Island Park.........................317
  Kiri Vihara..........................315
  Lankatilaka.........................315
  Menik Vihara......................314
  Pabula Vihara......................314
  Polonnaruwa Museum..........310
  Potgul Vihara......................317
  Quadrangle.................311–314
  Rankot Vihara......................314
  Royal Baths of Parakramabahu...310
  Royal Palace of Parakramabahu
 310
  Satmahal Prasada................313
  Shiva Devale no.1................311
  Shiva Devale no.2................314
  southern ruins.....................317
  Statue of Parakramabahu......317
  Thuparama...........................314
  Tivanka-patamaghara............316
  Vatadage.............................312
Popham Arboretum 294
port, Hambantota..................417
Portuguese in Sri Lanka
.... 379, 402
Poson Poya 42, 336
post....................................... 60
poya days 41, 424
poyage..................................430
Prabhakaran, Vellupilai........376,
  390, 416
precious stones...............49, 268
Premadasa, Ranasinghe........410,
  411
prickly heat 54
public holidays 40
pubs....................................... 39
Punkudutivu..........................392
Purana Totagama Raja
  Mahavihara 134

Q

Queen of the Sea train 134
Queen Vihara Maha Devi........185

R

rabies 55
Radawaduna...........................200
radio 40
rainforest, Hiyare 155
rainforest, Kottawa.................155
rainforest, Sinharaja.... 269–272
Rajapaksa, Mahinda................181
Rajapakse, Basil.....................418
Rajapakse, Gotabhaya 418

Rajapakse, Namal 418
Rajaraja...................................399
Rama 110
Ramayana, the.........110, 157, 246, 252, 306, 377
Ramboda..................................238
rambutan....................................38
Rangala....................................235
Rathgama lagoon......................134
Ratnapura 49, 266–269
Ratnapura............................ 266
Rawana Ella Cave.....................252
Rawana Ella Falls......................252
Rekawa...............................23, 180
religious souvenirs.....................49
reptiles....................................435
rice 36
rice and curry.......................14, 35
Richmond Castle.......................115
rickshaws...................................31
riddle of the mangoes..............336
Ridi Vihara 282
Ritigala....................................305
road traffic safety......................51
rotty 36
Ruhunu National Park.....see *Yala National Park*
Rumassala 157

S

safety...............................50–52
safety in the north 372
St Clair Falls............................246
salt...182
Saman......................................262
Samankanda.............................155
sambol 36
Sampur....................................415
Sangha, the.............................442
Sansoni, Barbara 146, 443
Saradiel, Deekirikevage...........202
Sasseruwa................................297
scams...51
seafood......................................37
security...............................50–52
Seenigama................................133
Selvadurai, Shyam....................441
Senanayake, D.S.......................406
Senanayake, Dudley..................408
Senanayake, Laki 443
Senanayake Samudra 360
Senarat....................................404
Senkadagala.............................205
service tax..................................57
Shiva..110
shopping 47–50
Sigiriya......17, 22, 297–303, 398
Sigiriya 297
Sigiriya Rock 298–301

singing fish, Batticaloa 358
Sinhala....................................444
Sinharaja 19, 23, 269–272
Sinharaja bird wave..................270
Sita Amman Temple 246
Sitawake..................................402
Situlpahuwa 189
Skanda.....................................191
sloth bear 434
snakebite...................................56
snorkelling 44
    Hikkaduwa 133
    Nilaveli...352
    Polhena...172
    Unawatuna......................................160
soft drinks 38
south, the 142
South Indian food 37
Southern Expressway 28
spice gardens...........................286
spices 49
spirits, alcoholic 39
sports.............................42–45
Spowers, Rory 155, 442
squirrels...................................434
Sri Jayawardenepura...................88
Sri Lanka Freedom Party (SLFP) 407
Sri Lankan English (language) 445
Sri Pada................see *Adam's Peak*
Sri Wickrama Rajasinha 210
STDs...56
stilt fishermen 162, 164
stings, jellyfish 55
string hoppers 36
Subha......................................328
sun, safety in 54
surfing.................................43, 164
    Arugam Bay 361
    Hikkaduwa 133
    Medawatta.......................................172
    Unawatuna......................................160
    Weligama..167
Swami Rock 347
sweets and desserts 37
swimming 55, 114

T

Talawila....................................112
Tamil (language) 445
Tamil Tigers..................... see *LTTE*
tampita.....................................429
Tangalla 176–179
Tangalla 177
Tangamalai Nature Reserve 260
tanks..322
Tantirimalai.............................335
Taprobane 166

Tarshish 143
taxes...57
Taylor, James............................438
tea.....38, 49, 240, 405, 438–440
Tea Museum 234
television 40
Tellipalai...................................388
temperature chart......................58
temple etiquette........................46
temples, Buddhist 428–430
tetanus.......................................55
Thai Pongol................................41
Thalpe......................................161
theft...50
Theravada Buddhism................423
Thiranagama.............................135
three-temples loop...................230
three-wheelers .... see *rickshaws*
time difference 62
tipping 57
Tissa Wewa...............................185
Tissamaharama 184–188
Tissamaharama.................. 184
toddy..39
Tooth Relic 208, 212, 329, 401
Totapolakanda..........................247
tour operators (UK)....................26
tour operators in Sri Lanka 27
tour operators, Tissa 186
tourist information.....................62
tourist prices 57
touts 51, 52
traffic, dangers...........................51
train timetables, from Colombo 89
train timetables, hill country 200
train timetables, south coast 143
trains 29
travel agents (UK).......................26
travel agents in Sri Lanka 27
travellers with disabilities..........62
travellers' cheques......................61
trekking......................................44
Trincomalee 345–349
Trincomalee........................ 346
Tripitaka...................................420
Tripitakaya, the 287
tsunami 134, 366, 413
Tsunami Honganji Vihara 134
tuktuks.................... see *rickshaws*
Turnour, George.......................180
Turtle Conservation Project 128, 180
turtle hatcheries 128
turtles................. 46, 128, 180, 435
typhoid......................................55
typhus.......................................55

U

Uda Walawe National Park......23, 272
Uddapu...111
Unawatuna 156–161
Unawatuna............................156
United National Party (UNP)...406
Unmadachitra.............................284
Uppuveli......................350–352
Uppuveli.................................351
Urundi Fort 391
uttapam...37
Utuwankanda...............................202

V

vaccinations.................................52
vadai..37
Vakarai.......................................415
Valli Amma..................................191
Vallipuram..................................390
Vanni, the 374–378
vatadage.....................................429
Vattagamani Abhaya.....290, 291, 329
Vavuniya.....................................375
Veddahs 236, 237, 397
vegetables.....................................36
vegetarian food.............................37
Vel 191
Vel festival 42
Velvettiturai...............................390
Vesak Poya...................................41
Victoria Reservoir and Dam...234
Vihara Maha Devi 185
Vijaya, Prince 397
Vijayabahu I.....................308, 399
villas, south coast 152
Villiers, Sir Thomas....................260
Vimala Dharma Surya 205, 403
visas...59
volunteering.................................62

W

Wadduwa 115
Waikkal......................................109
Wanniyala-aetto........see Veddahs
war crimes.....................................416
Wasgomuwa National Park....288
water, drinking 38, 53
water sports..................................43
watersports, Bentota................124
watersports, in Hikkaduwa....133
watersports, Negombo 102
wattalappam 37
weather....................................10, 58
Weddagala..................................271
weddings in Sri Lanka 63
Weherehena...............................172
Weligama 165–168
Weligama and Mirissa 166
Weligama Bay 166
Wellawaya 255
Wellington, Duke of...................347
west coast, the 100–137
Wewala..135
Wewurukannala.........................175
whales...437
whale-watching 17, 46, 113, 168
whitewater rafting 43, 265
Wickramasinghe, Martin.........163
Wickramasinghe, Ranil....412, 414
Wickramatunga, Lasantha 418
Wijeyeratne, Gehan de Silva ...443
wildlife......................................432–437
Wilpattu National Park 23, 111
wood apples..................................38
Woolf, Leonard 182, 441
World War II 406
World's End 14, 247

Y

Yala East National Park 366
Yala National Park.......14, 22, 188, 433
Yapahuwa 285, 400
Yasalalakatissa 328
yoga...44
Yudaganawa................................368

Beautifully diverse. Inherently Sri Lankan.

At your next getaway in the tropical isle of Sri Lanka, you could choose to relax by the beautiful blues of the Negombo sky and the sun kissed sands of its beaches where barefoot elegance reigns. Or you could drink in the iconic creations of architect Geoffrey Bawa at the neighbouring lagoon, or stand amongst royal bronze warriors along a magnificent Bawa staircase further south in Galle. Dive deep into historical lore at the fabled rock fortress of Sigiriya in the heart of the country, or recline in the misty mountains of Nuwara Eliya. Whatever captivates you, the Jetwing chain of hotels will always be there to greet you with a warm Sri Lankan smile.

HOTELS

www.jetwinghotels.com